Professional Open Source Web Services

Kapil Apshankar
Dietrich Ayala
Christopher Browne
Vivek Chopra
Tim McAllister
Dr Poornachandra Sarang

Wrox Press Ltd. ®

Professional Open Source Web Services

The authors and publisher have made every effort in the preparation of this book to ensure the accuracy of the information. However, the information contained in this book is sold without warranty, either express or implied. Neither the authors, Wrox Press nor its dealers or distributors will be held liable for any damages caused or alleged to be caused either directly or indirectly by this book.

Published by Wrox Press Ltd,
Arden House, 1102 Warwick Road, Acocks Green,
Birmingham, B27 6BH, UK
Printed in the United States
ISBN 1-861007-46-9

Trademark Acknowledgements

Credits

Author
Kapil Apshankar
Dietrich Ayala
Christopher Browne
Vivek Chopra
Tim McAllister
Dr Poornachandra Sarang

Technical Reviewers
Afrasiab Ahmad
Hemant Adarkar
Mathew Antony
Kapil Apshankar
Dietrich Ayala
Anil Balaram
Joshua Hoover
Pankaj Kumar
Neil Matthew
Ramesh Mani
Rob Sacciacco
Richard Stones
Bryan Waters

Author Agents
Shivanand Nadkarni
Safiulla Shakir

Commissioning Editors
Paul Cooper
Ranjeet Wadhwani

Technical Editors
Dipali Chittar
Kedar Kamat
Matthew Moodie
Shivanand Nadkarni

Indexers
Adrian Axinte
Andrew Criddle

Proof Reader
Agnes Wiggers

Production Coordinators
Rachel Taylor
Pip Wonson

Illustrations
Santosh Haware
Manjiri Karande

Cover
Dawn Chellingworth

About the Authors

Kapil Apshankar

Kapil has three years experience in knowledge management, i18n, L10n, and manufacturing domains. He works as a team leader for a major software corporation in India. Currently he is working with Web Services in all their forms to devise ways and means to take this nascent technology to its limits.

His other interests include Linux, networking, and distributed computing. When not dabbling with his computer, he can be seen playing the harmonica or drawing pencil portraits. Kapil can be reached at kapilapshankar@yahoo.co.in.

Dietrich Ayala

Dietrich Ayala has spent the past four years designing and developing web applications. He feels fulfilled when programming with PHP and XML. Dietrich currently works for NuSphere Corporation developing Web Services tools for PHP developers. NuSOAP, formerly known as SOAPx4, is distributed by him (http://dietrich.ganx4.com/nusoap/), and by the NuSphere Corporation (http://www.nusphere.com/). He holds certifications in E-commerce programming and XML technologies from the University of Washington. Dietrich's other interests include hiking through swamps, juggling sharp objects, and finding other fun things to do with his partner and daughter, who happen to be the coolest people in the whole world.

Christopher Browne

Christopher is a consultant specializing in Unix, Linux, and the SAP R/3 ERP system. He has been involved with numerous SAP R/3 installation projects at SHL Systemhouse, American Airlines, and Sabre. Chris holds a Bachelor of Mathematics degree from the University of Waterloo, Joint Honors Co-op Chartered Accountancy and Computer Science, and a Master of Science degree in Systems Science from the University of Ottawa, Canada.

Vivek Chopra

Vivek has eight years of experience in software design and development, the last two years of which have been in Web Services and various XML technologies. He is co-author of *Professional ebXML Foundations* and *Professional XML Web Services* (both Wrox Press). He is also a committer For UDDI4J, an open source Java API for UDDI. His other areas of experience and interest include compilers, middleware, clustering, GNU/Linux, and mobile computing. He is currently consulting in the domain area of Web Services.

Vivek holds a Bachelor's degree in Electronics and a Master's in Computer Science, both from Pune University, India. He lives and works in the beautiful San Francisco Bay Area, and can be reached at vivek@soaprpc.com.

Tim McAllister

Tim McAllister is a software architect, engineer, author, and conference speaker with over a decade of experience in the industry. His work is focused on object-oriented analysis and design, distributed systems, Web Services, Java, XML, and related Internet technologies.

Tim currently spends his days at Hewlett Packard, where he says they are "enabling pervasive interoperability of nomadic devices". Until recently he was a senior architect at Nike working with the B2C and B2B teams.

Tim lives in the Pacific Northwest, spending too much time in front of a computer. He should take more time to fish the rivers of Oregon and play guitar in a blues band. Tim enjoys helping his son build combat robots and takes his daughters shopping. He can be reached at tim@ObjectAnswers.com.

Dr Poornachandra Sarang

Dr Sarang is one of the leading software architects in the industry. With more than 20 years of IT experience, Dr. Sarang provides consulting in architecting and designing solutions to clients worldwide. He is an ex-professor of Computer Engg of University of Notre Dame, USA. Dr. Sarang is an invited speaker at many international conferences and has many research papers to his credit. He is a regular contributor of technical articles in many international journals and has co-authored several books for Wrox.

My special thanks to Chandan, Rahul, and Madhav for providing valuable inputs during this writing.

I dedicate this writing to my son Sanket who co-operated by not bothering me with his studies during the time of writing.

Table of Contents

Introduction

Since the start of the Internet, few other technologies have been adopted as quickly as Web Services. Its introduction more than a year ago generated great interest in the industry and Web Services is now seen as a big leap in distributed computing. In the open source arena, Web Services has made an indelible mark and programmers are already solving big problems with it.

Web Services represent the next generation of e-business applications. They make application functionality available over the Internet in a standardized programmatic manner. The key benefit of Web Services is that they allow incompatible applications to interoperate on the Web regardless of language, platform, and operating systems.

Who is this Book For?

This book targets programmers who have knowledge of programming, TCP/IP, HTTP, XML, and the concept of client-server applications. While the audience is expected to be experienced, we shall cover the basic aspects of installation and good examples. Since the area is still evolving and shall see many changes, we will discuss more on architecture and approaches. We are assuming the readers are programmers who are looking for viable solutions to Web Services implementations using open source technology. We also assume an interest in programming web applications and distributed applications.

The audience is expected to have good knowledge of languages they are interested in. Also the readers are expected to have a good knowledge of installation and configuration of various servers.

What's Covered in this Book?

In this book, we aim to give you the best possible understanding of the technologies involved in generating Web Services using various open source products.

In Chapter 1, we look at the traditional distributed computing and its drawbacks. We introduce Web Services and make a case for open source Web Services.

In Chapter 2, we look at the architecture of Web Services and discuss the various building blocks like XML, XML-RPC, SOAP, UDDI, WSDL, WSFL, and so on.

In Chapter 3, we present an in-depth discussion on the three most important technologies used to create Web Services – SOAP (Simple Object Access Protocol), WSDL (Web Service Description Language), and UDDI (Universal Description, Discovery and Integration).

In Chapter 4, we start dealing with the practical aspects of Web Services. We demonstrate how to do Web Services using popular open source products like Apache AXIS and Tomcat. We discuss the architecture of AXIS and also unfold its various aspects with practical examples.

In Chapter 5, we deal with security and see how it is relevant to Web Services. We discuss the various security techniques and show how to develop secure Web Services.

In Chapter 6, we deal with one of the most matured implementations – SOAP::Lite. We delve into SOAP::Lite by exploring various capabilities using real-life examples. We also demonstrate practical aspects of designing and developing Web Services clients and servers with the help of examples.

In Chapter 7, we go through various facilities available under Python and provide detailed discussion on the SOAP.py and ZSI infrastructure available for Python.

In Chapter 8, we see another popular language in action, PHP. We focus on various aspects of PHP-based Web Services using solutions from open source.

Chapter 9 caters to the need of C++ developers who want to create Web Services. C/C++ based applications are popular. We discuss the various aspects of Web Services using three different popular open source packages.

In Chapter 10, we see some other popular packages. SOAP4R facilitates SOAP-based Web Services for Ruby. XMLRPC4R provides XML-RPC based Web Services for Ruby. kSOAP is an open source product that enables Web Services in Java applets and devices.

Chapter 11 deals with the important task of making Web Services out of existing legacy applications. We use a case study to demonstrate a practical approach of converting a popular SQL-Ledger package to a web service.

Appendix A: Configuring Tomcat with Apache

Appendix B: Server.xml Attributes for Tomcat Configuration

Appendix C: TcpTunnelGui and Tcpmon

Appendix D: JBoss Installation

Appendix E: WSDL2Java Options

Appendix F: Java2WSDL Options

Appendix G: SOAP::Lite Classes

Appendix H: kSOAP API

What You Need to Use this Book

We also cover various third-party modules and utilities, details of which are mentioned in the relevant chapters.

The code included in this book can be downloaded from http://www.wrox.com/. More details are given in the *Customer Support* section.

Conventions

To help you get the most from the text and keep track of what's happening, we've used a number of conventions throughout the book.

For instance:

> **These boxes hold important, not-to-be-forgotten information, which is directly relevant to the surrounding text.**

While the background style is used for asides to the current discussion.

As for styles in the text:

- When we introduce them, we **highlight** important words
- We show keyboard strokes like this: *Ctrl-K*
- We show filenames and code within the text like so: `<Location>`
- Text on user interfaces and URLs are shown as: Menu

We present code in two different ways. Code that is new or important is shown as so:

```
In our code examples, the code foreground style shows new, important, and
pertinent code
```

Code that is an aside, or has been seen before is shown as so:

```
In our code examples, the code background style shows code that's less important
in the present context, or that has been seen before
```

Customer Support

We always value hearing from our readers, and we want to know what you think about this book: what you liked, what you didn't like, and what you think we can do better next time. You can send us your comments, either by returning the reply card in the back of the book, or by e-mail to feedback@wrox.com. Please be sure to mention the book title in your message.

How to Download the Sample Code for the Book

When you visit the Wrox site, http://www.wrox.com/ simply locate the title through our Search facility or by using one of the title lists. Click on Download in the Code column, or on Download Code on the book's detail page.

The files that are available for download from our site have been archived using WinZip. When you have saved the attachments to a folder on your hard-drive, you need to extract the files using a de-compression program such as WinZip or PKUnzip. When you extract the files, the code is usually extracted into chapter folders. When you start the extraction process, ensure your software (WinZip, PKUnzip, etc.) is set to use folder names.

Errata

We've made every effort to make sure that there are no errors in the text or in the code. However, no one is perfect and mistakes do occur. If you find an error in one of our books, like a spelling mistake or faulty piece of code, we would be very grateful for your feedback. By sending in errata you may save another reader hours of frustration, and of course, you will be helping us provide even higher quality information. Simply e-mail the information to support@wrox.com; your information will be checked and if correct, posted to the errata page for that title, or used in subsequent editions of the book.

To find errata on the web site, go to http://www.wrox.com/, and simply locate the title through our Advanced Search or title list. Click on the Book Errata link, which is below the cover graphic on the book's detail page.

E-Mail Support

If you wish to directly query a problem in the book with an expert who knows the book in detail then e-mail support@wrox.com, with the title of the book and the last four numbers of the ISBN in the subject field of the e-mail. A typical e-mail should include the following things:

- The **title of the book, last four digits of the ISBN**, and **page number** of the problem in the Subject field.
- Your **name, contact information**, and the **problem** in the body of the message.

We *won't* send you junk mail. We need the details to save your time and ours. When you send an e-mail message, it will go through the following chain of support:

- Customer Support – Your message is delivered to our customer support staff who are the first people to read it. They have files on most frequently asked questions and will answer anything general about the book or the web site immediately.
- Editorial – Deeper queries are forwarded to the technical editor responsible for that book. They have experience with the programming language or particular product, and are able to answer detailed technical questions on the subject.
- The Authors – Finally, in the unlikely event that the editor cannot answer your problem, they will forward the request to the author. We do try to protect the authors from any distractions to their writing; however, we are quite happy to forward specific requests to them. All Wrox authors help with the support on their books. They will e-mail the customer and the editor with their response, and again all readers should benefit.

The Wrox Support process can only offer support to issues directly pertinent to the content of our published title. Support for questions that fall outside the scope of normal book support is provided via the community lists of our http://p2p.wrox.com/ forum.

p2p.wrox.com

For author and peer discussion join the P2P mailing lists. Our unique system provides **programmer to programmer**™ contact on mailing lists, forums, and newsgroups, all in addition to our one-to-one e-mail support system. If you post a query to P2P, you can be confident that it is being examined by the many Wrox authors and other industry experts who are present on our mailing lists. At p2p.wrox.com you will find a number of different lists to help you, not only while you read this book, but also as you develop your applications.

To subscribe to a mailing list just follow these steps:

1. Go to http://p2p.wrox.com/
2. Choose the appropriate category from the left menu bar
3. Click on the mailing list you wish to join
4. Follow the instructions to subscribe and fill in your e-mail address and password
5. Reply to the confirmation e-mail you receive
6. Use the subscription manager to join more lists and set your e-mail preferences

Why this System Offers the Best Support

You can choose to join the mailing lists or you can receive them as a weekly digest. If you don't have the time, or facility, to receive the mailing list, then you can search our archives. Junk and spam mails are deleted, and your own e-mail address is protected by the unique Lyris system. Queries about joining or leaving lists, and any other general queries about lists, should be sent to listsupport@wrox.com.

1

Web Services – An Introduction

For quite some time now, web services have been hyped as the next big thing on the front of enterprise business applications. Simply put, web services are applications that interact with each other using web standards.

Web services are made available from a business' web server for users or other interconnected applications over the Internet. In a very short span of time, the industry has seen the emergence of web services for as varied and disparate applications as storage management, customer relationship management, and even specific areas like stock quotes and auctions. The current industry trend is accelerating the creation and availability of these services.

In this chapter, we cover an introduction to web services, their purpose, and a brief history of earlier technologies. We shall also see how the new Web Service technology could bring a radical change to current enterprise applications. Nonetheless, our approach throughout the chapter will be that of pragmatism. The chapter will cover the following points:

- Issues in enterprise and network computing
- Traditional distributed computing and its drawbacks
- The emergence of loosely coupled systems based on Industry Standards
- An introduction to web services
- Two platforms for web services – .NET and J2EE
- The case for open source web services

This chapter is a general introduction to web services so readers with this knowledge already can safely skip to Chapter 2.

Issues in Enterprise and Network Computing

Every major technology goes through a series of revolutions or "waves" with each wave building upon the generation before it, and computing is no exception. Over the decades, enterprise computing has moved away from a monolithic architecture to a distributed architecture. And now, we stand on the threshold of yet another wave, web services.

Distributed Computing

As a broad definition, distributed computing is any computing that involves multiple computers that are remote from each other. Each of these distributed computers has a role to play in a given computing or processing scenario.

In business enterprises, distributed computing generally has meant optimizing the business process methodology at the most efficient places in a network of computers. In the typical transaction using the 3-tier model, user interface processing is done on the user's desktop, business processing is done in an application server, and database access and processing is done in a database server that provides centralized access for many business processes. Typically, this kind of distributed computing has evolved from a client-server architecture into an n-tier distributed architecture.

In network computing, the Distributed Computing Environment is an industry standard for setting up and managing computing and data exchange in a system of distributed computers. It is typically used in a larger network of computing systems that includes geographically distributed processing units. A client-server model is typically used here. In such an environment, application users can use applications and data at remote servers. Application programmers need not be aware of where their programs will run or where the data will be located.

The Distributed Computing Environment makes use of distributed directories so that applications and related data can be located when they are being used. Some implementations provide support access to popular databases such as IBM's CICS, IMS, and DB2 databases.

The Open Software Foundation (OSF), using software technologies contributed by its member companies, developed the distributed computing environment. There has been an emergence of third-party service providers who provide some generalized services that fit into this model.

Component-Based Computing

One of the historical trends that have led us towards web services has its roots in component architecture. Developed over the course of the 1980s, components were originally used in the context of graphical user interfaces – they still form the core of most GUI architectures today. Before components, applications had to be more or less atomic: single entities containing all of the required functionality. Applications would also contain a lot of duplicated code, which would be expensive in both storage and memory.

Instead of compiling all of the code in an application into one entity, component architecture allows the code to be broken down into several independently compiled components with defined interfaces and semantics, which are constructed to be reusable, and communicate via an infrastructure provided by the operating system. This opens up the possibility of making use of components that have been pre-built externally.

To do this only the application needs to know about the component infrastructure calls and component interface. The application is also isolated from how the component infrastructure communicates with the external components.

The component infrastructure doesn't just manage communication between components on the same computer, but, by communicating with component infrastructures on other computers across a network, it manages communication between components on many different computers. This could be used to handle communications between client programs and databases, or between web servers and business applications. Distributed component architectures thus enabled the rapid development of complex, distributed applications. The software, which manages the communication in these systems, is what we call component middleware.

Over the years, three main component architectures have developed: EJBs, CORBA, and COM.

EJBs form part of Sun's J2EE framework which we will discuss later.

The Object Management Group (OMG) developed the first specification of CORBA (the Common Object Request Broker Architecture) in 1991, and Microsoft developed the distributed version of their COM component architecture, DCOM, in 1995. When Sun launched the Java platform, it included its own simple distributed component system, RMI (Remote Method Invocation). However, it still relied on CORBA for heavy-duty distributed systems and it has only come of age in the last couple of years.

Distributed components have one limitation: they can generally only be used across a tightly managed network, such as a corporate intranet. They don't play well in an open, fragile environment such as the public Internet. Web services are, in some ways, a development of distributed components onto the public Internet. In the same way that component middleware allows one piece of software to make use of functionality which is contained in another piece of software on another computer, web services use the Internet's protocols to provide a component infrastructure which does the same across the whole net.

Messaging

Distributed components offer a relatively low-level approach to distributed programming. Message-oriented middleware (MOM) is a new kind of distributed middleware. IBM MQSeries and Microsoft MSMQ are examples of this.

MOM is a much more disconnected architecture even than distributed component architectures, because it allows the disconnection of software not simply across space, but also over time. Message queuing, as the name implies, provides a mechanism for messages from one program to be queued, and then handled by another program at a later time. Messaging systems have been one of the most interesting developments in business middleware of recent times, and also provide some of the inspiration for web services.

In a similar way to components, message queuing systems are generally limited to operating in closed, managed networks, and in a similar way, web services offer the possibility of extending their benefits across the wider world of the open Internet.

B2B and B2C

As B2B and B2C assumed significance, web applications became more and more complex, giving rise to a separate area called middleware. Middleware typically is capable of doing complex jobs to serve consumers better, but the need for utilizing services from other vendors was felt consistently. This too fostered the emergence and growth of web services. B2B – business-to-business – is the exchange of products, services, or information between businesses rather than between businesses and consumers.

In the diagram below our client is talking to our corporate server, who in turn talks to the travel agent. The travel agent then books a hotel room and a hire car before talking to a credit card server to confirm the payment:

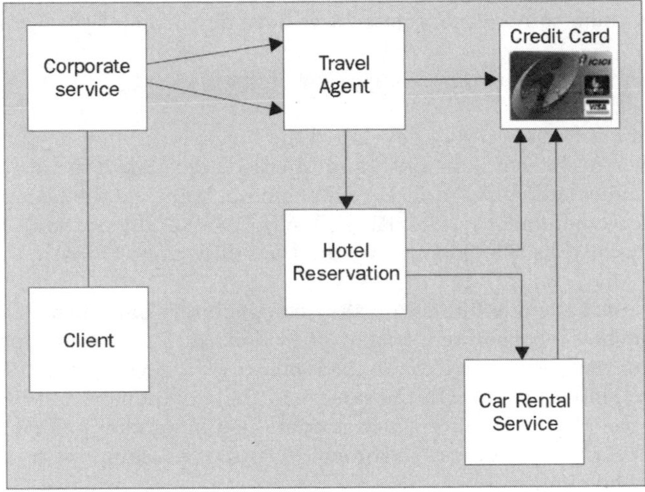

An earlier and much more limited kind of online B2B prior to the Internet was Electronic Data Interchange (EDI), which is still widely used. B2C is the retailing part of e-commerce on the Internet.

As the web services platform matures, we would see this paving the way for data exchange using web services. We will cover this again later in the chapter when we see the applications and advantages of web services.

EAI

EAI (enterprise application integration) is a business computing term for the plans, methods, and tools aimed at modernizing, consolidating, and coordinating the computer applications in an enterprise. Typically, an enterprise has existing legacy applications and databases and wants to continue to use them while adding or migrating to a new set of applications that exploit the Internet, e-commerce, extranet, and other new technologies. EAI may involve developing a new total view of an enterprise's business and its applications, seeing how existing applications fit into the new view, and then devising ways to efficiently reuse what already exists while adding new applications and data.

EAI encompasses methodologies such as distributed, cross-platform program communication using message brokers with CORBA and DCOM, the modification of enterprise resource planning (ERP) to fit new objectives, enterprise-wide content, and data distribution using common databases and data standards implemented with the XML, middleware, message queuing, and other approaches.

Web services also lend themselves to make EAI cheaper, faster, reliable, and effective. Since we are only dealing with the predecessors to web services here, we will come to this again later on in the chapter.

Traditional Distributed Computing

The major drawbacks of traditional distributed computing are:

- It is complex to develop and maintain
- It needs holes in the firewall

We will look at three distributed computing models:

- RMI
- DCOM
- CORBA

RMI

Remote Method Invocation (RMI) is a way in which components on different computers can interact in a distributed network using J2EE. RMI is the Java version of remote procedure calls. However it has the ability to pass one or more objects along with the request. The object can include information that will change the service that is performed in the remote computer. This helps in catching mistakes early in the process and also increases the maintainability of the code at large. In general, RMI is designed to preserve the object model and its advantages across a network:

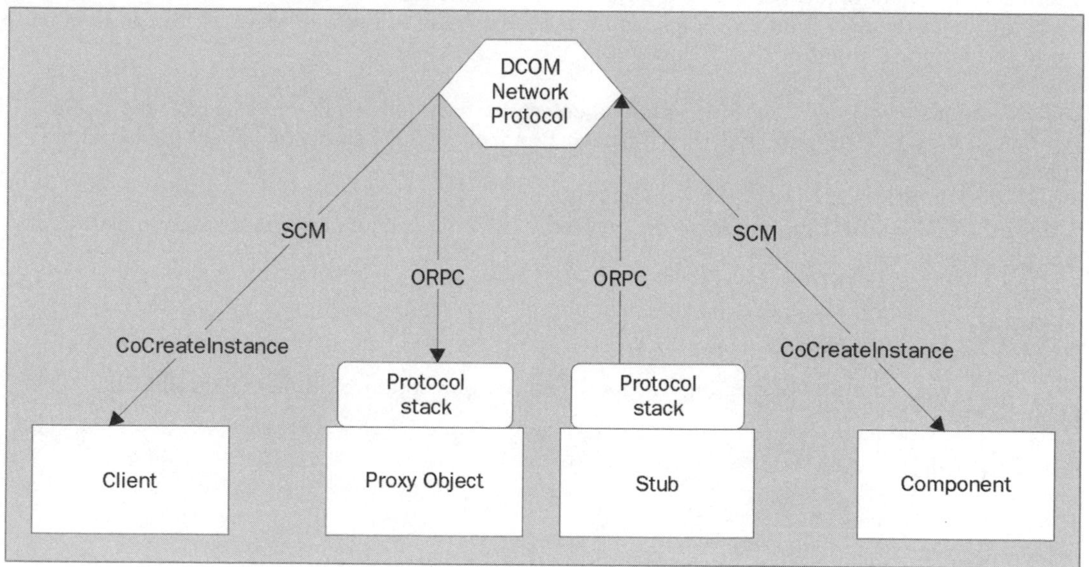

RMI is implemented as three layers:

- A proxy or stub at the client side of the client/server relationship, and a corresponding skeleton at the server end. The stub appears to the calling program to be the program being called for a service.
- A remote reference layer that behaves differently depending on the parameters passed by the calling program. For example, this layer can determine whether the request is to call a single remote service or multiple remote programs as in a multicast.
- A transport connection layer, which sets up and manages the request. A single request travels down through the layers on one computer and up through the layers at the other end.

The drawback of RMI technology is that in the process discussed above, the communication between the client and server is based on a proprietary protocol (JRMP – Java Remote Method Protocol), thereby mandating the use of Java for both client and server development. Thus, it is not easily possible to integrate distributed server components developed in different languages in a single application. The use of proprietary protocol reduces the possibility of interoperability between software components developed using a wide variety of technologies.

DCOM

Distributed Component Object Model (DCOM) is a set of Microsoft concepts and program interfaces in which client program objects can request services from server program objects on other computers in a network. DCOM is based on the COM framework.

Let us consider an example here. We could create a page for a web site that contains a script or program that can be processed on an application server that is not on the network. Using DCOM interfaces, the client object can forward a Remote Procedure Call (RPC) to the application server object, which provides the necessary processing and returns the result to the web server. This can then be sent out in the response object.

DCOM can also work on a network within an enterprise or on other networks besides the public Internet. It uses TCP/IP and Hypertext Transfer Protocol. DCOM comes as part of the Windows operating systems.

RMI and COM/DCOM did not solve the problems of the industry as it wanted an architecture for creating interoperable software.

CORBA

The market wanted a way of creating distributed applications that would meet the following requirements:

- Vendor neutral
- Platform neutral
- Network neutral
- Language neutral

Common Object Request Broker Architecture (CORBA) is an architecture and specification for creating, distributing, and managing distributed program objects in a network. It allows programs at different locations and developed by different vendors to communicate in a network through an interface broker. CORBA was developed by a consortium of vendors through the Object Management Group (OMG), which currently includes over 500 member companies. Both the International Organization for Standardization (ISO) and X/Open have ratified CORBA as the standard architecture for distributed objects. The latest version of CORBA is 3.0:

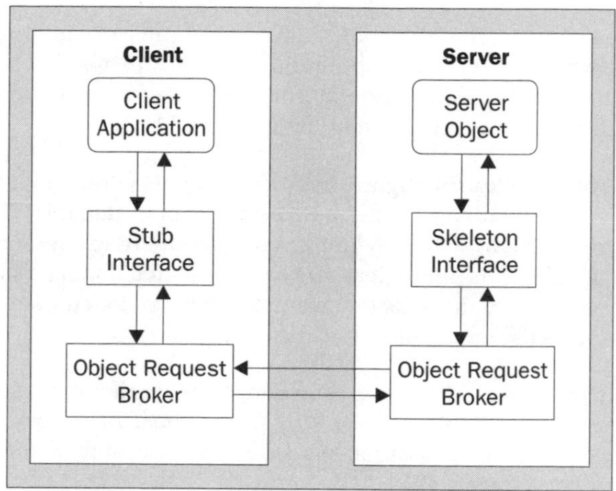

The essential concept in CORBA is the Object Request Broker (ORB). What do we mean by ORB support in a distributed network? It means that a client program can request services from a server program or object without having to understand where the server is located in a distributed network or what the interface to the server program looks like. To make requests or return replies between the ORBs, programs use the General Inter-ORB Protocol (GIOP) and, for the Internet, its Internet Inter-ORB Protocol (IIOP). IIOP maps GIOP requests and replies to the Internet's Transmission Control Protocol (TCP) layer in each computer.

A notable fact here is that CORBA and Microsoft support a gateway approach so that a client object developed with the Component Object Model will be able to communicate with a CORBA server and vice versa.

After these discussions, a natural question that may come to your mind is, have we ultimately attained the "technology maturity"? Unfortunately, the answer is still NO. After so many decades of computing, the industry has not yet achieved the complete maturity and is still evolving. Though CORBA is an excellent architecture for the development of distributed applications, it does not solve all the problems in this area. It has several limitations as listed below:

- CORBA uses IIOP (Internet InterORB Protocol) for communication between client and server. This requires the use of custom marshaling and security code and restricts the interoperability in the long run.
- Use of IIOP may require puncturing firewalls in your organization.
- CORBA implementation is usually complex and may require special skills to design, install, and maintain.

Loosely Coupled Systems

The concept of distributing application logic over a network isn't new. The concept of distributing and integrating application logic over the Web is. Previously, distributed application logic called for a distributed object model such as Microsoft's DCOM, the OMG's CORBA, or Sun's RMI. Using this infrastructure, developers can maintain much of the richness and precision that they're used to with the local programming model, yet still place services on remote systems.

The problem with these systems is that they don't scale to the Internet: their reliance on tightly coupling the consumer of the service to the service itself implies a homogeneous infrastructure, and often means that they are very brittle: if the implementation at one side changes, the other side breaks. For example, if the server application's interfaces change, then the client will break.

Many applications have been built using tightly coupled systems. Ultimately, however, this model won't scale over time. There is no guarantee that the service you want to talk to at the far end of your pipe will have all the infrastructure you want: you may not know what operating system, object model, or programming language it used. This often gives rise to shabby marshaling code and security features and repetition of mundane, redundant tasks that should ideally be taken care of by the operating system. This ultimately led to the emergence of web services.

Web services are loosely coupled – where you can change the implementation at either end of a connection and the application will continue working. This translates to using message-based, asynchronous technology to achieve robustness, and using Web protocols such as HTTP and SMTP, with XML, to achieve universal reach.

Messaging systems wrap up the fundamental units of communication into self-describing packages (called messages) that they put onto the network wire. The key difference between a messaging system and a distributed object system is how much knowledge of the recipient's infrastructure the sender requires. With a distributed object system, the sender makes many assumptions about the recipient – about how the application will be activated and torn down, what its interfaces are called, and so on.

Messaging systems, on the other hand, form the contract at the wire format level. The only assumption the sender makes is that the recipient will be able to understand the message being sent. The sender makes no assumptions about what will happen once the message is received, nor does it make any assumptions about what might happen between the sender and the receiver.

The advantages to creating the contract at the wire format level are pretty obvious. For example, it enables the recipient to change at any time without breaking the sender as long as it can still understand the same messages. The receiver is free to upgrade and improve without breaking any current applications. Further, the sender doesn't require any special software to be able to talk with the receiver: as long as it can emit properly formed messages, the receiver can respond.

RPC

RPC is a protocol that one program can use to request a service from a program located in another computer in a network without having to understand network details. RPC also uses the client/server model. Like a regular local procedure call, an RPC is a synchronous operation requiring the requesting program to be suspended until the results of the remote procedure are returned. However, the use of lightweight processes or threads that share the same address space allows multiple RPCs to be performed concurrently.

When program statements that use RPC are compiled into an executable program, a stub is included in the compiled code that acts as the representative of the remote procedure code. When the program is run and the procedure call is issued, the stub receives the request and forwards it to a client runtime program in the local computer. The client runtime program has the knowledge of how to address the remote computer and server application and sends the message across the network that requests the remote procedure. Similarly, the server includes a runtime program and stub that interface with the remote procedure itself. Results are returned the same way.

The RPC implementations are based on four basic tenets:

- Interface contract
- Binary standard
- Wire protocol
- Interoperability

Web Services

Gartner defines web services as "loosely coupled software components that interact with one another dynamically via standard Internet technologies". Forrester research defines web services as "automated connections between people, systems, and applications that expose elements of business functionality as a software service and create new business value".

Though the way different organizations define a web service differs, it is essentially a software component that interacts with other discrete software components using ubiquitous protocols. The remote clients and applications access web services via ever-present web protocols using the XML-based SOAP protocol. Due to the use of XML and SOAP, the access to the service becomes independent of its implementation. Thus, a web service offers the benefits of both component architecture and the web.

Like component development web services display the following two characteristics:

- Optional registration with a lookup service
- A public interface for the client to invoke the service

Each web service can register itself with a central repository so that clients can look up the registry for a desired service. Once a service is located, the client obtains a reference to the service. The client now uses the service by invoking various methods implemented in the service with the help of a published public interface. Thus, each service must publish its interface for clients to use:

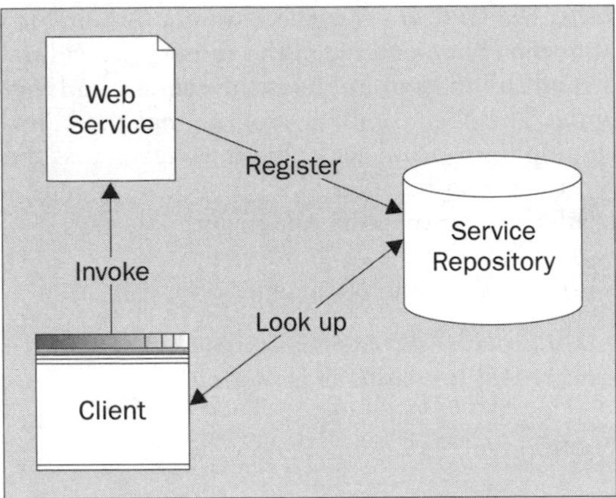

In addition, web services also possess the following characteristics:

- Use standard web protocols for communication, such as HTTP.
- Accessible over the web.
- Support loose coupling between uncoupled distributed systems so that the systems running on different platforms and based on different technologies can cooperate with each other to form a distributed system. A lightweight platform-, network-, and language-neutral protocol will allow the loose coupling between the systems.

The messages delivered by a web service are encoded using XML and the public interfaces are also described in XML, which provides a platform-neutral data transport. Thus, XML-enabled web services can theoretically interoperate with other XML-enabled web services provided the two services agree on a common protocol for communication. The protocols used by web services for communication are being standardized and we will discuss this in the following chapters. An essential requirement for a web service is that it should be easily accessible over the Web and thus allow the loose coupling between the distributed applications.

There are two main dialects of web services, SOAP and XML-RPC. Although both can perform RPC, SOAP is object-oriented and stateful while XML-RPC is procedural and stateless. This means that a SOAP Web Service can consist of several objects, and each of these objects handles RPC calls for that user, allowing the object to store information about the user between requests to the service. An XML-RPC service, on the other hand, handles all requests in isolation, and doesn't store information between requests. An example of an XML-RPC application would be a read-only Web Service interface to a proprietary database. Since no transactions are needed in this application, the limitations of XML-RPC are irrelevant.

SOAP might be a better choice for distributing application logic across several machines. It is likely that each SOAP message would need to maintain the application's state to know which task to perform next. Large companies like Microsoft and IBM are very interested in making SOAP the standard Web Service protocol, but XML-RPC has been adopted by a few languages recently, such as PHP and Perl. Another advantage is that the XML-RPC specification is complete, whereas the SOAP equivalent isn't. To try and avoid problems in the future, work is being done right now to make these protocols interoperate seamlessly.

UDDI

UDDI (Universal Description, Discovery, and Integration) is an XML-based registry for businesses worldwide to list themselves on the Internet. Its ultimate goal is to streamline online transactions by enabling companies to find one another on the Web and make their systems interoperable for e-commerce. UDDI is often compared to a telephone book's white, yellow, and green pages. The project allows businesses to list themselves by name, product, location, or the web services they offer. The service repository in the diagram opposite is a UDDI repository.

Microsoft, IBM, and Ariba spearheaded UDDI. The project now includes 130 companies, including some of the biggest names in the corporate world. While the group does not refer to itself as a standards body, it does offer a framework for web services integration. The UDDI specification utilizes World Wide Web Consortium (W3C) and Internet Engineering Task Force (IETF) standards such as XML, HTTP, and Domain Name System (DNS) protocols. It has also adopted early versions of the proposed Simple Object Access Protocol (SOAP) messaging guidelines for cross-platform programming.

In the next chapter we will see each of these web service components in detail and also how they fit into the broader picture of web services architecture.

WSDL

The Web Services Description Language (WSDL) is an XML-based language used to describe the services a business offers and to provide a way for individuals and other businesses to access those services electronically. WSDL is the cornerstone of the UDDI initiative spearheaded by Microsoft, IBM, and Ariba. The web service client uses WSDL to find a method to invoke on the target web service.

WSDL is derived from SOAP and IBM's Network Accessible Service Specification Language (NASSL). WSDL replaces both NASSL and SOAP as the means of expressing business services in the UDDI registry.

SOAP

Simple Object Access Protocol (SOAP) is a set of rules for a program running in one kind of operating system to communicate with a program in the same or another kind of an operating system by using the Hypertext Transfer Protocol and XML as the mechanisms for information exchange. Since Web protocols are installed and available for use by all major operating system platforms, HTTP and XML provide a handy solution to the problem of how programs running under different operating systems in a network can communicate with each other. SOAP specifies exactly how to encode an HTTP header and an XML file so that a program in one computer can call a program in another computer and pass it information. It also specifies how the called program can return a response.

SOAP was developed by Microsoft, DevelopMentor, and Userland Software and has been proposed as a standard interface to the Internet Engineering Task Force (IETF). It is somewhat similar to the Internet Inter-ORB Protocol (IIOP) and RMI.

An advantage of SOAP is that program calls are much more likely to get through firewall servers that screen out requests other than those for known applications through the designated port mechanism. Since HTTP requests are usually allowed through firewalls, programs using SOAP to communicate can be sure that they can communicate with programs anywhere.

XML-RPC

XML-RPC is a RPC protocol based on XML. It is a specification and a set of implementations that allow software running on disparate operating systems, running in different environments, to make procedure calls over the Internet.

It leads to remote procedure calling using HTTP POST as the transport and XML as the encoding. XML-RPC is designed to be as simple as possible, while allowing complex data structures to be transmitted, processed, and returned. A procedure executes on the server and the value it returns is also formatted in XML. The procedure parameters can be scalars, numbers, strings, dates as well as complex record and list structures.

XML-RPC is based on the following goals and strategies:

- **Firewalls**
  The goal of this protocol is to lay a compatible foundation across different environments, no new power is provided beyond the capabilities of the CGI interface. Firewall software can watch for POSTs whose `Content-Type` is `text/xml`.

- **Discoverability**
  XML-RPC is a clean, extensible format that's very simple.

- **Easy to implement**
  XML-RPC is an easy to implement protocol that could quickly be adapted to run in other environments or on other operating systems.

Benefits of Web Services

Let's now look in depth at the benefits of web services.

Interoperability

One major benefit that is described so far is interoperability. You could be a manufacturer, a service provider, an auctioneer, an insurance company, or simply a health care center. If you need to share business documents and allow others to access services offered by you, you need interoperability.

For example, if you run a health care center that would like to share patient's data with other health care centers, you may need XML for data exchange. You may allow the collaborating partners to search through your database for a patient's history or the case studies of patients you might have successfully treated for a particular disease. In this case, you can expose some functionality of your application with a small modification in your application. This will make your application accessible to other applications developed using an altogether different technology.

Integration

Integration is one of the main benefits of web services. Web services can help to integrate two separate applications into a single composite application. In a real-world scenario, if an organization had a wide variety of applications or custom software across various departments, it was impossible to exchange data between them. After a lot of investment in the development of old applications it was a difficult task to make them share data or create a standard function from these applications.

With web services it is possible to expose the functionality and data of each existing application as a web service. Then you could create a composite application that uses this collection of web services to enable interoperability between these applications. All this is made possible due to the use of SOAP for communication between components. SOAP, as it is XML-based, is easily adapted in the integration of various services.

Efficiency of Implementation

Web services are very efficient to implement since they support interoperability. By making applications interoperate between each other, we need not invest into a totally new system for our organization. We just have to re-develop the existing applications and make them web service-enabled. Web services are also an efficient way to expose legacy code to provide a new service to external consumers.

Code Recycling

Web services are made up of reusable components, so, if our existing applications are component-based, the migration to web services is easier.

Modularity

Web services also promote modularity. They help to assemble enterprise applications by consuming external web services, change implementations without affecting the interface and promote a plug-and-play architecture.

Architecture

Here is the final architecture of a web service:

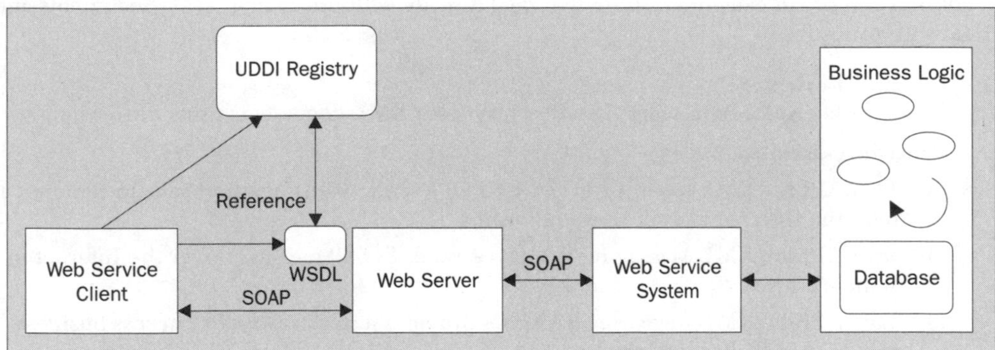

Why Develop Web Services?

Enterprise applications are typically characterized by aggregations. Although aggregation can take place without a Web Service, it's far easier and profitable to use a Web Service for this purpose.

Users can access some web services through a peer-to-peer arrangement rather than by going to a central server. Some services can communicate with other services and a class of software known as middleware generally enables this exchange of procedures and data. Services previously possible only with the older standardized service known as Electronic Data Interchange (EDI), increasingly are likely to become web services.

Two Evolving Platforms for Web Services

We will now discuss two major platforms for web services:

- J2EE
- .NET

J2EE

Web services depend on the ability of enterprises using different computing platforms to communicate with each other. This requirement makes the Java platform, which makes code portable, a good choice for developing web services. This choice is even more attractive as the new Java APIs for XML become available, making it easier and easier to use XML from the Java programming language. These APIs are summarized later in this introduction and explained in detail in the tutorials for each API.

In addition to data portability and code portability, web services need to be scalable, secure, and efficient, especially as they grow. J2EE meets such needs quite successfully. It facilitates the really hard part of developing web services, which is programming the infrastructure. This infrastructure includes features such as security, distributed transaction management, and connection pool management, all of which are essential for industrial strength web services. And because components are reusable, development time is substantially reduced.

Because XML and the Java platform work so well together, they have come to play a large role in web services. In fact, the advantages offered by the Java APIs for XML and the J2EE platform make them the ideal combination for deploying web services.

The Java APIs for XML let you write your web applications entirely in the Java programming language. They fall into two broad categories: those that deal directly with processing XML documents and those that deal with procedures:

- **Document-oriented**
  Java API for XML Processing (JAXP) – processes XML documents using various parsers
- **Procedure-oriented**
  - Java API for XML-based RPC (JAX-RPC) – sends SOAP method calls to remote parties over the Internet and receives the results
  - Java API for XML Messaging (JAXM) – sends SOAP messages over the Internet in a standard way
  - Java API for XML Registries (JAXR) – provides a standard way to access business registries and share information

Perhaps the most important feature of the Java APIs for XML is that they all support industry standards, thus ensuring interoperability.

Another feature of the Java APIs for XML is that they allow a great deal of flexibility. Users have flexibility in how they use the APIs. For example, JAXP code can use various tools for processing an XML document, and JAXM code can use various messaging protocols on top of SOAP.

Implementers have flexibility as well. The Java APIs for XML define strict compatibility requirements to ensure that all implementations deliver the standard functionality, but they also give developers a great deal of freedom to provide implementations tailored to specific uses. Sun Open Net Environment (Sun ONE) is a key constituent of J2EE web services.

.NET

Web services play a major role in the .NET application architecture. In the .NET vision, an application is constructed using multiple web services that work together to provide data and services for the application.

The definition of web services in the .NET platform is concerned with the external appearance of the web services. After all, we've said that as long as a client application can create and consume the appropriate messages, it doesn't need to know anything about the internals of the web services it uses. Developers of web services will obviously care about the internal structure as well.

The .NET framework also provides a collection of classes and tools to aid in development and consumption of XML web services applications. XML web services are built on standards such as SOAP, XML, and WSDL.

For example, the WSDL tool included with the .NET Framework SDK can query an XML web service published on the web, parse its WSDL description, and produce .NET binary code that your application can use to become a client of the XML web service. The sourcecode can create classes derived from classes in the class library that handle all the underlying communication using SOAP and XML parsing. Although you can use the class library to consume XML web services directly, the WSDL tool and the other tools contained in the SDK facilitate your development efforts with the .NET framework.

If you develop and publish your own XML web service, the .NET Framework provides a set of classes that conform to all the underlying communication standards, such as SOAP, WSDL, and XML. Using those classes enables you to focus on the logic of your service, without concerning yourself with the communications infrastructure required by distributed software development.

Microsoft's .NET platform provides an easy interface for creating web services using any of the .NET languages. Visual Studio.NET provides a new project type for creating a web service. When you use this project type, the wizard creates all the files required for creating and deploying web services and you simply need to define and implement the desired component interface. All the XML, SOAP, and WSDL code is automatically generated for you. This project option is available for .NET family languages – Visual Basic.NET, C#, and ASP.NET

Thus, developers can create a web service using their favorite language without the need to learn XML, SOAP, WSDL, or a new component development language. The ATL web service uses VC++ and creates an ISAPI and web application DLLs. As these DLLs are developed in VC++, they provide better performance and scalability as compared to the web services created using other .NET languages.

Comparison

Although we are moving into the open source arena for web services starting with the next section, we will look briefly at how the two technologies handle them before moving on.

Web services are bring in their wake four basic challenges:

- Service description
- Service implementation
- Service publishing, discovery, and binding
- Service invocation and execution

Service Description

J2EE	.NET
J2EE-enabled web services exchange information with interested parties using WSDL to come to an agreement on the proper format for each transferred XML document. Third parties who want to transact business with a J2EE-enabled Web Service company can look up information about the company's web services in a registry.	As with a J2EE Web Service, a .NET Web Service supports the WSDL 1.1 specification and uses a WSDL document to describe itself. In this case, however, an XML namespace is used within a WSDL document to uniquely identify the Web Service's endpoints. .NET provides a client-side component that lets an application invoke Web Service operations described by a WSDL document and a server-side component that maps Web Service operations to COM-object method calls as described by a WSDL and a web services Meta Language (WSML) file. This file is needed for Microsoft's implementation of SOAP.

Service Implementation

J2EE	.NET
Existing Java classes and applications can be wrapped using the Java API for XML-based RPC (JAX-RPC) and exposed as web services. JAX-RPC uses XML to make remote procedure calls (RPC) and exposes an API for marshaling (packing parameters and return values to be distributed) and un-marshaling arguments and for transmitting and receiving procedure calls. With J2EE, business services written as Enterprise JavaBeans are wrapped and exposed as web services. The resulting wrapper is a SOAP-enabled Web Service that conforms to a WSDL interface based on the original EJB's methods. The J2EE web services architecture is a set of XML-based frameworks, providing infrastructures that allow companies to integrate business-service logic that was previously exposed as proprietary interfaces. Currently, J2EE supports web services via the Java API for XML Parsing (JAXP). This API allows developers to perform any Web Service operation by manually parsing XML documents.	.NET applications are no longer directly executed in native machine code. All programs are compiled to an intermediate binary code called the Microsoft Intermediate Language (MSIL). This portable, binary code is then compiled to native code using a Just In Time compiler (JIT) at run time and run in a virtual machine called the Common Language Runtime (CLR). This is similar to the way that Java works, except .NET encompasses several languages; each is translated to MSIL, which is executed in the CLR using the JIT. With the .NET platform, Microsoft will provide several languages based on the Common Language Infrastructure (CLI), such as Managed C++, JScript, VB.NET, and C#.

Service Publishing, Discovery, and Binding

J2EE	.NET
Sun Microsystems is positioning its Java API for XML Registries (JAXR) as a single general-purpose API for interoperating with multiple registry types. JAXR allows its clients to access the web services provided by a web services implementer exposing web services built upon an implementation of the JAXR specification. There are three types of JAXR providers: The **JAXR Pluggable Provider**, which implements features of the JAXR specification that are independent of any specific registry type. The **Registry-specific JAXR Provider**, which implements the JAXR specification in a registry-specific manner. The **JAXR Bridge Provider**, which is not specific to any particular registry. It serves as a bridge to a class of registries such as ebXML or UDDI.	At first, Microsoft facilitated the discovery of web services with DISCO in the form of a discovery (DISCO) file. A published DISCO file is an XML document that contains links to other resources that describe the Web Service. Since the widespread adoption of UDDI, however, Microsoft has supported it to maximize interoperability between solutions in what is, after all, a set of specifications for interoperability. In addition to providing a .NET UDDI server, the UDDI SDK provides support for Visual Studio .NET and depends on the .NET framework. Products such as Microsoft Office XP offer support for service discovery through UDDI.

Service Invocation and Execution

J2EE	.NET
J2EE uses the Java API for XML-based RPC (JAX-RPC) to send SOAP method calls to remote parties and receive the results. JAX-RPC enables Java developers to build web services incorporating XML based RPC functionality according to the SOAP 1.1 specification. Once a JAX-RPC service has been defined and implemented, the service is deployed on a server-side JAX-RPC runtime system. The deployment step depends on the type of component that has been used to implement the JAX-RPC service. For example, an EJB based service is deployed in an EJB container. During the deployment of a JAX-RPC service, the deployment tool configures one or more protocol bindings for this JAX-RPC service. A binding ties an abstract service definition to a specific XML-based protocol and transport. An example of a binding is SOAP 1.1 over HTTP. A Web Service client uses a JAX-RPC service by invoking remote methods on a service port described by a WSDL document. Sun Open Net Environment (Sun ONE) is Sun's standards-based software vision, architecture, platform, and expertise for building and deploying Services on Demand. It provides a highly scalable and robust foundation for traditional software applications as well as current Web-based applications, while laying the foundation for the next-generation distributed computing models such as web services.	In Microsoft's .NET framework, interested parties can gain access to a Web Service by implementing a Web Service listener. To implement this, a system needs to understand SOAP messages, generate SOAP responses, provide a WSDL contract for the Web Service, and advertise the Service via UDDI. .NET developers creating SOAP-based Web Service listeners and consumers currently have three choices: Use the built-in .NET SOAP message classes. Construct a Web Service listener manually, using MSXML, ASP, or ISAPI, and so on. Use the Microsoft SOAP Toolkit version 2 to build a Web Service listener that connects to a business facade, implemented using COM. The Microsoft SOAP Toolkit 2.0 offers a client-side component that lets an application invoke Web Service operations described by a WSDL document.

The Case for Open Source Web Services

Having seen the crux of web services and the offerings from industry giants, we have moved into the world of open source. This is the place where we see why, in spite of all these, open source is still a good choice to consider while developing web services.

The basic idea behind open source is very simple: When programmers can read, redistribute, and modify the sourcecode for a piece of software, the software evolves. People improve it, people adapt it, people fix bugs. And this can happen at a speed that, if one is used to the slow pace of conventional software development, seems astonishing.

This rapid evolutionary process produces better software than the traditional closed model, in which only a very few programmers can see the source and everybody else must blindly use an opaque block of bits.

Open source software is an idea whose time has finally come. For twenty years it has been building momentum in the technical cultures that built the Internet and the World Wide Web. Now it's breaking out into the commercial world, and that's changing all the rules. This makes a solid case for exploiting the features, facilities, and advantages that open source software has to offer.

Let's revisit the main advantages of web services: interoperability, scalability, availability, and manageability. The savings in up-front costs, a high level of reliability, and the excellent support networks enhance the probability that our web services will fulfil these commitments.

In Java technology, the Apache Software Foundation provides support for the Apache community of open source software projects. The Apache projects are characterized by a collaborative, consensus based development process, an open and pragmatic software license, and a desire to create high quality software that leads the way in its field. Axis is an open-source implementation of the SOAP v1.1 and SOAP Messages with Attachments specifications in Java.

Axis can be used as a client library to invoke SOAP services available elsewhere or as a server-side tool to implement SOAP accessible services. As a client library it provides an API for invoking SOAP RPC services as well as an API for sending and receiving SOAP messages. As a mechanism to write new RPC accessible services or message accessible services, it expects to be hosted by a servlet container (such as Apache Tomcat, for example).

It does have some limitations in the current incarnation, but they should be removed soon enough, considering the commitment and the maturity of the Apache project. We will look at Axis in Chapter 4.

Similarly, kSOAP is an SOAP API suitable for the J2ME.

SOAP::Lite (covered in Chapter 6) for Perl is a collection of Perl modules that provides a simple and lightweight interface to SOAP both on the client and the server side. PHP support for web services is available from the PHP Extension and Application Repository for SOAP and is covered in Chapter 8.

As we shall see later in the book, exotic languages like Python and Ruby (Chapters 7 and 10 respectively) also have extensive support for web services. It is possible to develop and consume web services using these technologies as well. Which language to choose is a choice, yours for the taking.

Summary

Web services, while they may feel like a completely new way of doing things, have a certain feeling of inevitability about them – a sense that they are an evolution not a revolution.

Web services in open source offer tremendous opportunities for personal and professional growth. They also come cheap and could prove cost effective in the long run, especially with the staggering economy in mind. The reason why open source web services have not yet fully developed is because they lack the marketing strategies used by industry giants, huge investments made by software corporations, and active recommendation by solution providers. Open source web services will definitely come of age once solution architects start actively considering them a part of their architecture strategies and we have already started witnessing developments towards that end.

2

Web Services Architecture

We saw in Chapter 1 that several technologies are in use for the development of distributed applications. The major drawback of all these technologies is interoperability with each other. In a B2B scenario, interoperability is the most essential part of successful e-commerce. The interoperability requirement demands a lot of agreement and creation of shared contexts for reliable and effective business transactions. This turns out to be a lot of overhead to implement successful B2B e-commerce.

Also, the current trend is to move away from tightly coupled monolithic applications to loosely coupled multi-platform service-based architecture. The new service-based architecture uses loosely coupled components that may be dynamically discovered and bound to other components at real time. The next generation of software will be service-oriented. The applications will be composed of services that are discovered and marshaled dynamically at run-time. The run-time integration of these services demands a standard protocol for communication between various services.

The Web Services architecture defines standard ways of creating dynamic and loosely coupled service-oriented systems. A service itself may be implemented using any of the well-known technologies such as DCOM, EJB, and so on. The architecture defines a standard for coupling these incompatible services together. It also addresses the various supplementary requirements of a distributed application such as security and transactions.

In this chapter, you will become familiar with the Web Service architecture, its purpose, a brief history of the earlier architectures, and how the new Web Service architecture technologies are going to bring a radical change to the Internet. This chapter will cover the following essential points:

- Web Services architecture
- Technologies used for creation of Web Services
- Real-world case studies

New Service-Oriented Architecture

Service-oriented architecture provides a standard programming model that permits separately developed software components to be published, discovered, and invoked by one another. These components can reside in the same or different computer networks. They can interact with each other in a distributed architecture over the Internet or any other third-party extranet regardless of their network location.

The basic difference between other service-oriented architecture and the Web Service architecture lies in the underlying technologies involved in the development process. Other service-oriented architectures use some of the proprietary technologies, which restrict the components' use across some platforms and their interoperability with other software. In Web Service architecture, the technologies involved make a service accessible across any platform and can inter-communicate with any service components implemented in any language through a standard interface.

The Web Services architecture utilizes XML to build various messaging protocols. SOAP, WSDL, and UDDI are most popular amongst many other evolving standards. These technologies provide an additional layer between applications/modules and other popular protocols, giving rise to integration. XML-based messaging standards provide the required flexibility to build new standards to fulfil additional requirements that might arise as Web Services continue to evolve.

The diagram below makes this concept clearer:

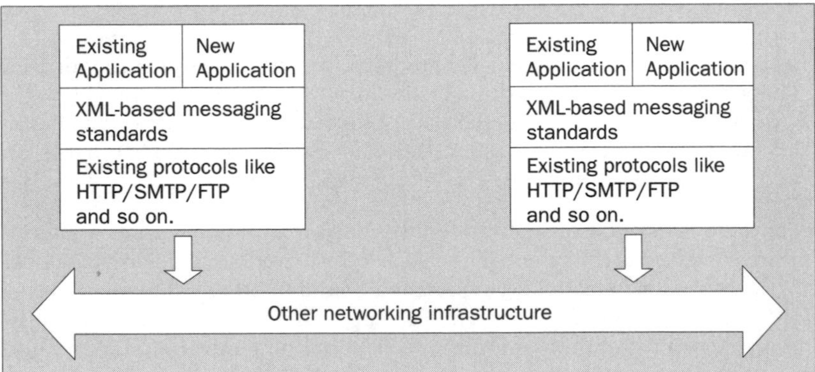

We shall now see how technologies supporting Web Services fit in to this service architecture. The figure given opposite provides us with a better picture of the Web Service architecture:

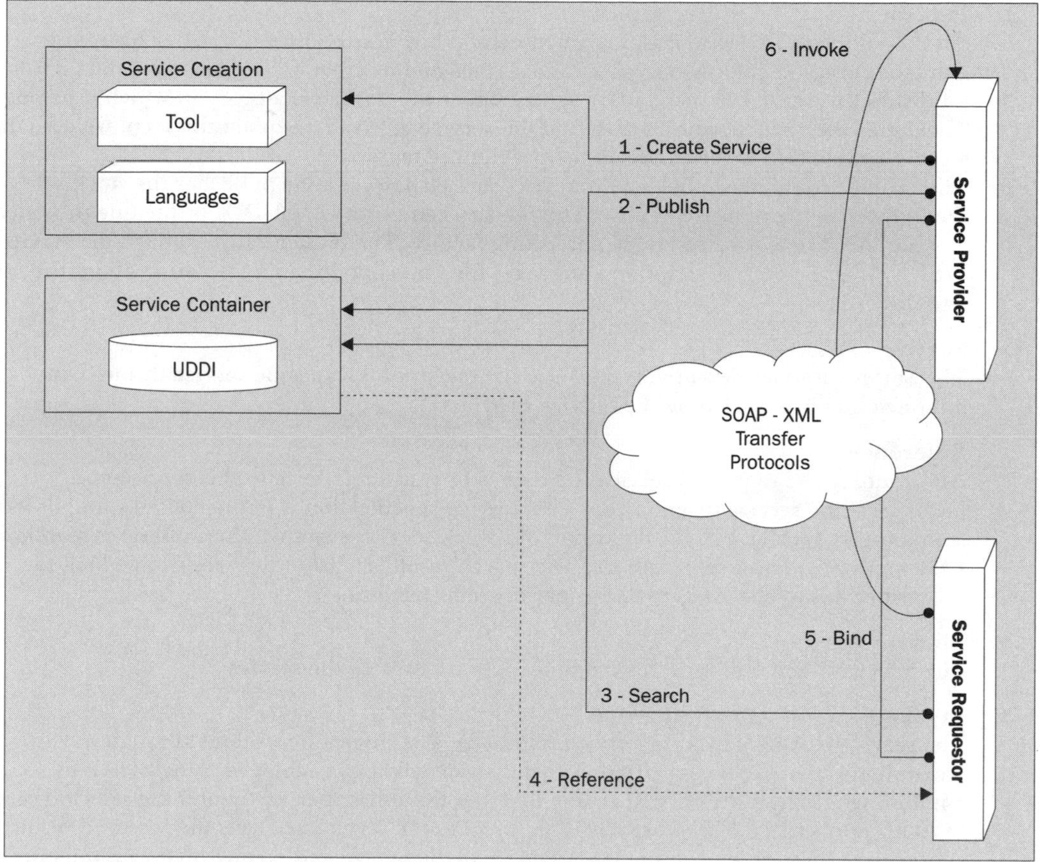

The Web Service architecture consists of three basic components:

- Service
- Service Requestor
- Service Container

Various service creation tools and languages support the Service component. The Service Requestor can be implemented in any language and on any platform. Similarly, the Service Container or Provider can be implemented as a server that provides information about the published service.

The Web Service architecture may be explained with the help of a description of events that take place in a typical Web Service. These are described below:

- **Create Service**
  A service is created as per the business requirements, using appropriate tools and languages that support Web Services. For a practical example, we take Stock Quote service as our Web Service. A broker may develop or have an existing component that provides stock quotes to its subscribers. This component can be developed in any languages such as C++, VB, Java, Perl, PHP, Python, and so on.

- **Publish**
  After creating this service, it is published on to a business registry (UDDI). This registry contains complete information about the service and its creator. The Service Container publishes this service in the UDDI registry under the business category in which it belongs. This helps the service requestors to find the service easily. To explain this step, we take the same example that we discussed in the previous paragraph.
  The broker would like to have a broader customer base, so s/he publishes the stock service in the registry in the money category. The registry can be an IBM UDDI or the one provided by any organizations, which provide publishing facility. The broker has to publish the service as a WSDL (Web Service Description Language) file that contains all information about the service and the broker.

- **Search**
  The Service Requestor searches this business registry for a specific service through an interface that is provided by the Service Provider.

- **Reference**
  After finding the requested service the requestor gets a reference to this service and introspects the service specification. This service specification is implemented using different technologies such as WSDL. Following our stock service example, the subscriber searches the IBM registry to find a stock service. The search result is a list of services from which the subscriber has to choose a service as per his requirements.

- **Bind**
  The Service Requestor uses this reference to bind itself to the service.

- **Invoke**
  The service is invoked via the service reference. The invocation is done through the technologies that are standardized. The data transmission is achieved using SOAP by combining XML and HTTP. Reaching this step the subscriber has bound the selected service in to his application. The subscriber then invokes the service and gets the required result. The subscriber's application can be developed in any language and on any platform; the only requirement is the implementation of SOAP for invocation.

The interesting part of Web Service architecture is that the technologies are used for data transmission and communication between applications. Since these technologies are standardized and accepted in the industry, the developers can develop their business logic and apply it in any language and on any platform keeping the standards in mind.

In the following sections, you will study different technologies that are used in the creation of Web Services.

XML

XML stands for e**X**tensible **M**arkup **L**anguage. It is text based. The difference between HTML and XML is that HTML tags are for presentation of data, while XML tags are for description of data. For example, an XML document describes data such as name of the employee, gender, and age. The data is described by creating human-understandable tags. These tags are helpful to create well-formed documents. XML is very effective in exchanging structured data between applications since XML documents have a definite structure to qualify as well-formed documents.

XML is defined by the World Wide Web Consortium (W3C) and is a subset of Standard Generalized Markup Language (SGML). The standardization by W3C guarantees vendor independence and portability across a wide variety of applications.

An element in XML contains a start tag, element content, and an end tag; for example, `<language>perl</language>`. An element could have other elements as its content. The element that contains the whole document is called the root element. An element with no content is called an empty element. The tags of elements are nested and cannot overlap. Elements can have attributes associated with them that can be declared by a pair of name and value. In the example below, `name` is an attribute of the `Employee` element:

```
<Employee name="John">
  <department>systems</department>
  <age>25</age>
</Employee>
```

The ambiguity of element names in XML is resolved by namespaces as it is resolved by scope in programming languages. A namespace identifier is added to turn a local name into a qualified name; for example `SavingAccount:balance`. This clearly makes it different from `Inventory:balance`. XML provides a mechanism for namespace declaration with the help of an attribute called `xmlns`. This declaration enables association of identifiers with URIs.

While using XML for building various global messaging standards, namespaces come in handy to ensure name resolution and to avoid collision. We shall soon see an example of this.

XML Schemas were brought in the picture to address some weaknesses DTD offered. Schemas provide a mechanism to convey the rules to the machine. They also provide meaning to the data by specifying type information and validation. It includes built-in primitive data types and provides a mechanism to derive user-defined data types. This ensures integrity as the receiver has the meaning of data properly conveyed. For example:

```
<count type="xsd:integer">25</count>
```

A complete discussion on XML is highly recommended for an in-depth understanding of the same. *Beginning XML 2nd Edition* from *Wrox Press (ISBN 1-861005-59-8)* is a good place to start.

Here is a sample XML document:

```
<?xml version='1.0' encoding='UTF-8'?>

<SOAP-ENV:Envelope xmlns:SOAP-ENV="http://schemas.xmlsoap.org/soap/envelope/"
      xmlns:xsi="http://www.w3.org/1999/XMLSchema-instance"
      xmlns:xsd="http://www.w3.org/1999/XMLSchema">
      <SOAP-ENV:Body>
             <ns1:getStockPrice xmlns:ns1="urn:stockquote-service"
       SOAP-ENV:encodingStyle="http://schemas.xmlsoap.org/soap/encoding/">
          <symbol xsi:type="xsd:string">IBM</symbol>
          </ns1:getStockPrice>
      </SOAP-ENV:Body>
</SOAP-ENV:Envelope>
```

As we have seen earlier, Web Services facilitate data exchange between vast varieties of legacy applications using ubiquitous protocols. Web Services use XML as a means of data exchange. For effective data exchange, the involved parties must agree on a common format. This is achieved by using shared DTDs (Document Type Definitions) and XML-Schemas. XML documents are delivered using standard HTTP protocol. These technologies help in creating complex searches that can span multiple platforms.

XML is just a data definition language and cannot solely provide solutions to all problems like integration of existing or newly developed applications. We need standards to allow seamless integration between businesses. Organizations and standard bodies such as RosettaNet, CIDX, and OASIS are creating standards for vertical industries so that different companies within these industry segments can easily collaborate to ease B2B integration.

XML-RPC

A distributed application like Web Services needs to invoke methods on a remote machine. This invoked method may be implemented in a different language than the calling method. It could also be running on a totally different platform than the client machine. We need standards for calling such remote methods. An invoked method may require arguments and may return a result to the caller.

We need a standard way to marshal and un-marshal such parameters and return types. Such standardization will help in achieving cross-platform integration. One way of creating such a standard is to define a format for XML documents for describing procedure calls, parameters, and return types. XML-RPC is about defining such a standard.

The XML-RPC standard allows cross-programming language integration. It also allows interoperability between different operating systems allowing various applications to seamlessly integrate into a unified distributed application. For example, it is possible for a client written in Perl to talk to a server written in C++ or Java. Programs using XML-RPC can also be developed in any language including the popular C. The translation of XML code to any of these languages is transparent to the application developer. Thus, it is easy to write XML-RPC code, as one has to simply follow the defined standard for calling and receiving the remote procedure. XML may be used for transporting data or information about the method invocations.

The XML-RPC standards use HTTP for transport. The conversation consists of requests and response packets both coded in XML. As of today, there is no support for transactions and encryption of data.

XML-RPC Architecture

In a typical client-server system, a client calls a remote procedure in a program running on a remote machine. Dave Winer, of Frontier and Userland fame, extended the concept of RPC with XML and HTTP. In XML-RPC, RPC requests are encoded in an XML document. The document itself is sent to the server over HTTP. At the server end, the server decodes the document, executes the requested procedure, packages the result, if any, in an XML document and sends it back to the client over HTTP. The client decodes the result and continues execution.

The diagram opposite shows a typical client-server conversation that uses XML-RPC:

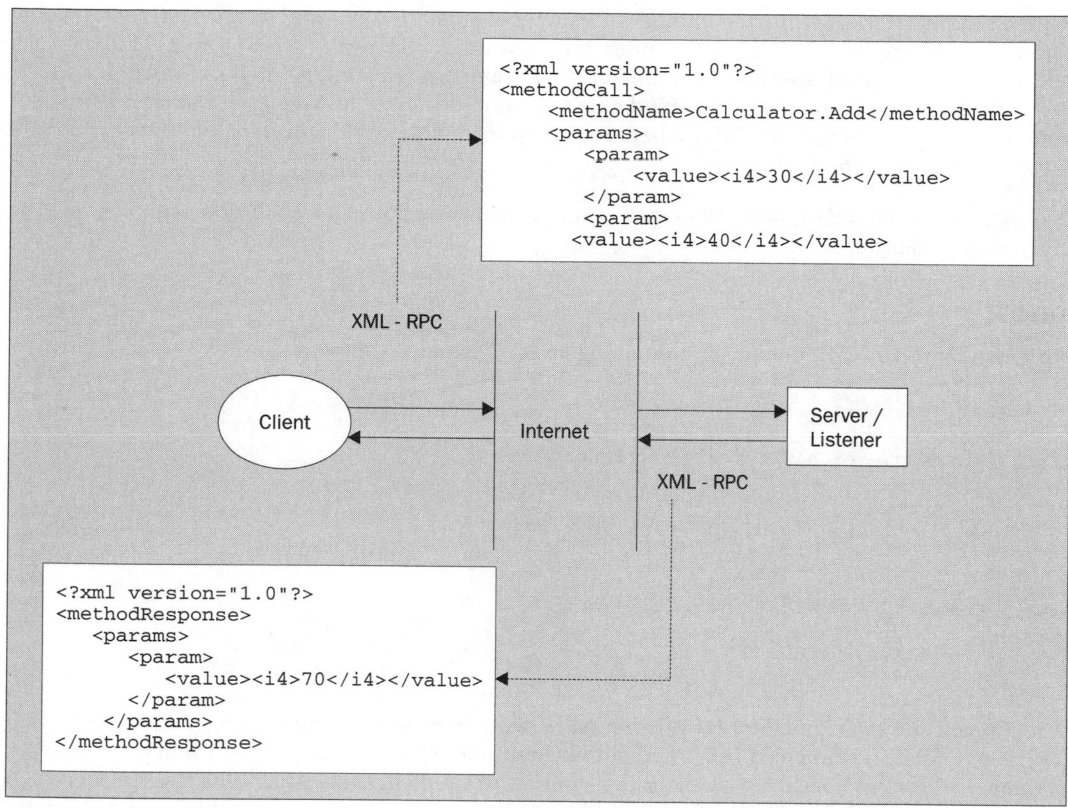

<?xml version="1.0"?>
<methodCall>
<methodName>Calculator.Add</methodName>
<params>
<param>
<value><i4>30</i4></value>
</param>
<param>
<value><i4>40</i4></value>
XML - RPC
Client
Internet
Server / Listener
XML - RPC
<?xml version="1.0"?>
<methodResponse>
<params>
<param>
<value><i4>70</i4></value>
</param>
</params>
</methodResponse>

XML-RPC Data Types

The XML-RPC standard defines only a few data types. These are listed in the table below:

XML-RPC tag	Description
`<string>`	An ASCII or Unicode sequence of characters
`<int>` `<i4>`	A signed 32-bit integer values
`<boolean>`	Either `true` (1) or `false` (0)
`<double>`	A double precision floating point number
`<dateTime.iso8601>`	A date and time (but no time zone, which makes it almost useless)
`<base64>`	A base64 encoded string (raw binary data of any length)
`<array>`	An one-dimensional array of values (individual values in the array can be of any types)
`<struct>`	A collection of key-value pairs (keys are strings, values may be of any type)

As seen in the overleaf table, the number of data types supported is really small. XML-RPC cannot define named structs and arrays and it does not allow-user defined data types. These disadvantages were addressed in the SOAP specifications and all these features were implemented in SOAP. If the requirement is of a complex user-defined data type and the ability to have each message define how it should be processeds then SOAP is a better solution than XML-RPC. For detailed information refer to http://www.xmlrpc.com/spec.

We shall study the use of these data types in the following sections. We shall now look into an XML-RPC request.

Request

An example of an XML document containing an RPC request is shown below:

```
<?xml version="1.0"?>
<methodCall>
   <methodName>Calculator.Add</methodName>
   <params>
      <param>
         <value><i4>30</i4></value>
      </param>
      <param>
         <value><i4>40</i4></value>
      </param>
   </params>
</methodCall>
```

The above code calls a method `Add()` that takes two parameters having values `30` and `40` respectively. The above XML document is generated at the client side representing the client request. The root element is the `<methodCall>` element that consists of child elements describing the method call. The `<methodName>` element defines the name of the method to be called. The method is called using the server alias `Calculator.Add`. The `Calculator` is the alias name for the server on which the method implementation is provided.

The method signature accepts two parameters, these parameters are represented in the document using `<param>` element. The `<param>` element has a child element `<value>` that defines the type of data accepted. Since the method accepts parameters as integers the data is defined using `<i4>` element. This element defines an integer type of data. The data type element specification is provided in the previous section.

Response

An example of an XML document containing a response to the above request is shown below:

```
<?xml version="1.0"?>
<methodResponse>
   <params>
      <param>
         <value><i4>70</i4></value>
      </param>
   </params>
</methodResponse>
```

The client receives a response containing value of `70`. We shall discuss an example based on Apache XML-RPC in Chapter 4.

SOAP

An emerging standard for calling procedures on remote objects is the SOAP (Simple Object Access Protocol). The basic difference between SOAP and XML-RPC is that the SOAP procedures take named parameters where the request must encode the method parameter names within its XML. The order of these parameters is irrelevant but, in XML-RPC, order is relevant and the parameters are not named.

SOAP is a simple, lightweight XML-based protocol. It enables the exchange of structured and typed information on the web. SOAP describes a messaging format for machine-to-machine communication. SOAP enables the creation of Web Services based on an open infrastructure. SOAP defines elements to specify the method name, its parameters, and the return type. It also defines various data types for exchanging parameters and return values.

SOAP can be used in combination with a variety of existing Internet protocols and formats including HTTP, SMTP, and MIME and can support a wide range of applications from messaging systems to RPC.

SOAP Architecture

The following diagram illustrates how a SOAP message is used in a request/response mechanism between client and server:

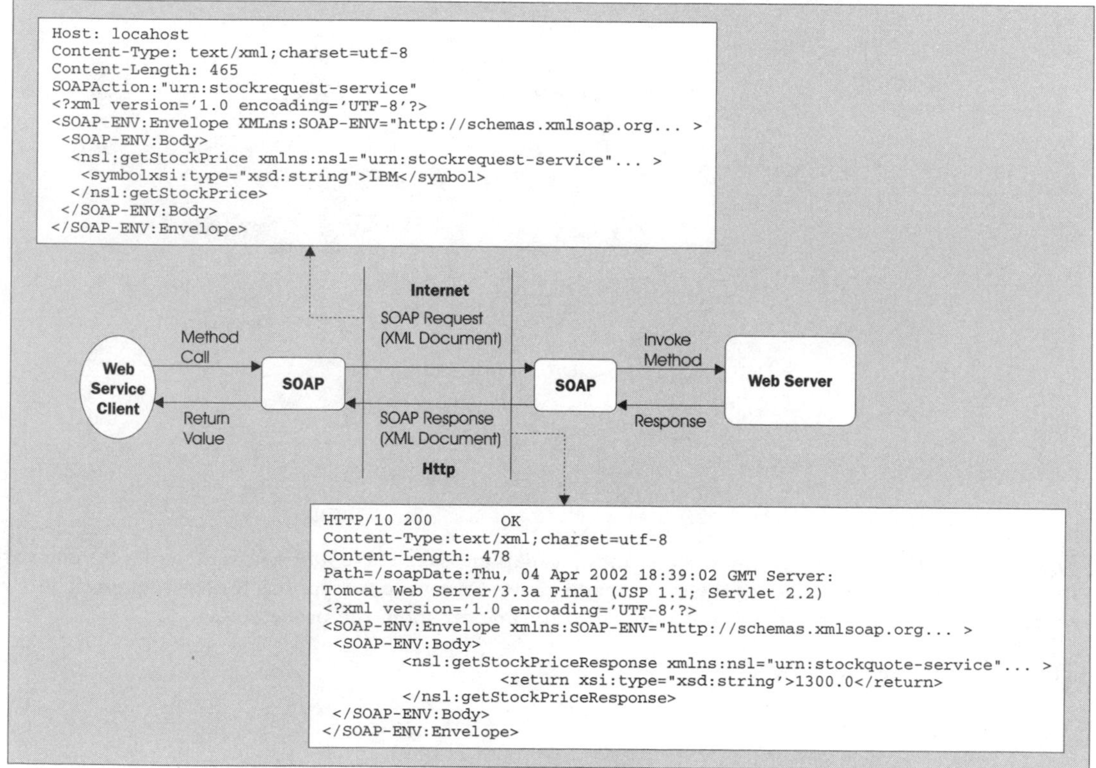

In the previous diagram, we demonstrate how a SOAP request is sent to the server and a response is generated by the server and sent back to the client or the requestor. To give a practical example of this process we can say that the request can be a purchase order request, or a product manufacturing information. The response for the request made will be the order confirmation or a production contract.

SOAP Message

The request/response flow can be described using the following diagram:

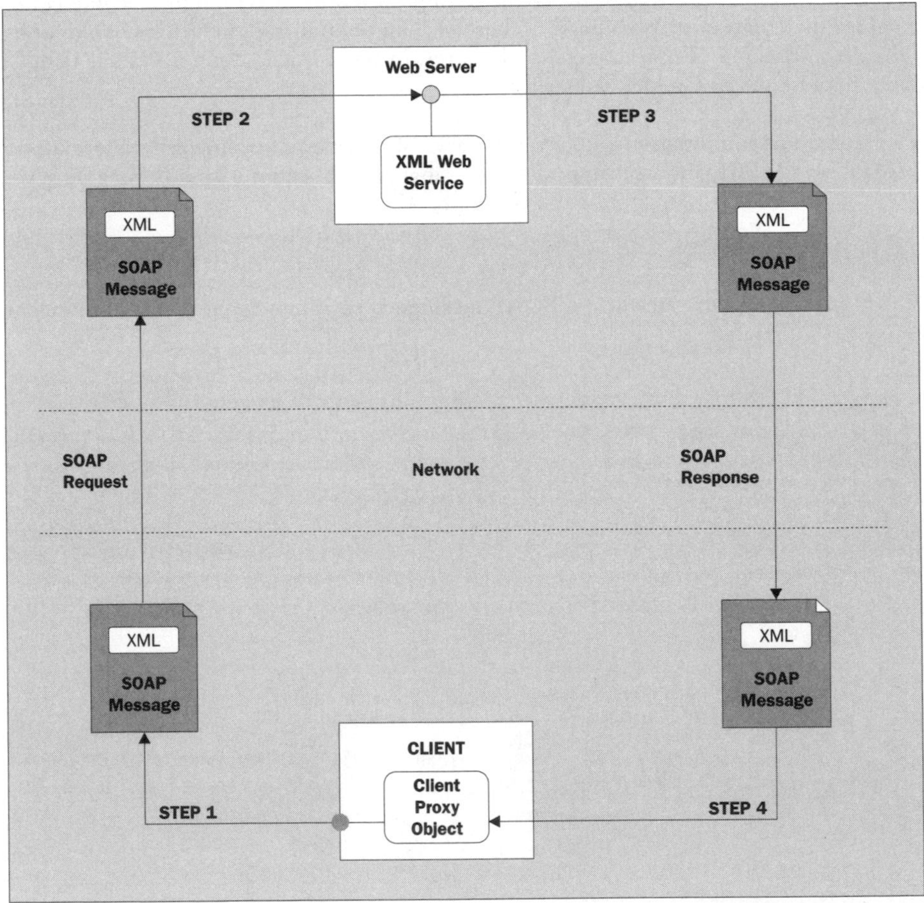

First, the client for the service makes a request; a soap message is created and sent across the network to the server. The server processes the request and generates a proper response for the request. The response can be a result of the request or error information about the processing.

The SOAP message consists of:

- SOAP envelope
- SOAP encoding rules
- SOAP RPC representation

The SOAP envelope defines an overall framework. The framework defines what is in a message, which is the message recipient, and whether the message is optional or mandatory. The encoding rules define a set of rules for exchanging instances of application-defined data types. The SOAP RPC representation defines a convention for representing remote procedure calls and responses.

We will discuss SOAP in greater depth in the next chapter.

SOAP Example

A typical SOAP message is shown below:

```
<IVORY:Envelope
  xmlns:IVORY="http://schemas.xmlsoap.org/soap/envelope/"
  IVORY:encodingStyle="http://schemas.xmlsoap.org/soap/encoding/">
   <IVORY:Body>
       <m:GetLastTradePrice xmlns:m="Some-URI">
           <symbol>DIS</symbol>
       </m:GetLastTradePrice>
   </IVORY:Body>
</IVORY:Envelope>
```

As seen from this example, a SOAP message is encoded using XML. SOAP defines two namespaces, one for the envelope (`http://schemas.xmlsoap.org/soap/envelope/`) and the other for encoding rules (`http://schemas.xmlsoap.org/soap/encoding/`). A SOAP message must not contain a DTD (Document Type Definition) or any processing instructions. In such a case, the message will be ignored or sent back as a fault by the SOAP receivers. The above SOAP message defines a method called `GetLastTradePrice` that takes the stock symbol as a parameter.

Embedding SOAP Messages in HTTP

The consumer of the Web Service creates a SOAP message as above and embeds it in an `HTTP POST` and sends it to the Web Service for processing as shown below:

```
POST /StockQuote HTTP/1.1
Host: www.stockquoteserver.com
Content-Type: text/xml;
charset="utf-8"
Content-Length: nnnn
SOAPAction:
"Some-URI"
     ...
      SOAP Message
     ...
```

The Web Service processes this message, executes the requested operation and returns the result to the client as another SOAP message. The returned message contains the requested stock price. A typical returned SOAP message may look like:

```
<SOAP-ENV:Envelope
  xmlns:SOAP-ENV="http://schemas.xmlsoap.org/soap/envelope/"
  SOAP-ENV:encodingStyle="http://schemas.xmlsoap.org/soap/encoding/">
   <SOAP-ENV:Body>
       <m:GetLastTradePriceResponse xmlns:m="Some-URI">
           <Price>34.5</Price>
       </m:GetLastTradePriceResponse>
   </SOAP-ENV:Body>
</SOAP-ENV:Envelope>
```

The message is returned to the client as an HTTP response and will contain the proper HTTP header block at the top of the message.

Interoperability

The major goal while designing the SOAP protocol was to allow easy interoperability amongst distributed Web Services. However, since a few details of the SOAP specifications are open to interpretation, the implementations across vendors do differ. Thus, the messages created by different applications differ in their conformance level resulting in non-interoperable applications.

Note that a valid XML document is not necessarily a valid SOAP message and similarly a valid SOAP message is not a conformant SOAP 1.1 message. To test for the conformance, third-party tools may be used. One such tool called SOAP 1.1 Validator is developed by Userland and is available at http://validator.soapware.org/. Using the Validator, you can test any SOAP code for conformance to SOAP 1.1 specifications.

Implementations

DevelopMentor, IBM, Lotus, Microsoft, and Userland developed SOAP technology. More than 50 implementations are currently available. The Apache Software Foundation (ASF) provides one of the most popular implementations. It is an open source Java-based implementation. Another is by Microsoft within their .NET platform. Unfortunately, these two implementations have a few discrepancies, and thus cannot interoperate. The SOAP specification has been submitted to W3C, which is now working on new specifications called XMLP (XML Protocol) that is based on SOAP version 1.1. XMLP is discussed in a later section. The information on XMLP can be obtained from the URL http://www.w3.org/TR/xmlp-reqs/.

SOAP Messages with Attachments (SwA)

Often, you find that you need to send a SOAP message with an attachment consisting of another document or an image. On the Internet, generally the GIF and JPEG data formats are treated as standards for image transmission. In general, the attachments are in text or in binary formats. Such attachments can be combined with a SOAP message by using a multipart MIME structure. This multipart structure is called SOAP message package. Hewlett Packard and Microsoft developed this new specification and submitted to the W3C. A sample SOAP message containing an attachment (`myimage.tiff`) is shown here:

```
MIME-Version: 1.0
Content-Type: Multipart/Related; boundary=MIME_boundary; type=text/xml;
        start="<myimagedoc.xml@mysite.com>"
Content-Description: This is the optional message description.

--MIME_boundary
Content-Type: text/xml; charset=UTF-8
Content-Transfer-Encoding: 8bit
Content-ID: <myimagedoc.xml@mysite.com>

<?xml version='1.0' ?>
<SOAP-ENV:Envelope
xmlns:SOAP-ENV="http://schemas.xmlsoap.org/soap/envelope/">
<SOAP-ENV:Body>
..
<theSignedForm href="cid:myimage.tiff@mysite.com"/>
..
</SOAP-ENV:Body>
</SOAP-ENV:Envelope>

--MIME_boundary
Content-Type: image/tiff
Content-Transfer-Encoding: binary
Content-ID: <myimage.tiff@mysite.com>

...binary TIFF image...
--MIME_boundary--
```

XMLP/SOAP 1.2

XMLP can be defined as a system where two or more nodes (computers) communicate in a distributed environment using XML as their encapsulation language. The XMLP structure consists of an open-ended set of XMLP modules defining a large variety of functions and services. The basic examples of XMLP functions and services are generic mechanisms for handling security, caching, routing, and event handling to specific functions like submitting a purchase order.

Since an XMLP implementation is simple and lightweight, XMLP modules can be designed and composed to perform complex operations allowing the core protocol to remain simple. The XMLP specifications are provided at http://www.w3.org/TR/SOAP-attachments.

The XMLP protocol addresses the following four components:

- **Envelope**
  This defines the envelope that encapsulates XML data to be transferred in an interoperable manner.
- **Convention**
  This defines the contents of the envelope for remote procedure calls.
- **Mechanism for serializing data**
  This consists of object graphs and directed labeled graphs based on data types of XML Schema.
- **Using HTTP as transport**
  Though HTTP is typically used as a transport for the XML protocol, one may use other transports. The working committee addressed HTTP as a transport since it is widely used.

XMLP is known as SOAP 1.2 today. The W3C XML Protocol Working Group initially used the name XMLP while drafting the new specifications for SOAP 1.1. Finally, they decided to call it SOAP 1.2 rather than XMLP to avoid confusion in the industry and technical community.

WSDL

The WSDL (Web Services Description Language) is an XML format for describing the Web Service interface. It defines the set of operations supported by the server and the format that a client must use when requesting the service. The WSDL file acts like a contract between the client and the service for effective communication between the two parties. The client has to request the service by sending a properly formatted SOAP request. The above statements are explained using the following diagram:

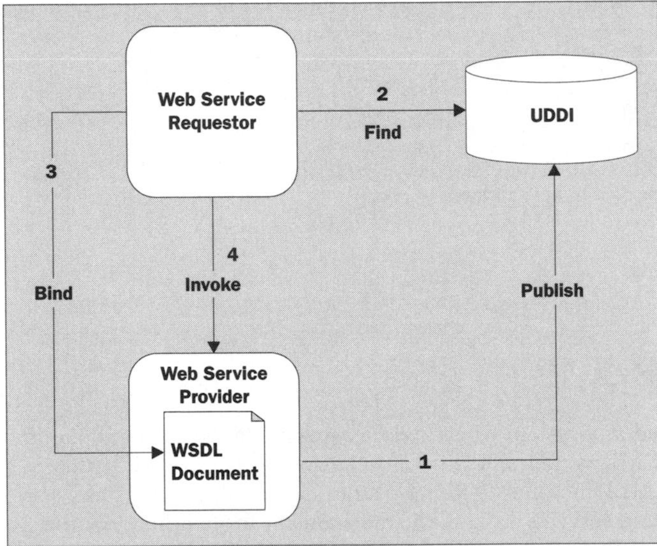

For example, if you are creating a Web Service that offers the latest stock quotes to the customers, you will need to create a WSDL file that describes the service. This file will be put on your server or published onto a UDDI registry. The client interested in the service first obtains a copy/reference of this file using a search on the registry, understands the contract, creates a SOAP request based on the contract, and dispatches a request to the server using (say) `HTTP Post`. The server validates the request and if found valid, executes the request by passing it to the applicable service. The result, which is the latest stock price for the requested symbol, is then returned to the client as a SOAP response.

WSDL Document Structure

A WSDL document is an XML document that consists of a set of definitions. The root element is `<definitions>` as shown here.

```
<wsdl:definitions name="nmtoken" targetNamespace="uri">
    <import namespace="uri" location="uri"/>*
    <wsdl:documentation .... />
...
</wsdl:definitions>
```

Within the <definitions> are other elements. There are six major elements in the document structure that describe the service. These are listed below:

- types
- message
- portType
- binding
- port
- service

We shall look at these elements in detail in Chapter 3.

Implementation

IBM and Microsoft developed the WSDL technology. The Microsoft SOAP Toolkit 2.0 is fully compliant with the WSDL 1.1 specification. To illustrate what the WSDL file looks like, we create a simple Web Service. The service is called HelloWorld and returns a string response to the caller. The generated XML code is shown below:

```
<?xml version="1.0" ?>
<serviceDescription xmlns:s0="http://tempuri.org/" name="WebService1"
targetNamespace="http://tempuri.org/" xmlns="urn:schemas-xmlsoap-org:sdl.2000-01-
25">
<soap xmlns="urn:schemas-xmlsoap-org:soap-sdl-2000-01-25">
<service>
<addresses>
  <address uri="http://ice6/WebServiceHello/WebService1.asmx" />
  </addresses>
<requestResponse name="HelloWorld" soapAction="http://tempuri.org/HelloWorld">
  <request ref="s0:HelloWorld" />
  <response ref="s0:HelloWorldResult" />
  </requestResponse>
  </service>
  </soap>
<httppost xmlns="urn:schemas-xmlsoap-org:post-sdl-2000-01-25">
<service>
<requestResponse name="HelloWorld"
href="http://ice6/WebServiceHello/WebService1.asmx/HelloWorld">
<request>
  <form />
  </request>
<response>
  <mimeXml ref="s0:string" />
  </response>
  </requestResponse>
  </service>
  </httppost>
```

```
<httpget xmlns="urn:schemas-xmlsoap-org:get-sdl-2000-01-25">
<service>
<requestResponse name="HelloWorld"
href="http://ice6/WebServiceHello/WebService1.asmx/HelloWorld">
  <request />
<response>
  <mimeXml ref="s0:string" />
  </response>
  </requestResponse>
  </service>
  </httpget>
<schema targetNamespace="http://tempuri.org/" attributeFormDefault="qualified"
elementFormDefault="qualified" xmlns="http://www.w3.org/1999/XMLSchema">
<element name="HelloWorld">
  <complexType />
  </element>
<element name="HelloWorldResult">
<complexType>
<all>
  <element name="result" xmlns:q1="http://www.w3.org/1999/XMLSchema"
type="q1:string" nullable="true" />
  </all>
  </complexType>
  </element>
  <element name="string" xmlns:q2="http://www.w3.org/1999/XMLSchema"
type="q2:string" nullable="true" />
  </schema>
  </serviceDescription>
```

UDDI

UDDI (Universal Description, Discovery, and Integration) or Business Registry is like the Yellow Pages of Web Services. It helps various business enterprises to publish their services thus making them available to partner enterprises. Information stored in the registry is organized according to the different business criteria. It stores information about the organization's activities and service-related information for the services published in the registry. Having all this information organized in one place helps other business enterprises and business partners to search for a service and conduct transactions quickly, easily, and dynamically with their respective trading partners.

The position of UDDI in the Web Service architecture is described using the following diagram:

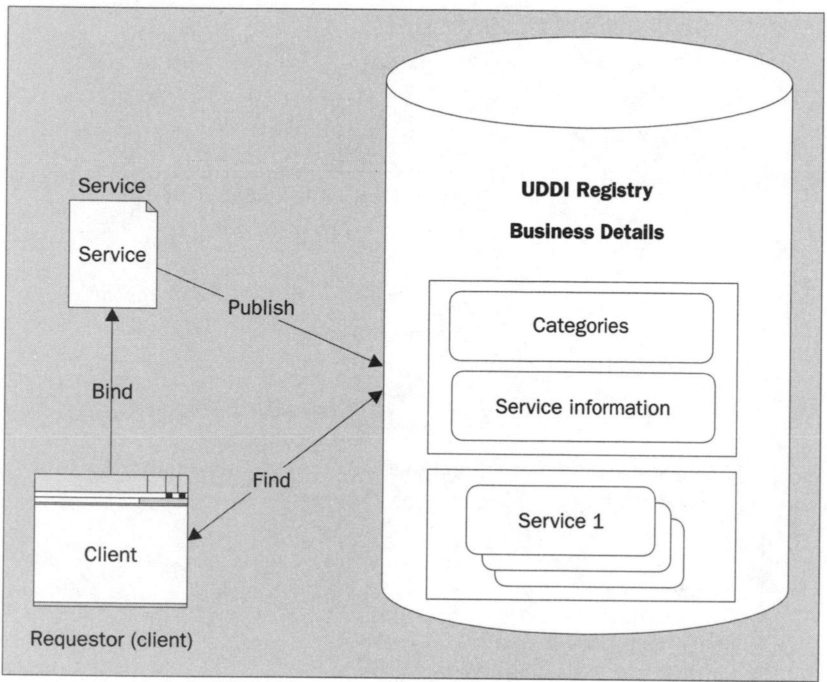

Software giants like Microsoft, IBM, Sun, HP, Ariba, and many more are currently backing this concept. UDDI is important to Web Services because it enables access to businesses from a single source. The basic idea behind the Web Services is that the web will be colonized with a wide range of small pieces of code, which can be published, located, and invoked across the web. To invoke these chunks of code, technologies such as SOAP are implemented to allow an application to interact with remote applications. But the problem here is that where and how to find these small chunks of code (or services) in the first place. This empty space problem is solved by UDDI. We shall see the basic functionalities of UDDI in Chapter 3.

There could be entries in the UDDI registries about Web Services that are no more active. Sometimes the service may be unavailable due to various reasons. UDDI servers shall become smarter to deal with this. Some of the existing client implementations follow an algorithm as described overleaf:

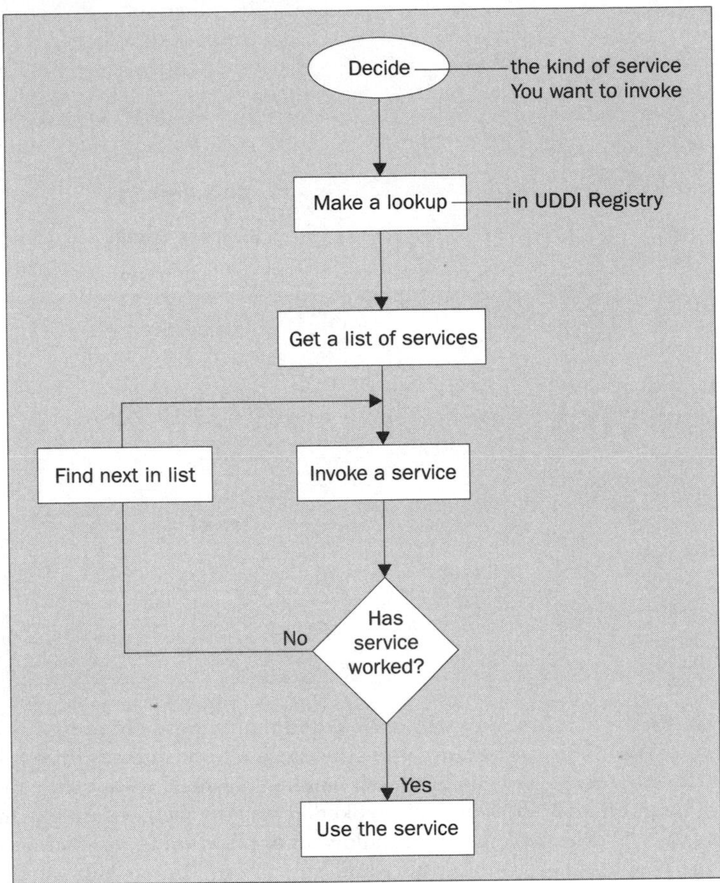

We will discuss UDDI in greater depth in the next chapter.

HTTPR

Reliable HTTP or HTTPR is a new protocol that offers the reliable delivery of a message between the client and server over HTTP. IBM invented this protocol and the first specifications were drafted on 13 July, 2001. The protocol addresses the deficiencies of HTTP by ensuring that all messages are delivered to the destination in their exact form and are not delivered more than once. If the delivery fails, the sender is reliably informed of the failure.

Consider a case where the sender sends a purchase order to some receiver over the Internet. The delivery of such a message should be reliable and made exactly once. If the message is not delivered and the sender does not know about it, the purchase order is effectively lost. If the message is delivered more than once and if the receiver is not aware of the multiple receipts of the same message, it will result in multiple purchase orders without the knowledge of the sender. Thus, the reliable delivery of the message to its intended recipient is highly desirable.

To achieve the reliable delivery of messages, a sender may send the same message repeatedly to the recipient until a positive acknowledgement is received. Each message should have a unique identifier associated with it, so that the receiver can discard all the duplicate messages. To implement reliable delivery, a message is stored in a persistent storage until an acknowledgement is received from the recipient. Reliable messaging exists and several middleware products such as Java Message Queue (JMQ), IBM MQSeries, Microsoft's MSMQ, and such do support reliable messaging. However, all these are based on vendor-dependent proprietary protocols. HTTPR provides an open standard that is vendor neutral.

The **reliable** in HTTPR is layered on top of HTTP. The messaging can be relied upon even in case of network failures or the failures of messaging agents. The HTTPR specification defines the format for encapsulating meta data and application messages within the payload of HTTP requests and responses.

The specifications also define rules for guaranteeing the delivery of a message only once; in case of failures it is reliably reported as undeliverable. A messaging agent uses the HTTPR protocol and persistent storage for providing reliable messaging. The specifications do not address the design of a messaging agent or the storage mechanism. However, it specifies when to store the message and what to store. HTTPR specifications can be referred at the following location http://www.webservices.org/article.php?sid=179.

HTTPR operates based on HTTP/1.1 and thus all the facilities of HTTP/1.1 such as SSL, session keep-alive, proxy, and firewall support are available in HTTPR. You may use any messaging interface such as SOAP or JMS with HTTPR. This does not alter the message format. Thus, the SOAP message, irrespective of whether it is transported over HTTP or HTTPR, remains the same. The additional information required for reliable messaging is put into HTTPR message context header. The header also carries additional information that may be required by other extension protocols such as ebXML. HTTPR stack can be described using the following diagram:

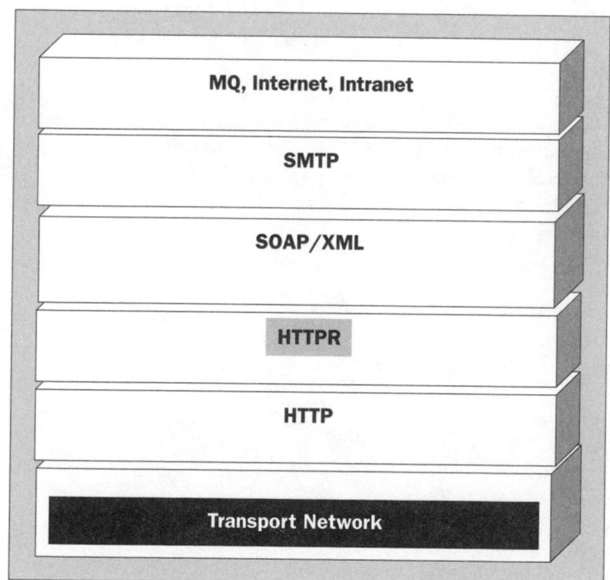

When HTTPR eventually matures, it provides reliable messaging on the Web without requiring major redevelopment of the existing applications. Using SOAP over HTTPR will allow Web Services to use this reliability feature.

RDF

RDF (Resource Description Framework) is a general-purpose language to represent meta data information about Web Services. It typically represents the title, author name of a web page, copyright information about a web site, and any other information that you may like to share with other web applications. RDF provides a common framework so that the web applications can share the information amongst them. Applications may use RDF parsers to extract information from a web document.

If you wish to generate an RDF page that contains your information, log on to the site http://swordfish.rdfweb.org/rweb/aboutme.

Here, the form will guide you through entering the required information. A typical XML page generated on completing the form is shown below:

```
<rdf:RDF
 xmlns:rdf="http://www.w3.org/1999/02/22-rdf-syntax-ns#"
 xmlns:dc="http://purl.org/dc/elements/1.1/"
 xmlns:foaf="http://xmlns.com/foaf/0.1/"
 xmlns:wn="http://xmlns.com/wordnet/1.6/" >
   <foaf:Person>
      <foaf:mbox rdf:resource="mailto: John@wrox.com ">
      <foaf:givenName>John</foaf:givenName>
      <foaf:surname>Hunt</foaf:surname>
      <foaf:projectHomepage rdf:resource="www.wrox.com/Webservices" />
      <foaf:workPlaceHomepage rdf:resource="www.wrox.com" />
      <foaf:img rdf:resource="John.jpg" />
      <foaf:interest rdf:resource="www.rediff.com/chat" />

      <foaf:knows>
         <foaf:Person>
            <foaf:mbox rdf:resource="mailto:Julia@yahoo.com">
            <foaf:givenName>Julia</foaf:givenName>
            <foaf:surname>Anderson</foaf:surname>
         </foaf:Person>
      </foaf:knows>
   </foaf:Person>

   <foaf:Document rdf:about="www.abcom.com">
      <dc:title>John Hunt</dc:title>
      <dc:description>About Me</dc:description>
      <dc:creator>
         <foaf:Person>
            <foaf:mbox="mailto: John@wrox.com " />
         </foaf:Person>
      <dc:creator>
      <dc:creator>
         <foaf:Person>
            <foaf:mbox="mailto:Greg@aol.com" /<
         </foaf:Person>
      </dc:creator;
   </foaf:Document>
</rdf:RDF>
```

RDF is being developed as part of W3C's Semantic Web Activity. The Semantic Web is an extension to the current Web. In Semantic Web, the information is well defined and allows both machines and humans to work cooperatively. As both machines and humans can process the information, it greatly enhances the usefulness of the Web.

The RDF specification consists of the following documents:

- The RDF model theory (and graph syntax)
- The RDF/XML syntax
- RDF schema (and data types)
- RDF test cases
- The RDF primer

The foundation of RDF is a model to represent named properties and property values. The RDF model draws on well-established principles from various data representation communities. RDF properties may be thought of as attributes of resources and in this sense correspond to traditional attribute-value pairs.

RDF also defines XML syntax for writing down and exchanging RDF graphs. This syntax is defined in the RDF/XML syntax specification. To encode a graph in XML, the nodes and arcs are turned into XML elements, attributes, element content, and attribute values. The URI labels for properties and object nodes are written in XML using XML namespaces (XML-NS) that give a namespace URI for a short prefix along with namespace-qualified elements and attribute names called local names.

The RDF schema specification is not represented by a specific vocabulary of descriptive elements such as "author". But it specifies the mechanisms needed to define such elements, to define the classes of resources they may be used with, and to restrict possible combinations of classes and relationships.

The complete specifications of RDF may be obtained from the W3C web site http://www.w3.org/RDF/.

DSML

The Directory Service Markup Language (DSML) is an XML-based language that addresses the interoperability issues in web applications. It provides an extensible, open, and standard-based format for publishing directory schemas and interchanging directory contents.

DSML is designed with Lightweight Directory Access Protocol (LDAP) directories in mind. LDAP is a TCP-based protocol used for accessing online directory services. DSML enables any XML-capable application to access the LDAP-enabled directories without having to write the LDAP interfaces or proprietary directory access APIs like Novell's NDAP (Novell Directory Access Protocol) or Microsoft's ADSI (Active Directory Service Protocol). DSML also gives a consistent way to work with multiple dissimilar directories.

The following diagram shows a typical DSML transaction:

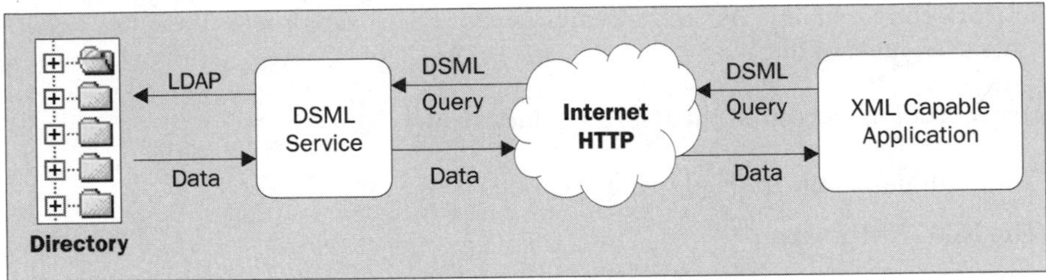

Any application that is capable of generating and reading an XML document can format a DSML query and send it over HTTP. This query is received by the DSML service, which then converts it into LDAP. The data is retrieved from the directory service via LDAP. This data is passed back to the application through HTTP.

The DSML protocol may use any of the standard transports such as HTTP or SMTP. Due to this, it is capable of penetrating firewalls where LDAP access is prohibited.

A DSML document is defined using the following statement:

```
<dsml:dsml xmlns:dsml="http://www.dsml.org/DSML">
```

A DSML document consists of directory **entries**, a directory **schema,** or both. Directory entries are universally unique. Every directory entry can have a number of property-value pairs called as attributes:

```
<dsml:directory-entries>
 <dsml:entry dn=
   "uid=prabbit,ou=development,o=bowstreet,c=us">...</dsml:entry>
  <dsml:entry dn="...">...</dsml:entry>
  <dsml:entry dn="...">...</dsml:entry>
  ...
</dsml:directory-entries>
```

Every directory entry describes a class that specifies the directory's attributes. The constraints on the attributes are specified in an XML Schema:

```
<dsml:directory-schema>
  <dsml:class id="..." ...>...</dsml:class>
  <dsml:attribute-type id="..." ...>...</dsml:attribute-type>
</dsml:directory-schema>
```

DSML is not an efficient way to talk to directory services as compared to the LDAP or any vender-specific approach. But DSML provides a common language for working with the directories independent of the platform and the programming language.

WSUI

The Web Service User Interface (WSUI) (http://www.wsui.org/) is a component model that enables us to add a presentation and interaction layer to the Web Services implemented in XML and SOAP. WSUI is the first proposed industry standard for the creation and delivery of Web Services as applications to end users. This standard enables us to design a basic model of a web site that exposes an application as an embeddable page component(s) to other web sites. WSUI architecture is described using the following diagram:

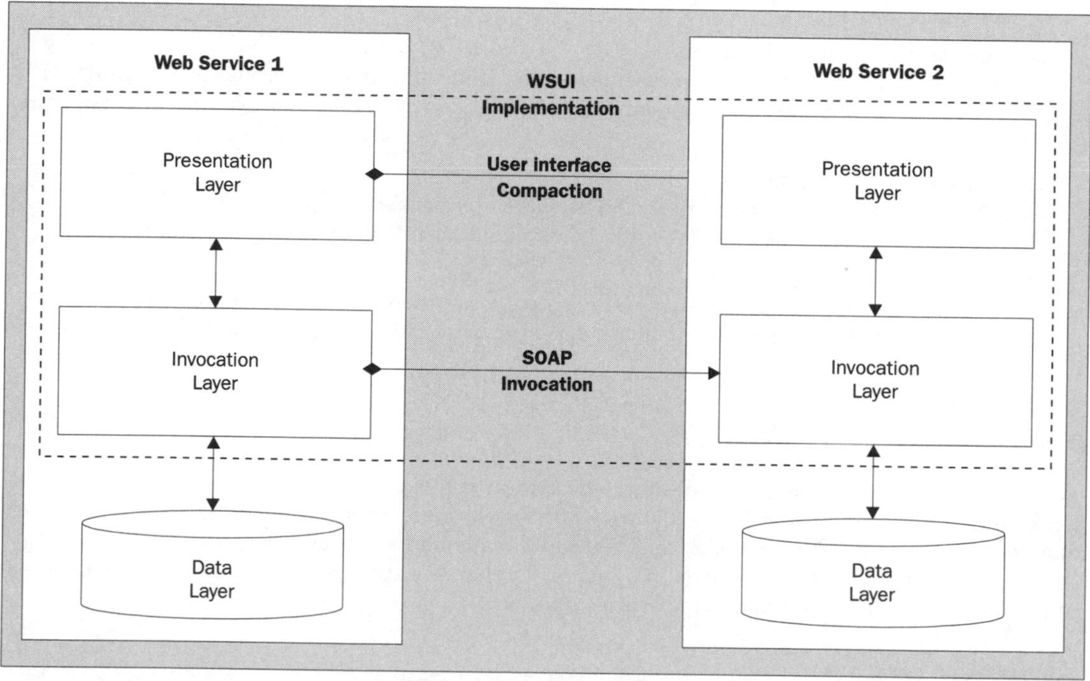

In the standard Web Service architecture, integration is done at the invocation layer. In the above diagram, we integrate the two services at the presentation layer. This integration is implemented using the WSUI component model. The whole application is compacted along with the user interface and the service methods. This entire application can then be embedded into another application.

To make this model work, the enterprises need to create a proprietary integration layer (Interface) which is built on top of the existing data transfer layers (Protocol) like XML or Simple Object Access Protocol (SOAP). For example, an enterprise that needs to deliver a service to another web site needs to build an interface to expose the service. This proprietary interface acts as an embeddable page component to the other web site. By using this model, interoperable and shareable applications can be developed. These applications can reside on web platforms implemented in entirely different languages such as Java, VB, and .NET languages.

Dynamic integration of Web Service applications into another web site is possible by packaging an application with a WSUI descriptor file along with an XSLT style sheet. The only requirement is that the web site must have a WSUI container implementation running on it.

WSUI is open to the Internet and Web Services community, and therefore can be integrated as a component of any web site. The benefits of this model are:

- **Standardization**
  WSUI is supported by technologies such as XML, SOAP, XSLT, XPATH, XHTML, and other XML-based technologies.
- **Ease of Implementation**
  Since WSUI is supported by standard technologies that are simple to understand it can be implemented easily. A programmer with basic XML and server-side knowledge can put this model to work.
- **Cross–platform integration**
  The WSUI model can be implemented in any languages that understand XML standards. Integration of applications developed in languages such as Java and .Net is also possible in this model.
- **Sharing of applications**
  As discussed above, applications can be shared by packaging applications as WSUI components. These components can be dynamically integrated into any other web site.
- **Server-side components**
  Since all WSUI components are server-side, the problem of browser dependency is eliminated. The entire implementation is done using XML messaging and thin-client XHTML to the client.

How Does WSUI Work?

WSUI implements a simple XML Schema to describe a WSUI component. This component calls the back-end support (SOAP and XML) that uses XSLT style sheets to develop interfaces (views), which enable users to interact with the service. This model implementation helps vendors, customers, and developers to gain the ability to develop dynamically sharable applications across web sites independent of the back-end implementation of the service interfaces.

Modeling WSUI

It is suggested that one should adhere to certain design parameters while modeling WSUI:

- The model should be easily implemented using the standards-based technologies.
- The model should have multi-language support that is HTML and WML should be supported within the same component.
- The model should be programming language-independent.
- The model should be entirely based on server-side technology.
- Single URL referencing, that is a WSUI component, should be referenced through a single URL. This helps installing the component just by knowing its URL.

Currently a number of vendor-specific approaches have emerged to facilitate non-developer integration of network services. Using these facilities, development of e-commerce and portal web sites is possible.

The concept of WSUI is an attempt to standardize the integration by defining a web component model that couples network services with interaction and presentation information. The WSUI components can be dynamically integrated or embedded into container applications at run-time by non-developers.

WSFL

The Web Service Flow Language (WSFL) is an XML-based language that describes compositions (business processes and overall partner interaction) of Web Services. The composition describes how to achieve a particular business goal. This WSFL implements two types of structures that define the composition:

- Flow Model
- Global Model

Here, composite Web Services combine many logically related services that are integrated to form an application or to perform a specific functionality. The above structures help the developers to design structure compositions properly.

The actual working of WSFL can be understood through a small example. Consider a shopping cart where we select some articles and add them to our cart. If we check the program logic of this process we need to call methods like `getCart()`, `addItem()`, `checkout()`, and such. This process has a specific flow of calling these methods. It makes no sense to call `checkout()` before calling `getCart()` method. So, by using the WSFL model, we can configure the calling process as per the requirements. This configuration feature is not available in the WSDL model and so using WSFL is a better option. We shall see the main parts of the WSFL model.

Flow Model

The model specifies a suitable implementation pattern for a collection of Web Services in such a way that the result composition describes how to achieve a particular business goal. The output from this structure represents a description of a business process.

In this model, we create a composition format. It describes how to use the functionality provided by the collection of composed Web Services. This process is also known as flow composition, orchestration, or choreography of Web Services. These compositions are modeled by WSFL as per the specifications of the execution sequence of the functionality provided by the composed Web Services. The execution orders or process are designed by defining the flow of control and data between Web Services. Lastly, flow models can be used to model the business processes or workflows based on Web Services.

Global Model

This model specifies the interaction pattern of a collection of Web Services. The output from this structure is the overall process of the partner interactions with the Web Services. The actual process of the two models is discussed below.

This model specifies how the composed Web Services interact with each other. The interactions between the services are modeled as links between the endpoints of the Web Services interface. We define this model as a global model, keeping in mind the decentralized or distributed nature of these interactions.

Recursive Composition

In WSFL, recursive composition specifies that a composition where every Web Service composition can itself become a new Web Service that is a flow model as a well as global model, both can become new services. This new Web Service can act as a component to other new compositions. This capability to do recursive composition of Web Services helps in improving the language scalability, improving top-down progressive refinement designing as well as for bottom-up aggregation. Due to these reasons the recursive composition plays an important role as a central requirement in the design of the WSFL language.

After studying the above model concepts, we can define WSFL as an ability to allow any Web Service provider to implement any of the activities defined in the business process. Also the ability to dynamically locate, and bind to providers based on a user-defined set of rules, adds a new dimension to conducting business on the web. This is one of the useful features that were not available initially.

Interaction Patterns

WSFL compositions support various interaction patterns between the business entities in a business process. The two basic interaction patterns supported are peer-to-peer and hierarchical. The peer-to-peer interaction pattern describes relationships that are formed or established dynamically on a per-instance basis. The hierarchical pattern describes a more stable and long-term relationship between the business entities.

Reference in the Web Service Stack

The Web Service stack is represented by different technologies that are XML, WSDL, SOAP, HTTP, and such. XML and WSDL form the first layer and SOAP along with HTTP forms the last layer. WSFL is layered on top of WSDL. The latter specifies the endpoint where the individual business operations can be accessed. WSFL makes use of WSDL for the description of interfaces and their protocol bindings. WSFL is supported by Web Service Endpoint Language (WSEL). This language helps WSFL to describe non-operational characteristics of service endpoints such as quality of service properties. The combination of WSDL, WSEL, and WSFL represent the core of the Web Service computing stack:

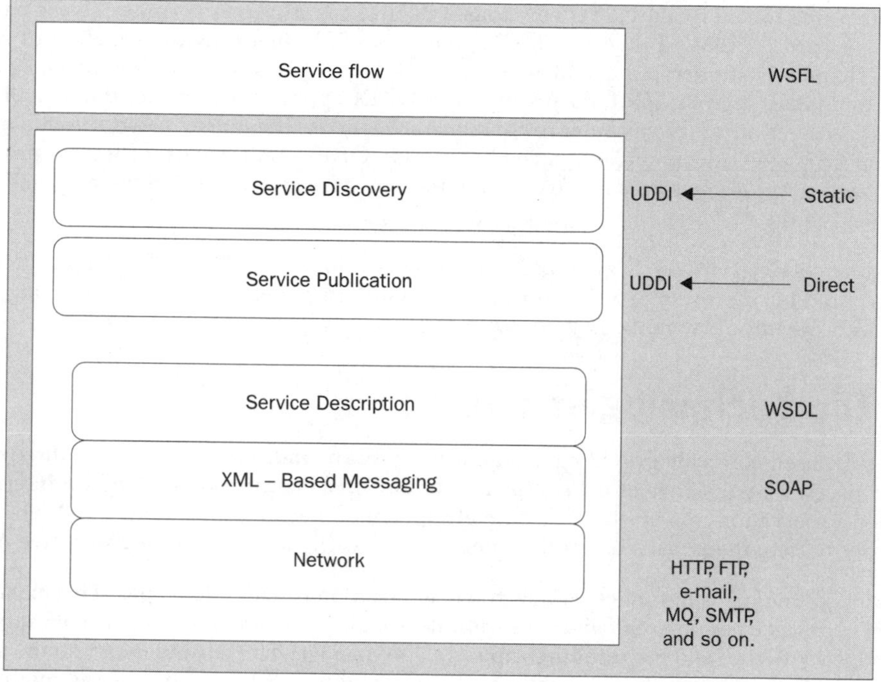

To summarize, a WSFL document specifies the composition of a Web Service as a flow model or a global model. These models declare a public interface and an internal composition structure. The composition assumes that the composed Web Service supports certain public interfaces that can be specified as a single port type or as a collection of port types. This collection of port types is called asService Provider.

Real-World Case Studies

In this section, we will discuss a few real-world case studies as implemented by different companies worldwide.

ORIX

This is a Japan-based company that provides a wide range of services in leasing, lending, rentals, life insurance, real estate financing and development, and many other sectors. Continuing to expand globally, today ORIX offers financial services in North America, Asia, the Middle East, and North Africa.

ORIX found that expanding its business over the Internet is a way to drive down cost, increase the customer base, and also improve customer services. But the B2B transactions over the Internet raised a concern over security. Along with secured messaging the authentication and identity of the original sender was the issue.

The problem was solved by the XSS4J component of IBM's XML Security Suite. This is basically a Web Service developed by IBM's Tokyo Research Laboratory (TRL) that provides capabilities such as digital signature, element-wise encryption, and access control. ORIX customers can use digital signature functions to digitally sign the XML documents. The ORIX applications transfer the digitally signed documents received from the customer to the signature service. It validates the document and retrieves the original message. This message is passed back to the ORIX applications for further processing. Similarly, the outbound messages are first sent to the signature service to sign them digitally before sending them to the customer.

The signature service is a Web Service-based solution developed by IBM. The TRL enabled ORIX to provide secured business transactions over the Internet. Further details on this project may be obtained from the web site http://www.orix.co.jp/index_e.htm.

Tripcentric Technologies Ltd.

This is a UK-based company providing e-commerce software and services to define, discover, and use travel resources. The objective of the company is to discover the true potential of the Internet as Distributed Reservation System (DRS) for travel suppliers. They are now in favor of Web Services technologies to help them make use of the Internet more easily and in a more productive manner.

Tripcentric Technologies introduced a new travel application called Tripkeeper. This makes it easy to buy travel supplies from different web sites with the use of a trip cart. Tripkeeper makes travel web sites fast to find, easy to use, and the resulting trip simple to manage. The customer can do the step-by-step bookings to plan the entire trip. The final trip plan is saved for further reference and modifications.

The company finds Web Services technologies helping in two major areas: intelligent discovery and ease of use. The UDDI would benefit Tripkeeper's DiscoveryEngine to quickly find the travel provider. With the help of Web Services, Tripkeeper can bind trip carts to the provider's service for modifications as well as the initial booking. This requires syntax to express complex business rules and workflow. Tripcentric believes that SOAP, WSDL, and WSFL are the obvious way to extend Tripkeeper's benefits to users.

Further details on this project may be obtained from the web site http://www.tripcentric.com/.

Hitachi Software

This is one of the leading system integrators in Japan. The main focus of the company is to develop the mission-critical applications in the finance, insurance, securities, authorities, and telecommunication sectors. The company works with 500 different companies to implement the different e-business strategies. This often requires the integration of applications across languages and platforms. Hence, the major concern for the Hitachi Software is the integration of a disparate world.

Hitachi Software believes that Web Services is an essential technology for developing distributed systems over the Internet. Looking forward to expand the business, Hitachi Software has launched an online shopping site called HitachiSoftware@Buy24. This site offers a wide range of products, hobby, and entertainment software for company use.

Their next plan is to use Web Services to further enhance the site. The work is underway to develop services that enable the customers to request quotations, sort the prices from the site, and submit the orders automatically. The Web Services will also provide another B2B feature to their customers. A variety of clients would be able to connect to the site since any SOAP-aware client applications can communicate with these Web Services.

Further details on this project may be obtained from the web site
http://www.Hitachi-sk.co.jp/English/index.html.

Summary

In this chapter, we have studied the Web Services architecture and the various components and technologies that facilitate its creation. We covered Web Service technologies such as SOAP, WSDL, UDDI, HTTPR, RDF, P3P, DSML, XMLP, WSUI, and WSFL. We briefly discussed XML, which is an integral part of Web Services.

At the end of the chapter, we looked at a few real-world case studies. In the next chapter, we will study the most important technologies in the Web Services architecture that are SOAP, WSDL, and UDDI, in greater depth.

3

Exploring SOAP, WSDL, and UDDI

In the last two chapters, we saw an overview of various technologies involved in the development of Web Services. The most important XML-based technologies used by Web Services are SOAP, WSDL, and UDDI. In Chapter 2, these were briefly introduced along with other related technologies. In this chapter, we will explain these technologies in depth.

A web-based application is required to call methods on remote objects. Such calls were previously made using RPC (Remote Procedure Calls). The well-known RPC-based systems are DCOM, RMI, EJB, and CORBA. Most of the RPC-based systems used proprietary protocols such as ORPC, JRMP, and IIOP for communication. These systems carry two major disadvantages:

- Proprietary protocol making interoperability between heterogeneous systems impossible
- Inability to penetrate firewalls making deployment difficult

Thus, there was a need for a standard protocol for calling the procedures on remote objects. The new protocol had to be vendor independent and capable to penetrate firewalls easily. This gave rise to SOAP (Simple Object Access Protocol).

SOAP and RPC

RPC is an excellent programming model that is used for developing distributed applications. The concept is to provide an abstraction so that invoking a method on an object deployed on a remote machine would appear like a simple local procedure call. The RPC protocol can be any standard protocol like SOAP or proprietary protocols like JRMP, ORPC, and IIOP.

The diagram below represents the high-level architecture of the RPC system:

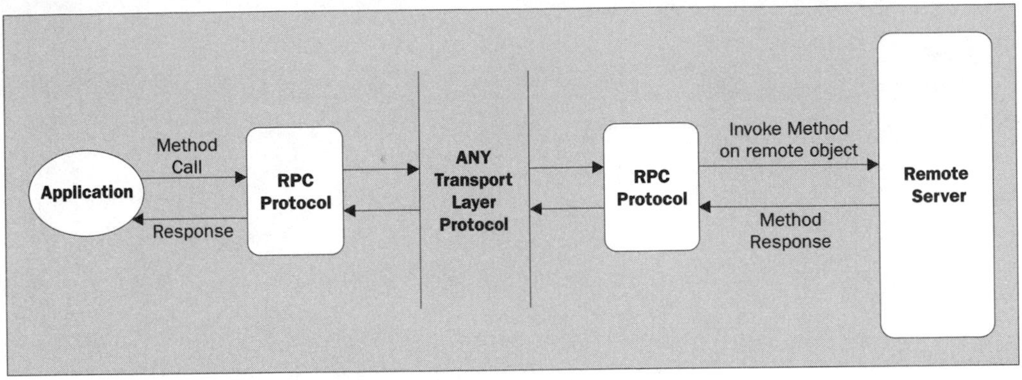

The current RPC-based systems obstruct the rapid development and deployment of web-based distributed applications. Most of the firewalls accept very few ports like the standard HTTP port 80. It limits the protocols like DCOM that use dynamically assigned ports for remote method invocation.

SOAP is an XML-based messaging protocol used for remote procedure calsl. The SOAP specification describes a way to represent the RPC call inside the SOAP message. SOAP solves the problems previously encountered in RPC. The advantage of SOAP is that the messages are embedded in HTTP requests, which allow them to easily penetrate through firewalls. In addition, SOAP implementations are easily available for any language on any platform, which allows the cross-language and cross-platform development of the distributed applications. Also, being an open standard, it enables interoperability between heterogeneous RPC systems that implement support for SOAP.

What is SOAP?

As seen in the earlier two chapters, SOAP is an XML-based protocol that is standardized by W3C. Many vendors including Microsoft and IBM have accepted this as a standard protocol for accessing remote objects. SOAP offers several benefits such as:

- Platform independence
- Vendor neutrality
- Programming language independence
- Extensibility
- Easy-to-use features
- Support of transport over HTTP

Though SOAP messages are transported over HTTP, you may use any other transport protocols such as FTP or SMTP.

SOAP essentially defines a format for a remote procedure call. The information required by a remote procedure is encoded in an XML document as a SOAP message. This is known as marshaling. At the other end, the information from the XML document is extracted and converted into a method call understood by the server object. This is known as un-marshaling. This reverse engineering is adapted if the server object wants to return a result to the client application.

Syntax Rules

As a SOAP message is an XML document, it adheres to the rules defined in an XML schema. A SOAP message must obey the following syntax rules:

- It must be encoded using XML
- It must have a SOAP envelope
- It must use the appropriate SOAP envelope namespaces
- It must use the appropriate SOAP encoding namespace
- It must have a SOAP body
- It must not contain a DTD reference
- It must not contain XML processing instructions

Optionally, a SOAP message may have a SOAP header. Let us now look at the structure of a SOAP document and its individual elements.

SOAP Message Structure

The template for a SOAP message is shown below:

```
<soap:Envelope
     xmlns:soap="http://schemas.xmlsoap.org/soap/envelope/"
     soap:encodingStyle="http://schemas.xmlsoap.org/soap/encoding/">
     <soap:Header>
...
            Header information goes here
...
     </soap:Header>
     <soap:Body>
...
            Body information goes here
...
     </soap:Body>
     <soap:Fault>
...
            Fault information goes here
...
     </soap:Fault>
</soap:Envelope>
```

The SOAP template contains the following elements:

- `Envelope` that defines the content of the message
- `Header` (optional) that contains header information
- `Body` that contains call and response information
- `Fault` that identifies the error condition

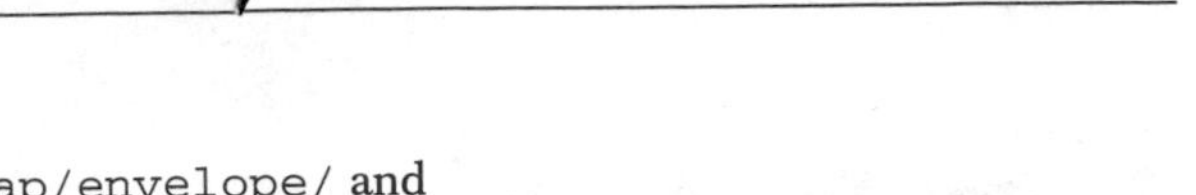

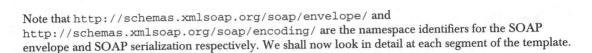

Note that http://schemas.xmlsoap.org/soap/envelope/ and http://schemas.xmlsoap.org/soap/encoding/ are the namespace identifiers for the SOAP envelope and SOAP serialization respectively. We shall now look in detail at each segment of the template.

Envelope

The Envelope is the root element and must be the first element in the document. It identifies the document as a SOAP message. It is used for specifying the version information about the message and for defining rules for serializing data, also called encoding rules. It defines two namespaces as shown in the code segment below:

```
<soap:Envelope
     xmlns:soap="http://schemas.xmlsoap.org/soap/envelope/"
     soap:encodingStyle="http://schemas.xmlsoap.org/soap/encoding/">
...
     Message information goes here
...
</soap:Envelope>
```

The default namespace for the SOAP Envelope recognized by SOAP 1.1 is http://schemas.xmlsoap.org/soap/envelope/. As per the working draft of SOAP 1.2, the namespace identifier is http://www.w3.org/2001/06/soap-envelope. The envelope namespace indicates the SOAP version. The SOAP message must use a valid namespace. Any invalid namespace at the endpoint would generate a SOAP fault. SOAP faults are discussed in detail in the section *Error Handling* later in the chapter.

The default namespace for SOAP encoding and data types is http://schemas.xmlsoap.org/soap/encoding/. This URI specifies the serialization rules defined by the SOAP specification. The SOAP message using the particular serialization must specify it using the encodingStyle attribute, which is explained later in the chapter.

Header

After the Envelope, the document may optionally contain the Header element, which may include additional application-specific information and is not tied to any understanding between the two communicating parties. If a Header element is defined, it must appear immediately after the Envelope. The Header is typically used for adding authorization or transaction information to a message.

Let us consider an example of a bank service for transferring money from one account to another. Before giving access to the service it is very important to authorize the user. Here, the user's account information such as the account number and password is passed in the SOAP Header and the appropriate validation is done before giving access to the Web Service.

The following code fragment illustrates the use of this element:

```
<soap:Header>
      <m:UserInfo xmlns:m="http://www.wrox.com/Info/">
            <m:UserID>123456</m:UserID>
            <m:Password>abcdefg</m:Password>
            <m:Email>john@wrox.com</m:Email>
      </m:UserInfo>
</soap:Header>
```

In this case, the `Header` element contains the user-login information. Here `UserInfo`, `UserId`, `Password`, and `Email` are user-defined elements. They are not part of the SOAP standard but declared in the namespace identified by the URI `http://www.wrox.com/Info/`.

Body

The `Header` is followed by the `Body` element. This is a mandatory element and contains application-specific data. Typically, it contains the name of a remote procedure along with its parameters.

The `Body` element contains the actual SOAP message payload and must be present in every SOAP document. The SOAP body element provides a simple mechanism for exchanging mandatory information intended for the ultimate recipient of the message. Typical uses of this element include marshaling RPC calls and error reporting.

The following code segment illustrates a simple use of this element:

```
<soap:Body>
   <GetStockPrice>
      <Symbol>IBM</Symbol>
   </GetStockPrice>
</soap:Body>
```

In this, the elements `<GetStockPrice>` and `<Symbol>` are application-specific. They are not part of the SOAP standard. Here, the `<GetStockPrice>` element represents the name of the method to be called and `<Symbol>` represents a single parameter to the method.

Fault

If the server encounters any errors while processing the message, it returns the error information by embedding it in a `Fault` element. This element is present only in the response SOAP document:

```
<soap:Fault>
   <faultcode>Client</faultcode>
   <faultstring>Invalid Stock Symbol</faultstring>
</soap:Fault>
```

The `<faultcode>` element used here is for identifying the type of the error. The value `Client` indicates that the message was incorrectly formed or the information provided was wrong. The `<faultstring>` element provides a human-readable explanation for the fault. We shall see the subelements of `Fault` and values of `<faultcode>` later in the chapter.

SOAP Attributes

SOAP elements can have the following attributes:

- `actor`
- `encodingStyle`
- `mustUnderstand`

Let us now look at each of these attributes in detail.

The Actor Attribute

A SOAP message travels from the originator to the ultimate destination, potentially by passing through a set of SOAP intermediaries along the message path. A SOAP intermediary is an application that is capable of both receiving and forwarding SOAP messages. Both intermediaries as well as the ultimate destination are identified by a URI.

The `actor` attribute defines the endpoint for header elements. The endpoint here is the intermediate node that receives the SOAP message for some processing. The `actor` attribute specifies the URI of this intermediate node for which the information in the soap header is targeted. Once the processing is done, this information is removed. If this namespace is `http://schemas.xmlsoap.org/soap/actor/next` then it indicates that this is targeted to the next endpoint that finds it. The `actor` attribute is not required in case of the payload since its target is the final endpoint.

The `actor` attribute has the following syntax:

```
soap:actor="URI"
```

The following code segment illustrates the use of this attribute:

```
<soap:Header>
      <m:UserInfo xmlns:m=http://www.wrox.com/Info/
soap:actor="http://www.abcom.com/authentication" />
            <m:UserID>123456</m:UserID>
            <m:Password>abcdefg</m:Password>
            <m:Email>john@wrox.com</m:Email>
      </m:UserInfo>
</soap:Header>
```

Here the `actor` attribute points to the URI `http://www.abcom.com/authentication`. It signifies that the information contained in the `<m:UserInfo>` element is targeted to this URI. This URI points to a SOAP intermediary that uses the content information for validating the user. Once the validation is done this information would be removed and the SOAP message would be forwarded to the next destination.

The encodingStyle Attribute

The `encodingStyle` attribute is used to define the data types that are used in the document. This provides the serialization rules defined in the SOAP message. The `encodingStyle` attribute appears on any element and is scoped to that element's contents and all child elements that do not contain such an attribute. There is no default encoding defined for a SOAP message. It has the following syntax:

```
soap:encodingStyle="URI"
```

The following code illustrates the use of the `encodingStyle` attribute:

```
<soap:Envelope
xmlns:soap="http://schemas.xmlsoap.org/soap/envelope/"
soap:encodingStyle="http://schemas.xmlsoap.org/soap/encoding/">
...
Message information goes here
...
</soap:Envelope>
```

This attribute may be set as follows:

```
soap:encodingStyle=http://www.w3.org/2001/06/soap-encoding
```

`http://schemas.xmlsoap.org/soap/encoding/` indicates the conformance with the SOAP encoding rules defined by W3C Note 08 May 2000 of SOAP 1.1. Alternatively, it may be declared as follows:

```
encodingStyle="http://example.org/encoding/restricted http://example.org/encoding/
"
```

`http://www.w3.org/2001/06/soap-encoding` indicates the conformance with the SOAP encoding rules defined by W3C Working Draft 17 December 2001 of SOAP version 1.2.

You may use a **`Null`** string for initializing the `encodingStyle` element:

```
encodingStyle=""
```

A value of the zero length URI ("") explicitly indicates that no claims are made for the encoding style of contained elements. This can be used to turn off any claims from containing elements. It means that there are no serialization rules defined for the data types used in the SOAP message.

The mustUnderstand Attribute

The `mustUnderstand` attribute is used to define if the receiver of a message must process a `Header` element. It has the following syntax:

```
soap:mustUnderstand="boolean"
```

The value of the `mustUnderstand` attribute is either `true` (1) or `false` (0). The absence of this attribute is semantically equivalent to its presence with the value `false`.

The following code illustrates the use of the `mustUnderstand` attribute. The value of 1 assigned to this attribute in the code example below indicates that the receiver must mandatorily process the header. The default for this attribute is zero; it means that if this attribute is not defined, it is not mandatory for the receiver to process this element. The purpose of this attribute is to ensure that the receiver does not silently or erroneously ignore the specified element:

```
<soap:Header>
      <m:UserInfo xmlns:m="http://www.wrox.com/Info/">
            <m:UserID soap:mustUnderstand="1">123456</m:UserID>
            <m:Password soap:mustUnderstand="1">abcdefg</m:Password>
            <m:Email soap:mustUnderstand="0">john@worx.com</m:Email>
      </m:UserInfo>
</soap:Header>
```

The above example demonstrates the SOAP `header` that is used for the user validation. The `mustUnderstand` attribute of `UserID` and `Password` elements is set to 1. It signifies the targeted endpoint that these two elements must understand for the validation process and they cannot be simply ignored.

HTTP Headers

One of the common transports used for SOAP messages is HTTP as this is in wide use. The following code fragment shows a typical HTTP header used for sending a SOAP message:

```
POST /soap/servlet/rpcrouter HTTP/1.1
Content-Length: 458
Content-Type: text/xml
SOAPAction: "urn:StockQuote"
Host: 175.25.25.155:8080
```

The first line specifies that the mechanism of sending SOAP message over HTTP is a standard `HTTP POST` method. It sends the message to the specified URI on the web server. The `Content-Type` header is `text/xml` since the SOAP message is in XML format. The `Content-Length` header indicates the length of the SOAP message. The `SOAPAction` header indicates the intent of the SOAP message. It tells the server that the particular `HTTP Post` contains a SOAP request. The reference of the service that is used while deploying the service should be set to the `SOAPAction` header.

Some SOAP receivers use this readily available information for optimizing the performance. Also, the presence and content of the `SOAPAction` header field can be used by firewalls to appropriately filter SOAP request messages in HTTP.

According to SOAP1.1 specifications, the `SOAPAction` header must be present in the SOAP HTTP request. However, the value of the header may be blank. As per the SOAP 1.2 specifications, the `SOAPAction` header is optional. The `HOST` header specifies the hostname and optionally the port on which the web server is running.

A Complete SOAP Request

As discussed previously, the remote method call is converted into an XML document. This document is called as a SOAP request. It consists of information required by the remote method. The following diagram shows the encapsulation of SOAP messages in HTTP requests:

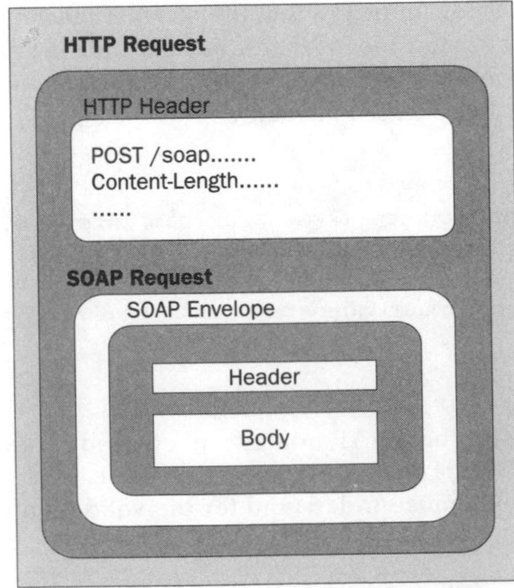

Let us consider a simple stock quote service deployed at `http://175.25.25.155:8080/soap/servlet/rpcrouter`. The service exposes a method, `getStockPrice` that takes `StockSymbol` as a parameter and returns a stock price. The following XML document represents the SOAP request for the `getStockPrice` method:

```
POST /soap/servlet/rpcrouter HTTP/1.1
Content-Length: 458
Content-Type: text/xml
SOAPAction: "urn:StockQuote"
Host: 175.25.25.155:8080
<?xml version='1.0' encoding='UTF-8'?>
<soap:Envelope xmlns:soap="http://schemas.xmlsoap.org/soap/envelope/"
xmlns:xsi="http://www.w3.org/1999/XMLSchema-instance"
xmlns:xsd="http://www.w3.org/1999/XMLSchema">
      <soap:Body>
            <ns1:getStockPrice xmlns:ns1="urn:StockQuote"
            soap:encodingStyle="http://schemas.xmlsoap.org/soap/encoding/">
                 <symbol xsi:type="xsd:string">MSFT</symbol>
     </ns1:getStockPrice>
     </soap:Body>
</soap:Envelope>
```

Note that the major difference in the previous example and this is the namespace used. In the previous examples we referred to some external schema that defines the type of the element and here we have explicitly specified the type of the elements.

The `xsi:type` is the attribute used by the element to indicate the type of the element in the SOAP payload. The prefix `xsi` is associated with the schema http://www.w3.org/1999/XMLSchema instance. This prefix indicates that the element type is borrowed from XML schema. The `xsd` prefix is used on the value of the type attribute, which indicates the type associated with the XML schemas URI http://www.w3.org/1999/XMLSchema.

SOAP XML Payload

SOAP XML Payload contains encoded method call information. This information consists of the SOAP envelope namespace, encoding style namespace, method name, and the parameters to be passed to the method as discussed earlier:

```
<?xml version='1.0' encoding='UTF-8'?>
<soap:Envelope xmlns:soap="http://schemas.xmlsoap.org/soap/envelope/"
xmlns:xsi="http://www.w3.org/1999/XMLSchema-instance"
xmlns:xsd="http://www.w3.org/1999/XMLSchema">
      <soap:Body>
            <ns1:getStockPrice xmlns:ns1="urn:StockQuote"
            soap:encodingStyle="http://schemas.xmlsoap.org/soap/encoding/">
                 <symbol xsi:type="xsd:string">MSFT</symbol>
            </ns1:getStockPrice>
      </soap:Body>
</soap:Envelope>
```

The above document represents the SOAP request for the `getStockPrice` method. This method accepts stock symbol as a parameter. The parameter type is `String`.

SOAP Response

The result of the remote method call is an XML-formatted document. It is called as a SOAP response. The following document represents the SOAP response for our stock service:

```
HTTP/1.0 200 ok
content-type: text/xml;charset=utf-8
content-length: 490
<?xml version='1.0' encoding='UTF-8'?>
<SOAP-ENV:Envelope xmlns:SOAP-ENV="http://schemas.xmlsoap.org/soap/envelope/"
xmlns:xsi="http://www.w3.org/1999/XMLSchema-instance"
xmlns:xsd="http://www.w3.org/1999/XMLSchema">
<SOAP-ENV:Body>
<ns1:getStockPriceResponse xmlns:ns1="urn:StockQuote"
SOAP-ENV:encodingStyle="http://schemas.xmlsoap.org/soap/encoding/">
      <return xsi:type="xsd:double">63.830000000000005</return>
</ns1:getStockPriceResponse>
</SOAP-ENV:Body>
</SOAP-ENV:Envelope>
```

Here, the first line of the HTTP header part indicates the successful execution of the method. If there were any execution errors this header would look like:

```
HTTP/1.0 500 Internal Server Error
```

The error details are provided in the SOAP `Fault` element inside the SOAP body.

The result of the `getStockPrice` method is specified by the `getStockPriceResponse` element. The name of this element may be any valid string, but appending the word `Response` at the end of the method name is the convention followed according to the SOAP specifications:

```
<ns1:getStockPriceResponse xmlns:ns1="urn:StockQuote" SOAP-
ENV:encodingStyle="http://schemas.xmlsoap.org/soap/encoding/">
      <return xsi:type="xsd:double">63.830000000000005</return>
</ns1:getStockPriceResponse>
```

The first child element of the `getStockPriceResponse` element contains the return value of the method. Here, the name of the element is `return`. This indicates that it contains the return value of the method. However, the method result may contain additional `OUT` parameters. In such a case, names of child elements should exactly match with the `OUT` parameters.

Data Serialization

Data Serialization is a technique of representing non-syntactic data models based on data types of XML schema. These data models can be any type of objects, object graphs, or directed labeled graphs. In short, it is a way of representing the typed data.

As we discussed before, all SOAP documents are XML documents with their own XML schema. This XML schema defines the encoding rules for serialization of data in the SOAP document. XML allows very flexible encoding of data, but SOAP defines a narrower set of encoding rules based on XML encoding. This set of encoding rules is referred to as SOAP encoding. The SOAP encoding URI is represented using `encodingStyle` attribute. According to the SOAP1.1 specifications, the SOAP encoding URI is http://schemas.xmlsoap.org/soap/encoding/. This URI points to the schema that defines the data encoding rules for SOAP.

SOAP adopts all the simple data types found in the XML schema http://www.w3.org/1999/XMLSchema. In the SOAP documents, the values can:

- Have accessor names with local or universal scope
- Be of simple type or compound type
- Be single-referenced or multi-referenced
- Be independent or embedded

Simple Types

Simple types are always represented in a single element in a SOAP message as shown below:

```
<EmpName xsi:type="xsd:string">Mike</EmpName>
```

The list of all simple types may be obtained from URL http://www.w3c.org/TR/xmlschema-0/. Here is an example of the schema with simple types:

```
<xs:schema xmlns:xs="http://www.w3.org/1999/XMLSchema" >
  <xs:element name="EmpCode" type="xs:int" />
  <xs:element name="EmpName" type="xs:string" />
  <xs:element name="Salary" type="xs:float" />
</xs:schema>
```

The valid instance elements referring to the above schema would be as follows:

```
<EmpCode>4354</EmpCode>
<EmpName>Mike</EmpName>
<Salary>2500</Salary>
```

The `xsi:type` attribute can be ignored if the application knows what type of the element is being sent and retrieved. This is possible by using some outside resources such as WSDL documents. But it is better to specify the `xsi:type` explicitly for interoperability since all languages may not support WSDL. For example, the scripting languages like Python, PHP, Perl, and so on may or may not support WSDL.

This example defines the type in a separate schema XML element but the previous example shows the same data encoded with the type embedded in an XML parameter.

Strings

SOAP borrows the string data type defined in XML Schema. This may not be same as any database or programming language string data type and hence may not support few of the characters.

A simple type element of string type can be represented in the XML Schema as follows:

```
<xs:element name="EmpName" type="xs:string" />
```

The instance element would be as follows:

```
<EmpName>Mike</EmpName>
<EmpName>John</EmpName>
<EmpName>Smith</EmpName>
```

A string may be encoded as a single-reference as well as a multiple-reference value. Multiple-reference data allows us to write more efficient XML documents to reduce the redundancy of data. This is covered in detail later in the chapter.

Enumerations

SOAP model adopts the enumeration mechanism supported by XML Schema. Enumeration is the set of distinct values with the same base type. For example, the set of currencies ("Dollar", "Euro", "Pound") can be defined as an enumeration. Here, the base type of the enumeration is the string built-in type:

```
<xs:simpleType name="Currency" >
  <xs:restriction base="xs:string" >
    <xs:enumeration value="Dollar" />
    <xs:enumeration value=" Euro" />
    <xs:enumeration value="Pound" />
  </xs:restriction>
</xs:simpleType>
```

The above enumeration can be used in the SOAP payload as shown in the following example:

```
<soap:Body>
      <m:ConcertCurrency xmlns:m=http://www.abcom.com/utils/>
         <m:cny xsi:type="m:Currency">Dollar</m:cny>
      </m:ConvertCurrency>
</soap:Body>
```

In the above code, the URI `http://www.abcom.com/utils/` points to the above declared XML Schema that contains the enumeration definition.

Enumerations are supported for all simple types except for Boolean.

Array of Bytes

SOAP and XML Schemas both provide the type for representing array of bytes. XML Schema uses `base64` encoding which is a recommended representation for binary data. Using this type, we can represent the binary data in the form of a byte array in the SOAP message. The `base64` type converts the binary data into text using the base64-encoding algorithm.

The following example shows the representation of an image using base64 encoding:

```
<Photo xmlns:xsi="http://www.w3.org/1999/XMLSchema-instance"
        xmlns:enc="http://www.w3.org/2001/09/soap-encoding"
        xsi:type="enc:base64" >
        trywjfHSBDjfnjdfaoidsjKJKJsdjasf093457'==23
</Photo>
```

SOAP does not directly support the base64 encoding of XML Schemas. However, it supplies the enc:base64 subtype for the encoding of binary data. Note here that xmlns:enc points to the URI http://www.w3.org/2001/09/soap-encoding that contains the base64 type definition.

An array of bytes may be encoded as a single-reference or multi-reference array.

Polymorphic Accessor

Like many other languages, SOAP also supports the use of accessors for accessing several types polymorphically. Polymorphic accessor is equivalent to the variant data type in COM or any type in CORBA. If the particular element is defined as a polymorphic accessor then the type of the element may vary depending upon the information. It is assumed that each type is available at run-time. In the following example, the EmpCode element is defined as being a polymorphic accessor:

```
<EmpCode xmlns:xsi="http://www.w3.org/2001/XMLSchema-instance"
xmlns:xs="http://www.w3.org/2001/XMLSchema"
xsi:type="xs:int">
     5654
</EmpCode>
```

The xsi:type must be explicitly specified in the polymorphic accessor to describe the type of the value. Since the type is xs:int the EmpCode is considered to be of type integer. However, the type of EmpCode could also be string as shown in the following example:

```
<EmpCode xmlns:xsi="http://www.w3.org/2001/XMLSchema-instance"
xmlns:xs="http://www.w3.org/2001/XMLSchema"
xsi:type="xs:string">
     5654
</EmpCode>
```

Without the use of the polymorphic accessor, it would look like:

```
<EmpCode>5654</EmpCode>
```

Here, the type of the value is invariant. In this, the application that receives message must know the type of EmpCode for explicit conversion.

Compound Types

Usually while accessing remote objects, simple data types are not sufficient. We need some mechanism to represent the complex real-world entities in the form of an XML message. The concept is similar to the programming languages where we use structures and arrays to represent the logically-related data. In a similar way, SOAP encoding also supports compound data types. SOAP encoding provides two compound types:

- Structs
- Arrays

These are represented as payload elements just like the simple types but the difference is that they have child elements. The child elements are the fields of elements of simple or compound type. Let us now look at each type in detail.

Structs

The struct is a compound value that uses an accessor to represent the members. The accessor name is the only distinction in the member values. In the same struct, no two accessors can have the same names. Let us consider an example of a student record, which stores a student's roll number, name, and grade.

The XML Schema for a `Student` struct is shown below:

```
<xs:element name="Student"
            xmlns:xs='http://www.w3.org/2001/XMLSchema' >
  <xs:complexType>
    <xs:sequence>
      <xs:element name="RollNo" type="xs:int" />
      <xs:element name="StudentName" type="xs:string" />
      <xs:element name="Grade" type="xs:string" />
    </xs:sequence>
  </xs:complexType>
</xs:element>
```

The instance of the struct declared above in the XML document would look like:

```
<e:Student xmlns:e="http://www.abcom.com/students" >
   <RollNo>343</RollNo>
   <StudentName>Henry</StudentName>
   <Grade>A</Grade>
</e:Student>
```

Here, the URI `http://www.abcom.com/students` points to the above given schema that contains the definition of the student record.

Arrays

An array is similar to the struct. The difference between these two types lies in the way of referencing the members. In a struct, the members are identified by their accessor name, but in case of arrays the members are identified by the ordinal position. SOAP arrays are defined using the special data type – `enc:Array`. Similar to all SOAP encoding, the namespace associated with the SOAP arrays is `http://schemas.xmlsoap.org/soap/encoding`.

Let us consider an example of an array that contains the marks of the students. Here is the XML Schema that declares the `StudentMarks` array:

```
<xs:schema xmlns:xs="http://www.w3.org/2001/XMLSchema"
           xmlns:enc="http://www.w3.org/2001/09/soap-encoding" >
  <xs:import namespace="http://www.w3.org/2001/09/soap-encoding" />
  <xs:element name="StudentMarks" type="enc:Array" />
</xs:schema>
```

The following code segment shows the array conforming to the preceding schema:

```
<StudentMarks xmlns:xs="http://www.w3.org/2001/XMLSchema"
                    xmlns:enc="http://www.w3.org/2001/09/soap-encoding"
                    enc:arrayType="xs:int[5]" >
  <marks>92</marks>
  <marks>95</marks>
  <marks>87</marks>
  <marks>89</marks>
  <marks>78</marks>
</StudentMarks >
```

The attribute `enc:arrayType` is used to declare the type of the array. SOAP also provides the attributes like `enc:offset` to set the starting offset for an array, `enc:position` attribute to set the absolute position of a particular element in the array:

```
<StudentMarks xmlns:xs="http://www.w3.org/2001/XMLSchema"
                    xmlns:enc="http://www.w3.org/2001/09/soap-encoding"
                    enc:arrayType="xs:int[5]" enc:offset=[10]>
```

In the above example the offset is set to `10`. Hence the data stored will be from 10 to 14. It can be very well used to transfer part of an array. All the values before the offset are assumed to contain default or `NULL` value depending upon the application.

Every element in the array can be of simple type or compound type and hence arrays can be used to represent more complex structures in the SOAP message.

Multi-Reference Values

SOAP allows us to write more efficient XML documents by reducing the data redundancy. This is achieved by allowing the values to be referenced multiple times. This avoids unnecessary repetition of the same information in the XML document. SOAP uses `id` and `href` attributes for this purpose. The attribute `href` specifies the URI that references the relevant serialized instance via its `id` attribute.

Let us take an example of an XML document that contains information relating to the books in a library. It uses the struct `bookCopy` that represents the information about a single copy of the book. The `bookCopy` attribute stores `bookNo` and other details such as ISBN, title, and publication that are represented using the `details` struct. The simple SOAP message representing the information of two different copies of the same book in the library could be as follows:

```
<e:Books xmlns:e="http://www.abcom.com/library"
>
    <bookCopy>
      <bookNo>342</bookNo>
      <details
>
        <ISBN>123456789</ISBN
>
        <title>Linux Web Services</title
>
        <publication>Wrox</publication
>
      </details
>
    </bookCopy>
      <bookNo>343</bookNo>
      <details
>
        <ISBN>123456789</ISBN
>
        <title>Linux Web Services</title
>
        <publication>Wrox</publication
>
      </details
>
    </bookCopy
>
</e:Books
>
```

Since other information is common except the bookNo, the XML document contains redundant data. Here, we can make the details field of the bookCopy a multi-reference value as follows:

```
<e:Books xmlns:e="http://www.abcom.com/library"
>
    <bookCopy>
      <bookNo>342</bookNo>
      <details href="#BookDetails-1"/
>
    </bookCopy
>
    <bookCopy>
      <bookNo>343</bookNo>
      <details href="#BookDetails"/
>
    </bookCopy>
```

```
</e:Books
>

<e:BookDetails xmlns:e="http://www.abcom.com/library" id="BookDetails-1">
    <ISBN>123456789</ISBN
>
    <title>Linux web Services</title
>
    <publicationWrox</publication
>
</e:BookDetails
>
```

This helps in removing the redundant data from the XML document.

Error Handling

So far, we have discussed how well-formatted SOAP messages are used for remote procedure calls in Web Services. We assumed that good and clean SOAP messages are exchanged between the client and the server. The SOAP request contains the name, parameters, and other related information about the remote method and the SOAP response contains the return value of the method. However, this will not be the realistic view for a real application. Some SOAP or application-specific problems cause errors that must be reported to the targeted endpoint. For this purpose, SOAP provides an error-handling model called the SOAP fault model.

This uses a single `Fault` element to represent the error inside the SOAP body. According to the SOAP specifications, this element should appear as the first child element of the body element and must appear only once in a SOAP body.

Here is an example of a SOAP response that indicates the failure in processing the SOAP request:

```
<?xml version='1.0' ?>
<env:Envelope xmlns:env="http://www.w3.org/2001/12/soap-envelope"
            xmlns:f='http://www.w3.org/2001/12/soap-faults'>
  <env:Body>
    <env:Fault>
      <faultcode>env:Sender</faultcode>
      <faultstring>Processing Error</faultstring>
      <detail>
        <e:myfaultdetails xmlns:e="http://www.abcom.com/faults" >
          <message>Invalid Account No</message>
          <line>105</line>
        </e:myfaultdetails>
      </detail>
    </env:Fault>
  </env:Body>
</env:Envelope>
```

faultcode Element

This element contains the information that indicates the type of error. The contents of this element must be a qualified name. This information is meant for the application and hence cannot be presented directly to the user.

The SOAP version 1.2 working draft the defines following `faultcodes`:

VersionMismatch

This indicates that the namespace specified in the SOAP request is invalid. For SOAP version 1.2 working draft, this namespace must be `http://www.w3.org/2001/12/soap-envelope`.

MustUnderstand

This indicates that the server could not understand the information in the SOAP header with the `MustUnderstand` attribute set to `true`.

DTDNotSupported

According to the SOAP specification, the SOAP message should not contain the Data type Definition. This `faultcode` is returned in the SOAP response if the SOAP request contains DTD.

DataEncodingUnknown

The current node does not support the data encoding specified by the SOAP request.

Sender

This indicates that the sender incorrectly formed the message. The information content in the message was inappropriate to continue the processing for the server. The possible cause could be a lack of proper authentication. It also indicates that the message should be modified before resending.

Receiver

This indicates that the error is due to the processing problem on the receiver. It could be due to the problem with some upstream node that the receiver is accessing. The same request would succeed at some other time.

faultstring Element

This is another child element of `Fault` element, which is intended for providing the human-readable information related to the SOAP fault. This information is meant for the end user and is of no use for the application processing. The `faultstring` element is mandatory in the `Fault` element.

faultactor Element

This attribute indicates the endpoint in the SOAP message that causes the fault to occur. This is similar to the actor attribute that points to an URI which is the destination for the SOAP header entity. Any SOAP node except the ultimate endpoint must add the `faultactor` element in the SOAP fault. If the SOAP fault does not contain this element we can consider that the error is generated at the ultimate endpoint.

detail Element

Though it is possible to provide the complete information regarding the SOAP fault using the elements discussed opposite, we can include some more information in the `detail` element. This additional information could be used in debugging the application. The server must include this element in the response message if the error is generated while processing the SOAP body.

We shall see language-specific implementations of error handling in the subsequent chapters.

SOAP Restrictions

As a protocol for remote object invocation, SOAP does not address many issues. Many aspects of building an object model are explicitly excluded from the SOAP specifications to maintain simplicity. SOAP defines only those aspects that are absolutely critical for developing a lightweight protocol. SOAP does not say anything about distributed garbage collection, type safety or versioning, bi-directional HTTP communications, message-box carrying or pipeline processing, object-by-reference or no-object activation. Despite these factors, this protocol could be implemented very easily in any language on any platform and also over other protocols apart from HTTP.

WSDL

WSDL (Web Service Description Language) is a format written in an XML file that describes a network service (http://www.w3c.org/TR/wsdl). The WSDL file consists of service interfaces and their respective bindings. The basic question here is why do we need WSDL? The answer to this question is addressed in one of Web Services proposed principles. This principle defines that a Web Service should be accessible across platforms and support interoperability. After we have built a service, how do clients access it? There should be an interface or a language that represents this service.

WSDL comes in the picture here since this technology is built using open standards like XML, XSD, SOAP, and MIME. In reality, it makes a Web Service platform- and device-independent. A client can look up for a published Web Service and receive a WSDL file. The client then introspects this file and calls the respective services programmatically without having to know on what platform or language the service is implemented.

The WSDL represents a description format in the Web Service architecture stack:

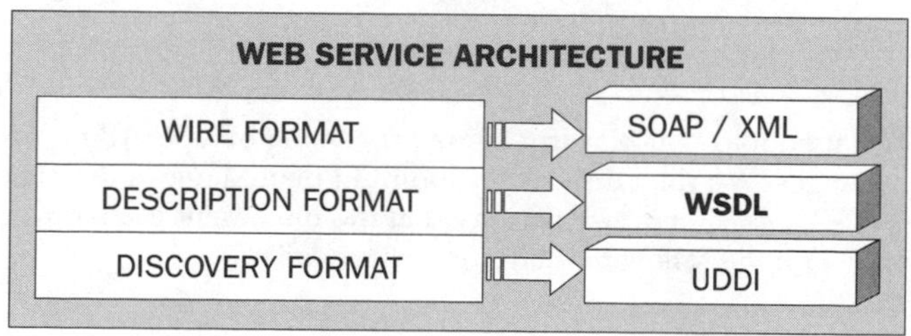

The invocation flow for a Web Service is depicted in the following flow diagram:

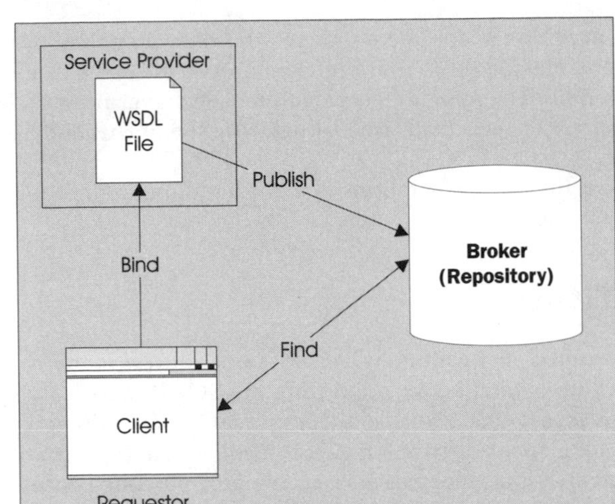

A WSDL file can be stored on the provider's Web Service server or can be published in a registry such as UDDI under its respective category. A requestor can search for the required service, get the WSDL document, and bind the service. After getting a WSDL file the requestor studies the WSDL document and understands the details about the service method, its parameters, and invocation. After introspecting the WSDL document the client invokes the service. The requestor needs to develop a client or a web application.

The client application requires a reference to the service which is done by generating a proxy class using the WSDL document. Proxy generation is done using toolkits such as Axis, SOAP Toolkit, and so on. We need to provide a WSDL file as an input parameter for the tool and in turn it generates a proxy class in the desired language. The proxy class consists of automatically generated SOAP invocation code for the service method.

After studying the WSDL flow process we shall study the WSDL document structure. Before starting the discussion on the WSDL document we rephrase the WSDL definition as:

A file in an XML format providing language rules for describing services as a set of endpoints that operate by exchanging messages containing document-oriented or procedure-oriented information.

Endpoints are the logical entities that perform some processing of a SOAP message. They are the receivers of SOAP messages. We shall discuss this point in detail later in the chapter. Getting back to our definition of the WSDL document, we can say that the document is a structure of definitions. This structure is represented with the following definitions:

- **Service**
  This is a set of one or more network endpoints or ports.

- **Bindings**
  Each port is linked with a specific binding. Bindings define how an abstract set of operations and messages are linked to a port according to a specific protocol.
- **Port type**
  As discussed above, the bindings map a specific protocol to a port type. A port type is composed of one or more operations. Port type is defined as an abstract set of operations supported by one or more endpoints.
- **Operations**
  Further in the document after defining the port type, we have to define the operations. Operations represent an abstract set of tasks that the service can perform. These operations are composed of an abstract set of messages.
- **Messages**
  Messages define the data that is transported or communicated to the other side during the operation. This message consists of pieces of data that are defined as types.

In the above element listing, each abstract definition can be bound to more than one concrete port so that the same message can be sent to different ports using different encoding. In other words, the operations and messages are specified abstractly and then bound to a concrete network protocol and message format to define an endpoint. The WSDL 1.1 specification right now defines how to use WSDL in conjunction with SOAP1.1, HTTP `GET/POST` methods, and MIME standards.

The WSDL Document

Normally, a WSDL document is generated using tools provided by many enterprises like IBM, SUN, and Microsoft. The tools include WSTK provided by IBM and Java2wsdl provided by Apache Axis. But to use the document, we need to know what the contents are and what they represent. We will not go into hand coding of the document but we shall discuss each of these elements in detail.

Document Structure

The structure of a WSDL document is implemented using XML Schema along with its supporting types. The WSDL document is easy to understand and it allows flexibility in defining your own types. The specifications for the WSDL document provide a set of six XML element definitions. The basic or root element in the document is `<definitions>`. The six nested elements are:

- `<types>`
- `<message>`
- `<porttype>`
- `<binding>`
- `<service>`
- `<port>`

(In addition to these, there is also the `<import>` element that is not a regular member of the WSDL document.) Let us see the use of these elements by looking at an example of a typical WSDL document. The WSDL document given oveleaf describes a Web Service that exposes a web method called `getStockRate` to clients:

```
<?xml version="1.0"?>
<definitions name="StockTrading"

targetNamespace="http://abcom.com/stocktrading.wsdl"
          xmlns:tns="http://abcom.com/stocktrading.wsdl"
          xmlns:xsd1="http://abcom.com/stocktrading.xsd"
          xmlns:soap="http://schemas.xmlsoap.org/wsdl/soap/"
          xmlns="http://schemas.xmlsoap.org/wsdl/">

    <types>
       <schema targetNamespace="http://abcom.com/stocktrading.xsd"
              xmlns="http://www.w3.org/2000/10/XMLSchema">
           <element name="StockRateRequest">
              <complexType>
                  <all>
                      <element name="StockScript" type="string"/>
                  </all>
              </complexType>
           </element>
           <element name="StockRate">
              <complexType>
                  <all>
                      <element name="rate" type="float"/>
                  </all>
              </complexType>
           </element>
       </schema>
    </types>

    <message name="GetStockRateInput">
        <part name="body" element="xsd1:StockRateRequest"/>
    </message>

    <message name="GetStockRateOutput">
        <part name="body" element="xsd1:StockRate"/>
    </message>

    <portType name="StockTradingPortType">
        <operation name="GetStockRate">
           <input message="tns:GetStockRateInput"/>
           <output message="tns:GetStockRateOutput"/>
        </operation>
    </portType>

    <binding name="StockTradingSoapBinding" type="tns: StockTradingPortType">
        <soap:binding style="document"
 transport="http://schemas.xmlsoap.org/soap/http"/>
        <operation name="GetStockRate">
           <soap:operation soapAction="http://abcom.com/GetStockRate"/>
```

```
            <input>
                <soap:body use="literal"/>
            </input>
            <output>
                <soap:body use="literal"/>
            </output>
        </operation>
    </binding>

    <service name="StockTradingService">
        <documentation>FIRST SERVICE</documentation>
        <port name="StockTradingPort" binding="tns:StockTradingBinding">
            <soap:address location="http://abcom.com/stocktrading"/>
        </port>
    </service>

</definitions>
```

We shall look at the above code example step-by-step discussing each of the elements used in the document.

<definitions>

The very first line of the example defines this document as an XML document:

```
<?xml version="1.0"?>
```

The second line defines a `<definitions>` element tag. This tag plays an important role in naming the service or the WSDL document. The name of the service can be defined using the `name` attribute in the WSDL document. The other attribute in this element is the `targetNamespace` attribute. This attribute specifies the attribute of type URI:

```
<definitions name="StockTrading"

targetNamespace="http://abcom.com/stocktrading.wsdl"
          xmlns:tns="http://abcom.com/stocktrading.wsdl"
          xmlns:xsd1="http://abcom.com/stocktrading.xsd"
          xmlns:soap="http://schemas.xmlsoap.org/wsdl/soap/"
          xmlns="http://schemas.xmlsoap.org/wsdl/">
```

Namespaces are used basically for maximizing the reusability of the components in the WSDL document. We shall see further in the chapter that many of the elements in the WSDL document contain attributes to refer to other elements defined in some other documents. A simple example of this will be the `<binding>` element of our example above. We can see here that there is an attribute type that refers to a `<portType>` element in the document. In the above case, namespace has a prefix of `tns` defined with it:

```
    <binding name="StockTradingSoapBinding" type="tns: StockTradingPortType">
```

Coming back to the `<definitions>` element, we summarize its definition as the root element of each WSDL document. It contains attributes defining the namespaces used in the WSDL document:

```
    <portType name="StockTradingPortType">
```

<import>

WSDL allows associating a namespace with a document location using an import statement. The specific use of the import statement here is to allow the separation of different elements of a service definition into independent documents, which can then be imported as needed. This technique helps writing clearer service definitions by separating the definitions according to their level of abstraction. It maximizes the ability to reuse service definitions of all kinds. We have not implemented the `<import>` element in the above example but here is an example of the same.

Assume that we have defined three separate documents as the data types definition document, abstract types definitions (Message, Port types, and so on), and the service definition file. The data type definition `.xsd` file is at a location, say:

```
http://abcom.com/stocktrading/stocktrading.xsd
```

The file definition is given below:

```
<?xml version="1.0"?>
<schema targetNamespace="http://abcom.com/stockquote/schemas"
      xmlns="http://www.w3.org/2000/10/XMLSchema">
    <element name="StockRateRequest">
        <complexType>
            <all>
                <element name="tickerSymbol" type="string"/>
            </all>
        </complexType>
    </element>
    <element name="StockRate">
        <complexType>
            <all>
                <element name="rate" type="float"/>
            </all>
        </complexType>
    </element>
</schema>
```

After writing our `.xsd` file, we refer it in our `.wsdl` file. The WSDL file consists of abstract type definitions like messages and the `portType`. An abstract definition file is given further below. This file is stored at the following location:

```
http://abcom.com/stocktrading/stocktrading.wsdl
```

The definition of the file is given below:

```
<?xml version="1.0"?>
<definitions name="StockTrading"

targetNamespace="http://abcom.com/stocktrading/definitions"
          xmlns:tns="http://abcom.com/stocktrading/definitions"
          xmlns:xsd1="http://abcom.com/stocktrading/schemas"
          xmlns:soap="http://schemas.xmlsoap.org/wsdl/soap/"
```

```
            xmlns="http://schemas.xmlsoap.org/wsdl/">

    <import namespace="http://abcom.com/stocktrading/schemas"
            location="http://abcom.com/stocktrading/stocktrading.xsd"/>

     <message name="GetStockRateInput">
          <part name="body" element="xsd1:StockRateRequest"/>
     </message>
  <message name="GetStockRateOutput">
          <part name="body" element="xsd1:StockRate"/>
     </message>

  <portType name="StockTradingPortType">
          <operation name="GetStockRate">
              <input message="tns:GetStockRateInput"/>
              <output message="tns:GetStockRateOutput"/>
          </operation>
     </portType>
  </definitions>
```

In the `targetNamespace` attribute, we provide the schema namespace along with other namespaces. We import the `.xsd` file using the `import` element assigning it the location of the file. In the `<message>` element we provide the reference for the data type definition in the `element` attribute. The `element` attribute is passed a namespace prefix and the type name:

```
     <message name="GetStockRateInput">
          <part name="body" element="xsd1:StockRateRequest"/>
     </message>
```

After importing the `.xsd` file in the `.wsdl` file, we write the final service definition along with its binding properties. This service definition is provided in the `stocktradingservice.wsdl` file. This file is stored in the following location:

```
http://abcom.com/stocktrading/stocktradingservice.wsdl
```

The definition of the file is given below:

```
<?xml version="1.0"?>
<definitions name="StockTrading"

targetNamespace="http://abcom.com/stocktrading/service"
          xmlns:tns="http://abcom.com/stocktrading/service"
          xmlns:soap="http://schemas.xmlsoap.org/wsdl/soap/"
          xmlns:defs="http://abcom.com/stocktrading/definitions"
          xmlns="http://schemas.xmlsoap.org/wsdl/">

    <import namespace="http://abcom.com/ stocktrading /definitions"
            location="http://abcom.com/ stocktrading / stocktrading.wsdl"/>

     <binding name="StockTradingSoapBinding" type="defs:StockTradingPortType">
          <soap:binding style="document"
transport="http://schemas.xmlsoap.org/soap/http"/>
```

```
        <operation name="GetStockRate">
            <soap:operation soapAction="http://abcom.com/GetStockRate"/>
            <input>
                <soap:body use="literal"/>
            </input>
            <output>
                <soap:body use="literal"/>
            </output>
        </operation>
    </binding>

    <service name="StockTradingService">
        <documentation>FIRST WEB SERVICE</documentation>
        <port name="StockTradingPort" binding="tns:StockTradingBinding">
            <soap:address location="http://abcom.com/ stocktrading "/>
        </port>
    </service>
</definitions>
```

In the above file, we import the stocktrading.wsdl file into targetNamespace xmlns:defs. The import namespace provides the location attribute that refers to the location of the file. This namespace is used in the <binding> element in the type attribute. The binding element requires a reference of the <portType> element. This reference is provided through the stocktrading.wsdl file. We use the stocktrading file because the definition of the <portType> is given in the stocktrading.wsdl file. We refer to the <portType> element using its name attribute. This is how we provide the reference:

```
<binding name="StockTradingSoapBinding" type="defs:StockTradingPortType">
```

The important point to note here is that in our stocktradingservice.wsdl file we do not have the <type> element. If an XML schema is included using the <import> element as in our case, there is no need of a <type> element wrapping the definition. In our case, we are using some basic data types, but if we want a data type such as a company with fields such as name, location, and so on, then we can have the type definition implemented directly in the WSDL document. An example for the company data type with fields name and location is given below:

```
<types>
    <xsd:schema xmlns="http://www.w3.org/2000/10/XMLSchema">
        <xsd:element name="CompanyDetails">
            <xsd:complexType>
                <xsd:sequence>
                    <xsd:element name="CompanyName" type="string"/>
                    <xsd:element name="Location" type="string"/>
                </xsd:sequence>
            </xsd:complexType>
        </xsd:element>
    </xsd:schema>
</types>
```

Having discussed the <definitions> and the <import> elements, we shall now discuss the <types> element or the type definition part of the WSDL document.

<types>

The `<types>` element provides data type definitions used to describe the messages exchanged. The basic use of this element is to make the service compatible, platform neutral, and interoperable. It makes different clients or services on different platforms or languages understand each other's data types easily. If we consider a distributed architecture, these types or objects are transported over a network in a binary format that is they are serialized/de-serialized on both sides of the network.

WSDL implements XSD (XML Schema Definition) as the standard type system for the data types and treats it as a native type system for maximum interoperability and platform neutrality. XSD-type system represents the data types in the message not considering whether the resulting XSD schema validates the particular wire format. Considering future development we cannot expect a single type system grammar to be used to describe all abstract types presently defined or expected in the future.

WSDL allows type systems to be added via extensibility elements. An extensibility element can be set under the types element to identify the type definition system being used and to provide an XML container element for the type definitions. The role of this element can be compared to that of the schema element of the XML Schema language. The syntax for the element is given below:

```
<definitions…>
<types>
<-- type-system extensibility element --> *
</types>
</definitions>
```

To understand this element, we take the `type` definition from our WSDL document:

```
    <types>
       <schema targetNamespace="http://abcom.com/stocktrading.xsd"
              xmlns="http://www.w3.org/2000/10/XMLSchema">
           <element name="StockRateRequest">
              <complexType>
                  <all>
                      <element name="StockScript" type="string"/>
                  </all>
              </complexType>
           </element>
           <element name="StockRate">
              <complexType>
                  <all>
                      <element name="rate" type="float"/>
                  </all>
              </complexType>
           </element>
       </schema>
    </types>
```

In the above code we specify the type system in the types element for the string and float data types. These are the basic types that are supported by the schema. For full listing of supported data types refer to http://www.w3.org/TR/xmlschema-2/. The list of data types consists of built-in data type and derived data types.

Up to this point, we have seen basic data type implementation in the <type> element. This element also supports implementation for the complex types. We have seen one of the complex type definitions in the previous element. Given below is an example for the complex types:

```
<types>
       <xsd:schema xmlns="http://www.w3.org/2000/10/XMLSchema">
           <xsd:element name="Employee">
              <xsd:complexType>
                  <xsd:sequence>
                      <xsd:element name="Identification" type="int"/>
                      <xsd:element name="Name" type="string"/>
                      <xsd:element name="Designation" type="string"/>
                  </xsd:sequence>
              </xsd:complexType>
           </xsd:element>
       </xsd:schema>
</types>
```

In the above example, we have `Employee` type with the fields `Identification`, `Name`, and `Designation`. These fields are represented by basic data types `int`, `string`, and `string` respectively. We can also define this in a separate `.xsd` file and use the <import> element to refer to it in the WSDL document. For example, we create:

```
<?xml version="1.0"?>
<schema xmlns="http://www.w3.org/2000/10/XMLSchema">
    <complexType name= Employee>
            <all>
                 <element name="Identification" type="int"/>
                 <element name="Name" type="string"/>
                 <element name="Designation" type="string"/>
            </all>
   </complexType>
</schema>
```

To summarize, we can say that the <types> element represent the data definitions or data types used in the WSDL service definition. Next, we have the <message> element in the WSDL document.

<message>

The <message> element represents an abstract definition of the data being transmitted. A message consists of logical parts, each of which is linked with a definition within some type system. WSDL defines a Web Service as a port that is similar to the ports used in TCP/IP for different protocols. The syntax for defining a message is given below:

```
<definitions...>
<message name="nmtoken"> *
<part name="nmtoken"? element="qname" type="qname"?/> *
</message>
</definitions>
```

In the previous syntax, the <part> element has three attributes:

- name
  This attribute defines a token or a unique name for the <part> attribute
- element
  This attribute refers to an XSD element using a qualified name
- type
  This attribute refers to an XSD simple type or complex type using a qualified name

A <message> element can have more than one <part> element. This element forms the actual message and it refers to the type defined in the <types> element on the document. We take our <message> element from the above WSDL document:

```
<message name="GetStockRateInput">
        <part name="body" element="xsd1:StockRateRequest"/>
</message>

<message name="GetStockRateOutput">
      <part name="body" element="xsd1:StockRate"/>
</message>
```

In the above code, element refers to an XSD element using a qualified name. The qualified namespace refers to the <types> element in the xsd1:StockRateRequest document. The xds1 prefix needs to be defined in the header block of the WSDL document. A unique name is provided by the message name attribute among all the messages defined within the enclosing WSDL document.

<portType> and <operation>

A collection of operations published or exposed by a service is called a Port Type. This is composed of one or more operations. The <portType> element represents a set of abstract operations exposed by a Web Service. Each of these operations refers to an input message and output messages. The <operation> element is the child element of the <portType> element. The <operation> element also defines one more attribute: the parameterOrder attribute. This attribute is optional and can be used to specify space-delimited listed part names to indicate the order of parameters when making the RPC call. The sample code using parameterOrder attribute is given below:

```
<operation name="GetStockRate" parameterOrder="StockSymbol StockRate" >
      <input message="tns:GetStockRateInput" />
      <output message="tns:GetStockRateOutput" />
</operation>
```

An <operation> element defines the message for sending and receiving. These messages are defined using the input and the output tags in the <operation> element. Each of these tags refers to the corresponding message by its fully qualified name as shown below:

```
<wsdl:definitions...>...>
<wsdl:portType name="nmtoken">
<wsdl:operation name="nmtoken".../>".../> *
</wsdl:portType>
</wsdl:definitions>
```

An extract of <portType> and <operation> elements from the WSDL document is given below:

```
<portType name="StockTradingPortType">
    <operation name="GetStockRate">
        <input message="tns:GetStockRateInput"/>
        <output message="tns:GetStockRateOutput"/>
    </operation>
</portType>
```

In the above code, the <operation> element has two child elements, <input> and <output>. The <operation> element has a name attribute that refers to the method to be invoked. The method accepts an input parameter of type string in the <input> element and the result is stored in the <output> element. The method accepts the stock symbol as the input parameter.

The WSDL document has four transmission primitives that endpoint supports.

One-Way Transmission

The message is received by the endpoint. A message is sent from the client to a service without any response from that service. The format of one-way transmission is given below:

```
<wsdl:definitions…>
      <wsdl:portType…>…> *
            <wsdl:operation name="nmtoken">
                  <wsdl:input name="nmtoken"? message="qname"/>
            </wsdl:operation>
      </wsdl:portType >
</wsdl:definitions>
```

The <input> element specifies the input message to the web method. As can be seen from the format we do not specify the <output> element in the operation. It means that the web method will not return anything to the client. Also, if there is any exception in the web method, the client will not be notified.

Request – Response Transmission

The endpoint receives a message and sends an interconnected message. A message is sent to the service and a response is returned as a result of that request:

```
<wsdl:definitions…>
      <wsdl:portType…> *
            <wsdl:operation name="nmtoken" parameterOrder="nmtokens">
                  <wsdl:input name="nmtoken"? message="qname"/>
                  <wsdl:output name="nmtoken"? message="qname"/>
                  <wsdl:fault name="nmtoken" message="qname"/>*
            </wsdl:operation>
      </wsdl:portType >
</wsdl:definitions>
```

Solicit – Response

The endpoint sends a message and receives an interconnected message. A message is sent from the service to the client and the client returns the response back to the service:

```
<wsdl:definitions…>
            <wsdl:portType…> *
                  <wsdl:operation name="nmtoken" parameterOrder="nmtokens">
                        <wsdl:output name="nmtoken"? message="qname"/>
                        <wsdl:input name="nmtoken"? message="qname"/>
                        <wsdl:fault name="nmtoken" message="qname"/>*
                  </wsdl:operation>
            </wsdl:portType >
</wsdl:definitions>
```

Notifications

The endpoint notifies the client by sending a message. A message is sent to the client that is registered with the service:

```
<wsdl:definitions…>
            <wsdl:portType…> *
                  <wsdl:operation name="nmtoken">
                        <wsdl:output name="nmtoken"? message="qname"/>
                  </wsdl:operation>
            </wsdl:portType >
</wsdl:definitions>
```

To summarize, we can say that `input` and `output` parameters can be mapped to the messages and use these operation messages that are enclosed in the `portTypes`. For example, one-way operation will be used when a client just wants to invoke a method and wait for the result. To understand the invocation procedure of a particular method, we need to study the `<binding>` element.

<binding>

A `<binding>` element is defined as a channel that is used by the service to communicate with an endpoint or a client. This element defines a structure and protocol specifications for operations and messages defined in a particular `portType`. This element plays an important role in making the Web Service independent of any invocation mechanism. The standard mechanisms used in this element are HTTP, MIME, and (most importantlt) SOAP. The syntax for the element is given below:

```
<wsdl:definitions…>
            <wsdl:binding name="nmtoken" type="qname"> *
                  <-- extensibility element (1) --> *
                        <wsdl:operation name="nmtoken"> *
                  <-- extensibility element (2) --> *
                             <wsdl:input name="nmtoken"?> ?
                                       <-- extensibility element (3) -->
                             </wsdl:input>
                             <wsdl:output name="nmtoken"?> ?
                                       <-- extensibility element (4) --> *
                             </wsdl:output>
                       <wsdl:fault name="nmtoken"> *
                             <-- extensibility element (5) --> *
                       </wsdl:fault>
                       </wsdl:operation>
            </wsdl:binding>
</wsdl:definitions>
```

The <binding> element has the following attributes:

- `name`
  This attribute defines a unique name among all bindings defined within the enclosing WSDL document
- `type`
  This attribute defines the binding references to the `portType` element

We take an extract from our WSDL document defined above:

```
<binding name="StockTradingSoapBinding" type="tns:StockTradingPortType">
        <soap:binding style="document"
              transport="http://schemas.xmlsoap.org/soap/http"/>
        <operation name="GetStockRate">
           <soap:operation soapAction="http://abcom.com/GetStockRate"/>
                 <input>
                      <soap:body use="literal"/>
                 </input>
                 <output>
                      <soap:body use="literal"/>
                 </output>
        </operation>
</binding>
```

In the above code, we have the binding name as `StockTradingSoapBinding`. The `type` attribute refers to the qualified namespace of the <portType> element. The `tns` namespace is defined in the document header. Since we are using SOAP as our access mechanism, our <binding> element is followed by a SOAP binding element:

```
<soap:binding style="document"
      transport="http://schemas.xmlsoap.org/soap/http"/>
```

SOAP Binding

SOAP is the basic mechanism that is used in the WSDL document. The syntax of the SOAP binding is given below:

```
<binding name="BindingName" type="PortType">
        <soap:binding style="rpc/document"
              transport="http://schemas.xmlsoap.org/soap/http"/>
        <operation name="Method Name">
           <soap:operation soapAction="action"/>
                 <input>
                      <soap:body encodingStyle="encoding"
                      use="encoded/literal"/>
                 </input>
                 <output>
                      <soap:body encodingStyle="encoding"
                      use="encoded/literal"/>
                 </output>
        </operation>
</binding>
```

The SOAP binding element has two important attributes:

- `style`
  There can be two values for the `style` attribute: `rpc` or `document`. These values are important since they define the communication type or procedure with the service. This attribute defines how a SOAP message is constructed for an application where a client accesses a service using SOAP.

  The default value for the `style` attribute is `document`. If we set the default value, all messages are directly copied into the envelope and no wrapper is generated.
  If it is set to `rpc` then all the parameters sent to the service will be wrapped in an XML element. This element is given the same name as that of the `<operation>` element. In our example, we have set the `style` value to `document`.
- `transport`
  As the name specifies, this attribute defines HTTP as the service network protocol over which the message will be sent by using the appropriate namespace.

The next statement in the binding element is the `<soap:operation>` element. This is the element that sends a request to the service:

```
<soap:operation soapAction="http://abcom.com/GetStockRate"/>
```

The element has an attribute `soapAction` that specifies the service method to be invoked. The question here is how does the receiver know which service method to invoke. This is answered in the `soapAction` attribute. This attribute has a header field which stores information about the service requested for invocation. This is a mandatory field for the SOAP requests that are sent via HTTP. The receiver's job becomes easier because it makes use of this field to invoke the requested service. This field can also act as a unique identifier that the server uses to direct the request to the right service implementation.

There are many other procedures used for calling the service. We can use a body tag to provide the same functionality as specified in the Apache SOAP implementation.

The `<input>` and `<output>` elements are the other two child elements in the `<soap:operation>` element:

```
<input>
      <soap:body use="literal"/>
</input>
<output>
      <soap:body use="literal"/>
</output>
```

These elements define how the request and the response envelopes are encoded. The `<soap:body>` element has an `encodingStyle` attribute that specifies which actual format is used for encoding. There are two basic SOAP schemes, which are used:

- SOAP encoding
  This is a style of encoding data as per the SOAP specifications.
- XML literal
  This specifies that data is simply sent and received as a simple XML document without any encoding. In the above example, we make use of this scheme.

As provided in the binding syntax above, we also have one more child element as <fault>. This element provides error information for the request response procedures. Further on, we shall discuss HTTP and MIME bindings as specified in the WSDL specifications.

HTTP 1.1 Bindings

This binding is one of the binding types specified in the WSDL specification. This binding is used mainly if the implementation is for invoking a Web Service from a web browser. Since we are using HTTP 1.1 it has two ways in which the implementation can be done:

- HTTP GET
- HTTP POST

To demonstrate an example of such an implementation, we shall have our StockTrading service implemented with HTTP GET bindings. We shall not discuss a full implementation, but only the binding part for the same.

In HTTP GET bindings, there are two different types, which are defined: GET with encoding and GET with replacement. We shall discuss each one of them.

Implementation for HTTP GET with urlEncoded is as follows:

```
<binding name="StockTradingHTTPBinding" type="tns:StockTradingPortType">
        <http:binding verb="GET"/>"/>
        <operation name="GetStockRate">
           <http:operation location="http://abcom.com/GetStockRate"/>
                 <input>
                      <http:urlEncoded/>
                </input>
                <output>
                      <mime:content type= "text/html"/>
               </output>
        </operation>
</binding>
```

In the above example, we have <http:binding> as the child element of the <binding> element. This element helps us to define which procedure is supported by the service that is either GET or POST. Procedure definition is provided in the verb attribute in the <http:binding> element.

The next element is the <operation> element. The element has a child element as <http:operation> that defines the location of the service. The location attribute specifies the URI for the operation. The URI value must be the relative URI. In our example, we have provided the location as http://abcom.com/GetStockRate.

The <input> element consists of an <http:urlEncoded> element. This element specifies that all the message parts be encoded into the HTTP request URI using the standard URI encoding rules. The rules define that the parameter names should be similar to the message part names and the values are assigned in the name- value pair. This grammar is used with GET to specify URI encoding. The ? is appended automatically to the string. A proper example to demonstrate a request string is given below:

```
GET, URL= "http://www.abcom.com/GetStockRate?stockscript=IBM"
```

The <output> element defines the response from the service. The response received from the service is presented in a format defined in the <mime:content type= "text/html"> element.

Implementation for HTTP GET with Replacement (urlreplacement)

Message parts are encoded into the HTTP request. This is indicated by `http:urlreplacement` element. Here we have an example that demonstrates the HTTP `GET` procedure with URL replacement bindings:

```
<binding name="StockTradingHTTPBinding" type="tns:StockTradingPortType">
        <http:binding verb="GET"/>
        <operation name="GetStockRate">
           <http:operation
            location="http://abcom.com/GetStockRate/(stockscript)"/>
                 <input>
                      <http:urlreplacement/>
                 </input>
                <output>
                <mime:content type= "text/html"/>
                </output>
        </operation>
</binding>
```

The process of this procedure and its attributes is similar to the previous example. The only difference is in the `<input>` element processing. Here, we use the `GET` verb but the encoding standard is not implemented. For the `location` attribute, we pass the `<input>` parameter name to the string as `(stockscript)`. When processed, this string will be replaced by the value of the message part with a similar name. The request string will be as given below:

```
GET, URL= "http://www.abcom.com/GetStockRate/IBM"
```

Implementation for HTTP POST

The code below illustrates `HTTP Post`:

```
<binding name="StockTradingHTTPBinding" type="tns:StockTradingPortType">
        <http:binding verb="POST"/>
        <operation name="GetStockRate">
           <http:operation location="http://abcom.com/GetStockRate/>
                 <input>
                 <mime:content type="application/x-www-form-urlencoded"/>
                 </input>
                <output>
                      <mime:content type= "text/html"/>
                </output>
        </operation>
</binding>
```

This kind of binding implementation is processed from a web page. In this binding, we make use of the `<mime:content>` element in the `<input>` element. The mime element specifies the value for the type attribute according to the process requirements and following standard MIME specifications. The request string is given below:

```
POST, URL= http://www.abcom.com/GetStockRate, PAYLOAD="stockscript=IBM"
```

A point to note here is that since our service returns the response in an XML format, the client is developed keeping in mind that it should be able to process the return value.

Next on the WSDL document block is the MIME binding.

MIME Bindings

MIME bindings can be implemented along with the SOAP and HTTP bindings. This adds an additional support or capability to our service. This allows us to send a multipart request/response encoded in the MIME format. We can send documents, images, and so on in the SOAP request/response. In this binding, we bind the abstract types to the defined messages in some MIME format. The frequently used binding formats are listed below:

- Text/XML
- Multipart related
- Others (by specifying the MIME type string)

Since we have not implemented MIME bindings in our WSDL example, we shall take a different example to demonstrate the above formats. Let us assume that we have a shopping site where we require displaying all the information relating to a particular product, that is, its documentation, image, and so on. We shall not see the full WSDL document but only the bindings for the same.

We have already seen the implementation for the first format text/XML. Our service always returns a response in a text/XML format. Let's now go on to the next format – multipart-related bindings.

The multipart bindings define a message with multiple parts all represented with different MIME types. All these message parts form a SOAP envelope's return value. Let us see how this is done with an example:

```
<binding name="ProductsBinding" type="tns:ProductsPortType">
        <operation name="GetProductsInfo">
           <soap:operation soapAction="http://abcom.com/GetProductInfo"/>
           <input>
               <soap:body use="literal"/>
           </input>
           <output>
               <mime:multipartRelated>
                    <mime:part>
                        <soap:body parts="Info" use="literal"/>
                   </mime:part>
                   <mime:part>
                        <mime:content part="docs" type="text/html"/>
                   </mime:part>
                   <mime:part>
                        <mime:content part="ProductPicture"
                         type="image/gif"/>
                   </mime:part>
               </mime:multipartRelated>
           </output>
        </operation>
    </binding>
```

The actual MIME bindings implementation is done in the <output> element. In this element, we specify different parts for our two responses: the product information and its picture. The first part is the <soap:body> element, which specifies that a normal SOAP envelope is returned and it consists of two parts: Info and the Picture. The second product information that will be in text format has the type attribute set to text/html. For the second part, we are having the product picture so the type attribute is set to image/gif.

To summarize, we can say that bindings define different message formats for the operations specified by a particular portType.

<service> and <port>

These are the last and important elements in the WSDL document representing our service. All the elements that we saw represent a specific functionality in the service document. With these elements, we created our service data types, the message, and the invocation mechanism in the operation element. Now, the question is where to send the request for the service. The <service> and the <port> elements provide the solution for this question.

The <service> element defines all this information for us. Technically, the definition of this element is that it groups a set of related ports together. For example, we take the service extract from our example:

```
<service name="StockTradingService">
    <documentation>FIRST SERVICE</documentation>
    <port name="StockTradingPort" binding="tns:StockTradingBinding">
       <soap:address location="http://abcom.com/stocktrading"/>
    </port>
</service>
```

In this, the service element has a child element called port. This element has all the information required for the request. The <port> element consists of type-specific binding for that service. The bindings attribute refers to the <binding> element we discussed in the previous section. This refers to SOAP binding that we have implemented. The <soap:address> element points to the actual service address.

According to the WSDL specifications, there can be more than one port element having different type bindings; that is, we can have bindings for SOAP and HTTP in the port element. The purpose of this type of implementation is to allow one Web Service to be accessible through multiple ports at the same time. The implementation sample is given below:

```
<service name="StockTradingService">
        <documentation>FIRST SERVICE</documentation>
        <port name="StockTradingPortSOAP"
         binding="tns:StockTradingSOAPBinding">
           <soap:address location="http://abcom.com/stocktrading"/>
        </port>
        <port name="StockTradingPortHTTP"
         binding="tns:StockTradingHTTPBinding">
           <soap:address location="http://www.abcom.com"/>
        </port>
    </service>
```

In this example, we have one Web Service being accessed from two different ports at the same time; one port points to the HTTP server and the other to the SOAP server.

UDDI

UDDI (Universal Description, Discovery and Integration) is an industry effort started in September 2000 by Ariba, IBM, Microsoft, and 33 other companies. Today, UDDI has over 200 community members.

The registries which follow the UDDI specifications, are known as UDDI-compliant registries. We shall discuss the specifications requirements in this section.

UDDI is a registry where businesses publish their Web Services for others to discover. A business publishes descriptive information about the various services it offers in a UDDI-compliant registry. Such information is provided in a neutral format that allows any kind of service to be published, regardless of the platform on which it is deployed or the technology used for the development. UDDI provides a framework for describing any kind of service, and allows storage of as many details about a service and its implementation as desired.

For example, a company may expose an invoicing Web Service that the company's suppliers use to send electronic invoices. Similarly, a vendor may expose a Web Service for placing orders electronically. If you wish to purchase computer equipment electronically, you may search for all vendors who sell computer equipment electronically. To do this, you will need to look up a "yellow pages"-type directory of all businesses that expose Web Services. UDDI provides such a directory.

Role of UDDI

UDDI (http://www.uddi.org/) provides the following basic services:

- **Publish**
  It deals with how the provider of the Web Service registers itself and its service with UDDI
- **Find**
  It deals with how a client can locate the desired Web Service
- **Bind**
  It deals with how a client can connect to and use the located Web Service

The companies that provide these services and host the UDDI global registry are called UDDI **operators**. These are responsible for synchronizing the registry information. Synchronizing registry information is called **replication**.

The companies publish their services and related information using these operators. Two of the well-known operators are Microsoft who provide UDDI service on http://uddi.microsoft.com and IBM who provide the same at http://www-3.ibm.com/services/uddi/protect/home.jsp. These registries are free. Your company may publish its services with any of these operators. Such company is called an operator node. An individual operator node may be comprised of several physical computers.

However, one unique ID, Universal Unique Identifier (UUID), must represent every operator node. SoapReplicationURL is used to represent the replication point for each operator node. This URL is unique for each operator node. Replication is used to ensure that the information stored at each operator node is consistent.

Businesses Benefit from UDDI

Businesses of all sizes can benefit from UDDI. The UDDI registry comprehensively addresses problems that limit the growth of B2B commerce and Web Services. The business can query any of the UDDI nodes available; they are guaranteed to get the same result. Since the UDDI project is not industry specific, any industry, worldwide, offering products and services can benefit from this open initiative. Before the UDDI project, there was no industry-wide approach for businesses to reach their customers and partners with information about their products and Web Services. Nor was there a method of how to integrate into each other's systems and processes.

The problems that the UDDI specification can help to solve are:

- Making it possible for organizations to quickly discover the right business from millions of them currently online
- Defining how to enable commerce to be conducted once the preferred business is discovered

Immediate Benefits of the UDDI Project for Businesses

These benefits include:

- Reaching new customers
- Expanding offerings
- Extending market reach
- Increasing access to current customers
- Solving customer-driven need to remove barriers to allow for rapid participation in the global Internet economy
- Describing their services and business processes programmatically in a single, open, and secure environment
- Using a set of protocols that enable businesses to invoke services over the Internet to provide additional value to their preferred customers

UDDI in Action

As we have seen, the UDDI describes a conceptual cloud of operator nodes and a programmatic interface that defines a simple framework for describing any kind of Web Service. This information can be added to the UDDI business registry either via a web site or by using tools that make use of the programmatic service interfaces. The UDDI business registry is a logically centralized, physically distributed service with multiple nodes that replicate data with each other on a regular basis. Once a business registers with a single instance of the business registry service, the data is automatically shared with other UDDI nodes and becomes freely available to anyone who needs to discover what Web Services are exposed by a given business.

The following diagram explains this process. The Service Provider publishes its service using any of the UDDI nodes. The added registry will be shared with all other nodes in the cloud. Finally, the Service Consumer locates the service with the help of any of the nodes in the cloud:

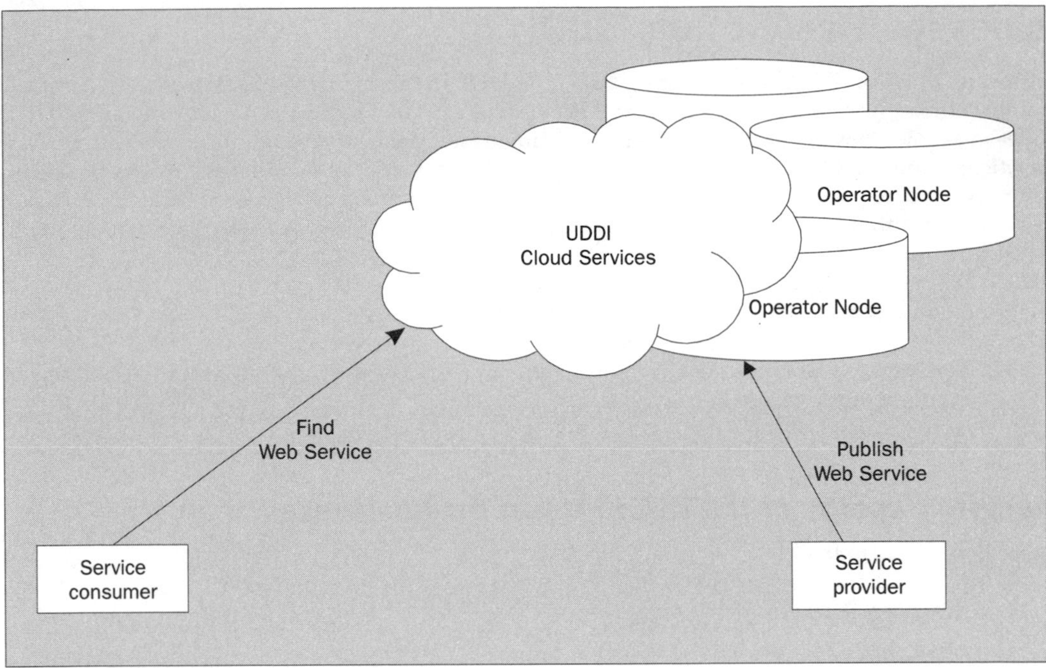

Data Custody

When a Web Service provider publishes the service at a particular node, that node keeps some part of the whole published data into its custody. This can be anything, a business entity, binding template, tModel, or assertion with business relationships. Other nodes do not know this part of the data. So, obviously only that node can change that data. In this case, the nodes are said to "originate changes". The node that keeps custody of such data can be changed. This multi-step process involves replication in the final stages. We will look at replication later in the chapter.

Data Structures of UDDI

We have seen that the UDDI registry contains information about the businesses and the services they offer. Logically, this information can be divided into three categories:

- **White pages**
  This contains information about the business names, contact information, and so on
- **Yellow pages**
  This contains the information related to the classification of business
- **Green pages**
  This contains the technical information like what services this business offers, their specifications, and so on

The operator node maintains five data structures to store the registered information as defined in the UDDI version 2.0 API schema.

These structures are listed below:

- businessEntity
- businessService
- bindingTemplate
- tModel
- businessAssertion

These structures help locating the information very fast. They also assist in the understanding of the registered information. All of these data structures are represented in XML format. These five structures constitute the complete information stored in the UDDI service description framework. The association of these structures is represented in the following diagram:

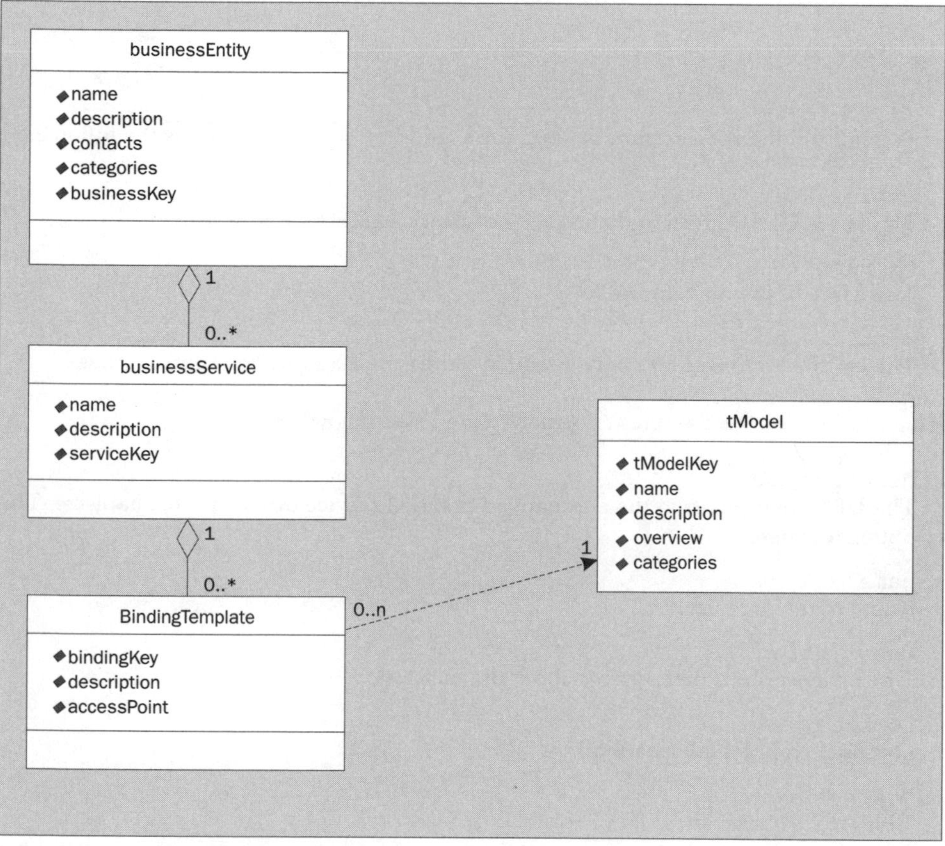

The Business Entity Structure

This is used to store all information about a publisher company, their contact information, and the services it offers. It also stores the unique business key, which is an identifier for the business entity. These are UUID (Universal Unique Identifier) keys and are guaranteed to be unique across all nodes. The `businessEntity` structure is a top-level data structure if you consider hierarchy of all data structures. These are also called the white pages of the registry.

Structure Specification

```
<element name = "businessEntity">
   <complexType>
      <sequence>
         <element ref = "discoveryURLs" minOccurs = "0"/>
         <element ref = "name" maxOccurs = "unbounded"/>
         <element ref = "description" minOccurs = "0" maxOccurs =
         "unbounded"/>
         <element ref = "contacts" minOccurs = "0"/> <element ref =
         "businessServices" minOccurs = "0"/> <element ref = "identifierBag"
          minOccurs = "0"/>
         <element ref = "categoryBag" minOccurs = "0"/>
      </sequence>
      <attribute ref = "businessKey" use = "required"/>
      <attribute ref = "operator"/>
      <attribute ref = "authorizedName"> </complexType>
</element>
```

As can be seen from the specification the `businessEntity` structure contains the following attributes:

- `businessKey`
  This is the UUID given to the instance of the `businessEntity` structure
- `operator`
  The name of the operator node
- `authorizedName`
  The certified name of the individual that published the `businessEntity` data

The elements of the `businessEntity` structure are listed below:

- `discoveryURLs`
  The URLs that points to the alternative file-based service discovery mechanisms. This is an optional element.
- `name`
  Name of the organization.
- `description`
  One or more short descriptions about the business.
- `contract`
  Optional contract information.
- `businessServices`
  Gives information about families of the services.
- `identifierBag`
  An optional list of name-value pairs that gives information about the common forms of identifications such as D-U-N-S (Dun & Bradstreet's Data Universal Numbering System) identifier, tax identifiers, Thomas Register ID, etc.

- categoryBag
  An optional list of name-value pairs allows the company's service to be categorized according to several taxonomy-based classifications. For example, NAICS (North American Industrial Classification System) that defines classification codes for industries in the US, Canada, Mexico. UNSPSC (Universal Standard Products and Services Classification), which is used for classifying products and services. Also, geographic taxonomies are used for location-based classification. It supports the ISO 3166 standard.

The Business Service Structure

The businessService structure is used to represent a logical service classification. This is contained in a businessEntity structure described earlier. A single businessEntity structure can contain more than one businessService structure. It contains the unique service key that identifies a particular service. The operator node assigns this key. These structures can be thought of as yellow pages about a company. The businessKey attribute is used to identify the parent businessEntity.

Some large companies may publish separate businessEntity structures. For such cases, there is a provision to share or reuse the services. This can be established by using the businessService structure managed by one businessEntity and others refer or project to the businessService.

Structure Specification

```
<element name = "businessService"> <complexType>
   <sequence>
     <element ref = "name" maxOccurs = "unbounded"/>
     <element ref = "description" minOccurs = "0" maxOccurs = "unbounded"/>
     <element ref = "bindingTemplates"/>
     <element ref = "categoryBag" minOccurs = "0"/>
   </sequence>
  <attribute ref = "serviceKey" use = "required"/>
  <attribute ref = "businessKey"/>
  </complexType>
</element>
```

The businessService structure contains the following attributes:

- serviceKey
  A unique key given for a businessService
- businessKey
  An optional key for a business entity

The elements in the businessService structure are as follows:

- name
  The name of the service family. It cannot be blank.
- description
  Optional description of the service family.
- bindingTemplates
  Technical description about the service family.
- categoryBag
  Optional list of name-value pairs specifying the classification.

The Binding Template Structure

The bindingTemplate structure is used to provide the technical details of the Web Service. It contains the information about the access point of the service. The businessService is identified using the serviceKey attribute. When this template is not the entry point of the service it gives the information about the remotely hosted services. These structures are also called green pages. It also maintains the list of tModels structures.

Structure Specification

```
<element name = "bindingTemplate">
   <complexType>
    <sequence>
      <element ref = "description" minOccurs = "0" maxOccurs = "unbounded"/>
      <choice>
          <element ref = "accessPoint" minOccurs = "0"/>
          <element ref = "hostingRedirector" minOccurs = "0"/>
      </choice>
      <element ref = "tModelInstanceDetails"/>
    </sequence>
    <attribute ref = "bindingKey" use = "required"/>
    <attribute ref = "serviceKey"/>
 </complexType>
</element>
```

The attributes of the bindingTemplate structure are listed below:

- bindingKey
  A UUID given for this structure
- serviceKey
  Used to identify the businessService

The elements of the bindingTemplate structure are listed below:

- description
  Description of the service entry point.
- accessPoint
  Used to specify the entry point address suitable for calling a Web Service.
- hostingRedirector
  Gives the reference of different bindingTemplates when the accessPoint is not specified.
- tModelInstanceDetails
  List of tModelInstanceInfo elements. It provides a fingerprint and can be used to identify a compatible service.

The tModel Structure

After locating the service the programmer needs the application-specific information of the Web Service. They need to know the behavior of the service, conventions followed by the service, expected data formats, and so on. This information is stored in the tModel structure. You can find references to specific tModel instances in many businessEntity structures.

There are two main uses of tModel:

- Defining the technical fingerprint
- Defining an abstract namespace reference

Defining the Technical Fingerprint

The main use of the tModel structure is to provide a technical service type. It provides the information about programming interface, data formats, wire protocols, and so on.

Defining an Abstract Namespace Reference

The tModelKey is also used in identifierBag, categoryBag, address, and publisherAssertion structures. These are used to define organizational identity and various classifications. The tModelKey used in a categoryBag defines the type of taxonomy, for example, NAICS, UNSPSC, and so on. In indentifierBag, the tModelKey describes the type of identifier. When used in the publisherAsssertion structure, it describes the type of relationship.

Structure Specification

```
<element name = "tModel">
    <complexType>
      <sequence>
         <element ref = "name"/>
         <element ref = "description" minOccurs = "0" maxOccurs =
         "unbounded"/>
         <element ref = "overviewDoc" minOccurs = "0"/>
         <element ref = "identifierBag" minOccurs = "0"/>
         <element ref = "categoryBag" minOccurs = "0"/>
      </sequence>
      <attribute ref = "tModelKey" use = "required"/>
      <attribute ref = "operator"/>
      <attribute ref = "authorizedName"/>
    </complexType>
</element>
```

The tModel structure contains the following attributes:

- tModelKey
  Unique key for the given tModel structure.
- operator
  The certified name of the UDDI node with which the Web Service Provider publishes its service.
- authorizedName
  The recorded name of the individual that published this tModel information.

The tModel structure contains the following elements:

- name
  Name of this tModel. It cannot be blank.
- description
  Description of this structure.

- `overviewDoc`
  Used to specify references to remote instruction and information related to this structure.
- `identifierBag`
  Used to record the identification number of this structure.
- `categoryBag`
  Used to specify the classification information.

The Publisher Assertion Structure

This structure is introduced in UDDI 2.0. Large companies or enterprises can publish several `businessEntity` structures. Since a single company may publish them, they form a relationship. The `publisherAssertion` structure is used for modeling this kind of a relationship in the UDDI registry. Both publishers have to publish exactly the same information to eliminate the possibility that one publisher claims a relationship between both businesses that is, in fact, not reciprocally recognized. Both publishers have to agree that the relationship is valid by publishing their own `publisherAssertion`. This structure consists of three elements:

- `fromKey`
  This represents the first `businessKey`
- `toKey`
  This represents the second `businessKey`
- `keyedReference`
  This designates the asserted relationship type

Structure Specification

```
<element name = "publisherAssertion">
   <complexType>
     <sequence>
       <element ref = "fromKey"/>
       <element ref = "toKey"/>
       <element ref = "keyedReference"/>
     </sequence>
   </complexType>
</element>
```

Managing Directory Information

To provide the services efficiently, UDDI registry needs to take care of the following things:

- Information storage
- Backup and recovery
- Updates and deletions
- Operator resignation from UDDI

Information Storage

The publisher registers its information using **publish** operations exposed by any one of the operator nodes. The publish operations and other services such as custody transfer are exposed by a web browser-based interface implemented by operator node. It is the responsibility of an operator node to allow the publisher to update or delete published information, which was entered through its interfaces. Thus, operator node is said to have 'custody' of the published information through its site. Other UDDI operator nodes are not permitted to make changes to the information that was not originally registered at their site.

The operator node also maintains the e-mail address for the publisher address in its custody for each of the following:

- `businessEntity`
- `tModel`
- Relationship assertion

These e-mail addresses are not exposed to other nodes.

Backup and Recovery

The operator node provides the durability for the information it stores. It also provides the backup facilities to the registries. The operator does not rely in this regard on the other nodes in the cloud to get the old changes in case of a system crash.

Updates and Deletions

The operator node always maintains the integrity of the registered information while making updates. It also needs to maintain the integrity of the information while deleting any information. To achieve this, the operator node follows certain rules for each type of data to delete:

- **businessEntity**
  After initiating the deletion of a `businessEntity`, the deletion of all related `businessServices` for that `businessEntity` is also initiated. The references to the `tModels` are not simply pointers and are not directly contained within the `businessEntity`. So the `tModels` referenced there are not automatically deleted.
- **businessService**
  After initiating the deletion of a `businessService`, the deletion of all contained `bindingTemplates` for that `businessService` is initiated. The referenced `businessServices` and `tModels` are not deleted automatically since they are simply pointers.
- **tModel deprecation**
  After deprecating a `tModel`, `find_tModel` request does not include it. Still the details of the `tModel` entry are returned as a result of a `get_tModelDetail` request.
- **tModel permanent deletion**
  This can be done in the **spam** event. An UDDI operator node may insert a delete operation into the replication stream in this event.

Operator Resignation from UDDI

The operator company may not want to continue its operations as operator node. In this case, the operator node needs to transfer the registered information to the other operator nodes in the replication cloud. For this, the operator follows certain steps as described below:

- When the company decides not to provide the registry services, it issues a notice of their shutdown schedule on their web site.
- It sends e-mails to all of the publishers to inform them that the node is no longer going to provide the registry services and will transfer their published information to other nodes.
- Each operator node provides the custody transfer service on their site. Using this the publishers need to initiate the custody transfer to some other node within 15 days.
- The operator node also needs to inform other nodes in the cloud.
- Once the notification that the operator is resigning from UDDI operation is sent to the publishers, the operator node does not accept any new registry entries. But the read, replication, and custody transfer operations are supported until the site is shut down.
- Finally, the operator node generates the final replication file. After generating this file no operations are allowed to perform.

Replication

As we have seen, the Service Provider can publish its service with any of the nodes in the cloud. And the Service Consumer can locate the Web Service from any of the nodes in the cloud. For this to happen successfully each node shares the published information with all the other nodes in the cloud. This process is called replication.

Update Sequence Numbers

While processing the changes the operator node tags information with a unique number. This unique number is called the Update Sequence Number (USN). Each node maintains this number inside a USN register. The size of this number is 63 bits. This number is incremented after it is assigned to a newly added record or updated record. So, the USNs generated by a node can be compared to each other to get the latest record.

Change Records

A change can be made to any of the data structures described earlier. After changing any of these data structures an operator node will create a change record. This record is used to store the details of the change.

Whenever any change is made, that change is replicated to all of the nodes in cloud. The changed data is passed from one node to the other. The originator of the change will create a change record. It contains three fields:

- The UUID of the originating node
- An originating USN
- A payload of data, which includes data structures described earlier

The receiver of the change record adds one more field to this record. That is a local USN. This whole process involves the following steps:

- The node that originates the changes, informs the other node about the availability of the Change Record
- The other node then requests the Change Record
- The originating node sends the Change Record, which includes the actual payload of data
- And finally the receiving node adds one more field to the Change Record that is the local USN and stores the Change Record to the local registry

This is represented in the following diagram:

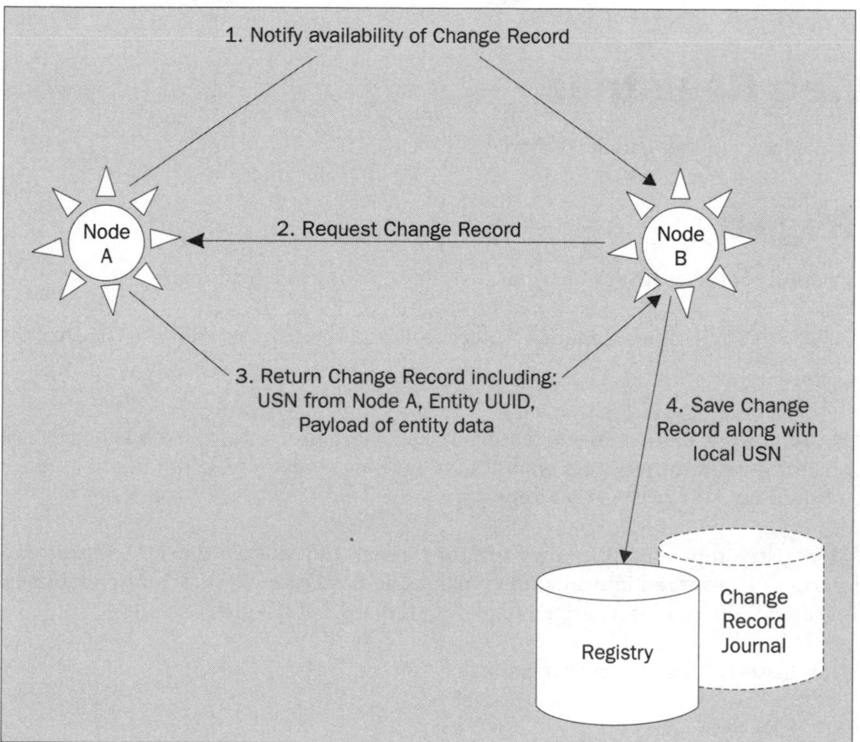

Change Record Journal

Each operator node maintains the XML file for all of the change records received from other operator nodes in the cloud. This file is called a Change Record Journal. The operator node may also store its own change records in this file. This journaling improves the overall performance of the UDDI service.

High Water Mark Vector

The operator node maintains a vector called High Water Mark Vector. Each entry in this vector contains the USN of the most recent change record that has been successfully processed by each operator node.

Each entry contains the following fields:

- **operatorNodeID**
  It contains the UUID of a node in the replication graph
- **originatingUSN**
  It contains the USN of the most recent change that originated on the `operatorNodeID`

Replication Processing

The replication process is nothing but propagating the changes to all of the nodes in the cloud. This is done by notifying the available changes and "pulling" them from other nodes. The request `get_changeRecords` is used to pull the changes. After changing the information or after getting changes from the other nodes, an operator node sends its High Water Mark vector to other nodes.

Other Web Registries

Now we will have a look at other parallel technologies.

ebXML Registry

ebXML represents collaborative efforts put together by two organizations:

- **UN/CEF/ACT** (United Nations Center for Trade Facilitation and Electric Business)
- **OASIS**

The ebXML framework defines specifications for the sharing of web-based business services. It includes specifications for a message service, collaborative partner agreements, core components, a business process methodology, a registry, and a repository.

The ebXML registry/repository provides a set of services that enable sharing of information between interested parties. The shared information is maintained as **Business Information Objects** (BIOs) in an ebXML repository. These objects are managed by the ebXML Registry Services.

The ebXML registry/repository may include:

- XML/EDI templates
- Links to GIS (Geographic Information System), NAICS (North American Classification System), and D-U-N-S (Data Universal Numbering System for companies)
- Links to taxonomies such as UDEF (Universal Data Element Framework)
- Specific user community data
- XML namespaces, and so on

The ebXML Registry Information Model (RIM) is founded on the use of classifications to manage and structure contents within the registry.

After a business has registered with the ebXML registry, other partners can look-up a registry to locate that business. Once the business partner (say, seller of services) is located, the core components of the located business can be downloaded. The buyer may then download the technical specifications for the service. Once the buyer is satisfied that the seller can meet its requirements, it negotiates a contract with the seller. Such collaborative partner agreements are defined in ebXML. Once both the parties agree on the contract terms, they sign the agreements and do a collaborative business transaction by exchanging their private documents.

JAXR

The Java API for XML Registries (JAXR) provides a convenient way to access standard business registries over the Internet. The first public draft of the specifications was released on August 10, 2001. Business registries are often described as electronic yellow pages because they contain listings of businesses and the products or services the businesses offer. JAXR tries to unify access to the following registries:

- eXML
- UDDI
- ISO 11179
- OASIS
- eCoFramework

Architecture

The following diagram illustrates the general architecture. The service provider implements the interface to a registry. A Java-based client then uses the JAXR API to access the registry using a standard Java interface:

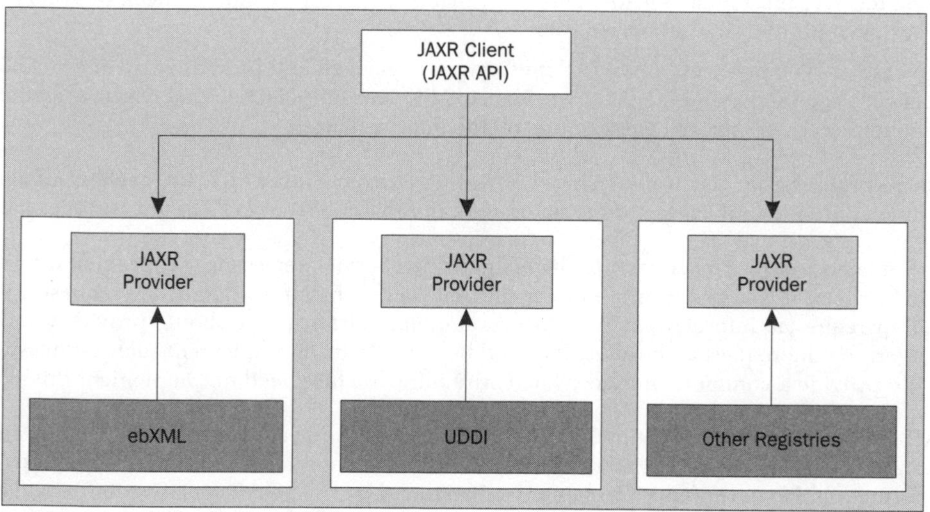

The JAXR service provider may use other XML-related APIs such as JAXP, JAXB, or JAXM to provide XML support to the existing registries. The JAXR provider is responsible for implementing the JAXR specifications. This will generally be implemented as a façade around the existing registry provider.

A JAXR client is a Java program that uses JAXR API to access the services provided by the JAXR provider.

DSML

DSML stands for Directory Service Markup Language. It is a XML schema for describing the structure and content of directories. This is designed for Lightweight Directory Access Protocol (LDAP), which is TCP based. We have discussed this technology in the last chapter.

Security

Security is one of the key issues to be addressed by the Web Services technology. The important point to consider here is whether this technology really needs to define a separate security model. The data exchange between a Web Service and a client takes place in an XML-formatted document. As this is a simple text message, secured communication can be taken care of by the underlying transport layer. There are many secured messaging mechanisms such as Secure Socket Layer (SSL) and Internet Protocol Security (IPSec). Also we need to consider whether the secured transport of messages would satisfy the security needs of Web Services. We shall be covering security in depth in Chapter 5.

Let us examine some real-time scenarios that a Web Service security layer must take care of:

- The information content inside the message is not made available to unauthorized users.
- Access must be given based on access rights. The sender and the receiver must have proper access rights for sending and receiving the message respectively.
- The data should not be changed or modified by an authorized user while it is being sent from sender to the receiver.
- The receiver must authenticate the sender, that is the, receiver should check whether the data is originated from the authorized user.
- In case of Web Services, the SOAP messages are received and processed by intermediaries between the sender and the receiver. Hence only point-to-point secured communication is not enough but there must be trust among all the intermediaries.

All the above goals are not achievable using the existing transport-layer security mechanism alone. If the communication does not have intermediates, we can rely on SSL or HTTPS for confidentiality.

In the case of Web Services for service providers and Web Service registries that provide information about Web Services, it is very important to decide who wants what and whether the requestor is authorized for requested information. Hence the underlying infrastructure should provide the flexible policies governing the request authorities. It would be a good idea to implement such services in XML, which would provide a common interface. The entire infrastructure need not implement this.

The SOAP request and response are defined in XML format. The header is a mechanism for adding features to the SOAP messages. The standardized header elements could be used to add the security-related information. However, no such elements are defined by the SOAP specifications yet. There are certain security-related issues that are under standardization by W3C such as support for digital signatures. The specifications provide an algorithm for generating the message digest and digitally signing the message. It uses public key algorithm where the receiver can authenticate the originator of the message.

The following are the XML-based security initiatives:

- **XML Key Management Services (XKMS)**
  This is used to distribute and manage the keys necessary for secured communication
- **Security Assertion Markup Language (SAML)**
  This is used by the sender and the receiver for populating the access control rights
- **XML Access Control Markup Language (XACML)**
  This is used by the receiver to parse the SAML assertion in the standardized manner

Summary

In this chapter we covered SOAP, WSDL, and UDDI in depth. These are the main constituents of a Web Service. In the next chapter, we will develop our first Web Service using open source technologies.

4

Java Web Services from Apache

In previous chapters we have studied the architecture of Web Services and the various technologies involved in the development of Web Services. Now it's time to develop our own Web Service. In this chapter, we will develop our first Web Service based on open source technologies. We will use Tomcat for the deployment of our Web Service using the Java-based open source implementation of SOAP, Axis. The latest version of Tomcat (Version 4.0.4 Beta 3, as of this writing) supports the Java Servlet 2.3 and JavaServer Pages (JSP) 1.2 specifications and also includes many additional features for developing and deploying web applications and Web Services.

We shall also look at two examples of EJBs that can be employed as Web Services in the JBoss EJB container. One is a stateless session bean and the other is a stateful session bean. We'll look at a traditional EJB client and then see how to use Axis to call them as a Web Service.

Finally, we'll look at a Java-based open source implementation of XML-RPC from the Apache Software Foundation.

Introduction To Axis

Apache Axis is the third generation Apache SOAP toolkit. As of this writing, the latest version that is available on the official Apache site is Beta 2. As we saw in earlier chapters, SOAP plays a vital role in the development of Web Services. Axis eases the generation of SOAP code for a Web Service.

The origins of Axis lie in the early development of Apache SOAP that began at IBM. The first version of the toolkit was called SOAP4J, the later version was named Apache SOAP version 2 in which SOAP 1.1 was used. The major problem with Apache SOAP v2 was that it did not have any support for WSDL. It also lacked flexibility; its RPC provider did not provide access to the headers in the SOAP envelope.

Because of these and several other issues the Apache SOAP project was abandoned. This was modified to incorporate both SOAP and upcoming XML Protocol (XMLP) specification and is now known as Apache Axis.

Axis offers several benefits over its predecessors as listed below:

- **WSDL support**
  The major advantage of Axis is the support for WSDL. It provides utilities to create WSDL files from a Java file (Java2WSDL) and generate proxy classes from existing Web Services (WSDL2Java). The WSDL support is explained in detail later in the chapter.
- **Speed**
  Axis uses SAX (event-based) parsing. This has significantly improved speed over earlier versions of Apache SOAP.
- **Flexibility**
  Axis is flexible; it allows us to insert extensions into the engine for custom header processing, system management, and so on. Custom classes can be passed to and returned from the web method. Also the service-level handlers can be used in between the Web Service and client, which can be used in request flow and response flow. Support for deployment of the Web Service is greatly improved with the help of the Web Service Deployment Descriptor (WSDD). In WSDD we can specify request/response handlers (and chains), serializers/deserializers, methods to be exposed, and so on.
- **Stability**
  Well-defined published interfaces make Axis more stable as compared to previous versions.
- **Component-oriented deployment**
  We can easily define reusable networks of handlers to implement common patterns of processing for our applications, or to distribute to partners. A handler is basically a class that is invoked when the central Axis processing logic runs. We can define more than a single handler during the message processing forming a network of handlers.
- **Transport framework**
  The Axis core engine is transport protocol-independent and one can easily design transports for SOAP over various protocols such as FTP, IIOP, and messaging, and plug them easily in the architecture.
- **Security**
  Axis has a great support for Web Service security. It supports authentication and authorization, but SOAP-level security is a work in progress. Transport-level security can be used by configuring Tomcat with SSL.

Axis Architecture

Axis' architecture is divided into the following subsystems:

- Message flow subsystem
- Administration subsystem

- Message model subsystem
- Encoding subsystem
- WSDL tools subsystem

Let's look at each of these subsystems in detail.

Message Flow Subsystem

Axis is a SOAP toolkit and revolves around processing SOAP messages. Axis processes the message in a different number of steps or layers. The actual transport of information is done using an instance of the `MessageContext` class. It contains the request and response message, properties of the message, service details, and so on. Each layer is nothing but a chain of **handlers**. A handler is a class that takes a message from the `MessageContext`, processes it, and gives the modified `MessageContext` to the next handler.

When a client invokes a service, the request first goes to the transport listener (`AxisServlet` in the case of HTTP). This will create the `MessageContext`, and pass it to the first chain of handlers. There are three kinds of chains used in Axis:

- Transport chains
- Global chains
- Service-specific chains

The `MessageContext` is passed from one chain to the next chain in a specific order. First it goes to the transport chain, then to the global chain, and finally to the service chain. The transport chain specifies the handlers that are specific to transport type. The global chain specifies the handlers that are applicable to all kinds of requests. Finally the service chain specifies the handlers that are specifically defined at the time of deployment of the service:

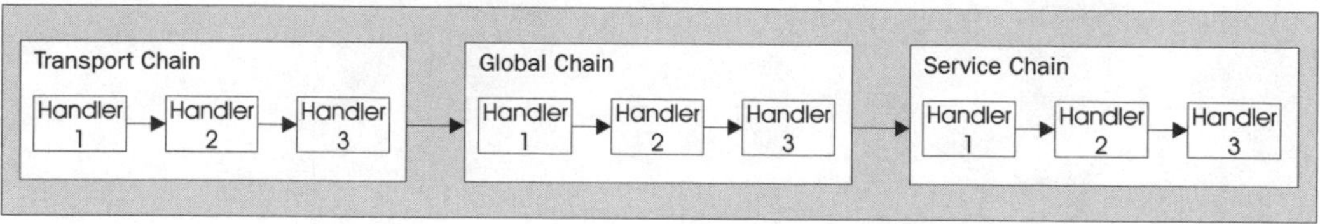

Then the `MessageContext` is passed to the **provider**. This is also a handler that takes responsibility for actually invoking a method on the target service object. This is also called a **pivot handler**. Generally the provider is RPC, which is the `RPCProvider` class in the `org.apache.axis.providers.java` package. In the case of SMTP, it uses `java:MSG` which uses the `MSGProvider` class in `org.apache.axis.providers.java`. We declare the type of provider at the time of deploying the Web Service.

Similar to the sequence of chains for the request we have the similar chains for the response, only the order of processing is reversed. First the response is passed to the service chain, then to the global chain, and finally to the transport chain.

We can now see why the pivot handler got its name:

When we install Axis, it creates the transport and global chains. The service chain is defined when we deploy the Web Service. We can get the information about this chain for all deployed services using the following command:

```
java org.apache.axis.client.AdminClient list
```

This will show the deployment descriptor of the Axis configuration. This whole process can be pictorially shown using the following diagram:

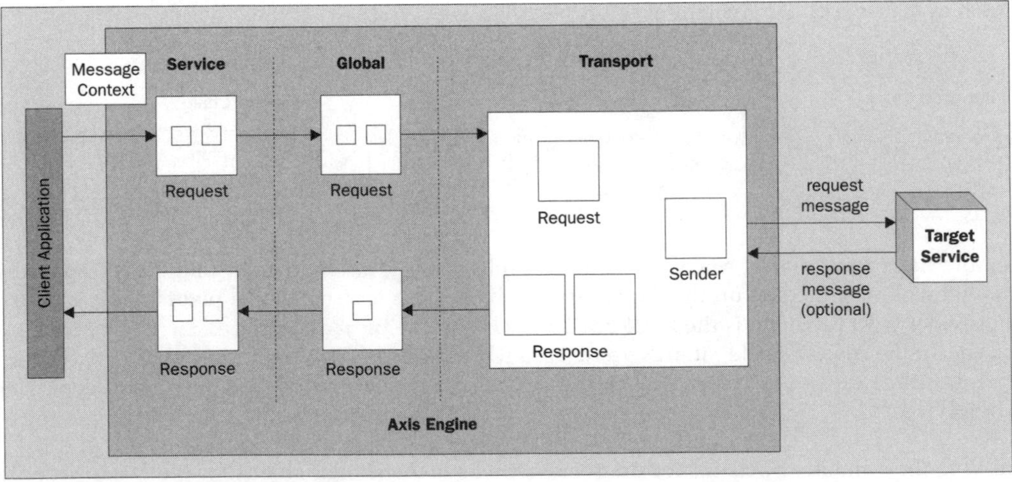

Axis has the following limitations:

- It does not allow RPC calls in SOAP headers
- It does not support multiple RPC calls in a single SOAP message

Administration Subsystem

The administration subsystem provides a way of configuring the Axis engine. The configuration information that the engine needs is a collection of factories for run time artefacts such as chains and `SOAPService` objects and a set of global configuration options for the engine.

The message flow subsystem's `EngineConfiguration` interface is implemented by the administration subsystem. `FileProvider` enables an engine to be configured statically from a file containing a deployment descriptor that is understood by the `WSDDDeployment` class. `SimpleProvider`, on the other hand, enables an engine to be configured dynamically. It allows the run time deployment of the components through program code. We will discuss the WSDD deployment in detail later in the chapter:

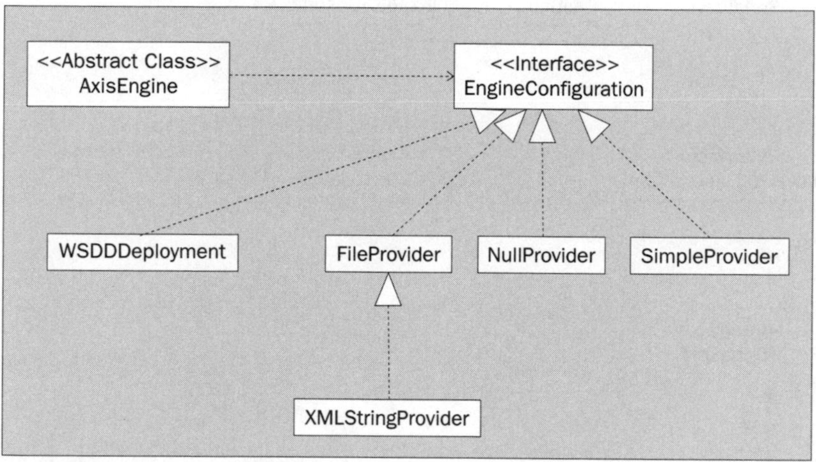

Message Model Subsystem

Axis uses the SOAP protocol to invoke the method on the service object. The service chain processes the `MessageContext` and passes it to the `RPCProvider`. The `RPCProvider` extracts the SOAP elements and invokes the `service()` method. The `DeserializationContextImpl` (DCI) class is used for deserialization of the SOAP document, that is, parsing the SOAP document. During deserialization a parse tree like the one shown below is constructed:

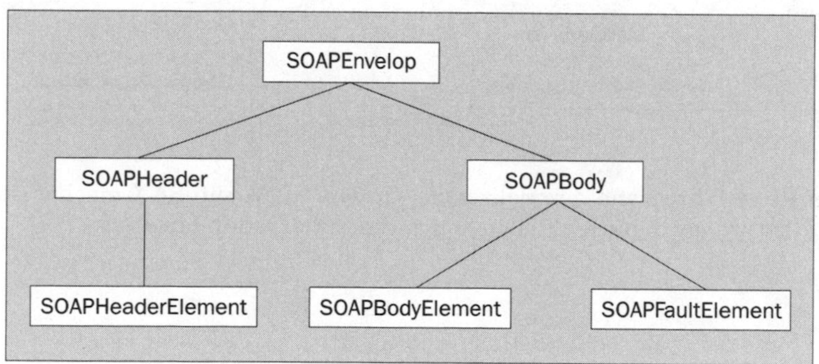

Encoding Subsystem

This subsystem is responsible for the mapping of Java data types to XML-based types. Basic Java data types can be mapped easily as Axis provides the XML type-mapping for them. For others, like arrays or custom Java classes, Axis uses different serializers and deserializers. To use type mapping on a particular message, Axis maintains a type-mapping registry. It maintains a map from encoding name (URI) to type mapping. This will be discussed with examples when we will learn WSDD. The class diagram of basic classes used for serialization and deserialization is shown below:

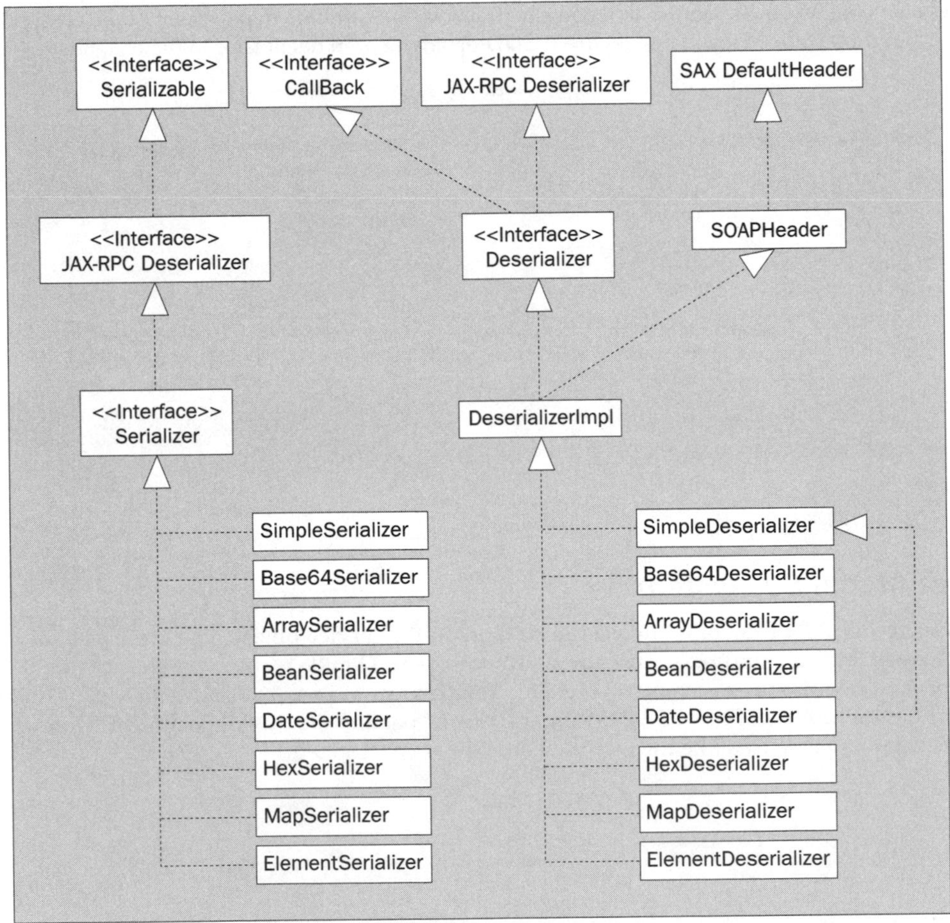

We can also create serializers and deserializers to support DOM and SAX mechanisms for XML processing. For that we need to use serialization and deserialization factories.

The class diagram is shown below:

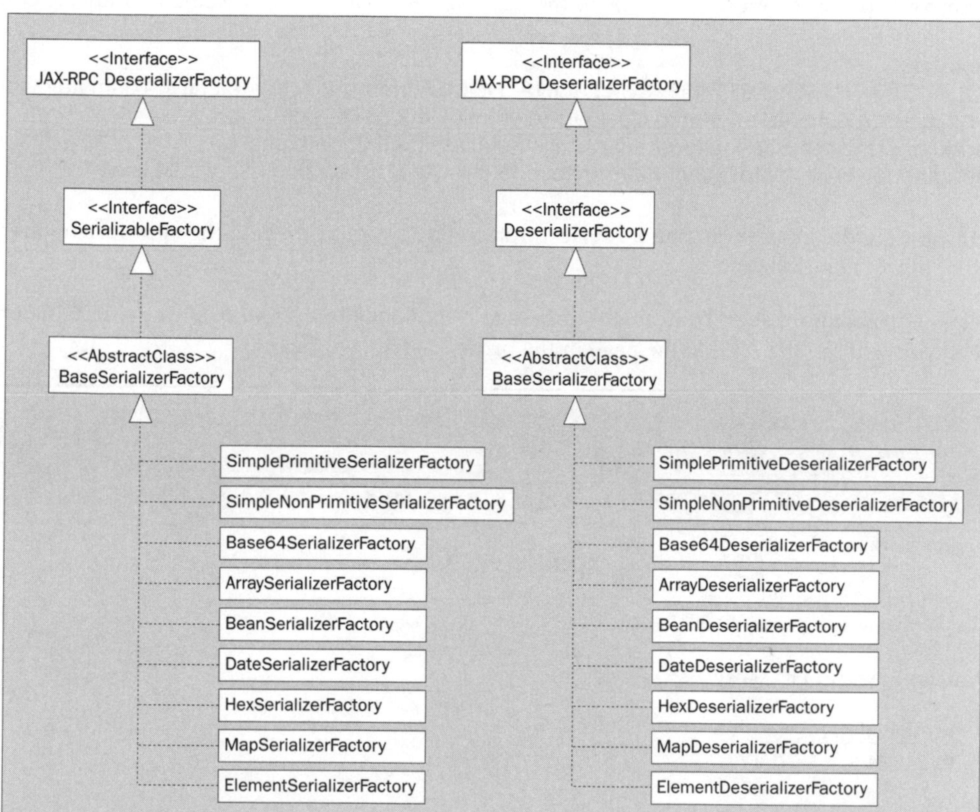

WSDL Tools Subsystem

Finally Axis provides the tools for using WSDL. WSDL is not an essential part of a Web Service, as it is possible for the cooperating client to consume a Web Service without looking up the WSDL. However, it is used to ease the programming of Web Services. Using WSDL we can generate proxy classes and stubs, which can be used by the client to locate the Web Service and invoke a method on it. Details of using WSDL with Axis are given later in the chapter.

Installing Axis

The Axis installation file may be downloaded from http://xml.apache.org/axis/. Extract the gzipped file to the desired folder. After extracting the files, we will need to configure Axis with Tomcat. Copy the newly created `AXIS_HOME/webapps/axis` folder to the `CATALINA_HOME/webapps` folder. We will configure our web applications in this folder. Now to configure the web application folder under Tomcat, add the following line under the `<Host>` element in the `CATALINA_HOME/conf/server.xml` file:

```
<Context path="/axis" docBase="axis" debug="0" reloadable="true"/>
```

Next, we need to add the .jar files in AXIS_HOME/lib directory to the CLASSPATH. Also we need to add the XML parser (xerces.jar) file in the CLASSPATH. This is done using the following command:

```
export
CLASSPATH=$CLASSPATH:$CATALINA_HOME/common/lib/xerces.jar:<AxisInstallation>/lib
/axis.jar:<AxisInstallation>/lib/clutil.jar:<AxisInstallation>/lib/jaxrpc.jar:
<AxisInstallation>/lib/log4j-core.jar:<AxisInstallation>/lib/commons-
logging.jar:<AxisInstallation>/lib/tt-bytecode.jar:<AxisInstallation>/lib/wsdl4j.jar
```

Before running the above command, replace <AxisInstallation> with the appropriate directory name of the Axis installation.

To test the installation, start Tomcat and browse to http://localhost:8080/axis/. If the installation is correct, you will see the Axis home page in the browser as shown below:

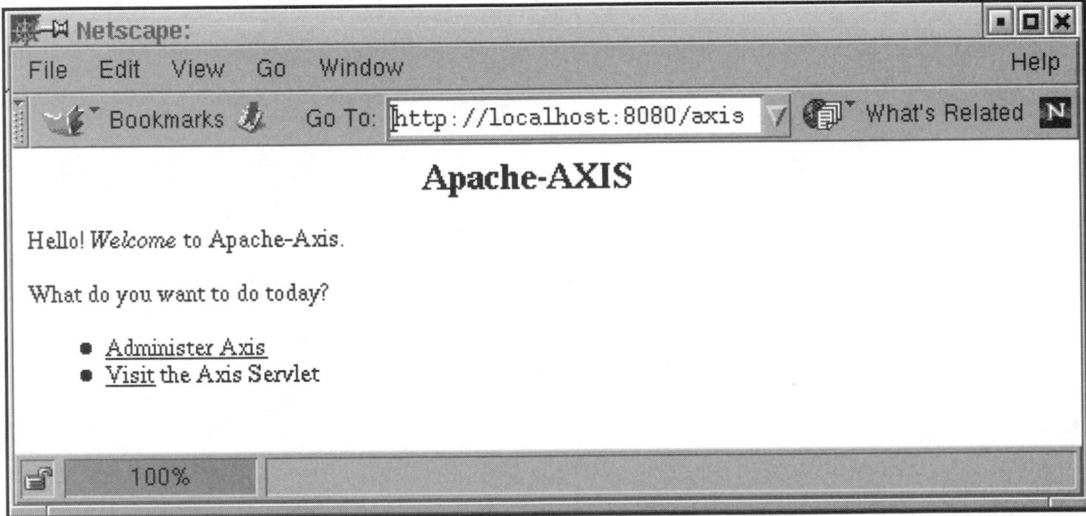

Now, follow the Visit link on this page; you will get the following page:

Now, let's develop a simple Web Service and deploy it using Axis.

Developing HelloService

We will create a simple Web Service that prints a greeting to the user. The Web Service will expose a method called `sayHello()` to the client. The method takes a `String` argument and returns a `String` message to the client. To create the Web Service, we will write a Java class called `HelloService` as shown below:

```
public class HelloService {
  public String sayHello(String arg) {
    return "Hello " + arg;
  }
}
```

This completes the development of the Web Service. We do not have to compile the above Java code.

Deploying HelloService

Axis provides two ways to deploy a service:

- Using a JWS file
- Passing a WSDD file to `AdminClient`

The first approach is much simpler. The only thing we have to do is copy the Web Service source file to `CATALINA_HOME/webapps/axis` and rename it as a `.jws` file. The second approach is a little more complicated; we will see deployment with WSDD later in the chapter.

For our first Web Service we will choose the first way. Copy the `HelloService.java` file to the `CATALINA_HOME/webapps/axis` directory and rename it to `HelloService.jws`.

When we invoke the service the `JWSHandler` sets the JWS filename and the service name in the `MessageContext`. The `JWSProcessor` then locates the JWS file and creates a temporary file with a `.java` extension. It then compiles this Java file. Finally `JWSProvider` is responsible for invoking this service. The `JWSProvider` also puts the response message into the `MessageContext` and sends it to the response flow service chain. This process is shown in the following diagram:

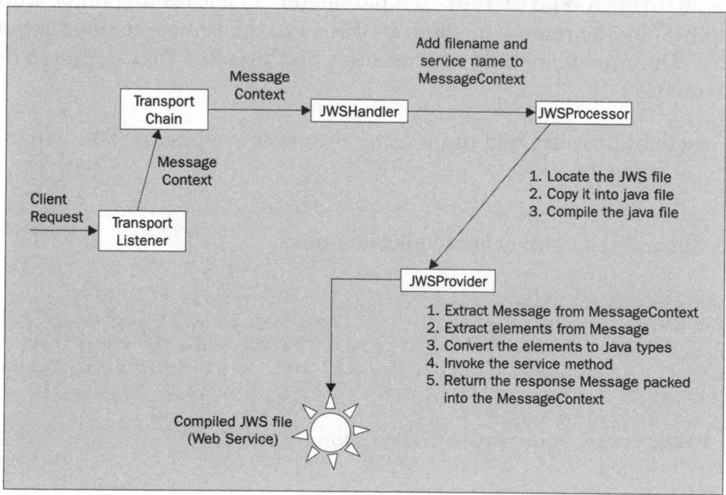

Writing a Client for HelloService

The client code that uses the HelloService is shown below:

```
import org.apache.axis.client.Call;
import org.apache.axis.client.Service;

import javax.xml.rpc.namespace.QName;

public class TestClient {
  public static void main(String[] args) {
    try {
      String endpoint = "http://localhost:8080/axis/HelloService.jws";

      Service service = new Service();
      Call call = (Call) service.createCall();

      call.setTargetEndpointAddress(new java.net.URL(endpoint));
      call.setOperationName("sayHello");

      String ret = (String) call.invoke(new Object[] {"John"});

      System.out.println(ret);
    } catch (Exception e) {
      System.err.println(e.toString());
    }
  }
}
```

This is a console-based application. In the main() method, we create an instance of the Service class and call its createCall() method to construct a SOAP call to the remote server. The Service class is used as the starting point for accessing SOAP Web Services. It is the Axis JAXRPC dynamic invocation interface implementation of the Service interface.

The setTargetEndpointAddress() method sets the URL for the Web Service to be called. The setOperationName() sets the method name to be called. The invoke() method calls the remote method and takes an array of type Object as a parameter. The array should be initialized with the list of parameters required by the remote method. In this case, the remote method requires only one single String parameter. The remote method returns a String message that is printed on the user console in the following statement.

Compile the above client program and run it using the java command. This will output as follows:

Hello John

The SOAP request generated by the client looks like this:

```
<?xml version="1.0" encoding="utf-8"?>
<SOAP-ENV:Envelope xmlns:xsd="http://www.w3.org/2001/XMLSchema"
                   xmlns:SOAP-ENV="http://schemas.xmlsoap.org/soap/envelope/"
                   xmlns:xsi="http://www.w3.org/2001/XMLSchema-instance">
  <SOAP-ENV:Body>
    <ns1:sayHello xmlns:ns1="">
      <testParam xsi:type="xsd:string">John</testParam>
    </ns1:sayHello>
  </SOAP-ENV:Body>
</SOAP-ENV:Envelope>
```

The client gets the response as a SOAP message. This is shown below:

```
<?xml version="1.0" encoding="UTF-8"?>
<SOAP-ENV:Envelope xmlns:xsd="http://www.w3.org/2001/XMLSchema"
                   xmlns:SOAP-ENV="http://schemas.xmlsoap.org/soap/envelope/"
                   xmlns:xsi="http://www.w3.org/2001/XMLSchema-instance">
  <SOAP-ENV:Body>
    <sayHelloResponse
         SOAP-ENV:encodingStyle="http://schemas.xmlsoap.org/soap/encoding/">
      <sayHelloResult xsi:type="xsd:string">Hello John!</sayHelloResult>
    </sayHelloResponse>
  </SOAP-ENV:Body>
</SOAP-ENV:Envelope>
```

Building an Advanced Web Service

Having seen how to develop a simple Web Service, we will now develop a slightly more advanced Web Service where the service provider uses a database to provide the service. We'll call the new service `StockQuoteServer`. The service will expose a web method that accepts a stock symbol as an argument and returns the current stock price to the client after looking up its database. The stock codes and the corresponding values are stored in a MySQL database.

Setting Up the Database

We'll use MySQL for storing the data. To access the database, we need a JDBC driver. The MySQL JDBC driver (`mm.mysql.jdbc-1.2c.tar.gz`) may be downloaded from the following URL http://www.mysql.com/downloads/. Extract this file to a convenient location.

Next, add the installation directory of this JDBC driver to the `CLASSPATH`. This is done using the following command:

```
export CLASSPATH=$CLASSPATH:<MySQL-JDBC Driver Directory>
```

Creating a Database Table

We will create a table called `StockTable` in the default `test` database provided by MySQL. First, start the MySQL server. Once the database is set, create the table using the following SQL statement:

```
CREATE TABLE StockTable (StockCode varchar(5), price double (6,2));
```

This creates the `StockTable` table in the default database. Once the table is successfully created, let's populate it with some sample data for testing the Web Service:

```
INSERT INTO StockTable(StockCode, price) VALUES('INFY', 1600.0);
```

Likewise, add some more records to `StockTable`.

Developing a StockQuote Web Service

We will now develop a Web Service that reads the stock price for a given stock symbol from the above database. The Web Service uses the mm-mysql JDBC driver for accessing data from MySQL. It will expose a method called `getStockPrice()` to the client. This method takes a `String` argument specifying the stock symbol and returns the current stock price as a `Double` to the client. The method will pass appropriate error codes to the client in the case of any errors while executing the service.

To create a Web Service, first we declare a class called `StockQuoteServer`:

```
// File : StockQuoteServer.java

import java.sql.Connection;
import java.sql.DriverManager;
import java.sql.ResultSet;
import java.sql.Statement;

public class StockQuoteServer {
```

In the class constructor, we load the JDBC driver:

```
  public StockQuoteServer() {
    try {
      // Load JDBC driver for MySql
      Class.forName("org.gjt.mm.mysql.Driver").newInstance();
    } catch (Exception e) {
      System.err.println("Unable to load driver.");
      e.printStackTrace();
    }
  }
```

The `getStockPrice()` is a web method that will be invoked by the client using the SOAP protocol. It receives one parameter of type `String` that specifies the stock symbol for which the current price is desired. The method returns a `double` value to the client. The value will be encapsulated in a SOAP response:

```
  public double getStockPrice(String symbol) {
```

In the method body, we first obtain the connection to the database using a `jdbc` URL:

```
    try {
      // Get Connection for 'test' database and
      // create Statement on the Connection
      Connection con =
              DriverManager.getConnection("jdbc:mysql://localhost/test");
```

Note that if the database is running on a server other than a local machine, you will need to specify the server IP or the name in the above connection string.

Once a connection to the database is established, the program creates a `Statement` object, constructs an appropriate SQL statement, and fires the query:

```
      Statement stmt = con.createStatement();
      String sql = "SELECT price FROM StockTable
                           WHERE StockCode=\'" + symbol + "\'";
      ResultSet rs = stmt.executeQuery(sql);
```

The query result is returned in a `ResultSet`. We retrieve the result from the `ResultSet` and assign it to a `Double` variable:

```
            rs.next();
            double price = (double) rs.getDouble(1);
            return price;
        } catch (Exception e) {
            e.printStackTrace();
        }
        return  -1.0;
    }
}
```

The retrieved value is then returned to the caller.

Publishing the StockQuote Service

Once the Web Service is created, it may be published in two different ways:

- Copy the `StockQuoteServer.java` file into the `webapps/axis` directory and rename it to `StockQuoteServer.jws`.
- Deploy the Web Service using Web Service Deployment Descriptor (WSDD). WSDD allows us to customize the deployment.

For the current example, we will use the first method of deployment. The WSDD deployment is discussed in the later examples. Thus, rename and copy the file in the appropriate web folder.

A StockQuote Client

In this section, we will develop a client that uses the `StockQuote` Web Service:

```
import org.apache.axis.client.Call;
import org.apache.axis.client.Service;
import org.apache.axis.encoding.XMLType;

import javax.xml.rpc.ParameterMode;
import javax.xml.rpc.namespace.QName;

public class StockQuoteClient {
  public static void main(String [] args) {
    try {
```

The `main()` method does all the work of calling the remote Web Service. The method first constructs the URL object that refers to the Web Service URL:

```
         String endpoint = "http://localhost:8080/axis/StockQuoteServer.jws";
```

Note that you will have to replace the above URL with the appropriate URL of your server.

Next, we will create a `Service` object:

```
         Service service = new Service();
```

The following code creates a `Call` object. The object of `Call` class is used for invoking the Web Service:

```
         Call call = (Call) service.createCall();
```

The following code sets the URL and the method name of the target Web Service:

```
        call.setTargetEndpointAddress(new java.net.URL(endpoint));
        call.setOperationName("getStockPrice");
```

Next, we add the parameter required by the remote web method using the `addParameter()` method of the `Call` class. The first parameter to the method specifies the parameter name, the second parameter specifies the data type for the parameter, and the third parameter specifies the `IN/OUT` mode for the parameter:

```
        call.addParameter("symbol", XMLType.XSD_STRING, ParameterMode.IN);
```

Other types in `XMLType` class are `SOAP_ARRAY`, `SOAP_BASE64`, `XSD_ANYTYPE`, `XSD_DATE`, and so on. These types are instances of the `QName` class.

The method return type is set by calling the `setReturnType()` method on the call object and sending the appropriate data type as the parameter to the method:

```
        call.setReturnType(XMLType.XSD_DOUBLE);
```

The remote method is invoked by calling the `invoke()` method on the `call` object. Parameters are passed as an array of type `Object`. The returned value that is the stock price is taken in an object of type `Double` and is printed on the user's console:

```
        Double ret = (Double) call.invoke(new Object [] {"INFY"});

        String price="";
        if(ret.doubleValue() == -1.0) {
          price = "Error in Server";
        } else {
          price = ret.toString();
        }

        System.out.println(price);
      } catch (Exception e) {
        e.printStackTrace();
      }
    }
  }
```

Running the Client

Test the client by calling the above client code. The remote web method will be invoked and you will see the current stock price displayed on the screen.

A JSP-Based Stock Client

Here is an alternative client using JSP:

```
<%@ page language="java"
         import="org.apache.axis.client.Call,
                 org.apache.axis.client.Service,
                 org.apache.axis.encoding.XMLType,
                 javax.xml.rpc.ParameterMode,
                 java.net.URL" %>
```

```
<html>
  <body>
    <form method="POST" action="StockClient.jsp">
      <table align="center" border="1">
        <tr align="center">
          <td>
            <br />
            <font size=5 color="red">
              Stock Quote Service <br />
            </font><br />
          </td>
        </tr>
        <tr align = "center" valign = "center">
          <td>
            Enter Stock Symbol:
            <input type="textbox" name="txtStockSymbol"
                   value="symbol"> <br /><br />

          </td>
        </tr>
        <tr align="center" valign="center">
          <td>
```

We have a <form> tag that defines the method attribute as POST and the action attribute refers to the StockClient.jsp file. In the above code we accept a stock symbol from the user. After accepting the value we get the value using the following code. The if statement is required when we invoke the JSP page for the first time. We check for the null value that is returned at the first invocation of the page:

```
            <%
            if (request.getParameter("txtStockSymbol")!=null) {
              String symbol= request.getParameter("txtStockSymbol");
              // Endpoint of the target Web Service
```

Code to create Call object and invoke the remote method is the same as in our client above:

```
              URL url =
                new URL("http://localhost:8080/axis/StockQuoteServer.jws");
              // Create Call Object
              Service service = new Service();
              Call call = (Call) service.createCall();

              // Set the endpoint of the target service
              call.setTargetEndpointAddress(url);
              // Set the name of the method to be invoked
              call.setOperationName("getStockPrice");
              // Add the parameters of the method
              call.addParameter("symbol", XMLType.XSD_STRING,
                                ParameterMode.IN);
              // Set the return type of the method
              call.setReturnType(XMLType.XSD_DOUBLE);
              // Invoke the method on the target service
              Double ret = (Double) call.invoke(new Object [] {symbol});
              // Print the price of the StockCode
              if (ret.doubleValue() == -1.0) {
                out.println("Error");
```

```
              } else {
                out.println("Stock Rate of " + symbol + " is: "
                            + ret.doubleValue());
              }
            }
            %>

          </td>
        </tr>
        <tr align = "center" valign = "center">
          <td>
            <input type="submit" name="submit" value="Submit">
            <br /><br />
          </td>
        </tr>
      </table>
    </form>
  </body>
</html>
```

Using the JSP Client

First we deploy the JSP page. Copy it to the `CATALINA_HOME/webapps/ROOT` directory. Then access the address of the JSP page http://localhost:8080/StockClient.jsp. After loading the JSP page enter the stock code and press the Submit button. The screenshot is given below:

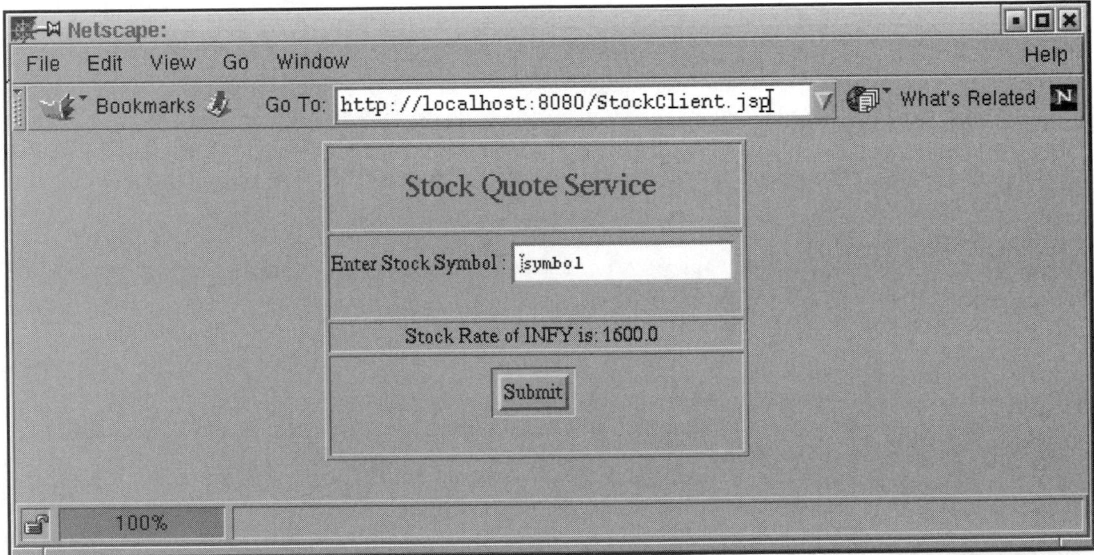

After the Submit button is clicked, the Web Service will be invoked. The result returned by the Web Service is displayed on the user screen as shown in the above screenshot.

The Web Service Deployment Descriptor

The JWS file provides us with the fastest and easiest way to deploy a Web Service in Axis. However, it does not allow us to customize the deployment of a Web Service. It also leaves the sourcecode open on the server for crackers to get their hands on and we cannot specify a custom type mapping or decide selectively to expose certain methods. To achieve this, Axis provides a way to customize our deployment: the **Web Service Deployment Descriptor** (WSDD).

The WSDD is an XML document. We may store those files anywhere, and we will have to provide the absolute path of the file at the time of deployment so the current directory is easiest. It contains information about the Web Service we want to deploy. It specifies the class name for the Web Service class, a list of methods to be exposed, and so on. The following XML file shows the sample format for a `<deployment>` tag:

```
<deployment xmlns="http://xml.apache.org/axis/wsdd/"
            xmlns:java="http://xml.apache.org/axis/wsdd/providers/java">
  <service name="SampleService" provider="java:RPC">
    <parameter name="className" value="SampleServer"/>
    <parameter name="allowedMethods" value="*"/>
  </service>
</deployment>
```

The `<deployment>` element includes the required namespaces. The `<service>` element specifies the details of the service to be deployed.

In the above `<deployment>`, `name` specifies the URI for the deployed service and `provider` specifies the handler, which calls the actual object of the service class. In our example, we will use `java:RPC` as a provider which is the `org.apache.axis.providers.java.RPCProvider` class. We have described `RPCProvider` earlier in the chapter. We may provide other providers such as `java:MSG` for message-based services. We will learn about the message-based service later in the chapter.

Inside the `<service>` element we specify different parameters by using the `<parameter>` tag.

In the above line parameter `className` is used to specify the actual Java class which provides the desired service. The name of the class is given as the `value` of the parameter. The `.class` file for this class should be located in the `CATALINA_HOME/webapps/axis/WEB-INF/classes` directory.

Next, we specify the `allowedMethods` parameter.

The `allowedMethods` parameter specifies the methods to be exposed to the outside world. The '*' in `value` field indicates that all methods of the class are exposed to the outside world. Alternatively, we can specify a list of the methods separated by spaces. For example:

```
<parameter name="allowedMethods" value="add multiply subtract"/>
```

Now we will deploy our `StockQuoteServer` using WSDD.

Deployment of StockQuoteServer Using WSDD

The following code segment shows the WSDD file for our `StockQuoteServer`:

```
<deployment xmlns="http://xml.apache.org/axis/wsdd/"
            xmlns:java="http://xml.apache.org/axis/wsdd/providers/java">

  <service name="StockQuoteServer" provider="java:RPC">
    <parameter name="className" value="StockQuoteServer"/>
    <parameter name="allowedMethods" value="*"/>
  </service>
</deployment>
```

The deployment descriptor is quite similar to the above general case. We expose all the public methods of our service as web methods. Save this configuration in the `stock.wsdd` file in the current directory. As stated earlier we may store this anywhere, but in that case we will have to provide the absolute path of the file in the following command. Note the success method telling us that the deployment was successful:

```
java org.apache.axis.client.AdminClient stock.wsdd
-Processing file stock.wssd
<Admin>Done processing</Admin>
```

The `AdminClient` is a utility provided by Axis that reads the specified WSDD and deploys the Web Service.

Modifying the StockQuote Client

We have earlier developed a client application for accessing our Web Service. We will need to make a few changes to it so that it can use the newly deployed Web Service.

There are two changes required in the `main()` method of the client application. First, we need to change the URL to the following one:

```
URL url = new URL("http://localhost:8080/axis/servlet/AxisServlet");
```

Here we specify the URL for the `AxisServlet`, rather than the URL of the target Web Service. Next, we need to change the parameter in the `call.setOperationName()` method call:

```
call.setOperationName(new QName("StockQuoteServer", "getStockPrice"));
```

Here we pass an object of `QName` class that takes two parameters in its constructor – the first parameter specifies the URI of the Web Service which is the same as the name specified in the `<service>` element and the second the name of the method to invoke.

Compile the client (`.java` file) and run it. You will see results similar to the one shown earlier.

Web Services with Deployment Descriptors

Now we will develop some advanced services that will show the actual strength of WSDD deployment. In this section, we will develop five Web Services:

- A service returning an array of type `String`
- A service taking a JavaBean as an argument
- Sending an attachment to the service
- Adding a custom handler to the service
- Using a message-based service

Returning an Array from a Service Method

We will create a Web Service that provides us with the address of its registered customers. For each customer, we will store an ID and the address as an array of strings. The customer ID is passed as an argument to the Web Service method. The customer address is returned as an array of `String` objects.

We construct the data by declaring an array of type `int` containing IDs and a 2-dimensional array of `String` objects containing the address of each employee. This is shown in the following code segment:

```
// File : AddressService.java

public class AddressService {
  private int[] id = {111, 222, 333};
  private String[][] addressBook = {{"Street 11", "London", "UK", "34534"},
                                    {"Lane 4", "New York", "USA", "53457"},
                                    {"Lane 5", "LA", "USA", "67635"}};
```

Next, we write a Web Service method for returning the address of the requested customer ID as shown below:

```
  public String[] getArray(int id) {
    for (int i=0; i<addressBook.length; i++) {
      if(this.id[i] == id) {
        return addressBook[i];
      }
    }
    String error[] = {"id not found!"};
    return error;
  }
}
```

Store this class in file `AddressService.java` file in the current directory and compile it.

Deployment Descriptor for AddressService

Now we will write a WSDD for our service and store it in the current directory. First we define the URI of the service, its class name, and exposed methods as shown overleaf:

```
<deployment xmlns="http://xml.apache.org/axis/wsdd/"
            xmlns:java="http://xml.apache.org/axis/wsdd/providers/java">

  <service name="AddressService" provider="java:RPC">
    <parameter name="className" value="AddressService"/>
    <parameter name="allowedMethods" value="*"/>
```

For mapping between the `String` array and an XML data type we use the <`typeMapping`> element. Since we cannot directly map the `String` array to an XML data type we have to use the `serializer` and `deserializer` attributes, which are used for serializing/deserializing of the parameter. The classes used for `serializer` and `deserializer` are provided by Axis:

```
    <typeMapping
        serializer="org.apache.axis.encoding.ser.ArraySerializerFactory"
        deserializer="org.apache.axis.encoding.ser.ArrayDeserializerFactory"
```

Inside `typeMapping`, we define another attribute called `encodingStyle` as follows:

```
        encodingStyle="http://schemas.xmlsoap.org/soap/encoding/"
```

This indicates the XML Schema used for SOAP encoding.

We also specify the type attribute as shown below:

```
        type="java:java.lang.String[]"
```

Finally we write the namespace and URI of the type mapping and close the <`service`> and <`deployment`> elements:

```
        qname="ns1:ArrayOfstring"
        xmlns:ns1="http://soapinterop.org/xsd"/>
  </service>
</deployment>
```

Save this in `address.wsdd`. To deploy the Web Service use the following command:

```
java org.apache.axis.client.AdminClient address.wsdd
```

You will get the same confirmation message as before.

Writing a Client for AddressService

This is a console-based Java application that requests a customer ID from the user. The `main()` method declares the required URL and prompts the user for the ID:

```
import org.apache.axis.AxisFault;
import org.apache.axis.client.Call;
import org.apache.axis.client.Service;
import org.apache.axis.utils.JavaUtils;

import org.apache.axis.encoding.ser.ArraySerializerFactory;
import org.apache.axis.encoding.ser.ArrayDeserializerFactory;
```

```
import org.apache.axis.encoding.XMLType;

import javax.xml.rpc.ParameterMode;
import javax.xml.rpc.namespace.QName;

import java.io.BufferedReader;
import java.io.InputStreamReader;

public class ArrayClient {
  public static void main(String [] args) throws Exception {
    String url = "http://localhost:8080/axis/servlet/AxisServlet";
    String id = null;
    try {
      BufferedReader reader = new BufferedReader(
                              new InputStreamReader(System.in));
      System.out.print("Enter id: ");
      id = reader.readLine();
    } catch (Exception e){
      e.printStackTrace();
    }
```

Next, we create the `Service` and `Call` objects as follows:

```
    Service service = new Service();
    Call call = (Call) service.createCall();
```

Then we create an object of `QName` that represents the namespace and URI of our type mapping:

```
    QName qn = new QName("http://soapinterop.org/xsd", "ArrayOfstring");
```

We have to register the type mapping information with our `Call` object for serialization and deserialization. We can do this using `registerTypeMapping()` in the `Call` class. We pass the Java class of the data type, object of `QName` class, and objects of `ArraySerializerFactory` and `ArrayDeserializerFactory` classes:

```
    call.registerTypeMapping(String[][].class, qn,
                             new ArraySerializerFactory(),
                             new ArrayDeserializerFactory());
```

We initialize an array of type `String` to store the return value of the method:

```
    String result[] = {""};
```

We set up the `call` object as follows:

```
    try {
      call.setTargetEndpointAddress(new java.net.URL(url));
      call.setOperationName(new QName("AddressService", "getArray"));
      call.addParameter("id", XMLType.XSD_INT, ParameterMode.IN);
      call.setReturnType(qn);
```

We invoke the remote method by calling `invoke()` on our `call` object, passing an array of type `Object` as a parameter. We store the return value in `resp`, which is of type `Object`:

```
Object resp = call.invoke(new Object[] {new Integer(id)});
```

Then we convert the `resp` object to an array of type `String`. This is done as shown below:

```
result = (String[])JavaUtils.convert(resp, String[].class);
```

Finally we catch any exceptions, and print the result:

```
    } catch (AxisFault fault) {
      System.out.println("Error : " + fault.toString());
    }
    System.out.println("Address of " + id);
    for(int i=0; i<result.length; i++)
      System.out.println("\t" + result[i]);
  }
}
```

Compile and run the client application. You will see a screen similar to the one shown below:

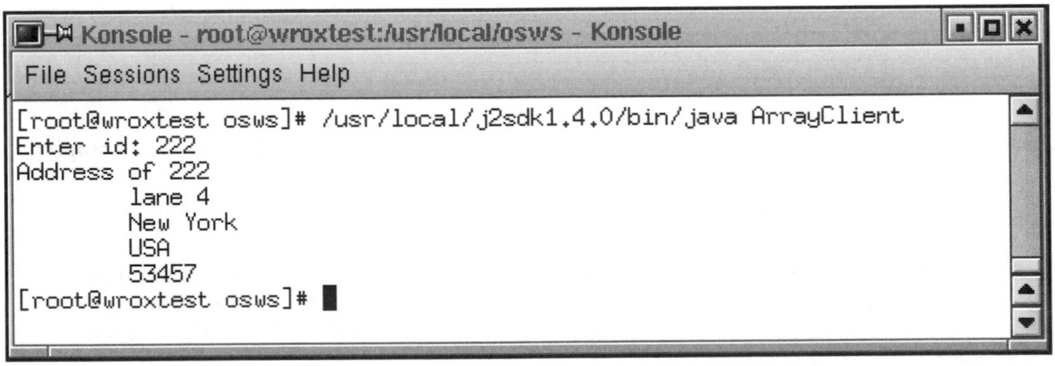
Konsole - root@wroxtest:/usr/local/osws - Konsole
File Sessions Settings Help
[root@wroxtest osws]# /usr/local/j2sdk1.4.0/bin/java ArrayClient
Enter id: 222
Address of 222
lane 4
New York
USA
53457
[root@wroxtest osws]#

JavaBean Parameters

In this section, we will develop a `SalaryManager` Web Service that calculates the net salary of an employee. The Web Service exposes a method that accepts a custom class as a parameter. This class follows the JavaBean standard.

First we will develop this custom class called `SalaryBean`. The instance of this class is passed as an argument to the `service()` method. We define three properties for this bean: `salary`, `tax`, and `bonus`. To access the attributes, we define accessor/mutator methods. The class definition is shown below:

```
import java.io.Serializable;

public class SalaryBean implements Serializable {
  private double salary;
  private double tax;
  private double bonus;
  public void setSalary (double salary) {
    this.salary = salary;
```

```
    }
    public double getSalary () {
      return salary;
    }

    public void setTax(double tax) {
      this.tax = tax;
    }
    public double getTax() {
      return tax;
    }

    public void setBonus(double bonus){
      this.bonus = bonus;
    }
    public double getBonus() {
      return bonus;
    }
  }
```

Now we will write code for our Web Service. The complete class code is shown below:

```
  public class SalaryManager {
    SalaryBean salBean;

    public double computeSalary(SalaryBean bean) {
      salBean= bean;
      double salary = salBean.getSalary ();
      double tax = salBean.getTax();
      double bonus = salBean.getBonus();

      salary = (salary+bonus)*(1-(tax/100));
      return salary;
    }
  }
```

Note that the `computeSalary()` method takes a custom Java class as a parameter.

Deployment Descriptor for Salary Manager

Now we will look at the deployment descriptor. First we write the service name, its provider, implementation class, and its exposed method as shown below:

```
<deployment xmlns="http://xml.apache.org/axis/wsdd/"
            xmlns:java="http://xml.apache.org/axis/wsdd/providers/java">

  <service name="SalaryManagerService" provider="java:RPC">
    <parameter name="className" value="SalaryManager"/>
    <parameter name="allowedMethods" value="*"/>
```

Next, we use `<beanMapping>` tag to map the JavaBean class to an XML `QName`. The qname attribute specifies the URI of the bean and `languageSpecificType` gives the name of the bean class:

```
    <beanMapping qname="myNS:SalaryBean" xmlns:myNS="urn:SalaryService"
                 languageSpecificType="java:SalaryBean"/>
  </service>
</deployment>
```

Save this WSDD in the salary.wsdd file in the current directory. Compile the SalaryBean and SalaryManager classes and copy them to the CATALINA_HOME/webapps/axis/WEB-INF/classes. We deploy the service using the following command:

```
java org.apache.axis.client.AdminClient salary.wsdd
```

Developing a Client for the SalaryManager Class

This is a console-based Java application. In the main() method, we instantiate a SalaryBean class and prompt the user for the various input values. The read values are stored as the bean's properties:

```
import org.apache.axis.client.Call;
import org.apache.axis.client.Service;

import org.apache.axis.encoding.ser.BeanSerializerFactory;
import org.apache.axis.encoding.ser.BeanDeserializerFactory;

import org.apache.axis.encoding.XMLType;

import javax.xml.rpc.ParameterMode;
import javax.xml.rpc.namespace.QName;

import java.io.BufferedReader;
import java.io.InputStreamReader;

public class SalaryClient {
  public static void main(String [] args) throws Exception {
    String url = "http://localhost:8080/axis/servlet/AxisServlet";
    SalaryBean slb = new SalaryBean();
    BufferedReader br = new BufferedReader(new
                                       InputStreamReader(System.in));
    System.out.print("Enter salary: ");
    double salary = Double.parseDouble(br.readLine());
    System.out.print("Enter Tax Rate: ");
    double taxRate = Double.parseDouble(br.readLine());
    System.out.print("Enter Bonus: ");
    double bonus = Double.parseDouble(br.readLine());

    slb.setSalary(salary);
    slb.setTax(taxRate);
    slb.setBonus(bonus);
```

Next we create Service and Call classes. We also create an object of QName as follows:

```
    Service service = new Service();
    Call call = (Call) service.createCall();
    QName qn = new QName("urn:SalaryService", "SalaryBean");
```

Then as in the previous example we call registerTypeMapping() on the call object. This time we use an instance of BeanSerializerFactory and BeanDeserializerFactory:

```
    call.registerTypeMapping(SalaryBean.class, qn,
                        new BeanSerializerFactory(SalaryBean.class, qn),
                        new BeanDeserializerFactory(SalaryBean.class, qn));
```

We set up the target endpoint and the operation name of the `call` object by calling the `setTargetEndpointAddress()` and `setOperationName()` methods respectively:

```
        call.setTargetEndpointAddress(new java.net.URL(url));
        call.setOperationName(new QName("SalaryManagerService",
                                        "computeSalary"));
```

The parameter and return type are set by calling the `addParameter()` and `setReturnType()` methods respectively:

```
        call.addParameter("slb", qn, ParameterMode.IN);
        call.setReturnType(XMLType.XSD_DOUBLE);
```

The remote method is invoked by calling the `invoke()` method on the `call` object:

```
        Double netSal = (Double) call.invoke(new Object[] {slb});

        System.out.print("Net Salary: " + netSal);
    }
}
```

When we run the client application, it asks for the three input values and prints the result as shown in the screenshot below:

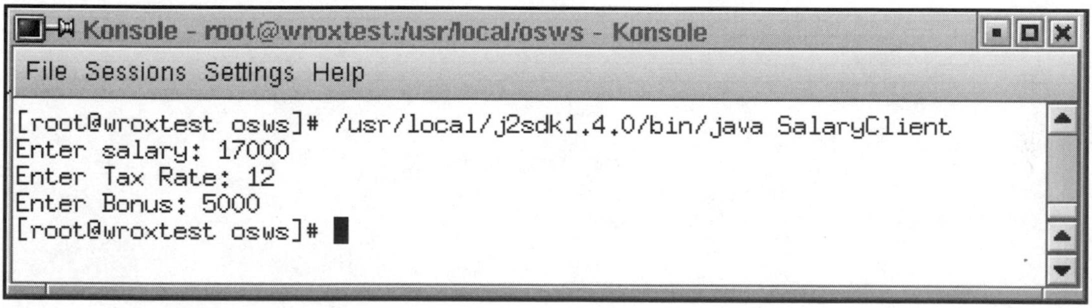

```
Konsole - root@wroxtest:/usr/local/osws - Konsole
File  Sessions  Settings  Help
[root@wroxtest osws]# /usr/local/j2sdk1.4.0/bin/java SalaryClient
Enter salary: 17000
Enter Tax Rate: 12
Enter Bonus: 5000
[root@wroxtest osws]#
```

Attachments with Axis

Additional data may be sent with the SOAP message as an attachment. This additional data can be a text or a binary file. Axis supports SOAP attachments based on the W3C specifications given at http://www.w3c.org/TR/SOAP-attachments/.

In this section we will develop a Web Service that accepts a purchase order as an attachment to a SOAP message. `PurchaseOrderService` is our Web Service class.

PurchaseOrderService

This class contains `placePurchaseOrder` method that retrieves the contents of the attached file from the `AttachmentPart` object. The retrieved file is stored at the location specified in the `Path` variable:

```
import org.apache.axis.attachments.AttachmentPart;

import javax.activation.DataHandler;
import java.io.File;
import java.io.FileOutputStream;
import java.io.BufferedInputStream;

public class PurchaseOrderService {
```

The `placePurchaseOrder()` method accepts two parameters; the first is the `FileName` of type `String` and the second `ap` of type `AttacmentPart`:

```
  public String placePurchaseOrder(String FileName, AttachmentPart ap) {
    try {
```

The `DataHandler` object is used to read and write the file contents. The `DataHandler` encapsulates the `Data` object and provides methods to access the data.

We create a `BufferedInputStream` object to read the contents from the `DataHandler` object and a `FileOutputStream` object to store the file to the specified location (in this case a hard-coded path):

```
      String Path = "/home/wrox/" + FileName;
      FileOutputStream fout = new FileOutputStream(new File(Path));
      BufferedInputStream in = new BufferedInputStream(dh.getInputStream());
      while (in.available() != 0) {
        fout.write(in.read());
      }
```

Finally, we close the streams:

```
      fout.close();
      in.close();
    } catch(Exception e) {
      e.printStackTrace();
      return "Error";
    }
    return "File received successfully";
  }
}
```

Deployment Descriptor for PurchaseOrderService

Once the service class is written the next step is to deploy the service. We will use the following deployment descriptor to deploy the service with the name `PurchaseOrderService`:

```
<deployment name="PurchaseOrder" xmlns="http://xml.apache.org/axis/wsdd/"
            xmlns:java="http://xml.apache.org/axis/wsdd/providers/java"
            xmlns:xsi="http://www.w3.org/2000/10/XMLSchema-instance">
  <service name="PurchaseOrderService" provider="java:RPC">
    <parameter name="className" value="PurchaseOrderService" />
    <parameter name="allowedMethods" value="placePurchaseOrder" />
  </service>
```

The <typeMapping> tag is added to explicitly specify the `serializer` and `deserializer` class:

```
    <typeMapping qname="ns1:DataHansdler" xmlns:ns1="PurchaseOrderService"
                 languageSpecificType="java:javax.activation.DataHandler"
  serializer="org.apache.axis.encoding.ser.JAFDataHandlerSerializerFactory"
  deserializer="org.apache.axis.encoding.ser.JAFDataHandlerDeserializerFactory"
                 encodingStyle="http://schemas.xmlsoap.org/soap/encoding/"/>
  </deployment>
```

Here the `serializer` and `deserializer` attributes specify the Java class name for `serializer` and `deserializer` factory classes. These classes are the part of JavaBean Activation Framework (JAF) that is used for providing support for MIME types. Axis uses the "multipart/related" content type for the SOAP attachments.

Now we are ready to deploy the service.

Deploying the Service

First compile the service class and copy the `PurchaseOrderService.class` file to the `/WEB_INF/classes` directory of the Axis deployment.

Then use the following command to deploy the service:

```
java org.apache.axis.client.AdminClient POServiceDeploy.wsdd
```

A PurchaseOrder Client

Now let's write the client application that accesses our Web Service. This application is a simple console-based application. It takes the complete path to the file and the filename as command line argument and sends the file as a SOAP attachment:

```
import org.apache.axis.client.Service;
import org.apache.axis.client.Call;

import org.apache.axis.encoding.XMLType;

import org.apache.axis.encoding.ser.JAFDataHandlerSerializerFactory;
import org.apache.axis.encoding.ser.JAFDataHandlerDeserializerFactory;

import javax.xml.rpc.ParameterMode;
import javax.xml.rpc.namespace.QName;

import javax.activation.FileDataSource;
import javax.activation.DataHandler;

public class PurchaseOrderClient {
  public static void main (String [] args) {
```

Here we check the command-line arguments. If two arguments are not set, we display the appropriate message to the user and exit:

```
    if (args.length!=2) {
      System.out.println("Usage => java PurchaseOrderClient <filepath>
<filename>");
      System.exit(0);
    }
```

Set the endpoint URI to http://localhost:8080/axis/services/PurchaseOrderService:

```
    try {
      String endpoint =
                "http://localhost:8080/axis/services/PurchaseOrderService";
```

Set up the RPC call and set the name of the service and the name of the method to be invoked:

```
      Service POService = new Service();
      Call POServiceCall = (Call) POService.createCall();
      POServiceCall.setTargetEndpointAddress(new java.net.URL(endpoint));
      POServiceCall.setOperationName(new QName("PurchaseOrderService",
                                                 "placePurchaseOrder"));
```

Here we set the parameter's type. The `placePurchaseOrder()` method accepts two parameters. First is the `filename`, which is of type `java.lang.String`, which is set using `XMLType.XSD_STRING` as the qualified name. `ParameterMode.IN` indicates that the parameter is an input parameter. The second parameter is the attached file as a `DataHandler` object.

```
      POServiceCall.addParameter("fileName", XMLType.XSD_STRING,
                                 ParameterMode.IN);
      QName qname = new QName("PurchaseOrderService", "DataHandler");
      POServiceCall.addParameter("PO", qname, ParameterMode.IN);
```

Create the `DataHandler` object that reads the contents of the file to be sent as the SOAP attachment:

```
      DataHandler dh = new DataHandler(new FileDataSource(args[0] +
                                                          args[1]));
```

Here we register the type mappings of the `DataHandler` using the class name, the qualified name, and `serializer` and `deserializer` classes:

```
      POServiceCall.registerTypeMapping(dh.getClass(), qname,
                                    JAFDataHandlerSerializerFactory.class,
                                    JAFDataHandlerDeserializerFactory.class);
```

Set the return type to `java.lang.String` using the `XMLType.XSD_STRING` as the qualified name:

```
      POServiceCall.setReturnType(XMLType.XSD_STRING);
```

Set the input parameters to the file's name and the file's data:

```
      Object[] params = new Object[] {args[1], dh};
```

Finally invoke the method, retrieve the result, and display it to the user:

```
      String result = (String) POServiceCall.invoke(params);

      System.out.println(result);
    } catch(Exception ex) {
      ex.printStackTrace();
    }
  }
}
```

Compile the above client, then use the following command to run the client:

```
java PurchaseOrderClient /home/po/ PO647.swd
```

Here is the output:

```
File received successfully
```

The file should also be stored in the location specified in the server code.

Writing Custom Handlers

Axis handlers are used to extend the behavior of Axis. The handler acts as an intermediary that can be used to pre-process or post-process the message. Axis defines an interface `org.apache.axis.Handler` for custom handler development. It includes the following methods.

public void init()

Executed when the Axis engine creates an instance of the handler. It is used for initializing members.

public void invoke(MessageContext messageContext) throws AxisFault

This is the most important method that contains the actual handler logic. The required information such as service name, target name, or value of any SOAP header can be retrieved from the `MessageContext` object and the necessary processing is done here.

public void inFault(MessageContext messageContext) trows AxisFault

The method is invoked if any error is generated. This method can be used to release resources or undo any changes.

public void cleanup()

The Axis engine calls this method when the object is no longer required.

Handler Options

Axis provides two options to build a custom handler, either implement the `Handler` interface and provide the implementation for all the methods or use the Axis provided class called `BasicHandler` that provides a default implementation for all the methods except `invoke()`. We can simply extend `BasicHandler` and provide the implementation for the `invoke()` method.

Here we develop a simple request handler that prints a message on the server console whenever a request is received. `RequestHandler` is the class that extends `BasicHandler` and provides an implementation of `invoke()`.

RequestHandler

The code listing of our `RequestHandler` class is given below:

```
import org.apache.axis.MessageContext;
import org.apache.axis.AxisFault;
import org.apache.axis.handlers.BasicHandler;
```

```
public class RequestHandler extends BasicHandler {
  public void invoke(MessageContext msgContext) throws AxisFault {
    System.out.println("New Purchase Order Received");
  }
}
```

Compile this class and copy the `.class` file to the `/WEB_INF/classes` folder of the Axis deployment.

Deployment Descriptor

The next step is to write a deployment descriptor. Here we will use the previously developed `PurchaseOrderService` to test the request handler.

Following are the required modifications in the descriptor:

```
<deployment name="PurchaseOrder" xmlns="http://xml.apache.org/axis/wsdd/"
            xmlns:java="http://xml.apache.org/axis/wsdd/providers/java"
            xmlns:xsi="http://www.w3.org/2000/10/XMLSchema-instance">
```

The handler is described using the `<handler>` element. The `name` attribute specifies a name for the handler and the `type` attribute specifies the Java class that implements the handler. The handler element may contain `<parameter>` as a subelement that can be used to pass parameters to the handler. Here we have not passed any parameters:

```
<handler name="RequestHandler" type="java:RequestHandler"/>
  <service name="PurchaseOrderService" provider="java:RPC">
    <requestFlow>
      <handler type="RequestHandler" />
    </requestFlow>
```

The handler can finally be attached to the service using the `<requestFlow>` element as shown above. This element specifies that the handler is to be invoked before processing the incoming request. Here we can also use `<responseFlow>` element, which will cause the handler invocation to be carried out after processing the request and before sending the response:

```
    <parameter name="className" value="PurchaseOrderService" />
    <parameter name="allowedMethods" value="placePurchaseOrder" />
  </service>
  <typeMapping qname="ns1:DataHansdler" xmlns:ns1="PurchaseOrderService"
               languageSpecificType="java:javax.activation.DataHandler"
serializer="org.apache.axis.encoding.ser.JAFDataHandlerSerializerFactory"
deserializer="org.apache.axis.encoding.ser.JAFDataHandlerDeserializerFactory"
               encodingStyle="http://schemas.xmlsoap.org/soap/encoding/"/>
</deployment>
```

Deploying the Service

Use the following command to deploy the service:

```
java org.apache.axis.client.AdminClient PORequestDeploy.wsdd
```

Running the Client

We will use the same client application used for the PurchaseOrderService.

Use the following command to run the client:

```
java PurchaseOrderClient /home/wrox/ PO647.swd
```

We should then also see a confirmation message on the Tomcat console.

Developing a Message-Based Service

So far we have been developing an RPC-based service. Now we will learn how to develop a message-based service. This type of service contains only one web method. In a message-based service the whole MessageContext is passed to the web method along with the vector of elements. This type of service may define its own set of commands and invoke an appropriate method on other objects.

We will develop a Web Service for placing orders to an OrderService class. The OrderService class contains one method called placeOrder(). This is the method that will be exposed by our service as a web method. The client will pass the order details to this method. In our sample service the web method will simply print the SOAP message on the Tomcat console. In a real-world scenario, the Web Service would store the order in the underlying database, update the inventory, ship the item, and finally send the appropriate response to the client. In our example the service will send a message to the client along with the date of shipping. The client then prints the response on the console.

Now we will walk through the server code. First we will import all the needed classes:

```
// File : OrderService.java

import org.w3c.dom.Element;
import org.w3c.dom.Document;
import org.w3c.dom.Text;
import org.apache.axis.MessageContext;
import javax.xml.parsers.DocumentBuilderFactory;
import javax.xml.parsers.DocumentBuilder;
import java.text.SimpleDateFormat;
import java.util.Vector;
import java.util.Date;
```

We define a Web Service class:

```
public class OrderService {
```

Then we will write the web method called placeOrder(). Note the parameter list and return type of the method. The method accepts a Vector of XML elements passed to the service.

The method returns an array of Element objects:

```
  public Element[] placeOrder(Vector elems) {
```

We get the current `MessageContext` and print the request message on the Tomcat server console:

```
      MessageContext msgC = MessageContext.getCurrentContext();
      System.out.println("Request Message");
      msgC.getRequestMessage().writeContentToStream(System.out);
```

We create an array of type `Element` of length 1. This array will be returned to the client:

```
      Element[] result = new Element[1];
```

Now we move on to build the response. First we create the `DocumentBuilder` object from `DocumentBuilderFactory`:

```
      try {
        DocumentBuilderFactory docFactory =
                                      DocumentBuilderFactory.newInstance();
        docFactory.setNamespaceAware(true);
        DocumentBuilder docBuilder = docFactory.newDocumentBuilder();
```

We create a DOM `Document` from `docBuilder` as shown below. We also create an XML `Element` from `responseDoc`. This is done by calling `createElementNS()` on the `responseDoc` object. We also pass the namespace name to the `createElementNS()` method. This will be the root element of the document:

```
        Document responseDoc = docBuilder.newDocument();
        Element resElem =
             responseDoc.createElementNS("http://www.abcom.com/OrderService",
                                         "OrderResponse");
```

Next we create elements to actually indicate the response. The `msg` element will just have a string. We also create an element for returning the shipping date. Both of the elements are text nodes:

```
        Element msg = responseDoc.createElement("Message");
        Text msgText = responseDoc.createTextNode("Thank you for placing your order
  with ABCOM's Web Service");

        Element date = responseDoc.createElement("ShippingDate");
        SimpleDateFormat dateFmt = new SimpleDateFormat("MM/dd/yyyy");
        Text dateText = responseDoc.createTextNode(
                                          dateFmt.format(new Date()));
```

We add these two elements to our root element. We set the root element in the `result` array:

```
        resElem.appendChild(msg);
        msg.appendChild(msgText);
        resElem.appendChild(date);
        date.appendChild(dateText);

        result[0] = resElem;
```

Finally we return the `result` array to the client:

```
      } catch (Exception e) {
        e.printStackTrace();
      }
      return(result);
          }
   }
```

Publishing the Message-Based Service

The following code segment shows the deployment descriptor used for our Web Service. Note the value of the `provider` attribute. Since we are using a message-based service we set the value of `provider` to `java:MSG`:

```
<deployment name="test" xmlns="http://xml.apache.org/axis/wsdd/"
            xmlns:java="http://xml.apache.org/axis/wsdd/providers/java"
            xmlns:xsi="http://www.w3.org/2000/10/XMLSchema-instance">
  <service name="OrderService" provider="java:MSG">
    <parameter name="className" value="OrderService" />
    <parameter name="allowedMethods" value="placeOrder" />
  </service>
</deployment>
```

Store the document shown above in the file `order.wsdd`. Use the following command to deploy the service:

```
java org.apache.axis.client.AdminClient order.wsdd
```

Developing a Message-Based Client Application

In our client application we create an array of type `SOAPBodyElement` to contain the request message elements. These elements will contain the order details. The elements will then be passed to the web method as a `Vector`. We'll now walk through the client code.

First we import all the needed classes:

```
import org.apache.axis.client.Service;
import org.apache.axis.client.Call;
import org.apache.axis.message.SOAPBodyElement;
import org.apache.axis.utils.Options;
import org.apache.axis.utils.XMLUtils;
import org.w3c.dom.Element;
import java.net.URL;
import java.util.Vector;
```

We then create `Service` and `Call` objects. As we did in our earlier example we set the URL of the Web Service by calling `setTargetEndpointAddress()` on the `call` object:

```
public class OrderClient {
  public String doit(String[] args) throws Exception {
    Options opt = new Options(args);
    opt.setDefaultURL("http://localhost:8080/axis/services/OrderService");

    Service service = new Service();
    Call call = (Call) service.createCall();
    call.setTargetEndpointAddress(new URL(opt.getURL()));
```

From here the code of an RPC-based client and our message-based client differs. In an RPC-based client we invoke a web method using an array of method parameters typed as an `Object` array. In this case we invoke the method using an array of type `SOAPBodyElement`. We are going to send three parameters to the web method so we create an array of three `SOAPBodyElement` objects:

```
    SOAPBodyElement[] input = new SOAPBodyElement[3];
```

Then we create each element using the `XMLUtils` class. We do this using the `StringToElement()` method of `XMLUtils` class. This method takes three parameters:

- A namespace
- An element
- The element's value

We create the element for the `CustomerID`, `Item`, and `Quantity` as shown below:

```
    input[0] = new
SOAPBodyElement(XMLUtils.StringToElement("http://www.abcom.com/",
                                         "CustomerID", "12345"));
    input[1] = new
SOAPBodyElement(XMLUtils.StringToElement("http://www.abcom.com/",
                                         "Item",
                                         "Hard Disk 40Gb : Samsung"));
    input[2] = new
SOAPBodyElement(XMLUtils.StringToElement("http://www.abcom.com/",
                                         "Quantity", "5"));
```

Next we call the `invoke()` method of `call`, passing it the array of `SOAPBodyElement` objects. We get the response into a `Vector`:

```
    Vector elems = (Vector) call.invoke(input);
```

Now we extract all the elements in the response. Each element is cast to `SOAPBodyElement`:

```
    SOAPBodyElement elem  = (SOAPBodyElement) elems.get(0);
```

Then we call `getAsDom()` method on the `elem` object to get an object of type `Element`:

```
    Element e = elem.getAsDOM();
```

Next we use `XMLUtils` to convert the element to a string. And finally we return the string to `main()`:

```
      String str = XMLUtils.ElementToString(e);

      return(str);
    }

    public static void main(String[] args) throws Exception {
      try {
        String res = (new OrderClient()).doit(args);
        System.out.println(res);
      } catch(Exception e) {
        e.printStackTrace();
      }
    }
  }
```

Now compile and run the client. The output of the client is shown below:

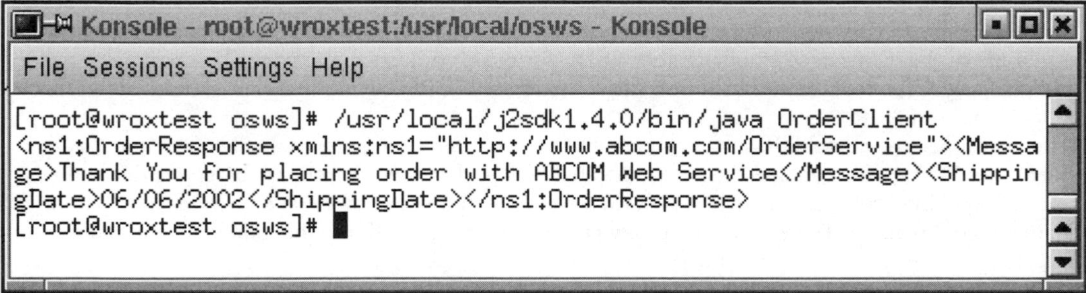

On the console of Tomcat you will get the SOAP message of the request. This is shown below.

Konsole - root@wroxtest:~ - Konsole
File Sessions Settings Help
[root@wroxtest root]# /usr/local/jakarta-tomcat-4.0.4-b3-LE-jdk14/bin/catalina.sh run
Using CATALINA_BASE: /usr/local/jakarta-tomcat-4.0.4-b3-LE-jdk14
Using CATALINA_HOME: /usr/local/jakarta-tomcat-4.0.4-b3-LE-jdk14
Using CATALINA_TMPDIR: /usr/local/jakarta-tomcat-4.0.4-b3-LE-jdk14/temp
Using JAVA_HOME: /usr/local/j2sdk1.4.0/
Starting service Tomcat-Standalone
Apache Tomcat/4.0.4-b3
Starting service Tomcat-Apache
Apache Tomcat/4.0.4-b3
Request Message
<?xml version="1.0" encoding="UTF-8"?>
<SOAP-ENV:Envelope xmlns:SOAP-ENV="http://schemas.xmlsoap.org/soap/envelope/" xmlns:xsd="
http://www.w3.org/2001/XMLSchema" xmlns:xsi="http://www.w3.org/2001/XMLSchema-instance">
<SOAP-ENV:Body><ns1:CustomerID xmlns:ns1="http://www.abcom.com/">12345</ns1:CustomerID><
ns2:Item xmlns:ns2="http://www.abcom.com/">Hard Disk 40Gb : Samsung</ns2:Item><ns3:Quanti
ty xmlns:ns3="http://www.abcom.com/">5</ns3:Quantity> </SOAP-ENV:Body>
</SOAP-ENV:Envelope>
New
Konsole

Here you can see the elements passed by our client inside the SOAP body.

Using WSDL with Axis

As discussed in Chapter 3, WSDL describes the interface exposed by a Web Service. WSDL describes the various web methods exposed by the Web Service, along with their parameters and return types.

Axis supports WSDL in three ways:

- After deploying the Web Service, an automatically-generated WSDL document may be obtained by accessing the service's URL from a standard web browser and by appending `?WSDL` to the end of the URL
- The WSDL2Java tool builds Java proxies and skeletons for services with WSDL descriptions
- A Java2WSDL tool builds WSDL from Java classes

Using WSDL2Java

We will use the earlier deployed `StockQuote` service here for generating proxies and skeletons using WSDL2Java. First, we need to obtain the WSDL for our `StockQuote` service. This is done by accessing the following URL from a web browser: http://localhost:8080/axis/StockQuoteServer.jws?WSDL.

When you open the above URL, the browser will ask you to save the output to a file. Save it to the file `stock.wsdl`. This file contains the auto-generated WSDL document for our Web Service that is the description of the Web Service. In a real-world scenario the publisher of the Web Service may put the WSDL file in a UDDI registry. To generate the proxy classes from this WSDL use the following command:

```
java org.apache.axis.wsdl.WSDL2Java -p osws stock.wsdl
```

This generates the following four Java files in a package named `osws`:

- `StockQuoteServer.java`
- `StockQuoteServerService.java`
- `StockQuoteServerServiceLocator.java`
- `StockQuoteServerSoapBindingStub.java`

The `StockQuoteServer.java` contains the proxy class for our Web Service. The proxy contains the signatures of the web methods exposed by the Web Service. The code is shown below:

```
package osws;

public interface StockQuoteServer extends java.rmi.Remote {
  public double getStockPrice(java.lang.String symbol) throws
java.rmi.RemoteException;
}
```

The `StockQuoteServerService.java` is an interface that contains the signatures for the methods used for locating the service. The interface code is shown below:

```
package osws;

public interface StockQuoteServerService extends javax.xml.rpc.Service {
  public String getStockQuoteServerAddress();

  public osws.StockQuoteServer getStockQuoteServer() throws
javax.xml.rpc.ServiceException;

  public osws.StockQuoteServer getStockQuoteServer(java.net.URL portAddress)
throws javax.xml.rpc.ServiceException;
}
```

The two getter methods return the reference to the server. The first method does not take any arguments while the second method accepts the URL of the Web Service as an argument.

The `StockQuoteServerServiceLocator` class implements the above interface and provides implementation for the above two get methods. The `StockQuoteServerSoapBindingStub` class implements the `StockQuoteServer` interface. This class creates the `Call` object and sets all the required parameters for the specified web method.

Creating a Client Using Generated Stubs

A client program that uses the above-generated classes can be written very easily. We will write a console-based client application that uses the generated stub classes:

```
import osws.*;

public class SimpleClient {
```

In the `main()` method of the class, we first create an instance of the service locator class:

```
  public static void main(String[] args) {
    StockQuoteServerServiceLocator locator =
                                     new StockQuoteServerServiceLocator();
```

We use the `locator` object to obtain a reference to the Web Service server:

```
  try {
    osws.StockQuoteServer server = locator.getStockQuoteServer();
```

Once a reference to the server is obtained, we invoke the web method `getStockPrice()` by passing an appropriate parameter to it. The value returned by the web method is printed on the user console:

```
      System.out.println("Price: " + server.getStockPrice("INFY"));
    } catch (java.lang.Exception e) {
      e.printStackTrace();
    }
  }
}
```

Using Java2WSDL

Now we demonstrate how to generate a WSDL file from a Java class with the Java2WSDL utility. We will use our `StockQuote` service example again. We will use the `StockQuoteServer.class` file for generating WSDL. To do so we will use the following command:

```
java org.apache.axis.wsdl.Java2WSDL -o mystock.wsdl -l
"http://localhost:8080/axis/services/StockQuoteServer" -n "urn:StockQuoteServer"
StockQuoteServer
```

The following list shows the meaning of each option used in the command shown above.

```
-o : Name of the WSDL file.
-l : Location of the service.
-n : Target namespace of the WSDL file.
```

It will generate the WSDL file as shown below:

```
<?xml version="1.0" encoding="UTF-8"?>
<wsdl:definitions targetNamespace="urn:StockQuoteServer"
                  xmlns:wsdlsoap="http://schemas.xmlsoap.org/wsdl/soap/"
                  xmlns:xsd="http://www.w3.org/2001/XMLSchema"
                  xmlns:SOAP-ENC="http://schemas.xmlsoap.org/soap/encoding/"
                  xmlns:intf="urn:StockQuoteServer"
                  xmlns:wsdl="http://schemas.xmlsoap.org/wsdl/"
                  xmlns:impl="urn:StockQuoteServer-impl"
                  xmlns="http://schemas.xmlsoap.org/wsdl/">

  <wsdl:message name="getStockPriceRequest">
    <wsdl:part name="in0" type="SOAP-ENC:string"/>
  </wsdl:message>

  <wsdl:message name="getStockPriceResponse">
    <wsdl:part name="return" type="xsd:double"/>
  </wsdl:message>

  <wsdl:portType name="StockQuoteServer">
    <wsdl:operation name="getStockPrice" parameterOrder="in0">
      <wsdl:input message="intf:getStockPriceRequest"/>
      <wsdl:output message="intf:getStockPriceResponse"/>
    </wsdl:operation>
  </wsdl:portType>

  <wsdl:binding name="StockQuoteServerSoapBinding"
                type="intf:StockQuoteServer">
    <wsdlsoap:binding style="rpc"
                      transport="http://schemas.xmlsoap.org/soap/http"/>
    <wsdl:operation name="getStockPrice">
      <wsdlsoap:operation soapAction=""/>
      <wsdl:input>
        <wsdlsoap:body use="encoded"
                      encodingStyle="http://schemas.xmlsoap.org/soap/encoding/"
```

```
                    namespace="getStockPrice"/>
      </wsdl:input>

      <wsdl:output>
        <wsdlsoap:body use="encoded"
                    encodingStyle="http://schemas.xmlsoap.org/soap/encoding/"
                    namespace="urn:StockQuoteServer"/>
      </wsdl:output>
    </wsdl:operation>
  </wsdl:binding>

  <wsdl:service name="StockQuoteServerService">
    <wsdl:port name="StockQuoteServer"
               binding="intf:StockQuoteServerSoapBinding">
      <wsdlsoap:address
          location="http://localhost:8080/axis/services/StockQuoteServer"/>
    </wsdl:port>
  </wsdl:service>
</wsdl:definitions>
```

Now we can use this WSDL file for generating proxy and client stubs like we did above.

EJB Web Services

This section is a primer on how to expose EJBs as Web Services using JBoss, Tomcat, and Axis. It is primarily focused on the "how", assuming you have a basic understanding of the related technologies. To this end our focus will include the following items:

- Configuring JBoss, Tomcat, and Axis as related to Web Services
- Deploying EJBs to JBoss
- Configuring these EJBs as Web Services
- Running a Web Service client

Installing the Sourcecode

The sourcecode and configuration files for this section can be downloaded from the Wrox web site at http://www.wrox.com/. You can install it in any directory you like, just remember to substitute it appropriately in the code. At the root of the distribution you will find a file called `build.xml`. This is the Ant build file and we will use it to build and deploy all our code.

Here are details of this distribution. These files are discussed in varying detail in this chapter:

```
build.xml
classes/
jars/
resources/
          deploy.wsdd
          ejb-jar.xml
          jboss-web.xml
          jboss.xml
          jndi.properties
```

```
            roles.properties
            undeploy.wsdd
            users.properties
    web.xml
    src/
        wrox/axis/Client.java
        wrox/ejb/Client.java
        wrox/ejb/StatefulService.java
        wrox/ejb/StatefulServiceHome.java
        wrox/ejb/StatefulServiceSessionBean.java
        wrox/ejb/StatelessService.java
        wrox/ejb/StatelessServiceHome.java
        wrox/ejb/StatelessServiceSessionBean.java
```

Required Configuration

There is a small amount of configuration required to enable JBoss to run Web Services.

Security

A discussion of security is beyond the scope of this chapter. However, its importance should not be overlooked. Default settings have been used in these examples to minimise security implications, but your production application will likely require serious consideration and application of security is not discussed in this section.

JBoss does not by default enforce restrictions provided for by the EJB specification. For our example, we have simply added the basic framework to get security elements in place in JBoss. Some of the default settings in JBoss are not secure, so be sure to read the JBoss security documentation carefully.

We'll specify a security domain in JBoss to run our Web Service EJBs. The JBoss `auth.conf` file is a Java Authentication and Authorization Service (JAAS) login configuration module. We will add the following lines to `auth.conf` which is found at `$JBOSS_HOME/jboss/conf/catalina/auth.conf`:

```
web-services {
org.jboss.security.auth.spi.UsersRolesLoginModule required
unauthenticatedIdentity="guest"
;
};
```

Here we are stating unauthenticated users will be granted the role of `guest`. This is convenient as it reduces complexity in our samples, but remember to consider your security needs and address them appropriately for your security needs.

jaxrpc.jar

Tomcat will not load JARs out of the webapps directories that start with `java` or `javax`. You will need to move `jaxrpc.jar` from `$JBOSS_HOME/catalina/webapps/axis/WEB-INF/lib` to `$JBOSS_HOME/catalina/lib`. This will allow Tomcat to load this JAR as required.

The Distribution Files

In this section we'll introduce each file in the distribution. Many of these are typical to all EJB deployments, and are not relevant to the scope of this section, so we won't spend much time on them.

build.xml

This is the Ant build script. In this file we have a number of targets defined to build, deploy, and run all the code in these examples. Let's look at the target elements in this file:

- build: calls compile and package targets.
- compile: compiles all classes defined in compile.classpath.
- package: builds WAR and JAR files. This includes directives that create the axis.war file that is deployed to JBoss.

  The code from the Ant build script that creates the axis.war file is shown below. Notice how the WAR file contains jboss-web.xml, users.properties, roles.properties, and ejb-client.jar. We'll discuss each of these files soon:

```
<war warfile="${jars}/${axis.war}" webxml="${resources}/web.xml">
  <webinf dir="${resources}">
    <include name="jboss-web.xml"/>
  </webinf>
  <classes dir="${resources}">
    <include name="users.properties"/>
    <include name="roles.properties"/>
  </classes>
  <lib dir="${jars}">
    <include name="ejb-client.jar"/>
  </lib>
  <lib dir="${axis.dist}/lib">
    <include name="*.jar"/>
  </lib>
</war>
```

- clean: deletes all created generated files (WARs, JARs, EARs, classes)
- deploy-jboss-axis: deploys Axis and sample EJBs into JBoss

  This target simply deploys the EJBs and Axis by copying their respective ejb.server.jar and axis.war files to the $JBOSS_HOME/jboss/deploy directory. JBoss automatically detects the files and deploys them immediately:

- undeploy-jboss-axis: undeploys Axis and the sample EJBs

  This Ant target simply deletes the ejb.server.jar and axis.war files from the JBoss $JBOSS_HOME/jboss/deploy directory. JBoss will automatically undeploy when they are deleted:

- deploy-ws: registers the sample EJBs as Web Services in Axis

  This Ant target runs org.apache.axis.client.AdminClient passing it the deploy.wsdd file. The deploy.wsdd file contains information describing how the EJBs are to be exposed as Web Services. We'll discuss the file in more detail later. Overleaf is the code from the target:

```
<target name="deploy-ws" description="Deploy Web Services to Axis">
  <java classname="org.apache.axis.client.AdminClient" fork="yes">
    <arg value="${resources}/deploy.wsdd"/>
    <classpath refid="axis.client.classpath"/>
  </java>
</target>
```

- undeploy-ws: registers the sample EJBs as Web Services in Axis.

  This Ant target again runs `org.apache.axis.client.AdminClient` but passes it the `undeploy.wsdd` file. The `undeploy.wsdd` file simply lists the names of the services to undeploy. In most cases, the services listed in `undeploy.wsdd` will be the same as those listed in `deploy.wsdd`. We'll discuss the file in more detail later. Below is the code from the target:

```
<target name="undeploy-ws" description="Undeploy Web Services from Axis">
  <java classname="org.apache.axis.client.AdminClient" fork="yes">
    <arg value="${resources}/undeploy.wsdd"/>
    <classpath refid="axis.client.classpath"/>
  </java>
</target>
```

- ejb-client: this target runs the Java EJB client. Standard fare for Ant users.
- ws-client: this target runs the Java Web Service client. We'll look at the Web Service client later. The Ant target should look familiar to Ant users.

resources/deploy.wsdd

The Axis Web Service deployment descriptor. This identifies our EJBs and defines how they will be exposed as Web Services. It is shown in its entirety below. Note how the Web Service name, corresponding EJB, and allowed methods are set:

```
<deployment xmlns="http://xml.apache.org/axis/wsdd/"
xmlns:java="http://xml.apache.org/axis/wsdd/providers/java">
  <!--Stateless session bean-->
  <service name="StatelessService" provider="java:EJB">
    <parameter name="scope" value="request"/>
    <parameter name="beanJndiName" value="wrox/ejb/StatelessService"/>
    <parameter name="homeInterfaceName"
               value="wrox.ejb.StatelessServiceHome"/>
    <parameter name="remoteInterfaceName"
               value="wrox.ejb.StatelessService"/>
    <parameter name="className" value="wrox.ejb.StatelessService"/>
    <parameter name="jndiContextClass"
               value="org.jnp.interfaces.NamingContextFactory"/>
    <parameter name="jndiURL" value="jnp://localhost:1099"/>
    <parameter name="allowedMethods" value="*"/>
  </service>

  <!--Stateful session bean-->
  <service name="StatefulService" provider="java:EJB">
    <parameter name="scope" value="session"/>
    <parameter name="beanJndiName" value="wrox/ejb/StatefulService"/>
    <parameter name="homeInterfaceName"
               value="wrox.ejb.StatefulServiceHome"/>
```

```
    <parameter name="remoteInterfaceName" value="wrox.ejb.StatefulService"/>
    <parameter name="className" value="wrox.ejb.StatefulService"/>
    <parameter name="jndiContextClass"
               value="org.jnp.interfaces.NamingContextFactory"/>
    <parameter name="jndiURL" value="jnp://localhost:1099"/>
    <parameter name="allowedMethods" value="*"/>
  </service>
</deployment>
```

Let's explain some of the settings in this file:

```
<service name="StatelessService" provider="java:EJB">
```

Two elements of the service element are shown. As in our earlier examples, the name element allows us to name the service and the provider element allows us to use one of several defined providers. In our example provider="java:EJB" specifies the EJBProvider class.

We then have a number of <parameter> elements that follow the name/value pattern; let's look at some of these. This first explains the scope of the service. In the case of a stateless EJB session bean, we will set this to request, meaning the service doesn't need to maintain any state between requests:

```
<parameter name="scope" value="request"/>
```

This <parameter> element tells the Web Service the JNDI name to use to look up the service. This JNDI name is defined in our EJBs deployment descriptor ejb-jar.xml:

```
<parameter name="beanJndiName" value="wrox/ejb/StatelessService"/>
```

The next few are straightforward; they are defining specific classes the Web Service might need to instantiate or use the EJB:

```
<parameter name="homeInterfaceName"
               value="wrox.ejb.StatefulServiceHome"/>
<parameter name="remoteInterfaceName" value="wrox.ejb.StatefulService"/>
<parameter name="className" value="wrox.ejb.StatefulService"/>
```

Next are some details on the JNDI context and URL to look up the EJBs:

```
<parameter name="jndiContextClass"
           value="org.jnp.interfaces.NamingContextFactory"/>
<parameter name="jndiURL" value="jnp://localhost:1099"/>
```

The final name/value pair for our StatelessService defines the methods this EJB is exposing through its Web Service interface:

```
<parameter name="allowedMethods" value="*"/>
```

The next <service> element is for the StatefulService with the only significant difference in its name/value pairs being scope. We define this as session, which makes sense as we want this EJB to maintain state across requests:

```
<parameter name="scope" value="session"/>
```

resources/ejb-jar.xml

The ejb-jar.xml is the EJB's deployment descriptor. It is used to specify most of the configuration details the EJB container will need. A snippet from that file is shown below. Notice the <session-type> element where we differentiate between stateful and stateless:

```
<session>
  <ejb-name>StatelessService</ejb-name>
  <home>wrox.ejb.StatelessServiceHome</home>
  <remote>wrox.ejb.StatelessService</remote>
  <ejb-class>wrox.ejb.StatelessServiceSessionBean</ejb-class>
  <session-type>Stateless</session-type>
  <transaction-type>Bean</transaction-type>
</session>
<session>
  <ejb-name>StatefulService</ejb-name>
  <home>wrox.ejb.StatefulServiceHome</home>
  <remote>wrox.ejb.StatefulService</remote>
  <ejb-class>wrox.ejb.StatefulServiceSessionBean</ejb-class>
  <session-type>Stateful</session-type>
  <transaction-type>Bean</transaction-type>
</session>
```

All EJB containers will use the ejb-jar.xml configuration file we just reviewed. You may want to specify vendor-specific configuration information to the EJB container. For JBoss, this additional configuration information is in jboss.xml. You are not required to use jboss.xml, but it is there if you need it.

Similarly, web applications use the standard web.xml file for configuration. Vendor-specific configuration information cannot be stored in this file, so jboss-web.xml contains JBoss-specific information you'd like to deploy with your web application.

resources/jboss-web.xml

jboss-web.xml contains JBoss-specific servlet deployment descriptor information. Below is the majority of the jboss-web.xml file in which you can see we're specifying the security domain and JBDI names for the EJBs:

```
<jboss>
  <!--Specify the security domain for EJBs
      this is declared in JBoss auth.conf file -->
  <security-domain>java:/jaas/web-services</security-domain>
  <!-- EJB JNDI names-->
  <enterprise-beans>
    <session>
      <ejb-name>StatelessService</ejb-name>
      <jndi-name>wrox/ejb/StatelessService</jndi-name>
    </session>
    <session>
      <ejb-name>StatefulService</ejb-name>
      <jndi-name>wrox/ejb/StatefulService</jndi-name>
    </session>
  </enterprise-beans>
</jboss>
```

resources/jboss.xml

This file contains JBoss-specific deployment information. It is shown in its entirety below. Here we are exposing the same security domain, EJBs, and JNDI names to the EJB container, as we exposed to the web application as specified in `jboss-web.xml`:

```
<?xml version="1.0" encoding="UTF-8"?>
<jboss>
  <!--Specify the security domain for EJBs
      this is declared in JBoss auth.conf file -->
  <security-domain>java:/jaas/web-services</security-domain>
  <!-- EJB JNDI names -->
  <enterprise-beans>
    <session>
      <ejb-name>StatelessService</ejb-name>
        <jndi-name>wrox/ejb/StatelessService</jndi-name>
    </session>
    <session>
      <ejb-name>StatefulService</ejb-name>
      <jndi-name>wrox/ejb/StatefulService</jndi-name>
    </session>
  </enterprise-beans>
</jboss>
```

resources/jndi.properties

Contains JNDI information for the EJB project. The entire file is shown below. The information is used by our client application to look up EJBs based on their JNDI names using the port defined:

```
# JNDI properties file used by the EJB client application to
# identify the JNDI server.
java.naming.factory.initial=org.jnp.interfaces.NamingContextFactory
java.naming.provider.url=jnp://localhost:1099
java.naming.factory.url.pkgs=org.jboss.naming:org.jnp.interfaces
```

resources/roles.properties

Defines the JAAS roles and assigns them to a user. Each user can be assigned one or more roles in this file:

```
# roles.properties file
guest=role1
user1=role1
```

resources/undeploy.wsdd

The Axis Web Services undeploy configuration file. We define all Web Services to undeploy in this file. It is used by `org.apache.axis.client.AdminClient` that undeploys all services listed in the file from Axis. The file is shown in its entirety below:

```
<!--Axis undeployment descriptor to remove StatefulService and
    StatelessService-->
<undeployment xmlns="http://xml.apache.org/axis/wsdd/">
  <service name="StatelessService"/>
  <service name="StatefulService"/>
</undeployment>
```

resources/users.properties

Defines JAAS users and their password:

```
# user.properties
guest=guest
user1=user1
user2=user2
```

resources/web.xml

This is the standard servlet deployment descriptor. As discussed, the content in this file is common to all servlet containers. JBoss-specific information is in `jboss-web.xml`:

```
<web-app>
  <display-name>Apache-Axis</display-name>
  <servlet>
    <servlet-name>AxisServlet</servlet-name>
    <display-name>Apache-Axis Servlet</display-name>
    <servlet-class>
      org.apache.axis.transport.http.AxisServlet
    </servlet-class>
  </servlet>
  <servlet>
    <servlet-name>AdminServlet</servlet-name>
    <display-name>Axis Admin Servlet</display-name>
    <servlet-class>
      org.apache.axis.transport.http.AdminServlet
    </servlet-class>
    <load-on-startup>100</load-on-startup>
  </servlet>
  <servlet-mapping>
    <servlet-name>AxisServlet</servlet-name>
    <url-pattern>/servlet/AxisServlet</url-pattern>
  </servlet-mapping>
  <servlet-mapping>
    <servlet-name>AxisServlet</servlet-name>
    <url-pattern>*.jws</url-pattern>
  </servlet-mapping>
  <servlet-mapping>
    <servlet-name>AxisServlet</servlet-name>
    <url-pattern>/services/*</url-pattern>
  </servlet-mapping>
</web-app>
```

src

The `src` directory holds our sourcecode. It's worth noting here that our sample EJBs are designed to be as simple as possible. This chapter is intended to be an installation, configuration, and deployment primer, so all other pieces are kept simple. We use stateful and stateless EJB session beans for our demonstration. Each will be covered as we explain the `src` directory.

src/wrox/axis/client

This is the Axis Web Service client code. It demonstrates how to access our EJB Web Service through Axis:

```
package wrox.axis;

import org.apache.axis.client.Service;
import org.apache.axis.client.Call;
import java.security.Security;
import java.rmi.RemoteException;
import java.net.MalformedURLException;
import javax.xml.rpc.namespace.QName;
import javax.xml.rpc.ServiceException;

public class Client {

  private static final String STATELESS_SERVICE_END_POINT_URL  =
"http://localhost:8080/axis/services/StatelessService";
  private static final String STATEFUL_SERVICE_END_POINT_URL =
"http://localhost:8080/axis/services/StatefulService";


  public static void main (String [] args) {

    System.out.println ("Test Web Service Client");

    System.out.println ("Test Stateless");
    System.out.println ("");
    testStateless();
    System.out.println ("");
    System.out.println ("Stateless done");

    System.out.println ("Test Stateful");
    System.out.println ("");
    testStateful();
    System.out.println ("");
    System.out.println ("Stateful done");

    System.out.println ("Web Service Client - Complete");
  }

  public static void testStateless() {
    try {
      Service service = new Service ();
      Call call = (Call) service.createCall ();
      call.setTargetEndpointAddress (new java.net.URL
(STATELESS_SERVICE_END_POINT_URL));
      call.setOperationName (new QName ("StatelessService", "glue"));

      System.out.println ("StatelessService.glue(): " + call.invoke (new Object
[]{"Boston","London"}));

    } catch (Exception e) {
      System.out.println("Exception:"+ e.getMessage());
    }
  }

  public static void testStateful() {
    try {
      Service service = new Service ();
```

```
      Call call = (Call) service.createCall ();

      call.setTargetEndpointAddress (new java.net.URL
(STATEFUL_SERVICE_END_POINT_URL));
      call.setMaintainSession (true);
      call.setOperationName (new QName ("StatefulService", "count"));
      for (int counter=0; counter<5; counter++) {
        System.out.println ("statefulService.count(): " +
                            call.invoke(new Object [] {}));
      }
    } catch (Exception e){
      System.out.println("Exception:"+ e.getMessage());
    }
  }
}
```

src/wrox/ejb/client

To test the EJBs apart from their deployment as Web Services, we will write an EJB client. You may find it interesting how the two different clients compare and contrast:

```
package wrox.ejb;

import java.rmi.RemoteException;
import javax.rmi.PortableRemoteObject;
import javax.naming.InitialContext;
import javax.naming.NamingException;
import javax.ejb.CreateException;
import javax.ejb.RemoveException;

// This is an EJB client test class.
public class Client {

  // JNDI names of the EJBs.
  private final static String STATELESS_SERVICE_JNDI_NAME  =
"wrox/ejb/StatelessService";
  private final static String STATEFUL_SERVICE_JNDI_NAME =
"wrox/ejb/StatefulService";

  public static void main (String[] args) {

    System.out.println ("Test EJB Client");
    System.out.println ("Test Stateless");
    testStateless();
    System.out.println ("Stateless done");
    System.out.println ("Test Stateful");
    testStateful();
    System.out.println ("Stateful done");
    System.out.println ("Test EJB Client - Complete");
  }

  public static void testStateless() {
    try {
      InitialContext jndiContext = new InitialContext ();
      Object statelessServiceRef  = jndiContext.lookup
(STATELESS_SERVICE_JNDI_NAME);
      StatelessServiceHome statelessServiceHome =
                        (StatelessServiceHome) PortableRemoteObject.narrow
(statelessServiceRef,StatelessServiceHome.class);
```

```
        StatelessService  statelessService  = statelessServiceHome.create();

        String result = statelessService.glue("Boston", "London");
        System.out.println("Result is:" + result);
        statelessService.remove();
      } catch (Exception e){
        System.out.println("Exception:" + e.getMessage());
      }
    }

    public static void testStateful () {
      try {
        InitialContext jndiContext = new InitialContext ();
        Object statefulServiceRef  = jndiContext.lookup
  (STATEFUL_SERVICE_JNDI_NAME);

        StatefulServiceHome statefulServiceHome =
                          (StatefulServiceHome) PortableRemoteObject.narrow
  (statefulServiceRef, StatefulServiceHome.class);

        StatefulService  statefulService  = statefulServiceHome.create  ();

        for (int counter=0; counter<5; counter++) {
          System.out.println ("statefulService.count(): " +
                              statefulService.count());
        }
        statefulService.remove ();
      } catch (Exception e) {
        System.out.println("Exception:"+e.getMessage());
      }
    }
  }
```

wrox/ejb/StatefulService.java

Next we will list our stateful session bean and its three EJB source files. In this case, we have a single method of interest called `count()` that increments a counter each time it is called and then returns the counter's current value.

`StatefulService.java` is the sourcecode for our stateful session bean's remote interface. It declares the `count()` method that we will use to demonstrate stateful behavior:

```
package wrox.ejb;

import javax.ejb.EJBObject;
import java.rmi.RemoteException;

//Standard remote interface for an EJB
public interface StatefulService extends EJBObject {

  // This demonstrates stateful behavior.
  // Increments a counter each time it is called and
  // then returns the counter's current value
  public int count() throws RemoteException;
}
```

wrox/ejb/StatefulServiceHome.java

StatefulServiceHome is our session bean's home interface. It is displayed below:

```
package wrox.ejb;

import java.rmi.RemoteException;
import javax.ejb.CreateException;
import javax.ejb.EJBHome;

//Standard home interface for an EJB
public interface StatefulServiceHome extends EJBHome {

  // Standard Home interface create method
  StatefulService create () throws RemoteException, CreateException;
}
```

wrox/ejb/StatefulServiceSessionBean.java

Finally StatefulServiceSessionBean.java is the actual implementation of our remote interface StatefulService.java:

```
// This demonstrates stateful behavior.
// Increments a counter each time it is called and
// then returns the counter's current value
public int count() {
  return count++;
}
```

wrox/ejb/StatelessService.java

The stateless session bean exposes a single method designed to demonstrate simple, generic behavior. The method we will be using is called glue() as it takes two strings and glues (concatenates) them together. Simple, but it clearly displays behavior.

StatelessService.java is the remote interface for the stateless service. It is listed below. It declares a single method for our use called glue():

```
package wrox.ejb;

import javax.ejb.EJBObject;
import java.rmi.RemoteException;

// A standard EJB remote interface
public interface StatelessService extends EJBObject {

  // Behavior exposed as a Web Service.
  public String glue(String stringOne, String stringTwo)
                                            throws RemoteException;
}
```

wrox/ejb/StatelessServiceHome.java

`StatelessServiceHome.java` is the EJB home interface for this service. It simply contains the single required `create()` method and is listed below:

```
package wrox.ejb;

import java.rmi.RemoteException;
import javax.ejb.CreateException;
import javax.ejb.EJBHome;

// Standard EJB home interface
public interface StatelessServiceHome extends EJBHome {
  StatelessService create() throws RemoteException, CreateException;
}
```

wrox/ejb/StatelessServiceSessionBean.java

`StatelessServiceSessionBean.java` is the implementation of our remote interface `StatelessService.java`. It contains the implementation of our `glue` method, as well as implementations for the required EJB methods. Below is the `glue()` method from the file:

```
// Method used to demonstrate generic behavior. It simply
// concatenates two strings and returns the result.
public String glue(String stringOne, String stringTwo) {
  return stringOne + "-and-" + stringTwo;
}
```

Running the Distribution

At the root of this distribution you will find the Ant `build.xml` file. We will use Ant, along with this file, to build and deploy the provided sourcecode.

You must edit `build.xml` to point to your JBoss and Axis distributions. Update the `jboss.dist` and `axis.dist` properties as appropriate, as shown below:

```
<!--Update the jboss.dist and axis.dist properties to match installation
    on your PC-->
<property name="jboss.dist" value="/usr/local/JBoss-2.4.6_Tomcat-4.0.3/jboss"/>
<property name="axis.dist" value="/usr/local/xml-axis-beta2"/>
```

Building the Source

At a command prompt, go to the root directory of this distribution and build the sourcecode:

```
$ANT_HOME/bin/ant build
```

After a few moments you should get a successful message telling you the source has been built:

```
[root@wroxtest osws]# $ANT_HOME/bin/ant build
Buildfile: build.xml

compile:
    [javac] Compiling 8 source files to /usr/local/osws/classes

package:
      [jar] Building jar: /usr/local/osws/jars/ejb-server.jar
      [jar] Building jar: /usr/local/osws/jars/ejb-client.jar
      [jar] Building jar: /usr/local/osws/jars/axis-client.jar
      [war] Building war: /usr/local/osws/jars/axis.war

build:

BUILD SUCCESSFUL

Total time: 8 seconds
[root@wroxtest osws]#
```

Next we'll deploy the code, so ensure JBoss is running before proceeding. If it is not running, start JBoss with the `run_with_catalina.bat` file.

Deploying the Code

Deploy the code into JBoss by typing `$ANT_HOME/bin/ant deploy-jboss-axis`:

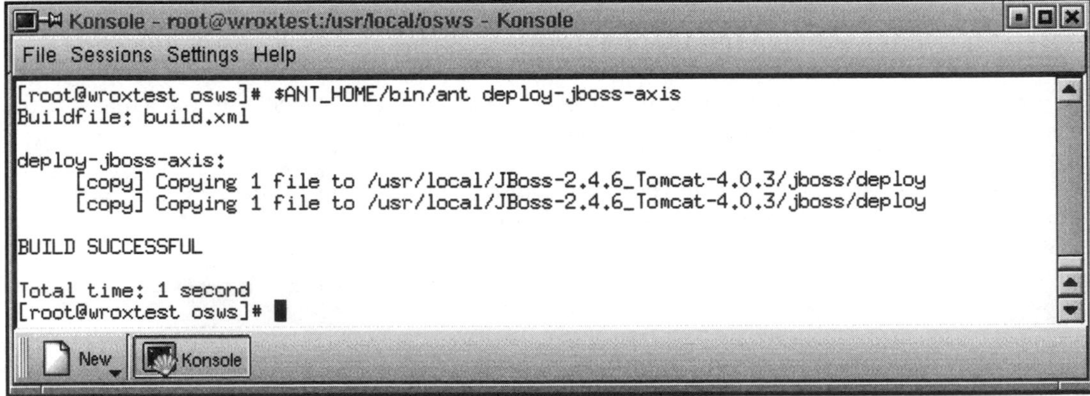

```
[root@wroxtest osws]# $ANT_HOME/bin/ant deploy-jboss-axis
Buildfile: build.xml

deploy-jboss-axis:
     [copy] Copying 1 file to /usr/local/JBoss-2.4.6_Tomcat-4.0.3/jboss/deploy
     [copy] Copying 1 file to /usr/local/JBoss-2.4.6_Tomcat-4.0.3/jboss/deploy

BUILD SUCCESSFUL

Total time: 1 second
[root@wroxtest osws]#
```

Notice this screen says it deployed two files. One was the EJB application, the other was Axis. As these were deployed in JBoss you may have noticed output in the JBoss console related to each of these deployments. You should not see any errors or exceptions.

Running the EJB Client

We are ready to run our EJB client. This will ensure our EJBs have been properly deployed. We'll again use Ant by executing the following command:

```
$ANT_HOME/bin/ant ejb-client
```

It should execute and display output similar to that shown below. Reading the output you can see the client has called the stateful and stateless EJBs successfully:

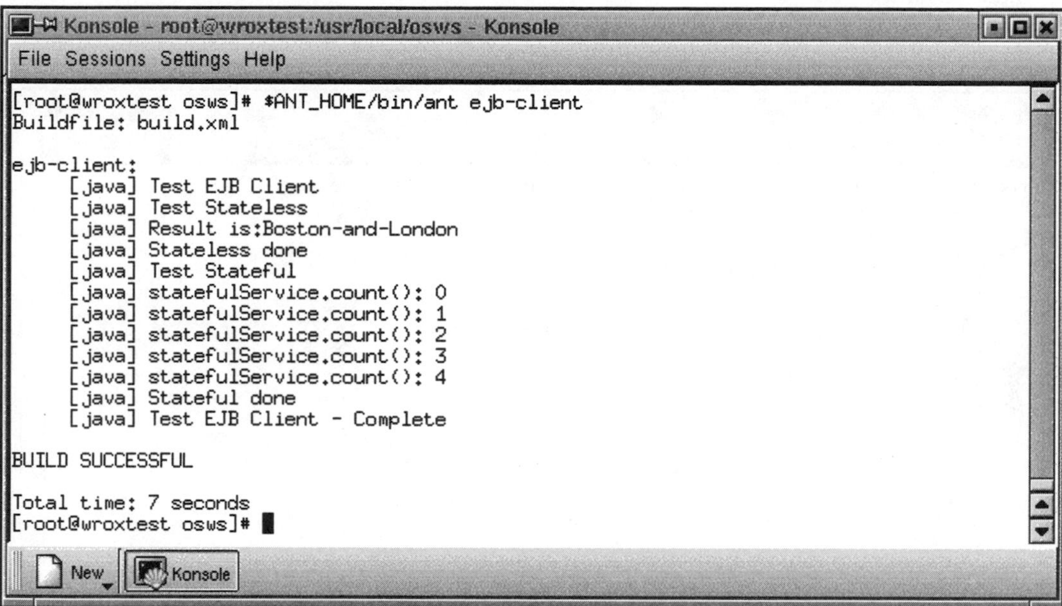
Konsole - root@wroxtest:/usr/local/osws - Konsole
File Sessions Settings Help
[root@wroxtest osws]# $ANT_HOME/bin/ant ejb-client
Buildfile: build.xml
ejb-client:
[java] Test EJB Client
[java] Test Stateless
[java] Result is:Boston-and-London
[java] Stateless done
[java] Test Stateful
[java] statefulService.count(): 0
[java] statefulService.count(): 1
[java] statefulService.count(): 2
[java] statefulService.count(): 3
[java] statefulService.count(): 4
[java] Stateful done
[java] Test EJB Client - Complete
BUILD SUCCESSFUL
Total time: 7 seconds
[root@wroxtest osws]#
New
Konsole

Deploy the Web Services

The next step will use the `deploy.wsdd` file to deploy the EJBs as Web Services in Axis:

```
$ANT_HOME/bin/ant deploy-ws
```

After a few moments you should receive a build successful message. The EJBs have been deployed as Web Services and are ready to use by our Web Service client:

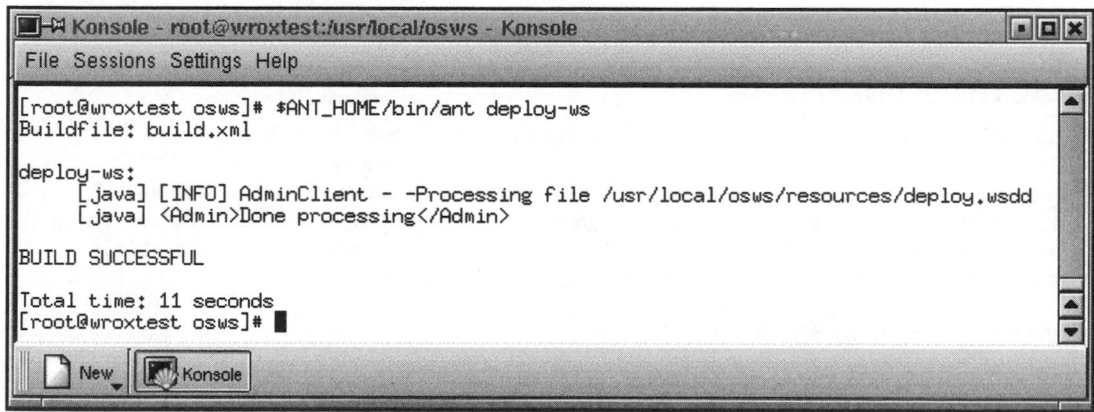
Konsole - root@wroxtest:/usr/local/osws - Konsole
File Sessions Settings Help
[root@wroxtest osws]# $ANT_HOME/bin/ant deploy-ws
Buildfile: build.xml
deploy-ws:
[java] [INFO] AdminClient - -Processing file /usr/local/osws/resources/deploy.wsdd
[java] <Admin>Done processing</Admin>
BUILD SUCCESSFUL
Total time: 11 seconds
[root@wroxtest osws]#
New
Konsole

Running the Web Service Client

Execute the following command to start the Web Service client:

```
$ANT_HOME/bin/ant ws-client
```

If all goes well you should see a screen similar to the following:

```
[root@wroxtest osws]# $ANT_HOME/bin/ant ws-client
Buildfile: build.xml

ws-client:
     [java] Test Web Service Client
     [java] Test Stateless
     [java]
     [java] StatelessService.glue(): Boston-and-London
     [java]
     [java] Stateless done
     [java] Test Stateful
     [java]
     [java] statefulService.count(): 0
     [java] statefulService.count(): 1
     [java] statefulService.count(): 2
     [java] statefulService.count(): 3
     [java] statefulService.count(): 4
     [java]
     [java] Stateful done
     [java] Web Service Client - Complete

BUILD SUCCESSFUL

Total time: 9 seconds
[root@wroxtest osws]#
```

We've deployed both stateful and stateless EJB session beans. We also have one Java client that accesses these EJBs directly, and a second Java client application that accesses them as Web Services.

Now that we've covered Axis and SOAP, we'll take a look at an open source Java XML-RPC implementation.

Apache XML-RPC

Apache XML-RPC is a Java implementation of XML-RPC. It provides a class called `org.apache.xmlrpc.XmlRpcClient` for creating client applications that use XML-RPC calls on a remote server. A client may call remote methods either synchronously or asynchronously. We will illustrate both these methods. First, we need to write a server application for this. Before writing the code we need to download the XML-RPC-1.1 `.jar` file required for XML-RPC. This file is downloadable at http://xml.apache.org/dist/xmlrpc/release/v1.1/.

Server Application for XML-RPC

We will develop a simple server application that returns a stock price for the requested abbreviation (symbol) to the client. To keep the application simple, we have used a `Hashtable` for maintaining the stock symbols and their prices. The full program listing is given below:

```
import java.util.Hashtable;
import org.apache.xmlrpc.WebServer;
```

The class constructor initializes this `Hashtable`:

```
public class MyServer {
  Hashtable StockQuotes;
  public MyServer () {
    StockQuotes = new Hashtable();
    StockQuotes.put("INSYS", new Double(120.00));
    StockQuotes.put("IBM", new Double(150.00));
  }
```

The `getStockPrice()` method takes a stock symbol as an input parameter and returns the current stock price to the caller:

```
  public Double getStockPrice(String symbol) {
    return (Double) StockQuotes.get(symbol);
  }
```

The `main()` method creates an instance of the `WebServer` class that listens to port 8080 for the client requests and creates a handler called `STOCKS` that clients use to call a method on the server. The `WebServer` class is provided by the XML-RPC package `org.apache.xmlrpc` that we import at the start of this program:

```
  public static void main (String [] args) {
    try {
      WebServer server = new WebServer(8080);
      server.addHandler("STOCKS", new MyServer());
      System.out.println("Server started :: invoke me on: http://localhost:8080");

    } catch (Exception exception) {
      System.err.println("MyServer: " + exception.toString());
    }
  }
}
```

When you compile and run the above server application, the server starts, prints a confirmation message on the console, and listens to port 8080 for client requests. The above application is shown in the screenshot below:

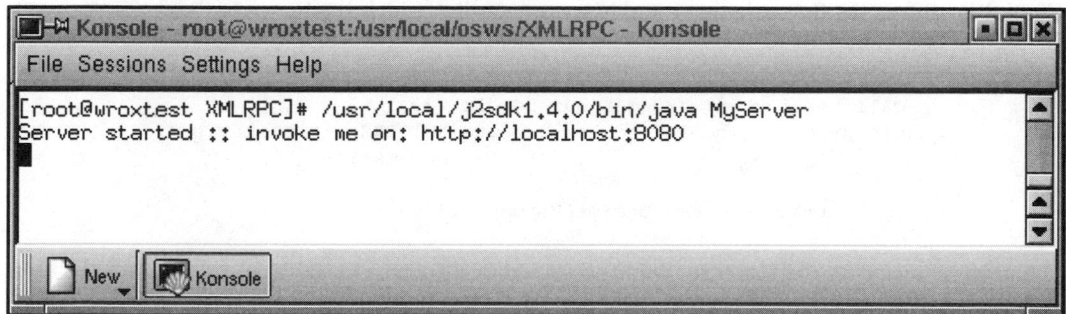

We will now write a client application that calls a method on the server by making a synchronous call to the server method.

A Synchronous XML-RPC Client Application

This is also a Java console application. The full class listing is as given below:

```
import java.util.Vector;
import java.text.DecimalFormat;
import org.apache.xmlrpc.XmlRpcClient;
import org.apache.xmlrpc.XmlRpcException;

public class SyncClient {
  // The location of our server.
  private final static String server_url = "http://localhost:8080";

  public static void main (String [] args) {
    if (args.length!=1) {
      System.out.println("Usage => java AsyncClient <StockSymbol>");
      System.exit(0);
    }
```

We first create an RPC client by instantiating the `XmlRpcClient` class:

```
    try {
      // Create an object that represents our Server (MyServer.java).
      XmlRpcClient server = new XmlRpcClient(server_url);
```

Note that we have specified the server URL as a parameter to the class constructor.

Next, we create a `Vector` object for storing the parameters to be passed to the server class methods. The server method `execute()` requires a `Vector` as one of its parameter types. In the current application, the `getStockPrice()` method requires only one parameter:

```
      // Build our parameter list.
      Vector params = new Vector();
      params.addElement(args[0]);
```

The server method itself is called by calling the `execute()` method. This call specifies the server method's name as the first parameter and its parameter list (which is why we have used a `Vector`) as the second argument:

```
      // Call the server, and get our result.
      Double price = (Double) server.execute("STOCKS.getStockPrice",
                                             params);

      DecimalFormat df = new DecimalFormat("##.00");
```

The value returned by the server method is assigned to a `Double` variable and printed on the user console. We use the `DecimalFormat` class to format our output:

```
            // Print out our result.
            System.out.println("Stock Price is: $" +
                               df.format(price.doubleValue()));

          } catch (XmlRpcException exception) {
            System.err.println("MyClient: XML-RPC Fault #" +
                               Integer.toString(exception.code) + ": " +
                               exception.toString());
          } catch (Exception exception) {
            System.err.println("MyClient: " + exception.toString());
          }
        }
      }
```

The program output is shown below:

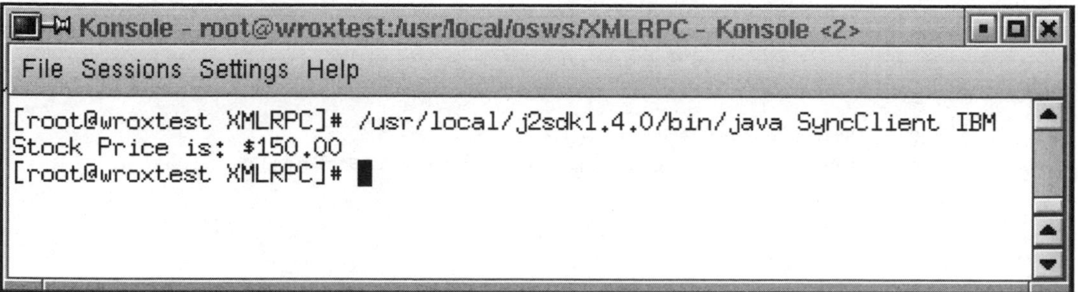

We will now write a client that calls the same method asynchronously.

An Asynchronous XML-RPC Client Application

The code to create a client with its parameter list remains the same as a synchronous application. The full code listing is given below:

```
import java.util.Vector;
import java.text.DecimalFormat;
import java.net.URL;
import org.apache.xmlrpc.AsyncCallback;
import org.apache.xmlrpc.XmlRpcClient;

public class AsyncClient {
  // The location of our server.
  private final static String server_url = "http://localhost:8080";

  public static void main (String [] args) {
    if (args.length!=1) {
      System.out.println("Usage > java AsyncClient <StockSymbol>");
      System.exit(0);
    }

    try {
      // Create an object that represents our Server ( MyServer.java ).
      XmlRpcClient server = new XmlRpcClient(server_url);

      // Build our parameter list.
      Vector params = new Vector();
      params.addElement(args[0]);
```

The server method is executed by calling `executeAsync()` rather than the `execute()` method. This method call requires one additional parameter that defines the callback handler. The server will call this handler after its method has executed. If the service has more than one method, then those method calls can be tracked using the `method` parameter in the `handleResult()` method of this class:

```
        // Call the server.
        server.executeAsync("STOCKS.getStockPrice", params,
                            new AsyncCallHandler());
```

After executing, a call is made to the server's remote method and the client is free to do any other job. In our example, the client simply prints a dot on the user console 2000 times:

```
        System.out.println("Request sent to the server");
        System.out.println("The main thread is free and can do more processing");
        for(int i=0; i<2000; i++)
          System.out.print(".");

      } catch (Exception exception) {
        System.err.println("MyClient: " + exception.toString());
      }
    }
  }
```

The handler class implements the `AsyncCallback` interface. We implement the `handleResult()` and `handleError()` methods of this interface as shown in the code below:

```
  class AsyncCallHandler implements AsyncCallback {

    public void handleResult (Object result, URL url, String method) {
      System.out.println("Returned");
      Double price = (Double) result;
      // Print out our result.
      DecimalFormat df = new DecimalFormat("##.00");

      System.out.println("Stock Price is: $" +
                         df.format(price.doubleValue()));
    }

    public void handleError (Exception exception, URL url, String method) {
      //print the error
      System.out.println("Error on server: " + exception);
    }
  }
```

While printing this dot on the user console, if the server method completes its execution, it will call the client handler. The typical output of the program is shown opposite:

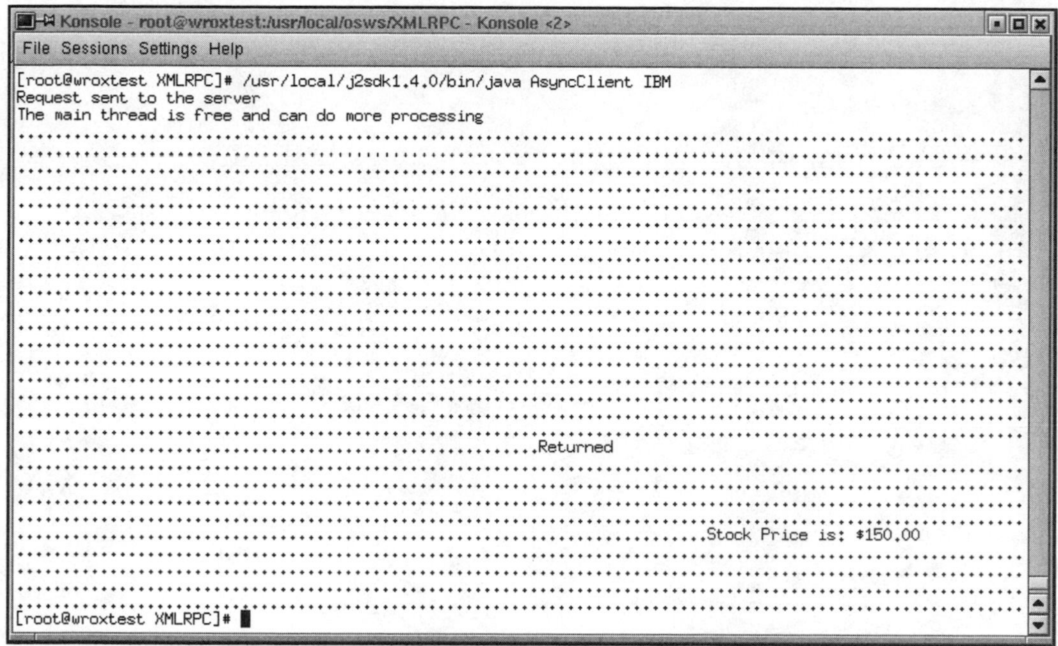

As can be seen from the output, while the client is counting up to 2000, sometime in between the server method returns the result to the client and it is printed on the client console. The counting resumes after this.

Summary

After discussing the architecture of Web Services, and related technologies in the previous chapters, in this chapter we covered how to develop an open source Web Service with Java. We used Tomcat to deploy our Web Services developed using Axis, the open source SOAP implementation from the Apache group.

First, we learned the architecture and features of Axis that is the successor of Apache SOAP. After we installed Axis, we developed a simple Web Service with Tomcat. We then stepped ahead to develop an advanced Web Service that uses a database, where we also saw how to develop a JSP-based client for the service.

Then we learned how to customize the Web Service deployment using WSDD, and demonstrated this with an example. We then discussed developing Web Services that accept attachments with the SOAP message. We also covered the handlers in Axis, and how we can write custom handlers and how to configure them using WSDD.

After talking about RPC-based Web Services, we studied how to develop a message-based service that contains only one web method. We then took a look at using WSDL with Axis, and learned using WSDL2Java, and Java2WSDL.

Then we developed an EJB Web Service using JBoss, Tomcat, and Axis. Finally, we covered developing Web Services using Apache XML-RPC.

5

Web Services Security

When Web Services were introduced, doubts were raised about their security on the Internet. There still needs some substantial development. We have discussed the technologies that support Web Services; we can now look at them and consider the security issues involved while developing a Web Service.

As we have seen in previous chapters, Web Services are supported by technologies such as XML, SOAP, UDDI, and so on. These technologies have some shortcomings that need to be addressed when we talk about a secured Web Service. Using the functionalities of XML and SOAP, a Web Service can go right through a firewall, which makes the Web Service more vulnerable to cracking and other security concerns.

Since SOAP is based on XML it is also prone to attacks; for example, a heavy document can cause buffer overflow, or a DoS (Denial of Service). DoS can cause networked computers to disconnect from the network, or just outright crash. DoS can affect a Web Service, if SOAP attachments of size 10 to 20 MB are used. Also, there could be the possibility of poisoning the UDDI registry; however digital signatures can rescue the Web Service from this. Hence, we need to take various security measures to develop a secured Web Service. We will discuss topics such as cryptography, PKI, digital signatures, client-server authentication, and encryption/decryption of data.

To implement security on the Internet and to secure the data transferred through the Web Service one needs to know what security is all about, and what measures we should take to make Web Services secure.

Security Issues

In today's world, privacy of important information is required at each and every step of business. While developing applications, developers should implement a well thought-out system architecture on which applications are deployed. Proper security systems need to be implemented to avoid data leaks or tampering of data, as the data flows over the open Internet. An application can be cracked even if there is a small loophole in the application structure. A cracker can tamper with the application data, and crash the system. There are many security systems and protocols that can be implemented to have secure system architecture. We need to select a proper system and protocol as per our needs.

The main security concerns that need to be considered while developing a Web Service include:

- Authentication
- Authorization
- Non-repudiation
- Integrity
- Privacy

Authentication

Many times a user, computer, or an application needs to ensure that another user, computer, or application is who or what they claim to be. Authentication represents the physical existence of an entity. Validation of a particular entity is required when we think of a secured system. After authentication, we can decide on how to authorize that particular entity.

Authentication can also be implemented in Web Services using various techniques. To have a secured transmission of data between the server and the client, the server or the client may need to authenticate each other. This may be achieved by using a simple username/password system, or techniques like cryptography, digital signatures, or digital certificates, which are discussed in detail later in the chapter.

Authorization

Authorization depends on authentication. After authenticating the client or the server, the client can be authorized to take any action depending on the privileges assigned to it. This can keep unauthorized entities from accessing resources or tampering with data. A standard implementation of this system is the operating system access in a network; valid users that are present in the access control list (ACL) are allocated system resources as per the privileges assigned to them.

In the case of Web Services, these specifications and techniques can be implemented using languages, or implementations such as Extensible Access Control Language (XACL) and Security Assertion Markup Language (SAML), which are discussed in detail later in the chapter.

Non-Repudiation

Non-repudiation is a service to ensure that the data sent by the client safely reaches the server. It generates and stores evidence of data transmission. The receiver certifies the information received from a sender and since the evidence of the transmission is available from a third party, the sender or the receiver can't deny the transmission. For example, a web site is certified by a certifying authority as a valid and trusted site. Hence, clients can rely on the confidentiality of the information provided to that web site, and if there is a dispute about the transmission, the third party can easily resolve it.

Non-repudiation is implemented by using digital signatures and digital certificates, and keeping the private keys secure. Non-repudiation is supported by Certification Authority (CA) that issues digital certificates for the generated signatures or keys by the user or any entity. The CA maintains all the information about the entity along with the life-cycle management of the certificate, which includes issuing and revoking certificates. The structures that support non-repudiation are Public Key Infrastructure (PKI) and XML Key Management Specification (XKMS), which we'll study later in the chapter.

Integrity

Integrity is the authenticity of the data, or proving that the data transmitted has not been tampered with. To have secure communication between the server and the client, the data should be intact, that is, the receiver should get the same data that was sent by the sender. Since the Internet is an unsecured communication channel, integrity of the data is a major concern.

To maintain the integrity of the data, we can use various techniques at various levels. We can implement various encryption algorithms to make the data unintelligible to others during the transmission. We can also use techniques like digital signatures, digital certificates, and other XML encryption techniques like XML signatures. More information about XML encryption can be found at http://www.w3.org/Encryption/2001.

Privacy

Privacy is closely related with integrity of data. Integrity is about tampering with the data, whereas privacy defines keeping data private from the outside world. Privacy is required when dealing with sensitive data like authorization codes, credit card numbers, and other important business documents.

The privacy of the data can be maintained by using a cautious approach in providing the data to others, and transferring data by using an encryption mechanism. There are many technologies that are proposed to support privacy. The W3C's Platform for Privacy Preferences (P3P) discussed in Chapter 2 is expected to be the possible way forward to dealing with some of the privacy concerns. More information about P3P can be found at htttp://www.w3.org/p3p/.

Security Techniques

Now, we will cover the techniques and technologies that are used to take the proper security measures for Web Services. First, we'll take a look at how data can be encrypted using cryptography algorithms to hide it from outsiders. Public Key Infrastructure, digital certificates, and many other techniques use these algorithms to ensure secured transactions.

Cryptography

Cryptography defines techniques for transmitted data securely by encrypting or decrypting it. Encryption means converting data into some unintelligible form, which is called **ciphertext**. Decryption is used to get the original data, that is, **plaintext** from ciphertext.

The encryption is done using some mathematical operation on data. This mathematical operation uses a key to convert data to ciphertext. Decryption is also performed using some mathematical operation on ciphertext that produces the original data, and it also uses a key to perform these operations.

There are two types of techniques used in cryptography. Those are as follows:

- Symmetric key cryptography
- Asymmetric key cryptography

We will describe both of these techniques along with their advantages and disadvantages.

Symmetric Key Cryptography

In symmetric cryptography, the logically same key is used by the sender and the receiver of the data. This key is used for encryption as well as decryption of data. The key that the sender uses for encryption is sent to the receiver of the data on a secured channel. The receiver uses this key to decrypt the ciphertext, and gets the data in its original form. Hence, the ciphertext can be sent on an unsecured channel. Since the key used for encryption can be calculated by a cracker during the transmission, it has to be sent on a secured channel:

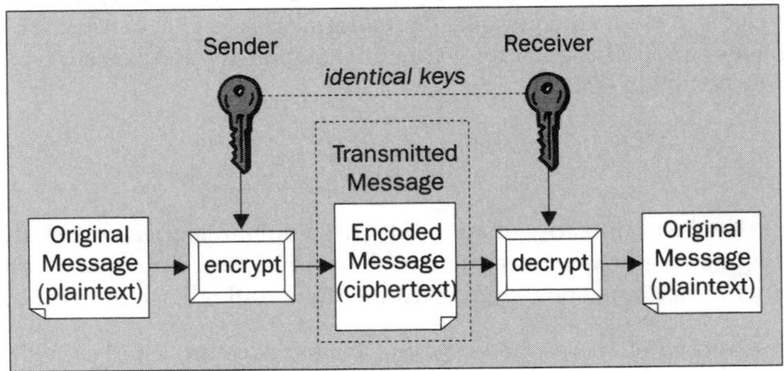

Symmetric key cryptography is also called **private key cryptography**, because the key used to perform encryption and decryption is a **private key** between the sender and the receiver. Only the sender and the receiver are aware of it. There are two types of symmetric key techniques – block ciphers and stream ciphers.

The block ciphers technique divides the plaintext into a fixed-size block over some alphabet and encrypts one block at a time. Stream ciphers are a special type of block ciphers that always have the block size as one character. Thus, encryption changes each character of plaintext. This helps in reducing transmission errors, since error propagation cannot take place. An example of symmetric key cryptography is the Data Encryption Standard (DES) algorithm that is still widely used for security in e-commerce applications.

Asymmetric Key Cryptography

Asymmetric key cryptography uses two totally different keys for encryption and decryption. The receiver generates a pair of keys; one is used for encryption and the other for decryption. The receiver sends an encryption key to the sender over the network. The sender then encrypts the data using this key, and sends it to the receiver.

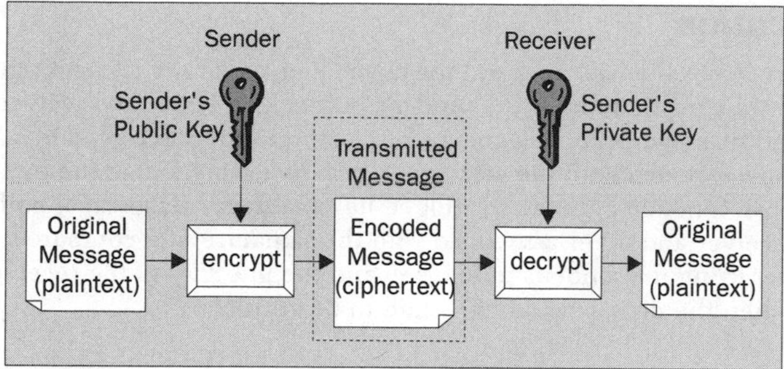

Here, the key can be transmitted over an unsecured network, and is assumed to be available to other senders who want to send data to that receiver. This key is called the **public key**. The receiver uses another undisclosed key to decrypt this data, and as such is called the **private key**. This technique of encryption is also known as **public key cryptography**. In this case, only the receiver's private key can be used to decrypt the data encrypted by its public key, since these two keys are mathematically linked.

Public Key Infrastructure (PKI)

With the presence of Internet and e-commerce technologies, online business transactions are increasing. The most important concern for such transactions is security and to maintain the customer's confidence, online commerce has to be secured. Public Key Infrastructure (PKI) provides powerful data encryption and services that support it.

PKI manages the digital certificates that consist of a public key and a private key. As we know, these keys are used to authenticate the users and data. Such identities are registered with the certificate authorities. The certificate authority acts as the trusted third party for the users and their identities.

Digital Signature

As a security measure, a digital signature is a code that can be attached to an electronically transmitted message. Digital signatures are used for verifying the non-repudiation of the received message. It allows the receiver to check who sent the message, and whether it was tampered with before receiving. Digital signatures use public key cryptography for encryption.

Signature Generation

When a message has to be sent, the sender uses a hash function that generates a hash value (or message digest) for that message. This hash function assigns specific bits (depending on the algorithm used) to very large messages. The hash function is guaranteed to generate a unique value for each message. A hash function that has a result shorter than the message can't be unique, in general; however, it is unlikely for the two values to be the same. Then public key cryptography is used to sign the hash value. The hash value is converted to a digital signature using the sender's private key, which is in unintelligible form. The signature is unique to the message and the private key of the sender, only the sender can sign the message, thus maintaining privacy.

This hash functions as a 'one-way' hash function; knowing the hash value, it is impossible to derive the original message. These are also called message digest algorithms. One such popular algorithm is MD5 (Message Digest 5). Generally, the signature is stored and transmitted with the message to the receiver. Alternatively, it can be sent as a separate element. However, the sender has to send its public key to the receiver as well.

Signature Verification

Once the receiver receives the message, and the associated signature, it checks for the tampering of the message during the transmission, using the sender's public key. First, the receiver calculates the hash value of the received message with the same hash function used by the sender. Then the receiver decrypts the signature received with the message to get the hash value of the message generated by the sender. Since the hash function generates a unique hash value for a message, both the hash values (one generated by the receiver and other associated with the signature) are compared. Doing so, the receiver can verify the sender using the sender's public key and the integrity of the received message. If the two hash values match then the digital signature is said to be verified.

Digital Certificates

We have seen that digital signatures can be used to verify the integrity of the message. With digital signatures, the receiver is relying on the fact that the public key is associated with the user it claims to be. In some cases, for more security, an enterprise may want to send its public key to its business partner by physical transport instead of an electronic one. However, the pair of private key and public key can be faked by a third party as the transmission can be intercepted. Hence, there is a need for some standard that can reliably associate a particular entity with the pair of keys. Digital certificates and digital signatures are used for verification of the entity and integrity of the data.

The enterprise issues digital certificates that contain the entity's details and its public key. Again the receiver of the certificate has to rely on the information published in the certificate provided by that entity. To trust the assertion in the digital certificate there has to be a trusted third party, which can associate the signer with its public key. This trusted third party is called a **Certification Authority** (CA). There are two kinds of CAs – enterprise-wide CAs and commercial CAs. For example, the US Postal Service acts as an enterprise-wide CA by involving itself and only its associated entities like employees, vendors, and clients. CAs like THAWTE (http://www.thawte.com/) and Verisign (http://www.verisign.com/) offer their services to any entity on a commercial basis, hence are called as commercial CAs.

The CA issues or endorses a Digital Certificate containing the signer's identity and its public key. The entity, which is issued a certificate, is called the **subject**, and the receiver is known as the **relying party**. The receiver can rely on this certificate and use the listed public key to verify the sender (subject).

The CA uses its own private key to sign the certificate. The signature of this certificate can be verified using the public key of the CA, which will be listed in another CA's certificate. Thus, the trust is transferred from a single entity to a CA and from one CA to a higher level CA, and so on, until the relying party is assured of the authenticity of the certificate. This is known as **certificate chaining**.

If the subscriber loses control over its private key, it is called a **compromise** of the private key. In such cases, the digital certificate of that subscriber becomes unreliable and the CA revokes the certificate. The CA also informs all relying parties about the revocation of that particular certificate. The subscriber may or may not be informed depending on the situation. Each CA periodically issues a signed and time-stamped data structure called a **Certificate Revocation List** (CRL).

The information stored in the certificate is encoded using two standards – Abstract Syntax Notation 1 (ASN.1) and Distinguished Encoding Rules (DER).

ASN.1 is a result of cooperative efforts by the ITU-T and ISO. It defines a standard to represent the data types and structures sent in the message transmitted over the network. DER is a set of rules for encoding data defined by ASN.1 as a stream of bits for external storage or transmission. Every ASN.1 object has exactly one corresponding DER encoding.

X.509 certificates (formally known as CCITT X.509) are widely used digital certificates. Many popular browsers support these certificates. The X.509 certificates contains the following information:

- Version – The version of the X.509 standard applies to this certificate.
- Serial Number – A unique number used to distinguish it from other certificates issued by a particular entity. When a certificate is revoked its serial number is placed in a Certificate Revocation List (CRL).
- Signature Algorithm Identifier – The algorithm used by the CA to sign the certificate.
- Issuer Name – Name of the entity that signed the certificate.
- Validity Period – The period for which the relying parties can rely on the listed public key. This is indicated by the start date and end date.
- Subject Name – This is the Distinguished Name (DN) of the entity; for example, Organizational Unit, Organization, or Country.
- Subject Public Key Information – The public key of the subscriber.

To date, there are three versions of X.509. The most recent version supports custom extensions for various tasks like sending files or e-mail. Digital certificates can also be used to tackle problems like domain cracking, IP or domain spoofing, or cache poisoning.

In the next section, we'll take a look at Web Services security from a different perspective. A basic principle of security is the need to secure all the levels involved in a Web Service. The system can be cracked even if any of the layers is weak. These levels include the low-level network layer, up to the transport layer, and finally the application layer itself.

Transport Layer Security

As we have seen, security should be taken care of at different layers. At the low-level network layer, the IP level, Internet Protocol Security (IPSec) takes care of it. As we learned earlier in the chapter, using cryptography we can securely transmit data over an insecure communication channel like the Internet. However, IPSec tries to secure the network, thus making the channel secured. More information on IPSec can be found at http://www.ss.com/products/ipsec/standards.html.

The security provided by the underlying protocols like HTTP has limitations, and can't make our Web Services completely secure. The HTTP/1.0 basic authentication scheme (http://www.w3c.org/protocols/http/1.0/spec.html#aa) is one of the security measures that require the user or the browser to authenticate themselves. Since the authentication is handled by HTTP we can't get a complete idea of what exactly happens underneath.

However, another approach to authentication called HTML forms is much more transparent, since we can see the exact interaction and decide on what data we can collect. However, HTML forms are unlikely to be supported by Web Services interfacing tools.

As we said earlier, HTTP has only modest support for the cryptographic mechanisms used for the client and server to authenticate each other and exchange data confidentially. Hence, it was extended to another secure message-oriented communication protocol called Secure HTTP (SHTTP). It provides a variety of security features for transmitting data, preserving the transaction model and implementation characteristics of HTTP. We can also use various cryptography algorithms with SHTTP. Since it supports symmetric key cryptography, a spontaneous transaction can take place without requiring the client to have a public key.

There is one more protocol called HTTPS that is based on SSL protocol; we'll learn more about SSL in the next section. The HTTPS protocol makes the URL start with `https://` instead of `http://`. The Internet Engineering Task Force (IETF) has approved and accepted these technologies as a standard. In the next section we shall see how the SSL protocol works.

The Secure Sockets Layer Protocol (SSL)

Secure Sockets Layer (SSL) has a very important role in the Transport Layer Security. The solution to the problem of transferring important information over the Internet is solved using the SSL protocol. This protocol was originally developed by Netscape to transfer important documents containing sensitive information over the Internet. The Internet Engineering Task Force has introduced a new standard call Transport Layer Security (TLS) which has been derived from SSL.

The SSL protocol specifies that a document can be transmitted over the SSL connection using a public key to encrypt a session key. The public key acts as a password for the document at the receiver's side. The receiver uses its private key to match it with the public key that is received with the document. The real-world example of SSL would be a credit card validation system in e-commerce, where SSL protocol is used to obtain the user's confidential information to validate the credit card number.

As shown in the figure below, TCP/IP is the underlying protocol, which governs the transmission and routing of data over the internet. Protocols like HTTP, Lightweight Directory Access Protocol (LDAP), or Internet Messaging Access Protocol (IMAP) that run on the top of TCP/IP (and hence are called 'high level' protocols). The SSL protocol also sits on the top of TCP/IP, but below these high-level protocols.

The SSL makes use of a TCP/IP layer on behalf of the high-level protocols that in turn allows an SSL-enabled server to authenticate itself to a client that is also SSL-enabled. In this process the client also authenticates itself to the server. After the authentication, a secure connection is established between the two machines on which the encrypted data can be transferred.

SSL Server Authentication

Server authentication allows the client to validate the server's identity. Public key cryptography is used to confirm the server's certificate and the Global Server ID against those issued by the Certificate Authority (CA) from the user's list of trusted CAs (we have discussed CAs earlier in the chapter). For example, if a user wants to send his credit card number to the server over the network, the server's identity can be verified.

Once the client receives the server's certificate, the validity period of that certificate is checked. Then it checks for the trusted Certificate Authority. If the certificate is valid the issuer is a trusted CA; the client compares the CA's key signature with the CA's key signature on the server's certificate. If they don't match, the client ceases to authenticate the server's identity. However, if they do match, the client checks for the server's domain name against the one in its certificate.

Now, that we have seen how the client can authenticate the server, let's see how the server authenticates the client to complete the secure transaction. However, the server can also validate the client for authentication following the same procedures as described above. The two extra validations performed by the server are listed in the client authentication section.

SSL Client Authentication

In SSL client authentication, a server confirms the user's identity using the same techniques used by the client for server authentication. The SSL-enabled server checks for the client's certificate and the global client ID issued by the CA. The SSL client authentication is optional and depends on the degree of security the transaction requires. For example, a bank server might want to check its customer's identity before sending some confidential information to him.

As we saw earlier, the client authentication occurs in the same manner as that of the server. However, sometimes the server needs more validations from the client before establishing a secure transaction. In such cases, the server looks for the user certificate in the LDAP directory, and can revoke the certificate if it doesn't match with that in the LDAP directory. The server can also check the client configuration; that is, it checks the resources allocated to the client as per the server's access control list (ACL); only then a connection is established using these specified properties allocated to the client.

An Encrypted SSL Connection

With SSL, a secure connection is established between the client and the server after they have been validated by each other. However, this connection needs the data to be encrypted before its transmission over the Internet to provide confidentiality. The encrypted SSL connection can keep the data integrity intact by verifying if the data has been tampered with in transit.

SSL consists of two subprotocols – the SSL Handshake Protocol and the SSL Record Protocol. The Handshake Protocol allows the server and the client to authenticate each other by having a negotiated encryption algorithm and the respective cryptographic keys before the data is exchanged. This protocol establishes a secure SSL connection between the client and the server.

The SSL Record Protocol defines the format for exchanging the data on the basis of the algorithms used by the SSL Handshake Protocol.

SSL Record Protocol

The SSL Record Protocol is the base protocol that is used by the upper-layer protocols of SSL such as the SSL Handshake Protocol. It keeps the SSL connections confidential by encrypting the messages to be transmitted and maintains the message integrity by using a Message Authentication Code (MAC).

Once the SSL Record Protocol takes the message to be transmitted, the data is fragmented into manageable blocks or compressed. Then using MAC the data is encrypted, and a header is added to the message. Finally, this unit is transmitted in a TCP segment.

SSL Handshake Protocol

The SSL Handshake Protocol uses the SSL Record Protocol to exchange a series of messages between the SSL-enabled server and the SSL-enabled client. When this exchange of messages begins, that is, the SSL session starts, it is called an SSL handshake. As we know, the SSL protocol uses a combination of symmetric and asymmetric encryption.

At the time of the SSL handshake, the client is allowed to verify the server's identity using public key cryptography. Then the server and the client use symmetric cryptography for encryption, decryption, and ensuring integrity of data during that particular SSL session. As mentioned earlier, the client can also authenticate the server, but it's optional.

XML Security Concerns

Though XML is used for Web Services, since it's simple and portable, it is a major security concern. Being verbose, XML can easily expose data, and it doesn't include any built-in security mechanism. Hence the chances of documents getting altered or inspected during transmission are higher. We need to ensure the security of the data at every point of the process. To prevent the tampering of data, we should be able to encrypt and sign only some parts of the XML document based on authentication.

There are many standards like SAML, XACL, and XKMS, which provide security for transmitting XML data over the Internet.

Security Assertion Markup Language (SAML)

In today's world, if we want to access any service we need to sign on for that service. These required services are not found or provided by a single provider. We need to sign on to different provider systems to access different services. For example, to book a plane ticket we need to sign on to the travel web site and for hotel reservation we again need to authenticate. In such cases, we need to sign on to use various Web Services from different but associated web sites. Security Assertion Markup Language (SAML) is an XML-based standard which can allow us to access multiple Web Services from different web sites by authenticating just once. The web sites may have their individual authentication system, but they accept users authenticated by other web sites.

SAML specifies an open and interoperable design for web-based single sign-on functionality for accessing multiple services. Implementing SAML for single sign-on helps users to authenticate in one domain and use the same resource in some other domain without authenticating again. The user's sign-on information from one provider consisting of authentication, authorization, and profile is transmitted across to the other provider during the same session. Note that in many cases the source and the destination of the service belong to the same federation. The service providers in the federation need to collaborate and agree to protect secure information that will be shared among them. For example, if we sign into a travel agency web site for a plane ticket and also require a hotel reservation, then the secured information can be shared only by the associates of that travel agency.

Specifications

SAML is a series of XML-based messages that describe if the user is authentic, their access permissions, and how they can use the data and resources. It works with protocols and technologies including HTTP, SMTP, FTP, and SOAP.

SAML is made of three main components – assertions, protocol, and binding. There are three types of assertions in SAML. As the name suggests, authentication assertions verify the user's identity. Information specific to the user, such as permissions, are contained in attribute assertions. Authorization decision assertions specify what the user is allowed to do. The protocol decides on the protocols to be used for getting assertions. The mapping of SAML message exchanges to SOAP message exchanges is described in the binding.

The important property of SAML is its interoperability. Different versions of single sign-on concept do exist in the market, but these versions were closed and not interoperable. On the other hand SAML implementations are fully interoperable.

SAML is proposed as a security service implementation for the Internet. The security service providers have accepted SAML specifications, in principle. These security service providers include Sun Microsystems (Sun ONE Platform for Network Identity) and iPlanet Directory Server, Access Management Edition (DSAME), Entrust (GetAccess portal), Systinet (WASP Secure Identity), Securant (RSA Cleartrust), Entegrity (AssureAccess), and Netegrity (AffiliateMinder).

The SAML 1.0 Specifications that were released in February 2002 have been submitted for standardization to Security Services Technical Committee of OASIS (Organization for the Advancement of Structured Information Standards) in March 2002. More information about this can be found at http://www.oasis-open.org/committees/security/.

XML Access Control Language (XACL)

XACL is one of the several development projects undertaken by the IBM Tokyo Research Library in the XML security area. XACL is aimed at providing XML documents with a sophisticated access control model and access control specification language. We can also specify the policies for transferring the document over the Internet. These policies ensure that the document is securely transferred.

Let's consider an example of an XML document that lists all the technical articles published on the Wrox web site. An access control policy could be written for the document so that only the registered user can read articles, and others can view only the list of articles and the overview of the article.

The policy written for the following document specifies that only Mike, being the registered user, has rights to view the list of the articles as well as read the article. However, all non-registered users can only view the list of the articles:

```
<document>
  <contents id="contents">
    ...
    ...
    ...
    ...
  </contents>
  <policy>
    <xacl>
      <object href="id(contents)"/>
      <rule id="rule1">
        <acl>
          <subject><uid>Mike</uid></subject>
          <privilege type="view" sign="+"/>
          <privilege type="read" sign="+"/>
        </acl>
      </rule>
      <rule id="rule2">
        <acl>
          <subject></subject>
          <privilege type="view" sign="+"/>
        </acl>
      </rule>
    </xacl>
  </policy>
</document>
```

The policy for a particular XML document involves subject, object, and action. The subject indicates the identity, group, and role. The object specifies the contents to which the policy is to be applied. The action specifies the different operations that could be performed with the XML document. XACL uses a provisional authorization model that allows specifying the provisional actions associated with the primitive actions. The primitive actions available currently are read, write, create, and delete.

Based on the condition and the privileges the user is authorized before giving access to the document. With the use of the provisional authorization model, the response from the system could be beyond 'grant' or 'deny'. Here, the system can inform the user about the reasons of the authorization failure, or the actions required to be taken for getting access to the document.

XML Key Management Specification (XKMS)

XML Key Management Specification (XKAMS) proposes a protocol for distributing and registering the public keys, following the proposed standard for XML Signature and XML Encryption. The XKMS specification defines two parts – XML Key Information Service Specification (X-KISS), and the XML Key Registration Service Specification (X-KRSS). Along with these two protocols XKMS is also supported by Trust Assertion Service Specification (X-TASS). XKMS was submitted to W3C in March 2001, the detailed specifications are available at http://www.w3.org/TR/xkms/.

XKMS is an XML-based way of managing the PKI. We define XKMS as a proposed protocol for the registration and management of keys. XKMS simplifies the outsourcing of this PKI functionality to remote trust services. This is done by integrating complicated PKI key management functionality into applications through toolkits. We should only know how to create and process the appropriate XML messages with which the remote services are invoked.

Here, a trust service is a Web Service that is invoked by other services to enable trust for their own transaction processes. Trust services implement foundations for security functions such as signing on, encryption, key registration, and validation. These functions are required by the other Web Services to guarantee the trust of their transactions. XKMS is the first proposed standard for such a trust service.

In XKMS, a key information element is designed to allow a signer to communicate proposals to the verifier, such as which public key to use. Another important feature of this element is that the information may or may not be cryptographically connected to the signature, that is, the services can be complemented by having cryptographic capabilities on the client, but the client cryptography is not required. The user can easily have the XKMS service generate the keys that are subsequently managed through the service.

Easily understandable syntax in XKMS eliminates PKI toolkits and proprietary plug-ins. Use of a common XML vocabulary to describe authentication, authorization, and profile information in XML documents makes XKMS services completely independent of the platform, the vendor, and the transport protocol.

As we defined earlier, XKMS comprises of two parts: X-KISS and X-KRSS. These protocols describe message exchanges that consist of a simple request and response exchange with a trust service.

X-KISS

X-KISS defines a protocol used for resolution of the public key contained in XML signature elements. It allows the client of a trust service to delegate all or some of the tasks required to process `<ds:KeyInfo>` elements. This protocol mainly makes the application implementations simpler, by allowing them to become clients, and keeps away from the complexity and syntax of the underlying PKI that is used to establish trust relationships. The PKI may be based upon a different specification such as X.509/PKIX, SPKI, or PGP.

X-KRSS

X-KRSS is a protocol that allows a Web Service to accept the registration of public key information. Once the public key information is registered, the public key may be used to work with X-KISS and other Web Services. The registered user may request additional information that is related to the public key such as name or attributes defined by the implementation.

Developing Secured Web Services

Until now, we have discussed different issues in web security and the technologies available for building the secured Web Services. In this section, we will actually develop the secured Web Services that provide functionality like client authentication, Web Service invocation over a secured channel and secured communication over unsecured channels.

Security By Client Authentication

As we discussed earlier, an important aspect of security in any application is client authentication. Web Services also need to be protected from unauthorized users. The Axis toolkit, which we learned about in the previous chapter, provides a facility to authenticate the client trying to access the Web Service. By using such a facility, we can control access to our Web Services. Thus, if a Web Service is retrieving sensitive data, we will only allow authorized users to access it. In case of a paid service, this facility can be used to authenticate the user before access to the service is granted.

In this section, we will describe how to add a client authentication security feature to a Web Service developed using Axis. For this purpose, we will use `AddressService` described in the previous chapter. The service returns the address of the employee specified by an ID. We will add a client authentication feature to this service. As a demonstration, we will create two users named `john`, and `andy` in our Axis engine. Only `john` will be given access to our `AddressService`.

Creating Users

First, we'll need to create users in the Axis engine. Axis maintains the list of users in a flat file `users.lst`. This file is located in the `CATALINA_HOME/webapps/axis/WEB-INF` directory (`CATALINA_HOME` is the installation directory of Tomcat). By default the file contains three usernames as shown below:

```
user1 pass1
user2
user3 pass3
```

Each line contains a username and a password separated by one whitespace. Note that `user2` has no password. We will add two more users for our Web Service, simply by appending the following two lines to the file:

```
john john
andy andy
```

We can add any number of users in the above manner. However, we need to protect such files at the server.

Setting Permissions

Axis allows setting service-level permissions for the users. The permissions are also stored in a flat file called `perms.lst` that resides in the `CATALINA_HOME/webapps/axis/WEB-INF` directory. By default, there are permissions for the default users:

```
user1 urn:xmltoday-delayed-quotes
user2 urn:xmltoday-delayed-quotes
user3 urn:cominfo
```

This indicates that `user1` and `user2` have access to the `xmltoday-delay-quotes` service, and `user3` has access to `cominfo` service. Let's add permissions for our Web Service by adding the following statements in the `perms.lst` file:

```
john urn:AddressService
andy
```

We allow `john` to access to our `AddressService` service, while andy is not given access to any of the Web Services.

Now, we need to modify the deployment descriptor of the Web Service to register the authorized users for it.

Deployment Descriptor

Let's copy the deployment descriptor of our `AddressService` to our current directory under the name `array.wsdd` just for the sake of simplicity. We'll now add the following statement in the descriptor to define the list of authorized users:

```
<parameter name="allowedRoles" value="john"/>
```

Next, we will need to add the handlers for performing client authentication. These handlers are added using the `<requestFlow>` tag, as these handlers are service-specific, and are invoked before the service method. The handlers are of two types, authentication handler and authorization handler.

The authentication handler is implemented in the `SimpleAuthenticationHandler` class and the authorization handler in the class `SimpleAuthorizationHandler`. Both these classes are defined in the `org.apache.axis.handlers` package. The authentication handler checks the username and password specified in the `MessageContext` parameter in the `users.lst` file. Once the user is authenticated, the `MessageContext` is passed to the authorization handler. The authorization handler then checks the user's permissions in `perms.lst` file. If the user is allowed to access that service, the Axis engine invokes a method on the service object.

These handlers are specified inside the `<service>` tag in the deployment descriptor as shown below:

```
<requestFlow name="checks">
    <handler type="java:org.apache.axis.handlers.SimpleAuthenticationHandler"/>
    <handler type="java:org.apache.axis.handlers.SimpleAuthorizationHandler"/>
</requestFlow>
```

We will need to redeploy the service to activate the above modifications. Now, our Web Service is secured and can be accessed only by authorized clients.

Developing a Client for the Authentication Service

We will now modify the client program (written in the previous chapter) to accept a username and password at the command line, and pass this authentication information to the Axis engine.

First, we import the various Java packages from the Axis toolkit:

```
import org.apache.axis.AxisFault;
import org.apache.axis.client.Call;
import org.apache.axis.client.Service;
import org.apache.axis.utils.Options;
```

We will now import the XML classes from the `javax` package:

```
import javax.xml.rpc.ParameterMode;
import javax.xml.rpc.namespace.QName;
import java.io.*;
public class ArrayClient {
```

In the `main()` function, we get the username and password by constructing an `Options` object, and calling the `getUser()` and `getPassword()` methods on it:

```
  public static void main(String [] args) throws Exception {
    Options opts = new Options( args );
    String user = opts.getUser();
    String passwd = opts.getPassword();
    String id = null;

    // Take input for id from console
    try {
      BufferedReader reader =
                     new BufferedReader(new InputStreamReader(System.in));
      System.out.print("Enter id: ");
      id = reader.readLine();
    } catch (Exception e) {
     e.printStackTrace();
    }
```

We then construct the call object by creating a Service instance, and calling the createCall() method on this instance. This code is similar to the one discussed in the previous chapter:

```
// Create Call object
Service  service = new Service();
Call call = (Call) service.createCall();
QName qn = new QName("http://soapinterop.org/xsd", "ArrayOfstring");

call.registerTypeMapping(java.lang.String[][].class, qn,
new org.apache.axis.encoding.ser.ArraySerializerFactory(),
new org.apache.axis.encoding.ser.ArrayDeserializerFactory());

String result[] = {""};

try {
  call.setTargetEndpointAddress( new java.net.URL
          ("http://localhost:8080/axis/servlet/AxisServlet"));
  call.setOperationName(new QName("AddressService", "getArray"));

  call.addParameter("id", qn, ParameterMode.IN);
  call.setReturnType(org.apache.axis.encoding.XMLType.XSD_INT);
```

Here, we set the target endpoint, the operation name, parameters for the method, and the return type on the call object.

To add the authentication information, we call the setUsername() and setPassword() methods on the call object:

```
  call.setUsername(user);
  call.setPassword(passwd);
```

The service is invoked by calling the invoke() method on the call object:

```
  Object resp = call.invoke(new Object[] { new Integer(id) });
```

This call will authenticate the user by checking the supplied credentials with the username and password information registered with the Axis engine. On successful invocation of the method, the return value is extracted in a String array:

```
  // Extract the returned value of the method
  result = (java.lang.String[])org.apache.axis.utils.JavaUtils.convert
  (resp, java.lang.String[].class);
```

Then we show the result on the console, using a for loop. This prints the complete address of the located customer. If an error occurs, we catch the exception:

```
  System.out.println("Address of " + id);
  for(int i=0; i<result.length; i++) {
    System.out.println("\t" + result[i]);
  } catch (AxisFault fault) {
    System.out.println("Error : " + fault.toString());
  }
}
```

Now, let's try to access the AddressService Web Service. To use the service, a valid username and password is required; we'll access it as user john. Tomcat and Axis will authenticate the username and password supplied by the client. After the user john is authenticated, the address information of the requested customer ID (for example, 222) is returned to the client:

```
java ArrayClient -ujohn -wjohn
Enter id: 222
Address of 222
         lane 4
         New York
         USA
         534574
```

If we try to access the service as the user andy, the system throws an exception. andy is a valid user, but he does not have permission to run the Web Service:

```
java ArrayClient -uandy -wandy
Enter id: 222
Error : Unauthorized
```

If we try to run the service as user guest, which doesn't exist in our users.lst file, we will get an error message as shown below:

```
java ArrayClient -uguest -wguest
Enter id: 222
Error : User 'guest' not authenticated
```

Note that all these exception messages are thrown by the system; we simply catch AxisFault exceptions, and print the message string on the user console.

Security Using SSL

The JSSE (Java Secure Socket Extension) is a set of Java packages that covers SSL implementations to ensure secured communication between the server and the client. As we learned earlier in the chapter, SSL facilitates data encryption, server authentication, message integrity, and optional client authentication. Hence, using JSSE transmission, the server and the client can have a secured data transmission over the Internet. We can easily integrate JSSE in the applications.

Since Java 2 SDK 1.4, JSSE has been integrated with SDK; for the previous versions of SDK (1.2 and 1.3), JSSE was available as an optional package. JSSE 1.0.2 is the recent release that provides SSL v3, TLS 1.0 for the Java 2 platform. More information, and downloads for JSSE can be found at http://java.sun.com/products/jsse/.

It comes in two versions – domestic that is restricted to the USA and Canada, and global that is meant for the rest of the world.

To install the JSSE version (for releases prior to Java 2 SDK 1.4), we need to extract the downloaded .jar file to the directory of our choice. Then we need to copy the jsse.jar, jcert.jar, and jnet.jar files in our $JAVA_HOME/jre/lib/ext folder. We then add the following line to our $JAVA_HOME/jre/lib/security/java.security file:

```
security.provider.3=com.sun.net.ssl.internal.ssl.Provider
```

Now that we have JSSE installed, we need to configure our server to work with SSL. The next section describes how to configure our server for SSL.

Configuring Tomcat for SSL

Let's begin to configure Tomcat to work with SSL. First, we need to generate a `keystore` and the certificate for the server, using the `keytool` (http://java.sun.com/j2se/1.4/docs/tooldocs/solaris/keytool.html) tool provided as a part of Java 2 SDK 1.4. Once we generate the `keystore` and the certificate, the self-signed certificate will be exported to the appropriate external file. The certificate within this file is then imported on the client's machine. The client program will use the certificate in the `keystore` to validate the server before passing on the sensitive information to the server.

Before creating the `keystores` and the certificates, we need to ensure that the `bin` directory of the SDK installation is available in the environment path. Now, we'll generate `keystore` for the server in the `server.keystore` file and generate a public/private key for the alias `wroxservice`:

```
keytool -genkey -alias wroxservice-sv -dname "CN=localhost, OU=X, O=Y, L=Z, S=XY,
C=YZ" -keyalg RSA -keypass wrox123 -storepass wrox123 -keystore server.keystore
```

We then export the generated certificate to `server.cer` file:

```
keytool -export -alias wroxservice-sv -storepass wrox123 -file server.cer -
keystore server.keystore
```

Now, we'll import the server's certificate in the client's `keystore`, using the following command on the client machine:

```
keytool -import -v -trustcacerts -alias wroxservice -file server.cer -keystore
client.keystore -keypass wrox123 -storepass wrox123
```

Now that the `keystore` and the certificate have been created, we have to set the path of `server.keystore` and the `keystore` password in the `server.xml` file. We also need to uncomment the SSL settings in the `server.xml` file:

```
<!-- Define an SSL HTTP/1.1 Connector on port 8443 -->
<Connector className="org.apache.catalina.connector.http.HttpConnector"
           port="8443" minProcessors="5" maxProcessors="75"
           enableLookups="true"
           acceptCount="10" debug="0" scheme="https" secure="true"<
    <Factory className="org.apache.catalina.net.SSLServerSocketFactory"
             keystoreFile="<filepath>"
             keystorePass="<password>"
             clientAuth="false" protocol="TLS"/>
  </Connector>
```

As shown in the above code, we need to provide the path for the `keystoreFile` and the `password` for the `keystore`. The `keystoreFile` contains the server `keystore`, and may also contain the client's certificate that is used by the server to validate the client.

Once we make the above changes, we need to restart the server. Let's test the SSL settings by accessing the URL https://localhost:8443/. The port number here is the default port used by SSL. The server may display a message saying that the certificate is not recognized if we don't sign our certificates from a CA. However, we can proceed by accepting the certificate via the wizard started by the browser; this wizard finally presents Tomcat's welcome page.

So far we have installed the JSSE on our system and configured the Tomcat server to work with SSL. Now we are ready to write, test, and deploy our service using SSL.

Writing the CreditCardAuthentication Service

We'll develop a simple server class that verifies the credit card number:

```
public class CreditCardValidationServer {
  public boolean validateCreditCard(String CardNo) {
    if (CardNo.equals("123456789")) {
      return true;
    } else {
      return false;
    }
  }
}
```

The above class implements the `validateCreditCard()` method. This web method accepts the credit card number in `String` format. For simplicity, we verify the received parameter with a hard-coded number instead of a server database.

We'll now compile the service class, and copy it into the `WEB-INF/classes` directory.

Deploying the CreditCardAuthentication Service

To deploy our Web Service, we create the following deployment descriptor:

```
<deployment xmlns="http://xml.apache.org/axis/wsdd/"
            xmlns:java="http://xml.apache.org/axis/wsdd/providers/java">

  <service name="CreditCardValidationService" provider="java:RPC">
    <parameter name="className" value="CreditCardValidationServer"/>
    <parameter name="methodName" value="*"/>
  </service>
</deployment>
```

This descriptor is available in the `CreditCardServicedeploy.wsdd` file. After creating the descriptor, the service is deployed using the following command:

```
java -Djava.protocol.handler.pkgs=com.sun.net.ssl.internal.www.protocol
-Djavax.net.ssl.trustStore= <filepath/client.keystore>
org.apache.axis.client.AdminClient
-lhttps://localhost:8443/axis/services/AdminService
<filepath/CreditCardServicedeploy.wsdd>
```

Note that you need to replace `<filepath/client.keystore>` *with the absolute path of the* `client.keystore` *file.*

We set the system property `java.protocol.handler.pkgs` to `com.sun.net.ssl.internal.www.protocol`, which is a URL handler for the HTTPS URL protocol type. We also set the system property `javax.net.ssl.trustStore` to point to the client's `keystore`, so that the trusted certificate may be located at the time of deployment.

Generating Stub Classes

Once the service is deployed, we can generate the stub classes (for the client) using the WSDL file obtained from the server. The WSDL file is obtained using the following URL in the browser https://localhost:8443/axis/services/CreditCardValidationService?wsdl. We'll save this to the file called `CreditCardService.wsdl`.

We'll then generate the stub classes with the following command:

```
java -Djavax.net.ssl.trustStore=<filepath/client.keystore>
org.apache.axis.wsdl.WSDL2Java -p wrox CreditCardService.wsdl
```

Here, we have specified the package as `wrox`, hence all the class will be generated in the `wrox` subdirectory under the working directory.

Developing a Client for the SSL Service

We'll now write a client that uses the above Web Service over the secured channel. Our client application is a console-based Java application that accepts the credit card number at the command line:

```
package wrox;
public class CreditCardValidationClient {
  public static void main(String[] args) {
    if (args.length!=1) {
      System.out.println ("Usage => java CreditCardValidationClient
             CardNo");
      System.exit(0);
    }

    try {
      CreditCardValidationServerServiceLocator serviceLocator =
            new CreditCardValidationServerServiceLocator();
      CreditCardValidationServer server =
            serviceLocator.getCreditCardValidationService();
      boolean result = server.validateCreditCard(args[0]);
      if (result) {
        System.out.println("The Card number is Valid.");
      } else {
        System.out.println("The Card number is Invalid.");
      }
    } catch(Exception ex) {
       ex.printStackTrace();
    }
  }
}
```

The client application simply creates an instance of `CreditCardValidationServerServiceLocator` and calls the `getCreditCardValidationService()` method on it to obtain the reference to the Web Service.

The `CreditCardValidationServerServiceLocator` has the following private declaration that points to the remote server where the Web Service is deployed. This was discussed in detail in the previous chapter. Note that the URL uses HTTPS rather than HTTP:

```
private final java.lang.String CreditCardValidationService_address =
        "https://localhost:8443/axis/services/CreditCardValidationService";
```

The program then invokes the web method `validateCreditCard()` on the obtained server object. The validation result is printed on the user console. After we compile the client application, we'll run it with a valid credit card number `123456789`:

```
java -Djava.protocol.handler.pkgs=com.sun.net.ssl.internal.www.protocol
-Djavax.net.ssl.trustStore=<filepath/client.keystore>
wrox.CreditCardValidationClient 1234567890
```

This will print The Card number is Valid.

If we enter a card number that does not exist, we will get a message saying that the card number is invalid:

```
java -Djava.protocol.handler.pkgscom.sun.net.ssl.internal.www.protocol
-Djavax.net.ssl.trustStore=/root/client.keystore wrox.CreditCardValidationClient
0987654321
The Card number is Invalid.
```

Security Over HTTP

We can develop secured Web Services that may use an unsecured communication channel like HTTP by using data encryption techniques. To demonstrate this, we will modify the `CreditCardAuthentication` web service developed earlier in the chapter. We will use the Asymmetric Cryptographic algorithm (RSA) for this purpose.

Our Web Service will generate a random pair of public/private keys. The Web Service will expose two methods called `getPublicKeyParams()` and `validateCardNo()`. The `getPublicKeyParams()` method returns the public key to the caller. The client uses this public key to encrypt the credit card number before sending it to the server. The encrypted card number is sent as a parameter in the `validateCardNo()` method. The server then decrypts the number using its private key. The method returns `true` or `false` to the client, depending on the card's validity.

We'll use a third-party service provider named `BouncyCastleProvider` for the RSA cryptography algorithm. The Bouncy Castle Crypto package (http://www.bouncycastle.org/latest_releases.html) is a Java implementation of cryptographic algorithms. It provides a lightweight API suitable for use in any environment with the additional infrastructure to make the algorithms conform to the JCE framework.

The MyRSACryptoServiceProvider Class

The `MyRSACryptoServiceProvider` class is a utility class used by our Web Service defined later. This class provides key pair generation, encryption, and decryption functionality to the Web Service class.

In the `MyRSACryptoServiceProvider` class, we first import the required packages including the classes provided by `BouncyCastleProvider`:

```
import org.bouncycastle.jce.provider.BouncyCastleProvider;
import java.security.*;
import javax.crypto.*;
```

We then declare a private variable of type `KeyPair` as an instance variable of the class. This variable will be used for holding randomly generated public and private keys:

```
public class MyRSACryptoServiceProvider {
  private KeyPair ServiceKeyPair;
```

In the class constructor, we register the `BouncyCastleProvider` with the security manager:

```
    Security.addProvider(new BouncyCastleProvider());
```

The key pair is generated using the following lines of code:

```
    KeyPairGenerator gen = KeyPairGenerator.getInstance("RSA");
    gen.initialize(1024, new SecureRandom());
    ServiceKeyPair = gen.generateKeyPair();
```

Since the object of this class is declared as static in the service, the key pair generation will not be done at every connection. Our Web Service class returns the randomly generated public key from the above step to the caller, by means of the return value of the public method `getPublicKey()`:

```
    public PublicKey getPublicKey()throws GeneralSecurityException {
      return ServiceKeyPair.getPublic();
    }
```

The class defines another method called `decrypt()`. This method accepts encrypted data in binary form. The data is decrypted using the private key from the `ServiceKeyPair`. The decrypted data is returned to the caller as a `byte` array:

```
    public byte[] decrypt(byte[] toDecrypt) throws GeneralSecurityException {
      byte[] result=null;
      Cipher deCipher = Cipher.getInstance("RSA");
      deCipher.init(Cipher.DECRYPT_MODE, ServiceKeyPair.getPrivate());
      deCipher.update(toDecrypt);
      result = deCipher.doFinal();
      return result;
    }
  }
```

The class may also provide the `setPublicKey()`, and `encrypt()` methods for more generalized use. By providing these methods, this class can be used even on the client side. The public key received from the server can be set using `setPublicKey()` method, and then the data is encrypted using the `encrypt()` method. This will hide the complexity of the key pair generation, encryption, and decryption, and provide an easy interface to the application.

Creating the CreditCardService Class

This is our Web Service class that exposes its methods as web methods. The class declares a private member `CryptPro` of type `MyRSACryptoServiceProvider`. This member is declared as `static`, since we want the keys to persist across multiple invocations (by the client):

```
private static MyRSACryptoServiceProvider CryptPro =
        new MyRSACryptoServiceProvider();
```

When we instantiate the `MyRSACryptoServiceProvider` class, the public and private keys are created and stored in the `static` member `CryptPro`.

The `getPublicKeyParams()` method first obtains the public key from the `CryptoPro` object. There are two standard public key parameters used by the RSA public key algorithm. These two parameters, `Modulus` and `PublicExponent`, together form the RSA public key. We'll extract these parameters from the public key; they are returned in the `HashMap` object.

We declare the `getPublicKeyParams()` method and the service provider is registered with the security manager:

```
public HashMap getPublicKeyParams() throws Exception
  Security.addProvider(new BouncyCastleProvider());
```

We then obtain the public key by calling the following lines of code:

```
KeyFactory kf= KeyFactory.getInstance("RSA");
RSAPublicKeySpec ksp = (RSAPublicKeySpec) kf.getKeySpec
(CryptPro.getPublicKey(), RSAPublicKeySpec.class);
```

Now, we'll extract the parameters, and put them in the `HashMap` object:

```
BigInteger m = ksp.getModulus();
BigInteger p = ksp.getPublicExponent();
HashMap params = new HashMap();
params.put("Modulus", m);
params.put("Public Exponent", p);
```

Finally, we return the `HashMap`:

```
return params;
```

Once the client obtains the public key from the server by calling the `getPublicKeyParams()` web method, it can use this public key to encrypt the sensitive information and send it to the server. The `validateCardNo()` method accepts the encrypted card number as a `byte` array, and returns `true` or `false` to the caller after verifying the card's credentials in the server database:

```
public boolean validateCardNo(byte[] bCardNo) {
```

In the method, we decrypt the card number by calling the `decrypt()` method of `CryptPro` object:

```
String sCardNo = new String(CryptPro.decrypt(bCardNo));
```

The method compares the decrypted number with the hard-coded number in the program. In real-world applications, this will be validated against the number stored in the database by using the payment gateway:

```
if (sCardNo.equals("1234567890")) {
  return true;
} else {
  return false;
}
```

Deploying the RSA Service

We now need to deploy our Web Service. We have already discussed different ways of deploying Web Services using Tomcat and Axis, in the previous chapter. Here, we will simply rename the `CreditCardService.java` file as `CreditCardService.jws`, and copy it to `CATALINA_HOME/webapps/axis` directory. Note that `CATALINA_HOME` points to the Tomcat installation directory.

The service uses the `MYRSACryptoServiceProvider` class, hence we also need to compile this class, and add it to the server classpath, so that it can be found at the time of execution. We also have to add the `bcpro-jdk14-113.jar` (the latest version of `BouncyCastleprovider` for SDK1.4) file in the class path of the Tomcat server.

Developing a Client for the RSA Service

Next we'll develop a simple client application that accesses the Web Service over HTTP. The application accepts the credit card number as command-ine parameter:

```
import org.apache.axis.client.*;
import org.bouncycastle.jce.provider.BouncyCastleProvider;
import java.security.*;
import java.security.spec.*;
import javax.crypto.*;
import java.math.*;
import java.util.*;

public class TestClient {
  public static void main(String [] args) {
    if (args.length!=1) {
      System.out.println("Usage => java TestClient CardNo");
      System.exit(0);
    }
    try {
```

We need to register the provider with the security manager:

```
      Security.addProvider(new BouncyCastleProvider());
```

Next, we obtain the reference to the Web Service:

```
        String endpoint = "http://localhost:8080/axis/CreditCardService.jws";
        Service  CardService = new Service();
```

We then create the `call` object, and set the endpoint URL to http://localhost:8080/axis/CreditCardService.jws (the URL will change depending on the setup):

```
        Call CardServiceCall = (Call) CardService.createCall();
        CardServiceCall.setTargetEndpointAddress(new java.net.URL(endpoint) );
```

Invoke the `getPublicKeyParams()` method to retrieve the public key parameters:

```
        CardServiceCall.setOperationName("getPublicKeyParams");
        HashMap params = (HashMap) CardServiceCall.invoke(new Object[]{});
```

Now, we'll create the public key object from the retrieved parameters:

```
        RSAPublicKeySpec ksp = new
                    RSAPublicKeySpec(((BigInteger)params.get("Modulus")),
                    ((BigInteger)params.get("Public Exponent")));

        KeyFactory kf = KeyFactory.getInstance("RSA");

        PublicKey pk =  kf.generatePublic(ksp);
```

The credit card number will be encrypted using the public key:

```
        Cipher cf = Cipher.getInstance("RSA", "BC");
        cf.init(Cipher.ENCRYPT_MODE, pk);
        byte[] enData = cf.doFinal(args[0].getBytes());
```

Finally, the `validateCardNo()` method is invoked to validate the card number:

```
        CredirServiceCall.setOperationName("validateCardNo");
        Boolean val = (Boolean) CreditServiceCall.invoke(new
                                                  Object[]{enData});
```

Display the appropriate message to the user depending upon the response.

```
        if (val.booleanValue()) {
          System.out.println("Valid card number.");
        } else {
          System.out.println("Invalid card number.");
        }
      } catch(Exception ex) {
        ex.printStackTrace();
      }
    }
  }
```

The credit card number is specified as a command-ine parameter. The screen output for a valid number would be:

```
java TestClient 1234567890
Valid card number.
```

Summary

As Web Services are becoming more popular day by day, developing secured Web Services has been a major concern. In this chapter, we reviewed various security issues. First we discussed security measures like authentication and authorization that can prevent invalid users from accessing the service, and non-repudiation that ensures safe delivery of the data to the intended receiver.

Though the receiver of the data is authentic, to have a secured communication, the data shouldn't be tampered with during transmission. Hence, we need to maintain the integrity of the data. We then looked at another security issue, privacy of data, which is closely related to integrity. During data transmission, we need to ensure that the data doesn't get leaked to outsiders, thus keeping it private between the sender and the reviewer.

We can use different algorithms and techniques to develop secured Web Services. As we learned, cryptography is one of the commonly used techniques that creates a base for many other techniques. Cryptography provides security by encrypting and decrypting the data to be transmitted. We discussed two types of cryptography called symmetric key cryptography and asymmetric key cryptography. As we studied in this chapter, symmetric key cryptography uses two identical keys for the sender and the receiver to have a secure communication. A set of private and public keys is used in asymmetric key cryptography.

We then learned another technique called Public Key Infrastructure (PKI) that uses cryptography techniques to provide security to Web Services. We then learned how a digital signature and digital certificate can be used to tackle security problems.

Security can be maintained at various layers of Internet protocols. In this chapter, we covered security issues at the transport layer. Apart from Internet Protocol Security (IPSec) and Secure HTTP (SHHTP), we looked at the Secure Sockets Layer Protocol (SSL) that is commonly used for ensuring secured transactions. We discussed the SSL connection, and the protocols involved.

Another security concern is XML-related security, since XML is verbose and can easily expose data. We talked about various security measures like SAML, XACL, and XKMS that can be used to take care of XML security.

Finally, to demonstrate a few of the techniques covered in the chapter, we developed some sample secured Web Services.

6

Perl and SOAP::Lite

Perl (Practical Extraction and Reporting Language) is the most popular scripting language used on Linux and other systems for building web applications. It was originally developed by Larry Wall in 1986 to help generate ad-hoc reports, combining text-processing features from Unix tools like awk and sed. Its original merit was that of being faster than these programs. Larry soon added Henry Spencer's Regular Expressions package, and provided syntax to make regular expressions into tightly integrated language operators.

Developers have been regularly adding goodies to Perl ever since. The immense set of libraries now available through the Comprehensive Perl Archive Network (CPAN) allows easy interface of Perl code to many network protocols, databases, Web Services, and such. For example, to use PalmOS database simply add `use Palm::PDB;` anywhere in the script file. Similarly, add `use Net::LDAP;` or `use SOAP::Lite;` for LDAP database and SOAP Web Services respectively. Here `Palm`, `Net`, and `SOAP` are directories containing `PDB.pm`, `LDAP.pm`, and `Lite.pm` files.

This chapter introduces the Perl's class that supports the construction of Web Services, namely the module SOAP::Lite. This module supports the implementation of both clients and servers with a diverse set of protocols by using the Jabber (XML-based instant messaging system) and IBM's MQSeries reliable message queuing system. It also supports a number of extensions, including client submission of messages using SMTP and FTP, client support of cookies, and server support for POP3.

Introduction to SOAP::Lite

The SOAP::Lite collection had its version 0.1 released in August 2000, and has seen fairly steady releases since then. The version 0.52 was released in October 2001 and supports most of the SOAP 1.1 and SOAP 1.2 specifications, as well as the SOAP messages with attachments specification.

SOAP::Lite is one of the most sophisticated open source implementations of SOAP that supports the following important extensions:

- **Partial support for WSDL schema**
  WSDL is particularly important for Perl as compared with other languages, since Perl is a weakly-typed language, where scalar values are coerced at run time into whatever form seems appropriate for the present value and operation. We shall see an example of this later in the chapter.
- **UDDI supporting both inquiry and publishing**
  SOAP::Lite may thus be used to search for Web Services, or to update your data on a UDDI server.
- **Supports a wide range of transport protocols**
  SOAP::Lite also supports the transfer of messages using additional protocols including Jabber, FTP, SMTP, POP3, and even supports "very reliable messaging" using IBM MQSeries.

It wouldn't be expected to interoperate with clients and servers that are not specifically aware of the use of those transports, but if your security or latency requirements mandate using a different transport method, it provides the freedom to do so. For the list of classes included in the SOAP::Lite module, refer to Appendix G.

A significant drawback to SOAP, as compared to other RPC schemes like ONC/RPC and CORBA, is in the verbosity of XML messages. A SOAP message has a base size of about 500 bytes and grows from there. This has two notable overheads:

- The size of SOAP messages means that you are moving a fairly large amount of data across the network
- Each XML message body must be processed using an XML parser, which consumes both time and memory

In a system where a huge number of SOAP messages are processed, either of these may become significant limitations to system performance.

An obvious and relatively simple modification, already directly supported by `SOAP::Lite`, is for the data transport to compress messages using the common `zlib` compression library. This can compress SOAP-related messages to around a quarter of their original size. Unfortunately, this comes at the cost of increasing CPU usage, so if the CPU is the bottleneck, compression worsens the problem.

Another alternative for message types, for which WSDL is already available, would be to compile the WSDL to generate a pair of specialized parsers: one to accept arguments and generate a binary encoded message consisting of crucial signatures and serialized data, and another to read that binary message format. There already exists a mature technology exactly like this in the form of CORBA, where function arguments may be specified in a language called IDL, and then compiled into code that encodes/decodes arguments in a compact transmission form called IIOP.

The SOAP::Lite functionality:

- Supports SOAP 1.1 specification, and has initial support for SOAP 1.2
- Allows interoperability with a wide array of SOAP implementations
- Allows a COM interface on Win32
- Includes `XMLRPC::Lite`, a client and server implementation of XML-RPC

Data type:

- Supports transmission and receipt of SOAP faults including custom faults
- Supports transmission and receipt of arrays
- Supports the map data type
- Supports circular-linked lists and multiple references
- Supports `Base64` encoding
- Supports multipart/form-data MIME attachments using `MIME::Base64`
- Supports embedding of encoded XML entities
- Supports custom serialization and customization of header attributes

Protocols support:

- Includes a TCP server implementation using `HTTP::Daemon` and URI
- Includes a server implementation accepting requests from files or `stdin` and `stdout` using `IO::File`
- Provides CGI, daemon, `mod_perl`, and `Apache::Registry` server implementations
- Supports HTTPS protocol using `IO::Socket::SSL`
- Provides FTP client implementation using `Net::FTP` and `IO::File`
- Supports client message transmission using SMTP protocol with `MIME::Lite` and URI
- Supports POP3 server implementation using `Net::POP3`
- Provides compatiblity with CGI accelerators using `FCGI`
- Provides Apache `mod_soap` module allowing implementation of a SOAP server with a few lines in `.htaccess` or `.conf` using the `Apache` module
- Provides IBM MQSeries transport for both client and server
- Provides Jabber "instant messaging" transport for both client and server

Protocol variations:

- Provides transparent compression support for HTTP transport using `libzlib` and `Compress::Zlib`
- Provides proxy support
- Provides an option of a regexp-based XML parser, `XML::Parser::Lite`, which may run in places where `XML::Parser::Expat` is not available
- Supports Basic/Digest server authentication
- Supports M-POST and redirects in HTTP transport
- Parses single/multipart MIME attachments using `MIME::Parser`

Function binding:

- Supports WSDL schema, including a stub generator, `stubber.pl`, as well as run time access
- Supports dynamic and static binding of classes and methods
- Implements server-side support for objects by reference
- Provides `SOAPsh.pl` shell to run interactive SOAP sessions

UDDI supports:

- UDDI interface on client side
- UDDI publishing API

SOAP::Lite has a few limitations:

- Limited support for WSDL schema
- `XML::Parser::Lite` relies on Unicode support in Perl and doesn't do entity decoding
- Limited support for `mustUnderstand` and `Actor` attributes

Installation of SOAP::Lite

As is true for almost all things relating to Perl, "There's more than one way to do it", so it is for the installation of Perl. Packages have been constructed for a number of Linux distributions and BSD operating systems, thus offering the possibility to use the package management tools for your favorite distribution if you are using:

- RPM-based (RedHat Package Manager) Linux distribution
  There are RPM packages available. For example, Red Hat software makes available `perl-SOAP-Lite-0.50-1.i386.rpm` (http://ftp.interchange.redhat.com/perl/perl-SOAP-Lite-0.50-1.i386.rpm).
- Debian
  For Debian, the command apt-get install libsoap-lite-perl will download and install SOAP::Lite, assuming you have entries in `/etc/apt/sources.list` pointing to either the testing or unstable release (and the package should ultimately enter a stable release).
- BSD-related systems
  The package `p5-SOAP-Lite` is available at http://www.freshports.org/ and may also be included in the Ports tree for your favorite flavor of BSD.
- Microsoft Windows
  The package `ActivePerl` is available at http://downloads.activestate.com/ActivePerl/Windows/5.6/ and is also available for Linux and Solaris.

Assuming you have the `CPAN.pm` Perl module tool installed, you may install SOAP::Lite using the command `perl -MCPAN -e 'install SOAP::Lite'`. Alternatively, you might download it from http://www.soaplite.com/download/ or from CPAN (http://www.cpan.org/), pulling down a tar file such as `SOAP-Lite-latest.tgz`.

The installation steps are then:

- Extract the archive: `tar xfvz SOAP-Lite-latest.tgz`
- Enter the directory via (at the time of writing) `cd SOAP-Lite-0.55`

The command following this is:

```
perl Makefile.PL
```

This step allows you to choose which transport protocols are to be made available. A `Makefile.PL` session might look something like the following:

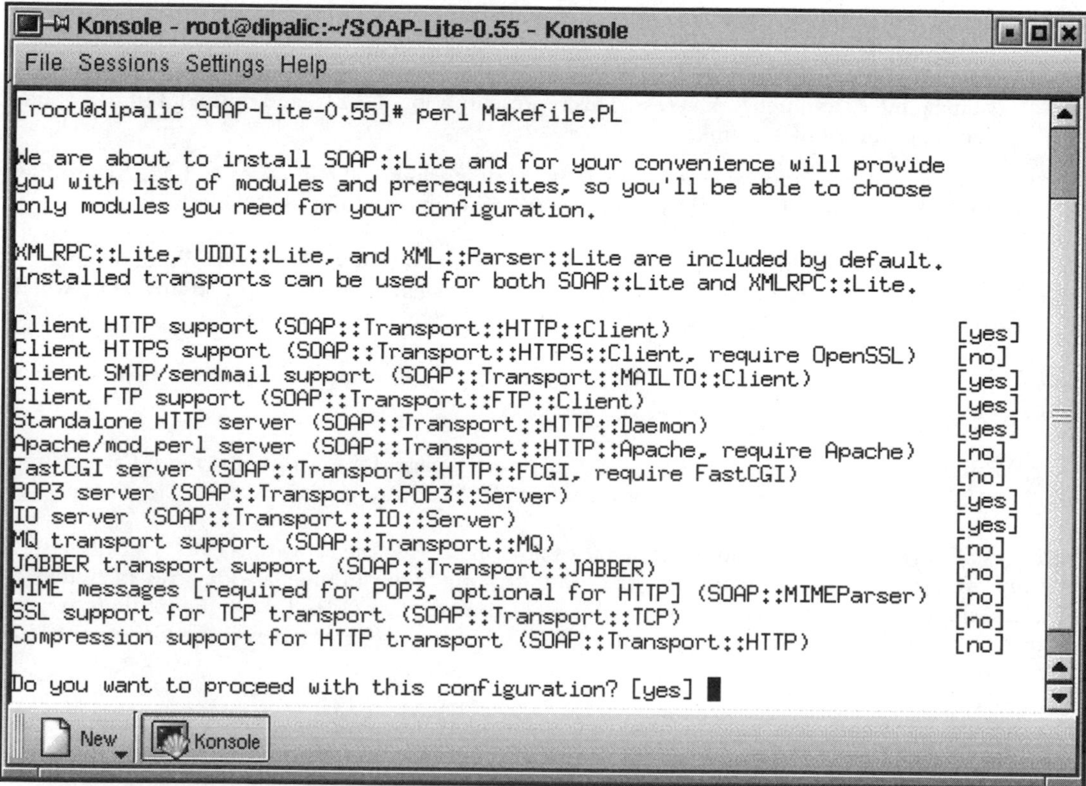

Konsole - root@dipalic:~/SOAP-Lite-0.55 - Konsole
File Sessions Settings Help
[root@dipalic SOAP-Lite-0.55]# perl Makefile.PL
We are about to install SOAP::Lite and for your convenience will provide
you with list of modules and prerequisites, so you'll be able to choose
only modules you need for your configuration.
XMLRPC::Lite, UDDI::Lite, and XML::Parser::Lite are included by default.
Installed transports can be used for both SOAP::Lite and XMLRPC::Lite.
Client HTTP support (SOAP::Transport::HTTP::Client) [yes]
Client HTTPS support (SOAP::Transport::HTTPS::Client, require OpenSSL) [no]
Client SMTP/sendmail support (SOAP::Transport::MAILTO::Client) [yes]
Client FTP support (SOAP::Transport::FTP::Client) [yes]
Standalone HTTP server (SOAP::Transport::HTTP::Daemon) [yes]
Apache/mod_perl server (SOAP::Transport::HTTP::Apache, require Apache) [no]
FastCGI server (SOAP::Transport::HTTP::FCGI, require FastCGI) [no]
POP3 server (SOAP::Transport::POP3::Server) [yes]
IO server (SOAP::Transport::IO::Server) [yes]
MQ transport support (SOAP::Transport::MQ) [no]
JABBER transport support (SOAP::Transport::JABBER) [no]
MIME messages [required for POP3, optional for HTTP] (SOAP::MIMEParser) [no]
SSL support for TCP transport (SOAP::Transport::TCP) [no]
Compression support for HTTP transport (SOAP::Transport::HTTP) [no]
Do you want to proceed with this configuration? [yes]
New
Konsole

If the defaults seem acceptable, it would be reasonable to proceed with the configuration by answering yes to the question shown above in the screenshot. Unfortunately, not all of the prerequisite Perl modules were installed here, as some relating to SSL are missing. The `Makefile.PL` script gives warnings about missing modules. If you wish to add in support for Jabber, POP3, SSL, and `Compress::Zlib`, answer `no` to the question displayed in the screenshot, and `Makefile.PL` will proceed to a questionnaire to ask which transport options to change.

The parenthesized descriptions indicate the Perl classes that the installation process proposes to set up. The code for the `SOAP::Transport::HTTP::Client` module is likely to be installed in `/usr/share/perl5/SOAP/Transport/HTTP.pm`. The Perl `.pm` modules supporting other protocols fall into the same directory, in files such as `LOCAL.pm`, `MAILTO.pm`, `MQ.pm`, `POP3.pm`, and `TCP.pm`. Many of the modules and their files will never need to be explicitly referenced in your code as they are automatically drawn in when needed. For example, HTTPS support (including a number of related modules outside of SOAP::Lite) is drawn in automatically by the client when the `proxy()` method is invoked on a URL starting with `https://`.

Perl Module Configuration

Traditionally, Perl components have the most sophisticated installation schemes amongst other tools available. The problems requiring this sophistication have been twofold:

- Perl provides fairly direct access to operating system services including file access, process management, and network access. This represents a lot of APIs, and thus a lot of `#include` files and library files to link.
- Perl runs on a very diverse set of operating systems, hence the libraries and `#include` files reside in a lot of different places and provide different capabilities.

Perl runs on just about anything that looks reasonably similar to Unix, along with Windows and MacOS. In addition, it runs on various mainframe systems, such as OS/390 and Stratus VOS, which most definitely do not look like Unix.

Since there are many different flavors of Unix, it cannot quite be treated as a uniform platform, and hence you get a great deal of configuration complexity.

Larry Wall, the creator of Perl, created `metaconfig` to manage these variations, and it has inspired a number of descendants, the best known of which is most likely `autoconf`.

Perl's install is rather large spreading its tentacles not only across the array of scripts typically installed in `/usr/share/perl5` or `/usr/lib/perl5` but, drawing in at run time, a wide array of system libraries, since it uses services in many libraries in `/lib` and `/usr/lib`. Due to the resultant large disk footprint, it is challenging to get Perl into devices with limited storage such as embedded systems and handheld computers.

The benefit is that once you have the base Perl components installed, the process of installing additional components like SOAP::Lite becomes relatively straightforward, and there is little need to manually work with the configuration files. You will not need to modify the configuration to indicate where files are to be installed, as has been a longstanding Unix tradition, because the Perl environment already has paths set up that are more than likely to be satisfactory.

Each transport protocol has some dependencies on other Perl modules, which obviously need to be installed for your SOAP::Lite installation to work properly. If some are not installed, the configuration process reports errors indicating the missing modules, and gives suggestions to search for those particular modules at CPAN. This might lead to a need for additional runs of `perl -MCPAN -e install Missing::Module` to load and install additional modules, such as `MailTools`. For SOAP::Lite as well as any other modules that prove necessary, the installation procedure proceeds thus:

- `make`
  This step builds the server
- `make test`
  This step is arguably not necessary, but it is certainly a good idea to check that the module works
- `make install`
  This final command will have to be run as the root user to install files into `/usr/lib/perl5` or `/usr/share/perl5`
- `perl -v`
  This step is just a check and will show the version and copyrights of the Perl installed
- `perl -V`
  This step (note the V in uppercase) will display all the configuration information like compilers, operating system, and `@INC`

> **SOAP::Lite supports a large number of transport protocols; if you require one (for example, Jabber or SSL) that is not included in the packaging of SOAP::Lite, you could install it directly from the source distribution.**

A more sophisticated approach would be to build your own custom RPM or dpkg package or customize a BSD Port. Package construction is generally a fairly involved process, and the approach might sound a little extreme at first glance, but if you need to support running SOAP clients on a large number of hosts, automating the installation of the customized SOAP software will be an important part of keeping the system manageable.

It is easier to download (at the time of writing) http://soap.ourhost.com/packages/perl-lite_1.75_i386.rpm and install it using `rpm -i perl-lite_1.75_i386.rpm` than to set up installation instructions that require widespread installation of development tools and customize the installation to include the transport protocols that are required.

There is considerable documentation and software freely available on how to construct packages for various Unix-like systems. Unfortunately, the tools typically used to create Windows packages such as InstallShield are not available in open source form, as having 'package-oriented' installation is more important to system administrators on Windows than on Linux. A few reference guides are:

- Constructing Debian Packages: http://www.debian.org/doc/maint-guide/
- Constructing BSD Ports:
  http://www.freebsd.org/doc/en_US.ISO8859-1/books/porters-handbook/index.html
- Constructing RPMs: http://www.rpm.org/

SOAP::Lite Client Usage

Let us now look at the client usage of SOAP::Lite with the help of an example.

Accessing Stock Prices Using a Simple WSDL-Based Call

We will start with a simple example that accesses time-delayed US stock prices via a web server hosted at http://www.xmethods.net/. It searches for stock prices for 7 companies traded on US NYSE and NASDAQ stock exchanges, and displays a formatted list of security symbols and prices:

```
#!/usr/bin/perl -w
use SOAP::Lite;
my $wsdl = 'http://www.xmethods.net/sd/StockQuoteService.wsdl';
print "Stock    Price\n";
print "================\n";
foreach $el (sort ("RHAT", "IBM", "MSFT", "AMR", "LNUX", "NT", "TSG")) {
  my $result =
    SOAP::Lite
      -> service($wsdl)
        -> getQuote($el);
  printf ("%6s %8.3f\n" , $el, $result);
}
```

Let's now dissect the SOAP::Lite call:

- To use the SOAP::Lite class functions, the statement starts with a reference to SOAP::Lite.
- The Web Service must be referenced; when a WSDL reference is available, it may be used via the `service()` method, as shown in the code above. This method requests the WSDL document at the specified URL, thus providing information on the location of the Web Service and the set of methods provided by the service. If the WSDL document has been downloaded to a local location, the URL might change to something like file:///tmp/local-WSDL/StockQuoteService.wsdl.
- Finally, a specific Web Service method must be referenced. The only one supported by the `StockQuoteService` is `getQuote()`.When this method is requested, SOAP::Lite transforms it into a SOAP method call using the access information drawn by `service()` from the WSDL document.
- Once the call has been executed, the value is placed in the Perl scalar variable `$result`.

To run this, the script sourcecode should be entered into a file such as `perl-stocks-wsdl.pl`, and then the script may be executed using a shell command like `perl perl-stocks-wsdl.pl`. The code in this chapter can also be downloaded from the code bundle on our web site http://www.wrox.com/.

Notice the initial `-w` option in the first line of the script where `w` is for "warning"; the Perl interpreter will, as a result, generate somewhat more verbose warning messages if it notices dubious code constructs such as variables whose values are never used or used before being set. This is similar to the GCC–`wall` option, or the traditional C tool, `lint`.

The output of the above code shall look like:

```
Stock    Price
================
   AMR   24.580
   IBM   99.250
  LNUX    1.480
  MSFT   56.330
    NT    3.930
  RHAT    5.050
   TSG   45.500
```

Notice that it takes a fair amount of time to run this script. On a system with a reasonably quick DSL (Digital Subscriber Line ~ 1.5Mbps) connection, it takes around 9 seconds to pull in the 7 stock prices and while there is a fair bit of latency involved, it does keep the Internet connection fairly busy. Increasing the number of securities would certainly make it run longer.

This implies that when you use SOAP to provide services across the Internet, it is important to design the APIs carefully so that the application does not have performance bottlenecks designed into it.

We could alternatively tie the WSDL to the initialization of SOAP::Lite, which loads the WSDL earlier, tying the methods it finds to the Perl `main` namespace, allowing us to simply run `getQuote()` calls which would look like the code shown below. This approach will lead to significantly shorter and more readable code, particularly if a whole lot of the SOAP methods used in a particular Perl script are associated with one WSDL instance:

```
#!/usr/bin/perl -w
use SOAP::Lite service => "http://www.xmethods.net/sd/StockQuoteService.wsdl";
print "Stock    Price\n";
print "================\n";
foreach $el (sort ("RHAT", "IBM", "MSFT", "AMR", "LNUX", "NT", "TSG")) {
  my $result = getQuote($el);
  printf ("%6s %8.3f\n" , $el, $result);
}
```

This variation of the `service()` method draws in all the methods specified in the WSDL document, putting them into the Perl `main` namespace, and associates them with the server information specified in the WSDL document. As a result, not only is the code shorter, but also it runs faster since it is not repeatedly requesting the WSDL document.

The same SOAP method is also accessible by specifying the proxy location and the URI. Instead of specifying the `service()`, this version specifies `proxy()` and `uri()`:

```
#!/usr/bin/perl -w
use SOAP::Lite;
my $soap = SOAP::Lite
  -> proxy("http://services.xmethods.com:80/soap")
  -> uri("urn:xmethods-delayed-quotes");

print "Stock    Price\n";
print "================\n";
foreach $el (sort ("RHAT", "IBM", "MSFT", "AMR", "LNUX", "NT", "TSG")) {
  printf ("%6s %8.3f\n" , $el, $soap->getQuote($el)->result);
}
```

In many situations with SOAP::Lite, the order of methods in the Perl statement is not significant, particularly with those methods that set up configuration information. You may safely reorder the `uri()` and the `proxy()` as shown below without affecting the way the SOAP message is submitted:

```
my $soap = SOAP::Lite
  -> uri("urn:xmethods-delayed-quotes")
  -> proxy("http://services.xmethods.com/soap");
```

These methods are essentially orthogonal to one another, the `uri()` call indicating the namespace in which the method lies, while the `proxy()` call indicates the network address. The meaning of the URI depends on how the server interprets it, which will vary from language to language. With SOAP::Lite, the `xmethods-delayed-quotes` portion would indicate the Perl namespace in which the SOAP methods reside. The http://www.xmethods.com/ site implements methods in Java, so the URI indicates how the implementers have organized their services.

If you are behind a proxy firewall there are different ways to tell the client to take this into account. It could be done programmatically which we shall see later in the code. If you wish, you could set a global environment variable `HTTP_proxy` and all SOAP::Lite functions will understand how to get around the proxy server. The environment variable `HTTP_proxy` is specified like: `HTTP_proxy=http://url.of.proxy/`. In case the proxy server has authentication in place, you may specify `HTTP_proxy_user` and `HTTP_proxy_pass` environment variables for user and password and SOAP::Lite should know how to handle it properly.

Accessing Book Prices Using SOAP::Lite

The script `Books.pl` demonstrates how to look up pricing information about books through a SOAP service provided by bookseller Barnes and Noble:

```
#!/usr/bin/perl -w
use SOAP::Lite;
use strict;
my ($uri, $proxy) = ("urn:xmethods-BNPriceCheck",
    "http://services.xmethods.net/soap/servlet/rpcrouter");
my $squidproxy = ['http' => "http://localhost:3128"];
my $soap = SOAP::Lite -> proxy($proxy, proxy => $squidproxy)
                      -> uri($uri);

my %ISBNS = ( '0596000278' => 'Programming Perl',
              '0716715872' => 'Linear Programming',
              '1861003013' => 'Professional Linux Programming',
              '0131103628' => 'The C Programming Language',
              '1555581234' => 'The Unix Philosophy',
              '1568842031' => 'The Unix-Haters Handbook',
              '0201379279' => 'Advanced CORBA Programming with C++'
            );

&header;
foreach my $isbn (sort (keys(%ISBNS))) {
  my $code = $isbn;
  my $title = $ISBNS{$isbn};
  display_book($title, $soap->getPrice($code)->result);
}
&footer;
&header;
foreach my $isbn (sort (keys(%ISBNS))) {
  my $code = SOAP::Data->type(string => $isbn);
  my $title = $ISBNS{$isbn};
  display_book ($title, $soap->getPrice($code)->result);
}
&footer;
```

```
sub display_book {
  my ($title, $price) = @_;
  printf ("%35s  %8.2f\n", $title, $price);
}
sub header {
  print "-----------------------------------------------\n";
  print "      Book                                 Price\n";
  print "-----------------------------------------------\n";
}

sub footer {
  print "-----------------------------------------------\n\n";
}
```

While there is a `getPrice(ISBN)` method, there is no `getTitle(ISBN)`, nor is there any method (at least not yet) to allow searching for ISBNs based on author or title, which is why the program has to maintain its own little database of ISBN and title information.

There are three common methods for finding additional SOAP methods:

- If the organization publishing the Web Service has registered it in a UDDI registry, it could be found using a UDDI search, discussed later in the chapter
- If the service is being provided through a WSDL document, the WSDL document could be examined to find additional methods
- Also, methods are found through more ad-hoc forms of communication, like looking at public web sites that collect lists of SOAP services such as http://www.xmethods.com/ or providing greater authority by direct contact with Web Service providers to determine what methods are available

It is possible to submit HTTP requests to bookseller web sites to request web pages based on the ISBN, but unfortunately that provides a plain HTML web page, which would then have to be parsed to extract bibliographic information. This approach represents a throwback to the days before the existence of SOAP, completely vulnerable to any changes that the website maker might make to web page formats.

With the rapid evolution of SOAP standards and the changes in availability of layered services such as UDDI and WSDL, it is difficult to guarantee that services will continue to remain available. The popular 'Google' search engine has recently released WSDL and other tools to allow conducting web searches using SOAP, as documented at http://www.google.com/apis/. This presently represents a beta service for personal use, and there are no ongoing guarantees of its permanent availability. The same is true for any such service; if there is no formal contract guaranteeing continued service, there is likely to be no recourse if service ceases.

One of the UDDI examples discussed later in the chapter demonstrates how to look up the `getPrice()` method using UDDI, which would be useful in finding the new location of a Web Service should the service provider change names, as often happens as a result of corporate acquisitions. If Barnes and Noble joined with another publisher, there is some hope that UDDI registries would be updated to reflect the new location of `getPrice()`.

Use of Proxy Servers

This example makes further use of the `proxy()` functionality, referring requests through a proxy server. On some networks, traffic needs to pass through a firewall to get out to the public Internet. On the network in which this was run, there was a host with (as one of its aliases) the name **cache**, running the Squid caching proxy server on its default port 3128:

```
my $squidproxy = ['http' => "http://cache:3128"];
my $soap = SOAP::Lite -> proxy($proxy, proxy => $squidproxy)
                      -> uri($uri);
```

If you need to run this in an environment where there is no proxy server, you may simply omit the `proxy => $squidproxy` clause.

If you haven't fixed a proxy server at the specified location, you will get a message:

```
500 Can't connect to cache:3128 (Timeout) at Books.pl line 23
```

There is no particularly useful way to distinguish this from other error messages but it may be obtained by modifying the proxy settings:

- `404 Not Found at Books.pl line 23`
  This occurs if the URL is modified to reference an invalid location at a legitimate web site
- `503 Service Unavailable at Books.pl line 23`
  This occurs if an invalid Web Service server is referenced, for example, www.nosuchaddress.com

Note that the loop is executed twice: once with the ISBN being passed as a raw value, and again with it being transformed into a `SOAP::Data` reference. This is provided to demonstrate a common issue encountered when using SOAP services using Perl. Notice that all of the first set of entries in the output reports back prices of 0.00, and you will likely see warnings similar to:

```
Use of uninitialized value in printf at Books.pl line 36.
```

This demonstrates one difficulty commonly encountered with Perl-based SOAP code, that Perl has a very weak typing system. The problem that occurs with `getPrice()` calls on just straight ISBN numbers is that Perl recognizes them as integers, and passes them as such to the SOAP server, which expects to receive a string. Since they consist of decimal digits, they may appear to be numbers but are intended to indicate identity and are not to be treated as the mathematical constructs that are manipulated using addition, subtraction, and other such operators.

As a rule, Perl code should use references to `SOAP::Data` objects to make the typing manifest rather than implicit, thereby eliminating this problem.

In the second loop, the ISBNs are explicitly presented to `getPrice()` with the SOAP string type, which allows the client to successfully communicate them to the server and receive back rather more useful price information.

At the time of writing, the results (interspersed with error messages to STDERR) looked something like the following:

```
----------------------------------------------
        Book                                Price
----------------------------------------------
           The C Programming Language       0.00
Advanced CORBA Programming with C++         0.00
                     Programming Perl       0.00
                   Linear Programming       0.00
                  The Unix Philosophy       0.00
             The Unix-Haters Handbook       0.00
        Professional Linux Programming      0.00
----------------------------------------------

----------------------------------------------
        Book                                Price
----------------------------------------------
           The C Programming Language      40.00
Advanced CORBA Programming with C++        57.95
                     Programming Perl      49.95
                   Linear Programming      42.95
                  The Unix Philosophy      29.99
             The Unix-Haters Handbook      -1.00
        Professional Linux Programming     59.99
----------------------------------------------
```

Using SMTP as the Transport Method

An alternative transport mechanism is to use SMTP to send messages. Here, messages are submitted asynchronously to an SMTP server such as sendmail, Postfix, or qmail to forward via some series of mail servers in the process. It might be thought of as a "poor man's alternative to MQSeries". It is very much analogous to the CORBA one-way operation.

Note in the diagram overleaf that the process ends with the message sitting in a mail queue at a remote server. It does not display delivery to the remote SOAP server; there is quite a critical disconnection in the process as soon as the message is passed on to the local SMTP server:

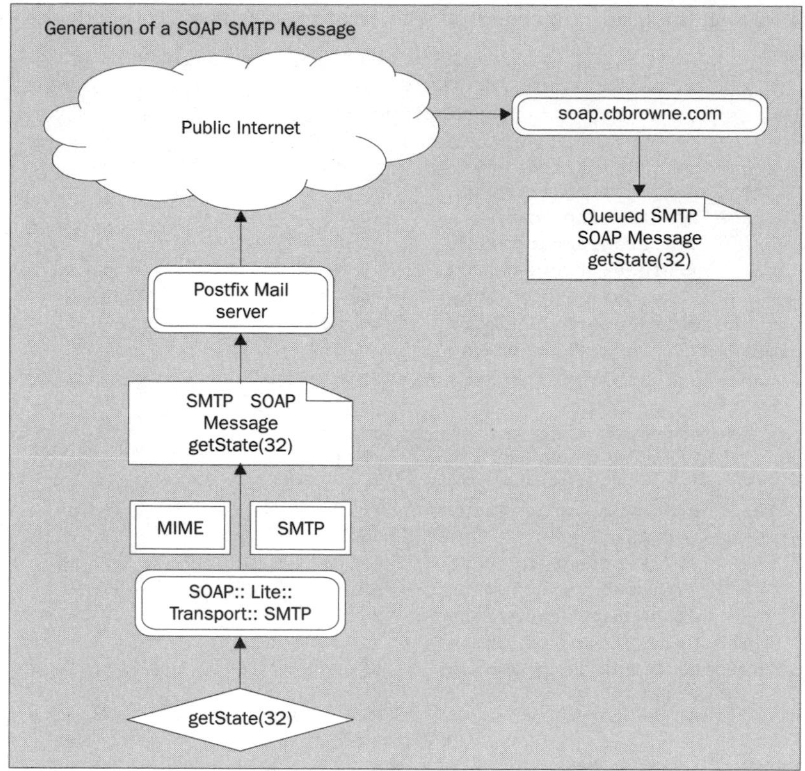

Disadvantages of SMTP Over HTTP

SMTP has several disadvantages, as compared to HTTP. Let us look at them in detail.

Standards

There is no widely used standard for this SOAP transport, so its use is likely to be limited to SOAP::Lite. Messages consist simply of the SOAP-XML message encoded using MIME, and since all of the components involve widely used protocols and formats, this is certainly not a design demonstrating any particular disregard for portability. Thus, all that SOAP::Lite directly implements in this regard is the client side of the transaction. Nothing prevents using SOAP::Lite or some other SOAP implementation such as ZSI (Zolera SOAP Infrastructure) to process the messages, but whatever that process would be, it would need to be integrated together manually.

A proposal for ebXML Message Service Specification has been presented to the OASIS ebXML messaging committee; see http://www.oasis-open.org/committees/ebxml-msg/.

There is no security implementation available to correspond to the use of SSL with HTTPS and to ensure that messages are not read or modified by intruders along the way. There are efforts underway to try and address security of SOAP messages, but nothing has reached the point of common implementation.

Function Return Values

There is no ability for any values to be returned by the SOAP method. The message gets bundled into an e-mail message, and is passed on to the SMTP server, which stores it in a file before forwarding it. Nothing can be returned. The payload is quite properly described as a message, and SOAP behaves as a messaging system rather than as an RPC system. This precisely parallels CORBA one-way methods, which are forbidden to return a result.

Configuration of SMTP SOAP

Configuring the server side to receive SMTP-SOAP requests requires rather a lot of configuration. First, ensuring there is a suitable user account to receive mail, and second, if there are to be multiple mail queues, then this could be handled by setting up a Unix user ID and one or more Perl scripts for each queue.

An alternative that would not require such a proliferation of user IDs would be to use a POP3 server (such as Cyrus pop3d or Solid pop3d or GNU Mailutils pop3d) and configuring a POP3 account for each SOAP message queue. A POP3 client like Fetchmail may be used to process each named mail queue, or the `SOAP::Transport::POP3` module may be used to process input on a POP3 account. Either way, IDs must be set up on a mail server for each mail queue.

The third step would be to configure some processor to evaluate each message. For example, a mail filter might be attached using Procmail, thus:

```
:0:
* ^Subject: SOAP Message
|/usr/bin/metamail | /usr/local/SOAP/message-processor
```

If the `SOAP::Transport::POP3` module is in use, there would be a daemon configured to periodically query the POP3 server where mail resides.

Returning results requires either SOAP methods to be implemented to put results in a predetermined location that may be accessed later, or that the arguments to SMTP SOAP methods include some sort of non-SOAP address to which results might be addressed. An example of the latter would be for one of the SOAP arguments to be a return e-mail address to which a message might be returned, sending a SOAP-over-SMTP message back to the client. Unfortunately, this approach means that clients need to implement and configure their own SOAP-over-SMTP servers, which doubles the reliability and complexity issues.

Reliability of Transport

Reliability of the transport is difficult to evaluate. This is most likely the issue that would disqualify SMTP as an option. The problem is that SMTP provides no way to guarantee or verify message delivery. The similarity with CORBA one-way continues; these operations are deprecated in part because it is legitimately argued as "correctly implemented" by simply throwing the requests away. That would be an unfriendly treatment of such messages, just as it would be for SMTP-SOAP messages.

The problem demonstrated for both protocols is that there is no conceivable way to either ensure or validate message delivery. For example, if a message sits in a queue on a laptop for five days and it is never delivered, then Sendmail delivers a warning to a disused root account. Suppose the warning gets ignored, then there is no obvious mechanism to make either the client or the server aware of this.

Managing this would be problematic even if all the components were under local control; if e-mail is travelling through the public Internet, there is no possibility of controlling the quality of message delivery. The sort of messages that would queue up in this manner would be like accounting transactions which, on one hand, don't need to be processed right away, but on the other hand, represent important data that cannot be lost. SMTP systems have not been designed as transactional systems. In effect, if message delivery is important, SMTP should only be used if the SMTP servers involved are very closely managed, and are known to be working reliably.

Timing of Message Delivery

The timing of message delivery is also unpredictable. There is no "a priori" reason to expect messages to be delivered with any specific timing or in any particular order, as their flow to the destination depends on combination of the policies of each mail server along the way. It might take only a few seconds for messages to reach the destination. It is more reasonable to expect delivery to take a minimum of several minutes. It is unsafe, however, to assume such short times (for example, on a disconnected laptop, messages could stay queued for hours or even days).

These messages may wait in queue for a number of reasons:

- A busy server anywhere in the chain may build up a queue of messages waiting to be passed on, or otherwise processed.
- There may be no connection available between source and destination, blocking delivery attempts. This will happen, for example, if messages are queued from a laptop that is not connected to the Internet.
- Latency times may leave messages waiting in queues.

If mail delivery cannot be accomplished immediately, it is common for SMTP servers to leave messages queued for a while before retrying. This may happen several times, on multiple mail servers, if the message must go across the open Internet to reach the destination server.

It is typical for the Fetchmail POP3 client to wait between polls, which mean that if the final step is for SOAP messages to be pulled off a POP3 server, it might introduce a 5-minute wait. Alternatively, a SOAP server might consciously choose to defer processing much longer than that.

Consider a web-based sales and distribution application using SOAP to submit accounting transactions to be added to the General Ledger. If the accounting staff works 9am to 5pm in Chicago, it would not be unreasonable for General Ledger transactions submitted outside those hours to be held in a queue overnight to be applied to the General Ledger at 8am CST, a little before the accounting staff comes in to work.

Advantages of SMTP

Despite these significant caveats, there are merits to the idea of using SMTP as the message transport. It decouples client from server. A user may submit an SMTP-SOAP message while completely disconnected from the server to process the message. For example, a salesman might fill in order information on the laptop while out at a customer site, and set up requests for sales. The sales transaction could be submitted as a SMTP-SOAP message, and stay queued on the salesman's computer until a link is made to update his e-mail, at which point queued SOAP messages could flow on to their targets.

Notice in the diagram below that SOAP messages may be submitted by the salesman at any time, and will be held by the SMTP server in its own queue, waiting to be transmitted to the recipient POP3 server back at the main office. The mail queue might also include traffic not related to SOAP. Notice also from the directions of the arrows that there is no flow of data back from the Sales Management systems; at least no flow involving SOAP messages:

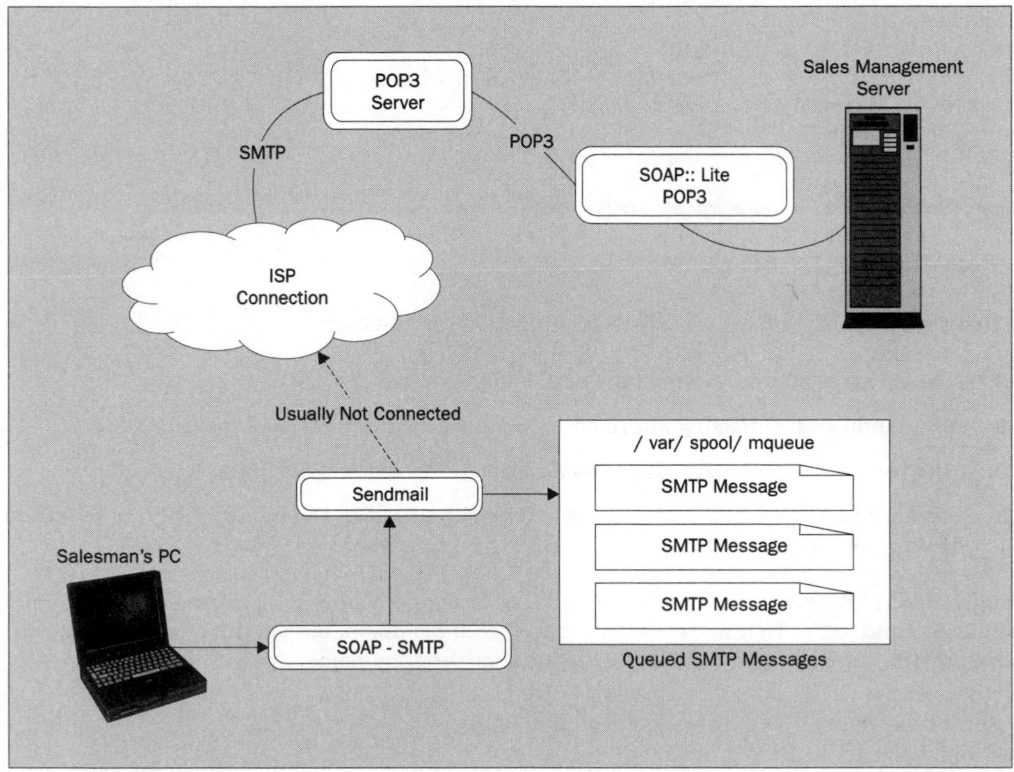

On the server, it may also allow messages to be processed in an asynchronous manner. For example, by having the messages in a single POP3 mail queue, the server may be assured that it will process messages serially, avoiding locking and other concurrency complications associated with supporting multiple threads of execution.

Using the SOAP::Transport::SMTP Class

The following script demonstrates the use of the `SOAP::Transport::SMTP` class:

```
print "First: lots of parms\n";
SOAP::Lite
  -> uri($uri)
  -> proxy("mailto:$to\@$domain", From => "$from\@$domain",
           Subject => "$subject - lots of parms",
           sendmail => $sendbin)
  -> getStateName(12);
```

The scripts start by loading in the needed classes, and by setting up various variables indicating routing information:

```
#!/usr/bin/perl
use SOAP::Lite;
my ($from, $to) = ("tester", "roosta");
my $domain = "127.0.0.1";
my ($uri, $subject, $sendbin) =
   ('http://www.soaplite.com/My/Examples',
    "SOAP message",
    "/usr/lib/sendmail");
my $smtp = 'chvatal';

my ($proxyinfo) = assemble($from, $to, $domain);

print "Proxy: $proxyinfo\n";
```

The first request demonstrates the full array of `proxy()` arguments:

- The initial argument passes in the destination as a `mailto` URL
- `From` indicates addressing information to be attached to the e-mail message header
- `Subject` indicates what subject should be attached to the e-mail message header
- `Sendmail` indicates that messages will be submitted to the binary program specified in this argument

Virtually all SMTP servers running on Unix-like systems allow submitting messages using the program `/usr/lib/sendmail`. That name was introduced with Sendmail, but alternatives such as qmail and Postfix provide equivalent functionality with the same program name:

```
print "Second: $proxyinfo, sendmail\n";
SOAP::Lite
   -> uri($uri)
   -> proxy($proxyinfo,
            sendmail => $sendbin)
   -> getStateName(12);
```

The second call uses `$proxyinfo`, which can merge `From` and `Subject` into a single argument, like:

```
mailto:toaddr@todomain.org?From=from@fromdomain.org#&38;Subject=A%20Subject
```

A careless analysis might suggest that using this string representation might be a bit more efficient as it submits two rather than four arguments to `proxy()`. In fact, the `SOAP::Transport::MAILTO` function `send_receive()` pulls the arguments apart again. There seems to be little value in assembling this data format manually when using named parameters makes the code much clearer and eliminates accidental format errors on the part of the programmer. The third call uses a socket-based SMTP connection to the specified server. This allows submitting messages to a remote SMTP server rather than trying to route messages via a local `/usr/lib/sendmail`:

```
print "Next: $proxyinfo, smtp via $smtp\n";
SOAP::Lite
  -> uri($uri)
  -> proxy("mailto:$to\@$domain", From => "$from\@$domain",
           Subject => "$subject - using SMTP",
           smtp => $smtp)
  -> getStateName(12);
```

The final attempt to send a message will fail, as it specifies neither `smtp` nor `sendmail`, with the result that the system does not know which method to use to submit the message:

```
print "Next: $proxyinfo, nothing more - fails due to no smtp or sendmail parm\n";
SOAP::Lite
  -> uri($uri)
  -> proxy($proxyinfo,
           Subject => "$subject - using nothing")
  -> getStateName(12);
```

Finally, the function `assemble()` provides a wrapper to build a complex `mailto` URL, escaping space characters:

```
 sub assemble {
  my ($from, $to, $domain, $subject) = @_;
  $subject =~ s/ /\%20/g;   # Can't have spaces in the proxy
  return "mailto:$to\@$domain?From=$from\@$domain&Subject=";
}
```

A resulting message, in raw form, is not really illuminating, as it is encoded using the `base64` type:


```
Return-Path: <root@sample.org>
Content-Disposition: inline
Content-Transfer-Encoding: base64
Content-Type: text/xml
MIME-Version: 1.0
Date: Thu, 28 Mar 2002 18:55:31 UT
To: sample@sample.org
From: tester@sample.org
Subject: >SOAP message
X-Mailer: SOAP::Lite/Perl/0.52
Soapaction: "http://www.soaplite.com/My/Examples#getStateName"
Message-Id: <20020328185531.A0D83355AB@sample.org>

PD94bWwgdmVyc2lvbj0iMS4wIiBlbmNvZGluZz0iVVRGLTgiPz48U09BUC1FTlY6RW52ZWxvcGUg
eG1sbnM6U09BUC1FTkM9Imh0dHA6Ly9zY2hlbWFzLnhtbHNvYXAub3JnL3NvYXAvZW5jb2Rpbmcv
IiBTT0FQLUVOVjplbmNvZGluZ1N0eWxlPSJodHRwOi8vc2NoZW1hcy54bWxzb2FwLm9yZy9zb2Fw
L2VuY29kaW5nLyIgeG1sbnM6U09BUC1FTlY9Imh0dHA6Ly9zY2hlbWFzLnhtbHNvYXAub3JnL3Nv
YXAvZW52ZWxvcGUvIiB4bWxuczp4c2k9Imh0dHA6Ly93d3cudzMub3JnLzE5OTkvWE1MU2NoZW1h
LWluc3RhbmNlIiB4bWxuczp4c2Q9Imh0dHA6Ly93d3cudzMub3JnLzE5OTkvWE1MU2NoZW1hIj48
U09BUC1FTlY6Qm9keT48bmFtZXNwMTpnZXRTdGF0ZU5hbWUgeG1sbnM6bmFtZXNwMT0iaHR0cDov
L3d3dy5zb2FwbGl0ZS5jb20vTXkvRXhhbXBsZXMiPjxjLWdlbnN5bTMgeHNpOnR5cGU9InhzZDpp
bnQiPjEyPC9jLWdlbnN5bTM+PC9uYW1lc3AxOmdldFN0YXRlTmFtZT48L1NPQVAtRU5WOkJvZHk+
PC9TT0FQLUVOVjpFbnZlbG9wZT4=
```

When MIME is decoded using `metamail`, the XML message emerges like:

```
Date: Thu, 28 Mar 2002 18:55:31 UT
To: sample@sample.org
From: tester@sample.org
Subject: >SOAP message

<?xml version="1.0" encoding="UTF-8"?><SOAP-ENV:Envelope xmlns:SOAP-
ENC="http://schemas.xmlsoap.org/soap/encoding/" SOAP-
ENV:encodingStyle="http://schemas.xmlsoap.org/soap/encoding/" xmlns:SOAP-
ENV="http://schemas.xmlsoap.org/soap/envelope/"
xmlns:xsi="http://www.w3.org/1999/XMLSchema-instance"
xmlns:xsd="http://www.w3.org/1999/XMLSchema"><SOAP-ENV:Body><namesp1:getStateName
xmlns:namesp1="http://www.soaplite.com/My/Examples"><c-gensym3
xsi:type="xsd:int">12</c-gensym3></namesp1:getStateName></SOAP-ENV:Body></SOAP-
ENV:Envelope>
```

It is then necessary to have a POP3 server to access this. Note that the client side of the process never appears in the diagram. While some address information is contained in the e-mail "envelope", there is no actual connection between the server and the client:

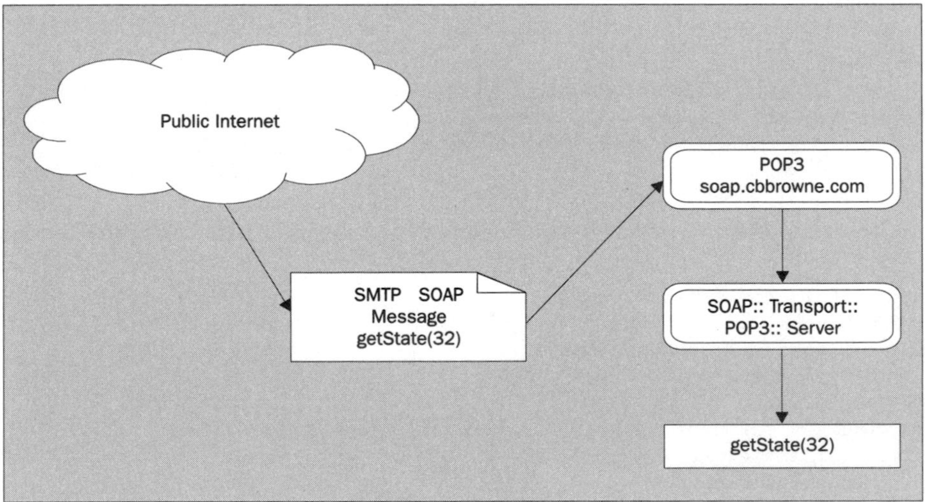

The script begins by loading in the `SOAP::Transport::POP3`, and setting up the authentication information required to connect to the POP3 server. Instead of instantiating an HTTP daemon, it instantiates a `SOAP::Transport::POP3::Server`, connecting to the specified POP3 server and allowing dispatch of the SOAP method `getStateName()`:

```
#!/usr/bin/perl
use SOAP::Transport::POP3;
my $popserver = "soap.cbbrowne.com";
my $id = "soapsamp\@soap.cbbrowne.com";
my $password = "tooeasytoguess";
my $server = SOAP::Transport::POP3::Server
  -> new("pop://$popserver")
  -> dispatch_to ( qw(getStateName) );
```

In this case, the server must authenticate itself for the connection to the POP3 server using the `login()` method. This method could also have been tied to the initialization by separating them; this makes it possible for the server to detect an authentication failure:

```
$server->login($id => $password)
  or die "Authentication failed when connecting as $id to $popserver\n";
```

This is actually the "meat" of the server. This loop invokes `$server->handle` to process the contents of the POP3 queue, sleeps 20 seconds, and repeats this indefinitely:

```
  do {
  print "Walking through messages!\n";
  print `date`;
  $server->handle;
} while sleep 20;
```

Finally, `getStateName()` provides a method to process the input. The function logs what was passed in; that is about the most useful action available for this particular method. There is no return value, and it would not be meaningful to return a fault, as there is no way to pass anything back to the client:

```
  sub getStateName {
  my ($arg) = @_[1];
  print "getStateName: Got $arg\n";
  print `date`;
  open (OUT, ">>/tmp/states.log");
  print OUT time(), $arg, "\n";
  close OUT;
}
```

The only way to potentially pass something back would be for one of the method parameters to provide some sort of "callback" location indicating where this server function might send back an e-mail or perhaps behave as a SOAP client, submitting a request to another SOAP server.

The SMTP transport is an interesting one. Unfortunately, the difficulties associated with establishing verifiable levels of reliability make it a poor choice for the sort of deferred transaction processing for which it might seem most attractive. The lack of implementations of this protocol in conjunction with other SOAP implementations would also somewhat discourage its use if there might be a need to implement clients and servers in other languages.

The reliability issues might be resolved by using a system like IBM MQSeries that provides reliable message queuing, or other similar systems, such as Microsoft MSMQ or SunSoft JMS. SOAP::Lite includes modules to support MQSeries, making its use a plausible proposition. The lack of open source implementations of these systems renders further discussion out of the scope of this book.

Using FTP as a Transport Protocol

The FTP protocol has been in use for many years for file transfer. The SOAP::Lite usage of it allows pushing out SOAP messages to a destination FTP site. Like HTTP (and unlike SMTP), FTP represents a **synchronous** protocol where the client has a connection going all the way from client to server.

The `SOAP::Transport::FTP` implementation behaves rather like the `SOAP::Transport::SMTP`, where message submission is a one-way operation, offering no ability to receive any result. This synchronous connection has an advantage over SMTP that the client can have a good degree of certainty that a message has in fact been submitted. In the diagram, the file `/home/cbbrowne/foo.xml` is at the end of the line. Once the connection is complete, this allows the client to be aware that the message has been delivered, but there is no feedback from the server:

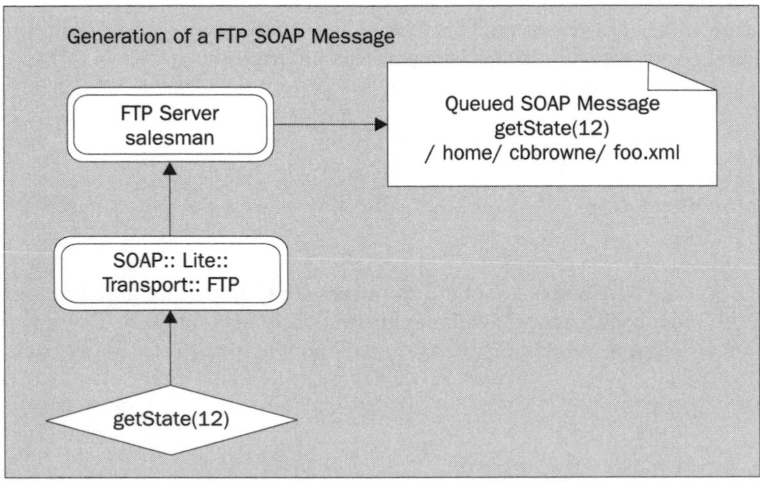

Using SOAP::Transport::FTP Class

Here is a simple example that demonstrates the use of the SOAP method `getStateName()` by transmitting an XML message to a destination FTP site:

```
#!/usr/bin/perl
use SOAP::Lite;
my $uri = 'http://www.soaplite.com/My/Examples';

my ($site, $id, $password, $path)
  = ("salesman", "cbbrowne", "noneofyourbeeswax",
     "/home/cbbrowne/foo.xml");

print SOAP::Lite
  -> uri($uri)
  -> proxy(mkftp($site, $id, $password, $path))
  -> getStateName(12);

sub mkftp {
  my ($site, $id, $password, $path) = @_;
  return "ftp://$id:$password\@$site$path";
}
```

Disadvantages of FTP

Note that this FTP-based protocol has a number of demerits which means that it may not be suitable in all circumstances:

- The FTP protocol (RFC 959) transmits ID and password in plain-text format. As a result, messages transmitted over the public Internet are vulnerable to an adversary grabbing the initial authentication messages and thereby gaining the ID and password to read and/or modify whatever data is accessible on the FTP server. Furthermore, data is also transmitted in plain-text form, which makes the contents of SOAP messages vulnerable to interception during transmission. FTP and Telnet are increasingly being deprecated in favor of protocols using encrypted channels.
- Messages are associated with a specific filename on the server. To submit ten messages, and have them queued, it is necessary to have some method- and server-specific protocol for naming them.
- As with the SMTP protocol, there are no guarantees of specific timing on the processing of messages. Unlike with SMTP, the client may not be certain that the message has been delivered, but there is no guarantee of instant processing, nor is there any way of receiving values back, aside from some fault indicating delivery failure.
- Unlike the SMTP process, for which there is a `SOAP::Transport::POP3` module to support server side, there is no server-side process for `SOAP::Transport::FTP`. The server side will involve some sort of polling process that looks for messages in the specified directories, processes them, and then deletes the messages.

Since no values may be returned by `SOAP::Transport::POP3` methods, this protocol should only be used to support messages that supply data to the server, requiring no return of values. Using `SOAP::Transport::POP3` will only be appropriate under specific circumstances where the reliability of the mail transport system is understood well, and where the reliability that is available matches what is needed.

The SOAPsh.pl Interactive Shell

SOAP::Lite includes a tool called `SOAPsh.pl` which allows you to interactively try out methods. When running it, you specify:

- A mandatory endpoint, that being what is passed to the SOAP::Lite method `proxy()`
- An optional URI, which is what is passed to the SOAP::Lite method `uri()`

Thus, if a Perl call would read:

```
$server = SOAP::Lite -> proxy('http://localhost:1234/') -> uri
('http://www.soaplite.com/Temperatures');
```

then the command to connect using `SOAPsh.pl` would be:

```
SOAPsh.pl http://localhost:1234/ http://www.soaplite.com/Temperatures
```

This is useful for exploring the methods on a SOAP server, providing the ability to test things out without having to write client code. Here is an example of the use of `SOAPsh.pl` to access some methods from one of the examples described earlier:

```
% SOAPsh.pl http://localhost:7938/
Usage: method[(parameters)]
> action2()
--- SOAP RESULT ---
'That'

> action6()
--- SOAP RESULT ---
{
  '0' => '3',
  'n1' => 'name 1',
  '1' => '2',
  '2' => '6',
  'n2' => 'name 2',
  '3' => '14',
  '-1' => '7',
  '4' => '30'
}
>
```

Using stubber.pl for Package Generation

The SOAP::Lite toolkit includes a script called `stubber.pl` which generates a Perl package based on the WSDL input. This eliminates the need to explicitly write code to access the function `getQuote()`; the stubber generates functions for all the methods specified by the WSDL. For example, you might try `perl.stubmaker.pl http://www.xmethods.net/sd/StockQuoteService.wsdl` that generates the package file `net_xmethods_services_stockquote_StockQuoteService.pm` which defines the package of the same name containing `getQuote()`. The package name is rather long but nothing prevents you from renaming the file and the package to suit your needs.

Alternatively, if you have the WSDL in the file `/tmp/StockQuoteService.wsdl`, you may instead use the command `stubber.pl file:///tmp/StockQuoteService.wsdl` which would generate the package file `StockQuoteService.pm`, defining `StockQuoteService`.

The file `StockQuoteService.pm` reads as follows:

```
package StockQuoteService;

# -- generated by SOAP::Lite (v0.52) for Perl -- soaplite.com -- Copyright (C)
2000-2001 Paul Kulchenko --
# -- generated from
file:///home/cbbrowne/public_html/publishing/stocks/StockQuoteService.wsdl [Sun
Mar 10 13:10:56 2002]

my %methods = (
  getQuote => {
    endpoint => 'http://services.xmethods.net:80/soap',
    soapaction => '',
    uri => 'urn:xmethods-delayed-quotes',
    parameters => [
```

```
      SOAP::Data->new(name => 'symbol', type => 'xsd:string', attr => {}),
    ],
  },
);

use SOAP::Lite;
use Exporter;
use Carp ();

use vars qw(@ISA $AUTOLOAD @EXPORT_OK %EXPORT_TAGS);
@ISA = qw(Exporter SOAP::Lite);
@EXPORT_OK = (keys %methods);
%EXPORT_TAGS = ('all' => [@EXPORT_OK]);

no strict 'refs';
for my $method (@EXPORT_OK) {
  my %method = %{$methods{$method}};
  *$method = sub {
    my $self = UNIVERSAL::isa($_[0] => __PACKAGE__)
      ? ref $_[0] ? shift # OBJECT
                  # CLASS, either get self or create new and assign to self
                  : (shift->self || __PACKAGE__->self(__PACKAGE__->new))
      # function call, either get self or create new and assign to self
      : (__PACKAGE__->self || __PACKAGE__->self(__PACKAGE__->new));
    $self->proxy($method{endpoint} || Carp::croak "No server address (proxy)
specified") unless $self->proxy;
    my @templates = @{$method{parameters}};
    my $som = $self
      -> endpoint($method{endpoint})
      -> uri($method{uri})
      -> on_action(sub{qq!"$method{soapaction}"!})
      -> call($method => map {@templates ? shift(@templates)->value($_) : $_} @_);
    UNIVERSAL::isa($som => 'SOAP::SOM') ? wantarray ? $som->paramsall : $som-
>result
                                        : $som;
  }
}

sub AUTOLOAD {
  my $method = substr($AUTOLOAD, rindex($AUTOLOAD, '::') + 2);
  return if $method eq 'DESTROY';

  die "Unrecognized method '$method'. List of available method(s): @EXPORT_OK\n";
}

1;
```

We may thus shorten the script that runs `getQuote()` to the following:

```
#!/usr/bin/perl -w
use StockQuoteService;
print "Stock    Price\n";
print "===============\n";
foreach $el (sort ("RHAT", "IBM", "MSFT", "AMR", "LNUX", "NT", "TSG")) {
  my $result = StockQuoteService::getQuote($el);
  printf ("%6s %8.3f\n" , $el, $result);
}
```

The stub generator does not do much about parameter handling. The single parameter you pass generates a `SOAP::Data` bundle, thus:

```
SOAP::Data->new(name => 'parameters', type => '', attr => {})
```

If all that needs to be passed in is a string, `getQuote($some_string)` will do the trick; if the data is of greater complexity (such as with ISBN codes that are not SOAP integers), you will need to write your own marshaling code.

Perl UDDI Query Searching for Company Information

SOAP::Lite includes a set of functions in the class `UDDI::Lite` to access UDDI registries. Here is a sample that searches the UDDI registry at Microsoft (http://uddi.microsoft.com/) looking for information on some companies:

```
#!/usr/bin/perl
# $Id: bizsearch.pl,v 1.3 2002/03/29 21:38:47 cbbrowne Exp $
### Script to search for UDDI information for some companies
use UDDI::Lite +autodispatch =>
  #proxy => 'http://www-3.ibm.com/services/uddi/inquiryapi';
  proxy => 'http://uddi.microsoft.com/inquire';

my @COMPANIES = ('microsoft', 'ibm', 'redhat', 'cbbrowne Computing Inc');

foreach my $csearch (@COMPANIES) {
  my $companyname = find_business(name => $csearch);
  if ($companyname) {
    my $bis = $companyname->businessInfos;
    print "\n$bis\n";
    print "
      Name                      UDDI Key
-----------------------------------------------------------------\n";
    foreach my $b ($bis->businessInfo) {
      my $service = $b->serviceInfos->serviceInfo;
      if ($service) {
        my ($name, $bkey) = ($service->name, $service->businessKey);
        printf ("%25s %s\n", $name, $bkey);
      }
    }
  } else {
    print "\n\nNo UDDI Entry found for company [$csearch]!\n";
  }
}
```

This script walks through Microsoft's public UDDI repository searching for companies matching four company names, and then lists what Web Services the members of the result set offer:

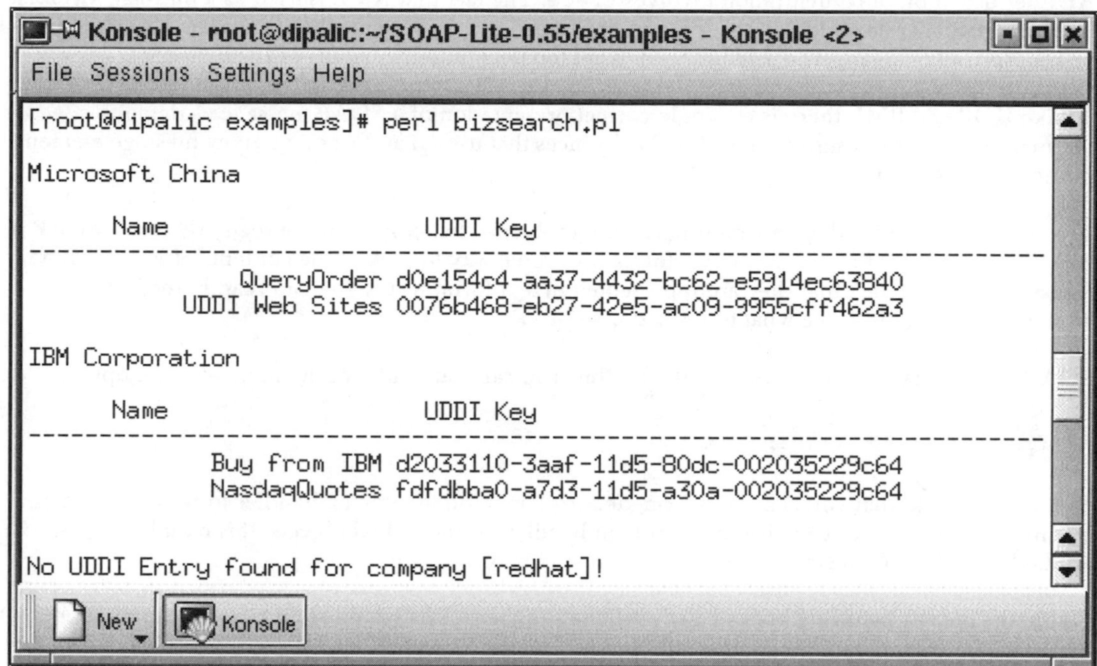

If you look at the results carefully, you'll find a somewhat unexpected company name: `Microsoft China`. Apparently, someone decided to change the company name, and further searches found other fields that have been modified, indicating that the information is unreliable. This underlines the principle that it is important to be very careful about how you trust a UDDI registry.

Just because information is out on the web does not mean that it is true. Ted Nelson coined the term **cybercrud** in his book *Computer Lib/Dream Machines* from *Aperture (ISBN 0-893470-02-3)* back in the early 1970s to describe the way computers get quietly used to apply a patina of credibility to otherwise worthless information. Unfortunately, what was a problem then, namely that people would blindly believe whatever a computer printed out, is still a problem today.

Just a note: the `UDDI::Lite` module offers a variety of idioms to shorten queries. With UDDI queries, for example, it is unlikely that you will be accessing multiple servers in any given session, so you will typically want to use the `+autodispatch` to indicate the favored proxy:

```
use UDDI::Lite +autodispatch =>
  proxy => 'http://uddi.microsoft.com/inquire';
```

Without this, each and every UDDI query would need to include the method call:

```
-> proxy('http://uddi.microsoft.com/inquire')
```

Tracing and Debugging with SOAP::Lite

Another useful bit of configuration involves trace. The fact that XML is used as a message format is an implementation issue which, in theory, you don't need to worry much about; similar to users of CORBA or Enterprise JavaBeans who seldom need to get too deep into the details of IIOP or RMI.

Unlike IIOP and RMI, there is no single correct presentation of a SOAP message as demonstrated by the many variations in support for SOAP references that use id and href to allow message elements to point to one another.

If you are struggling with some interoperability problems that crop up quite regularly (since SOAP is still somewhat immature), it is very useful to have some way to look at the contents of SOAP-message transmissions. The fact that they are represented in text form means you can readily read the raw contents of messages to see what is going on.

SOAP::Lite offers considerable control over this; you can start with adding in its +trace option, like:

```
use SOAP::Lite +trace;
```

You will also find that you can use the on_debug() method to attach a handler to process on_debug events. Unlike on_fault() that attaches fault handlers to individual objects, this handler will be applied to all SOAP objects.

Often, the default behavior from +trace will be sufficient. You would need to set up an on_debug() handler if you wanted to trace some calls and not others. You might either modify the handler to turn it on and off, write the handler to check a global flag, or perhaps do something really clever like having the handler look at the objects being worked with, and pick the interesting ones that are to be reported on, and ignore the boring ones.

There are a number of manual pages included with SOAP::Lite, containing a great deal of additional example code. Each of the module scripts also contains documentation in the Perl POD format, so if you are encountering problems with a particular transport mechanism, you may find it useful to load the sourcecode into your favorite editor and examine the documentation there, or use the perldoc command to extract and view it. Commands like perldoc SOAP::Transport::HTTP or perldoc SOAP::Transport::MQ will display the module's documentation.

A UDDI Query to Find Methods

Here is a more sophisticated UDDI query that searches a UDDI repository to find WSDL and proxy information for the stock and book price quotes previously described. The UDDI lookup is encapsulated in the function lookup_method(criteria, bizname), where criteria is used to determine which service is to be extracted, and bizname indicates the name of the business where we expect to find the service:

```
sub lookup_method {
my ($criteria, $bizname) = @_;
use UDDI::Lite import => 'UDDI::Lite', import => 'UDDI::Data',
  # proxy => 'http://uddi.microsoft.com/inquire';
  proxy => 'http://www-3.ibm.com/services/uddi/inquiryapi';
```

Notice that there are lines to support the use of UDDI registries at both Microsoft and IBM. It so happens that XMethod, the organization for which we are drawing service information, has services registered in both UDDI registries.

The query starts by searching for entries where the business name matches `$bizname`, retrieving all of the `$serviceInfo` entries. The call to `grep()` extracts the element that matches the search criteria:

```
    my($Query) = grep { $_->name =~ /$criteria/i }
    UDDI::Lite::find_business(name($bizname)) -> businessInfos ->
    businessInfo
        -> serviceInfos -> serviceInfo;
```

This searches the `Query`'s service details, walking down the tree of UDDI data to locate the `$bindingTemplate`, from which proxy and WSDL information is to be extracted:

```
    my $Template =
    get_serviceDetail($Query->serviceKey)
      -> businessService -> bindingTemplates -> bindingTemplate;
```

This walks from the `$bindingTemplate` to get the `accessPoint`, or `proxy`, and walks the tree to get the `$ModelKey`:

```
    my ($Proxy, $ModelKey) =
    ($Template->accessPoint->value,
     $Template -> tModelInstanceDetails -> tModelInstanceInfo
     -> tModelKey);
```

Finally, a call to `get_tModelDetail()` using the `$ModelKey`, walks through methods `tModel`, `overviewDoc`, and `overviewURL` to find the location of the WSDL, and the proxy and WSDL locations are returned:

```
    my $wsdl = get_tModelDetail($ModelKey) -> tModel -> overviewDoc ->
    overviewURL -> value;
  return ($Proxy, $wsdl);
}
```

The main body of the program is similar to what has already been seen in the earlier SOAP clients:

```
#!/usr/bin/perl
# $Id: bigsamp1.pl,v 1.1 2002/03/25 20:57:01 cbbrowne Exp $
($proxy, $wsdl) = lookup_method("Barnes and Noble", "XMethods");
print "WSDL for Book Pricing may be found at:\n   $wsdl \n";
print "Proxy: $proxy\n";

%ISBNS = ( '0596000278' => 'Programming Perl',
           '0716715872' => 'Linear Programming',
           '1861003013' => 'Professional Linux Programming',
           '0131103628' => 'The C Programming Language',
           '1555581234' => 'The Unix Philosophy',
           '1568842031' => 'The Unix-Haters Handbook',
```

```
        '0201379279' => 'Advanced CORBA Programming with C++' );

@STOCKS = ("RHAT", "IBM", "MSFT", "AMR", "LNUX", "NT", "TSG");

print "-----------------------------------------------\n";
print "      Book                                Price\n";
print "-----------------------------------------------\n";

foreach my $isbn (sort (keys(%ISBNS))) {
  my $code = SOAP::Data->type(string => $isbn);
  printf ("%35s  %8.2f\n", $ISBNS{$isbn},
          SOAP::Lite-> service($wsdl) -> proxy($proxy)
          -> getPrice($code));
}

print "-=" x 35, "\n\n";
($proxy, $wsdl) = lookup_method("stock quote", "XMethods");
print "WSDL for Stock Quote may be found at:\n   $wsdl \n";
print "Proxy for Stock Quote may be found at: $proxy \n";
print "-=" x 35, "\n\n";
print "Stock    Price\n";
print "===============\n";
foreach $el (sort @STOCKS) {
  my $result = SOAP::Lite->service($wsdl)->proxy($proxy)
    ->getQuote($el);
  printf ("%6s %8.3f\n" , $el, $result);
}
```

The main difference is that rather than hard coding the locations of proxies and WSDL service information, they are found on a UDDI server using `lookup_method("Barnes and Noble","XMethods")`. It is a fact that at some point, it is necessary to reference some specific servers; UDDI allows the number of public servers needing to be referenced in your programs to be reduced.

Security and UDDI

The quality of the data in a particular UDDI registry is only as good as the controls in place on updates to that registry.

The entries you can find by browsing the Microsoft UDDI sample server (http://uddi.microsoft.com/inquire) demonstrate this nicely. For example, suppose you search for businesses based on the criteria:

```
my @parameters =
   (findQualifiers(findQualifier('sortByNameAsc',
                                  'caseSensitiveMatch')),
    name('Sample'));
```

This will find over a dozen entries, none of which correspond to any existing company, let alone anyone you should have any reason to want to trust with any important data.

There is nothing from a technical perspective to prevent a nefarious user from trying to register a UDDI entry providing an unfortunate duplicate of the name of a company you might want to deal with. Since publishing the interface distributes the ability to update such fields as `businessInfo-name`, responsibility for the quality of the registry information jointly rests on everyone with the ability to update a given registry. The presence of `Microsoft China` in Microsoft's UDDI database should underline this point.

As a result, before you try doing any automatic exploration of UDDI registries to find would-be business partners, you need to be very clear on how well the registries are managed.

It would do no good to perform a UDDI search for a server providing a `getQuote()` method that is to be used to get stock prices you plan to use to make financial decisions on, only to find that the method you found was hooked up to a server feeding you deliberately wrong information.

Server Programming Using SOAP::Lite

We now get to the core of the matter – how to use Perl to construct SOAP services? This involves the following four topics:

- How to set up methods to be accessible?
- How to set up faults?
- How to read input parameters?
- How to write export parameters?

These four matters apply similarly to both client and server, so the examples will present a server along with a client to demonstrate their functionality.

Making Perl Methods Accessible

A simple example may be demonstrated like:

```
my $SoapServer = SOAP::Transport::HTTP::Daemon
   -> new (LocalPort => 4213)
   -> dispatch_to qw(function1 function2 function3)
   -> options ({compress_threshold => 800});
```

This attaches the three Perl functions `function1()`, `function2()`, and `function3()` to the Perl HTTP daemon, to be accessible on port `4213`.

The `options()` method adds the ability of compressing return messages. It assumes that the other side is able to cope with compressed messages, which means that you should not use it unless you know both parties involved can cope with compression.

Fault Handling

In Chapter 3, we skimmed the topic on SOAP faults but shall look at it in detail here. While walking through parameters to extract data from input parameters generating output parameters may get somewhat lengthy, it is very easy to throw SOAP faults. You need to only execute the function `die()`, passing in a string of the exception message.

This generates a SOAP fault that reports back:

- Fault code of `Server`
- Fault actor is the server URL
- Fault string is the string passed to `die()`
- No fault details are passed back

If you need to pass back fault details, the way to do this would involve the `SOAP::Fault` class, demonstrated in `faults.pl`:

```
#!/usr/bin/perl
use SOAP::Lite;
use SOAP::Transport::HTTP;

my ($port, $action) = (4422, "http://localhost");
my $Actions = qw( InherentlyFaultyMethod );

my $SoapServer = SOAP::Transport::HTTP::Daemon
  -> new (LocalPort => $port)
  -> dispatch_to ($Actions);

$SoapServer->handle;

sub InherentlyFaultyMethod {
  die SOAP::Fault
    -> faultcode('Server Custom')
      -> faultstring('InherentlyFaultyMethod produces a custom fault')
        -> faultactor('http://foo.frobozz.com/soap/')
          -> faultdetail(bless {code => 42} => 'UltimateError');
}
```

The interesting bit is the subroutine `InherentlyFaultyMethod()` at the end. Note the four methods that it calls, one for each `Fault` component:

- `faultcode()`
  If this method is omitted, the fault code that is passed back defaults to server.
- `faultstring()`
  This is the most necessary method of all; when you raise a fault, this should contain a brief but useful message to describe the error.
- `faultactor()`
  This method ordinarily does not need to be called; a default value will be returned indicating information about the server on which the failure took place, and the default value is usually correct. Adding an `actor`, explicitly, would most likely be useful if there are multiple hosts on which the code could be running, or if the host has multiple names, and the default value that results provides internal network configuration information that you do not wish to release to clients.

- `faultdetail()`
  This allows passing back more complex fault details.

Specifying the actor manually using the method `faultactor()` would primarily be needed if a particular server is hosting multiple domains, as is seen with Apache virtual hosting. For example, let's suppose domains www.foo.org and www.bar.org are being hosted by a server at the service provider http://www.foobar-isp.com. If you are "publishing" a SOAP service for www.foo.org, it would be appropriate to use `faultactor()` to ensure that any faults report back to www.foo.org.

The method `faultdetail()` would be useful when processing complex accounting transactions. It would be useful for the SOAP server to examine a transaction, and report back all of the problems it finds, all at once. This approach is necessary when using SOAP in the context of asynchronous messaging, submitting messages with no intent of dealing with immediate feedback.

Suppose a message contains an invoice document (or perhaps ten of them), and the server finds that there are the following problems:

- The date is formatted badly
- The customer code doesn't correspond to a valid customer
- The product requested is not available in sufficient quantities to ship out

The method `faultdetail()` allows us to pass back a list detailing all these problems at once, so that the user may resolve them together rather than discover just one problem at a time, and having to repetitively resubmit messages with minor changes. This leads to severe performance problems down the road.

Here is a client, `faultc.pl`, which accesses `faults.pl` and reports the fault information passed back:

```
#!/usr/bin/perl -w
use SOAP::Lite;

my ($proxy) = ("http://localhost:4422/");
my $soap = SOAP::Lite
  -> proxy($proxy);

$f = $soap->InherentlyFaultyMethod();
if ($f->fault) {
  ($code, $string, $actor) = ($f->faultcode, $f->faultstring, $f->faultactor);
  $~ = FAULT_TOP;
  write;
  if ($f->faultdetail) {
    %D = %{$f->faultdetail};
    foreach $t (values(%D)) {
      %T = %{$t};
      print " Main key: $t\n";
      foreach $k (keys %T) {
        ($key, $value) = ($k, $T{$k});
        $~ = FAULT_DETAIL;
        write;
```

```
        }
      }
    }
}

format FAULT_TOP =
==============================================================
                       Fault Found
==============================================================
 Code:   @<<<<<<<<<<<<<<<<<<<<<<<<<<<<<<<<<<<<<<<<<<<<<<<<<<<
$code
 String: @<<<<<<<<<<<<<<<<<<<<<<<<<<<<<<<<<<<<<<<<<<<<<<<<<<<
$string
 Actor:  @<<<<<<<<<<<<<<<<<<<<<<<<<<<<<<<<<<<<<<<<<<<<<<<<<<<
$actor
.

format FAULT_DETAIL =
 Key: @<<<<<<<<<<<<<<<<  Value: @<<<<<<<<<<<<<<<<<<<<<<<<<<<
$key, $value
```

Enumerations

SOAP supports a number of schema information, typically encoded in WSDL, for which support is either limited or non-existent in the Perl bindings. For example, if we have a field that is to contain only the allowable currencies, we might define enumeration types similar to the following:

```
<simpleType name='allowableCurrencies'>
  <restriction base='xsd:string'>
    <enumeration value='USD'/>
    <enumeration value='CDN'/>
    <enumeration value='UKP'/>
    <enumeration value='EUR'/>
    <enumeration value='FRF'/>
  </restriction>
</simpleType>
```

These enumerations would be placed in the WSDL file, and would be intended to indicate restrictions on those fields to which they are applied. If you create a SOAP request for an `allowableCurrencies` that contains the value `MXP`, it would be legitimate for some component of the message transport infrastructure to generate an exception indicating that the value does not conform to the schema, perhaps even at the client level, doing some validation before messages get to the network. Unfortunately, SOAP::Lite does not make any beneficial use of that information.

SOAP References

SOAP::Lite has slightly more meaningful support for SOAP references. SOAP can use `id` and `href` references to allow values to be referenced multiple times in a document.

Here is an example of an XML document containing several references:

```
<?xml version="1.0" encoding="utf-8"?>
<Employees>
  <Employee>
    <id xsi:type="xsd:integer">441716</id>
    <fname>Chris</fname>
    <sname id="sbrowne">Browne</sname>
    <province id="pon">Ontario</province>
  </Employee>
  <Employee>
    <id xsi:type="xsd:integer">441717</id>
    <fname>David</fname>
    <sname href="#sbrowne" />
    <province>Manitoba</province>
  </Employee>
  <Employee id="bigguy">
    <id xsi:type="xsd:integer">441718</id>
    <fname>Bradley</fname>
    <sname href="#sbrowne" />
    <province>Nova Scotia</province>
  </Employee>
  <Employee id="biggerguy">
    <id xsi:type="xsd:integer">441719</id>
    <fname>Douglas</fname>
    <sname>Fir</sname>
    <province>British Columbia</province>
  </Employee>
</Employees>
<Managers>
  <Employee href="#bigguy" />
  <Employee href="#biggerguy" />
  <Managers />
</Managers>
```

Using `href` references has two effects:

- There is an elimination of redundant data, recognizing that different parts are referencing the same thing. This allows the data payload to accurately reflect the data that it represents.
- There may be a reduction in the amount of data in the message.

In the above XML document, there wasn't data excessive enough to make the document smaller.

In a SOAP message transferring payroll data for 150 employees, many of them in the same city with a lot of data elements that are used repeatedly, more substantial savings might be possible. Maximum wins would result from whole trees of elements being able to be referenced and thus eliminated. What is easy both in terms of coding effort as well as in the amount of computational skill required to detect patterns are elements that encapsulate single strings. Unfortunately, reference tags themselves consume some space, so the expected savings may be limited.

There have been considerable variations in the degree of support for multi-reference values, sometimes not interoperating too well. At one extreme, Microsoft's .NET framework took the approach of generating multi-reference values to represent every element of an array. SOAP::Lite sits more at the other extreme, not bothering to generate multi-references.

Fortunately, sufficient time and interoperability tests have shown that even if SOAP::Lite doesn't generate such references, it does recognize them.

SOAP::SOM Client Return Values

The values returned by a SOAP::Lite call actually return an object of type `SOAP::SOM`, and you may access the results in a number of different ways. Consider the call:

```
my $result = $soapserver->GetInformation();
```

There are a host of `SOAP::SOM` methods that may be attached to `$result` to return different aspects of the results. For example, we have already seen the fault-handling methods earlier in the chapter. The following code shows their implementation:

```
my $result = $soapserver->GetInformation();
if ($result->fault) {
  print "Fault Code:", $result->faultcode, "\n";
  print "Fault Actor:", $result->faultactor, "\n";
  print "Fault Description:", $result->faultstring, "\n";
  if ($result->faultdetail) {
    print Dumper($result->faultdetail);
  }
}
```

The `SOAP::SOM` module also contains some interesting functions for return values or results of a function call like the following:

- `$result->result;`
  This returns the result of the call; the first argument passed back by the server
- `$result->paramsout;`
  This returns the `OUT` parameters; the remaining arguments passed back by the server
- `$result->paramsall;`
  This returns the whole combination of result and `OUT` parameters

Look at how these method behaviors differ in the following code sample:

```
# Server function:
sub sample {
  return ([1, 2], 3, 4);
}
```

Here is a set of client code to display the three different output parameter methods:

```
$result = $ssrv->samp();
print "result: ", Dumper($result->result);
print "paramsall: ", Dumper($result->paramsall);
print "paramsout: ", Dumper($result->paramsout);
```

The output from these three calls looks like:

```
result: [
  '1',
  '2'
]
paramsall: [
  '1',
  '2'
]
'3'
'4'
paramsout: '3'
'4'
```

A set of `SOM` methods is available to search the `Envelope` returned by the SOAP message, allowing applications to base their search on node paths using an argument format similar to the notation used with XPath, where / is interpreted as the root node, // indicates a relative location path, `[num]` allows selecting numbered nodes, and `[op num]` allows the use of comparison operators (<, >, <=, >=, `!`, =). These methods are:

- `$result->match('/Envelope//addr1')`
  This accepts a node path, returning true/false or a SOM object representing the matched node path.
- `$result->valueof()`
  This returns the value of a previously matched node. This value may either be, in a scalar context, the first element in a matched set, or, in an array context, the whole list of matched elements.
- `$result->dataof()`
  This behaves similar to `valueof()`, but instead of simply returning values, it returns a SOAP::Data object, allowing you to access the name, type, and other elements of the previously-matched node.
  Note that it does not return a tree of SOAP::Data elements; only the root element is of that type.
- `$result->headerof()`
  This is the same as `dataof()`, but returns a `SOAP::Header` object, which is preferable if there is a need to access `Header` elements.
- `$result->namespaceuriof()`
  This returns the URI for the element.
- `$result->root()`
  This method is exactly equivalent to `$result->valueof('/')`.
- `$result->envelope()`
  This returns, generally as a hashtable, the value of the `Envelope` element, often including `Header`, `Body`, and any other custom elements.
- `$result->header()`
  This returns the `Header` element as a hashtable.
- `$result->headers()`
  This returns the set of header elements inside the `Header` element.
- `$result->body()`
  This returns the value of the `Body` element.

A SOAP Sampler

We now look at an extended example to demonstrate various SOAP programming techniques. It consists of a server, `pserver.pl`, which provides a wrapper for a set of SOAP methods, a number of classes, and a client to make use of them.

The Price Server – pserver.pl

The code for the `pserver.pl` is as follows:

```
#!/usr/bin/perl
# $Id: pserver.pl,v 1.7 2002/03/25 22:57:28 cbbrowne Exp $
use SOAP::Lite ;
use SOAP::Transport::HTTP;
use Actions;
use ComplexAction;
use ComplexSchema;
my $port = 7927;
my $SoapServer = SOAP::Transport::HTTP::Daemon
  -> new (LocalPort => $port)
  -> dispatch_to qw(action1 action1a action1b action2 action3
                    action3a action3b action4 action5 action6
                    action7 methods country phonenums
                    priceitems foo)
  -> options ({compress_threshold => 800});
print "Server at $port bound to: ", $SoapServer->dispatch_to(), "\n";

$SoapServer->handle;

# And we define one local function, not in a class...
sub foo {
  return "foo";
}
```

This server program largely consists of references to modules and methods that are to be imported from other scripts, and then exported as a set of SOAP methods. The modules imported are:

- SOAP::Lite draws in the generic aspects of SOAP support
- `SOAP::Transport::HTTP` draws in support for using the HTTP protocol; this server will be running as a daemon attached to the specified port number
- The modules `Actions`, `ComplexAction`, and `ComplexSchema` draw in the set of methods that this SOAP server will be publishing

Using the class `SOAP::Transport::HTTP::Daemon` the server object is created and attached to a specific port, supporting dispatch to the listed set of methods with the specified compression option. The server does not start handling requests until the `handle()` method is invoked, so this is the final action taken.

Compression

One interesting bit of SOAP::Lite functionality that is demonstrated here is the addition of the compression option. This can enable compression of SOAP messages when both client and server support it:

```
-> options ({compress_threshold => 10000});
```

The compression is handled in a manner that is transparent to client and server code, although if a compressed message is submitted to a server that cannot recognize it, or is returned to a client that cannot recognize it, the requests will fail. Compression should certainly not be enabled for services that are to be made publicly accessible.

The actions are defined in `Actions.pm`, `ComplexAction.pm`, and `ComplexSchema.pm`. There are quite a number of tricks presented in the `Actions` package.

Test Actions – Actions

We start `Actions` with a set of Perl declarations describing the class:

```
#!/usr/bin/perl
# $Id: ActionHeader.pm,v 1.1 2002/03/20 04:17:41 cbbrowne Exp $
package Actions;
require 5.000;
require Exporter;
use Carp;

@ISA = qw(Exporter);

@EXPORT = qw(methods foo action1 action1a action1b action2
             action3 action3a action3b action4
             action5 action6 action7);
```

Note that the `@EXPORT` of function names includes `foo()` which does not actually occur in this package. This has the result that if you want to actually use `foo()`, you'll have to use a suitable Perl namespace to avoid the call failure.

To satisfy that, `foo()` is defined in the main body of `pserver.pl`. This approach wouldn't tend to work out very well in languages that involve static compiling, such as C or C++, which are likely to complain at compile time if `foo()` is missing. It also wouldn't work well in dynamic languages like Python or Ruby, which observe stricter "class hierarchies" and which would be likely to complain about the function not being defined within class `Actions`.

We then proceed to define some generic methods for class `Actions`:

```
sub mkdata {
  my ($value, $name, $type) = @_;
  $name = 'return' unless $name;
  $type = 'string' unless $type;
  return SOAP::Data -> name($name) ->type($type) ->value($value);
}
```

```
sub methods {
  return \@EXPORT;
  return mkdata (\@EXPORT, "return", "array");
}
```

The `mkdata()` function is not exported via SOAP; it is kept internal to `Actions`. It is a helper function that provides a shorthand for using `SOAP::Data` to explicitly declare the SOAP types for return values. In more strongly typed languages than Perl, it may be practical to simply pass back values based on the implicit mappings of local language types to SOAP types but, in Perl, types will often need to be explicitly declared.

> **While Perl is readily able to silently coerce scalar values into whatever sort of data type it is trying to manipulate, the same cannot be said for all languages you might use with a SOAP service.**

It is critical for any sort of service that is to be provided to a potentially hostile world, to carefully coerce values using `SOAP::Data` methods into the types that are specifically intended to be returned. This may not always be critical for dynamically typed scripting languages like Perl or Python that are able to attach values of almost any type to variables. It is, however, critical for languages that attach types to variables at compile time such as Java, C, and C++. And it can be important, even in Perl, if values are going to be used with strongly typed interfaces; for example, if the value is to be used to populate a query to a SQL database.

The `method()` function returns an array consisting of the function names defined in `Actions`. This allows the server to explicitly broadcast a list of available methods to a client. The client may then call them using:

```
$soapserver->call('somemethodname' => @PARMS);
```

For the purpose of this example, it allows us to have the client run all exported methods, and if we add additional methods, there is no need to change the client. In effect, this is "poor man's white pages", providing some of the information that would be provided by a WSDL document resembling what the `SOAP::Lite stubmaker.pl` utility would provide.

Methods `action1()`, `action1a()`, and `action1b()` demonstrate the ability for a SOAP method to return a simple string:

```
sub action1 {
  return "That";
}
sub action1a {
  return mkdata("This", "return", "string");
}

sub action1b {
  return SOAP::Data->type('string')->value('Other Thing');
}
```

Compare the XML messages that they respectively generate:

```
<?xml version="1.0" encoding="utf-8"?>
<SOAP-ENV:Envelope
xmlns:SOAP-ENC="http://schemas.xmlsoap.org/soap/encoding/"
SOAP-ENV:encodingStyle="http://schemas.xmlsoap.org/soap/encoding/"
xmlns:SOAP-ENV="http://schemas.xmlsoap.org/soap/envelope/"
xmlns:xsi="http://www.w3.org/1999/XMLSchema-instance"
xmlns:xsd="http://www.w3.org/1999/XMLSchema">
  <SOAP-ENV:Body>
    <action1Response xmlns="">
      <s-gensym10 xsi:type="xsd:string">That</s-gensym10>
    </action1Response>
  </SOAP-ENV:Body>
</SOAP-ENV:Envelope>
```

The message for `action1()`, shown above, has virtually the same structure as the message for `action1a()`:

```
<?xml version="1.0" encoding="utf-8"?>
<SOAP-ENV:Envelope
xmlns:SOAP-ENC="http://schemas.xmlsoap.org/soap/encoding/"
SOAP-ENV:encodingStyle="http://schemas.xmlsoap.org/soap/encoding/"
xmlns:SOAP-ENV="http://schemas.xmlsoap.org/soap/envelope/"
xmlns:xsi="http://www.w3.org/1999/XMLSchema-instance"
xmlns:xsd="http://www.w3.org/1999/XMLSchema">
  <SOAP-ENV:Body>
    <action1aResponse xmlns="">
      <return xsi:type="xsd:string">This</return>
    </action1aResponse>
  </SOAP-ENV:Body>
</SOAP-ENV:Envelope>
```

Lastly, `action1b()` generates:

```
<?xml version="1.0" encoding="utf-8"?>
<SOAP-ENV:Envelope
xmlns:SOAP-ENC="http://schemas.xmlsoap.org/soap/encoding/"
SOAP-ENV:encodingStyle="http://schemas.xmlsoap.org/soap/encoding/"
xmlns:SOAP-ENV="http://schemas.xmlsoap.org/soap/envelope/"
xmlns:xsi="http://www.w3.org/1999/XMLSchema-instance"
xmlns:xsd="http://www.w3.org/1999/XMLSchema">
  <SOAP-ENV:Body>
    <action1bResponse xmlns="">
      <s-gensym15 xsi:type="xsd:string">Other Thing</s-gensym15>
    </action1bResponse>
  </SOAP-ENV:Body>
</SOAP-ENV:Envelope>
```

Note that both `action1()` and `action1b()` have the result tagged using an internally conjured `s-gensym` tag. Across all the variations of specifying or not specifying types, the values are all tagged with the same `xsd:string` type.

When the action of a SOAP method fails, it is necessary to generate a failure. This is done, in Perl, using the `die()` function. You may typically expect `die()` to cause the Perl server process to terminate, but what happens is that the request dies, returning fault information:

```
sub action2 {
  die SOAP::Fault -> faultcode('Action 2 fault')
    -> faultstring('This page is intentionally blank (and the method intentionally
faulty :-)');
}
```

Next, the `action3()` family shows different treatments of the return of the value `275`:

```
sub action3 {
  return 275.0;
}

sub action3a {
  return mkdata(275.0, "return", "float");
}
```

Take a look at the message below that is generated by `action3()`. The value returned was `275.0`, which we might have thought would have been treated as a `float` value. Unfortunately, Perl coerces this value into a string, after noticing and dropping the unnecessary `.0` at the end, and then SOAP::Lite notices that `275` looks like an integer, and the result passed back is an integer.

This result may be fine if the client is written using a dynamically typed language like Perl, Python, or Lisp where values can dynamically be coerced into appropriate types at run time. However, it would be entirely unsuitable to pass to a client written in C that expects a `float` and where the value may get passed in, copied straight from memory, through a pointer, so that passing back an integer will provide quite unexpected results:

```
<?xml version="1.0" encoding="utf-8"?>
<SOAP-ENV:Envelope
SOAP-ENV:encodingStyle="http://schemas.xmlsoap.org/soap/encoding/"
xmlns:xsi="http://www.w3.org/1999/XMLSchema-instance"
xmlns:xmlsoap="http://xml.apache.org/xml-soap"
xmlns:SOAP-ENC="http://schemas.xmlsoap.org/soap/encoding/"
xmlns:SOAP-ENV="http://schemas.xmlsoap.org/soap/envelope/"
xmlns:xsd="http://www.w3.org/1999/XMLSchema"
xmlns:namesp1="http://namespaces.soaplite.com/perl">
  <SOAP-ENV:Body>
    <action3Response xmlns="">
      <s-gensym64 xsi:type="xsd:int">275</s-gensym64>
    </action3Response>
  </SOAP-ENV:Body>
</SOAP-ENV:Envelope>
```

Compare this to `action3a()` which passes back the same value, `275.0`. Since it attaches the `SOAP::Data type(float)` method, the result is passed back as a `float`:

```
<?xml version="1.0" encoding="utf-8"?>
<SOAP-ENV:Envelope
SOAP-ENV:encodingStyle="http://schemas.xmlsoap.org/soap/encoding/"
xmlns:xsi="http://www.w3.org/1999/XMLSchema-instance"
xmlns:xmlsoap="http://xml.apache.org/xml-soap"
xmlns:SOAP-ENC="http://schemas.xmlsoap.org/soap/encoding/"
xmlns:SOAP-ENV="http://schemas.xmlsoap.org/soap/envelope/"
xmlns:xsd="http://www.w3.org/1999/XMLSchema"
xmlns:namesp1="http://namespaces.soaplite.com/perl">
  <SOAP-ENV:Body>
    <action3aResponse xmlns="">
      <return xsi:type="xsd:float">275</return>
    </action3aResponse>
  </SOAP-ENV:Body>
</SOAP-ENV:Envelope>
```

Notice the third method, `action3b()`, which shows an alternative way of indicating type and value:

```
sub action3b {
  return SOAP::Data->type(float => 275.0) -> name('return');
}
```

Method `action4()` demonstrates the return of some randomly selected values embedded in an array:

```
sub action4 {
  my @ARRAY;
  foreach $i (0..6) {
    $ARRAY[$i] = int($i * $i + 3 * rand(4) - 2) / 4.0;
  }
  push @ARRAY, ("this", "that", "other", "that", "that", "42");
  return mkdata (\@ARRAY, "return", "array");
}
```

There are two special things particularly worth looking at in `action4()`. The values in the array get coerced automatically into their assorted types. Some of the numbers wind up as `floats`, others as `ints`. As with `action3()`, this may not interoperate well with SOAP clients that aren't expecting this kind of dynamic:

```
<?xml version="1.0" encoding="utf-8"?>
<SOAP-ENV:Envelope
SOAP-ENV:encodingStyle="http://schemas.xmlsoap.org/soap/encoding/"
xmlns:xsi="http://www.w3.org/1999/XMLSchema-instance"
xmlns:SOAP-ENC="http://schemas.xmlsoap.org/soap/encoding/"
xmlns:SOAP-ENV="http://schemas.xmlsoap.org/soap/envelope/"
xmlns:xsd="http://www.w3.org/1999/XMLSchema"
xmlns:namesp1="http://namespaces.soaplite.com/perl">
  <SOAP-ENV:Body>
    <action4Response xmlns="">
```

```
        <return SOAP-ENC:arrayType="xsd:ur-type[11]"
        xsi:type="namespl:array">
          <item xsi:type="xsd:float">1.5</item>
          <item xsi:type="xsd:int">1</item>
          <item xsi:type="xsd:float">2.5</item>
          <item xsi:type="xsd:int">4</item>
          <item xsi:type="xsd:int">6</item>
          <item xsi:type="xsd:int">6</item>
          <item xsi:type="xsd:float">11.25</item>
          <item xsi:type="xsd:string">this</item>
          <item xsi:type="xsd:string">that</item>
          <item xsi:type="xsd:string">other</item>
          <item xsi:type="xsd:int">42</item>
        </return>
      </action4Response>
    </SOAP-ENV:Body>
  </SOAP-ENV:Envelope>
```

The array is returned as `\@ARRAY`, using the hard link reference operator. This is necessary because `\@ARRAY` was declared as a local variable and it gets discarded as soon as the function goes out of scope. Without the hard link, the values would be de-allocated before being passed back.

Note that Perl's hard links may be most easily understood by thinking about Unix file links, which come in two varieties: hard and symbolic. With a hard link, the reference is quite indistinguishable from the original. Technically, with file systems, a hard link is one which shares the same inode with the original. If you then `unlink()` the original, the hard-linked reference still remains, and the inode with the contents of the file is kept.

Compare that with a symbolic link, which does not point to the inode, but rather to the name of the original file. With a symbolic link, if the original file is unlinked, the inode is also deleted, and the symbolic link is left pointing at nothing but a file name that no longer exists.

In Perl, this approach is used for variable references. A hard link creates a counted reference separate from the one Perl manages in its symbol tables, and the object that is referenced will not be de-allocated until all such references go away. An example of a soft or symbolic reference would be in the code where `$$a` is a symbolic reference to `$foo`:

```
$foo = 1; $a = 'foo'; $b = $$a;
```

This is quite critical in this example, as `@ARRAY` is created as a local variable in `action4()`. When returning from the function, all local references are de-allocated, and without the hard link indicated by the backslash operator \ to keep the contents around, the contents of `@ARRAY` would disappear on return from `action4()`, not lasting long enough to be passed out as part of a SOAP message.

Method `action5()` demonstrates what happens when a Perl hashtable is passed back. As with `action4()`, it is necessary to keep a hard link to the hashtable so that it is retained long enough to generate the outgoing XML message.

The hashtable has been made rather large to provide an example of a large, highly compressible SOAP message. The Perl client is able to negotiate a compressed session using the `compress_threshold` option. A sample run showed the message compressing from about 42K to about 3.6K. That may not always be representative, but it certainly demonstrates that SOAP is amenable to modifying transport methods to improve its behavior. Here is method `action5()`:

```
sub action5 {
  my (%FOO);
  foreach $i (-17..472) {
    $FOO{$i} = int($i*$i * rand(2) + rand(7)) ;
  }
  $FOO{"n1"} = "name 1";
  $FOO{"n2"} = "name 2";
  return \%FOO;
}
```

The hashtable transforms into the SOAP Map type. Notice the order of the items does not correspond to any particular ordering; they may as well be considered to be in a random order. The following extract shows just a few elements:


```
<?xml version="1.0" encoding="utf-8"?>
<SOAP-ENV:Envelope
SOAP-ENV:encodingStyle="http://schemas.xmlsoap.org/soap/encoding/"
xmlns:xsi="http://www.w3.org/1999/XMLSchema-instance"
xmlns:xmlsoap="http://xml.apache.org/xml-soap"
xmlns:SOAP-ENC="http://schemas.xmlsoap.org/soap/encoding/"
xmlns:SOAP-ENV="http://schemas.xmlsoap.org/soap/envelope/"
xmlns:xsd="http://www.w3.org/1999/XMLSchema"
xmlns:namesp1="http://namespaces.soaplite.com/perl">
  <SOAP-ENV:Body>
    <action5Response xmlns="">
      <s-gensym31 xsi:type="xmlsoap:Map">
        <item>
          <key xsi:type="xsd:string">n1</key>
          <value xsi:type="xsd:string">name 1</value>
        </item>
        <item>
          <key xsi:type="xsd:int">0</key>
          <value xsi:type="xsd:int">5</value>
        </item>
        <item>
          <key xsi:type="xsd:int">1</key>
          <value xsi:type="xsd:int">6</value>
        </item>
        <item>
          <key xsi:type="xsd:string">n2</key>
          <value xsi:type="xsd:string">name 2</value>
        </item>
        <item>
          <key xsi:type="xsd:int">2</key>
          <value xsi:type="xsd:int">8</value>
        </item>
        <item>
          <key xsi:type="xsd:int">3</key>
          <value xsi:type="xsd:int">14</value>
        </item>
        <item>
          <key xsi:type="xsd:int">4</key>
          <value xsi:type="xsd:int">17</value>
```

```
        </item>
        <item>
          <key xsi:type="xsd:int">-1</key>
          <value xsi:type="xsd:int">3</value>
        </item>
      </s-gensym31>
    </action5Response>
  </SOAP-ENV:Body>
</SOAP-ENV:Envelope>
```

Method `action6()` is much more representative of what an industrial strength method should return than the preceding methods. It ties specific types to each element as well as the array:

```
sub action6 {
  my @PROVS = ( 'ON', 'QC', 'NB', 'NF', 'NS', 'MB', 'SK', 'AB', 'BC', 'PE');
  my $prov1 = mkdata($PROVS[int(rand(10))], "province", "string");
  my $prov2 = mkdata($PROVS[int(rand(10))], "province", "string");
  my @PROVRES = ($prov1, $prov2);
  return mkdata(\@PROVRES, "provinces", "array");
}
```

Method `action7()` is consciously faulty, passing a `date` in an illegitimate format:

```
sub action7 {
  return mkdata("2002/07/01", "return", "date");
}
```

A Dysfunction Module – ComplexSchema

Another module, `ComplexSchema`, is introduced to demonstrate one of the limitations of SOAP::Lite; it does not support complex objects:

```
#!/usr/bin/perl
# $Id: ComplexSchema.pm,v 1.1 2002/03/16 04:27:01 cbbrowne Exp $
package ComplexSchema;
require 5.000;
require Exporter;
use Carp;

@ISA = qw(Exporter);

@EXPORT = qw(phonenums country);

sub phonenums {
  return SOAP::Data
    -> name("numbers")
    -> value (mkphonenum("+011", 800, 123, 4567, "homephone"),
              mkphonenum("+011", 800, 123, 6789, "faxphone"),
              mkphonenum("+011", 800, 123, 1234, "officephone"));
  # See the mixture of integers and strings; while it may function in
  # the cases here, leading zeros would get dropped, demonstrating
  # that these aren't really 'numbers.'
}

# mkphonenum is a helper function that shortens the repeated
# generation of phone numbers
```

```
sub mkphonenum {
  my ($cntry, $ac, $ex, $num, $name) = @_;
  return SOAP::Data
    -> type("abc:telephoneNumber")
      -> name($name)
        -> value (mkdata($cntry, "country", "abc:country"),
                  mkdata($ac, "area", "abc:area"),
                  mkdata($ex, "exchange", "abc:exchange"),
                  mkdata($num, "number", "abc:number"));
}

sub country {
  return mkdata("+011", "country", "abc:country");
}
sub mkdata {
  my ($value, $name, $type) = @_;
  $name = 'return' unless $name;
  $type = 'string' unless $type;
  return SOAP::Data -> name($name) ->type($type) ->value($value);
}
1;
```

The `ComplexSchema` module defines method `country()`, which returns a telephone country code as type `country`, a private `mkphonenum()` which tries to define a phone number with the not uncommon international elements: `country`, `area`, `exchange`, `number`, and method `phonenums()`, which generates and tries to return a set of phone numbers using `mkphonenum()`.

Generation of the phone numbers works out fine, but unfortunately, SOAP::Lite will report back faults for the call to `mkphonenum()` since it is unable to resolve the typing of these objects.

The essential problem is that `SOAP::Lite` is not able to deal with complex XML Schemas. The same is true for many of the open source SOAP implementations. This may change as SOAP implementations mature, though people may alternatively work around the limitation by not using more complex data types, which would make it pointless to implement support for them.

A Pricing Server – ComplexAction

In contrast, module `ComplexAction` provides the most complex SOAP method that we have seen so far, `priceitems()`, which accepts messages containing:

- An integer ID number, `$id`, indicating a customer number based on which `priceitems()` will apply discounts. In this implementation, customers with ID numbers below 10000 receive a 15% discount.
- Then there is an array of line items. Each line item consists of an alphanumeric product ID consisting of four letters followed by four digits. If the format differs from that, it is treated as an error. A WSDL schema might be used to formalize the constraint. Better still, this constraint might be validated at the SOAP client, so that erroneous product IDs would lead to `SOAP-ENV:Client` faults that would never even get submitted to the server. Unfortunately, since such validation is not supported by SOAP::Lite and cannot be guaranteed to be supported by all SOAP implementations, responsible server programming needs to assume a lack of validation, and therefore that `priceitems()` must validate the format of this element.
- Lastly, it contains an integer quantity of product. As with the product ID, it is important to validate that the type and value match expectations.

The module begins by indicating packages and other module information that are used, declared, and required:

```
#!/usr/bin/perl
# $Id: ComplexActionHead.pm,v 1.2 2002/03/23 08:14:08 cbbrowne Exp $
package ComplexAction;
require 5.000;
require Exporter;
use DB_File;
@ComplexAction::ISA = qw(SOAP::Server::Parameters Exporter);
@ComplexAction::EXPORT = qw(priceitems);
```

The function `priceitems()` begins by drawing the expected parameters, `lineitems` and `id`, from the function's input parameters:

```
sub priceitems {
my $self = shift;
my $lineitems = pop;
my $id = pop;
my ($discount, @FAULTS);
```

The `$id` is evaluated, and this is used to determine the discount rate. The quality of the data is evaluated if the line items do not consist of an array; fault information is collected in `@FAULTS`. It is used to put together a whole set of fault information, so that if many problems are found, they may all be reported back together:

```
# Evaluate inputs
  if ($id < 10000) {    # Folks with low ID numbers get discounts
    $discount = 0.15;
  } else {
    $discount = 0;
  }
  my $t = lc(ref($lineitems));
  if ($t ne 'array' && $t ne 'hash') {
    push @FAULTS, 'lineitems not an array - was [' . ref($lineitems) . ']';
    push @FAULTS, 'lineitems contained [' . $lineitems . ']';
    push @FAULTS, $lineitems;
    die SOAP::Fault -> faultcode("priceitems fault in $self")
    -> faultstring('illegal data passed to priceitems()')
      -> faultdetail (mkdata(\@FAULTS, "faultdetails", "array"));
  }
```

Next, the line items are individually evaluated for validity. Faults are reported if the product ID does not match the required format, or if the quantity is not a positive integer:

```
my (%QUANTITIES, $num, $product, $quantity);
my @ARR;
if (lc($t) eq 'array') {
  @ARR = @{$lineitems};
} else {   # Unravel hashtable into array...
  foreach my $v (values %{$lineitems}) {
```

```
        push @ARR, $v;
      }
    }
    foreach my $lineitem (@ARR) {
      my $ltype = lc(ref($lineitem));
      if ($ltype ne 'hash' && $ltype ne 'array') {
        push @FAULTS, "lineitem not an array";
        push @FAULTS, $lineitem;
      } elsif ($ltype eq 'hash') {
        my %H = %{$lineitem};
        $product = $H{product};
        $quantity = $H{quantity};
      } elsif ($ltype eq 'array') {
        my %H = %{$lineitem};
        $product = $H{product};
        $quantity = $H{quantity};
        my %P = %{$product};
        my %Q = %{$quantity};
        $product = $P{product};
        $quantity = $Q{quantity};
      }
      my $pfound;
      if ($product =~ /^[A-Z][A-Z][A-Z][A-Z]\d\d\d\d$/) {
        # OK thus far...
      } else {
        push @FAULTS,
          "product ID should have format ZZZZ0000 - was [$product] [$quantity]";
        $pfound = 'yup';
      }
      if (($quantity == int($quantity)) && ($quantity > 0)) {
        # quantity is OK - positive integer
        $QUANTITIES{$product} += $quantity;
        } else {
          push @FAULTS, "quantity was [$quantity] for product [$product] - must be a
positive int - lineitem [$num]";
        }
    }
```

Note that the valid entries are collected together into a hashtable. This has the (disputable) result that if multiple line items are set up for a single product, the results reported back consolidate those into a single entry. That could be right-that could be wrong; when designing such a service, it is important to be careful about the handling of these sorts of semantics.

Next comes an opportunity to check if problems have been observed, and to return the `@FAULTS`, if that is the case:

```
  if (@FAULTS) {
      push @FAULTS, "ID: [$id] discount: [$discount]";
      die SOAP::Fault -> faultcode("priceitems fault in $self")
        -> faultstring('illegal data passed to priceitems()')
          -> faultdetail (mkdata(\@FAULTS, "faultdetails", "array"));
    }
```

If no problems have been encountered so far, the Web Service opens a database to get a new transaction identifier. In a more realistic application, connecting to a relational database such as PostgreSQL and Oracle would typically do this. Here, `DB_File` is used to get at a simple on-disk hashtable:

```
# Get new transaction ID
 my $dbmtier = new DB_File::HASHINFO;
 my %final;
 tie %final, 'DB_File', "/tmp/counter", O_RDWR|O_CREAT or
   die SOAP::Fault->faultcode('priceitems DB fault')
     ->faultstring('Could not open /tmp/counter counter file');
 my $txn_no = $final{"final"};
 if ($txn_no < 1500) {
   $txn_no = 1500;
 }
 $txn_no ++;
 $final{"final"} = "$txn_no";
 untie %final;

 # turn transaction ID into a SOAP data object
 $txn_no = &mkdata($txn_no, 'transactionid', 'int');
```

Failure leads to returning a fault, otherwise the script pulls the final entry in the database, increments it, and sets it up as a `SOAP::Data` object to be returned later to the client:

```
my %PRICES;
# Access price DB
tie %PRICES, 'DB_File', "/tmp/prices", O_RDWR|O_TRUNC|O_CREAT or
  die SOAP::Fault->faultcode('priceitems DB fault')
    ->faultstring("Could not open /tmp/prices price file " .
                  $txn_no->value());

# Attach some prices...
($PRICES{ABCD1236}, $PRICES{ABCD1235}, $PRICES{ABCD1234})
  = ("42.50", "72.75", "2742");
```

Similar to the transaction tracker, this service connects to a simple price database using a DBM style database. The script sets up a few prices by hand; in a more extensive example, it would be a neat idea to add additional SOAP methods to add, modify, and delete prices, storing data in a more sophisticated relational database. In a production environment, this would be more than just a neat idea; it would be a necessary design practice:

```
my @PRICING;
foreach my $product (keys %QUANTITIES) {
  my $price = $PRICES{$product};
  if ($price) {
    push @PRICING, mklineitem($product, $quantity, $discount, $price);
  } else {
    push @FAULTS, "No price available for product [$product]";
  }
}
untie %PRICES;
```

Processing moves on, examining entries in the database to get prices for the products for which pricing has been requested, either adding line items to what is to be returned to the client, or adding faults to the @FAULTS list:

```
  if (@FAULTS) {
      push @FAULTS, "ID: [$id] discount: [$discount]";
      die SOAP::Fault -> faultcode("priceitems fault in $self")
      -> faultstring('illegal data passed to priceitems()')
        -> faultdetail (mkdata(\@FAULTS, "faultdetails", "array"));
    }
    return [\$txn_no,
            mkdata(\@PRICING, 'prices', 'array')];
  } # End of function priceitems()
```

The function priceitems() checks the @FAULTS once more to see if there are any outstanding faults. If so, it passes back a fault. Otherwise, it passes back the transaction number and the set of prices.

In a system based on an SQL database, it is likely that success would lead to a COMMIT WORK to finalize database updates, or that failure would lead to ROLLBACK WORK to take back any database updates that are partially done.

You might expect this sort of SOAP method to be used to support "order fulfilment", where inventory quantities would be checked, and where, if products were all available as required, requests might also be put in to reserve products for the customer:

```
sub mkdata {
  my ($value, $name, $type) = @_;
  $name = 'return' unless $name;
  $type = 'string' unless $type;
  return SOAP::Data -> name($name) ->type($type) ->value($value);
}

sub mklineitem {
  my ($product, $quantity, $disc, $price) = @_;
  my ($product, $cost) =
     (mkdata($product, 'product'),
      mkdata(sprintf("%.2f", $price * $quantity * (1 - $disc)),
             'cost', 'float'));
  return SOAP::Data
    ->name('lineitem')
      ->value([\$product, \$cost])
        ->type('Array');
}
1;
```

The class ends with a mkdata() helper function, which provides a shorthand method for generating SOAP::Data values, and mklineitem(), which takes all of the data associated with a price line item, computes the cost, and builds, using SOAP::Data and mkdata(), nicely typed results that will be returned to the client.

The Sampler Client – pclient.pl

The script `pclient.pl` provides a sample client, testing out the methods implemented in `pserver.pl`. This wouldn't be too useful without having a client program to call it. So, here is a client that tries to exercise the functions – `pclient.pl`:

```
#!/usr/bin/perl -w
use SOAP::Lite #+trace;
;
use Data::Dumper; $Data::Dumper::Terse = 1; $Data::Dumper::Indent = 1;
my $port = 7927;
my $host = "localhost";
my $proxy = "http://$host:$port/";
my $csize = 800;
my $ssrv = SOAP::Lite -> proxy($proxy,
                              options => {compress_threshold => $csize}
                            );
print "Soap Server: $ssrv at $proxy\n";
```

The script starts by setting up variables for each of the various SOAP parameters that are used, and by loading in classes `SOAP::Lite` for SOAP support and `Data::Dumper` to provide a convenient generic method to display message contents.

It connects to a SOAP service on the localhost. Note that the client adds in the SOAP::Lite option to support message compression for messages 800 characters in size or larger:

```
print "Now, explore all the exported methods\n";
print "-" x 75, "\n";
$methods = $ssrv->methods();  # Get list of method names
#print "Methods: $methods\n";
#&reportresults("methods", $methods);
print "-" x 75, "\n";
```

Next, the client uses the `methods()` method to request a list of method names, and uses `reportresults()` to display the list:

```
print "Try each method: \n";
print "-" x 75, "\n";
my $mlist = $methods->result;
my @METHODS = @{$mlist};
foreach my $method (@METHODS) {
  print "   Method: $method\n";
  my $res = $ssrv->call($method);
  &reportresults($method, $res);
}
print "-" x 75, "\n";
```

Next, the methods are extracted into an array, `@METHODS`, and a loop goes through each method name, in order, and executes the SOAP method. It demonstrates a new way of invoking a method that allows storing the name of the method in a variable. Rather than having to code the client for each of `$ssrv->action1()`, `$ssrv->action2()`, `$ssrv->action3()`, and so on, they may be requested via `$ssrv->call('action1')`. If a parameter list is to be passed in, that may be handled via `$ssrv->call('action1' => $SOAP::Data ->type (string ->'this')`:

```
print "And try out foo, which wasn't on the list...\n";
print "-" x 75, "\n";
&reportresults('foo', $ssrv->foo());
print "-" x 75, "\n";
```

Looking back at the server implementation, `foo()` was referenced as part of module `Actions`, but actually implemented in `pserver.pl`. It shows that this somewhat unusual linkage worked:

```
# print "Try country() that tries to assert a simple schema type\n";
# &reportresults('country()', $ssrv->country());

# print "Try phonenums() that tries to assert a complex schema type\n";
# &reportresults('phonenums()', $ssrv->phonenums());
```

Unfortunately, SOAP::Lite does not support customized attributes of this sort, and therefore complains about both methods thus:

```
Unresolved prefix 'abc' for attribute
value 'abc:country'
```

The method `priceitem()` presents a rather more sophisticated example, passing in a somewhat complex set of line items, each consisting of a product ID and a quantity, as well as an ID number indicating who the customer is. It then passes back a table indicating pricing information for that customer (the point of the ID being that discount policies are able to vary by customer):

```
print "Try priceitem() with a bunch of parameters...\n";
@ITEMSET = (['ABCD1234',int(rand(5) + rand(47))+ 3],
            ['ABCD1235',int(rand(5) + rand(14))+ 3],
            ['ABCD1235',int(rand(5) + rand(14))+ 3],
            ['ABCD1236',int(rand(5) + rand(24))+ 3],
);
@LINEITEMS = ();
foreach $ITEM (@ITEMSET) {
  my ($q, $v) = @{$ITEM};
  push @LINEITEMS, mklineitem($q, $v);
}
my $lineitems = SOAP::Data
  ->value(\@LINEITEMS)
  ->name('lineitems')
  ->type('ARRAY');

for ($i = 500; $i <= 15000; $i+= 7000) {
  my $id = mkdata($i, 'id', 'int');
  print "Try: $i\n";
  print "Lineitem:", $lineitems, "\n";
  &reportresults('priceitems', $ssrv->priceitems(id => $id, lineitems =>
$lineitems));}
```

Another run of `priceitem()` is done, this time introducing several intentional data errors, including invalid formatting of the product ID and trying to price negative quantities of products. All these errors are reported back together as a set of `Fault` details, which, in a more realistic application, might allow the client/user to look at fixing all of the errors that are reported:

```
# Second example of priceitems () with some invalid values
@ITEMSET = (['ABCD124', -2],
            ['ABCD1235', -3],
            ['ABCD1234', 2.5],
            ['ABCD1235',int(rand(5) + rand(14))+ 3],
            ['ABCF1239', 42]);

@LINEITEMS = ();
foreach $ITEM (@ITEMSET) {
  my ($q, $v) = @{$ITEM};
  push @LINEITEMS, mklineitem($q, $v);
}
$lineitems = SOAP::Data
  ->value(\@LINEITEMS)
  ->name('lineitems')
  ->type('ARRAY');

  &reportresults('priceitems', $ssrv->priceitems(id => 175, lineitems =>
$lineitems));
```

Suppose this pricing function were being used to submit prices from an invoice in some sort of "purchasing" application, this indicates that system processes should be designed to allow the user to fix the whole invoice, as opposed to just working on one line item at a time. The function `reportresults()` provides a generic function that can dump out the results returned by any of the SOAP methods. Note that it produces formatted output when the results indicate a SOAP fault:

```
===================================================================
  Fault Found
===================================================================
 Code:   SOAP-ENV:priceitems fault in main
 String: illegal data passed to priceitems()
 Actor:  http://salesman:7912/
{
  'faultdetails' => bless( [
    'product ID should have format ZZZZ0000 - was [ABCD124] - lineitem [1]',
    'quantity was [-2] for product [ABCD124] - must be a positive int - lineitem
[1]',
    'quantity was [-3] for product [ABCD1235] - must be a positive int - lineitem
[2]',
    'quantity was [2.5] for product [ABCD1234] - must be a positive int - lineitem
[3]',
    'ID: [175] discount: [0.15]'
  ], 'array' )
}
''

  sub reportresults {
  my ($method, $ssrv_result) = @_;
  if ($ssrv_result->fault) {
    ($code, $string, $actor) = ($ssrv_result->faultcode,
                                $ssrv_result->faultstring,
                                $ssrv_result->faultactor);
    $~ = FAULT_TOP;
```

```
    write;
    print Dumper($ssrv_result->faultdetail, '');
  } else {
    print "-" x 70, "\n";
    print "Result from : $method\n";
    print "-" x 70, "\n";
    my $result = $ssrv_result->result;
    print Dumper($result, '');
  }
}

format FAULT_TOP =
=======================================================================
  Fault Found
=======================================================================
 Code:   @<<<<<<<<<<<<<<<<<<<<<<<<<<<<<<<<<<<<<<<<<<<<<<<<<<<<<<<
  $code
 String: @<<<<<<<<<<<<<<<<<<<<<<<<<<<<<<<<<<<<<<<<<<<<<<<<<<<<<<<
  $string
 Actor:  @<<<<<<<<<<<<<<<<<<<<<<<<<<<<<<<<<<<<<<<<<<<<<<<<<<<<<<<
  $actor
```

The client script finishes off with a couple of helper functions. First, there is `mkdata()`, which wraps the call parameters into a `SOAP::Data` value, with default name and type. Second, there is `mklineitem(product, quantity)`, which generates a product line for use with `priceitem()`, attaching type information and structuring it so that it is ready for transmission as part of a SOAP message:

```
sub mkdata {
  my ($value, $name, $type) = @_;
  $name = 'return' unless $name;
  $type = 'string' unless $type;
  return SOAP::Data -> name($name) ->type($type) ->value($value);
}

sub mklineitem {
  my ($p, $q) = @_;
  my $product = mkdata($p, 'product');
  my $quantity = mkdata($q, 'quantity', 'integer');
  return SOAP::Data->name('lineitem')->
    value({'product' => \$product, 'quantity'=> \$quantity})
      ->type('Array');
}
```

Using XMLRPC::Lite

The `XMLRPC::Lite` module provides a simple interface to the XML-RPC protocol using the transport modules from SOAP::Lite. By using them, it supports the same set of diverse mechanisms starting with HTTP but also including SMTP, HTTPS, and so on.

Just as with SOAP, servers may be run either as daemon processes, using the `XMLRPC::Transport::HTTP::Daemon` method, or may be managed by a web server as CGI processes, using `XMLRPC::Transport::HTTP::CGI`. Here, we will illustrate its use with `XMLRPC::Transport::HTTP::CGI` by building a server that supports the same `Actions` module used in the previous examples:

```
#!/usr/bin/perl
use XMLRPC::Lite;
use XMLRPC::Transport::HTTP;
use Actions;

XMLRPC::Transport::HTTP::CGI
  -> dispatch_to('Actions')
  -> options ({compress_threshold => 800})
  -> handle;
```

The only difference between a SOAP and XML-RPC version is the switch from SOAP to XML-RPC. The CGI module necessitates some additional configuration relating to the web server. In this case, we will use Apache, which is the most widely used open source web server. There are other web servers available such as WN, BOA, AOLserver, and Roxen Challenger.

The first step is to decide on a location to install SOAP components that will be serviced by the web server. The directory for the script files in this case will be `/var/www/soap`. For Apache to invoke Perl scripts as CGI handlers, it is necessary to configure three things in `/etc/apache/httpd.conf`.

Apache needs to be aware that files with the `.pl` suffix are to be treated as CGI scripts, thus:

```
# CGI files may have the following suffixes
AddHandler cgi-script .pl
```

Secondly, there needs to be a mapping to indicate where the scripts actually reside. It is typical for some CGI scripts to reside in `/usr/lib/cgi-bin`, and for that to be associated with URLs looking like http://foo.com/cgi-bin/frobozz.pl. The following `ScriptAlias` allows the SOAP code to reside in `/var/www/soap` and accessed by URLs looking like http://foo.com/soap/soapmethods.pl:.

```
# http://server.org/soap/foo.pl accesses script in file /var/www/soap/foo.pl
ScriptAlias /soap/ /var/www/soap/
```

Lastly, permission needs to be established to execute CGI scripts in directory `/var/www/soap`, which is accomplished by the following `<Directory>` directive:

```
# Allow running CGI scripts in /var/www/soap
<Directory /var/www/soap>
    Options ExecCGI
</Directory>
```

After adding these directives to the Apache `httpd.conf` file, it will be necessary to request that Apache reload its configuration. This may be accomplished by a command similar to `/etc/init.d/apache reload` or `/etc/rc.d/init.d/apache restart` depending on the Linux distribution.

Then, we need a client to make use of the XML-RPC methods. The following client bears a marked resemblance to the sample client presented earlier, the characteristic substitution being that XML-RPC is substituted for SOAP in various module names:

```
#!/usr/bin/perl
use XMLRPC::Transport::HTTP;
use SoapTools;
my $host = "salesman";
my $proxy = "http://$host/soap/xserver.pl";
my $csize = 800;
my $xsrv = XMLRPC::Lite
  -> proxy($proxy, options => ({compress_threshold => $csize}));
print "XML-RPC Server: $xsrv at $proxy\n";
```

Unlike earlier servers using `SOAP::Transport::HTTP::Daemon`, where the proxy is simply a hostname combined with a socket number, the CGI-based software must be referenced via a URL that accesses the CGI script. Thus, when the server resides in `/var/www/soap/xserver.pl`, the URL used for `proxy()` is http://hostname/soap/xserver.pl. There is a bit of a change in the function call used to call the method; the "namespace" must be specified specifically, so that instead of calling `$ssrv->call("methods")`, as done in previous SOAP calls, the call becomes `$xsrv->call("Actions.methods")`:

```
print "Now, explore all the exported methods\n";
UnderLine;
$methods = $xsrv->call("Actions.methods");  # Get list of method names
UnderLine;
```

Given the set of methods, which are the result of `$xsrv->call("Actions.methods")`, the loop goes through each of the methods, running them one by one. Just as with the call to `Actions` method, it is necessary to append `Actions` to each of the methods; `$xsrv->call("Actions.".$method)`:

```
print "Try each method: \n";
UnderLine;
my $mlist = $methods->result;
my @METHODS = @{$mlist};
foreach my $method (@METHODS) {
  print "   Method: $method\n";
  my $res = $xsrv->call("Actions.".$method);
  &reportresults($method, $res);
}
UnderLine;
```

Nonetheless, the code is otherwise nearly the same as it would be for invoking SOAP methods. Here is the implementation of the `UnderLine()` function that generates a line of dashes to improve the appearance of the report:

```
sub UnderLine {
  print "-" x 75, "\n";
}
```

In addition to `Actions.pm` we require another module, `SoapTools.pm`:

```
#!/usr/bin/perl
# $Id: SoapTools.pm,v 1.1 2002/05/13 20:36:21 cbbrowne Exp $
package SoapTools;
require 5.000;
use Exporter;
use Data::Dumper; $Data::Dumper::Terse = 1; $Data::Dumper::Indent = 1;
use SOAP::Lite;
use vars qw(@ISA);
@ISA = (Exporter);
@EXPORT = qw(mkdata reportresults connect_db);

sub connect_db {
    my $dbh = DBI->connect( $dbi_access, $db_user, "", {AutoCommit => 0})
    || die "DB Error\n";
 }

sub mkdata {
  my ($value, $name, $type) = @_;
  $name = 'return' unless $name;
  $type = 'string' unless $type;
  return SOAP::Data -> name($name) ->type($type) ->value($value);
}

sub reportresults {
  my ($method, $ssrv_result) = @_;
  if ($ssrv_result->fault) {
    ($code, $string, $actor) = ($ssrv_result->faultcode,
                               $ssrv_result->faultstring,
                               $ssrv_result->faultactor);
    $~ = FAULT_TOP;
    write;
    print Dumper($ssrv_result->faultdetail, '');
  } else {
    print "-" x 70, "\n";
    print "Result from : $method\n";
    print "-" x 70, "\n";
    my $result = $ssrv_result->result;
    print Dumper($result, '');
  }
}

format FAULT_TOP =
=================================================================
  Fault Found
=================================================================
 Code:  @<<<<<<<<<<<<<<<<<<<<<<<<<<<<<<<<<<<<<<<<<<<<<<<<<<<<<<<<<
  $code
 String: @<<<<<<<<<<<<<<<<<<<<<<<<<<<<<<<<<<<<<<<<<<<<<<<<<<<<<<<<
  $string
 Actor:  @<<<<<<<<<<<<<<<<<<<<<<<<<<<<<<<<<<<<<<<<<<<<<<<<<<<<<<<<
  $actor
.
1;
```

With SoapTools.pm, Actions.pm, and xserver.pl residing in the directory /var/www/soap, the client code may be put in a file, xclient.pl; the output is thus:

```
XML-RPC Server: XMLRPC::Lite=HASH(0x82f3348) at http://salesman/soap/xserver.pl
Now, explore all the exported methods
Try each method:
   Method: methods
----------------------------------------------------------------------
Result from : methods
----------------------------------------------------------------------
[
  'methods',
  'foo',
  'action1',
  'action1a',
  'action1b',
  'action2',
  'action3',
  'action3a',
  'action3b',
  'action4',
  'action5',
  'action6',
 ...

     Method: action2
====================================================================
  Fault Found
====================================================================
 Code:  Action 2 fault
 String: This page is intentionally blank (and the method inten
 Actor:
''
   Method: action3
----------------------------------------------------------------------
Result from : action3
----------------------------------------------------------------------
'275'
''
   Method: action3a
```

Secure Connections Using Apache and HTTPS

If sensitive information is to be transferred across open networks, it is important to have the ability to submit messages in an encrypted manner. The SOAP::Lite daemon functionality does not directly support SSL/HTTPS, but the typical web server such as Apache does, and may be readily pressed into duty to manage HTTPS transport.

To use HTTPS requires configuring a web server to support this. With Apache, this is likely to involve installing an additional apache-ssl package. With the popularity of Apache, there is probably such a package already set up for any distribution in use. For more information on Apache documentation, refer to the book *Professional Apache 2.0* from *Wrox Press (ISBN 1-861007-22-1).*

To use the HTTPS protocol, it is necessary to generate a RSA certificate. Apache comes with a tool called `ssl-certificate` to generate a self-signed RSA certificate:

```
salesman:/tmp# /usr/sbin/ssl-certificate
creating selfsigned certificate
replace it with one signed by a certification authority (CA)

enter your ServerName at the Common Name prompt

If you want your certificate to expire after x days call this programm
with -days x
Using configuration from /usr/share/apache-ssl/ssleay.cnf
Generating a 1024 bit RSA private key
..++++++
..++++++
writing new private key to '/etc/apache-ssl/apache.pem'
-----
You are about to be asked to enter information that will be incorporated
into your certificate request.
What you are about to enter is what is called a Distinguished Name or a DN.
There are quite a few fields but you can leave some blank
For some fields there will be a default value,
If you enter '.', the field will be left blank.
-----
Country Name (2 letter code) [GB]:CA
State or Province Name (full name) [Some-State]:Ontario
Locality Name (eg, city) []:Scarborough
Organization Name (eg, company; recommended) []:Wrox Canada
Organizational Unit Name (eg, section) []:SOAP Services
server name (eg. ssl.domain.tld; required!!!) []:salesman.cbbrowne.com
Email Address []:root
salesman:/tmp#
```

If the web server were to be made accessible on the public Internet, it would be appropriate to purchase a certificate signed by a public certification authority such as VeriSign or Thawte. It is then necessary to configure `apache-ssl` to be aware of where the CGI scripts will be located, and to configure it to permit their access.

The server script resides in `/var/www/soap/pserver.pl`. The steps for this are the same as described earlier:

```
#!/usr/bin/perl
use SOAP::Transport::HTTP;
use Actions;

SOAP::Transport::HTTP::CGI
  -> dispatch_to('Actions')
  -> options ({compress_threshold => 800})
  -> handle;
```

This server script draws in the `SOAP::Transport::HTTP` class, allows it to use the CGI methods, and draws in `Actions`, providing a set of methods to be invoked. The `dispatch_to('Actions')` method draws in all the public methods of the `Actions` class, allowing their use as SOAP methods. The `compress_threshold` attribute allows large messages to be compressed, if the client supports that. The server resides in `/var/www/soap/pserver.pl` and the URL used for `proxy()` is http://hostname/soap/pserver.pl, similar to the code, as seen in the previous example:

```
#!/usr/bin/perl
use SOAP::Lite;
use SOAP::Transport::HTTP;
use SoapTools;
my $host = "salesman";
my $ssrv = SOAP::Lite
  -> uri("http://www.cbbrowne.com/Actions")
  -> proxy("https://$host/soap/pserver.pl",
           options => ({compress_threshold => 800}));
print "Soap Server: $ssrv at $proxy\n";
```

We specify a `uri()` which ends with the suffix `Actions`, which sets the service identifier for the call. The server uses this to dispatch the call to the appropriate object on the server side. SOAP::Lite expects the URI to take one of the two forms:

- `urn:CLASSNAME`
- `http://urlname/CLASSNAME`

Also, SOAP::Lite will treat `CLASSNAME` as the name of the Perl class to invoke methods.
The `proxy()` call indicates an HTTPS URL, which results in the use of the HTTPS protocol to access the server. This requires having an adequate set of SSL modules installed along with Perl; in the test environment, this requires adding in `libcrypt-ssleay-perl`.

The `libcrypt-ssleay-perl` contains the `Crypt::SSLeay` module. It may be found at CPAN in the Crypt section. Compiling it requires that one of the SSL libraries OpenSSL (http://www.openssl.org/) or SSLeay be installed, though OpenSSL seems to be the preferred library for it to work with.

Note that if the `proxy()` URL is changed to use HTTP rather than HTTPS, the same method can function without any particularly visible change in behavior:

```
print "Now, explore all the exported methods\n";
UnderLine;
$methods = $ssrv->call("methods");  # Get list of method names
UnderLine;
```

Unlike the XML-RPC call, the namespace was specified by the `uri()` call when the connection was set up, so there is no need to specify any namespace. So we have `$ssrv->call("methods")`:

```
print "Try each method: \n";
UnderLine;
my $mlist = $methods->result;
my @METHODS = @{$mlist};
foreach my $method (@METHODS) {
  print "   Method: $method\n";
  my $res = $ssrv->call($method);
  &reportresults($method, $res);
}
UnderLine;
```

Given the set of methods, the result of `$ssrv->call("methods")`, the loop goes through each of the methods, running them one by one. The code is nearly the same as it would be for invoking XML-RPC methods. Here again is the implementation of the `UnderLine()` function that generates a line of dashes to improve the appearance of the report:

```
sub UnderLine {
  print "-" x 75, "\n";
}
```

With SoapTools.pm, Actions.pm, and pserver.pl residing in the directory /var/www/soap, the client code may be put in a file, pclient.pl, and the output is thus:

```
Soap Server: SOAP::Lite=HASH(0x8100918) at
Now, explore all the exported methods
Try each method:
   Method: methods
---------------------------------------------------------------------------
Result from : methods
---------------------------------------------------------------------------
[
  'methods',
  'foo',
  ...

     Method: action6
---------------------------------------------------------------------------
Result from : action6
---------------------------------------------------------------------------
bless( [
  'BC',
  'QC'
], 'array' )
''
   Method: action7
---------------------------------------------------------------------------
Result from : action7
---------------------------------------------------------------------------
'2002/07/01'
''
```

User Authentication

The HTTP protocol provides a way of managing authentication. When a resource is protected, the web server will initially come back with a 401 Authentication Required response, notifying the client that credentials need to be presented in order to receive the requested resource.

A suitably configured client will see this response, and if it supports authentication, it will request a username and password. With a web browser, this would typically involve popping up a box that requests a name and password. With a SOAP method that might be embedded deep inside an application, this is not much of an option.

In Perl, SOAP::Lite makes use of the LWP::UserAgent WWW user agent class, which has methods credentials (netloc, realm, uname, pass) and get_basic_credentials (realm, uri, proxy) for assigning and retrieving credentials for different web sites and realms. The SOAP::Lite side of this is very simple, requiring only a user ID and password to associate with the server connection:

```
#!/usr/bin/perl
use SOAP::Lite;
use SOAP::Transport::HTTP;
use SoapTools;
my $host = "salesman";
my ($user, $password) = ("cbbrowne", "easytoguess");
my $proxy ="https://$user:$password\@$host/soap/pserver.pl";
$ssrv = SOAP::Lite
  -> uri("http://www.cbbrowne.com/Actions")
  -> proxy($proxy,
           options => ({compress_threshold => 800}));
print "Soap Server: $ssrv at $proxy\n";
```

The bigger question is of how to configure authentication on the web server. Apache offers a variety of methods of configuring this, including storing credentials in a file configured in `/etc/apache/httpd.conf`, storing them in each web server directory in a file called `.htaccess`, or if using the `mod_auth_dbm` module in a Berkeley DB file, in some central location.

There are additional modules that allow authenticating clients respectively against an LDAP database, a PostgreSQL or MySQL database against a SMB server using PAM, or against passwords in `/etc/passwd`. Few, if any, other web servers offer that degree of diversity of choice, but do tend to offer similar capabilities regarding how access is to be granted or denied to particular directories or documents.

Authentication is, on one hand, somewhat independent of the transport protocol, working equally well with HTTP and HTTPS. On the other hand, transmitting credentials over the Internet as plain text might not be considered to be very wise, which would encourage sensitive services to only be supported using HTTPS.

Using HTTP::Cookies

If the server hosting the Web Service manages authentication using cookies, SOAP::Lite may use the `HTTP::Cookies` to manage the cookies. This has the benefit that the authentication process can take place once, at the beginning of a session, and SOAP methods will not need to contain any authentication information, as the server may request a cookie containing the credentials on demand.

Cookies are a general mechanism that a web server can use to store and retrieve a block of information on the client side of the connection.

Their use has proven somewhat controversial, as web applications have sometimes used them poorly. Server applications sometimes store substantial data on the client, which certainly is not necessary; this data then points to a security risk since an adversary server might try to pull information from a client's **cookie jar**.

The proper use for a cookie would be storing a randomly generated session ID and providing a somewhat more elegant way for a web server to track user sessions than alternatives such as embedding the ID in a URL or in a hidden HTML FORM field.

Unfortunately, people tend to get a bit edgy when web sites pass on information via cookies to advertisers' traffic-tracking systems. There are concerns of private information being exposed using cookies; it only happens when cookies themselves are used to store substantial data. A session ID, useless to anything other than the one web application, which expires in an hour or two is not a huge security exposure; if a web application stored your credit card number in a cookie, that should be a matter for concern.

If a cookie contains a seemingly random jumble of data, how can you prove that it doesn't contain important private information in some encrypted form? A random session ID cannot be easily distinguished from an encrypted credit card number. For more information on cookies, refer to the Netscape Cookie Specifications at http://www.netscape.com/newsref/std/cookie_spec.html and http://www.cookiecentral.com/.

The SOAP::Lite Perl module offers the ability for client-side management of cookies. It uses the `HTTP::Cookies` class that is usually found in a package called `libwww-perl`. Look at the following diagram:

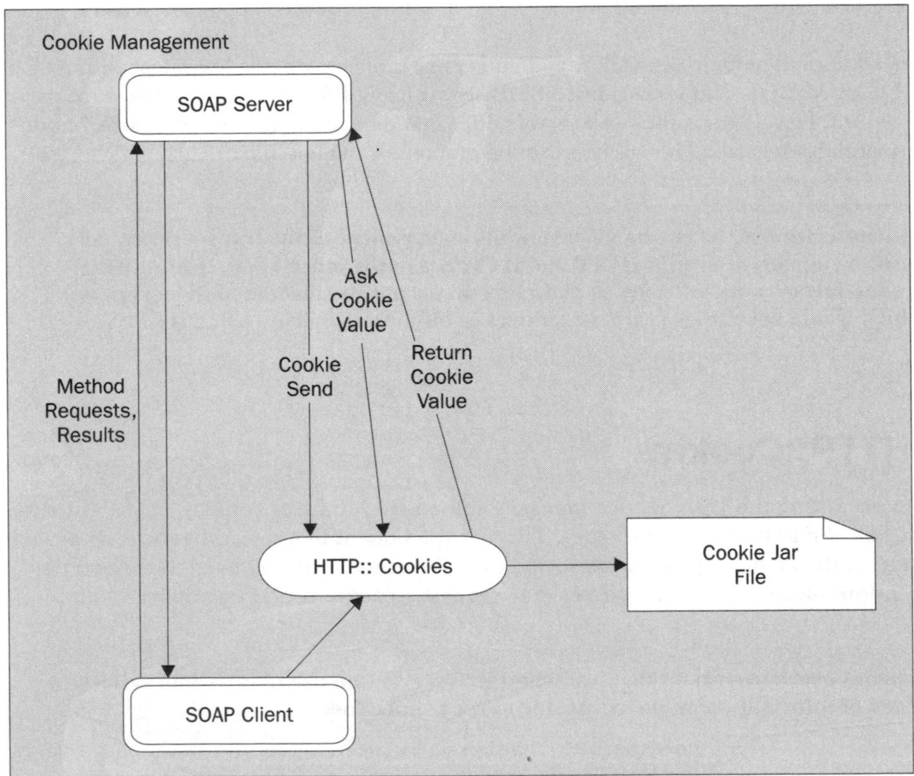

When the client attaches the `HTTP::Cookies` object to its transport method, it allows the cookie object to intercept any HTTP cookie requests made by servers, thus allowing servers to add cookies, or request their values. If a cookie jar file is attached to this, cookies may persist across sessions:

```
#!/usr/bin/perl -w
use SOAP::Lite;
use HTTP::Cookies;

$uri = "foo";
my $soap = SOAP::Lite
  -> proxy("http://localhost:8072")
  -> uri($uri);
```

This script uses a simple calendar service, which unfortunately doesn't support cookies. The special cookie configuration here starts by instantiating a cookie jar. In this case, the file parameter results in cookies being stored between sessions in the file `/home/cbbrowne/.perlcookies`, and the parameters `autosave` and `ignore_discard` are configured to maximize the cookie information that is to be stored, including keeping the cookies that the server requests to be discarded:

```
my $CookieJar = HTTP::Cookies
  -> new( file => "/home/cbbrowne/.perlcookies",
          autosave => 1,
          ignore_discard => 1,
        );
$soap->transport->cookie_jar($CookieJar);
```

Given a `$CookieJar`, it may then be attached to the SOAP requests using the `cookie_jar()` method. Any server requests that ask for or provide cookies will use this cookie jar:

```
print "Get year:\n";
print $soap->getYear(2002)->result;
print "Get month:\n";
print $soap->getMonth(2002, 2)->result;
```

The script then proceeds to request some SOAP methods from the server, processing any cookies as they come along:

```
#LWP-Cookies-1.0
```

Since the particular server accessed did not request to store any cookies, the resulting cookie jar doesn't contain much. Unfortunately, the SOAP::Lite module does not yet provide any server-specific support for the use of cookies.

Summary

This chapter has provided an introduction to the use of SOAP::Lite to implement SOAP clients and servers in Perl. We also saw examples showing the use of `XMLRPC::Lite` module. This module provides a simple interface to the XML-RPC protocol using the transport modules from SOAP::Lite.

The essential points covered in the chapter are:

- SOAP::Lite provides a large set of functions to support the use of Perl to build and use SOAP services
- Additional SOAP::Lite utilities were used, including an interactive test shell, `SOAPsh.pl`, and a WSDL stub generator `stubber.pl`
- SOAP::Lite includes a set of methods to access and even update UDDI repositories
- A server and client were constructed to show various techniques of service construction

For additional information on SOAP and Perl, you may want to refer to the following web links:

- http://www.soaplite.com/ – home site of SOAP::Lite development
- http://www.perl.com/pub/a/language/admin/whats_new.html
- The Perl Institute (http://www.perl.org/)
- CPAN – Comprehensive Perl Archive Network (ftp://ftp.sedl.org/pub/mirrors/CPAN/ROADMAP.html)

7

Python and Web Services

Python is one of the popular high-level languages for building web-based applications. It was developed in the early 1990s as a scripting component for the Amoeba distributed operating system.

In this chapter we will talk about the implementation of the Web Service technologies like SOAP, and XML-RPC using Python. We will start by taking a brief look at the language features and see how compatible it is with Web Services. We then look at the installation and usage of the popularly used Python libraries.

Lastly, we will discuss the advantages and disadvantages of XML-RPC over the SOAP protocol.

Python

Python was designed with emphasis on concepts like quality, productivity, portability, and integration. The design forces a programmer to write readable code that helps to maintain and reuse software. Since the Python interpreter handles declarations, memory management, and such, it helps in writing scripts faster. Also, since it is portable across platforms from IBM mainframes to handheld PDAs and integrates with other languages like C, C++, and Java along with components like COM, CORBA, and SOAP, it is viable for a wide variety of domains.

In addition, Python also provides some object-oriented features, where all the variables in a program are represented as objects having identity and type. Similar to other object languages, the identity of a Python object is represented by the memory address of the object, and type information is stored at the address to determine the methods to be used to manipulate the object. Both types and method bindings are assigned to objects dynamically at run time, similar to dynamic languages such as Lisp and Smalltalk.

Python uses automatic reference counting of objects to manage their life cycle, so that programmers do not spend extra time writing memory management code. When the number of references to an object drops to zero, Python's run time environment automatically discards it.

Dynamic languages like Python use "introspection" – programs that manipulate types, values, methods, and (may even) construct method bindings at run time. This allows native Python function calls to intercept a SOAP handler function that transforms the function arguments into XML messages and in turn submit it to the SOAP server. The XML message that is returned is then transformed into a return value for the method.

In contrast, in languages that lack this sort of dynamic introspection, such as C and C++, code that calls a SOAP method using an ordinary function call such as `Price = SOAP::getPrice("RHAT")`, must be created when the program is initially compiled.

Python uses strong dynamic typing where strings are not automatically coerced into numbers and vice-versa; conversions must be expressly requested. Python does not take this to the extreme that the ML family of languages (such as Standard ML and Objective CAML) do, where, to add an integer variable to a float, one must be coerced to match the other, but it certainly behaves in a much stricter manner than Perl. The various standard SOAP types of integers, strings, floats, and such, map quite directly to Python types.

The SOAP implementations discussed later contain code marshaling both to transform values from Python types into SOAP data (for transmission) and to transform XML message data back into the native Python data types.

Python and SOAP

There is a large set of open source SOAP libraries developed for Python. Unfortunately, this includes a number of abandoned projects as well. The implementation that is most 'mature' at the time of writing, SOAP.py, is no longer being actively developed. The company sponsoring development for it, actzero, went out of business. However, some efforts have gone in to keep it working with Python 2.1, and the Python2 SAX XML parser. These are quite widely released in packaged forms like RPMs and Debian's `.deb`.

The other implementation that is undergoing significant development effort is ZSI (The Zolera SOAP Infrastructure), produced by Rich Salz, who is probably best known as the author of INN that succeeded C-News as the "industrial strength news server." Version 1.2 of ZSI was released in March 2002. Though ZSI is not mature yet, the Python community expects it to ultimately become dominant.

On the other hand the XML libraries have been under heavy development during the year 2001 and 2002, making them something of a "moving target" for applications depending on their use. It has proven fairly easy to implement basic Python libraries to provide support for some parts of SOAP. As a result, a number of projects have recreated the same relatively rudimentary parts of SOAP. The implementation of additional layered standards such as WSDL requires considerably effort and interest. These projects have come down before getting WSDL support working.

Another implementation called SOAPy (http://www.sourceforge.net/projects/soapy/) claims that given a WSDL or SDL document, SOAPy parses the published API to expose it to Python applications as transparently as possible. Unfortunately, SOAPy had its sole release in April 2001, and is no longer compatible with the Python XML tools available in 2002.

The developers of the Zope Framework (http://www.zope.org/) also have efforts under way to implement Web Services. Zope already has support for an XML-RPC transport layer, so developers are considering how they might use WSDL and UDDI for service discovery. There is some preliminary documentation for Zope Web Services (http://cvs.zope.org/~checkout~/Packages/WebService/doc/WebService.html). However, no code has yet been released; just a discussion of what ought to be implemented.

ZSI Interoperability Issues

As of early 2002, ZSI has not yet gone through a full spectrum of interoperability tests, and does not yet interoperate well with a number of common SOAP platforms. For example, it submits messages to both the `getQuote()` and `getPrice()` servers (used in a number of the examples in this book) that some servers cannot cope with.

Here is an XML message that it submits for a book price query `getPrice('0716715872')`:

```
<?xml version='1.0' encoding='utf-8'?>
<SOAP-ENV:Envelope
xmlns:SOAP-ENV="http://schemas.xmlsoap.org/soap/envelope/"
xmlns:SOAP-ENC="http://schemas.xmlsoap.org/soap/encoding/"
xmlns:xsi="http://www.w3.org/2001/XMLSchema-instance"
xmlns:xsd="http://www.w3.org/2001/XMLSchema"
xmlns:ZSI="http://www.zolera.com/schemas/ZSI/"
SOAP-ENV:encodingStyle="http://schemas.xmlsoap.org/soap/encoding/"
xmlns="urn:xmethods-BNPriceCheck">
  <SOAP-ENV:Body>
    <getPrice>
      <xsd:string id="8089f28">0716715872</xsd:string>
    </getPrice>
  </SOAP-ENV:Body>
</SOAP-ENV:Envelope>
```

Compare the above message with the equivalent XML message generated by `SOAP::Lite` (Perl and SOAP) below:

```
<?xml version="1.0" encoding="utf-8"?>
<SOAP-ENV:Envelope
xmlns:SOAP-ENC="http://schemas.xmlsoap.org/soap/encoding/"
SOAP-ENV:encodingStyle="http://schemas.xmlsoap.org/soap/encoding/"
xmlns:SOAP-ENV="http://schemas.xmlsoap.org/soap/envelope/"
xmlns:xsi="http://www.w3.org/1999/XMLSchema-instance"
xmlns:xsd="http://www.w3.org/1999/XMLSchema">
  <SOAP-ENV:Body>
    <namesp5:getPrice xmlns:namesp5="urn:xmethods-BNPriceCheck">
      <c-gensym15 xsi:type="xsd:string">0131103628</c-gensym15>
    </namesp5:getPrice>
  </SOAP-ENV:Body>
</SOAP-ENV:Envelope>
```

The XML generated by ZSI looks quite a lot cleaner than what SOAP::Lite produced, with far fewer namespace attributes. This simplicity doesn't make it a functional query. The interoperability problem appears to result from a bug on the server side, where the server expects a `xmlns` attribute with the URN to be enclosed in the `getPrice` element tag, not taking into consideration the URN in the attribute `xmlns` of the `SOAP-ENV:Envelope` element.

The SOAP specification permits the URN to appear in both places, and indeed examples in the specification show `xmlns` attributes in both places. ZSI omits this element, under the assumption that servers will draw the namespace from the envelope. It seems that a number of servers implemented require the namespace attribute to be part of the method element. This can be argued to be incorrect.

Since the server implementation does not lie under our control, the inability of a server to pick up namespaces from the envelope might never get fixed. It seems more likely that ZSI will ultimately be modified to conform interoperability to other SOAP implementations.

This represents a good example of the "not-so-clean" side of SOAP. There is a great deal of variance in the ways different implementations go about implementing the standards. There isn't (even in theory) a single, unambiguous, "correct" representation for the XML messages being transferred. While sometimes there are pleasant surprises, as with ZSI's ability to generate multiple-reference links, interoperability is a goal that is not accomplished with complete success. Though ZSI works quite well as a server library, its behavior for implementing clients still leaves gaps.

Installing Python Libraries

The widespread popularity of Python has led to a great deal of distribution support for Python and extension libraries. The Debian distribution, for instance, has around 200 Python-related packages available. There is a good chance that pre-packaged libraries might be available for whatever service is needed, and it has some significant advantages over installing packages from source:

- Running a package installation command like `rpm -i python-soap_1.6-i386.rpm` is a lot simpler than locating sourcecode, extracting it from an archive file, customizing, and installing it.
- If there is a need to have Python libraries installed on a large number of systems, installing them manually becomes time consuming, especially if they need to be upgraded later.

As a result, it is an excellent idea to start by investigating the availability of packages for Python libraries for your systems. However, if you do not have suitable package files for your distribution available, you will find it necessary to install some set of Python modules manually. If there is a need to deploy SOAP-related Python modules on a large number of systems, it may prove necessary to build packages for the systems on which the applications are to be used.

The good news is that Python comes with a `distutils.core` module which often makes manual installation as easy as running the command `python setup.py install`.

The `distutils.core` module might be left out of a default Python install on Linux distributions that make extensive use of package management, since the makers often assume that all software will be installed using the package management system. On Debian, `distutils.core` is found in the `python2.1-dev` package; on Red Hat 7.3 it is found in the `Distutils` package. As of Python 2.0, `distutils` is part of the "core" install of Python on FreeBSD, and hence should already be there.

The `setup()` function is able to examine Python configuration to determine where the package ought to be installed, and can invoke scripts to customize the installed package for your system's configuration.

Once you get Python installed, with its large quantities of links to UNIX libraries and a sizeable set of Python modules, it becomes very easy to support the installation of additional modules written in Python.

For example, the script that performs installation of ZSI consists of the following Python code, most of which represents documentation about the ZSI module:

```
#!/usr/bin/env python
import sys
from distutils.core import setup

_url = "http://www.zolera.com/resources/opensrc/zsi"

import ConfigParser
cf = ConfigParser.ConfigParser()
cf.read('setup.cfg')
_version = "%d.%d" % \
    ( cf.getint('version', 'major'), cf.getint('version', 'minor') )

try:
    open('ZSI/version.py', 'r').close()
except:
    print 'ZSI/version.py not found; run "make"'
    sys.exit(1)

setup(
    name="ZSI",
    version=_version,
    licence="Python",
    packages=[ "ZSI", ],
    description="Zolera SOAP Infrastructure",
    author="Rich Salz",
    author_email="rsalz@zolera.com",
    maintainer="Rich Salz",
    maintainer_email="rsalz@zolera.com",
    url=_url,
    long_description='For additional information, please see ' + _url
)
```

With the amount of meta data stored in `setup.py` and `setup.cfg`, it would not be surprising to see tools emerge to automatically generate package files based on this. This has not yet been done with Python tools, but there is a tool for FreeBSD of just this sort to help install Perl modules called `BSDPAN`. This module causes Perl extensions to register themselves in the FreeBSD package database in much the same manner that they would be had they been installed from a BSD "port," effectively merging the Perl and FreeBSD packaging systems. Hopefully, similar tools will emerge to help manage Python extensions.

Installing XML Support – PyXML

PyXML is a toolkit for Python comprising of several XML parsers, a SAX interface, and DOM interfaces. This package is a collection of libraries to process XML with Python. The official location of development of the XML library used by both SOAP.py and ZSI is PyXML at SourceForge (http://pyxml.sourceforge.net/).

Typically, the simplest way of managing packages on Linux and BSD is to use a distribution's native packaging scheme, thereby automating installation and management of upgrades. There are versions of PyXML downloadable in pre-packaged form for a wide variety of systems:

- **RPM-based systems**
  Many Linux distributions use the RPM format for management of the installation of software packages. Downloads available at SourceForge include versions 0.6.6, 0.7.0, and 0.7.1 as RPM files that may be usable on your RPM-based distribution

- **PyXML for SuSE - 0.6.2-16**
  (http://www.suse.com/en/products/suse_linux/alpha/packages/pyxml.html)

- **PyXML 0.7-4 for Red Hat 7.3**
  The web site http://rpmfind.net/ lists versions compiled for several platforms (http://rpmfind.net//linux/RPM/redhat/7.3/i386/PyXML-0.7-4.i386.html). For RPM-based Linux distributions, the installation process involves downloading a RPM package file suitable for your distribution, and then installing that file via a command similar to `# rpm -i PyXML-0.7-4.i386.rpm`

- **Debian**
  Debian offers multiple versions of the distribution; the stable version at the time of writing offers Python 1.5 with python-xml version 0.5.1. The testing and unstable versions offer Python 2.1 with python2.1-xml version 0.7. With Debian systems, the installation process can be as simple as running the command `# apt-get install python-xml` or `# apt-get install python2.1-xml`

Console and graphical applications such as dselect, aptitude, kpackage, gnome-apt, and synaptic are also available, providing interactive applications to manage packages.

The BSD family of systems are prominent for their use of the Ports system to manage the installation of software packages, providing a set of tools to automate the process of downloading sourcecode and compiling the resulting applications:

- NetBSD Ports includes pyxml (ftp://ftp.netbsd.org/pub/NetBSD/packages/pkgsrc/textproc/pyxml/README.html)
- FreeBSD Ports includes py-xml (http://www.freebsd.org/cgi/url.cgi?ports/textproc/py-xml/pkg-descr/)
- OpenBSD Ports also includes a py-xml package

Hopefully, one of these options will provide a managed way of installing PyXML. If none of them provide a suitable version, it will be necessary to download the package and install it manually:

- First, download the source code, from the downloads of PyXML at SourceForge (http://sourceforge.net/projects/pyxml/)
- Extract the sources from the sourcecode download, typically with a command similar to tar xfvz PyXML-0.7.1.tar.gz
- Build a C extension and set up all *.py files using the command python setup.py build. This step requires having a C compiler available, as several files related to the Expat XML and SGML parser must be compiled

- Finally, install everything in the /site-packages/ directory for your system using the command python setup.py install. This must be done by a privileged user such as 'root' who has write access to the directory where the Python libraries will be installed, commonly in /usr/lib/python2.1/site-packages/ or /usr/local/lib/python2.1/site-packages/.

Using SOAP.py

In this section, we will take a look at the SOAP.py implementation. We will start with the installation of SOAP.py and then move on to some practical examples. This will involve accessing stock prices, book prices, server-side programming, programming with SSL connection, and lastly some client-side programming. We will also look at the unique feature of SOAP.py – the multiple references facility.

Installing SOAP.py

The SOAP.py package can use several XML parsers, including the DOM and SAX implementations that are part of PyXML. Packaged versions are available for some Linux and BSD distributions; it is worth checking for packages for Linux distributions that use RPM.

On Debian, the installation process is as simple as the command:

```
$ apt-get install python-soappy
```

Alternatively, you may download sourcecode (`SOAPpy097.tgz`) from the development site SourceForge – Web Services for Python, and then copy the file SOAP.py from the archive into the location of Python packages, commonly `/usr/lib/python2.1/site-packages/` or `/usr/local/lib/python2.1/site-packages/`.

There may also exist directories on your system for older or newer versions of Python, such as `/usr/local/lib/python2.0/site-packages/` or `/usr/lib/python2.1/site-packages/`; it may prove necessary to alter the location accordingly.

SOAP.py can make use of `M2Crypto` and `SSL` classes to permit encrypted access using SSL, including support of SSL certificates. This requires building Python with support for OpenSSL, and, if you wish to use an SSL server with SOAP.py, installing M2Crypto which also depends on the Simplified Wrapper and Interface Generator (SWIG). Some distributions may include packages to support SSL with Python. For instance, Debian comes with a package called `python2.1-pyopenssl`.

The availability of pre-packaged M2Crypto support is rather limited. The package available for Red Hat Linux 7.2 is configured only for use with Python version 1.5, which is not suitable for use with SOAP.py that prefers Python 2.1.

All these packages can be found at:

- Web Services for Python
  http://sourceforge.net/projects/pywebsvcs/
- SOAPpy097.tgz
  http://prdownloads.sourceforge.net/pywebsvcs/SOAPpy097.tgz

- M2Crypto
  http://www.post1.com/home/ngps/m2/
  http://www.pobox.org.sg/home/ngps/m2/
- m2crypto-0.05_snap4-2.i386 RPM
  http://rpmfind.net/linux/RPM/redhat/7.2/i386/m2crypto-0.05_snap4-2.i386.html
- OpenSSL
  http://www.openssl.org/
- SWIG
  http://www.swig.org/

Accessing Stock Prices

The SOAP.py class of primary interest here while building a SOAP client is called `SOAPProxy`. Depending on the parameters provided, it sets up the destination address as an instance of `SOAPAddress`, and sets up message transport using `HTTPTransport`. There is normally no need to consider these classes, as `SOAPProxy` dispatches them automatically. If later SOAP.py supports additional transport protocols such as SMTP or Jabber, then we would expect to see additional classes such as `SMTPTransport` or `JabberTransport`.

The diagram below shows the class objects with their various functionalities and relationships. All the classes make use of the `HTTPTransport` class for transmission. The various keywords that are used with the `SOAPProxy` class are shown in the table below. The SOAP method is invoked by the `call()` function through the `SOAPProxy` object as we shall see in the diagram below:

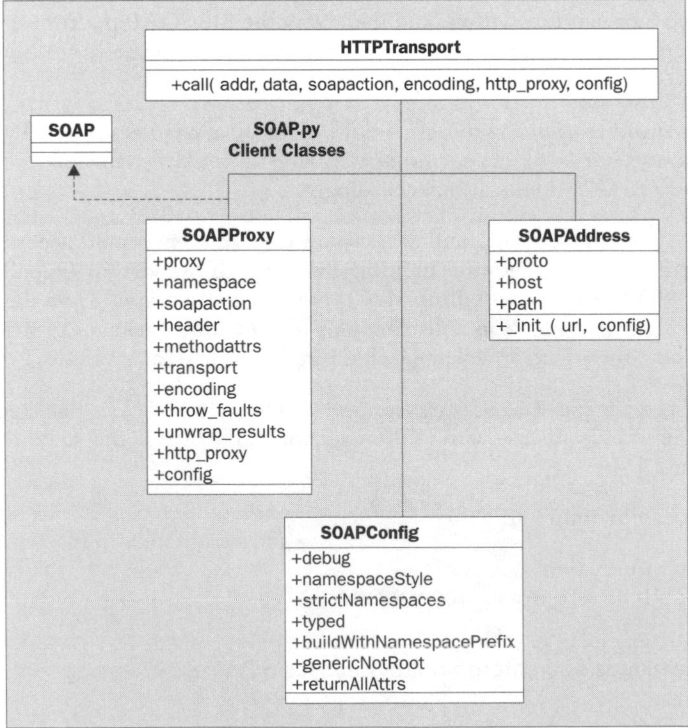

This program submits messages to a SOAP service at http://services.xmethods.com/soap/ that provides time-delayed access to prices of securities trading on NYSE and NASDAQ:

```
#!/usr/bin/env python
import SOAP
from SOAP import *
server = "http://services.xmethods.com/soap"
namespace= "urn:xmethods-delayed-quotes"
serv = SOAP.SOAPProxy(server, namespace=namespace)
stocks = ["LNUX", "NT", "TSG", "RHAT", "IBM", "MSFT", "AMR"]
print "Stock     Price"
print "==============="
stocks.sort
for el in stocks:
    print "%6s %8.3f" % (el, serv.getQuote(symbol=el))
```

The method that sets up the connection to the SOAP server is `SOAPProxy()`, which is a member of the `SOAP` class. The table below shows the various parameters accepted by `SOAPProxy()`:

Keyword	Default Value	Description
`proxy`	none	URL to the SOAP server
`namespace`	none	Namespace for the `xmlns` attribute
`soapaction`	`''`	Value for HTTP SOAPAction
`header`	none	Set of Python tuples to attach to envelope header
`methodattrs`	none	Set of Python tuples to attach to method tag
`transport`	`HTTPTransport`	Python class providing a `call()` method to transmit messages
`encoding`	`UTF-8`	Character set encoding
`throw_faults`	`1`	If true, SOAP fault is raised as a Python fault
`unwrap_results`	`1`	Should the results be unwrapped from XML form?
`http_proxy`	none	A proxy through which messages should be tunneled
`config`	`Config`	Python object containing SOAP.py configuration

Accessing Book Prices Using Python SOAP

The script `Books.py` demonstrates the process of looking up the pricing information about books using a SOAP service provided by the bookseller Barnes and Noble:

```
#!/usr/bin/env python
import SOAP
server = "http://services.xmethods.net/soap/servlet/rpcrouter"
namespace="urn:xmethods-BNPriceCheck"
serv = SOAP.SOAPProxy(server, namespace=namespace)

ISBNS = {  '0596000278' : 'Programming Perl',
```

```
            '0716715872' : 'Linear Programming',
            '1861003013' : 'Professional Linux Programming',
            '0131103628' : 'The C Programming Language',
            '1555581234' : 'The Unix Philosophy',
            '1568842031' : 'The Unix-Haters Handbook',
            '0201379279' : 'Advanced CORBA Programming with C++'
        }

print "      Book                              Price"
print "------------------------------------------"
for el in ISBNS.keys():
    print "%32s  %8.2f" % (ISBNS[el], serv.getPrice(el))
```

In a weakly typed language, it proves necessary to explicitly present the ISBN as a string for the SOAP message to recognize it. In Python, a strongly typed language, the ISBN type is recognized as a string.

Server Programming with SOAP.py

Here is a simple server that exports a set of functions in a class called `Actions`, running as an HTTP daemon:

```
#!/usr/bin/python
import SOAP
import Actions
import ComplexAction
from Actions import *
from ComplexAction import *
port = 7452
server=SOAP.SOAPServer(("localhost", port))
server.registerFunction(action1)
server.registerFunction(action2)
server.registerFunction(action3a)
server.registerFunction(action3b)
server.registerFunction(action3c)
server.registerFunction(action3d)
server.registerFunction(action3e)
server.registerFunction(action4)
server.registerFunction(action5)
server.registerFunction(action6)
server.registerFunction(action6a)
server.registerFunction(methods)
server.registerKWFunction(priceitems)
print "Start server on port ", port
server.serve_forever()
```

The diagram below shows some of the relationships between the classes that are connected to the `SOAPServer` class:

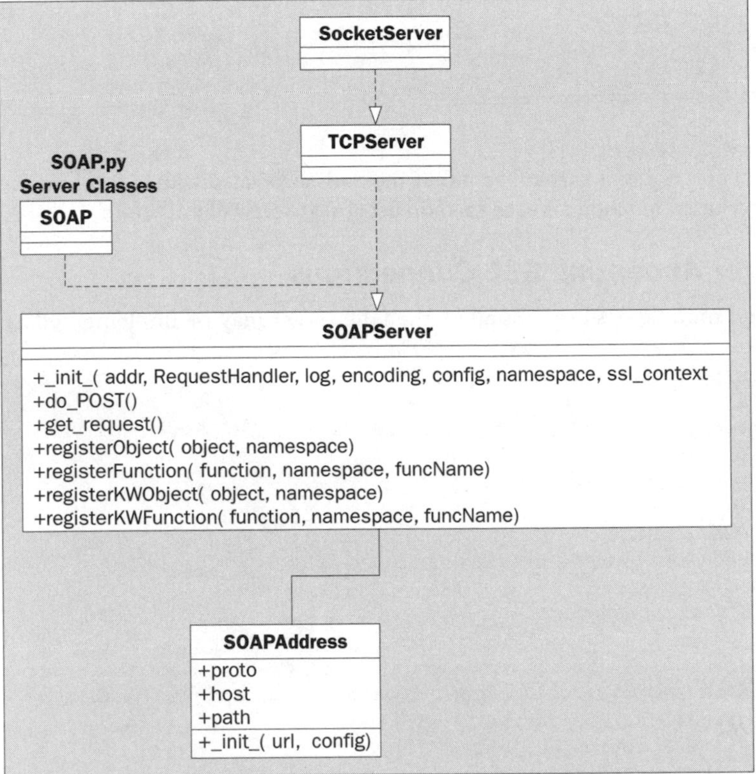

This class has several methods used to set up its connections to SOAP methods. The server is initialized with an indication of what protocols it can accept, and how it is to be configured overall. A set of registration functions is then used to attach Python methods to the `SOAPServer` object, indicating what namespaces they are to use. Objects as well as functions can be registered; in the case of a Python object, each of the public methods associated with that object will be added as SOAP methods.

The server draws in a set of functions from the class `Actions` that accept no parameters, and pass back different types of values; these functions are discussed in greater detail later in the chapter.

The server runs on the local host, accepting connections on port 7452. Notice that the methods are registered with the server using the method. There are four ways of registering methods:

- `registerFunction(function, namespace)`
  Add in the namespace parameter to allow functions to be associated with different URNs.
- `registerObject(obj)`
  This registers every method associated with the object instance obj.
- `registerKWFunction(f1)`
  This registers function `f1()`, passing in a Python dictionary of named arguments.

The implementation of function `f1()` looks like:

```
def f1 (**kw):
    first = kw['first']
    second = kw['second']
    third = kw['third']
    return first + second + third
```

- `registerKWObject(obj)`
  This function registers each of the public methods associated with object instance obj, setting up a keyword-based function for each method using registerKWFunction().

SOAP.py Server Accepting SSL Connections

If the `M2Crypto` module has been installed, then the server may be implemented as follows:

```
#!/usr/bin/python
import SOAP
import Actions
from Actions import *
from M2Crypto import SSL

# Set up SSL context
apachecert= '/etc/apache-ssl/apache.pem'
ssl_c = SSL.Context()
ssl_c.load_cert(apachecert)

port = 7452
server=SOAP.SOAPServer(("localhost", port), ssl_context = ssl_c)
server.registerFunction(action1)
server.registerFunction(action2)
server.registerFunction(action3a)
server.registerFunction(action3b)
server.registerFunction(action3c)
server.registerFunction(action3d)
server.registerFunction(action3e)
server.registerFunction(action4)
server.registerFunction(action5)
server.registerFunction(action6)
server.registerFunction(action6a)
server.registerFunction(methods)
print "Start server on port ", port
server.serve_forever()
```

The differences between this and the previous server have to do with the set-up of `ssl_c`:

- `SSL.Context()` initializes an SSL context object
- `load_cert()` loads a SSL certificate from the named file

SOAP.py does not offer any way to generate such certificates; a certificate for public use that would provide users with some assurance of authenticity of identity would need to be requested from a certificate authority such as VeriSign or Thawte Consulting.

Alternatively, if the service is to be used privately, and the only concern is to ensure that traffic is transmitted with encryption, Apache-SSL package includes a tool called `ssl-certificate` that is used to generate a self-signed SSL certificate. Once the certificate is loaded, it must be tied to the SOAP server instance through the `ssl_context` parameter to `SOAPServer()`.

In the long run, it would likely be preferable for this functionality to be managed in a centralized manner through a web server like Apache or Roxen; but unfortunately SOAP.py does not offer a transport scheme whereby it can be invoked as a CGI method.

Client –Implemented Using SOAP.py

We now look at an extended example to demonstrate many SOAP programming techniques. It connects to the server, `pserver.py`, and demonstrates the use of the methods. The script starts by importing the SOAP module, as well as others that are used, then configures the connection to the SOAP server, attaching it to the server:

```
#!/usr/bin/env python
from SOAP import *
import types
import sys
#(host, port) = ('salesman', 7927)
#url="http://%s:%d/" % (host, port)
url="http://salesman/soap/pserver.pl"
action="http://www.cbbrowne.com/Actions"

#Config.debug=1
Config.BuildWithNoType=1
Config.BuildWithNoNamespacePrefix=1
print "SOAP server at ", url
server=SOAPProxy(url,action)
```

Functions `DisplayResult(name, res)` and `unravel(res)` provide somewhat similar functionality to Perl's `Data::Dumper` class, and are used to display the results returned by SOAP messages:

```
  def DisplayResult(name, res):
  print '--------------------------------------------------------------'
  print ' Method: ', name
  print '--------------------------------------------------------------'
  unravel(res)

def unravel(res):
  if type(res) == type('string'):
      print res
  elif isinstance(res, arrayType):
      print "List: ["
      for foo in res:
          unravel(foo)
      print "]"
  elif isinstance(res, typedArrayType):
      print "List: ["
      for foo in res:
          unravel(foo)
```

```
        print " ]"
    elif isinstance(res, structType):
        print "Structure: {"
        for foo in res:
            unravel(foo)
        print " }"
    else:
        print res
```

This calls the SOAP `methods()`, and lists the methods listed therein. There is no easy equivalent with ZSI or SOAP.py to the Perl's `call()` method, so this isn't as useful as it was in Perl. In the future, methods might be added to these SOAP libraries to harness this sort of functionality:

```
methods = server.methods()
DisplayResult('method', methods)
```

This section runs through each of the SOAP methods defined in the `Actions` class, displaying the results. Each call is wrapped in a `try` / `except` exception handler so that the script will not abort early if one or another of the methods should happen to fail:

```
try:
    res = server.action1()
    DisplayResult('action1', res)
except:
    'Failure of method: action1'
try:
    res = server.action2()
    DisplayResult('action2', res)
except:
    'Failure of method: action2'
try:
    res = server.action3a()
    DisplayResult('action3a', res)
except:
    'Failure of method: action3a'
try:
    res = server.action3b()
    DisplayResult('action3b', res)
except:
    'Failure of method: action3b'
try:
    res = server.action3c()
    DisplayResult('action3c', res)
except:
    'Failure of method: action3c'

try:
    res = server.action3d()
    DisplayResult('action3d', res)
except:
    'Failure of method: action3d'
```

```
try:
    res = server.action3e()
    DisplayResult('action3e', res)
except:
    'Failure of method: action3e'

try:
    res = server.action4()
    DisplayResult('action4', res)
except:
    'Failure of method: action4'

try:
    res = server.action5()
    DisplayResult('action5', res)
except:
    'Failure of method: action5'

try:
    res = server.action6()
    DisplayResult('action6', res)
except:
    'Failure of method: action6'

try:
    res = server.action6a()
    DisplayResult('actiona', res)
except:
    'Failure of method: action6a'

try:
    res = server.action7()
    DisplayResult('action7', res)
except:
    'Failure of method: action7'
```

The `try` / `except` structure allows trapping errors. In the block of code in the `try` section, there is code that we intend to try to run. If an error is raised within that block, program control moves to the `except` section. In this case, `except` has no arguments, and so will trap any sort of error that is raised in the `try` section. If a specific type of error were specified, then the specified sort of error would be trapped, while other errors would be left to propagate to any other exception handlers that might also be watching.

Within each `try` block, a statement like `res = server.actionsomething()` passes a pretty empty SOAP message to the method `actionsomething()` on the SOAP server. The result is bound to the variable `res`.

The result in `res` is then displayed using the local function `DisplayResult(name, result)`. This function uses `unravel()` to pull apart and display the contents of `res`. If the result is a complex data structure like an array, `unravel()` recursively unravels it and displays each element.

In case the SOAP method fails, an exception is raised and the method is listed as having failed. This is repeated for each of the methods that have been implemented in the server.

The types represented in this table reflect transformations of values into specific SOAP types:

SOAP Type	Python Type	Class in SOAP.py
`xsd:string`	`StringType`, `UnicodeType`	`StringType`
`xsd:Boolean`	`0`, `'0'`, `'false'`, `''`, `1`, `'1'`, `'true'`	`booleanType`
`xsd:decimal`	`IntType`, `LongType`, `FloatType`	`decimalType`
`xsd:float`	`IntType`, `LongType`, `FloatType`	`floatType`
`xsd:double`	`IntType`, `LongType`, `FloatType`	`doubleType`
`xsd:duration`	List of up to 6 numeric elements	`durationType`
`xsd:datetime`	timestamp as numeric or as list of numerics	`dateTimeType`
`xsd:time`	numeric timestamp, list of numeric elements	`timeType`
`xsd:date`	numeric timestamp, list of numeric elements	`dateType`
`xsd:yearmonth`	numeric timestamp, list of numeric elements	`gYearMonthType`
`xsd:year`	numeric timestamp, list of numeric elements	`GYearType`
`xsd:hexbinary`	`StringType`, `UnicodeType`	`hexBinaryType`
`xsd:base64binary`	`StringType`, `UnicodeType`	`base64BinaryType`
`xsd:binary`	any type	`binaryType`
`xsd:integer`	`IntType`, `LongType`	`IntegerType`
`xsd:long`	`IntType`, `LongType`	`longType`
`xsd:int`	`IntType`, `LongType`	`intType`
`xsd:short`	`IntType`, `LongType`	`shortType`
`xsd:byte`	`IntType`, `LongType`	`byteType`
`xsd:unsignedlong`	`IntType`, `LongType`	`unsignedLongType`
`xsd:unsignedshort`	`IntType`, `LongType`	`unsignedShortType`
`xsd:unsignedbyte`	`IntType`, `LongType`	`unsignedByteType`
`xsd:array`	`ListType`, `TupleType`	`arrayType`
`xsd:array[type]`	`ListType`, `TupleType`	`typedArrayType`

This section shows a set of Python class definitions that may be used to set up structured requests for SOAP.py using the SOAP structure type:

```
class ID(structType):
    def __init__(self, id):
        structType.__init__(self, name='id')
        self.id = id

class LineItems(structType):
    def __init__(self, items):
        structType.__init__(self, name='lineitems')
        self.lineitems = items

class Product(structType):
    def __init__(self, product):
        structType.__init__(self, name='product')
        self.product = product

class Quantity(structType):
    def __init__(self, quantity):
        structType.__init__(self, name='quantity')
        self.quantity = quantity

class LineItem(structType):
    def __init__(self, product, quantity):
        structType.__init__(self, name='lineitem')
        self.product = Product(product)
        self.quantity = Quantity(quantity)
```

These classes are defined solely with an initialization method, which, in Python, is always named `__init__()`, and which is used to attach attributes to instances of the object.

Each of these classes inherits structure from the SOAPpy class `structType`, which is used to associate a name with the structure. For instance, by initializing the parent class with `structType.__init__(self, name='lineitems')`, the name of the structure is set up.

Then each attribute that we wish to pass must be set. Thus, for a `LineItem`, which will have a product ID and a quantity, the initializer function `__init__` must be passed the two values, and the attributes `self.product` and `self.quantity` will be appropriately set. These attributes are actually set to instances of the `Product` and `Quantity` classes, so that `LineItem` objects will refer to `Product` and `Quantity` objects. An interesting extension of this would be for the initializer functions to contain code to validate the values that are passed in.

Class `ID` inherits from the SOAP.py class `structType`, attaching the parameter name/ID to the object via the call to `structType.__init__(self, name='id')`. This results in having no identifier, in which case the system might generate something like:

```
<xsd:integer> 4521 </xsd:integer>
```

By attaching the name to `structType`, the XML that is generated looks more like:

```
<xsd:id xsi:type="xsd:integer"> 4521 </xsd:id>
```

Similarly, `LineItems` attaches the name `lineitems` to any instances that are created of that class, `Quantity` generates `quantity` instances, and `Product` generates `product` instances. Finally, `LineItem` generates (not too surprisingly) `lineitem` entries. It uses `Product` and `Quantity` to generate the elements that make up a `lineitem`. It is used as shown below:

```
#Config.debug=1
id = ID(2705)
lineitems = LineItems([LineItem('ABCD1234', 7),
                       LineItem('ACE1234', -8),
                       LineItem('ACDE134', -19),
                       LineItem('ACDE1234', -11),
                       LineItem('ACDE1234', -12),
                       LineItem('ACDE1234', 13),
                       ])
try:
    res = server.priceitems(id, lineitems)
    DisplayResult('Priceitems', res)
except:
    print 'Pricing failed'

id = ID(2750)
print 'ID:', id
lineitems = LineItems([LineItem('ABCD1234', 7),
                       LineItem('ABCD1235', 87),
                       LineItem('ABCD1236', 37),
                       LineItem('ABCD1234', 29)
                       ])

try:
    res = server.priceitems(id, lineitems)
    DisplayResult('Priceitems', res)
except:
    print 'Pricing failed...'
```

Multiple References in SOAP.py

Where SOAP::Lite (SOAP implementation in Perl) took the approach of largely ignoring the XML capabilities of compression from the use of `id` and `href`, SOAP.py may be considered to head to the other extreme. Take a look at the following XML generated by a request to submit prices to `priceitems`. It lays out the message in a very different order, making extensive use of references. Most of the elements contain references to elements defined later in the XML document:

```
<?xml version="1.0" encoding="utf-8"?>
<SOAP-ENV:Envelope
SOAP-ENV:encodingStyle="http://schemas.xmlsoap.org/soap/encoding/"
xmlns:xsd="http://www.w3.org/1999/XMLSchema"
xmlns:SOAP-ENV="http://schemas.xmlsoap.org/soap/envelope/"
xmlns:xsi="http://www.w3.org/1999/XMLSchema-instance"
xmlns:SOAP-ENC="http://schemas.xmlsoap.org/soap/encoding/">
  <SOAP-ENV:Body>
    <priceitems SOAP-ENC:root="1">
      <id href="#i1" />
      <lineitems href="#i2" />
```

```
    </priceitems>
    <xsd:id id="i1" SOAP-ENC:root="0">
      <id xsi:type="xsd:int">2750</id>
    </xsd:id>
    <xsd:lineitems id="i2" SOAP-ENC:root="0">
      <lineitems href="#i3" />
    </xsd:lineitems>
    <lineitems SOAP-ENC:arrayType="ns1:SOAPStruct[4]"
    xsi:type="SOAP-ENC:Array"
    xmlns:ns1="http://soapinterop.org/xsd" SOAP-ENC:root="0"
    id="i3">
      <item href="#i4" />
      <item href="#i5" />
      <item href="#i6" />
      <item href="#i7" />
    </lineitems>
    <xsd:item id="i4" SOAP-ENC:root="0">
      <product href="#i8" />
      <quantity href="#i9" />
    </xsd:item>
    <xsd:item id="i5" SOAP-ENC:root="0">
      <product href="#i10" />
      <quantity href="#i11" />
    </xsd:item>
    <xsd:item id="i6" SOAP-ENC:root="0">
      <product href="#i12" />
      <quantity href="#i13" />
    </xsd:item>
    <xsd:item id="i7" SOAP-ENC:root="0">
      <product href="#i14" />
      <quantity href="#i15" />
    </xsd:item>
    <xsd:product id="i8" SOAP-ENC:root="0">
      <product href="#i16" />
    </xsd:product>
    <xsd:quantity id="i9" SOAP-ENC:root="0">
      <quantity xsi:type="xsd:int">7</quantity>
    </xsd:quantity>
    <xsd:product id="i10" SOAP-ENC:root="0">
      <product href="#i17" />
    </xsd:product>
    <xsd:quantity id="i11" SOAP-ENC:root="0">
      <quantity xsi:type="xsd:int">87</quantity>
    </xsd:quantity>
    <xsd:product id="i12" SOAP-ENC:root="0">
      <product href="#i18" />
    </xsd:product>
    <xsd:quantity id="i13" SOAP-ENC:root="0">
      <quantity xsi:type="xsd:int">37</quantity>
    </xsd:quantity>
    <xsd:product id="i14" SOAP-ENC:root="0">
      <product href="#i16" />
    </xsd:product>
    <xsd:quantity id="i15" SOAP-ENC:root="0">
```

```
      <quantity xsi:type="xsd:int">29</quantity>
    </xsd:quantity>
    <product xsi:type="xsd:string" id="i16" SOAP-ENC:root="0">
    ABCD1234</product>
    <product xsi:type="xsd:string" id="i17" SOAP-ENC:root="0">
    ABCD1235</product>
    <product xsi:type="xsd:string" id="i18" SOAP-ENC:root="0">
    ABCD1236</product>
  </SOAP-ENV:Body>
</SOAP-ENV:Envelope>
```

However, the result of this extensive referencing does not seem to make the SOAP messages much shorter. It may be helpful with large elements, or in cases where the transport system is able to find larger compound patterns (which SOAP.py does not support).

Using ZSI

The SOAP implementation for Python that continues to attract significant development effort is ZSI, part of the 'Web Services for Python' project at SourceForge. ZSI provides a SOAP client/server and comes with a toolkit that can generate SOAP messages and build applications utilizing SOAP messages with attachments and also translate between SOAP syntax and Python data types.

Installing ZSI

ZSI is now available with RPM files, but the new library packages might not be included as a part of any Linux or BSD distribution, so there is a possibility of installing it manually.

Fortunately, the modern Python tool chain includes the `distutils.core` module, which contains a `setup()` function that makes installation of Python modules a quite straightforward and clean process. At the time of writing, the latest version of ZSI was 1.22-6. The installation proceeds as follows:

- Download sources from SourceForge – Web Services for Python (http://sourceforge.net/projects/pywebsvcs)
- Extract archive via tar xfvz ZSI-1.2.tgz
- Move to directory /ZSI-1.2/ where the files are extracted
- Use command python setup.py install

This command mostly needs a `'root'` user, so that suitable permissions are available to create and update files in `/usr/lib/` or `/usr/local/lib/`.

Note: ZSI requires Python 2.0 or later, and PyXML 0.6.6 or later.

Since both ZSI and PyXML are undergoing active development, version and compatibility issues will certainly change by the time you read this.

Using ZSI to Construct SOAP Clients

The messages generated by ZSI are not (at present) compatible with all the servers on which the Web Service resides. As development efforts are ongoing, some of the interoperability issues may have been remedied by the time this reaches print. These libraries do not (at this point) include any WSDL parsing support, therefore there is no ability to simply specify the service; it is necessary to specify proxy and URI.

Here is a sample SOAP client that uses ZSI to access a "Bible query" service published by an Indian Orthodox church in the Washington DC area:

```
#!/usr/bin/env python
import sys
from ZSI import TC
from ZSI.client import Binding
url = "/cgi/websvcbible.cgi"
namespace = "http://www.stgregorioschurchdc.org/Bible"
host="www.stgregorioschurchdc.org"
soapaction=namespace + "#read_bible"
b=Binding(host=host, ns=namespace, url=url, soapaction=soapaction)
try:
    print b.read_bible("John 3:16; Jude 1:17; Mark 1:3")
except: pass
```

Some SOAP implementations could access the service via the single reference to the WSDL at Bible WSDL (http://www.stgregorioschurchdc.org/wsdl/Bible.wsdl). Many implementations could access the service by a reference to just the server URL combined with the URI indicating the namespace.

In contrast, ZSI does not offer a WSDL processor, and accessing the service requires specifying all of `host`, `url`, `namespace`, and `soapaction`. There is considerable sharing of information between these parameters: the `host` and `url` might readily be combined, and the `soapaction` is calculated by combining the method name `read_bible` with the namespace variable.

The verbosity of this may initially appear repelling, as it is common for other SOAP implementations to only require two of the parameters, computing the others (typically `host` and `soapaction`) from the URL and URI based on the usual behavior of server implementations. Unfortunately, the treatment of the `SOAPAction` attribute in the SOAP is something that varies considerably between implementations.

SOAP implementations from Microsoft commonly require an empty `SOAPAction` attribute, whereas the "IBM approach" often involves combining the namespace with the method name. SOAP implementations that silently compute these sorts of values often make it awkward to specify a `SOAPAction` value other than what implementation assumes to be the appropriate calculation. ZSI requires a little more awareness of these components, but treats the `SOAPAction` in a more neutral manner.

The table below lists the things discussed:

Keyword	Default Value	Description
`host`	`localhost`	Host to connect to for service
`url`	blank	URL to post SOAP requests to
`port`	defaults to `80` or `443`	Port to attach to for service
`ns`	blank	Namespace for requests
`nsdict`	optional Python dictionary	Namespace dictionary to include in SOAP `envelope`
`soapaction`	`http://www.zolera.com`	Value in HTTP header for `SOAPAction`
`readerclass`	none	Python class used to create XML readers
`ssl`	0	Use SSL connection if non-zero
`tracefile`	none	An object with a `write()` method where SOAP message traces will also be submitted
`auth`	none	Python tuple with authentication information

A Larger Example

This section implements a larger example, involving both a SOAP client and a SOAP server implemented in Python.

It begins with a set of simple methods that simply pass back values of all sorts of different types, demonstrating how values may be passed and the way that the SOAP libraries map various Python types onto SOAP types.

There is a `methods()` method, which lists all of these methods, providing a loosely defined sort of "white pages." The Python SOAP implementations do not support WSDL, so there is no centralized way of registering methods in that manner. The `methods()` method provides something somewhat analogous.

Then the server implements a more sophisticated method, `priceitems()`, where the client passes a set of data about an order, and where the server looks up price information, passing back a complex data structure describing the results.

Note that this example parallels the extended example in the chapter on SOAP::Lite. You might wish to try pointing a Python client at a Perl server to see how they interoperate.

Server – Implemented Using ZSI

The main server script file is `pserver.py`; you may wish to compare this with the Perl implementation, `pserver.pl`, in the earlier chapter:

```
#!/usr/bin/env python
from ZSI import *
from ZSI.dispatch import *
from Actions import *
from ComplexAction import priceitems

def foo():
    return "foo"

port = 7911
print 'Pserver on port: ', port
s = dispatch.AsServer (port=port)
```

This server supports a set of methods in the Python class `Actions`, which provide a set of simple methods that demonstrate how values are transferred by the SOAP implementation, as well as a class `ComplexAction` implementing a more complex method, `priceitems()`, which transfers a complex set of data in both directions.

The local definition of `foo()` provides another simple function, defined in the main file, but which is referenced in the `methods()` list in class `Actions` (Chapter 6 contains a similar example).

The server will accept connections on port 7911, and run any functions found in the "main" namespace, which includes the functions in classes `Actions` and `ComplexAction`.

The final statement runs `dispatch.AsServer()`, indicating that the server should now wait for SOAP requests on port 7911:

```
#!/usr/bin/env python
from ZSI import *
from ZSI import resolvers
import types

# Define a random number generator instance to be used by various
# methods
from random import Random
rand = Random()
```

The header for `Actions` begins by indicating the Python classes it needs to use. The ZSI classes are declared, but could be left commented out here, since they are declared in the main script.

Several of the methods require random numbers, so class `random` is drawn in, and `rand` is set up as a `Random()` instance. Python's use in the scientific community for simulation work has resulted in its random number generator being quite sophisticated. It may be a bit more sophisticated than is needed for this application, but it only introduces a few lines of additional complexity.

The `action1()` method demonstrates how easy it is to build a simple SOAP method in Python; a mere two lines of code, the minimum amount of code needed to implement a Python function in any case, were all that was required to implement the method:

```
def action1():
  return 'action1() returns a simple string'
```

The difference between this and Perl is fairly minor, but languages like Java or C++ require considerably more extensive declarations. The fault is not returned as a fault, as that is not yet supported by ZSI. That will hopefully change as additional efforts go into ZSI:

```
def action2():
    from ZSI import Fault
    import sys
    message='This page is intentionally blank (and the method intentionally
faulty',
    actor='foo'
    detail = ['A set' , 'of details']
    nhd = 'no header detail'
    return Fault(Fault.Server, message, detail=detail,
                 headerdetail=nhd,actor = 'http://chvatal:7890/')
```

Method `action3a()` generates an integer result, as the Python is an integer. `action3b()` and `action3c()` both demonstrate the way that floating point operations are treated as a sort of "contagion;" once a computation has been "infected" by association with a float, it stays as a float, and is returned as a decimal:

```
def action3a():
    return 275

def action3b():
    return 275 + 0.0

def action3c():
    total = 5.0
    for i in range(0,27):
        total = total + 10
    return total
```

`action3d()` demonstrates a reasonable way of ensuring that the marshaled output value is a SOAP decimal. The other methods here are largely 'toys' to demonstrate different approaches to type coercions; this method is reasonably representative of how you might ensure appropriate typing of output:

```
def action3d():
    value = 275
    return float(value)
```

Method `action3e()` demonstrates that nothing prevents you from using methods internally as well as externally. The call that is made to `action3c()` is done locally, requiring no marshaling of data into XML:

```
def action3e():
    return int(action3d())
```

This method demonstrates how you pass a Python list out as a return argument, which is marshaled by the ZSI SOAP code into the SOAP array type:

```
def action4():
    array = []
    for i in range(0,7):
        array.append(int(i * i + 3 * int(r.random()*4) - 2) / 4.0)
    array.extend(["this", "that", "other", "42", 42])
    return array
```

The SOAP type of each element in the SOAP array is based on the Python types for that element, with scalar values translating naturally into SOAP types, integers into `xsd:int`, strings into `xsd:string`, and such:

```
<?xml version="1.0" encoding="utf-8"?>
<SOAP-ENV:Envelope
xmlns:SOAP-ENV="http://schemas.xmlsoap.org/soap/envelope/"
xmlns:SOAP-ENC="http://schemas.xmlsoap.org/soap/encoding/"
xmlns:xsi="http://www.w3.org/2001/XMLSchema-instance"
xmlns:xsd="http://www.w3.org/2001/XMLSchema"
xmlns:ZSI="http://www.zolera.com/schemas/ZSI/"
SOAP-ENV:encodingStyle="http://schemas.xmlsoap.org/soap/encoding/">
  <SOAP-ENV:Body>
    <action4Response>
      <None SOAP-ENC:arrayType="xsd:anyType[12]">
        <E80936cc xsi:type="xsd:decimal">1.000000</E80936cc>
        <E80936bc xsi:type="xsd:decimal">1.250000</E80936bc>
        <E80936ac xsi:type="xsd:decimal">1.250000</E80936ac>
        <E809369c xsi:type="xsd:decimal">4.000000</E809369c>
        <E809368c xsi:type="xsd:decimal">4.250000</E809368c>
        <E809367c xsi:type="xsd:decimal">5.750000</E809367c>
        <E809366c xsi:type="xsd:decimal">10.750000</E809366c>
        <xsd:string id="80dc998">this</xsd:string>
        <xsd:string id="815fbb0">that</xsd:string>
        <xsd:string id="816fd30">other</xsd:string>
        <xsd:string id="815fbd0">42</xsd:string>
        <E805ef7c xsi:type="xsd:integer">42</E805ef7c>
      </None>
    </action4Response>
  </SOAP-ENV:Body>
</SOAP-ENV:Envelope>
```

Note that there is a combination of Python float numbers treated as SOAP decimal values, the number `42` provided as a Python string, which is passed back as a SOAP string, and the `int` value `42`, passed back as a SOAP integer.

The method `action5()` assigns values to a Python dictionary, `dict`, which is a hashtable analogous to the associative arrays used in awk and Perl. A loop accesses the elements in the dictionary in a single operation. A second loop rewrites the dictionary into the list, `dict2`. ZSI passes that back as a SOAP array, each element of which is itself a SOAP array consisting of keys and values. The 492 elements result in a SOAP message of 73Kbytes in size. `gzip` can compress that message down to about 10K, a substantial reduction; but ZSI does not support any compression scheme:

```
def action5():
    dict = {}
    for i in range(-17, 473):
        dict[i] = int(i * i + 3 * int(r.random()*2) +int(r.random() * 7))
    dict['n1'] = 'name 1'
    dict['n2'] = 'name 2'
    # ZSI can't return a dictionary directly, hence it is unravelled
    # into a list...
    dict2 = []
    for key in dict.keys():
        value = dict[key]
        dict2.append([key, value])
    return dict2
```

Method `action6()` demonstrates an example of where ZSI moves a little ahead of the curve, having the ability to automatically generate `href` references:

```
PROVS = ( 'ON', 'QC', 'NB', 'NF', 'NS', 'MB', 'SK', 'AB', 'BC', 'PE')
def action6():
    prov1 = PROVS[int(r.random() * 10)]
    prov2 = PROVS[int(r.random() * 10)]
    provres = (prov1, prov2)
    return provres

def action6a():
    LIST = []
    for a in range(0, 23):
        LIST.append(PROVS[int(r.random() * 10)])
    return LIST
```

It takes the approach where every string has an `id` attached to it; later instances to the same string may refer to the earlier instance.


```
<?xml version="1.0" encoding="utf-8"?>
<SOAP-ENV:Envelope
xmlns:SOAP-ENV="http://schemas.xmlsoap.org/soap/envelope/"
xmlns:SOAP-ENC="http://schemas.xmlsoap.org/soap/encoding/"
xmlns:xsi="http://www.w3.org/2001/XMLSchema-instance"
xmlns:xsd="http://www.w3.org/2001/XMLSchema"
xmlns:ZSI="http://www.zolera.com/schemas/ZSI/"
SOAP-ENV:encodingStyle="http://schemas.xmlsoap.org/soap/encoding/">
  <SOAP-ENV:Body>
    <action6Response>
      <None SOAP-ENC:arrayType="xsd:anyType[2]">

        <xsd:string id="815e6c8">ON</xsd:string>
        <xsd:string href="#815e6c8" />
      </None>
    </action6Response>
  </SOAP-ENV:Body>
</SOAP-ENV:Envelope>
```

Method `action6a()` provides a larger example of this, where the array is choosing elements randomly from a list of ten Canadian provinces. Since they are chosen randomly, the message will contain different results each time, unless the random number generator has somehow become deranged.

Since there are to be 23 elements in the array, it is guaranteed that there will be at least 13 that will be repeated, and in this case, province PE (Prince Edward Island) was not included, so there are 14 elements that are `href` references to the nine unique province elements. In this case, the use of references reduces the size of the SOAP message slightly; if there were more data in each element, the savings would increase:

```
<?xml version="1.0" encoding="utf-8"?>
<SOAP-ENV:Envelope
xmlns:SOAP-ENV="http://schemas.xmlsoap.org/soap/envelope/"
xmlns:SOAP-ENC="http://schemas.xmlsoap.org/soap/encoding/"
xmlns:xsi="http://www.w3.org/2001/XMLSchema-instance"
xmlns:xsd="http://www.w3.org/2001/XMLSchema"
xmlns:ZSI="http://www.zolera.com/schemas/ZSI/"
SOAP-ENV:encodingStyle="http://schemas.xmlsoap.org/soap/encoding/">
  <SOAP-ENV:Body>
    <action6aResponse>
      <None SOAP-ENC:arrayType="xsd:anyType[23]">
        <xsd:string id="815f368">MB</xsd:string>
        <xsd:string id="819dfe0">BC</xsd:string>
        <xsd:string id="8160690">NF</xsd:string>
        <xsd:string id="813b2b8">NS</xsd:string>
        <xsd:string id="81606d8">QC</xsd:string>
        <xsd:string id="819dfa0">SK</xsd:string>
        <xsd:string href="#813b2b8" />
        <xsd:string id="819d748">ON</xsd:string>
        <xsd:string href="#81606d8" />
        <xsd:string href="#819dfe0" />
        <xsd:string href="#8160690" />
        <xsd:string href="#813b2b8" />
        <xsd:string id="819dfc0">AB</xsd:string>
        <xsd:string id="819dc00">NB</xsd:string>
        <xsd:string href="#815f368" />
        <xsd:string href="#813b2b8" />
        <xsd:string href="#819dfa0" />
        <xsd:string href="#813b2b8" />
        <xsd:string href="#819dfa0" />
        <xsd:string href="#819dfe0" />
        <xsd:string href="#819dfa0" />
        <xsd:string href="#819dc00" />
        <xsd:string href="#813b2b8" />
      </None>
    </action6aResponse>
  </SOAP-ENV:Body>
</SOAP-ENV:Envelope>
```

Notice also that instead of returning an array of type `xsd:string`, which would be theoretically possible, the array is of type `xsd:anyType[23]`, as it consists of both strings and references.

Finally, methods() returns the list of methods that we wish to 'publish' on this SOAP server:

```
def methods():
  return ['action1', 'action2', 'action3a', 'action3b',
          'action3c', 'action3d', 'action3e', 'action4',
          'action5', 'action6', 'action6a']
```

The ComplexAction class implements the priceitems() method, accepting a numeric ID and an array of items each indicating product IDs and integer quantity. Low customer IDs lead to a discount of 15%; so long as the data was found to be valid, the method passes back an array with total costs for each product.

Note that if you are typing this in Python, indentation is used to control where the ends of blocks of code are, so that whitespace and indentation need to be the same as you see in the code listing for the code to work. There is no obfuscated code here to be particularly worried about, but it is important to take care in indenting code.

First, class anydbm is loaded in to support loading price data from a dbm file, and maintaining a transaction counter:

```
#!/usr/bin/env python
import anydbm
import re

def mklineitem(product, quantity, discount, price):
    cost = price * quantity * (1 - discount)
    return (product, cost)
```

Method priceitems(id, items) starts by calculating the discount, then setting up a couple of 'work tables' as well as the regular expression to be used to validate product IDs:

```
def priceitems (id, items):
  discount = 0
  if id < 10000:
      discount = 0.15
  else:
      discount = 0.00
  Q = {}          # Quantity table
  errors = []     # List of errors
  anums = re.compile('^[A-Z][A-Z][A-Z][A-Z][0-9][0-9][0-9][0-9]$')
```

The next step is to go through the input parameters in items to see if they are legitimate. It does not abort immediately upon finding a problem; it instead walks through the whole table of items so that a full set of problems can be reported back:

```
    for lineitem in items['lineitems']:
      product =  lineitem['product']
      product = product['product']
      quantity = 0
      try:
          q - lineitem['quantity']
          quantity = quantity + q['quantity']
      except:
          errors.append("quantity not a number [%s] for product [%s]" %
                        (quantity, product))
      if Q.has_key(product):
          Q[product] += quantity
      else:
          Q[product] = quantity
      if quantity <= 0:
          errors.append("quantity was negative [%.2f] for product [%s]" %
                        (quantity, product))
      if quantity > int(quantity):
          errors.append("quantity [%.2f] not integer for product [%s]" %
                        (quantity, product))
      if not(anums.match(product)):
          errors.append("Invalid product code: [%s]" % product)
```

Notice that the values have to be converted between integers and strings in order to be properly serialized to and from the database:

```
  tdb = anydbm.open("/tmp/counter", 'c')
if tdb.has_key('final'):
    txn_no = int(tdb['final'])
else:
    txn_no = 1500
txn_no = txn_no + 1
tdb['final'] = "%d" % txn_no  # Cast to string
tdb.close()
  pdb = anydbm.open("/tmp/prices", 'c')
(pdb['ABCD1236'], pdb['ABCD1235'], pdb['ABCD1234']) = ("42.50", "72.75",
                                                       "2742")
for i in range(7825, 7903):
    name = "RAND%04d" % i
    value = i % 23 + i % 17 + i % 59 + (i%7 + i%13 + i%29 + i % 37) / 100.0
    pdb[name] = "%.2f" % value
```

If you try this out on the same host on which you have run the Perl version, be aware that the Python dbm libraries may be at different version levels from those used by Perl and thus may not accept the same file formats.

There is no guarantee that this code is safe under conditions of concurrency: if you need to maintain real transactional information, it is crucial to use a database system that supports transactions, whether an SQL engine, or a non-relational database like Berkeley DB which, in recent versions, supports transactional updates.

The RAND7825 through RAND7903 entries use a series of modulus operations based on a series of values that are relatively prime to generate prices that appear random. This code connects to the price table and makes sure that there is a set of products and prices provided in the table:

```
        PRICING= []
      for i in Q.keys():
          q = Q[i]
          price = float(pdb[i]) * (1 - discount)
          PRICING.append({'product' : i,
                          'cost' : float (q * price)})
      return txn_no, PRICING
```

Finally, we reach the stage where we have available all the information needed to generate the data to be passed back:

- Prices are available in the table pdb[]
- The discount has been computed
- Quantities by product have been collected into Q[]

Note that as Q[] is a hashtable, the results are not necessarily computed or returned in any predictable order. When building distributed applications, it is very important for the software to expect results to be received "out of order."

Indeed, if it is expected that SOAP requests may take a substantial period of time for a server to respond to them, that suggests an argument for using asynchronous transport schemes such as e-mail or MQ Series, or simply for separating transmission from receipt of the results, and designing the application around some form of message queuing rather than treating SOAP requests simply as "procedure calls".

IBM sells a "message queueing" middleware system called IBM MQSeries (http://www-4.ibm.com/software/ts/mqseries/), which provides a reliable message transfer system where messages may be placed in named queues, and "work processes" pull messages off the queue for processing, often returning the results via another queue. A variety of vendors sells systems based on MQSeries, including Microsoft's MSMQ, Talarian MQexpress, Oracle Advanced Queueing, Falcon MQ.

Sun has designed, for Java, an analagous service, the Java Message Service, or JMS. Several vendors have implemented versions of this, including SwiftMQ and SonicMQ.

Some open source systems that are similar to one degree or another include Isect Message-Oriented Middleware (http://pweb.netcom.com/~tgagne/index.html), OpenQueue (http://openqueue.sourceforge.net/), the POSIX message queues whose API is found in /usr/include/linux/msg.h.

Another highly relevant system would be the Spread (http://www.spread.org/) messaging toolkit, providing a high-performance messaging service, available under an open source license similar to those used with BSD systems, which has language bindings to a number of languages including Spread Module 1.2 for Python (http://www.python.org/other/spread/).

If it is important for the results of a SOAP method to be returned in a specific order, then that needs to be part of the specification of the SOAP interface. Unfortunately, different clients may have different expectations, and if processing takes place in an asynchronous manner, there can be no guarantee of the results coming back in any particular order.

The client presented earlier written using SOAP.py is well suited to connect to this server.

Running ZSI Server as a CGI Application

Another way to invoke a ZSI server is via CGI, supported by some web server. This has several advantages over running SOAP servers as scripts. Installing new copies of scripts does not require stopping and restarting a Python server; the web server can immediately invoke new versions. A web server that supports running multiple processes will more readily scale to large numbers of users concurrently accessing a service than a single Python process can. Security can also be managed at the web server level, both for authentication and encryption.

The web server may also handle support for encrypted connections via SSL. This eliminates the need for a sizable set of library dependencies required to allow SOAP.py to directly support server certificates. A web server is typically used to serve information about server certificates, and if the web server is managing connections to the SOAP application, that holds true for SOAP requests as well as other HTTP requests.

Access controls may also be implemented using the web server's authentication management system. The Apache and Roxen Challenger web servers both offer the ability to manage authentication using a variety of methods including files typically named `.htaccess`, as well as more sophisticated systems such as LDAP and PostgreSQL.

We will discuss here how to run the ZSI application via CGI using the popular Apache web server. Many other open source web servers are available, including Boa, Roxen Challenger, and WN; they all offer ways of invoking CGI code, with their own slightly different configuration schemes.

Some additional configuration must be done in order to get the application running as a set of CGI scripts. For Apache to be able to invoke Python scripts as CGI handlers, it is necessary to configure three things in `/etc/apache/httpd.conf`. Apache needs to be aware that files with the `.py` suffix are to be treated as CGI scripts, thus:

```
# CGI files may have the following suffixes
AddHandler cgi-script .py
```

Secondly, there needs to be a mapping to indicate where CGI programs actually reside. It is typical, for instance, for some CGI scripts to reside in `/usr/lib/cgi-bin/`, and for that to be associated with URLs looking like `http://foo.com/cgi-bin/frobozz.py`.

The following `ScriptAlias` allows the SOAP code to reside in `/var/www/soap/` and be accessed by URLs looking like `http://foo.com/soap/soapmethods.py`.

```
# http://server.org/soap/foo.py accesses script in file /var/www/soap/foo.py
ScriptAlias /soap/ /var/www/soap/
```

Lastly, permission needs to be established to execute CGI scripts in directory /var/www/soap/, which is accomplished by the following <Directory> directive:

```
  # Allow running CGI scripts in /var/www/soap
<Directory /var/www/soap>
   Options ExecCGI
</Directory>
```

After adding these directives to the Apache httpd.conf file, it will be necessary to request that Apache reload its configuration. This may be accomplished by a command similar to /etc/init.d/apache reload or /etc/rc.d/init.d/apache restart; precise requirements will vary somewhat based on which init system is in use.

The Python script files are put in /var/www/soap/, including the method module Actions.py and the server script PythonCGI.py. The PythonCGI.py script required to support the application is as follows:

```
#!/usr/bin/python
from ZSI import *
from ZSI.dispatch import *
from Actions import *

def foo():
    return "foo"

dispatch.AsCGI()
```

Rather than having to establish a port to attach to, the script merely needs to draw in the set of methods that are to be supported by the web service, and execute via dispatch.AsCGI(). The web server manages network connections; the Python CGI script need only accept environment variables indicating HTTP header information (notably the SOAPAction value), read message input from standard input, and submit results back to standard output.

If a request is submitted using SSL, with an https:// URL, the web server manages encryption and decryption, perhaps even including compression, all invisible to the ZSI Python code.

Note: At the time of writing, support for the CGI dispatcher dispatch.AsCGI() is still fairly shaky. Once resolved, this is likely to be a preferable way to manage SOAP services, for all the reasons described above.

Tracing SOAP Messages with ZSI and SOAP.py

Virtually all SOAP implementations provide some scheme for tracing the contents of messages, so that you may see both the raw contents (in XML) of messages being sent to a server as well as the raw contents of the messages received back from the server. With the wide variations in permissible formatting of SOAP messages, and the permissible variations in element typing, it is often very valuable to be able to look at messages in raw form in order to try to figure out what went wrong with a message transmission.

ZSI offers SOAP message tracing in the following manner. Control over tracing is attached to the ZSI `Binding()`, as shown in the following function call:

```
b = Binding(url=u, host='localhost', port=port,
            tracefile=sys.stdout)
```

The `tracefile` variable allows you to hook in any Python output stream. This may be easily used to have verbose raw output only for those methods that are of interest, that is, the ones currently causing problems, as follows.

`bverbose` provides a verbose binding to the SOAP server which lists the XML messages to `sys.stdout`, that is, to the "standard output" device:

```
bverbose = Binding(url=u, host='localhost', port=4567,
            tracefile=sys.stdout)
```

`bquiet` provides a "quiet binding" to the SOAP server, not showing the XML messages:

```
bquiet = Binding(url=u, host='localhost', port=4567)
```

If a particular method is well debugged, or their output is otherwise not particularly interesting, you might call them using `bquiet`, the "quiet" binding, thus:

```
r1 = bquiet.boringmethod()
r2 = bquiet.anotherboringmethod()
for i in 1..50:
   r3 += bquiet.stillanotherboringmethod(i)
```

Calls to the "interesting" methods would be done using the "verbose" binding, `bverbose`, thus:

```
r5 = bverbose.interestingmethod()
r6 = bverbose.problematicmethod()
r7 = 0
for i in 1..r6:
   r7 += bquiet.stillanotherboringmethod(i)
r8 = bverbose.buggymethod(r7)
```

In the above code fragment, `bquiet` is used with the method `stillanotherboringmethod()` so that the repeated messages for that method are not displayed.

SOAP.py provides a different tracing mechanism whereby debugging messages are emitted when the variable `SOAP.Config.debug` is set, as with `SOAP.Config.debug = 1`, and may be turned off by setting it to `0`.

Thus, the equivalent code, with SOAP.py, would look like the following (where the server was set up as bs):

```
SOAP.Config.debug = 0
r1 = bs.boringmethod()
r2 = bs.anotherboringmethod()
for i in 1..50:
    r3 += bs.stillanotherboringmethod(i)
SOAP.Config.debug = 1
r5 = bs.interestingmethod()
r6 = bs.problematicmethod()
r7 = 0
SOAP.Config.debug = 0
for i in 1..r6:
    r7 += bs.stillanotherboringmethod(i)
SOAP.Config.debug = 1
r8 = bs.buggymethod(r7)
```

XML-RPC

The RPC scheme that predated SOAP was called XML-RPC created by Dave Winer of Userland Software. The protocol is documented at XML-RPC.com (http://www.xmlrpc.com/). It is a similar protocol to SOAP, bundling messages in XML format, transferring messages using the HTTP protocol.

The principal Python implementation is called xmlrpc, and is found at XML-RPC for Python (http://www.pythonware.com/products/xmlrpc/). It is licensed under the GNU Lesser General Public License, meaning that you are free to use it in your applications without influencing your own code's licensing, and is available in pre-packaged form as RPM and `.deb` files for a number of Linux distributions as well as for BSD ports.

We will now look at the difference between SOAP and XML-RPC protocol.

Advantages and Disadvantages of XML-RPC

The XML-RPC protocol is very similar to the SOAP protocol; it arguably has better claim to the moniker of "Simple" than SOAP. However, clients and servers for XML-RPC will not interoperate directly with those for SOAP even though the XML messages are structured similarly. The difference in message format prevents direct interoperability. The principal differences between XML-RPC and SOAP include:

- XML-RPC mandates the use of HTTP; there is no intent to allow using alternative transport protocols, as is the case for SOAP. This has the benefit that it is simpler to be sure that an implementation handles all aspects of XML-RPC, but limits its usefulness.
- XML-RPC has a fixed set of data types, not using the extensible XML schema approach of SOAP. The XML schema was not nearly ready for use when XML-RPC was created. Again, this has benefits as well as disadvantages when compared to SOAP. The simple set XML-RPC data types are easier to implement and verify than the more complex layers of standards associated with SOAP.

- On the other hand, XML-RPC does not support references, with the result that the resultant messages are more verbose than the SOAP equivalents. Since it lacks XML Schema, there is no way to describe sparse arrays.
- Major vendors such as IBM and Microsoft have been quick to embrace SOAP instead of XML-RPC, with the result that there are far more commercial tools and servers for use with SOAP. XML-RPC has none of the "layered" standards associated with SOAP such as WSDL and UDDI. Looking at this from the perspective of Web Services used with Python, this is not, at present, a difference of any practical importance. While `python-xmlrpc` offers no support for WSDL or UDDI, none of the SOAP implementations available for Python have any support for these standards either.

Overall, XML-RPC is somewhat better supported for use with Python than SOAP at this point in time, having two more mature and complete implementations. There are two major open source implementations of XML-RPC for Python:

- The `py-xmlrpc` or `python-xmlrpc` package that provides classes suitable for embedding in Python applications.
- XML-RPC support in the Zope Application Framework, where any Zope script that is configured to be called from a URL, may be called using XML-RPC.

The general idea is that every Zope object is able to respond to HTTP requests. What that usually involves is pointing a web browser at Zope objects that are built to generate web pages. But some Zope objects are described as "Zope script objects", and encapsulate chunks of code typically written in Python that are used in Zope to control application logic.

Here is a somewhat fanciful way to do a mass firing of employees in the janitorial department:

```
import xmlrpclib
server = xmlrpclib.Server('http://www.zopezoo.org/')
for employeeID in server.JanitorialDepartment.personnel():
    server.sackEmployee(employee)
```

The Zope server for this fictitious example is located at `http://www.zopezoo.org/` (not a real site). The object, `JanitorialDepartment`, has various methods attached to it, including a script object called `personnel()`, which lists employee ID numbers for each employee in the department. The object `sackEmployee` references a script object to which an employee ID may be passed, and has the effect of terminating the employee.

This process isn't something you would want to be highly accessible, certainly not to any random individual out on the Web. XML-RPC does not directly provide any detailed security framework, however Zope does. The URL `http://www.zopezoo.org/sackEmployee/` should be restricted for use to a very small group of people. Fortunately, Zope's security framework is applied at the HTTP level, and would thus apply just as well to XML-RPC calls as it would to the use of a Zope web form that used the `sackEmployee` object.

The size and complexity of the Zope framework makes it unfeasible to present a detailed example of its use. Visit the Zope XML-RPC HOWTO document for further details (http://www.zope.org/Members/Amos/XML-RPC/).

Summary

This chapter has reviewed the set of available SOAP implementations for Python, as well as how to install the Python libraries required for two of these implementations, SOAP.py and ZSI. Some sample client and server programs for SOAP.py and ZSI were constructed. We then saw how Web Services could also be implemented and used with a protocol called XML-RPC. There are two notable implementations of this for Python: A library called `xmlrpc`, as well as support in the Zope Web Application Framework. However, the Python implementations of SOAP have not settled down to maturity yet.

For more information about SOAP and Python, consult the following web links:

- http://www.python.org/
- Python Web Services – SOAP.py (http://sourceforge.net/projects/pywebsvcs)
- ZSI at Zolera Systems (http://www.zolera.com/opensrc/zsi/zsi.html)
- Zope Application Framework (http://www.zope.org/)
- xmlrpc (http://www.pythonware.com/products/xmlrpc/)

8

PHP and Web Services

PHP Hypertext Processor (PHP) is a widely-used general-purpose scripting language that is specially suited for web development as it was designed to work on the Web and can be embedded into HTML. It is a procedural language, with some object-oriented capabilities and has syntax similar to C, Perl, and Java. PHP was first released on June 8, 1995. PHP version 4, which was released in May 2000, was a major milestone, with its explosive performance increase and many features, such as native session support.

In this chapter, we will first present PHP with its advantages for Web Services development. Then we will cover the installation and configuration of PHP on a Unix system.

The second section will concentrate on SOAP usage in PHP. We'll look at the NuSOAP toolkit, and learn how to use it for both consumption and deployment of SOAP Web Services. We'll also explore NuSOAP's functionality for several advanced Web Services scenarios such as using HTTP proxy, SOAP over HTTPS, and document style messaging. We'll discuss some of the issues facing Web Service development in PHP, such as security and language to data type mapping, and how NuSOAP solves them.

The final section covers XML-RPC in PHP. We'll explore the particular features of XML-RPC, as well as discuss scenarios for using XML-RPC versus using SOAP. We will then use the Useful, Inc. implementation to create XML-RPC client and server applications.

PHP Features

Several of PHP's features are advantageous for Web Service development. The first would be its object-oriented programming capabilities. This may be limited in comparison to other natively object-oriented languages, but it provides the support needed to create extendable and reusable tools for PHP. It also allows SOAP and XML-RPC toolkits to be split into a group of classes each supporting parts of the entire Web Service transaction, but which on its own can be reused to accomplish the plethora of different kinds of transactions that are possible and tasks that may be necessary, such as native type serialization, network operations, XML parsing, and XML generation.

Another advantage of PHP is its XML support. The Expat parser is bundled with PHP, providing SAX capability out of the box. There are several PHP extensions available for expanded XML functionality, such as the `domxml` extension that use the libxml library to provide DOM, Xpath, and Xlink support. The `xslt` extension is a wrapper for different third-party XSLT libraries such as Sablotron and libxslt. There are also experimental extensions for XML-RPC and SOAP.

A very helpful PHP extension for Web Service development is the `CURL` extension, described as a Client URL Library. CURL allows you to communicate via various different protocols such as HTTP, HTTPS, FTP, telnet, and LDAP. The HTTPS support is particularly helpful for Web Service usage in PHP as it allows a (Web Service) client to make a secure connection with the server.

PHP and Web Services

PHP Web Service newbies can experiment with Web Services using PHP by writing only a few lines of code, without having to set up a special environment, and without needing to know anything about how Web Services actually work. But this ease-of-use is a double-edged sword and general advice is to know as much as possible about the technologies used, to stay abreast of security issues especially, considering that by nature Web Services are exposed to the network.

PHP is already broadly deployed for data-centric web applications. If you are planning to develop Web Services using PHP, your PHP-driven web sites may have components that may be reused by exposing their methods using XML-RPC or SOAP. The conversion from wrapping your data in HTML to serving it as SOAP messages is trivial using the tools available today.

An excellent reason to use PHP for Web Services is that sometimes it's the only choice you've got. Web sites that are hosted by PHP hosting services and want to use Web Services to share data with their partners to access services cannot do so, since they have no control over their PHP installation. They cannot install Java, don't have compiler access, and have no permissions to restart Apache if assuming they could install new software on the server. Now users in such a scenario can easily consume and deploy Web Services in short order if the server has PHP.

Currently PHP does not have standard SOAP or XML-RPC support. There are several different implementations each of SOAP and XML-RPC and the stable ones are written in pure PHP. There has been a recent push by developers to create standard support for SOAP in PHP. Several of the PHP core developers have expressed interest in seeing this happen, and a PHP-SOAP mailing list was started to pursue the effort. Hopefully, this activity will culminate in a SOAP extension that will be compiled into PHP by default, thereby being available out of the box to developers everywhere, regardless of system-related limitations such as permissions or compiler access.

The XML-RPC support in PHP has increased with Epinions opening the source to their XML-RPC extension. The extension has been in the main PHP CVS repository for quite some time, yet is still marked experimental and is not recommended for production use.

There are several advantages and disadvantages in using SOAP against XML-RPC for Web Services:

- Strong and extensible typing – SOAP allows user- and schema-defined types to be passed in SOAP message bodies. XML-RPC is very limited in the types of data it supports.
- Character set – SOAP allows the user to define the character set used in the message (like US-ASCII, UTF-8, UTF-16) while XML-RPC does not.
- Specifies recipient – SOAP can specify the recipient of a message, as well as can be routed through intermediaries.
- Failure if not understood – SOAP allows the sender to force a recipient to fail if the recipient cannot understand its message.
- Ease of use – Both PHP and XML-RPC have a short learning curve. It is easy for users new to PHP and Web Services to consume and deploy Web Services quickly and easily.
- Simplicity by design – XML-RPC was designed to be simple; to accomplish remote procedure calls with a minimum of infrastructure. SOAP is overkill for many Web Services that pass only simple or complex values.

Configuring PHP

Installing and configuring PHP for the examples in this chapter requires the Apache web server. To compile and configure PHP for Apache, we first download the PHP source from http://www.php.net/downloads.php and unpack it. Then change your directory to the root directory of the PHP source distribution. To run the configure script type `./configure` on the command line. You can add options to this command to compile PHP with non-standard functionality. Some useful options are listed below:

- **Apache**
  To enable PHP to be run as an Apache module, use the `--with-apxs` option, adding the path to your APXS binary as is appropriate for your server. For example:
  `--with-apxs=/www/bin/apxs`
- **DOMXML**
  This extension provides XML DOM, Xpath, and Xlink functionality. Currently, this extension is not required in Web Services, but is useful for reading and manipulation XML documents. Domxml support requires a version of the libxml libraries to be present on the system (with a version number greater than or equal to 2.4.2). For example, `--with-dom=DIR`. Here `DIR` is the `libxml` install directory, which defaults to `/usr`.
- **XSLT**
  This extension is also not necessary for using Web Services with PHP, but is useful for transforming XML data returned in Web Service messages into other types of documents. The configure option for this extension is `--enable-xslt --with-xslt-sablot`. The Sablotron XSLT library from Gingerall (http://www.gingerall.com/) must be installed in a location where your compiler can find it, usually `/usr/lib` or `/usr/local/lib`.

- **CURL**
  The CURL extension provides the ability to initiate secure socket connections using SSL. This is a necessary extension if you want to conduct SOAP client operations using SSL. The configure option is `--with-curl=DIR` where `DIR` is the location of the CURL libraries on your system. The CURL extension requires version 7.0.2-beta or higher of the CURL libraries.

Finally, run `make` and then `make install` on the command line, and the installation is complete. The final installation process on the command line using the previous options would look like this:

```
> cd PHP-xxx
> ./configure --with-apxs=/www/bin/apxs --with-dom=/usr/local/lib --enable-xslt
--with-xslt-sablot --with-curl=/usr/local/lib
> make
> make install
```

The PHP web site at http://www.php.net/manual/en/installation.php provides instructions for installing PHP with many other options on a variety of platforms.

PHP Web Services Using NuSOAP

NuSOAP is a collection of PHP classes that allow users to send and receive SOAP messages over HTTP. NuSOAP, formerly known as SOAPx4, is distributed by the NuSphere Corporation (http://www.nusphere.com/). It is open source, licensed under the GNU LGPL. SOAPx4 has been used as the core of several Web Services toolkits for PHP, including PEAR-SOAP and Active State software's simple Web Services API project.

One of the benefits of NuSOAP is that it's not a PHP extension, but is written in pure PHP. This means that nearly all PHP developers, regardless of the web server or permissions restrictions, can use NuSOAP.

NuSOAP is a component-based Web Services toolkit. It employs a base class that provides utility methods such as variable and envelope serialization, as well as namespace information and mappings of different types to different namespaces. Web Service interaction is achieved through a high-level client class called `soapclient`. This high-level class allows users to specify options such as HTTP authorization credentials, HTTP proxy information, as well as managing the actual sending and receiving of the SOAP message itself. It uses several helper classes to accomplish the sending and receiving of SOAP messages.

SOAP operations may be executed by passing the name of the operation you'd like to execute to the `call()` method. If the service to be consumed provides a WSDL file, the `soapclient` class takes the URL of the WSDL file as an argument to its constructor, and uses the `wsdl` class to parse the WSDL file and extract all the data. The WSDL class has methods that extract data on a per-operation or per-binding basis.

The `soapclient` uses this data from the WSDL file to encode parameters and create the SOAP envelope when the user executes a call to a service. When the call is executed, the `soapclient` class uses the `soap_transport_http` class to send the outgoing message and receive the incoming message. The incoming message is parsed using `soap_parser` class. The diagram opposite describes the process of consuming a SOAP Web Service using NuSOAP.

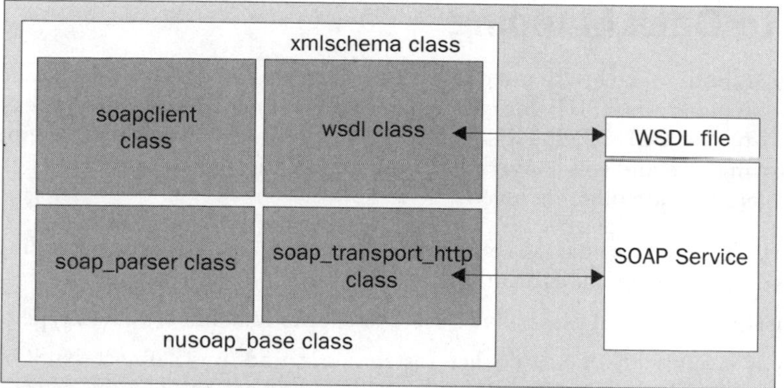

If the Web Service to be consumed does not provide a WSDL file, then the process is different. The URL of the service is passed to the `soapclient` class constructor. Operations are still executed using the call method of the `soapclient` object, but details that are otherwise provided by the WSDL file must be passed as arguments. Parameters that are custom types can be represented using the `soapval` class, which allow users to customize a parameter's serialization.

Installation and Configuration

The installation of NuSOAP is a pretty straightforward process. It can be achieved in a few steps as follows:

- Download the files from http://dietrich.ganx4.com/nusoap/.
- Extract the file `nusoap.php` from its zip.
- For easy access, copy the classes to a location in your include path, or into the directory in which you'll be using the classes.
- Include the class in your script. The path to `nusoap.php` can be relative or absolute:

```
include('nusoap.php');
```

In this example, we have used the `include()` function to include the NuSOAP classes in our script. This function will generate a warning if the path to `nusoap.php` is incorrect, but will continue to process the rest of the script. There are several other alternatives:

- `require()`
  This function is identical to `include()`, but handles failure by emitting a fatal error, which will halt processing of the script
- `require_once()`
  Identical to `require()`, except that if the file to be included is already included in the script, it will not repeat the inclusion
- `include_once()`
  Identical to `include()`, except that if the file to be included has been previously included in the script, it will not include it again

Language to Data Mapping

SOAP and WSDL both make heavy use of the data types described in the XML Schema specification. This can be problematic since PHP does not natively support most of the data types defined in the specification. Also, the XML Schema data types are fine-grained and explicitly defined, whereas PHP is a loosely-typed language and will convert data types automatically when deemed appropriate. NuSOAP solves this problem at three different levels:

- In WSDL, NuSOAP's `soapclient` class will encode a value's type according to the type specified in the WSDL document.
- The NuSOAP `soapval` class allows users to explicitly define a value's type.
- If no type is explicitly declared when instantiating a `soapval` object, NuSOAP will analyze the value passed to it using PHP's built-in variable introspection functions as well as regular expressions and other means where necessary, and classify it as a valid XML Schema data type, or a valid type as described in Section 5 of the SOAP 1.1 specification.

A Simple PHP SOAP Client Example

In this example we will pass a string to a SOAP server that echoes the same string back. This example demonstrates the basic process of creating a SOAP client, calling a SOAP service and passing it parameters, and receiving the response. We will name this file `echoStringClient.php`.

In this chapter to start a script in a standard way would be to include the NuSOAP classes first. We'll use the `require()` function in our examples because we'd like the script to halt execution if it cannot find the NuSOAP file:

```
<?php
require('nusoap.php');
```

Let's create a variable for the string we'd like to send.

```
$myString = 'Dietrich Ayala';
```

Our parameters must be passed as an array to the SOAP client, so let's create one:

```
$parameters = array($myString);
```

Now we can instantiate the `soapclient` object. It takes the URL of the server as an argument to its constructor:

```
$s = new soapclient('http://localhost/wrox/nusoap/echoStringServer.php');
```

This step is where all the magic takes place. Using the `call()` method, we tell the `soapclient` object which service we'd like to access, then pass our array of parameters, and the method then returns the response from the server. This response is a PHP native type, such as a string, integer, or array. It is the result of the decoding that takes place when NuSOAP parses the response message:

```
$result = $s->call('echoString',$parameters);
```

NuSOAP offers error detection through the `getError()` method. If an error has occurred this method returns a string describing the error, and returns `false` otherwise. In our example, we print our result after checking for errors if there are none. If there are errors, we'll print the error message:

```
if(!$err = $s->getError()){
    echo 'Result: '.$result;
} else {
    echo 'Error: '.$err;
}
```

This final bit of code is very helpful for debugging SOAP operations. The `request` and `response` properties of the `soapclient` class contain strings of the respective messages, including the HTTP headers sent with each:

```
echo '<xmp>'.$s->request.'</xmp>';
echo '<xmp>'.$s->response.'</xmp>';
?>
```

SOAP Request and SOAP Response

Here is the request message from the previous example:

```
POST /wrox/nusoap/echoStringServer.php HTTP/1.0
User-Agent: NuSOAP v0.6.1
Host: localhost
Content-Type: text/xml
Content-Length: 569
SOAPAction: ""

<?xml version="1.0" encoding="ISO-8859-1"?>
<SOAP-ENV:Envelope
  SOAP-ENV:encodingStyle="http://schemas.xmlsoap.org/soap/encoding/"
  xmlns:SOAP-ENV="http://schemas.xmlsoap.org/soap/envelope/"
  xmlns:xsd="http://www.w3.org/2001/XMLSchema"
  xmlns:xsi="http://www.w3.org/2001/XMLSchema-instance"
  xmlns:SOAP-ENC="http://schemas.xmlsoap.org/soap/encoding/"
  xmlns:si="http://soapinterop.org/xsd">
<SOAP-ENV:Body>
  <nu:echoString xmlns:nu="http://testuri.org">
    <soapVal xsi:type="xsd:string">Dietrich Ayala</soapVal>
  </nu:echoString>
</SOAP-ENV:Body>
</SOAP-ENV:Envelope>
```

This is the server's response message from the previous example. Notice that the first element in the body of the message is the name of the operation we called, with `Response` appended to it. Also, the element name of the return value is called `return`. Both of these are standard practice for serializing SOAP responses:

```
HTTP/1.1 200 OK
Server: Microsoft-IIS/5.0
Date: Tue, 04 Jun 2002 18:47:53 GMT
X-Powered-By: PHP/4.1.2
Status: 200 OK
Server: NuSOAP Server v0.6.1
Connection: Close
Content-Type: text/xml; charset=UTF-8
Content-Length: 1525

<?xml version="1.0" encoding="ISO-8859-1"?>
<SOAP-ENV:Envelope
  SOAP-ENV:encodingStyle="http://schemas.xmlsoap.org/soap/encoding/"
  xmlns:SOAP-ENV="http://schemas.xmlsoap.org/soap/envelope/"
  xmlns:xsd="http://www.w3.org/2001/XMLSchema"
  xmlns:xsi="http://www.w3.org/2001/XMLSchema-instance"
  xmlns:SOAP-ENC="http://schemas.xmlsoap.org/soap/encoding/"
  xmlns:si="http://soapinterop.org/xsd">
<SOAP-ENV:Body>
  <echoStringResponse>
    <soapVal xsi:type="xsd:string">Dietrich Ayala</soapVal>
  </echoStringResponse>
</SOAP-ENV:Body>
</SOAP-ENV:Envelope>
```

A Simple PHP SOAP Server Example

This example is the server that was accessed by our client example. It implements the `echoString` service.

The first step as usual is to include the NuSOAP classes:

```
<?php

require('nusoap.php');
```

Now we can instantiate the server object, provided by the `soap_server` class:

```
$s = new soap_server;
```

To allow our function to be called remotely, we must register it with the server object. If this is not done, the server will generate a fault indicating that the service is not available if a client accesses the service. In the absence of such a registration process, any PHP functions would be remotely available, which would present a serious security risk:

```
$s->register('echoString');
```

Now we can define our function that we are exposing as a service. Notice that we first check to make sure a string was passed. If the parameter is not a string, we use the `soap_fault` class to return an error to the client indicating that they must pass a string value as the parameter to this function:

```
function echoString($inputString){

     if(is_string($inputString)){
         return $inputString;
     } else {
         return new soap_fault('Client','','The parameter to this service must be a
string.');
     }
}
```

The final step is to pass any incoming posted data to the SOAP server's `service` method. This method processes the incoming request, and calls the appropriate function. It will then formulate the response, and print it:

```
$s->service($HTTP_RAW_POST_DATA);

?>
```

Fault Handling

The `soap_fault` class provides a way to specify errors and return them when developing services with NuSOAP.

The properties of the `soap_fault` class are below. These are also the arguments to the `soap_fault` constructor, in the same order as below:

Fault	Description
`faultcode`	This property must have a value. The values available to the user are `Client` and `Server`. Client class errors indicate that the message didn't contain the information required for the operation to succeed. Server class errors indicate processing problems on the server.
`faultactor`	This property is not functional yet in NuSOAP, and can be left empty. Its purpose is to indicate the location of the fault among multiple actors in a message path.
`faultstring`	This is a human-readable error message. This is the best place for you to describe errors.
`faultdetail`	The value of the `faultdetail` property is XML data used to detail the application-specific errors related strictly to the `Body` element of the SOAP message. You can insert your own XML markup here.

The `soap_fault` class has only one method besides the constructor that is `serialize()`. The `serialize()` method takes the fault information and serializes it, returning a complete SOAP message.

An example of using the `soap_fault` class is shown here:

```
$fault = new soap_fault(
     'Client','','The inputString parameter must not be empty');

echo $fault->serialize();
```

The SOAP message below is what is returned by the `serialize()` method of the `soap_fault` object instantiated above:

```
<?xml version="1.0"?>
<SOAP-ENV:Envelope
SOAP-ENV:encodingStyle="http://schemas.xmlsoap.org/soap/encoding/"
  xmlns:SOAP-ENV="http://schemas.xmlsoap.org/soap/envelope/"
  xmlns:xsd="http://www.w3.org/2001/XMLSchema"
  xmlns:xsi="http://www.w3.org/2001/XMLSchema-instance"
  xmlns:SOAP-ENC="http://schemas.xmlsoap.org/soap/encoding/"
  xmlns:si="http://soapinterop.org/xsd">
<SOAP-ENV:Body>
<SOAP-ENV:Fault>
  <faultcode>Client</faultcode>
  <faultactor></faultactor>
  <faultstring>The inputString parameter must not be empty</faultstring>
  <detail></detail>
</SOAP-ENV:Fault>
</SOAP-ENV:Body>
</SOAP-ENV:Envelope>
```

Using Arrays

Transmitting and receiving arrays is transparently done in NuSOAP. You can pass PHP arrays in the parameters array argument to the `soapclient` class's call method, and NuSOAP will detect the type of the array contents, and serialize accordingly. This script uses a service called `echoArray` that accepts an array and returns the same array. While running this example, try modifying the parameter array by adding different data types, and see how the serialization changes.

First, include the NuSOAP classes:

```
<?php

require('nusoap.php');
```

Create the array we'd like to send:

```
$arr = array('string1','string2');
```

Create the array of parameters:

```
$parameters = array($arr);
```

Instantiate the `soapclient` object, passing it the endpoint URL:

```
$s = new soapclient('http://localhost/wrox/nusoap/echoArrayServer.php');
```

Now we call the echoArray operation, passing it our array of parameters, and receive the result. Then print the result on the screen, and view the request and response messages, as follows:

```
$result = $s->call('echoArray',$parameters);

if(!$err = $s->getError()){
     echo 'Result: '.$result;
} else {
     echo 'Error: '.$err;
}

echo '<xmp>'.$s->request.'</xmp>';
echo '<xmp>'.$s->response.'</xmp>';

?>
```

Creating Complex Types

SOAP allows users to define their own types, called "general compound types" in the specification. NuSOAP provides the soapval class for defining custom types, or for situations where you want to override NuSOAP's default serialization behavior. An example of overriding NuSOAP's behaviors would be where let's say NuSOAP would type the value 2.3433 as a float, but the service requires it to be typed as a double. You could create the parameter like:

```
$param = new soapval('','double',2.3433);
```

NuSOAP would then serialize the parameter like this:

```
<soapVal xsi:type="xsd:double">2.3433</soapVal>
```

Here is an example of using the soapval class to create a custom type for some contact information:

```
<?php

include('nusoap.php');

$address = array(
     'street' => '123 Freezing Lane',
     'city' => 'Nome',
     'state' => 'Alaska',
     'zip' => 12345,
    'phonenumbers' => array('home'=>'1234567890','mobile'=>'0987654321')
);

$s =new soapval('myAddress','address',$address,'','http://myNamespace.com');

print "<xmp>".$s->serialize()."</xmp>";

?>
```

Here is the result of running the above code:

```
<myAddress xmlns:ns8467="http://myNamespace.com" xsi:type="ns8467:address">
<street xsi:type="xsd:string">123 Freezing Lane</street>
<city xsi:type="xsd:string">Nome</city>
<state xsi:type="xsd:string">Alaska</state>
<zip xsi:type="xsd:int">12345</zip>
<phonenumbers>
<home xsi:type="xsd:string">1234567890</home>
<mobile xsi:type="xsd:string">0987654321</mobile>
</phonenumbers>
</myAddress>
```

Using WSDL and soap_proxy

WSDL is an XML language used to describe a Web Service. It is a machine-readable format that provides Web Service clients with all the information necessary to access the service. NuSOAP provides a class for parsing WSDL files, and extracting data from them. The `soapclient` object uses the `wsdl` class to ease the burden of the developer calling a service. With the help of the WSDL data to create messages, a programmer only needs to know the name of the operation to call, and the parameters required by the operation.

Using WSDL with NuSOAP provides several benefits:

- All service meta data such as namespaces, endpoint URLs, parameter names, and much more are read from the WSDL, allowing the client to dynamically cope with changes from the server. This information no longer needs to be hard-coded into the user's script since it's on the server.
- It allows us to use the `soap_proxy` class. This class is an extended `soapclient` class with new methods for each of the operations detailed in the WSDL file. Now the user can call these methods directly. This process is described below.

The `soapclient` class contains a method called `getProxy()`. This method returns an object of the class `soap_proxy`. The `soap_proxy` class extends the `soapclient` class with methods that correspond to the operations defined in the WSDL document, and allows users to call the remote methods of an endpoint as if they were local to the object. This is only functional when the `soapclient` object has been instantiated using a WSDL file and has the advantage of easy access for a user. The disadvantage though is the performance – object creation is expensive in PHP – and this functionality serves no utilitarian purpose.

Here is an example of using WSDL to call a stock quotes service from Xmethods, using the `soap_proxy` class. We start by including the NuSOAP classes:

```
<?php

include('nusoap.php');
```

When instantiating the client object using WSDL, we pass the URL or path to the WSDL file as an argument to the constructor, as well as an argument that lets the client know we've passed it WSDL and not a SOAP endpoint:

```
$s = new soapclient(
'http://services.xmethods.net/soap/urn:xmethods-delayed-quotes.wsdl', 'wsdl');
```

Now we'll generate the proxy class. This is achieved by invoking the `getProxy()` method of the `soapclient` class:

```
$p = $s->getProxy();
```

We can now invoke the remote method as a method of the proxy class, and pass our parameters directly. The proxy object will handle the details such as matching up parameter values to their names, assigning namespaces, and types:

```
$sq = $p->getQuote('ibm');
```

Lastly let's check for errors, and if none are present print out the results:

```
if(!$err = $p->getError()){
     print "IBM current stock price: $sq.";
} else {
     print "ERROR: $err";
}

print '<xmp>'.$p->request.'</xmp>';
print '<xmp>'.str_replace('><',">\n<",$p->response).'</xmp>';

?>
```

Using an HTTP Proxy Server

The `soapclient` class has a method called `setHTTPProxy()`, which allows you to use an HTTP proxy server. It takes two arguments: the proxy hostname and the port address. For example:

```
$s = new soapclient('http://www.remoteserver.com/soap_server.php');
$s->setHTTPProxy('proxy.myCompany.com',8080);
```

You can then continue your SOAP calls as we did above. Calling this method will force all requests to be sent to the specified proxy server, which then forwards the request to its intended recipient.

HTTP Authentication

The `soapclient` object provides a method called `setCredentials()`. This method is used when HTTP authentication is needed to access a SOAP server. The two arguments to the method are a username and password. Its functionality is shown in the example below:

```
$s = new soapclient(
'http://www.remoteserver.com/protected_directory/soap_server.php');

$s->setCredentials('myUsername','myPassword');
```

You can then continue your SOAP calls, as you would normally do. The most common way of implementing this level of security on the server is to use Apache's `.htaccess` files to implement required authorization to protect a directory or file.

SSL

Using SSL with the NuSOAP client requires the CURL extension, which was discussed earlier in the chapter, to be installed. The CURL functions provide a way to make a secure connection to a URL. Standard PHP doesn't provide this functionality. If you have the CURL extension, and you would like to connect to a secure Web Service using SSL, you need do nothing other than enter the URL as you normally would. If the URL is secure, you'll notice it starts with `https` instead of the normal `http`:

```
$s = new soapclient('https://mySecureServer.com');
```

Implementing SSL on the server side is outside the scope of PHP's abilities. Check your web server's documentation for instructions on how to achieve this.

Using Document Style Messaging

All of the examples we have seen so far were remote procedure calls, or SOAP RPC, in which we call remote methods, and pass them, encoded parameters. There is another style of message exchange in SOAP, which is known as document style. Document style messaging involves the exchange of literal XML documents. This means that the message bodies are not modeled after procedure calls, and the elements in the message bodies do not have attributes containing type information.

This section provides two examples of document/literal usage using NuSOAP: one using WSDL and one without WSDL. The more common scenario would be to use a WSDL document, but it is useful being able to send arbitrary XML documents and document fragments via SOAP. The service used in the examples is a simple service that allows users to pass a ZIP code, and it returns a listing of 10 ATM cash machines in the ZIP code. The service is listed on Xmethods (http://www.xmethods.net/), and is provided by ServiceObjects (http://www.serviceobjects.com/).

The initial step, as usual, is to include the NuSOAP classes:

```
<?php

require('nusoap.php');
```

Next let's set the URL or path to the WSDL file:

```
$wsdlfile = 'http://ws.serviceobjects.net/gc/GeoCash.asmx?WSDL';
```

Now we'll create the XML document to be sent to the service. This document can be created manually by examining the schema defined in the WSDL document, or by using an XML writing tool, or a PHP class that supports the generation of document skeletons from an XML Schema:

```
// set parameters
$msg =
'<GetATMLocations xmlns="http://www.serviceobjects.com/">
  <strInput>32804</strInput>
  <strLicenseKey>0</strLicenseKey>
</GetATMLocations>';
```

We can now instantiate our `soapclient` object, and pass it the WSDL location:

```
$s = new soapclient($wsdlfile,'wsdl');
```

Finally, we make the call and get the result (which will be an XML document). When using document style messaging with NuSOAP, the document is available as a string via the document property of the `soapclient` class. Here we are printing out the document, and the request and response messages:

```
$s->call('GetATMLocations',array($msg));

print 'RESULT:<xmp>';
var_dump($s->document);
print '</xmp>';

print 'REQUEST:<xmp>'.$s->request.'</xmp>';
print 'RESPONSE:<xmp>'.$s->response.'</xmp>';

?>
```

Sometimes no WSDL is available for a service, or you just need to send arbitrary XML documents via SOAP. The method for sending arbitrary documents is described below:

```
<?php

require('nusoap.php');
```

First we create the XML messages we would like to send:

```
$body =
'<GetATMLocations xmlns="http://www.serviceobjects.com/">
  <strInput>32804</strInput>
  <strLicenseKey>0</strLicenseKey>
</GetATMLocations>';
```

Now we will instantiate the `soapclient` object by passing the service endpoint to the constructor, like this:

```
$s = new soapclient('http://ws.serviceobjects.net/gc/GeoCash.asmx');
```

The `serializeEnvelope()` method can be used to wrap a SOAP envelope around XML content:

```
$msg = $s->serializeEnvelope($body);
```

Use the `send()` method to actually send the message. The method takes two arguments: the message content, and the `SOAPAction` header value. Once again, we can examine the result via the document property of the `soapclient` class, and we'll print out our request and response messages:

```
$s->send($msg,'http://www.serviceobjects.com/GetATMLocations');

print 'RESULT:<xmp>';
var_dump($s->document);
print '</xmp>';

print 'REQUEST:<xmp>'.$s->request.'</xmp>';
print 'RESPONSE:<xmp>'.$s->response.'</xmp>';

?>
```

Other PHP SOAP Implementations

The following are PHP Web Services toolkits for sending and receiving SOAP messages.

Active State SWSAPI

Active State, a software company in Vancouver, Canada, used SOAPx4 as the core for their SOAP and WSDL toolkit for PHP, which is Web Service API called the Simple Web Services API (SWSAPI). It is a unified API for Web Service programming for Active State's Perl, Python, and PHP distributions.

PEAR

PHP Extension and Add-on Repository or PEAR is a group of classes bundled with the PHP distribution. PEAR is a community effort to create a set of tools that provide functionality common to the many uses of PHP. Shane Caraveo recently converted the SOAPx4 classes to meet the PEAR standards, and the toolkit was added to the repository. He also added many new features, such as HTTPS, SMTP support, and function overloading.

Krysalis

Krysalis is an application development platform for PHP from Interakt. It is similar in design to the Cocoon Application Framework, and was inspired by it. In the latest version of Krysalis, 1.0.4, Interakt has implemented a simple SOAP client and SOAP server. Until now, much of the message creation is done manually. Use of Krysalis requires PHP's XSLT Sablotron extension, and access to the PEAR classes. http://www.interakt.ro/products/Krysalis/.

PHP Web Services and XML-RPC

XML-RPC in PHP provides a simple and accessible alternative to SOAP. It is widely used, and there are several implementations to choose from. For many PHP developers, XML-RPC serves their RPC needs, without the complexity and infrastructure required by other RPC methods.

XML-RPC Data Types

As discussed above, XML-RPC specification defines a limited number of supported data types. The supported types are listed below with their PHP equivalents and examples:

XML-RPC	PHP	Example
`i4`	Integer	`23`
`int`	Integer	`23`
`boolean`	Boolean	`true, false`

XML-RPC	PHP	Example
`string`	String	`'Dietrich Ayala'`
`double`	Double or float	`23.3`
`dateTime.Iso8601`	no native PHP equivalent	-
`base64`	Base64 encoded string	`base64 ('Dietrich Ayala')`
`array`	Array	`array ( 1, 2, 'red', 'blue');`
`struct`	Associative array	`array ('color' => 'red', 'number'=> 2)`

Useful Inc. XML-RPC Implementation

The XML-RPC toolkit that we'll be using for our examples is a set of PHP classes authored by Edd Dumbill of Useful, Inc. The code and documentation can be found at Sourceforge.net (http://phpxmlrpc.sourceforge.net/). The toolkit contains both client and server implementations of XML-RPC.

The toolkit comes with two important classes: the `xmlrpc_client` class for the client and the `xmlrpc_server` class for server-side programming. These classes are mainly used for sending and receiving the XML-RPC messages. An `xmlrpcval` class is used to encode the PHP variables into their XML-RPC equivalents and is used to pass parameters to a remote method. The reverse process of decoding back into the PHP equivalent is done using the `xmlrpc_decode()` function. An XML-RPC message is created using the `xmlrpcmsg` class by passing a parameter list to it.

The `xmlrpc_client` class sends XML-RPC messages that are created by the `xmlrpcmsg` class. On the server side, the `xmlrpc_server` class parses these incoming messages back into an `xmlrpcmsg` object. This message object is then passed as the single argument to the user's deployed function. This function must return a response in the form of an `xmlrpcresp` object that the `xmlrpc_server` class uses to serialize and return back to the client. This basic architecture of the toolkit is shown in the diagram below:

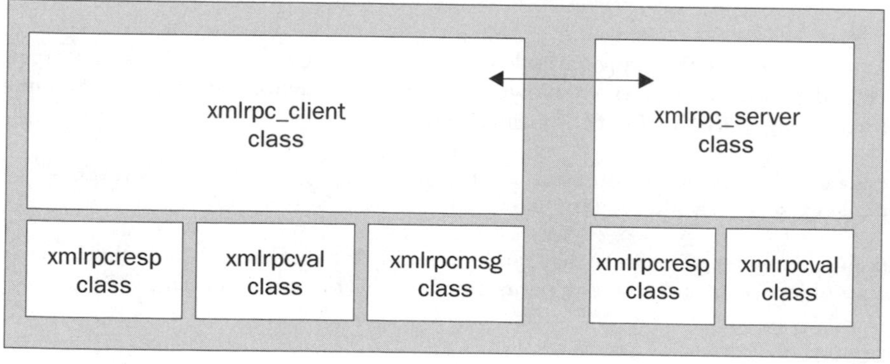

Installation and Configuration

The installation can be achieved in a few steps as follows:

- Download XML-RPC for PHP from http://phpxmlrpc.sourceforge.net/
- Unpack it
- Move `xmlrpc.inc` and `xmlrpcs.inc` to a location in your include path, or save them to the same directory as the script(s) in which you expect to use them

To use the XML-RPC client you must include the client code that is done by adding the following line at the top of your script. Here, the argument to the `include()` function is the path to the `xmlrpc.inc` file:

```
include('xmlrpc.inc');
```

To use the XML-RPC server class – to create and deploy your own XML-RPC Web Services – you must include the client and the server code:

```
include('xmlrpc.inc');
include('xmlrpcs.inc'); //server code
```

A Simple XML-RPC Client Example

This example demonstrates an XML-RPC client that passes a string variable to an XML-RPC server that echoes the string back to the client.

The first step is to include the XML-RPC client code:

```
<?php

// include the xml-rpc classes
require('xmlrpc.inc');
```

Now we can create a client object, and pass it our connection information. The `xmlrpc_client` class is a high-level class that serializes parameters and messages. It is also responsible for sending the messages to the server. Its constructor takes three arguments: the path, hostname, and port address of the server:

```
$s = new xmlrpc_client('/wrox/xmlrpc/xmlrpc_server.php','localhost',80);
```

The next step is to create the string variable that we would like to send to the `echoString` service. We do this using the `xmlrpcval` class. It allows us to create abstractions of PHP variables into XML elements according to the XML-RPC specification:

```
// create xmlrpcval object, which allows the encoding of our variable
$inputString = new xmlrpcval('Dietrich Ayala','string');
```

Let's add our parameter to an array that can hold multiple parameters. We do this because the `xmlrpcmsg` object constructor takes a parameter list as its second argument:

```
// create an array of parameters
$parameters = array($inputString);
```

The final preparatory step is to create the XML-RPC message using the `xmlrpcmsg` object. Its constructor takes the method name we are calling as its first argument, and our array of parameters as its second:

```
// create the message object
$msg = new xmlrpcmsg('echoString',$parameters);
```

Now we are ready to send our message. To do this we use the `send()` method of the `xmlrpc_client` object. It takes our `xmlrpcmsg` object as an argument and returns an `xmlrpcresp` object. The `xmlrpcresp` object has three methods of use to the client:

- `faultCode()`
  This method returns the code associated with any errors returned
- `faultString()`
  This method returns a string description of the error
- `value()`
  This method returns the value contained in the response in the form of an `xmlrpcval` object

If no errors occur, the `faultCode()` method will return a zero. This is an easy way to check for errors and this is what we'll do in our example:

```
// send the message, get the response
$rsp = $s->send($msg);

// check for errors
if($rsp->faultcode() == 0){
```

If no errors occurred, we can go ahead and retrieve the value returned by the server. To do this, we will first call the `value()` method of the response object, which returns an `xmlrpcval` object. To convert this into its equivalent PHP type, we use the `xmlrpc_decode()` function that returns the value converted into a PHP type:

```
    // decode the response to a PHP type
    $response = xmlrpc_decode($rsp->value());
```

Let's print the result, or any errors, and view the messages:

```
    // print results
    print '<pre>';
    var_dump($response);
    print '</pre>';
```

```
} else {
    // print errors
    print 'Error: '.$rsp->faultcode().', '.$rsp->faultstring().'<br>';
}

// show messages
$msg->createpayload();
print 'REQUEST:<xmp>'.$msg->payload.'</xmp>';
print 'RESPONSE:<xmp>'.$rsp->serialize().'</xmp>';

?>
```

XML-RPC Request and Response

This is the request message generated in the previous code sample. Notice the readability of the message. Though verbose, it is intuitive and easy to decipher its meaning:

```
<?xml version="1.0"?>
<methodCall>
<methodName>echoString</methodName>
<params>
<param>
<value><string>Dietrich Ayala</string></value>
</param>
</params>
</methodCall>
```

Here is the response message from the server:

```
<methodResponse>
<params>
<param>
<value><string>Dietrich Ayala</string></value>
</param>
</params>
</methodResponse>
```

A Simple XML-RPC Server Example

This example implements the service that we used in our client example that is the `echoString` service. Here we'll see how to use the `xmlrpc_server` class to create and deploy a service and then serve requests using the `xmlrpcresp` class to encapsulate and return responses.

We must first include the XML-RPC files. Note the inclusion of `xmlrpcs.inc`, which provides the code necessary for the server:

```
<?php

// include the client and server classes
require('xmlrpc.inc');
require('xmlrpcs.inc');
```

Let's define our function that will handle the incoming request. The function to be deployed must take only one argument, which is an `xmlrpcmsg` object:

```
// service that echoes a string
function echoString($msg){
```

The first step in our function is to take the parameters from the message object and decode them into PHP types. The decoding is done using the `xmlrpc_decode()` function that we discussed above:

```
    // decode parameters into native types
    $inputString = xmlrpc_decode(array_shift($msg->params));
```

Here we check the parameter's type to see that it is valid. If it is, we return it using the `xmlrpcresp` object. To return a value, the `xmlrpcresp` class constructor takes one argument of type `xmlrpcval`. Thus, any returned value must first be encoded as an `xmlrpcval`:

```
    // check for input parameter validity
     if(is_string($inputString)){
        return new xmlrpcresp( new xmlrpcval($inputString, 'string') );
}
```

If the parameter is invalid, we may use the `xmlrpcresp` object again to return a fault. This is done by passing zero to the `xmlrpcresp` constructor as its first argument followed by the error code. The XML-RPC specification says that fault codes are to be user-defined. XML-RPC for PHP defines a constant named `$xmlrpcerruser`, which sets an error level. For errors taking place outside of the XML-RPC classes themselves, the standard convention recommended by the author of these classes is to increment the value of this variable by one. The last argument is the fault code, which is a human-readable string describing the error:

```
    else {    // or return a fault

      return new xmlrpcresp(0, $xmlrpcerruser+1,
      "Parameter type ".gettype($inputString)." mismatched expected type.");

    }
}
```

The final step in the process is to instantiate the server class, and register our function in it. The `xmlrpc_server` constructor takes an associative array as its first argument. This array is what is called the "dispatch map." It is an associative array of associative arrays. The key values of the outer array are the public names of the functions being deployed that are the names by which XML-RPC clients would call them. The inner array contains three members:

- `function`
  This is a mandatory entry and its value is the name of the PHP function you've defined to handle this service. In our example above this is the same as the service name that is `echoString`. For example, you could deploy a service called `reverser` that maps to a PHP function `strrev()` that takes a string as an argument and returns the string reversed. The most important point to note is that the value of `function` must be a valid function in the global scope.
- `signature`
  This is an optional member. A `signature` is defined by creating an array of parameter types for each input and output parameters. It is an array of possible signatures to validate requests against. The value of this member takes an array in which each member is a possible signature. Here, the last one is the output parameter while all the previous ones are input parameters.
- `docstring`
  This is an optional member that may contain the documentation for your service, and may even have HTML contents.

Instantiating the server class initiates the processing of any incoming requests. The second parameter to the `xmlrpc_server` constructor is optional. When this is set to zero, the server will not immediately process requests. The processing can be executed later by using the server's `service()` method:

```
// instantiate the server object and register our functions
$s = new xmlrpc_server(array(
            'echoString' => array(
                  'function' => 'echoString',
                  'signature' => array( array('string','string') ),
                  'docstring' => 'This service echoes the input string back to the
client.'
            )
      ));

?>
```

Other PHP XML-RPC Implementations

The other open source implementations of the XML-RPC protocol for PHP are either experimental or not well documented. Here we list a couple of them.

XMLRPC-EPI

XMLRPC-EPI is an XML-RPC implementation written in C. It was originally developed for internal use at Epinions (hence the -EPI). Epinions (http://epinions.com/) released XMLRPC-EPI as open source in March 2000. Since then the project has been hosted and managed on Sourceforge.net. Epinions also donated a PHP module for the code, written by Dan Libby. This module has since been folded into the PHP core distribution and has been available in PHP since version 4.1.0. It is currently labeled experimental in the PHP manual.

Noyade

This is a pure PHP implementation by Matt Bean. It has no documentation available. The source is available at http://rpc.lemurpants.com/noyrpc.phps. The script for testing the implementation against Userland Software's Validator is provided at http://rpc.lemurpants.com/rpc-validator1.phps.

Future of PHP Web Services

The momentum of Web Services in PHP is growing rapidly. The core PHP developers are discussing the possibility of having standard SOAP support bundled with the main PHP distribution. This would enable Web Service usage in PHP to explode by making it available in every new PHP installation.

Brad LaFountain has recently released the first version of a SOAP extension for PHP. It looks very promising, and will probably end up being PHP's standard SOAP extension. It uses the `libxml` library, which provides implementations of XML DOM, Xpath, and XLink. If it were bundled with PHP it would be a double win for PHP developers who use XML.

Other Web Services activity in PHP is the creation of PEAR-SOAP. PEAR (PHP Extension and Application Repository) is a collection of reusable PHP components. Shane Caraveo, primary developer of the initial port of PHP to Windows, ported SOAPx4 (NuSOAP's predecessor) to PEAR, which became PEAR-SOAP.

Summary

With NuSOAP we've been able to create a client that retrieves content by consuming services offered by remote servers using SOAP, and guided by WSDL. We've also deployed our own service that is accessible by a multiplicity of clients of all different platforms and languages. These basic operations are boilerplates for your imagination as you can use them to create robust interoperable Web Services for yourself.

We have also seen how to use XML-RPC for PHP to create a client that can pass encoded data to a server and detect success or failure from the response. We have seen how to create an XML-RPC server and deploy services using it. These examples demonstrate how PHP and XML-RPC can be used together to access remote applications, as well as to create your own.

Though the question that arises is "which is a better choice: SOAP or XML-RPC?", actually there is no black-and-white answer to this question. The best solution is the one that solves the stated problem best, or achieves the goals of your application. Both XML-RPC and SOAP have different abilities, different strengths and weaknesses. You should weigh these against the needs of your application to make your decision.

XML-RPC is designed for simplicity. It contains limitations that some developers might welcome, such as a small number of types to support and a small XML vocabulary. It may perform faster as it requires much less infrastructure than SOAP.

SOAP is designed to accomplish much more complex messaging problems than XML-RPC. It allows users to define a near limitless amount of types, as well as different styles of messaging. You can specify the character set of the message, as well as specify a recipient, and force the recipient to reply with a fault if it can't understand the message. All in all, SOAP provides a much richer set of features than XML-RPC, but at the cost of more complexity. The final decision of which is better will be decided by the needs of your application or project.

This chapter has demonstrated the use of PHP tools to consume and deploy Web Services with XML-RPC and SOAP, which is not only possible, but robust and interoperable as well. The examples in this chapter have shown that PHP and Web Services can turn your web applications into distributed systems that can provide interoperable services to others.

9

Web Services with C++

As in the case of other languages we have seen in the previous chapters, we can also develop Web Services in C++. In this chapter, we will see how to develop Web Services using C++ SOAP implementations. There are many SOAP implementations for C++. However, in this chapter, we'll discuss three popular open source implementations –WASP Server Lite for C++, EasySoap++, and gSOAP.

For each of these SOAP implementations, we will begin with the installation, and then build a SOAP Web Service, and a client for the same. This would help us to compare the process of developing applications in these implementations. Finally, we will also go over the details of how each SOAP implementation maps C++ data to XML.

Later in the chapter, we'll compare these three implementations for the features present and missing from them. We'll also cover some design and implementation issues that would help us choose the right implementation for our needs.

WASP Server Lite for C++

WASP Server Lite for C++ is a SOAP implementation developed by Systinet (formerly Idoox), and available under the BSD Open Source licence. WASP (Web Applications and Services Platform) is designed as a solution that can be embedded in C++ applications, and consists of a multi-threaded SOAP server, C++ client library, and WSDL tools. Unfortunately, the WSDL tools that exist in open source C++ SOAP implementations are a bit limited in functionality.

In this chapter, we'll use WASP Server 3.0 Beta 2 Lite for C++, an early release, which offers significant improvements over its predecessor (version 1.2). Some of these are:

- Support for WSDL 1.1 standards and 2001 XML schema version
- Native WSDL2CPP tools for generating C++ code from WSDL (version 1.2 had Java-based WSDL tools)
- Better performance due to pull parser-based SOAP message processing instead of depending on Xerces
- Better portability as it doesn't use the STLPort library and Xerces

However, this version is still in beta, and at the time of writing lacked some features present in the earlier 1.2 versions, such as HTTP proxy support, and complete support for WSDL 1.1 (it currently has no support for document style messaging).

This version also does not support SSL, or have an UDDI client API. These features will not be available in the open source version, but instead as a part of Systinet's non-open source product WASP Server for C++.

Installing WASP Server Lite for C++

WASP Server 3.0 Beta 2 Lite for C++ can be downloaded from http://www.systinet.com/eap/waspc_30/index.html. We'll extract the gunzipped file in the directory of our choice:

```
$ gunzip WASP-CPP-3.0-beta2.tar.gz
$ tar xvf WASP-CPP-3.0-beta2.tar
```

We now need to run the `configure` script. This analyzes the system that we are installing on, and generates the `Makefile`:

```
$ ./configure --prefix=/home/vivek/install/WASP30 --with-
waspc=/home/vivek/install/WASP30
```

Here, we use the `--prefix` option to specify the installation directory for WASP, and the `--with-waspc` option to point to the WASP C++ installation directory. Once this is done, we'll build and install WASP with the `make` command followed by `make install`:

```
$ make
$ make install
```

Along with the `Makefile`, the `configure` script also generates a `config.log` file that contains the log of the `configure` commands that were run as well as a log of the system information the command was able to detect. Now, we have WASP ready, and we can proceed with developing the Web Service.

Before we move ahead, let's set the `$WASP_HOME` environment variable to the WASP install directory for our convenience though it's not required by WASP:

```
$ export WASP_HOME=/home/vivek/install/WASP30
```

Building the Web Service Using WASP

Let's take an example of an ice cream cone manufacturer that sells various kinds of cones to its retail outlets. It has a number of legacy applications running at geographically distributed locations. These applications do not work well with each other as they have proprietary interfaces. Many of the legacy applications are written in C. Some of the newer code has been written in C++, and the resultant application is linked together with a C++ compiler.

We'll integrate its warehouse inventory system with the order processing system. The warehouse inventory system is a C++ application. The order processing system will check the availability of the item before accepting a new order. Since these systems are geographically distributed, and don't have a common interface, we'll develop a Web Service that checks the availability for a particular item from the warehouse inventory system.

We'll develop our `warehouseService` Web Service, which will have a method called `checkAvailabilty()`, which takes a purchase order item as input. The purchase order item contains the type of ice cream cone, and the required quantity. This method checks the warehouse inventory database, and returns an availability status indicating if the required cones are in stock, out of stock, or partially in stock.

In case of partial stock, it returns the number of cones it has in stock, as a part of the availability status report. The order processing system then has the option of either placing an order for the complete or partial number of cones, or advising the customer to place a back order.

Building the WSDL File

Since we are using WASP to develop our Web Service, we need to build a WSDL file to get the client stub, and server implementation ancestor classes. The 3.0 Beta 2 release of WASP does not come with a tool to generate a WSDL file from a C++ class/header, nevertheless it has a tool that consumes a WSDL file, and generates client stubs and service skeletons.

One of the ways to get the WSDL for a service is to write its interface in terms of a Java class, and use any one of the freely available Java-to-WSDL conversion tools to generate the WSDL file. Another way would be to use gSOAP's stub and skeleton compiler (described later in the chapter) to build a WSDL file template from the C++ header (actually a header file following gSOAP's conventions) for the service. We could otherwise just write the WSDL manually, especially if the service is simple enough.

For our `warehouseService` Web Service, we'll write the WSDL file (`warehouse.wsdl`) as given below:

```
<?xml version="1.0" encoding="UTF-8"?>
<definitions name="warehouseService"
  xmlns="http://schemas.xmlsoap.org/wsdl/"
  xmlns:SOAP-ENV="http://schemas.xmlsoap.org/soap/envelope/"
  xmlns:SOAP-ENC="http://schemas.xmlsoap.org/soap/encoding/"
  xmlns:SOAP="http://schemas.xmlsoap.org/wsdl/soap/"
  xmlns:WSDL="http://schemas.xmlsoap.org/wsdl/"
  xmlns:xsd="http://www.w3.org/2001/XMLSchema"
  targetNamespace="http://www.wrox.com/warehouse"
  xmlns:tns="http://www.wrox.com/warehouse">

  <types>
```

```
    <schema
      xmlns="http://www.w3.org/2001/XMLSchema"
      xmlns:SOAP-ENV="http://schemas.xmlsoap.org/soap/envelope/"
      xmlns:SOAP-ENC="http://schemas.xmlsoap.org/soap/encoding/"
      targetNamespace="http://www.wrox.com/warehouse"
      xmlns:tns="http://www.wrox.com/warehouse">

      <complexType name="AvailabilityStatus">
       <sequence>
        <element name="status" type="xsd:string" minOccurs="0"
                 maxOccurs="1" nillable="true"/>
        <element name="quantity" type="xsd:int" minOccurs="0"
                 maxOccurs="1"/>
       </sequence>
      </complexType>
    </schema>
  </types>

  <message name="checkAvailabilityRequest">
    <part name="itemName" type="xsd:string"/>
    <part name="quantity" type="xsd:int"/>
  </message>

  <message name="AvailabilityStatus">
    <part name="status" type="tns:AvailabilityStatus"/>
  </message>

  <portType name="warehouseServicePortType">
    <documentation>
      Service definition of function checkAvailability
    </documentation>
    <operation name="checkAvailability">
      <input message="tns:checkAvailabilityRequest"/>
      <output message="tns:AvailabilityStatus"/>
    </operation>
  </portType>

  <binding name="warehouseServiceBinding"
           type="tns:warehouseServicePortType">
    <SOAP:binding style="rpc"
                  transport="http://schemas.xmlsoap.org/soap/http"/>
    <operation name="checkAvailability">
      <SOAP:operation soapAction=""/>
      <input>
        <SOAP:body use="encoded" namespace="http://www.wrox.com/warehouse"
                encodingStyle="http://schemas.xmlsoap.org/soap/encoding/"/>
      </input>
      <output>
        <SOAP:body use="encoded" namespace="http://www.wrox.com/warehouse"
                encodingStyle="http://schemas.xmlsoap.org/soap/encoding/"/>
      </output>
    </operation>
  </binding>

  <service name="warehouseService">
    <port name="warehouseServicePort" binding="tns:warehouseServiceBinding">
      <SOAP:address location="localhost:6070"/>
    </port>
  </service>
</definitions>
```

Developing the Web Service

Once we have this WSDL file, we can now run the WSDL compiler, `wsdlc`, to generate WASPC client-side stubs, and service skeletons for us:

```
$ $WASP_HOME/bin/wsdlc warehouse.wsdl warehouse
```

As we can see, the `wsdlc` command takes two parameters – the name of the WSDL file, and the name of the project (in this case, `warehouse`). It also has an optional argument `--config` through which we can pass the configuration file pathname. We'll see the WASPC configuration files in more detail later in the chapter. The above command generates the following files:

- The client-side stub code and header –
  `warehouse.cpp`
  `warehouse.h`
- The service skeleton code and header –
  `warehouseImpl.cpp`
  `warehouseImpl.h`
- The serializers and deserializers for the `AvailabilityStatus` data structure used by the service and client –
  `warehouseStructs.cpp`
  `warehouseStructs.h`

Now that these files have been generated for us, let's start implementing the actual service logic and write a client.

The service skeleton class (`warehouseServicePortImpl`) generated in the service skeletons `warehouseImpl.cpp` and `warehouseImpl.h` has a virtual public method for each SOAP method. In our case, the SOAP method generated will be as shown below:

```
    // Abstract implementation method headers
    virtual AvailabilityStatus * checkAvailability (WASP_String * itemName,
            int quantity) = 0;
```

We need to implement this method in a class that derives from `warehouseServicePortImpl` class. For this implementation, we'll write the header file (`warehouseServiceImpl.h`) as given below:

```
#ifndef _WAREHOUSE_SERVICE_IMPL_H_
#define _WAREHOUSE_SERVICE_IMPL_H_

#include <waspc/config/config.h>
#include "warehouseImpl.h"

class warehouseServiceImpl:public warehouseServicePortImpl {
  public:
  virtual AvailabilityStatus* checkAvailability (WASP_String*, int);
};

#endif /*  _WAREHOUSE_SERVICE_IMPL_H_ */
```

Now, we will write the implementation class (`warehouseServiceImpl.cpp`) that provides the implementation of the `checkAvailability()` method:

```
#include <waspc/common.h>
#include "warehouseServiceImpl.h"

#if defined(WASP_MEMORY_DEBUGGER)
# define new WASP_DEBUG_NEW
# undef THIS_FILE
  static char THIS_FILE[] = __FILE__;
#endif

AvailabilityStatus* warehouseServiceImpl::checkAvailability
                   (WASP_String* itemName, int quantity) {
  cout << "\nWarehouse inventory service got an status check for ";
  cout << quantity << " cases of " << itemName->transcode()<< " cones.\n";

  if (quantity <= 0) {
    // return SOAP FAULT - Not yet supported
  }
```

The current release of WASPC does not provide support for SOAP faults. This is a work in progress, and it is expected that it will appear in subsequent releases.

The `WASP_String` class is a WASP representation of Unicode character string. This class comes with `create()` methods that can take a `char*`, or a `wchar*` (wide character set) and convert it to a `WASP_String` type:

```
  AvailabilityStatus* availabilityStatus = new AvailabilityStatus ();

  // A database lookup would come here. However, we are going to fake it.
  int regular_amt = 10000;
  int sugar_amt = 0;
  int waffle_amt = 10;

  WASP_String* regularString = WASP_String::create ("regular");
  WASP_String* sugarString = WASP_String::create ("sugar");
  WASP_String* waffleString = WASP_String::create ("waffle");
```

In a real-world application, we can query the inventory database to determine the availability status. However, we are using hardcoded values to simulate the database look up, just to keep our example simpler. We'll now compare the quantity for the particular kind of cone with the hardcoded value (that simulates the available stock) for the same kind.

For example, we compare the request quantity for 'regular' cones against the available stock (hard coded to be 10000 above), and return an availability status. The 'quantity' attribute of the availability status is set to an actual number that can be fulfilled. If there is a request for 50 cases, we can fulfill an order for all 50 (status is `INSTOCK`). However, if there is a request for 50000 cases, we can fulfill a request for only 10000 (status is `PARTIALSTOCK`):

```
    if (itemName->equals (regularString)) {
    if (quantity == 0) {
      //We have no stock.
      availabilityStatus->quantity = 0;
      availabilityStatus->status = WASP_String::create ("OUTOFSTOCK");
    }
    else if (quantity < regular_amt)
    {
      // We have the required quantity.
      availabilityStatus->quantity  = quantity;
      availabilityStatus->status = WASP_String::create ("INSTOCK");
    }
    else
    {
      // We have inadequate stock.
      availabilityStatus->quantity  = regular_amt;
      availabilityStatus->status = WASP_String::create ("PARTIALSTOCK");
    }
  }
  else if (itemName->equals (sugarString)) {
    if (quantity == 0) {
      availabilityStatus->quantity = 0;
      availabilityStatus->status = WASP_String::create ("OUTOFSTOCK");
    }
    else if (quantity < sugar_amt) {
      availabilityStatus->quantity = quantity;
      availabilityStatus->status = WASP_String::create ("INSTOCK");
    }
    else
    {
      availabilityStatus->quantity  = sugar_amt;
      availabilityStatus->status    = WASP_String::create ("PARTIALSTOCK");
    }
  }
  else if (itemName->equals (waffleString)) {
    if (quantity == 0) {
      availabilityStatus->quantity  = 0;
      availabilityStatus->status    = WASP_String::create ("OUTOFSTOCK");
    }
    else if (quantity < waffle_amt) {
      availabilityStatus->quantity  = quantity;
      availabilityStatus->status    = WASP_String::create ("INSTOCK");
    }
    else {
      availabilityStatus->quantity  = waffle_amt;// That's all we have
      availabilityStatus->status    = WASP_String::create ("PARTIALSTOCK");
    }
  }
  else {
    // return SOAP FAULT - Not yet supported
  }

  regularString->removeRef();
  sugarString->removeRef();
  waffleString->removeRef();

  return availabilityStatus;
}
```

When an object of type `WASP_String` is created, its reference count is set to `1`. Users can bump this up by `1` via the `addRef()` method of `WASP_String` (not used here). As we can see in the above code, this object is removed from memory by calling the `removeRef()` method, when its reference count goes down to `0`.

A WASP service implementation class, like the one we just wrote, is not responsible for cleanup of the parameters, or the return values. The WASP server performs this task, as we'll see in the next section. This means that if the service needs to store any parameters, such as for maintaining state information across calls, it needs to make a copy of them. The exception to this is reference-counted parameters (such as the `WASP_String` above). The service can increase its reference count as we discussed earlier. The service can then store this as is, without the risk of it being deleted by the server.

Implementing the Server

Once the service has been written, we need to deploy it in a server. WASP supports a standalone, multi-threaded SOAP server. Let's write the server (`server.cpp`). First, we need to include our service implementation header file along with the header files `common.h`, `Runtime.h`, and `SuperFactory.h`:

```
#include <waspc/common.h>
#include <waspc/runtime/Runtime.h>
#include <waspc/runtime/SuperFactory.h>

// Include files for all our service implementations
#include "warehouseServiceImpl.h"

#if defined(WASP_MEMORY_DEBUGGER)
# define new WASP_DEBUG_NEW
# undef THIS_FILE
  static char THIS_FILE[] = __FILE__;
#endif
```

We then add definitions for the factory method for each of our service implementations. The macro `WASP_FACTORY_DEFINE` expands to a factory method that returns a new `warehouseServiceImpl` object. Next, we create a table mapping the service class name to the factory method. The `WASP_FACTORY_ENTRY` macro that we add in the `demoFactory` array does this for us:

```
// Define factories for all our service implementations

WASP_FACTORY_DEFINE (warehouseServiceImpl);

// Add the factories to the factory definition

WASP_FactoryDefinition demoFactory[]=
{
  WASP_FACTORY_ENTRY (warehouseServiceImpl),
  WASP_FACTORY_END ()
};
```

This server first initializes the SOAP standalone server using the `WASP_Runtime::serverInitialize()` method, and then registers the array of service implementation factory methods (`WASP_SuperFactory::registerFactory()`).

We then run `WASP_Runtime::serverStart()` to start the server. It takes a server configuration file (`server_config.xml`) as a parameter, and calls blocks until the server is shut down:

```
int main (int,char *[])
{
  // Initialize the server
  WASP_Runtime::serverInitialize ();

  // Register the demo factory
  WASP_SuperFactory::registerFactory (demoFactory);
  TRY (ee) {
    printf ("Starting WASP SOAP Server\n");
    WASP_Runtime::serverStart("server_config.xml",ee);
    CHECX_NESTED (ee);
  }
  catch_all (exc,ee) {
    // Some exception occurred during server run
    char *trace=GET_TRACE (exc);
    printf ("Exception during server startup:
            '%s'\n%s\n",exc->getCharMessage (),trace);
    delete trace;
    delete exc;
  }
  stop_catch_all (ee);
    // Stop all services, terminate the server
    WASP_Runtime::serverTerminate ();
    return 0;
}
```

Configuring the Server

The service configuration file (`server_config.xml`) that is passed as a parameter to the `serverStart()` method is listed below:

```
<?xml version="1.0"?>

<waspcServer
  xmlns:wasp="urn:WaspServer"
  xmlns:disp="urn:DispatcherRepository"
  xmlns:trans="urn:TransportRepository"
  xmlns:xprot="urn:XMLProtocolHandlerRepository"
  xmlns:adap="urn:AdaptorFactory"
  xmlns:xpa="urn:XMLProtocolAdaptor"
  xmlns:cppa="urn:CppAdaptor"
  xmlns:sbnd="urn:ServiceBinding"
  xmlns:svci="urn:ServiceInstanceRepository"
  xmlns:header="urn:HeaderProcessorRepository"
  xmlns:ser="urn:Serialization"
  xmlns:del="urn:DeleterRepository">

  <!-- Module TransportRepository -->
  <wasp:module wasp:class="WASP_TransportRepositoryImpl"/>
```

```
<trans:transport
       trans:class="WASP_FileTransportClient" trans:scheme="file"
       xmlns:ftc="urn:FileTransportClient" ftc:extout=".out"/>

<trans:transport
         trans:class="WASP_HTTPTransportClient" trans:scheme="http"
         xmlns:htc="urn:HTTPTransportClient"/>
```

The configuration directives for WASP seen in this configuration file are described later in the chapter in the *WASP Configuration File Directives* section.

Now, we do the HTTP transport settings for our server. These contain the `hts:hostname` and `hts:port` attributes that point to the host and port that the server listens to. We set them as `localhost` and `6070` respectively:

```
<trans:transport
       trans:class="WASP_HTTPTransportServer" trans:scheme="server-http"
       xmlns:hts="urn:HTTPTransportServer" hts:dispatcher="DispatcherA"
       hts:singleThread="0"
       hts:hostname="localhost"
       hts:port="6070"/>

<!-- Module XMLProtocolHandlerRepository -->
<wasp:module wasp:class="WASP_XMLProtocolHandlerRepositoryImpl"/>

<xprot:protocolHandler xprot:class="WASP_SOAPProtocolHandler"
                       xprot:name="SOAP"/>

<!-- Module AdaptorFactory -->
<wasp:module wasp:class="WASP_AdaptorFactoryImpl"/>

<!-- XMLProtocol adaptor default config -->
<adap:adaptor adap:class="WASP_XMLProtocolAdaptorImpl"
adap:name="XMLProtocolAdaptorA" xmlns:xpa="urn:XMLProtocolAdaptor"
      xpa:nestedAdaptor="" xpa:xmlProtocolHandler="SOAP"/>

<!-- Module HeaderProcessorRepository -->
<wasp:module wasp:class="WASP_HeaderProcessorRepositoryImpl"/>

<!-- Cpp adaptor default config -->
<adap:adaptor adap:class="WASP_CppAdaptorImpl" adap:name="CppAdaptorA"
      cppa:nestedAdaptor="XMLProtocolAdaptorA"/>

<!-- Modules related to serialization -->
<wasp:module wasp:class="WASP_DeleterRepositoryImpl"/>
<wasp:module wasp:class="WASP_SerializationRepositoryStorageImpl"/>

<!-- Basic deleters -->
<del:deleter del:class="WASP_PrimitiveTypeDeleter"/>
<del:deleter del:class="WASP_AbstractStructureDeleter"/>

<!-- SOAP 1.1 (de)serializers -->
<ser:serialization ser:name="http://schemas.xmlsoap.org/soap/encoding/">
```

```
    <ser:resolver ser:class="WASP_SOAP11_Resolver"/>
    <ser:deserializer ser:class="WASP_SOAP11_PrimitiveTypeDeserializer"/>
    <ser:serializer ser:class="WASP_SOAP11_PrimitiveTypeSerializer"/>
  </ser:serialization>

  <!-- Module DispatcherRepository -->
  <wasp:module wasp:class="WASP_DispatcherRepositoryImpl"/>

  <!-- Displatcher config -->
  <disp:dispatcher disp:class="WASP_DispatcherImpl"
                   disp:name="DispatcherA" xmlns:dispi="urn:DispatcherImpl"
                   dispi:shutdownURL="/Admin/Shutdown/"/>

  <!-- Module ServiceInstanceRepository-->
  <wasp:module wasp:class="WASP_ServiceInstanceRepositoryImpl"/>
```

We also need to add settings for the service we are deploying in this configuration file. These settings are specified as `serviceBindings` and `serviceInstance` bindings:

```
  <!-- Service bindings -->

  <!-- Service binding - warehouseService -->
  <sbnd:serviceBinding
        sbnd:dispatcherRef="DispatcherA" sbnd:adaptorRef="CppAdaptorA"
        sbnd:wsdl="./warehouse.wsdl" sbnd:url="/WarehouseService/">
    <cppa:instance cppa:ref="warehouse"/>
  </sbnd:serviceBinding>

  <!-- Service instances - implementation classes -->
  <svci:serviceInstance svci:class="warehouseServiceImpl"
                        svci:name="warehouse"/>

</waspcServer>
```

Here, the `sbnd:wsdl` attribute has the pathname of the WSDL file for the service, and `sbnd:url` contains the fragment of the URL for the service. The URL fragment specified here when combined with the `hts:hostname` and `hts:port` attributes specified in the transport element earlier, gives the complete URL for our Web Service (http://localhost:6070/WarehouseService/). The SOAP client uses this URL to connect to the service.

We then add a `serviceInstance` binding element for our Web Service. This element has the name of the C++ class that implements the service (`svci:class` attribute), and the name of the service (`svci:name` attribute) that is the same as the `cppa:ref` attribute in the `serviceBinding` element.

Developing the Client

We now can start writing the client application (`warehouseClient.cpp`). First, we need to initialize the WASP client:

```
#include <waspc/common.h>
#include <waspc/runtime/Runtime.h>

#include "warehouse.h"

#if defined(WASP_MEMORY_DEBUGGER)
```

```
#   define new WASP_DEBUG_NEW
#   undef THIS_FILE
    static char THIS_FILE[] = __FILE__;
#endif

int main (int argc,char *argv[])
{

  // Initialize WASP client
  WASP_Runtime::clientInitialize ();
  WASP_String *wasp_string = NULL;
  AvailabilityStatus* availabilityStatus = NULL;

  int   quantity;
  char* coneType;
  char* serviceURL;

  if (argc != 4) {
    printf ("usage: %s <coneType> <quantity> <URL>\n", argv[0]);
    printf ("Cone type is one of regular, sugar or waffle.\n");
    exit (1);
  }

  coneType   = argv[1];
  quantity   = atoi (argv[2]);
  serviceURL = argv[3];
```

We first start the WASP runtime using the `WASP_Runtime::clientStart()` call, and pass it the client configuration file (`client_config.xml`):

```
  TRY (ee) {
    // Start client using the specified XML configuration file
    WASP_Runtime::clientStart ("./client_config.xml",ee);
    CHECX_NESTED (ee);
```

The client stub (`warehouseServicePort`) generated for us by the `wsdlc` tool has a `setAddress()` method through which we can set the URL for the Web Service. This is the URL that we specified to the server via the `server_config.xml` file when it starts up. As shown below, we pass this URL via the command line to the client:

```
    warehouseServicePort wservice;

    if (argc>=2) {
      // Set a user supplied 'connect to' address
      wservice.setAddress (serviceURL,ee);
      CHECX_NESTED (ee);
    }
    else {
      printf ("You can supply service URL as parameter\n");
    }

    // Prepare parameter (see WASP_String documentation)
    wasp_string = WASP_String::create (coneType);
```

We then call the `checkAvailability()` on the client stub. This stub method has the code required to serialize the request method and its input parameters (cone type and quantity), into a SOAP method call, and POST it to the Web Service URL (`serviceURL`). It then takes the response, and returns it after deserializing:

```
// Call the service
    availabilityStatus =
                service.checkAvailability (wasp_string, quantity, ee );

    // Check if an exception was thrown
    CHECX_NESTED (ee);
```

We can now display the result of the SOAP call. The `transcode()` call shown below returns the `WASP_String` data as an 8 bit `char*` string that we display:

```
// Now check if we received expected data
    printf ("Status   = %s\n", availabilityStatus->status->transcode());
    printf ("Quantity = %d\n", availabilityStatus->quantity);

  }
  catch_all (exc,ee) {
    // Get exception stack trace and print it out
    char *trace=GET_TRACE (exc);
    printf ("Exception during call:
             '%s'\n%s\n",exc->getCharMessage (), trace);
    delete trace;

    // Destroy the exception instance
    delete exc;
  }
  stop_catch_all (ee);

  // Terminate client
  WASP_Runtime::clientTerminate();

  return 0;
}
```

Configuring the Client

The client configuration file (`client_config.xml`) passed to the `clientStart()` method call will look like this:

```
<?xml version="1.0"?>

<waspcServer
  xmlns:del="urn:DeleterRepository"
  xmlns:scec="urn:StubConfigEntryContent"
  xmlns:scr="urn:StubConfigRepository"
```

```
    xmlns:ser="urn:Serialization"
    xmlns:trans="urn:TransportRepository"
    xmlns:wasp="urn:WaspServer"
    xmlns:xprot="urn:XMLProtocolHandlerRepository">

    <!-- Module TransportRepository -->
    <wasp:module wasp:class="WASP_TransportRepositoryImpl"/>

    <trans:transport trans:class="WASP_FileTransportClient"
                     trans:scheme="file" ftc:extout=".out"
                     xmlns:ftc="urn:FileTransportClient"/>

    <trans:transport trans:class="WASP_HTTPTransportClient"
           trans:scheme="http" xmlns:htc="urn:HTTPTransportClient"/>

    <!-- Module XMLProtocolHandlerRepository -->
    <wasp:module wasp:class="WASP_XMLProtocolHandlerRepositoryImpl"/>

    <xprot:protocolHandler
          xprot:class="WASP_SOAPProtocolHandler" xprot:name="SOAP"/>

    <!-- Module HeaderProcessorRepository -->
    <wasp:module wasp:class="WASP_HeaderProcessorRepositoryImpl"/>

    <!-- Modules related to serialization -->
    <wasp:module wasp:class="WASP_DeleterRepositoryImpl"/>
    <wasp:module wasp:class="WASP_SerializationRepositoryStorageImpl"/>

    <!-- Basic deleters -->
    <del:deleter del:class="WASP_PrimitiveTypeDeleter"/>
    <del:deleter del:class="WASP_AbstractStructureDeleter"/>

    <!-- SOAP 1.1 (de)serializers -->
    <ser:serialization ser:name="http://schemas.xmlsoap.org/soap/encoding/">
      <ser:resolver ser:class="WASP_SOAP11_Resolver"/>
      <ser:deserializer ser:class="WASP_SOAP11_PrimitiveTypeDeserializer"/>
      <ser:serializer ser:class="WASP_SOAP11_PrimitiveTypeSerializer"/>
    </ser:serialization>

    <!-- Client config module -->
    <wasp:module wasp:class="WASP_StubConfigRepositoryImpl"/>

    <!-- Default client configuration -->
    <scr:stubConfig scec:xmlProtocolHandler="SOAP"/>

  </waspcServer>
```

Now that we have written the client, service, and the server to deploy the service, we are ready to build our applications.

Deploying the Web Service

The following commands build the server and client, from all the generated stubs, skeletons code, and the client/server-side code that we wrote. We might want to create a script for these commands:

```
$ export WASP_HOME=/home/vivek/install/WASP30
$ g++ -I. -I$WASP_HOME/include -c warehouseStructs.cpp
$ g++ -I. -I$WASP_HOME/include -c warehouseImpl.cpp
$ g++ -I. -I$WASP_HOME/include -c warehouseServiceImpl.cpp
$ g++ -I. -I$WASP_HOME/include -c warehouse.cpp
$ g++ -I. -I$WASP_HOME/include -c server.cpp
$ g++ -I. -I$WASP_HOME/include -c warehouseClient.cpp
$ g++  -o server  server.o warehouseServiceImpl.o warehouseImpl.o
warehouseStructs.o $WASP_HOME/lib/libwasp.a -lpthread -lm
$ g++  -o client warehouseClient.o warehouse.o warehouseStructs.o
$WASP_HOME/lib/libwasp.a -lpthread -lm
```

Now that we have the server and the client ready, let's run our server with the following command:

```
$ ./server
```

Let's send a request for `100` cases of regular cones to the `warehouseService` Web Service accessible at the URL `http://localhost:6070/WarehouseService`:

```
$ ./client regular 100 http://localhost:6070/WarehouseService
status = INSTOCK
Quantity = 100
```

For the above request, the server will output:

```
Warehouse inventory service got an status check for 100 cases of regular cones.
```

We'll now send another request to check availability of `100` cases of waffle cones:

```
$ ./client waffle 100 http://localhost:6070/WarehouseService
status = PARTIALSTOCK
Quantity = 10
```

For this request for waffle cones, the server will give the following output:

```
Warehouse inventory service got an status check for 100 cases of waffle cones.
```

WASP Configuration File Directives

In the sample application above, we had seen examples of the WASP configuration file directives in the server and client programs (`server_config.xml` and `client_config.xml`). We will look at the various elements of the configuration file that we had listed, but not explained earlier. There are ten types of element settings that can be configured in a WASP configuration file. All these elements are specified within the root `<waspcServer>` element.

Modules

Modules elements have the name `module`, and belong to the `urn:WaspServer` namespace. Specifying a module in a configuration file (client or server) causes it to get loaded during startup. The predefined modules provided along with WASPC are listed below:

- `WASP_DispatcherRepositoryImpl` – dispatcher repository
- `WASP_TransportRepositoryImpl` – transport repository
- `WASP_AdaptorFactoryImpl` – adaptor factory
- `WASP_XMLProtocolHandlerRepositoryImpl` – XML protocol repository
- `WASP_ServiceInstanceRepositoryImpl` – service instance repository
- `WASP_HeaderProcessorRepositoryImpl` – header processor repository
- `WASP_DeleterRepositoryImpl` – deleter repository
- `WASP_SerializationRepositoryStorageImpl` – serialization repository storage
- `WASP_StubConfigRepositoryImpl` – stub configuration repository

An example module declaration is:

```
<waspcServer
    xmlns:wasp="urn:WaspServer"
   ...
/>
   <wasp:module wasp:class="WASP_TransportRepositoryImpl"/>
   ...
```

Dispatcher Settings

The dispatcher specifies the endpoint to which requests are dispatched. It is referenced by the transport layer, as we shall see next. The rules for the dispatcher are defined in the service binding configuration (also described later).

The dispatcher settings are present only in the server-side configuration file. They have the element name `dispatcher`, and belong to the `urn:DispatcherRepository` namespace.

An example of the dispatcher settings is given below:

```
<waspcServer
  ...
  xmlns:disp="urn:DispatcherRepository"
  ...
>

  <!-- Dispatcher config -->
  <disp:dispatcher disp:class="WASP_DispatcherImpl" disp:name="DispatcherA"
   xmlns:dispi="urn:DispatcherImpl"  dispi:shutdownURL="/Admin/Shutdown/"/>
```

Transport Settings

The transport settings specify the low-level transport attributes for SOAP messages. These settings have the element name `transport`, and are in the `urn:TransportRepository` namespace. There are two attributes in the `trans` namespace – the scheme that identifies the transport name, and the class specifing the C++ class that implements this transport.

The different types of transport provided by WASPC are listed below:

- `WASP_FileTransportClient` – file transport setting
  This transport setting uses the `extin` and `extout` configuration options for specifying the input and output file extensions.
- `WASP_HTTPTransportClient` – HTTP client transport setting
  The client application uses this to create new connections to server. It has an attribute called `reuseCount` that is used to specify the number of requests that can use an HTTP connection. A reuse count of `1` will close the HTTP connection after every request.
- `WASP_HTTPTransportServer` – multi-threaded HTTP server setting
  This specifies the options for the server. The mandatory `dispatcher` attribute specifies the dispatch target to which all requests are directed. In the example given below, this is set to `DispatcherA` that we had defined earlier in the previous section. The `port` and `hostname` attributes specify the port and host endpoints that the server listens to. Finally, the `singleThead` attribute specifies if the server is single-threaded or multi-threaded.
- `WASP_StringTransport` – debugging transport setting
  This transport setting is used for debugging purposes only, and requires the client and server to be in one executable.

The example below demonstrates the usage of these transport settings:

```
<waspcServer
  xmlns:trans="urn:TransportRepository"
  ...
>
...

  <trans:transport trans:class="WASP_FileTransportClient"
         trans:scheme="file" xmlns:ftc="urn:FileTransportClient"
         ftc:extin=".in" ftc:extout=".out"/>

  <trans:transport trans:class="WASP_HTTPTransportClient"
         trans:scheme="http" xmlns:htc="urn:HTTPTransportClient"
         htc:reuseCount="10"/>

  <trans:transport trans:class="WASP_HTTPTransportServer"
         trans:scheme="server-http" xmlns:hts="urn:HTTPTransportServer"
         hts:dispatcher="DispatcherA" hts:singleThread="0"
         hts:hostname="localhost" hts:port="6070"/>

   <trans:transport xmlns:st="urn:StringTransport"
          xmlns:trans="urn:TransportRepository"
          trans:class="WASP_StringTransport" trans:scheme="string"
          st:dispatcher="MyDispatcher" st:baseURL="string://localhost/"/>
```

WASP allows users to implement their own transport classes, and configure them in the same way the transports above are configured.

Adaptor Settings

Adaptor settings are also used only in the server-side configuration. The adaptors provided by WASP are:

- WASP_XMLProtocolAdaptorImpl – XML protocol adaptor
- WASP_CppAdaptorImpl – C++ adaptor

The XML protocol adaptor can bind to three types of header processors – inputHeaderProcessor (for incoming request messages), outputHeaderProcessor (for outgoing response messages), and outputFaultHeaderProcessor (for outgoing response messages containing SOAP Faults). An example adaptor declaration for XML and C++ adaptors is given below. More on header processors is described later in the chapter:

```
<adap:adaptor xmlns:adap="urn:AdaptorFactory"
    xmlns:xpa="urn:XMLProtocolAdaptor"
    adap:class="WASP_XMLProtocolAdaptorImpl"
    adap:name="XMLProtocolAdaptorA"
    xpa:nestedAdaptor=""
    xpa:xmlProtocolHandler="SOAP"
    xpa:inputHeaderProcessor="inputHeaderProcessorName"
    xpa:outputHeaderProcessor="outputHeaderProcessorName"
    xpa:outputFaultHeaderProcessor="outputFaultHeaderProcessorName"/>

  <adap:adaptor adap:class="WASP_CppAdaptorImpl"
        xmlns:adap="urn:AdaptorFactory" xmlns:cppa="urn:CppAdaptor"
        adap:name="CppAdaptorA" cppa:nestedAdaptor="XMLProtocolAdaptorA"/>
```

Service Bindings

Each service needs to be bound to the server using the service binding settings. The following is the service binding that we had written for our example:

```
<waspcServer
  ...
  xmlns:sbnd="urn:ServiceBinding"
  ...
>

  <sbnd:serviceBinding sbnd:dispatcherRef="DispatcherA"
    sbnd:adaptorRef="CppAdaptorA" sbnd:wsdl="./warehouse.wsdl"
    sbnd:url="/WarehouseService/"> <cppa:instance cppa:ref="warehouse"/>
  </sbnd:serviceBinding>
```

As can be seen, the service binding element is named serviceBinding, and belongs to the urn:ServiceBinding namespace. The attributes for this element are:

- sbnd:dispatcherRef – Name of the dispatcher
- sbnd:adapterRef – Name of the adapter
- sbdn:wsdl – Location of the WSDL file describing the service
- sbnd:url – URL for the Web Service. The complete URL is constructed by combining with the transport settings. In our example, since we are using HTTP transport, the complete service URL is http://localhost:6070/WarehouseService/.

The example given above also has a `<cppa:instance>` element that is used to override the default settings of the C++ adapter.

Service Instances Settings

Service instances have the element name `serviceInstance`, and belong to the `urn:ServiceInstanceRepository` namespace. They have two attributes – the `svci:class` which specifies the implementing class, and `svci:name` that specifies the name of the instance. This name is the same as the `cppa:ref` attribute defined earlier in the `ServiceBinding`.

The example below gives the service instance settings from our sample application:

```
<waspcServer
  ...
  xmlns:svci="urn:ServiceInstanceRepository"
>

  <!-- Service instances - implementation classes -->
  <svci:serviceInstance svci:class="warehouseServiceImpl"
        svci:name="warehouse"/>
```

Header Processor Settings

Header processors are used to handle SOAP header data. The format of a header processor directive looks like the following:

```
<header:headerProcessor header:class="className" header:name="headerName"
  xmlns:header="urn:HeaderProcessorRepository">
  <custom header processor configuration/> *
</header:headerProcessor>
```

Users can write their own header processors. The following is an example configuration for a client-side header processor class:

```
<header:headerProcessor header:class="ClientHeaderProcessor"
        header:name="BasicAuthHP"/>
```

The class that implements the header processor (`ClientHeaderProcessor`) needs to be a base class of the `WASP_HeaderProcessor` class.

We would need a corresponding server-side header processor, if we want the server to respond to this header:

```
<header:headerProcessor header:class="ServerHeaderProcessor"
  header:name="ServerBasicAuthHP" xmlns:hpns="demo:ServerHeaderProcessor">
  <hpns:understandHeader hpns:name="BasicAuth"
   hpns:ns="http://soap-authentication.org/basic/2001/10/"/>
</header:headerProcessor>
```

We need to write a server-side header handler class (`ServerHeaderProcessor`) in a similar manner as the client, and register it with the server:

```
// Define factories for all implementations
WASP_FACTORY_DEFINE (ServerHeaderProcessor);

// Put them to factory definition

WASP_FactoryDefinition demoFactory[] = {
  ...
  WASP_FACTORY_ENTRY (ServerHeaderProcessor),
  WASP_FACTORY_END ()
};
```

Deleter Repository Settings

The deleter repository provides a store of object deleters. These deleters contain `remove()` methods for freeing up the memory allocated for objects of various types allocated. The `WASP_PrimitiveTypeDeleter` class for example, deletes the primitive objects such as floats, and doubles. These deleters are important for complex objects, such as those that are multi-referenced. In case of multi-referenced objects, deleters remove the object when the reference count is `0`.

An example of these settings is shown below:

```
<waspcServer
  ...
  xmlns:del="urn:DeleterRepository"
>
  <!-- Basic deleters -->
  <del:deleter del:class="WASP_PrimitiveTypeDeleter"/>
  <del:deleter del:class="WASP_AbstractStructureDeleter"/>
```

Stub Repository Settings

This repository manages the client stub settings such as header processors, serializers, and so on. This needs to be only in the client configuration file. The format specified for this setting is shown below:

```
<scr:stubConfig [scr:portName="portName" scr:portNamespace="portNamespace"
[scr:url="serviceURL"]]
  scec:xmlProtocolHandler="SOAP"
  scec:inputHeaderProcessor="inputHeaderProcessorName"
  scec:outputHeaderProcessor="outputHeaderProcessorName"
  scec:inputFaultHeaderProcessor="inputFaultHeaderProcessorName"
  scec:serializationRep="serializationRepositoryName"
/>
```

These settings can be common for all client stubs, or specific for stubs with a particular 'Qname'. A Qname is a fully qualified name that consists of a name plus a namespace.

Serialization Repository Storage Settings

The serialization repository is an experimental feature in WASP Server Lite for C++ 3.0 Beta2 release. It allows for binding another serializer and deserializer to arbitrary data types. This allows the use of encoding mechanisms other than SOAP encoding. A sample of this setting looks like the following:

```
<ser:serialization ser:name="http://schemas.xmlsoap.org/soap/encoding/"
  xmlns:ser="urn:Serialization">
  <ser:resolver ser:class="WASP_SOAP11_Resolver"/>
  <ser:deserializer ser:class="WASP_SOAP11_PrimitiveTypeDeserializer"/>
  <ser:serializer ser:class="WASP_SOAP11_PrimitiveTypeSerializer"/>
</ser:serialization>
```

WASP API

A reference list the WASP classes and methods used in this chapter is given below. For a complete list, please refer to the online API documentation at http://www.systinet.com/eap/waspc_30/doc/api/index.html:

Class	Description	Usage
`WASP_String`	Wrapper class for Unicode character strings	
	Returns pointer to new `WASP_String` created as substring from current one	`WASP_String* substring(const int iOffset, const int iLength=-1)`
	Creates deep copy of string including copying of internal representation	`WASP_String* clone()`
	Increments internal reference counter	`void addRef()`
	Decrements internal reference counter	`void removeRef()`
	Compares current string with second one	`bool equals(WASP_String *psSecond)`
	This method returns a copy of the data as 8 bit `char *` string	`char * transcode() const`
	This method returns a copy of the data as `wchar_t *` string	`wchar_t * transcodewc() const`
	Returns length of current string	`int length() const`

Table continued on following page

Class	Description	Usage
`WASP_Runtime`	Initialize and configure the client	`static void clientInitialize ()`
	Start the client. The client configuration file is passed as a parameter to this call.	`static void clientStart (const char *configurationFileName, EXCENV_DECL);`
	Stop the client.	`clientTerminate ()`
	Initialize and configure the WASP server.	`static void serverInitialize ()`
	Start the WASP server and all configured modules and listeners.	`static void serverStart(const char *configurationFileName, EXCENV_DECL);`
	Stop server explicitly. Notify all threads for termination and wait for them.	`static void serverTerminate()`
	Notify all threads for termination and wait for them to finish the task they have in progress.	`static void serverShutdown()`
`WASP_SuperFactory`	This class has a lookup map of class names and their instances. It is able to create an instance of a class.	
	Registers factory methods into the 'super factory' lookup table.	`static void registerFactory (WASP_FactoryDefinition *factoryDefinition)`

Mapping Between C++ and XML Types

Some of the primitive data types like `int`, `float`, or `double` are mapped to corresponding C++ types. Most of the other primitive XML types are converted to a `WASP_String` class. In the future releases, special C++ types are expected for some XML types like `decimal`, `integer`, or `base64Binary`.

Complex XML types are mapped to C++ classes. These are common classes or classes with special methods giving them the behavior of arrays. The complex types derived from `SOAP-ENC:Array` are converted to these classes.

Character Strings

WASP provides a `WASP_String` class for holding Unicode character strings. C++ data types of type `char*` or `wchar*` (wide character set) need to be stored as `WASP_String`. The client stub calls serializer methods on these `WASP_String` objects to write them out as XML string (`xsd:string`) types.

WASP_String is created via the create() method call as shown below:

```
WASP_String aString = WASP_String::create ("This is a string");
```

Refer to the WASP API for the other important methods in this class.

User-Defined Structures

All XML structure types get mapped to C++ classes with the same name as that of the structure. Let's study our example of our warehouseService Web Service.

The wsdlc tool takes this XML structure definition from the WSDL file, and generates a class called AvailabilityStatus:

```
<complexType name="AvailabilityStatus">
  <sequence>
    <element name="status" type="xsd:string" minOccurs="0"
          maxOccurs="1" nillable="true"/>
    <element name="quantity" type="xsd:int" minOccurs="0" maxOccurs="1"/>
  </sequence>
</complexType>
```

This class gets generated in the <projectName>Structs.cpp/.h file (warehouseStructs.cpp/.h in our example). Users can declare objects of this C++ type, and set values to its data elements as shown below:

```
AvailabilityStatus availabilityStatus = new AvailabilityStatus ();
availabilityStatus->quantity  = 0;
availabilityStatus->status = WASP_String::create ("OUTOFSTOCK");
```

This class has serialize() and deserialize() methods for AvailabilityStatus that get invoked by the client stub/service skeleton.

Once the application is done with a structure, it can delete it. We need to declare a WASP_DeleteContext for this. This class takes care of reference counts, and is also able to locate the deleter for a particular C++ type:

```
WASP_DeleteContext dc;
availabilityStatus->remove (dc);
```

Arrays

XML array types get mapped into C++ classes based on the type of the array element. For example, an array of integers gets mapped into an IntArray class.

The wsdlc tool starts with the WSDL file declaration of the array, and generates a C++ class for it:

```
<!-- int[] -->
<complexType name='IntArray'>
  <complexContent>
    <restriction base='SOAP-ENC:Array'>
      <sequence>
        <element name='item' type='int'
```

```
                    minOccurs='0' maxOccurs='unbounded'/>
          </sequence>
          <attributeGroup ref="SOAP-ENC:commonAttributes"/>
          <attribute ref="SOAP-ENC:offset"/>
          <attribute ref="SOAP-ENC:arrayType" wsdl:arrayType="int[]"/>
        </restriction>
      </complexContent>
    </complexType>
```

This class gets generated in the `<projectName>Structs.cpp/.h` file, just as the user-defined structures. We can use these array objects in the client, or the service code. We can declare them, and put and get data to them, as shown below:

```
IntArray* intArray = new IntArray (10);
intArray->put(0, 7); // put '7' at index 0 in the array
cout << "Integer at index 0 is " << intArray->get(0);
```

When we use it in a SOAP method call, the `serializer()` or `deserializer()` methods generated for us in the `<projectName>Structs.cpp` file get invoked to convert to or from the XML representation.

Care should be taken with the arrays of data types that involve reference counts (for example, `WASP_String`). For these arrays, it is the user's responsibility to increase or decrease the reference count, if these elements are added or removed from the array.

Arrays are deleted in a manner similar to structures:

```
WASP_DeleteContext dc;
intArray->remove (dc);
```

EasySoap++

EasySoap++ is yet another open source SOAP implementation in C++. It is available for download at http://sourceforge.net/projects/easysoap/ under the GNU Lesser General Public License (LGPL). This license, unlike the standard GPL license, does allow for commercial use of EasySoap++ as a part of other proprietary products.

Installing EasySoap++

EasySoap++ requires the Expat open source XML parser library which can be downloaded from http://sourceforge.net/projects/expat/. It is a stream-oriented parser, that is, for things like start tags that a parsrer finds in the XML document, the application registers handlers. Expat is written in C, and underlies various open source XML parsers like Perl's XML::Parser, and the Mozilla project. We'll use Expat version 1.95.2 in this chapter.

To install from source, we'll download the `tar.gz` file of Expat, and extract it in the directory of our choice:

```
$ gunzip expat-1.95.2.tar.gz
$ tar -xvf expat-1.95.2.tar
$ cd expat-1.95.2
```

We now need to run the `configure` script which generates the `Makefile` based on the system it is running on. Invoking `configure` without any options generates a `Makefile` that installs Expat in the standard location (`/usr/local`). However, this requires the `make install` to be run as `root`. If we are not logged in as `root`, or wish to install Expat in another location, we need to pass the directory prefix to `configure` via the `--prefix` option as shown below:

```
$ ./configure --prefix=/home/vivek/install/expat
```

This script will correctly guess the system it is being installed on, and generate an appropriate `Makefile`. Now, all we need to do is build, and then install. A `make install` will do both the operations in the directory specified:

```
$ make install
```

Now, we download, and extract the `tar.gz` file of EasySoap++ 0.6 in directory of our choice, and then build the sourcecode:

```
$ gunzip EasySoap++-0.5.tar.gz
$ tar xvf EasySoap++-0.5.tar
$ cd EasySoap++-0.5
```

We now have to run the `configure` script to generate the `Makefile` for our system. Since we had installed Expat in a non-standard place earlier, we need to set the `CPPFLAGS` and `LIBS` environmental variables before running `configure`. These variables allow for setting the parameters to be passed to the C++ pre-processor, and linker respectively, in the generated `Makefile`. We will pass the installation directory for the EasySoap++ via the `--prefix` option:

```
$ LIBS="-L/home/vivek/install/expat/lib"
$ CPPFLAGS="-I/home/vivek/install/expat"
$ export CPPFLAGS LIBS
$ ./configure --prefix=/home/vivek/install/EasySoap
```

Now that the `Makefile` is generated, we can build and install EasySoap++:

```
$ make install
```

This would compile and install EasySoap++ in the installation directory we specified via the `--prefix` option. We are now ready to start building our Web Service, and the client.

Building the Web Service Using EasySoap++

Now, we'll develop the same `warehouseService` Web Service using EasySoap++. This provides serializers and deserializers for only the basic C++ types. We need to write the serializers for the complex types. Refer to the *Mapping between C++ and XML types* section, for more discussion on this.

The code overleaf has the serializers for our `AvailabilityStatus` structure. We put this code in a header file, `AvailabilityStatus.h`, which we will include in our client and the service:

```
/* Availability status: serializers and deserializers */

class AvailabilityStatus {

public:
  SOAPString status;
  int quantity;

  AvailabilityStatus ()
  {
    quantity = 0;
  }

  AvailabilityStatus (const char* _status, int _quantity)
  {
    status   = _status;
    quantity = _quantity;
  }
```

The public AvailabilityStatus class contains the data types elements of the availability status – the status string (INSTOCK, OUTOFSTOCK, or PARTIALSTOCK), and the quantity. The status string is declared to be of type SOAPString, which is the EasySoap++ data type for a C++ string. We also define the constructors for this data type, which we will use later to build objects of AvailabilityStatus type.

We'll then have the following two constants that contain the name for the structure when it is serialized into XML, and the encoding namespace. The encoding style determines how data is represented in the XML message. Since we are using SOAP encoding, we set it to http://schemas.xmlsoap.org/soap/encoding/:

```
  static const char* soap_name;
  static const char* soap_namespace;
};

const char* AvailabilityStatus::soap_name = "AvailabilityStatus";
const char* AvailabilityStatus::soap_namespace =
          "http://schemas.xmlsoap.org/soap/encoding/";
```

According to the EasySoap++ convention, the serializer and deserializer are nothing but overloaded << and >> operators. The serializer sets the name for the structure, the namespace, and adds information that it is a structure type (SetIsStruct()). It then serializes the included basic types (status, quantity) via the overloaded << operators, and adds them to a serialized form of the structure via the AddParameter() method. The parameters passed to AddParameter (status and quantity) are the names of these parameters:

```
// Serializers and Deserializers for the struct
inline SOAPParameter& operator
       << (SOAPParameter &parameter, const AvailabilityStatus& value)
{
  parameter.SetType (value.soap_name, value.soap_namespace);
  parameter.SetIsStruct ();

  parameter.AddParameter ("status") << value.status;
  parameter.AddParameter ("quantity") << value.quantity;

  return parameter;
}
```

The deserializer for this structure type does the reverse. It calls the `GetParameter()` method to extract the values from the SOAP message, and calls the >> operator to deserialize it back into the basic C++ types:

```
inline const SOAPParameter& operator
       >> (const SOAPParameter &parameter, AvailabilityStatus& value)
{
  parameter.GetParameter ("status") >> value.status;
  parameter.GetParameter ("quantity") >> value.quantity;

  return parameter;
}
```

Now that we have the header file ready, we can write the Web Service and the client.

Developing the Web Service

The service code (`WarehouseService.cpp`) is listed below:

```
/* Server (and Service) for handing the checkAvailability request for
 * the warehouse inventory. */

#include <iostream.h>
#include <string.h>
#include <SOAP.h>
#include <SOAPCGIServer.h>

#include "AvailabilityStatus.h"
```

The service class needs to be a base class of the `SOAPDispatchHandler` class. The `SoapDispatchHandler` is a template class that has methods that a service needs to have, and that are internally invoked by the EasySoap++ server.

The constructor for the service sets the `DispatchMethod` to the `checkAvailability()` method as shown below. This causes any request for a method named `checkAvailability()` to be routed to this method:

```
class WarehouseService : public SOAPDispatchHandler <WarehouseService>
{
public:

  WarehouseService ()
  {
    const char* ns = "http://www.wrox.com/warehouse";
    DispatchMethod ("checkAvailability", ns,
                    &WarehouseService::checkAvailability);
  }

  ~WarehouseService () {}

  WarehouseService* GetTarget (const SOAPEnvelope& request)
  {
    return this;
  }
```

The method below is the actual service method. This is the method that we set earlier in the `DispatchMethod()` call. Here, we'll extract the input parameters from the `request`, perform the service logic as before, and serialize the result into the `response` object. We use the custom serializer for the `AvailabilityStatus` to build the response:

```
void checkAvailability (const SOAPMethod& request, SOAPMethod& response) {
    SOAPString itemName;
    int quantity;

    request.GetParameter ("itemName") >> itemName;
    request.GetParameter ("quantity") >> quantity;

    cout << "Received an order for " << quantity
         << " cases of " << itemName << " cones.";
```

In case of any error, such as an illegal value of the quantity of cases, we can return back a SOAP fault by throwing a `SOAPException`:

```
    if (quantity <= 0) {
      throw SOAPException ("Illegal quantity:Quantity has to be
            greater than 0");
    }

    // A database lookup would come here. We are going to fake it however.
    int regular_amt = 10000;
    int sugar_amt = 0;
    int waffle_amt = 10;

    AvailabilityStatus availabilityStatus;

    if (!strcmp (itemName, "regular")) {
      if (quantity == 0) {
        availabilityStatus.quantity = 0;
        availabilityStatus.status   = "OUTOFSTOCK";
      }
      else if (quantity < regular_amt) {
        // We have the required number
        availabilityStatus.quantity = quantity;
        availabilityStatus.status = "INSTOCK";
      }
      else {
        // that's all we have.
        availabilityStatus.quantity = regular_amt;
        availabilityStatus.status = "PARTIALSTOCK";
      }
    }
    else if (!strcmp (itemName, "sugar")) {
      if (quantity == 0) {
        availabilityStatus.quantity = 0;
        availabilityStatus.status = "OUTOFSTOCK";
      }
      else if (quantity < sugar_amt) {
        // We have the required number
```

```
            availabilityStatus.quantity = quantity;
            availabilityStatus.status = "INSTOCK";
        }
        else {
            // that's all we have
            availabilityStatus.quantity = sugar_amt;
            availabilityStatus.status    = "PARTIALSTOCK";
        }
    }
    else if (!strcmp (itemName, "waffle")) {
        if (quantity == 0) {
            availabilityStatus.quantity = 0;
            availabilityStatus.status = "OUTOFSTOCK";
        }
        else if (quantity < waffle_amt) {
            // We have the required number
            availabilityStatus.quantity = quantity;
            availabilityStatus.status    = "INSTOCK";
        }
        else {
            // that's all we have
            availabilityStatus.quantity = waffle_amt;
            availabilityStatus.status = "PARTIALSTOCK";
        }
    }
    else {
        throw SOAPException ("Illegal cone type:Cone type is
              one of regular, sugar or waffle.");
    }
    response.AddParameter ("availabilityStatus") << availabilityStatus;
  }
};
```

Again as before, we have thrown a `SOAPException` in case of a service error.

The EasySoap++ Web Service runs as a CGI script in a web server. For this, we register our service handler method with the CGI processing `SOAPCGIServer` class via the `DispatchTo()` method. The `Handle()` method sends the incoming request to the service handler:

```
int main (int argc, char* argv[])
{
  SOAPCGIServer server;
  WarehouseService warehouseService;

  return server.DispatchTo (&warehouseService).Handle();
}
```

Now that we have the code for our Web Service ready, let's move on to developing the client for our service.

Implementing the Client

The client code (WarehouseClient.cpp) is listed below:

```
#include <iostream.h>
#include <string.h>
#include <SOAP.h>
#include "AvailabilityStatus.h"

static const char *ns = "http://www.wrox.com/warehouse";

int main(int argc, const char *argv[])
{
  if (argc < 3) {
    cout << "usage: " << argv[0] << " <coneType> <quantity> [endpoint]\n";
    cout << "Cone type is one of regular, sugar or waffle.\n";
    exit (1);
  }

  try {
    const char *endpoint;
    const char* itemName = argv[1];
    int quantity    = atoi (argv[2]);

    cout << "Checking availability of " << quantity << " cases of "
         << itemName << " cones.\n";
```

In the client, we first build the SOAPProxy object, and set the endpoint for the service. We'll assume that the service will be deployed as a CGI script in a web server running at port 8080. Hence the default endpoint URL is http://localhost:8080/cgi-bin/warehouseServer.cgi:

```
    if (argc > 3) {
      endpoint = argv[3];
    }
    else
    {
      endpoint = "http://localhost:8080/cgi-bin/warehouseServer.cgi";
    }
    SOAPProxy proxy (endpoint);
```

We now set the name of the method (checkAvailability) that we wish to call, and its parameters (itemName, quantity). Note the use of the default serializer for these types, which is invoked via the overloaded << operators:

```
    SOAPMethod method ("checkAvailability", ns);

    method.AddParameter("itemName") << itemName;
    method.AddParameter("quantity") << quantity;
```

Now we'll invoke Execute() on the proxy. This POSTs the SOAP request onto the service endpoint, and returns the response. We can then use the deserializer we wrote earlier in AvailabilityStatus.h for the AvailabilityStatus class to deserialize this object from the SOAP response into a C++ object:

```
      const SOAPResponse& response = proxy.Execute(method);
      AvailabilityStatus availabilityStatus;

      response.GetReturnValue() >> availabilityStatus;

      cout << "Availability status is " << availabilityStatus.status << ".\n";
      if (!strcmp (availabilityStatus.status, "PARTIALSTOCK")) {
        cout << "Sorry, we have only " << availabilityStatus.quantity
             << " cases. Would that do?\n";
      }
      else if (!strcmp (availabilityStatus.status, "OUTOFSTOCK")) {
        cout << "Sorry, we are out of stock. You would need to
                 place a back order\n";
      }
      else
      { // INSTOCK
        cout << "Yes, we are in stock. Shall we place the order?\n";
      }
      return 0;
    }
    catch (SOAPException& ex) {
      printf("Caught SOAP exception: %s\n", ex.What().Str());
      return 1;
    }

    return 0;
}
```

We are now ready to build, and run our Web Service, and client. Let's build the service using the following command:

```
$ g++ -I/home/vivek/install/EasySoap/include/easysoap -static -o
warehouseServer.cgi WarehouseService.cpp -L/home/vivek/install/EasySoap/lib -
L/home/vivek/install/EasySoap/lib -leasysoap -lexpat
```

In our example, it is assumed that we have Apache 2.0 running as our web server. For more information on Apache 2.0, and enabling CGI scripts, you can refer to http://httpd.apache.org/docs-2.0/ or *Professional Apache 2.0* from *Wrox Press* (*ISBN 1-861007-22-154999*).

Now, we should copy the `warehouseServer.cgi` executable under the `cgi-bin` directory of the Apache web server:

```
$ cp warehouseServer.cgi /path/to/Apache/cgi-bin
```

Let's build our client application now:

```
$ g++ -I $EASYSOAP_HOME/include/easysoap -static -o warehouseClient
WarehouseClient.cpp -L $EASYSOAP_HOME/lib -L $EXPAT_HOME/lib -leasysoap -lexpat
```

We'll ensure that our Apache server is running. Now, we'll run the `warehouseClient` program to check for the availability for `100` cases of `regular`, and then `waffle` cones:

```
$ ./warehouseClient regular 100
Checking availability of 100 cases of regular cones.
Availability status is INSTOCK
Yes, we are in stock. Shall we place the order?

$ ./warehouseClient waffle 100
Checking availability of 100 cases of waffle cones.
Availability status is PARTIALSTOCK
Sorry, we have only 10 cases. Would that do?
```

Building a Standalone Service

Our `warehouseService` Web Service shown above (`WarehouseService.cpp`) requires to be run as a CGI script within a web server. However, we can also run this standalone. This kind of configuration would be useful in the scenarios where the SOAP service needs to be embedded inside an application. The drawback, at least in the case of EasySoap++, is that the incoming requests are handled sequentially as the EasySoap++ standalone server is not multi-threaded.

Changing `WarehouseService.cpp` to be standalone is remarkably easy. All we need to do are two changes:

- Change the include file from `SOAPCGIServer.h` to `SOAPHTTPServer.h`
- In the `main()` method, use the `SOAPHTTPServer` class instead of the `SOAPCGIServer` class

The `SOAPHTTPServer` class from the new `SOAPHTTPServer.h` will look as follows:

```
int main (int argc, char** argv []) {
  SOAPHTTPServer server (8080);
  WarehouseService warehouseService;
  return server.DispatchTo (&warehouseService).Handle();
}
```

Now, all we have to do is rebuild the service and run it independent of the web server:

```
$ g++ -I/home/vivek/install/EasySoap/include/easysoap -static -o
warehouseServer.cgi WarehouseService.cpp -L/home/vivek/install/EasySoap/lib -
L/home/vivek/install/EasySoap/lib -leasysoap -lexpat
$ ./WarehouseServerStandalone
```

Since we have specified the port number `8080` for the standalone server, the client can connect to it via the URL `http://localhost:8080`. If checked for the availability for `100` cases of `regular` cones using this standalone service, we'll get the same result:

```
$ ./warehouseClient regular 100 http://localhost:8080
Checking availability of 100 cases of regular cones.
Availability status is INSTOCK
Yes, we are in stock. Shall we place the order?
```

Connecting via a Proxy Server

I f we need to connect via a proxy server, EasySoap++'s `SOAPProxy` class has a `SetEndpoint()` method to set the service endpoint. An overloaded version of this method also takes a proxy server URL as a parameter along with the endpoint URL:

```
SOAPProxy proxy;
proxy.SetEndpoint(endpointURL, proxyURL);
```

Alternatively, we could pass the proxy URL while building the `SOAProxy` object as shown:

```
SOAPProxy proxy (endpointURL, proxyURL);
```

EasySoap++ API

A reference list of some commonly used EasySoap++ classes, and methods is given below. This is not however, an exhaustive list. For a complete list, we can look at the respective header file(s) in the `include` directory:

Class	Description	Usage
`SOAPException`	The class for SOAP-related Exceptions	
	Build a SOAP Exception with a Fault string	`SOAPException(const SOAPString& what)`
	Extracts out the Fault string from a SOAP Exception	`const SOAPString& What()`
`SOAPEnvelope`	Encapsulates a SOAP `Envelope`	
	Returns the SOAP `Header`	`SOAPHeader& GetHeader()`
	Returns the SOAP `Body`	`SOAPBody& GetBody()`
`SOAPProxy`	The client-side proxy object representing the remote service.	
	Construct a `SOAPProxy` with the given service endpoint.	`SOAPProxy (const SOAPUrl& endpoint)`
	Construct a `SOAPProxy` with the given service endpoint and proxy URL.	`SOAPProxy (const SOAPUrl& endpoint, const SOAPUrl& proxy)`
	Set the service endpoint for a `SOAPProxy`.	`void SetEndpoint(const SOAPUrl& endpoint)`
	Set the service endpoint and proxy URL for a `SOAPProxy`.	`void SetEndpoint(const SOAPUrl& endpoint, const SOAPUrl& proxy);`

Table continued on following page

Class	Description	Usage
	Set the remote method name and namespace.	`SOAPMethod& SetMethod(const char *name, const char *ns)`
	Execute the remote method.	`const SOAPResponse& Execute()`
`SOAPResponse`	Encapsulates the SOAP response.	
	Checks if there was a SOAP Fault.	`bool IsFault()`
	Returns a `SOAPParameter` by name	`const SOAPParameter& GetReturnValue(const char *name)`
`SOAPArray <T>`	Template class for arrays of type T. Used for handling array parameters and result types.	
	Returns size of the array.	`size_t Size()`
	Append an element at the end of the array.	`template <typename X) T& Add(const X& val)`
	Insert an element at the given index location in the array.	`template <typename X) T& AddAt(size_t index, const X& val)`
	Get the element at the specified index location.	`T& GetAt(size_t index)`

Mapping Between XML and C++ Types

As we discussed earlier, EasySoap++ provides serialization and deserialization methods for the basic C++ types including `bool`, `int`, `float`, `double`, `Strings (char*)`, and `Arrays`. In addition, there is support for a `SOAPBase64` type. This can be used to send binary data over SOAP packets.

The serialization and deserialization in EasySoap++ is done via overloaded << and >> operators. Hence, a client can pass an integer argument using the following simple piece of code:

```
int i, j;
i = 5;
j = 6;
SOAPProxy proxy (serviceEndpoint);
SOAPMethod method ("addTwoIntegers", ns);
method.AddParameter("integerOne") << i;
method.AddParameter("integerTwo") << i;
```

This can be deserialized using the >> operator after receiving it:

```
const SOAPResponse& response = proxy.Execute(method);
int sum;
response.GetReturnValue() >> sum;
```

The same works for any other basic type. This serialization and deserialization code works because of the overloaded << and >> operators defined in the `SOAPParameter.h` include file. These operators serialize the basic types into `SOAPParameters`. We don't have to include `SOAPParameter.h` explicitly since it is included through `SOAP.h`.

> **EasySoap++ assumes by default that all strings are `UTF-8`. However, it does support `UTF-16` too. It has serializers and deserializers for the wide character set (`wchar`).**

User-Defined structures

For user-defined C++ types, we need to write custom serializers and deserializers. The sample application above is a good example of how this is done. It is important to note that we need to define the name and the namespace of the structure type (C++ `struct` or `class`), for example:

```
const char* AvailabilityStatus::soap_name = "AvailabilityStatus";
const char* AvailabilityStatus::soap_namespace =
      "http://schemas.xmlsoap.org/soap/encoding/";
```

We then need to write the overloaded << and >> operator serializers and deserializer, as before:

```
// Serializers and Deserializers for the struct
inline SOAPParameter&operator <<
      (SOAPParameter &parameter, const AvailabilityStatus& value)
{
  parameter.SetType (value.soap_name, value.soap_namespace);
  parameter.SetIsStruct ();

  parameter.AddParameter ("status") << value.status;
  parameter.AddParameter ("quantity") << value.quantity;

  return parameter;
}

inline const SOAPParameter&operator >>
      (const SOAPParameter &parameter, AvailabilityStatus& value)
{
  parameter.GetParameter ("status") >> value.status;
  parameter.GetParameter ("quantity") >> value.quantity;

  return parameter;
}
```

Arrays

Array support in easySOAP++ is done via the `SOAPArray` template class. The following code declares two arrays of integers:

```
SOAPArray <int> requestIntArray;
SOAPArray <int> responseIntArray;
```

A client that needs to send an integer array as a parameter to a method would build it in the following manner:

```
requestIntArray.AddAt (0, 5); // Insert number 5 at location 0 in array
requestIntArray.Add (6);      // Append number 6 at the end
```

The client can then use the overloaded << operator to map the `SOAPArray` to a `SOAPParameter`, and make the RPC method call:

```
...
SOAPParameter& param = method.AddParameter ("someMethod");
param << requestIntArray;
const SOAPResponse& response = proxy.Execute(method);
```

If the response is an integer array too, the client can deserialize the content using the overloaded >> operator:

```
response.GetReturnValue() >> responseIntArray;
cout << "Size of response array is " << responseIntArray.Size();

// print it all out.
for (int i = 0; i < (int) responseIntArray.Size(); i++) {
  cout << "Array element at index " << i << " is "
       << responseIntArray.GetAt(i) << "\n";
}
```

This service has a similar code (it declares a variable of type `SOAPArray <int>`, and uses the overloaded << and >> operators, and the `Get()`, and `Add()` methods) to manipulate the array data types.

gSOAP

gSOAP is a complete SOAP 1.1 implementation in C++. It provides a set of compiler tools for generating SOAP-based Web Services and clients in C and C++. It comes with its own XML pull parser, and hence doesn't have the memory overheads that a DOM-based XML parser has.

It has been developed by Robert A. Van Engelen at the Department of Computer Science, Florida State University. gSOAP is available as open source under the Mozilla Public License 1.1 (MPL 1.1) at http://www.cs.fsu.edu/~engelen/soap.html. The MPL 1.1 license does allow a commercial use of gSOAP as a part of other products. We'll be using gSOAP 2.1.3 version in this chapter.

Installing gSOAP

The installation described below was done on Linux (specifically Redhat 7.1, with gcc 2.96). The compilation of gSOAP on non-Linux platforms (or for that matter the other SOAP implementations discussed earlier in this chapter) may differ, since most of them require linking of additional C++ libraries. For example, on Solaris, we need to link with `socket` and `nsl` libraries (`-lsocket -lnsl`).

First, let's download gSOAP `.zip` file from http://www.cs.fsu.edu/~engelen/soapdownload.html, and extract it in a directory of our choice:

```
$ unzip soapcpp.linux.2.1.3.zip
```

Next we switch to the soapcpp-linux-2.1.3 directory we created, and run make. The Makefile uses the soapcpp2 binary while building. We'll then add the current directory to the PATH, if it is not there; now make can find soapcpp2:

```
$ cd soapcpp-linux-2.1.3
$ PATH=$PATH:.
$ export PATH
$ make
```

soapcpp2 is the gSOAP compiler, and it generates the client-side stubs, service skeletons, and the WSDL file for us. Currently, it is available only in binary (soapcpp2.exe) form.

Building the Web Service

Using gSOAP to develop SOAP applications is a five-step process:

- First, we describe the interface for the service in a header file
- We then generate the client stubs and service skeletons using gSOAP's compiler
- Then we have to write code to implement the service
- Next, we write client-side code to invoke it
- And finally we develop a server that can be deployed either as standalone server or as a CGI program in a web server

Here, we'll develop our warehouseService again to demonstrate the use of gSOAP. We begin by writing a C++ header file that describes the service interfaces. This header file needs to follow gSOAP conventions. The purpose of the header file is to be an input to the gSOAP stub, and skeleton compiler (soapcpp2).

In the convention specified by gSOAP, each class and C++ method name in the interface header file needs to be prefixed by the namespace that it belongs to. This is explained in more detail later in the chapter.

The header defines the method ns1__checkAvailability() that takes as input the itemName and the quantity. We then determine its availability in the warehouse inventory. The result value for the method (the availability status) is passed by reference as the last parameter for the method. The return type of the method is an integer that indicates to the calling program if the method succeeded or failed. All this is gSOAP convention for SOAP method calls, which is discussed in later sections. The header file (warehouse.h) is listed below:

```
/* Header file for Warehouse Service. */

typedef char* xsd__string;
typedef int   xsd__int;

/* Availability status for ice cream cones. */
class ns1__AvailabilityStatus
{
  // One of "INSTOCK", "OUTOFSTOCK", or "PARTIALSTOCK"
  xsd__string status;

  // Quantity in stock. Useful for"PARTIALSTOCK" items
  xsd__int quantity;
```

```
};

int ns1__checkAvailability (xsd__string itemName, xsd__int quantity,
                            ns1__AvailabilityStatus &response);
```

The header file that we have above has just one method listed. If we have a service with multiple methods, we would list all in the same header file.

Note the method names and class names prefixed by the string `ns1__` (`ns1` followed by a pair of underscore characters). This is a convention for letting the gSOAP compiler know that these names belong to a particular XML namespace, in this case the `ns1` namespace. However, we could have chosen any prefix (for example, `wrox__`) instead of `ns1`.

`xsd_int` and `xsd_string` are the `thypedefs` for integers and strings respectively. These `typedefs` will cause the gSOAP compiler to generate serializers and deserializers for the primitive C++ data types like integer and string (`char*`).

Now, let's run the gSOAP compiler on this header file as shown below:

```
$ soapcpp2 warehouse.h
```

This compilation generates the following files:

- `soapH.h`
  Common header file to be included by all the clients and services. This contains, among other things, all gSOAP include files required by the client and the service, and the method declarations for the client stub and service skeletons.

- `soapC.cpp`
  Serializer and deserializers for the data types.

- `soapClient.cpp`
  Stub routines for the client-side proxy.

- `soapServer.cpp`
  Skeleton routines of the service.

- `soapStub.h`
  A modified header file produced from the input header file.

- `ns1.wsdl`
  The WSDL template file for the service. This WSDL file contains patterns delimited by `%{}%`. If we wish to publish these externally, we would need to replace them with actual values. This means that we need to replace `%{Service}%` with the name of the service application, `%{URL}%` with the endpoint URL of the service, and `%{URI}%` with the namespace URI of the service.

  However, we don't have to do this for building our SOAP application. It is required if the interface of our web application is to be shared with other users (for example, by publishing in a UDDI registry).

- `ns1.nsmap`
  Namespace mapping file (see oppsite). This contains the mappings from the namespace prefixes to the actual namespaces. The order of the namespaces is important, and the first four namespaces (`SOAP-ENV`, `SOAP-ENC`, `xsi` and `xsd`) are standard namespaces used by SOAP 1.1 specifications:

```
struct Namespace namespaces[] =
{
  {"SOAP-ENV", "http://schemas.xmlsoap.org/soap/envelope/"},
  {"SOAP-ENC", "http://schemas.xmlsoap.org/soap/encoding/"},
  {"xsi", "http://www.w3.org/2001/XMLSchema-instance",
          "http://www.w3.org/*/XMLSchema-instance"},
  {"xsd", "http://www.w3.org/2001/XMLSchema",
          "http://www.w3.org/*/XMLSchema"},
  {"ns1", "%{URI}%"},
  {NULL, NULL}
};
```

However, we need to replace the pattern `%{URI}%` with the actual namespace URI for our service. In this case, we'll change it to http://www.wrox.com/warehouse:

```
  {"ns1", "http://www.wrox.com/warehouse"},
  {NULL, NULL}
```

- `ns1.xsd`
  XML Schema descriptions for the service.

Now that the client-side stub, and the service skeleton code, along with serializers and deserializers have been generated for us, we can begin implementing our service.

The service we are developing is a standalone service, and not one that needs to be deployed as a CGI program inside a web server. We will see a CGI-based service using gSOAP later in the chapter.

Let's start writing the code for the service (`warehouseService.cpp`). We also include the common header (`soapH.h`), and `ns1.nsmap` file. The `ns1.nsmap` file, as we mentioned earlier, contains the mapping for all the namespace schemas:

```
/* Service for Warehouse inventory system. */

#include <iostream.h>
#include <sys/socket.h>
#include <netinet/in.h>
#include "soapH.h"
#include "ns1.nsmap"
```

The `soap` structure contains the gSOAP runtime environment. This is initialized via the `soap_init()` method call. The initialization needs to be done just once, and then this environment can be reused any number of times:

```
int main ()
{
  struct soap gSoapEnv;
  int master, slave; // master and slave sockets

  soap_init(&gSoapEnv);
```

We can also dynamically allocate or heap-allocate via the soap_new() method call. The soap_new() method also initializes the soap structure.

The soap_bind() method call binds the gSOAP server to the specified host and the port. In our example, the host and port are localhost and 8001 respectively. The soap_bind() method internally makes calls to the bind() and listen() Berkeley socket API methods.

The last parameter to soap_bind() is the maximum queue length (backlog), and this is passed through to the listen() BSD API method. If the number of incoming requests pending reaches the value specified by the queue length, the next incoming client request will fail. On Linux systems this can be as large as SOMAXCONN (128 on Linux 2.x), some older systems (such as BSD Unix) limit this to 5:

```
    master = soap_bind(&gSoapEnv, "localhost", 8001, 5);
    if (master < 0) {
      soap_print_fault(&gSoapEnv, stderr);
      exit(-1);
    }

    fprintf(stderr, "Socket connection successful:
            master socket = %d\n", master);
```

The Web Service client requests an infinite loop. The loop index i, keeps track of the number of requests coming in. The soap_accept() call blocks until there is a client request. This gSOAP API call internally calls the accept() Berkeley socket API method:

```
    for (int i = 1; ; i++) {
      slave = soap_accept(&gSoapEnv);
      if (slave < 0) {
        soap_print_fault(&gSoapEnv, stderr);
        exit(-1);
      }

      struct in_addr in;
      in.s_addr = htonl (gSoapEnv.ip);

      fprintf(stderr, "%d: accepted connection from IP = %s socket = %d",
              i, inet_ntoa (in), slave);
```

We then call the soap_serve() method that comes with the service skeleton (soapServer.cpp) generated for us by the soapcpp2 compiler. This method call contains the code that deserializes the SOAP request, and calls ns1__checkAvailability(). It then takes its response, and serializes it as a SOAP response message. In short, it does the major chunk of the work for us:

```
      // process RPC skeletons
      soap_serve(&gSoapEnv);
      fprintf(stderr, "request served\n");
```

Finally, we are ready to clean up after processing a request. The soap_end() method does this for us:

```
      soap_end(&gSoapEnv); // clean up everything and close socket
    }
    exit (0);
  }
```

The actual implementation for the service happens in the `ns1__checkAvailability()` method. Its method signature must match that defined in the `warehouse.h` file. Since this is a demo application for gSOAP, the service doesn't do a whole lot. It has hardcoded levels of the inventory database (as in our earlier examples), and it matches the incoming requests with them. It then builds and returns a status response via the last (reference) parameter.

If the service needs to return an error, it can build a SOAP Fault, for which it calls the `soap_fault()` method to allocate memory for storing SOAP Fault data. Calling `soap_fault()` multiple times has no effect, as it only allocates memory, if required. We can then update the fault string, and detail values in the `soap` structure. We then exit from the service method, returning the error indicator of `SOAP_FAULT`:

```
// Service implementation
int ns1__checkAvailability (struct soap* gSoapEnv,
                            xsd__string itemName, xsd__int quantity,
                            ns1__AvailabilityStatus &response)
{
  if (quantity <= 0) {
    soap_fault(gSoapEnv); // allocate space for fault (if necessary)
    gSoapEnv->fault->faultstring = "Illegal quantity";
    gSoapEnv->fault->detail = "Quantity has to be greater than 0";
    return SOAP_FAULT;
  }
```

These and other return status codes for a gSOAP service are listed in the *gSOAP Stub and Skeleton Return Codes* section, later in the chapter.

The rest of the implementation logic is the same as that in the previous examples. The service has hardcoded values for the number of `regular`, `sugar`, and `waffle` cones in the inventory. The client request is compared with the amount in the warehouse inventory, and we return an availability status of `INSTOCK`, `OUTOFSTOCK`, or `PARTIALSTOCK`, as the case may be. The `quantity` attribute of the availability status is set to the actual number that can be fulfilled:

```
  cout << "\nWarehouse inventory service got an status check for "
       << quantity << " cases of " << itemName << " cones.\n";

  // A database lookup would come here. We are going to fake it however.
  int regular_amt = 10000;
  int sugar_amt = 0;
  int waffle_amt  = 10;

  if (!strcmp (itemName, "regular")) {
    if (quantity == 0) {
      response.quantity = 0;
      response.status   = "OUTOFSTOCK";
    }
    else if (quantity <= regular_amt) {
      // We have the required number.
      response.quantity = quantity;
      response.status   = "INSTOCK";
    }
    else {
```

```
      // that's all we have.
      response.quantity = regular_amt;
      response.status = "PARTIALSTOCK";
    }
    return SOAP_OK;
  }
  else if (!strcmp (itemName, "sugar")) {
    if (quantity == 0) {
      response.quantity = 0;
      response.status = "OUTOFSTOCK";
    }
    else if (quantity < sugar_amt) {
      // We have the required number.
      response.quantity = quantity;
      response.status = "INSTOCK";
    }
    else {
      response.quantity = sugar_amt; // that's all we have
      response.status = "PARTIALSTOCK";
    }
    return SOAP_OK;
  }
  else if (!strcmp (itemName, "waffle")) {
    if (quantity == 0) {
      response.quantity = 0;
      response.status = "OUTOFSTOCK";
    }
    else if (quantity < waffle_amt) {
      // We have the required number.
      response.quantity = quantity;
      response.status = "INSTOCK";
    }
    else {
      // that's all we have.
      response.quantity = waffle_amt;
      response.status = "PARTIALSTOCK";
    }
      return SOAP_OK;
  }
```

As we can see in the above code, a return code of `SOAP_OK` from the service method indicates a successful SOAP method call invocation.

The following is another error situation, this one caused by an unrecognized ice cream cone type. We return a SOAP Fault in a manner similar to that described earlier:

```
  // this by default is an else statement
  {
    soap_fault(gSoapEnv);
    soap->fault->faultstring = "Illegal cone type";
    soap->fault->detail = "Cone type is one of regular, sugar or waffle.";
    return SOAP_FAULT;
  }
}
```

Now that we have the Web Service ready, we need to build it.

```
$ GSOAP_HOME=/path/to/gSOAP_install
$ export GSOAP_HOME
$ g++ -I$GSOAP_HOME -o warehouseService warehouseService.cpp soapServer.cpp
soapC.cpp $GSOAP_HOME/stdsoap2.cpp
```

Here, `$GSOAP_HOME` is the location where gSOAP is installed. `$GSOAP_HOME` is not a variable that is set (or required to be set) by gSOAP; we have defined it for our convenience.

Implementing the Client

We now write a simple client (`warehouseClient.cpp`) that invokes our Web Service:

```
/* Client program for Warehouse inventory system. */

#include <iostream.h>
#include "soapH.h"
#include "ns1.nsmap"
```

Note the service endpoint of `localhost:8001`. This needs to be the same as that the server is waiting on. We had specified this earlier in the `soap_bind()` call while writing the service:

```
#define SERVICE_ENDPOINT "localhost:8001"
#define SOAP_ACTION ""
```

The client program takes the parameters of the `checkAvailability()` SOAP method that we are going to invoke as its input parameters. These are the cone type name, and the quantity of cases required. We could also pass the service endpoint (`SERVICE_ENDPOINT` macro) as an input to the program instead of defining it in our program. This way we don't have to change the code and recompile, if the endpoint changes:

```
int main (int argc, char* argv[])
{
  if (argc != 3) {
    cout << "usage: " << argv[0] << " <coneType> <quantity>" << endl;
    cout << "Cone type is one of regular, sugar or waffle." << endl;
    exit (1);
  }

  // gSOAP runtime environment.
  struct soap gSoapEnv;
  soap_init (&gSoapEnv);
  ns1__AvailabilityStatus availabilityStatus;

  char* itemName = argv[1];
  int quantity   = atoi (argv[2]);

  cout << "Checking availability of " << quantity << " cases of "
       << itemName << " cones." << endl;
```

gSOAP's soapcpp2 compiler generates a client stub for us (soapClient.cpp). This generated client stub method is called soap_call_ ns1__checkAvailability (where ns1__checkAvailability is the name of the remote SOAP method). The stub does all the work of serializing the method parameters as a SOAP packet, sending it to the remote service, deserializing the return value, and returning it to us. The result, by gSOAP's convention, is returned in the last parameter to the method call. This parameter is passed by reference. The return value of the method is the status code of the SOAP call:

```
    if (soap_call_ns1__checkAvailability (&gSoapEnv, SERVICE_ENDPOINT,
            SOAP_ACTION,itemName, quantity, availabilityStatus) == SOAP_OK) {

      char* status = availabilityStatus.status;
      cout << "Availability status is " << status << ".\n";
      if (!strcmp (status, "PARTIALSTOCK")) {
        cout << "Sorry, we have only " << availabilityStatus.quantity
             << " cases. Would that do?\n";
      }
      else if (!strcmp (status, "OUTOFSTOCK")) {
        cout << "Sorry, we are out of stock. You would need to
                  place a back order\n";
      }
      else {
        // INSTOCK
        cout << "Yes, we are in stock. Shall we place the order?\n";
      }
    }
    else {
      // SOAP error
      cout << "Error making SOAP call\n";
      // dump error to stderr.
      soap_print_fault (&gSoapEnv, stderr);
    }

    return 0;
  }
```

As we can see above, we call the gSOAP API method soap_print_fault(), in case of an error. This method takes FILE* as input, and dumps the contents of the SOAP Fault onto it.

Now, we can build our client using the following command:

```
$g++ -I$GSOAP_HOME -o warehouseClient warehouseClient.cpp soapC.cpp soapClient.cpp
$GSOAP_HOME/stdsoap2.cpp
```

We now are ready to start the standalone server:

```
$ ./warehouseService
```

We can now run the client, first to check availability of 100 cases of regular ice cream cones, and then 100 cases of waffle ice cream cones:

```
$ ./warehouseClient regular 100
Checking availability of 100 cases of regular cones
Avalability status is INSTOCK.
Yes, we are in stock, Shall we place the order?
```

```
$ ./warehouseClient waffle 100
Checking availability of 100 cases of waffle cones
Avalability status is PARTIALSTOCK.
Sorry, we have only 10 cases. Would that do?
```

We can see the two requests being sent, and the response received back from the service:

```
1: accepted connection fromn IP = 127.0.0.1 socket = 4
Warehouse inventory service got an status check for 100 cases of regular cones
reuest served
2 accepted connection fromn IP = 127.0.0.1 socket = 4
Warehouse inventory service got an status check for 100 cases of waffle cones
reuest served
```

Building a Multi-threaded, Standalone Web Service

If we are having a single-threaded Web Service, our major concern could be the performance. A client request has to wait for the previous requests to get served, before it can get a response back. gSOAP 2.1 is thread-safe, and hence we can write a multi-threaded SOAP service that can handle multiple clients concurrently.

Now, let's develop the multi-threaded version (`warehouseServiceMultithreaded.cpp`) of our `warehouseService` Web Service.

As can be seen from the listing below, we provide for 8 (`MAX_THREADS`) threads. Increasing the `MAX_THREADS` macro would allow for the server to handle more concurrent connections. However, adding each new thread would have a memory overhead; at the least, each thread has its own gSOAP environment (`struct soap`). This memory versus number of concurrent connections is a design issue for a real-world Web Service.

The rest of the code is pretty much a straightforward multi-threaded program. First, we block on an `soap_accept()` call, and when there is a client request, we start off a thread using `pthread_create()`. The `pthread_create()` API call creates a new 'thread of control' that executes concurrently with the calling thread. This thread serves up the client request by running the service implementation code via the `soap_serve()` method. While this is being done, the service (main thread) has gone back to the `soap_accept()` call, and waits for the next incoming request:

```
/* Service for Warehouse inventory system. */

#include <iostream.h>
#include <sys/socket.h>
#include <netinet/in.h>
#include <pthread.h>
#include "soapH.h"
#include "ns1.nsmap"

// Maximum number of threads to serve requests.
#define MAX_THREADS 8

int
main () {
```

```
struct soap gSoapEnv;

// One runtime environment per thread
struct soap* soap_thr[MAX_THREADS];
pthread_t tid[MAX_THREADS];

// master and slave sockets.
int master, slave;

soap_init(&gSoapEnv);
master = soap_bind(&gSoapEnv, "localhost", 8001, 5);
if (master < 0) {
  soap_print_fault(&gSoapEnv, stderr);
    exit(-1);
}

fprintf(stderr, "Socket connection successful:
                 master socket = %d\n", master);

for (int i = 0; i < MAX_THREADS; i ++) {
{
  soap_thr[i] = NULL;
}

// infinite loop
for (;;) {
  for (int i = 0;i < MAX_THREADS; i++) {
    slave = soap_accept(&gSoapEnv);
    if (slave < 0) {
      soap_print_fault(&gSoapEnv, stderr);
      break;
    }
    struct in_addr in;
    in.s_addr = htonl (gSoapEnv.ip);

    fprintf(stderr, "%d: accepted connection from IP =
                    %s socket = %d", i, inet_ntoa (in), slave);

    // first time
    if (soap_thr[i] == NULL) {
      soap_thr[i] = soap_new ();
      if (soap_thr[i] == NULL) {
        soap_print_fault(&gSoapEnv, stderr);
        exit (-1);
      }
    }
    else {
      // already initialized, reuse soap environment
      pthread_join (tid[i], NULL);
      fprintf (stderr, "Thread %d completed\n", i);
      soap_end (soap_thr[i]); // free up the old thread data
    }
```

```
            soap_thr[i]->socket = slave;
            pthread_create(&tid[i], NULL, (void*(*)(void*))soap_serve,
                           (void*)soap_thr[i]);
            fprintf(stderr, "request served by thread #%d\n", i);
        }
    } // for (;;)

    exit (0);
  }

  // Service implementation
  int ns1__checkAvailability (struct soap* gSoapEnv,
                              xsd__string itemName, xsd__int quantity,
                              ns1__AvailabilityStatus &response)
  {
      // The service implementation code...
  }
```

We can now build this service as shown below:

```
$ g++ -I$GSOAP_HOME -o warehouseServiceMultithreaded
warehouseServiceMultithreaded.cpp soapServer.cpp soapC.cpp
$GSOAP_HOME/stdsoap2.cpp -lpthread
```

Let's run the multi-threaded service that is serving up multiple client requests:

```
$ ./ warehouseServiceMultithreaded
Socket connection successful: master socket = 4
Thread 0 accepted connection from IP = 127.0.0.1 socket = 5
request served by thread #0

Warehouse inventory service got an status check for 100 cases of reguar cones.
Thread 1 accepted connection from IP = 127.0.0.1 socket = 5
request served by thread #1

Warehouse inventory service got an status check for 100 cases of waffle cones.
```

The above output shows our multi-threaded service being run, and serving up multiple client requests. There are two incoming requests, and two different threads that are handled by the service concurrently.

Building a CGI Web Service

If we wanted a service that would be deployed inside a web server (like a CGI executable) instead of a standalone service, our `main()` function would be the following:

```
int main ()
{
  soap_serve (soap_new());
  return 0;
}
...// rest of the code as earlier
```

Comparing this code with that written earlier for the standalone server, we see that we have done away with the calls to bind to a host and port, and wait for incoming client connections (`soap_bind()` and `soap_accept()`). These are not required here as the web server does this work for us. We just need to call `soap_serve()`, passing it the gSOAP runtime environment that is created and initialized by the `soap_new()` call.

The rest of the program, and the command to compile it would remain the same. The CGI executable for the service can be deployed in the `CGI` directory of the web server (for example, Apache). The access point for the service would now be `http://host:port/cgi-bin/ServiceName` (assuming that the `http://host:port` is the URL for the web server, and `cgi-bin` is the directory for CGI scripts).

The complete code for this example as well as for other program listings in this chapter can be downloaded from http://www.wrox.com/.

Building a Secure Web Service

Web Services that expose confidential information (such as credit card numbers) require some level of security. gSOAP supports HTTPS/SSL in its clients and services.

To enable SSL, we need to download the OpenSSL software from http://www.openssl.org. This is available in source form, as well as binary form for some platforms. It also comes preinstalled on many Linux distributions. The version used here is OpenSSL 0.9.6b [engine].

Client-Side Changes

To enable SSL on the client-side, we need to make the following changes in our client code (`warehouseClient.cpp`):

- Change the service URL from `http` to `https`
- Enable server authentication using the `require_server_auth` attribute of the gSOAP runtime environment:

```
struct soap gSoapEnv;
...
gSoapEnv.require_server_auth = 1;
```

- Add a signal handler to catch broken connections (`SIGPIPE`). This is required for a known OpenSSL problem in which peers often close the connection as soon as they have read the HTTP response:

```
#include <signal.h>
...
void sigpipe_handle (int n) {}

main()
{
  ...
  signal (SIGPIPE, sigpipe_handle);
```

- If the Web Service requires the connecting clients to be authenticated too, we need to set the SSL-related attributes in the gSOAP runtime environment. This feature allows services to control access to their functionality. Typically, it is the server alone that needs to authenticate itself, and clients are not authenticated:

```
gSoapEnv.keyfile = "client.pem";
gSoapEnv.password = "password";
gSoapEnv.cafile = "cacert.pem";
```

The `keyfile`, `password`, and `cafile` specified above are the client key, the keystore password, and client certificate (self-signed, or signed by a known CA like Verisign). gSOAP comes with sample certificate files in PEM-encoded format that we can use for testing. For a real-world application, we would need to generate these, using the `openssl` command line tool, and the `CA.pl` Perl script. More information on generating these files is given in *Server-Side Changes* section below.

We now need to rebuild the client with the `-DWITH_OPENSSL` option. This enables the SSL-related code in `stdsoap2.cpp` that was not compiled earlier as it was protected by `#ifdef WITH_OPENSSL` macros:

```
$ g++ -DDEBUG -DWITH_OPENSSL -I.. -o warehouseClientSecure warehouseClient.cpp
soapC.cpp soapClient.cpp $GSOAP_HOME/stdsoap2.cpp -lssl -lcrypto
```

This code does all the behind-the-scene work to get the SSL connection working. It creates the SSL object, performs the SSL handshake, writes the HTTP request using the OpenSSL `SSL_write()` API call, and reads the response using `SSL_read()` and performs many other tasks.

Server-Side Changes

If the service is installed as a CGI program, the SSL support needs to be configured in the web server. We won't be discussing the configuration here; you can refer to your web server documentation for this.

If the service is for a standalone server, we need to make few changes to the server. First, the SSL parameter needs to be changed in the gSOAP runtime enviroment:

```
gSoapEnv.keyfile = "server.pem";
gSoapEnv.cafile = "cacert.pem";
gSoapEnv.dhfile = "dh512.pem";
gSoapEnv.password = "password";
```

gSOAP comes with sample certificate file that we can use for testing. For a real-world application, we would need to generate new certificates.

The following commands show, in brief, how these certificates are created. See the OpenSSL documentation at http://www.openssl.org, for more information on this.

First, a new unencrypted server key is created by the command:

```
$ openssl genrsa -out server.key 1024
```

Next, we create a server certificate request with this unencrypted key; for example:

```
$ openssl req -new -days 365 -key server.key -out newreq.pem
```

This certificate request needs to be submitted to a Certificate Authority (CA) like Verisign, and after paying some money, we get a properly signed certificate. Alternatively, we could self-sign our certificates as shown overleaf:

We'll first create a certificate authority, and then self-sign the certificate:

```
$ perl CA.pl -newca
$ perl CA.pl -sign
```

The default certificate name is `newcert.pem`. Finally, we generate the DH (Diffie-Hellman parameters) file. The Diffie-Hellman method allows two hosts to create, and share a secret key:

```
$ openssl gendh -out dh 1024
```

We also need to add a `soap_ssl_accept()` call. This call has the server-side OpenSSL code that creates an SSL object, and then calls `SSL_accept()` to complete the server-side portion of the SSL handshake:

```
slave = soap_accept(&gSoapEnv);
if (slave < 0) {
  soap_print_fault(&gSoapEnv, stderr);
  exit(-1);
}
if (soap_ssl_accept(&gSoapEnv)) {
  soap_print_fault(&gSoapEnv, stderr);
  exit(-1);
}
soap_serve(&gSoapEnv); // process RPC skeletons
```

We also need to add a signal handler to catch broken connections (`SIGPIPE`) like that done in the client. Now we can rebuild the server with the `-DWITH_OPENSSL` option:

```
$ g++ -DDEBUG -DWITH_OPENSSL -o warehouseServiceSecure -I..
warehouseServiceSecure.cpp soapServer.cpp soapC.cpp $GSOAP_HOME/stdsoap2.cpp -lssl
-lcrypto
```

Now, we have the SSL-enabled service and the client ready for use.

gSOAP Header Processing

gSOAP's stub and skeleton compiler generates a default header file for its applications. This looks like the following:

```
struct SOAP_ENV__Header
{
  char* transaction;
}
```

The idea here is that this header attribute (transaction) can be used for transaction control. The service would generate a transaction ID in some application-specific way. This ID would be passed back in the SOAP header to the client, and the client can use this transaction ID in the next SOAP call. SOAP is stateless, and this mechanism is an example of how transaction control can be built on top of it. Sample code for doing this on the server side is listed below:

```
struct soap gSoapEnv;
...
if (gSoapEnv.header) {
  my_transaction_id = gSoapEnv.header->transaction;
}
else {
  gSoapEnv.header = soap_malloc (sizeof (struct SOAP_ENV__Header));
  gSoapEnv.header->transaction = some_transaction_id;
}
```

The client-side can similarly manipulate the SOAP header attribute. The SOAP message fragment shown below is an example of how this would look on the wire:

```
<SOAP-ENV:Envelope ...>
  <SOAP-ENV:Header>
    <transaction xsi:type="int">23</transaction>
  </SOAP-ENV:Header>
  <SOAP-ENV:Body>
    ...
  </SOAP-ENV:Body>
</SOAP-ENV:Envelope>
```

If we wish to have our own, application-specific, SOAP header attributes, we need to define a `SOAP_ENV__Header struct` in our header file (for example, `warehouse.h`) that is passed to the stub and skeleton compiler.

Connecting Via a Proxy Server

The gSOAP runtime environment `struct` has attributes for specifying the proxy (the host and the port). This allows SOAP clients running behind a proxy server to access an external service.

The following client-side code example illustrates this use:

```
struct soap gSoapEnv; // gSOAP runtime environment
soap_init (&gSoapEnv);
gSoapEnv.proxy_host = "myproxyhost"; // the proxy host
gSoapEnv.proxy_port = 8088;          // the proxy port
... // make soap method calls
```

Debugging gSOAP Applications

In order to turn the debugging on for gSOAP applications (client and server), we need to rebuild them using the `-DDEBUG` option as shown below:

```
$ g++ -DDEBUG -I$GSOAP_HOME -o warehouseService warehouseService.cpp
soapServer.cpp soapC.cpp $GSOAP_HOME/stdsoap2.cpp

$ g++ -DDEBUG -I$GSOAP_HOME -o warehouseClient warehouseClient.cpp soapC.cpp
soapClient.cpp $GSOAP_HOME/stdsoap2.cpp
```

Now when the client and server application are run, the log messages are sent to the following log files by default:

- `SENT.log` – The SOAP messages sent by the application.
- `RECV.log` – The SOAP messages received by the application.
- `TEST.log` – The activity messages log file. This contains a log of internal debug messages from gSOAP.

The name of the files can be changed via the `soap_set_sent_logfile()`, `soap_set_recv_logfile()`, and `soap_set_test_logfile()` methods. The following code fragments show how this is done (`warehouseService.cpp`) for setting the debug files:

```
struct soap gSoapEnv; // gSOAP runtime environment
soap_init (&gSoapEnv);
soap_set_recv_logfile (&gSoapEnv, "/tmp/SERVICE_RECV.log");
soap_set_sent_logfile (&gSoapEnv, "/tmp/SERVICE_SENT.log");
soap_set_test_logfile (&gSoapEnv, NULL);// not interested in these
// rest of the code
...
```

Here, the service should have appropriate permissions for the directory that these log files get written (`/tmp` in this case).

We'll see a similar code from the `warehouseClient.cpp` file:

```
struct soap gSoapEnv; // gSOAP runtime environment
soap_init (&gSoapEnv);
soap_set_recv_logfile (&gSoapEnv, "/tmp/CLIENT_RECV.log");
soap_set_sent_logfile (&gSoapEnv, "/tmp/CLIENT_SENT.log");
soap_set_test_logfile (&gSoapEnv, NULL);// not interested in these
// rest of the code
...
```

Now, let's rebuild `warehouseService` and `warehouseClient` as shown above. When we run the service and the client, the log messages get appended to the trace files that we set above. The contents of the `CLIENT_SENT.log` should match that of the `SERVICE_RECV.log`. Similarly, the contents of `SERVICE_SENT.log` should match that of `CLIENT_RECV.log`.

Let's use the `warehouseClient` to query for the availability of `100` cases of `regular` cones:

```
$ ./warehouseClient regular 100
```

This will show the following trace messages (formatted for readability):

```
<?xml version="1.0" encoding="UTF-8"?>
<SOAP-ENV:Envelope
  xmlns:SOAP-ENV="http://schemas.xmlsoap.org/soap/envelope/"
  xmlns:SOAP-ENC="http://schemas.xmlsoap.org/soap/encoding/"
  xmlns:xsi="http://www.w3.org/2001/XMLSchema-instance"
```

```
    xmlns:xsd="http://www.w3.org/2001/XMLSchema"
    xmlns:ns1="http://www.wrox.com/warehouse"
    SOAP-ENV:encodingStyle="http://schemas.xmlsoap.org/soap/encoding/">
    <SOAP-ENV:Body>
      <ns1:checkAvailability>
      <itemName xsi:type="xsd:string">regular</itemName>
      <quantity xsi:type="xsd:int">100</quantity>
      </ns1:checkAvailability>
    </SOAP-ENV:Body>
  </SOAP-ENV:Envelope>
```

First, we list the SOAP request from `CLIENT_SENT.log`. We can see the namespace declarations in the SOAP `Envelope`. These are picked up from the `ns1.nsmap` generated by gSOAP, and that we included in our code. The `Body` of the SOAP message has the serialized form of the SOAP method call (`checkAvailability`) with its two parameters – the string valued cone type (`regular`), and the integer valued quantity of cases required (`100`).

Let's take a peek inside `SERVICE_RECV.log` too. It has the SOAP message received by the service, and it should be the same as that shown above.

The `warehouseService` does the processing required for `checkAvailability()` call, and then returns the `AvailabilityStatus` structure back in response. This, as can be see below in the extract from `SERVICE_SENT.log`, contains the status string (`INSTOCK`), and the quantity (which is the same `100`, since the item is in stock):

```
<?xml version="1.0" encoding="UTF-8"?>
<SOAP-ENV:Envelope
  xmlns:SOAP-ENV="http://schemas.xmlsoap.org/soap/envelope/"
  xmlns:SOAP-ENC="http://schemas.xmlsoap.org/soap/encoding/"
  xmlns:xsi="http://www.w3.org/2001/XMLSchema-instance"
  xmlns:xsd="http://www.w3.org/2001/XMLSchema"
  xmlns:ns1="http://www.wrox.com/warehouse"
  SOAP-ENV:encodingStyle="http://schemas.xmlsoap.org/soap/encoding/">
  <SOAP-ENV:Body>
    <ns1:AvailabilityStatus xsi:type="ns1:AvailabilityStatus">
    <status xsi:type="xsd:string">INSTOCK</status>
    <quantity xsi:type="xsd:int">100</quantity>
    </ns1:AvailabilityStatus>
  </SOAP-ENV:Body>
</SOAP-ENV:Envelope>
```

If we also check the `CLIENT_RECV.log`, we'll find the same content.

Let's, as an experiment, see what happens if an error occurs. To demonstrate this, we'll invoke the client with an illegal value for the input parameters:

```
$ ./warehouseClient regular -10
```

The service detects this to be an illegal value, and executes the following piece of code (from the server `warehouseService.cpp`) to build, and send back a SOAP Fault message:

```
soap_fault(gSoapEnv); // allocate space for fault (if necessary)
gSoapEnv->fault->faultstring = "Illegal quantity";
gSoapEnv->fault->detail = "Quantity has a to be greater than 0";
return SOAP_FAULT;
```

The client receives back this SOAP Fault message, and prints it to the console using the `soap_print_fault()` API call.

If we look in the `CLIENT_RECV.log` for the SOAP message received from the service, we should be able to see the `Fault` element in the SOAP body as shown below:

```
<?xml version="1.0" encoding="UTF-8"?>
<SOAP-ENV:Envelope
  xmlns:SOAP-ENV="http://schemas.xmlsoap.org/soap/envelope/"
  xmlns:SOAP-ENC="http://schemas.xmlsoap.org/soap/encoding/"
  xmlns:xsi="http://www.w3.org/2001/XMLSchema-instance"
  xmlns:xsd="http://www.w3.org/2001/XMLSchema"
  xmlns:ns1="http://www.wrox.com/warehouse"
  SOAP-ENV:encodingStyle="http://schemas.xmlsoap.org/soap/encoding/">
  <SOAP-ENV:Body>
    <SOAP-ENV:Fault>
      <faultcode>Client</faultcode>
      <faultstring>Illegal quantity</faultstring>
      <detail>Quantity has a to be greater than 0</detail>
    </SOAP-ENV:Fault>
  </SOAP-ENV:Body>
</SOAP-ENV:Envelope>
```

gSOAP API

We used some gSOAP API calls in our code. These, and some other commonly used API calls are listed below. These API calls come from `stdsoap2.cpp`, which is then compiled, and linked with all gSOAP services and clients. As can be seen, this is pure C API. This is especially useful if we wish to expose a legacy application in C, and don't want to write a C++ wrapper to expose the service interface:

Data Structure	Description
`void soap_init (struct soap* gSoapEnv)`	Initializes the gSOAP runtime environment. This call is required only once.
`struct soap *soap_new()`	Allocates, initializes and returns a pointer to the gSOAP runtime environment.
`int soap_bind(struct soap*gSoapEnv, char* host, char* port, int backlog)`	Returns the master socket. The backlog is the max queue length.
`int soap_accept (struct soap* gSoapEnv)`	Returns slave socket.
`void soap_begin (struct soap* gSoapEnv)`	
`void soap_end (struct soap* gSoapEnv)`	Cleans up deserialized data (except class instances).

Data Structure	Description
`void soap_free (struct soap* gSoapEnv)`	Cleans up temporary data only.
`void soap_destroy (struct soap* gSoapEnv)`	Cleans up deserialized class instances.
`void soap_set_recv_logfile (struct soap* gSoapEnv, const char* filename)`	Sets the log file's name used for logging SOAP messages received by an application.
`void soap_set_sent_logfile (struct soap* gSoapEnv, const char* filename)`	Sets the log file for SOAP messages sent by an application.
`void soap_set_test_logfile (struct soap* gSoapEnv, const char* filename)`	Sets the log file for the activity log messages.
`soap_print_fault(struct soap *gSoapEnv, FILE *fd)`	Dumps the SOAP Fault information onto the FILE stream.

gSOAP Runtime Environment Configuration

A data structure that is used a lot in gSOAP is `struct soap`. This contains the gSOAP runtime environment. It is initialized via the `soap_init()` method call, as we had seen earlier. Some important data members of this structure are listed below. These data members allow for configuring the behaviour of gSOAP clients and services (for a complete list, please refer to the `stdsoap2.h` header file):

Data Member	Description
`http_version`	The HTTP version attribute. This defaults to `1.0` for HTTP 1.0.
`encodingStyle`	The encoding style to be used for the SOAP messages. If it is `NULL`, it defaults to SOAP encoding. The default encoding style is http://schemas.xmlsoap.org/soap/encoding/.
`defaultNamespace`	If `NULL`, no default namespace is set. The default value is `NULL`.
`keep_alive`	The `KEEP_ALIVE` HTTP attribute. A non-zero value sets the `KEEP_ALIVE` to `TRUE` (that is, keep alive packets are sent to keep the connection open). The default value is `0`.
`disable_href`	This option controls serialization of C++ data elements. When this is non-zero, `hrefs` are disabled. This results in copies being made of the data in the SOAP payload. The default value is `0`.
`enable_embedding`	This option controls serialization of C++ data elements. When this is non-zero, it enables `hrefs` within embedded elements instead of encoding them as independent elements. The default value is `0`.

Table continued on following page

Data Member	Description
enable_null	This option controls serialization of C++ data elements. When it is non-zero, the NULL C++ elements (for example, pointers) are serialized. The xsi:nil attribute for these elements is set to TRUE. The default value is 0.
enable_utf_string	This option controls serialization of C++ data elements. When it is non-zero, it assumes that all character strings are already UTF-8/16 and emits them without translation. The default value is 0.
disable_request_count	When this is non-zero, the HTTP Content-Length is not calculated and emitted for the request. The default value is 0.
disable_response_count	When this is non-zero, the HTTP Content-Length is not calculated and emitted for the response. The default value is 0.
enable_array_overflow	When this is non-zero, elements that do not fit in a fixed-sized array are ignored. The default value is 0.
namespaces	The namespace mapping table
send_timeout	Used to control socket communication timeout. A value > 0, sets the socket send timeout in seconds. The default value is 0 (not timeout).
recv_timeout	Used to control socket communication timeout. A value > 0, sets the socket recv timeout in seconds. The default value is 0 (not timeout).
require_serv_auth	Related to HTTPS/SSL support. Setting it to non-zero value in the client's gSOAP environment enables server authentication. The default value is 0.
keyfile	SSL-related parameter. This is set to the resident key filename.
cafile	SSL-related parameter. This is set to the resident CA filename.
dhfile	SSL-related parameter. This is set to the resident DH filename
cookie_domain	Cookie-related parameter. Set to the domain (host) of the service. Cookies are useful in SOAP for implementing sessions.
cookie_path	Cookie-related parameter. Set to the default path of the service.
cookie_max	Cookie-related parameter. Set to the maximum cookie database size. The default value is 32.

Let's take a look at some of these configuration options in use.

Setting the HTTP Protocol Version

We can set the HTTP protocol version as shown below:

```
struct soap gSoapEnv;
soap_init (&gSoapEnv);

gSoapEnv.http_version = "1.1";
```

The default value of HTTP_VERSION is HTTP 1.0.

Setting the keep_alive Flag

We can also set the HTTP keep_alive flag for keeping the socket connections alive:

```
gSoapEnv.keep_alive = 1;
```

The keep_alive option can be switched off by setting it to 0.

gSOAP Stub and Skeleton Return Codes

In the code examples earlier, we had seen some gSOAP standard macros used for return codes from gSOAP services. The complete list of these is reproduced below:

Macro	Description
SOAP_OK	No error
SOAP_CLI_FAULT	The service raised a client Fault exception
SOAP_SVR_FAULT	The service raised a server Fault exception
SOAP_TAG_MISMATCH	An XML element didn't correspond to anything expected
SOAP_TYPE_MISMATCH	An XML schema type mismatch
SOAP_SYNTAX_ERROR	An XML syntax error occurred on the input
SOAP_NO_TAG	Start tag of an element expected, but not found
SOAP_IOB	Array index out of bounds
SOAP_MUSTUNDERSTAND	Service encountered a mandatory header entry that it did not understand.
SOAP_NAMESPACE	Namespace name mismatch (validation error)
SOAP_OBJ_MISMATCH	Mismatch in the size and/or shape of an object
SOAP_FATAL_ERROR	Internal error
SOAP_FAULT	An exception raised by the service
SOAP_NO_METHOD	Skeleton error: the skeleton cannot serve the method
SOAP_EOM	Out of memory
SOAP_NULL	An element was Null, when it is not supposed to be Null
SOAP_MULTI_ID	Multiple occurrences of the same element ID in the input
SOAP_MISSING_ID	Element ID missing for an HREF on the input
SOAP_HREF	Reference to object is incompatible with the object refered to
SOAP_TCP_ERROR	A TCP connection error occured
SOAP_HTTP_ERROR	An HTTP error occurred
SOAP_EOF	Unexpected end of file

Mapping Between C++ and XML Types

The default encoding for the C and C++ data types in gSOAP is SOAP Encoding. For example, integer (C++ type int) gets mapped to the SOAP Encoding type int, and would get represented as <int xsi:type="int">...</int> in the generated SOAP message. You can refer to the gSOAP user's guide for a complete list of this mapping.

We can also change the default encoding style to any XML schema type encoding (literal encoding) by adding typedefs in the header file passed as input to the gSOAP stub and skeleton compiler. For example:

```
typedef int xsd__intType;
```

Then, any data type used as an input or an output in a method call, and declared to be of xsd__intType type, gets serialized as:

```
<param xsi:type="xsd:intType">34243</param>
```

gSOAP can also handle complex data types, such as arrays, and structures. The sample application listed earlier is a good example of how this is specified in the header file passed as an input to the gSOAP compiler.

Interoperability

In the examples we have studied in this chapter, the service and the client have been written in the same implementation. This is not necessary; the client and the service could be implemented using different SOAP implementations. For example, we could have a client written with the EasySOAP++ API running against a service written, and deployed in WASP Server Lite for C++. This can be illustrated as shown below:

```
$ ./warehouseClient regular 100 http://localhost:6070/WarehouseService/
Checking availability of 100 cases of regular cones.
Availability status is INSTOCK.
Yes, we are in stock. Shall we place the order?
```

Here, the EasySOAP++ client connects to the service that we had written earlier in WASP, and deployed at the service endpoint http://localhost:6070/WarehouseService/. We do not require any code change in the client or the service. In fact, both are oblivious to the platform that the other is implemented on.

All the three SOAP implementations discussed in this chapter can interoperate with other popular SOAP implentations. The interoperability results for these and other implementations can be found at http://www.whitemesa.com/interop.htm, and http://www.xmethods.net/ilab/.

Selecting the Right Implementation

In this section, we will compare features from the three implementations discussed in the chapter – WASP Server Lite for C++, gSOAP, and easySOAP++.

- **WSDL tools support**
  gSOAP has a stub and skeleton compiler (`soapcpp2`) that generates client-side stubs, the service skeletons, and a WSDL file for the service. It takes as an input a header file describing the service interface in a specified convention.

  WASP 3.0 has a WSDL compiler tool (`waspc`) that can generate the client-side stubs, and the service skeletons from an input WSDL file. It currently does not have any tools to generate the WSDL file itself.

  EasySOAP++ does not have any WSDL tools.

- **Interoperability**
  As discussed in the previous section, all the three SOAP implementations discussed in the chapter run interopability tests against other SOAP implementations.

- **Use of fast and memory-efficient XML parsers**
  The more commonly used mechanisms of XML parsing are DOM (Document Object Model), and SAX. In DOM-based parsing, the XML parser builds an entire parse tree representation of the document. While this allows a lot of flexibility in manipulating complex XML documents, it is very expensive in terms of memory.

  Unlike the tree-based API of DOM, a SAX (Simple API for XML) parser offers an event-based API. The parser reports back parsing events, such as the start or the end of an XML element tag, to the application through using a callback mechanism. SAX has significant memory, and speed advantages over DOM as it deals with XML documents on the fly, and does not need to read the entire XML document into memory.

  SAX parsers are ideally suited for applications that wish to perform a few simple operations in a large XML document. However the application code can become fairly involved if complex XML operations need to be performed.

  XML Pull Parsers are a relatively new approach to parsing XML documents. In Pull Parsers, instead of the parser calling the applications handler methods when an event (like an element tag start) occurs, the application itself calls for the next parse event from the input XML document. Thus, a Pull Parser is similar to a tokenizer. This approach lends itself to a simpler programming style than a SAX parser, but with comparable performance and low memory footprint.

  Both WASP and gSOAP come with inbuilt Pull Parsers. EasySOAP++ uses James Clark's Expat XML parser library. This is a SAX-like stream-based parser.

- **C language support**
  gSOAP has a pure C-like API, and is the only implementation that can be used by C as well as C++ programs. The gSOAP stub and skeleton compiler creates `.cpp` files. However, these files contain C code, and all we need to do is to rename them as `.c` files, and compile with the client written in C.

  The following commands show how the files generated by gSOAP stub and skeleton compiler (`soapcpp2`) are renamed as `.c` files. Finally, the application is linked with a C client program (`warehouseClient.c`), and the C version of the gSOAP library (`stdsoap2.c`):

```
$ soapcpp2 warehouse.h
$ mv soapC.cpp soapC.c
$ mv soapClient.cpp soapClient.c
$ mv soapServer.cpp soapServer.c
$ gcc -I$GSOAP_HOME -o warehouseClient warehouseClient.c soapC.c soapClient.c
$GSOAP_HOME/stdsoap2.c
```

The other two implementations, WASP and EasySoap++ are for C++ only.

- **SSL support**
  Both gSOAP as well as EasySOAP++ support secure Web Services using SSL, though gSOAP's SSL API is better documented. The open source version of WASP, WASP Server Lite for C++ does not support SSL.
- **HTTP-based SOAP server**
  Web Services written in both gSOAP and EasySOAP++ can be run as CGI programs in any web server. The earlier version of WASP (version 1.2) has plugin modules for Apache and IIS. These modules are still under development for WASP 3.0.
- **Standalone SOAP server**
  All three SOAP implementations allow for developing standalone Web Services (that is, one that does not need a web server, but instead has networking method calls in its code to handle client connections).

  A standalone server allows users to embed a SOAP-based service inside its application. This has better performance (assuming the Web Service is multi-threaded, and can handle multiple concurrent client connections). However, only WASP and gSOAP support a multi-threaded standalone server.
- **Configurability**
  Both WASP and gSOAP allow for a number of configuration options for its clients and services. However, in WASP, this configuration is through an XML-based configuration file. This is unlike gSOAP where this is done through modifying the data attributes of the gSOAP environment structure (`struct soap`), and thus the code needs to be changed and recompiled.

  WASP is clearly the most configurable SOAP implementation of the three, and has a lot of pluggable modules, such as user-defined header processors, transports. EasySoap++ does not provide a lot of configurability; however, it is relatively very simple to use.
- **Document style or RPC style messaging**
  The current version of WASP 3.0 has a support for only RPC style messaging. gSOAP supports both RPC as well as Document style.
- **Open Source licenses**
  All the three implementations are available under an open source license that allow for commercial use. These licenses are BSD Open Source license for WASP, GNU LGPL for EasySoap++, and Mozilla Public License for gSOAP. However, gSOAP's stub and skeleton compiler (`soapcpp2`) is still not available under open source.

Summary

In this chapter, we covered how to develop Web Services in C++. We discussed three open source SOAP implementations – WASP Server Lite for C++, EasySoap++, and gSOAP.

We learned that WASP provides a solution that can be embedded in C++ applications and comes with a multi-threaded SOAP server, C++ client library, and WSDL tools. We discussed WASP Server 3.0 Beta 2 Lite for C++ in this chapter. It has some limitations; it doesn't have complete support for WSDL 1.1, HTTP proxy. The version we covered doesn't have an UDDI client API, and doesn't support SSL; but these features are available with its non-open source version. We developed a sample Web Service to demonstrate WASP's usage.

We then learned another open source C++ SOAP implementation, EasySoap++ that requires Expat XML parser library. We looked at Web Services development using EasySoap++ with the help of an example. After these two implementations, we reviewed gSOAP, a complete SOAP 1.1 implementation. We discussed how it can be used to develop Web Services in C++ and C. To illustrate its features, we studied an example of a Web Service.

We also saw the interoperability issues with these implementations. Finally, we compared the features of all these three implementations. We learned that we can use any of these implementations depending on our needs and the features provided by the implementation.

Even though these implementations lack some features, they are pretty usable, and as the SOAP interoperability results indicate (http://www.whitemesa.com/interop.htm), all three work well against other SOAP implementations.

C++ (and C) implementations of the Web Services stack are important as there is a lot of code, legacy or otherwise, written in these languages. This code can be exposed to other applications in a portable manner via SOAP. These implementations also are useful in environments that have performance requirements or are memory constrained. For example, both gSOAP and WASP run on WinCE platforms.

10

Other SOAP Implementations

Since SOAP was first introduced, dozens of implementations have appeared for a whole host of languages. Virtually any system that can handle XML data and communicate using HTTP can be a viable platform to use SOAP, and the wide interest in integrating XML and "web capabilities" means that many languages are viable for use as clients and as servers.

In this chapter, we take a detailed look at the use of SOAP with the Ruby language, looking at:

- An example client to access services on the Internet using SOAP4R
- A client/server using SOAP4R
- A client for Google search using SOAP4R
- A basic client/server application using xmlrpc4r

We later move on to the practical application and use of Web Services in embedded systems like mobile phones and PDAs. In this section we will explore the following:

- Use of XML Pull Parsers
- Using kSOAP with applets
- Using kSOAP in embedded systems

Introduction to Ruby

Ruby is an object-oriented language and its semantics are derived largely from Smalltalk, where everything, including numbers, iterators, and closures, is an object. Ruby then drops Smalltalk syntax in favor of a more traditional Algol-like syntax, borrowing syntax from languages such as Perl, Eiffel, and Ada. In Ruby, absolutely everything you manipulate is an object and ultimately everything is inherited from the `Object` class, including complex data structures, functions, control structures such as iterators, and even numbers.

In Ruby, there are no standalone functions; all functions are associated with some object class, and are thus methods, which makes it a true object-oriented language. More information about Ruby can be found at http://www.ruby-lang.org/ and http://dev.rubycentral.com/faq/rubyfaq.html.

The language design attempts to follow the *Principle of Least Surprise* or *Law of Least Astonishment*, where things are designed to work the way one would expect, aiming to minimize the incidence of special rules or exceptions. This may be contrasted with the designs of other languages:

- Perl was originally designed to combine the syntaxes of a number of languages and text processing tools such as awk, sed, tr, C, grep, and sh, with the result that a lot of the language represents "special rules" indicating the similarities to and differences between Perl and the languages from which it was derived.
- C++, as an extension of C, as well as a codification of numerous extensions developed by many C++ vendors, similarly involves a lot of special rules and exceptions.
- The design of Java, almost exclusively influenced by one vendor, leads to it having somewhat fewer "design exceptions" than Perl or C++. Nevertheless, there are irregularities in Java particularly relating to the differing treatments of numeric types such as `int` versus `Integer`, which sometimes does lead to some degree of astonishment.

Ruby did not start with the same sorts of expectations of compatibility with existing languages in its design, and as a result the designers could choose features they liked without any pressure to force particular features to fit. And unlike Python and Java, Ruby starts and ends with all data structures being objects, which improves the consistency of behavior.

One of the characteristic advantages of scripting languages over traditional compiled language families like C and Pascal is that they provide automatic dynamic memory allocation, allocating space for values on demand, and de-allocating them when they are no longer referenced. Perl and Python use reference counting, which is simple to understand and implement, but it leaks memory if self-referencing data structures do not manually break those self-references. Ruby goes further than that, using a mark and sweep garbage collection approach much like those used in Lisp, and does not suffer from such leaks.

The object model of Ruby is different than those of C++, Java, and such, and a fair bit of insight may be gotten by looking at Ruby's handling of the traditionally controversial problem of multiple inheritances. The problem comes when an object is created that inherits attributes and methods from multiple parent classes; here sometimes the inheritance hierarchy becomes ambiguous.

C++ supports multiple inheritances, and some of its considerable complexity arises from the need to provide ways to refer to the multiple methods and attributes. On the other hand Java *rejects* multiple inheritance, allowing classes to inherit only from a single immediate parent. Ruby uses the notion of **mixins**, allowing a class to include methods from additional modules, with the result that methods are *mixed in* together.

Ambiguity is dealt with by the notion that the last method included is what is used. Here is an example of this. We start by defining three modules that modify an attribute `@Value`. Here is the first module:

```
#!/usr/bin/ruby
module Mod1
  def foo
    @Value = 1
    @V1 = 1
  end
end
```

Here is the second module:

```
module Mod2
  def foo
    @Value = 2
    @V2 = 2
  end
end
```

And here is the third module:

```
module Mod3
  def foo
    @Value = 3
    @V3 = 3
  end
end
```

All the three modules above have the same method, `foo()`, modifying the same attribute, `@Value`, and each setting up its own attribute. Now, we will mix them together:

```
class Bar
  include Mod1
  include Mod3
  include Mod2
  def initialize
    self.foo
  end
  def getValue
    return [@Value, @V1, @V2, @V3]
  end
end

a = Bar.new;
v = a.getValue
print "Result of getValue:\n"
v.each do |value|
  print value, " "
end
print "\n"
```

Since the three modules have the same method, `foo()`, the final one included, `Mod2`, is what provides the `foo()` method, and so `@Value` takes the value 2, and of `@V1`, `@V2`, and `@V3`, the only one defined is `@V2`. To run this, use the command `ruby mixinsamp.rb`, that produces the output as follows:

```
Result of getValue:
2 nil 2 nil
```

Switching to a different module to be included last changes the output variously to `3 nil nil 3`, `2 nil 2 nil`, or `1 1 nil nil`.

This fits in quite well with the *Principle of Least Surprise* for a module mixed in last to override methods and values from earlier modules is certainly a logical approach.

The authors of the book *Programming Ruby* from *Addison-Wesley (ISBN 0-201710-89-7)* introduce the language with the comment: 'Use Ruby, and you'll write better code, be more productive, and enjoy programming more.' Such dramatic results cannot be guaranteed for everyone, but there certainly is a lot to like about Ruby.

SOAP4R

The SOAP implementation available for Ruby is called SOAP4R. SOAP4R was first released in July 2000, and has had over a dozen updates including fixes based on interoperability testing. Its latest version at the time of writing was version 1.4.4 released in May 2002.

SOAP4R does not yet support the following SOAP 1.1 features:

- SOAP `actor` attribute
- SOAP `mustUnderstand` attribute
- SOAP Fault codes
- SOAP XML Schema encoding
- SOAP transports other than HTTP

Nor does it support SSL, HTTP Authentication, layered standards like WSDL or UDDI, or the sorts of extended transport mechanisms (such SMTP, POP3, `libz` compression, and `Jabber`) found in SOAP::Lite. Some of these mechanisms should come as development progresses.

Development has been quite active, but expecting WSDL or UDDI support immediately may be too much to ask. Updates are frequently improving functionality and interoperability, which is quite encouraging.

Installation of SOAP4R

SOAP4R is written in Ruby and works on Ruby 1.6.x series and later. Ruby has an authoritative place to look for additional modules, the Ruby Application Archive (RAA at http://www.ruby-lang.org/en/raa.html). To use SOAP4R, we require a number of modules and classes that are available at RAA:

- Any one of the following XML processors which is automatically detected by SOAP4R at runtime:
  - NQXML (http://nqxml.sourceforge.net/)
  - XMLParser (http://www.ruby-lang.org/en/raa-list.rhtml?name=XMLParser)
  - REXML (http://www.ruby-lang.org/en/raa-list.rhtml?name=REXML)
- `Devel::Logger`
  A class that implements a message logger (http://www.ruby-lang.org/en/raa-list.rhtml?name=Devel%3A%3ALogger).
- `http-access2`
  Version F or later of this HTTP access class (http://www.ruby-lang.org/en/raa-list.rhtml?name=http-access2).
- `date2`
  Version 3.2 or later of this alternative date class (http://www.ruby-lang.org/en/raa-list.rhtml?name=date2). This module is scheduled to be included in the standard distribution of Ruby 1.7, so you may not need to install this module.
- `Uconv`
  Unicode Conversion Module (http://www.ruby-lang.org/en/raa-list.rhtml?name=Uconv).

Some packages may have been packaged for your favourite distribution; Debian includes `nqxml`, `Uconv`, and `rexml`, for example. As packages mature, it is reasonable to expect versions of many of these modules to become available as RPM or Debian or Ports packages, which would make managing the installation somewhat simpler.

Ruby classes are typically installed using the command `ruby install.rb`, which typically copies the class files to a system-dependent location such as `/usr/local/lib/site_ruby/1.6`.

On a typical system, the class `rbconfig.rb`, in `/usr/lib/ruby/1.6/i386-linux/rbconfig.rb` defines a Ruby class containing a whole array of configuration information, indicating where the Ruby system is configured to look for information. Install scripts named `install.rb` that can use this and related information to indicate where new classes may be installed.

Here is a diagram showing the basic SOAP4R architecture:

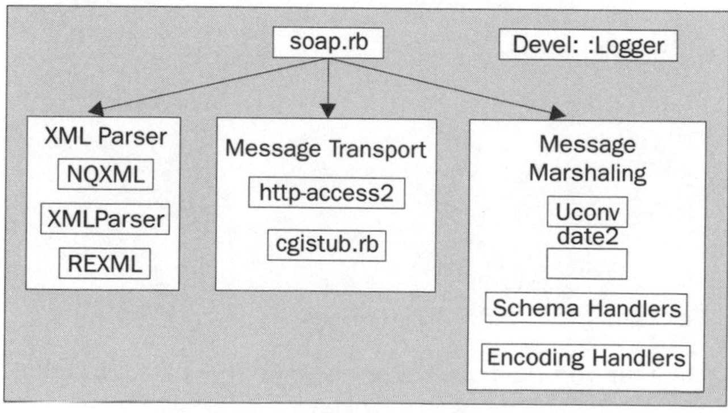

Here are scripts showing the installations of the date2, http-access2, devel/logger, and soap4r classes:

date2

```
/SOAP# tar xfvz date_2-3.tar.gz
/SOAP# cd date2-3
/date2-3# ruby install.rb config
/date2-3# ruby install.rb setup
/date2-3# ruby install.rb install
```

http-access2

```
/SOAP# tar xfz http-access2_D.tar.gz
/SOAP# cd http-access2_D
/http-access2_D# ruby install.rb
```

devel/logger

```
/SOAP# tar xfz devel-logger-1_0_0.tar.gz
/SOAP# cd devel-logger-1_0_0
/devel-logger-1_0_0# ruby install.rb
```

soap4r

```
/SOAP# tar xfz soap4r-1_4_3.tar.gz
/SOAP# cd soap4r-1_4_3
/soap4r-1_4_3# ruby install.rb
```

SOAP4R Stock Client

This program is very similar to sample programs presented in Perl and Python that access time-delayed stock quotes via http://services.xmethods.com/soap/. Here is a diagram showing the general flow of the client request to the remote service:

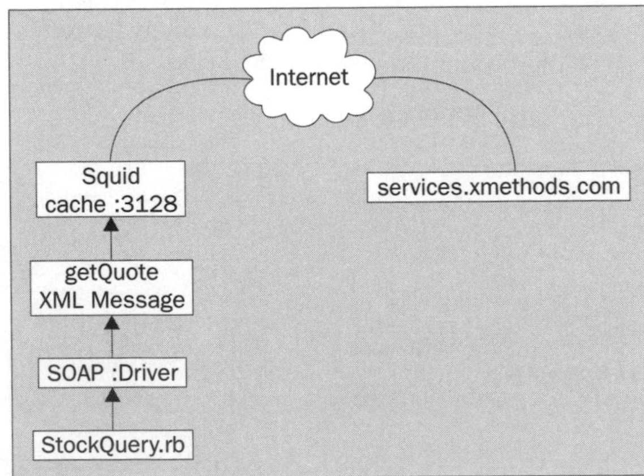

We start by including the required modules and setting variable passes to the SOAP::Driver class constructor:

```
#!/usr/bin/env ruby
require "soap/driver"

log = Log.new("/tmp/getquote.log")

logId = 'getQuote'
server = "http://services.xmethods.com/soap"
namespace = "urn:xmethods-delayed-quotes"
proxy = "http://cache:3128/"
```

We use the `SOAP::Driver` object below to point to the remote SOAP server and set its various parameters. This is quite similar to that used in other implementations and it is well worth comparing this script to, the ones presented in Python. The function prototype is:

```
SOAP::Driver.new(log, logId, namespace, endPoint, proxy, soapAction)
```

- `log`, `logID`
  These allow logging SOAP activity using the simple logging API defined in the `devel-logger` Ruby package. If `nil` values are passed in, no logging is done; if a `log` object is passed in, that will be used to manage the output.
- `namespace`
  This represents the URN that allows accessing different groupings of SOAP methods that may be supported on a server.
- `endpoint`
  This indicates the URL to which SOAP requests are to be passed.
- `proxy`
  This may be used to indicate a proxy server through which requests should be routed. This is generally used when the client sits behind a firewall, and all web requests going to the Internet pass through a proxy such as Squid.
- `soapAction`
  This indicates the `SOAPAction` value to be passed as part of the HTTP header. The `log`, `proxy`, and `SOAPAction` parameters may be left as `null`, and SOAP4R will use default/blank values.

We create the `SOAP::Driver` object and set it to `drv` as follows:

```
drv = SOAP::Driver.new( log, logId, namespace, server, proxy )
```

In Ruby, it is necessary to explicitly attach the methods that are to be used to the driver object using `addMethod()`. That differs from other scripting languages, where it may not even be necessary to name the methods before calling them. When this method is invoked, the method `getQuote(symbol)` is attached to `drv`:

```
drv.addMethod( "getQuote", "symbol" )
stocks = ["RHAT", "IBM", "MSFT", "AMR", "LNUX", "NT", "TSG"]

print "Stock    Price\n"
print "===============\n"

stocks.sort.each do |stock|
  printf("%6s %8.3f\n", stock, drv.getQuote(stock))
end
```

Running this script using the command `ruby StockQuote.rb` should produce the following output:

```
Stock    Price
================
   AMR   20.000
   IBM   80.550
  LNUX    0.840
  MSFT   51.660
    NT    1.600
  RHAT    5.000
   TSG   38.690
```

A sample SOAP message submitted by the script looks like the following:

```
<?xml version="1.0" ?>
<env:Envelope xmlns:xsd="http://www.w3.org/2001/XMLSchema"
xmlns:env="http://schemas.xmlsoap.org/soap/envelope/"
xmlns:xsi="http://www.w3.org/2001/XMLSchema-instance">
<env:Body>
<n2:getQuote xmlns:n1="http://schemas.xmlsoap.org/soap/encoding/"
xmlns:n2="urn:xmethods-delayed-quotes"
env:encodingStyle="http://schemas.xmlsoap.org/soap/encoding/">
<symbol xsi:type="xsd:string">AMR</symbol>
</n2:getQuote>
</env:Body>
</env:Envelope>
```

The response messages returned by the remote server runs a Java-based application server and isn't of any particular interest here. We will look at the response message in the later section when we explore our deployed service.

A Server Sampler Using SOAP4R

We now move on to the server side, constructing a set of SOAP services using SOAP4R. The server `pserver.rb` provides a wrapper for a set of SOAP methods, along with a client to access them.

The example here provides a server that supports a set of simple actions that demonstrate how values are transformed when they are passed from server to client, as well as a more complex method that performs some calculations on a more complex set of data that is passed in by the client, returning a combination of values and, perhaps, faults.

The following UML diagram characterizes the set of classes that are implemented in the server:

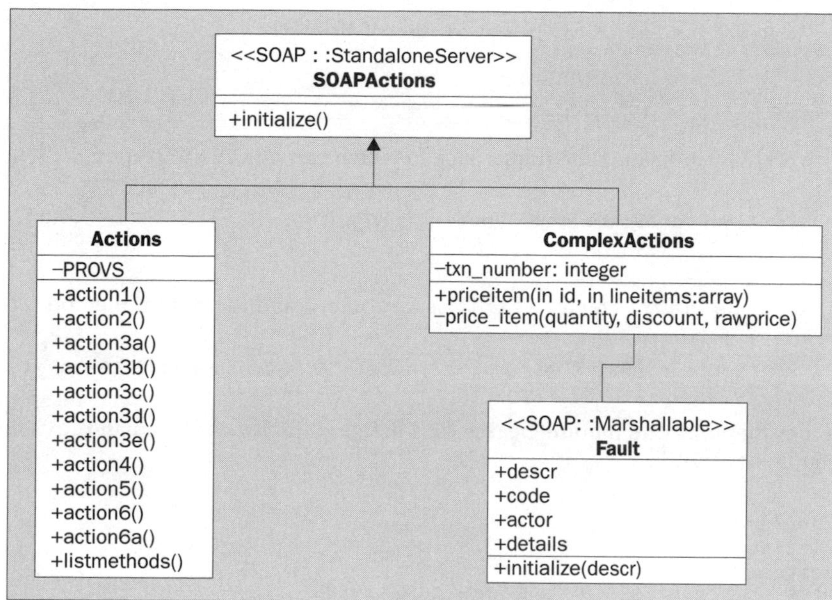

We will be going into more details off the implementations of the assortment of methods a little later.

Test Actions – Actions

We will start by discussing the 'driver' code. It imports SOAP modules as well as the Ruby module files in which the `Actions` and `ComplexActions` classes are implemented. It then creates a class, `SoapActions`, which mixes these methods together to create a combined class as shown below:

```
#!/usr/bin/env ruby
require 'soap/standaloneServer'   # Draw in SOAP methods
require 'Actions'                 # Draw in our methods to export
require 'ComplexActions'          # Draw in pricing method
class SoapActions                 # Now, create a class combining the sets of
  include Actions                 # actions to be supported.
  include ComplexAction
end
```

`SOAPActions` ultimately becomes the object serving SOAP requests from the clients. Its initialization method creates an instance of the 'mixed-in' class, `SoapActions`, and adds each of the methods from `SoapActions` to generate a 'dispatch table' that indicates which SOAP methods are supposed to exist:

```
class SOAPActions < SOAP::StandaloneServer
  def initialize (*arg)
    super             # Perform inherited initialization for superclass
    aServant = SoapActions.new   # Create servant instance
    aServant.listmethods.each do |method|
      addMethod(aServant, method)   # Add all methods from Actions
    end
```

It also explicitly adds in a SOAP method for `priceitems(id, lineitems)`:

```
addMethod(aServant, 'priceitems', 'id', 'lineitems')
    addServant(aServant)
  end
end
```

Then it sets up a URN, indicating the namespace to which this object will respond:

```
urn = 'http://www.cbbrowne.com/sample'
port = 7928
```

Finally, `SOAPActions.new()` creates a SOAP server object, and the `start` method sets it going:

```
status = SOAPActions.new('SOAPActions', urn, '0.0.0.0', port).start
```

The definition of the `Actions` module begins with defining the list of Canadian provinces as an instance variable, `@PROVS`:

```
#!/usr/bin/env ruby
module Actions
  def initialize
    @PROVS = ['ON', 'QC', 'NB', 'NF', 'NS', 'MB', 'SK', 'AB', 'BC', 'PE']
  end
```

The method `action1()` is about the most basic SOAP method possible, returning a simple string:

```
def action1
    return 'action1() returns a simple string'
end
```

Unfortunately, SOAP4R does not yet support SOAP Faults, so the method is left as just a placeholder. Eventually, there may be an appropriate Fault method for `action2()` to return:

```
def action2
    # SOAP4R does not support returning faults
end
```

Methods `action3a()`, `action3b()`, and `action3c()` compute and return the value `275` in three different ways to demonstrate the differences in the values returned:

```
def action3a
  return 275
end
```

Ruby works in much the same manner as Python, where types are associated with values, not variables, but where those values are (fairly) strongly typed:

```
def action3b
  return 275 + 0.0
end
```

Notice in `action3c()` the use of a sequence; the sequence is itself an object, with associated methods, notably `each()`:

```
def action3c
    total = 5.0
    (0..26).each do
      total = total + 10
    end
    return total
  end
```

Two additional methods show how Ruby values may be forcibly coerced into a specified type in much the same manner as would be used in Python:

```
def action3d
  value = 275
  return Float(value)
end
```

Notice how `action3e()` makes reference to the `action3d()` method, and how that reference looks like either a reference to a function or to a variable. If there were a variable called `action3d()`, that value would be used instead of calling the function:

```
def action3e
    return Integer(action3d)
  end
```

Method `action4()` returns a set of randomly selected values embedded in a Ruby array. It uses both array indexing to add items to the array, as well as the `concat()` method. There are over 60 Ruby methods available to manipulate arrays:

```
def action4
  array = Array.new
  (0..7).each do |v|
    array.push (Integer(v * v + 3 * rand(4) - 2) / 4.0)
  end
  array.concat(["this", "that", "other", "42", 42])
  return array
end
```

Method `action5()` sets up a hashtable, equivalent to an awk associative array or a Python dictionary, assigning a mixture of integers and strings as keys and values:

```
def action5
  dict = Hash.new
  (-17..473).each do |val|
    dict[val] = val * val + 3 * rand(2) + rand(7)
  end
  dict['n1'] = 'name 1'
  dict['n2'] = 'name 2'
  return dict
end
```

The analogous method in the Perl example that we saw in Chapter 6 was able to use libzlib compression to diminish message size; at this point, SOAP4R offers no such capability, so the resulting message, with over 500 elements, turns out to be quite large, and you may find that it takes quite some time for the method to run and for results to be returned and processed.

Method action6() selects two provinces randomly from the instance variable, @PROVS, collecting them together to be returned:

```
def action6
  prov1 = @PROVS[rand(@PROVS.length)]
  prov2 = @PROVS[rand(@PROVS.length)]
  provres = [prov1, prov2]
  return provres
end
```

Method action6a() puts together a list of 24 randomly-selected provinces, pushing them onto list one by one:

```
def action6a
  list=Array.new
  (0..23).each do
    list.push(@PROVS[rand(@PROVS.length)])
  end
  return list
end
```

We finish off with a method, listmethods(), which returns an array consisting of all of the names of the functions associated with this module. In some of the previous languages, the methods method was defined to handle this purpose; in Ruby, this conflicts with a standard Ruby class method called methods() which is used to return all the methods found in a class, so the function is renamed to listmethods(). It generates the list of methods automatically using the module method, instance_methods():

```
def listmethods
    return Actions.instance_methods
  end
end
```

The instance_methods() method winds up returning just the methods associated with the Actions module; that is true even when the methods are mixed in with those from ComplexAction to generate the class instance that is actually used as the SOAP server. Methods from ComplexAction are not included on the list.

A Pricing Class

Module ComplexAction begins by drawing in module bdb, an interface to the Berkeley database system, used to store price data, and a soap/driver interface that allows mixing the SOAP::Marshallable class into PriceLine.

The bdb class may be needed and may be found at RAA (Ruby Application Archive) as bdb (http://www.ruby-lang.org/en/raa-list.rhtml?name=bdb). There are two Berkeley DB interfaces, bdb1 for the version 1 API; here we use the newer one, API version 2.

Sleepycat Software (http://www.sleepycat.com/) has recently released version 4 of the open source Berkeley DB, which has significantly more featured than earlier versions, now offering multi-node storage supporting load balancing and the ability for applications to survive some failures of database nodes. The basic APIs for data access have not changed dramatically since version 2, a positive sign of good design. If you are using prepackaged libraries from your Linux distribution, it may prove necessary to install additional development libraries for Berkeley DB in order to install bdb.

The attribute txn_number is used to store a transaction ID that is stepped after each price request:

```
#!/usr/bin/env ruby
module ComplexAction
  require 'soap/driver'
  require 'bdb'
  attr :txn_number
```

The module ComplexAction provides the method priceitems, accepting messages as given below.

An integer ID number, id, indicating a customer number. Based on this customer number, priceitems() will apply discounts. In this implementation, customers with ID numbers below 10000 receive a 15% discount.

An array of line items – each line item consists of:

- **An alphanumeric product ID**
  It consists of four letters followed by four digits. If the format differs from that, this is to be considered an error.
- **An integer quantity for product**
  As with the product ID, it is important to validate that the type and value match as expected.

Let's get into the method priceitems(), drawing from the input parameters: the customer ID, id, and the set of products and quantities, in lineitems:

```
  # Only priceitems is a public method
    def priceitems (id, lineitems)
    if id.is_a? (Fixnum)
      # Already a number; keep it that way...
    else
      # SOAP Object with .id attribute
      id = id.id
    end
    # Evaluate inputs
    if (id < 10000)
      discount = 0.15
    else
      discount = 0
    end
```

The ID that is passed in might consist of either of the two:

- A `Fixnum` value
- A SOAP Object value

In Perl-based SOAP::Lite, values generally come in without any of the *tree* information about the attributes of the entity being passed in. In contrast, SOAP4R allows passing in trees of SOAP values as objects of type `SOAP::RPCUtils::Object`. At runtime, the method `instance_variables()` may be used to examine the set of attributes; the `methods` method can be used to examine the set of methods that can be invoked on the object.

Then, a discount rate is determined based on the value of `id`:

```
quantities = Hash.new
faults = nil
faultList = Array.new
# Product Regular expression
preg = Regexp.compile('^' + ('[A-Z]'*4) + ('[0-9]' * 4) + '$')
lineitems.each do |lineitem|
  print "Lineitem: #{lineitem}\n"
  fault = nil
  product = lineitem[0]
  quantity = lineitem[1]
  # validate that product looks like
  # /^[A-Z][A-Z][A-Z][A-Z]\d\d\d\d$/
  if product.instance_of? (String)
    unless preg.match(product) then
      fault = true
      faultList.push(Fault.new("Bad Product id format: #{product}"))
    end
  else
    faultList.push(Fault.new("Product Type Wrong: #{product}"))
    fault = true
  end
  # validate that quantity is a positive integer
  if quantity.instance_of? (Fixnum)
    if quantity < 0
      faultList.push(Fault.new("Quantity < 0: %d" % quantity))
      fault = true
    end
  else
    faultList.push(Fault.new("Quantity not integer "))
    fault = true
  end
  if fault
    # report fault
    faults = true
  else
    if quantities[product]
      quantities[product] = quantities[product] + quantity
    else
      quantities[product] = quantity
    end
  end
end
```

Now, quantities is set up as a hashtable to store the quantity of each product requested for pricing, and faults and faultList are set up to collect information about any problems that occur.

The Regexp class is used to compile preg, a regular expression matcher used to validate the format of the product codes, making sure they look like FGHI1234 or ZYXW987, where four uppercase letters must be followed by four digits.

Each line item from lineitems is drawn out of Array, into product and quantity, and the data is validated against the requirements:

- The product ID is validated against the regular expression in preg
- The quantity is required to be a positive integer

If any problems are found, the items in error are added to faultList. Otherwise, the quantities are added into quantities[]:

```
class Fault
  include SOAP::Marshallable
  attr_reader :descr, :code, :actor, :details
  def initialize (*iTems)
    @descr = iTems[0]
  end
end
```

The Fault class generates an object-structured return value to pass back fault information. The natural future extension would be for it to support the same sort of structure supported by SOAP, with fault code, actor, string, and details. To that end, there are attributes code, actor, descr, and details. Only the descr attribute is used at present.

If any problems were encountered in the first phase of the process, evaluation ends, and faults are returned:

```
    # If there's a problem, return with some sort of fault...
    if faults
      return "Fault found in Phase 1\n", faultList
    end
```

Next, the transaction number is set up. The method accesses @txn_number, the ComplexAction instance variable, initializing it to 1500 if it hasn't been initialized, and transforming it into a Transactionid to pass back to the requesting process:

```
    if @txn_number
      @txn_number += 1
    else
      @txn_number = 1500
    end
    # Turn txn_no into a "transactionid" object
    txn_no = Transactionid.new(txn_number)
```

Here is the class `Transactionid` that is used to generate this output object:

```
  class Transactionid
  include SOAP::Marshallable
  attr_reader :transactionid
  def initialize (*iTems)
    @transactionid = iTems[0]
  end
end
```

Now, class `BDB::Btree` is used to connect to the Berkeley database, used as the repository for product prices. Notice that the prices are stored as `String` values, not as `Fixnum` values:

```
      pdb = BDB::Btree.open '/tmp/prices', nil, BDB::CREATE |
                                                 BDB::TRUNCATE,
      0644, "set_pagesize" => 1024, "set_cachesize" => [0, 32 * 1024, 0]

    # Attach some prices...
    pdb['ABCD1236'] = '42.50'
    pdb['ABCD1235'] = '72.75'
    pdb['ABCD1234'] = '2742'
```

Now comes the work of the method. The arrays `pricing` and `faultList` are respectively used to store the pricing information, or, if no pricing is found, a report of errors is stored:

```
    pricing = Array.new
    faultList = Array.new
    faults = nil
    quantities.each_key do |product|
      price = pdb[product]
      if price
        pricing.push([product, price_item(quantities[product],
                                          discount, price.to_f),
                     quantities[product]])
      else
        faults = true
        faultList.push(Fault.new("Price not found for %s" % product))
      end
    end
    pdb.close
```

The private method `price_item()` performs the price calculation. Note that it won't be visible outside the `ComplexAction` module:

```
  private
    def price_item (quantity, discount, rawprice)
      return quantity * rawprice * (1 - discount)
    end
  end
```

Finally, it is time to return the results. If a fault was found in the second phase, it is returned along with the valid results:

```
  # If there's a problem - gripe!
    if faults
      return txn_no, pricing, faultList
    end
    return txn_no, pricing
  end
```

If the main script was named `server.rb`, then you may start up the server using the following command:

```
% ruby server.rb
```

This will block awaiting client requests. You might instead push it into a background process with the command:

```
% ruby server.rb &
```

There is also an option of running SOAP4R applications as CGI scripts; the examples bundled in the SOAP4R distribution includes samples of it. A web server such as Apache will invoke a CGI script on demand. Running SOAP services as CGI scripts has both advantages and disadvantages, as follows:

- The web server is responsible for running the CGI code, so there is no need to manually run the server, or to set up a script to automate starting up the server process.
- If CGI server code is modified, the new code will immediately be used the next time a client accesses the service. There is no need to restart the SOAP server.
- Scalability may improve, as web servers often may be configured to have specific policies about what processes they start up.
- If a lot of Ruby classes need to be loaded in each time a SOAP request comes in, the CGI approach will add some latency time as compared to a `SOAP::StandaloneServer` which already has all the code and application configuration data loaded.
- If the server manages some form of 'persistent state' that needs to be shared across all use of the service, such as the transaction ID `txn_no` in the example, it may be necessary for a CGI version to use some transactional storage system to manage that data.

For a more complex set of SOAP services, ensuring high scalability likely involves running the services as CGI scripts that use a relational database with transaction support to manage any persistent data.

A Sampler Test Client

To go along with the server, we will develop a test client `pclient.rb`, which tests out the methods implemented in `pserver.pl` above.

You might also wish to try one of the client scripts from one of the other chapters written in Perl or Python to see how they interoperate with the server written in Ruby, or use the Ruby client with one of the other servers. Minor changes may be needed to the URL, namespace, and port number in order to establish communications with the appropriate SOAP server.

The script starts by setting up variables containing all of the parameters needed to set up access to the SOAP server using the Ruby `SOAP::Driver` class:

```
#!/usr/bin/env ruby
require "soap/driver"
log = Log.new('/tmp/RubyClient.log')
logId = 'Sampler'
host='localhost'
port = 7928
url="http://#{host}:#{port}/"
namespace = 'http://www.cbbrowne.com/sample'
proxy = nil
print "SOAP Server at: #{url}\n"
srv = SOAP::Driver.new( log, logId, namespace, url, proxy )
```

The script then proceeds to use the `methods` method to get a list of registered SOAP methods, storing them in `Methods`, and adds them to the current namespace using the SOAP4R method, `addMethod()`:

```
srv.addMethod('listmethods')
Methods = srv.listmethods()

# Add the methods from 'listmethods' to Ruby namespace
Methods.each do |method|
  srv.addMethod( method )
end

# Add ComplexActions method 'priceitems'
srv.addMethod('priceitems', 'id', 'lineitems')
```

Notice the methods in `Methods` are sorted before attaching them to `method`; if that is not done, the methods would be tested out in a more or less random order since the `listmethods()` function does not pass them in any particular order.

A `begin` / `rescue` / `end` block is introduced to cope with any exceptions that might be raised by the SOAP methods. If one of the SOAP methods raises an exception, the program will transfer control to the `rescue` block instead of aborting. That way, if one method happens to be troublesome, the script does not stop dead in its tracks:

```
  Methods.sort.each do |method|
  begin
      res = srv.call(method);
      print "run #{method}\n Result: #{res}\n"
      print " type: ", res.type, "\n"
      if res.is_a? (Array)
        res.each do |item|
          print "  item: #{item}  type: #{item.type}\n"
        end
      end
      print "\n"
  rescue
    print "Error: ", $!, "\n"
  end
end
```

The class CustomerID will be a wrapper to pass structured values in to SOAP methods:

```
  class CustomerID
  include SOAP::Marshallable
  attr_reader :id
  def initialize (*iTems)
    @id = iTems[0]
  end
end
```

The nested set of arrays, lineitems1, lineitems2, lineitems3, and lineitems4 contain a set of products and quantities:

```
lineitems1 = [['ABCD1234', 9], ['ABCD1234', 1],
              ['ABCD1434', 7], ['ABCD1236', 7]]
lineitems2 = [['ABCD1234', 92], ['ABCD134', 1],
              ['ABCD1434', 7], ['ABCD1236', -7]]
lineitems3 = [['ABCD1234', 9], ['ABCD1234', 107],
              ['ABCD1434', 7], ['ABCD1236', 7]]
lineitems4 = [['ABCD1234', 9], ['ABCD1234', 1],
              ['ABCD1236', 7]]
```

Now, the client sets up to submit requests to the priceitems() method. A customerid is generated using the previously presented CustomerID class, randomly generating a customer ID in the range from 5000 to 14998:

```
 [lineitems1, lineitems2, lineitems3, lineitems4].each do |lineitems|
customerid = CustomerID.new(rand(5000) + rand(5000) + 5000)
print "Evaluating customer: #{customerid}\n"
plist = srv.priceitems(customerid, lineitems)
```

If all that is returned by priceitems() is a string, this indicates that priceitems() has passed back a simple string indicating a fault:

```
if plist[0].is_a?(String)
  print "Fault: #{plist}\n"
  dump_fault(plist[1])
```

Otherwise, the result is an array. The first element is the transaction ID, processed, by SOAP4R, as a SOAP::RPCUtils::Object. The transaction ID is drawn out from the transactionid attribute. Then the report begins like this:

```
else
  tobj = plist[0]
  print "\n\nTransaction ID: #{tobj.transactionid}\n",
        "-=" * 35, "\n"
  lineItems = plist[1]
  print "Product          Quantity              Price\n"
  print "-=" * 35, "\n"
```

Each line item is extracted from the SOAP results, and product ID, quantity, and total price is reported on, followed by a summary total:

```
    total = 0
  lineItems.each do |lineItem|
    product, pricing, quantity = lineItem
    print "%8s       %9d      %9.2f\n" % [product, quantity, pricing]
    total += pricing
  end
  print "-=" * 35, "\n"
  print "%8s                          %9.2f\n" % ["Total:", total]
  print "==" * 35, "\n"
```

If a value is found as a third element of the return values (remember, Ruby uses zero-based addressing), `plist[2]`, then the fault information is displayed using `dump_fault()`:

```
      if plist[2]
        dump_fault(plist[2])
      end
      print "\n\n"
    end
end
```

Method `dump_fault()` takes values passed back from structured fault values, pulling out the `descr` attributes:

```
def dump_fault (fault)
  print "Fault:\n", "-=" * 35, "\n"
  fault.each do |element|
    print "FaultElement: #{element.descr}\n"
  end
  print "=-" * 35, "\n"
end
```

We now take a look at the output of the above code. This is done by running the command `ruby pclient.rb` and the output generated is as follows:

```
SOAP Server at: http://localhost:7928/
run action1
 Result: action1() returns a simple string
 type: String

...
run listmethods
action6 ...

type: Array
  item: action6  type: String
  item: action2  type: String
  ...
```

```
Evaluating customer: #<CustomerID:0x402c9fd0>


Transaction ID: 1500
-=-=-=-=-=-=-=-=-=-=-=-=-=-=-=-=-=-=-=-=-=-=-=-=-=-=-=-=-=-=-=-=-=-=-=-=
Product        Quantity           Price
-=-=-=-=-=-=-=-=-=-=-=-=-=-=-=-=-=-=-=-=-=-=-=-=-=-=-=-=-=-=-=-=-=-=-=-=
ABCD1234              10       27420.00
ABCD1236               7         297.50
-=-=-=-=-=-=-=-=-=-=-=-=-=-=-=-=-=-=-=-=-=-=-=-=-=-=-=-=-=-=-=-=-=-=-=-=
  Total:                       27717.50
========================================================================
Fault:
-=-=-=-=-=-=-=-=-=-=-=-=-=-=-=-=-=-=-=-=-=-=-=-=-=-=-=-=-=-=-=-=-=-=-=-=
FaultElement: Price not found for ABCD1434
=-=-=-=-=-=-=-=-=-=-=-=-=-=-=-=-=-=-=-=-=-=-=-=-=-=-=-=-=-=-=-=-=-=-=-=-
...
```

The SOAP messages received and submitted are pretty much as would be expected; the one particularly worth taking a look at is the one returned by `action6a()`, which is the method that returns 23-odd 'province' codes. Just looking at the body, we find the following:

```
<n2:action6aResponse
 xmlns:n1="http://schemas.xmlsoap.org/soap/encoding/"
 xmlns:n2="http://www.cbbrowne.com/sample"
 env:encodingStyle="http://schemas.xmlsoap.org/soap/encoding/">
  <return xsi:type="n1:Array" n1:arrayType="xsd:anyType[24]">
    <item href="#id538651402"></item>
    <item href="#id538651152"></item>
    <item href="#id538651402"></item>
    <item href="#id538651402"></item>
    <item href="#id538650702"></item>
   ...
  </return>
</n2:action6aResponse>
  <item
   xmlns:n3="http://schemas.xmlsoap.org/soap/encoding/"
   id="id538651402" xsi:type="xsd:string"
   env:encodingStyle="http://schemas.xmlsoap.org/soap/encoding/">
     AB
  </item>
  <item
   xmlns:n4="http://schemas.xmlsoap.org/soap/encoding/"
   id="id538651152" xsi:type="xsd:string"
   env:encodingStyle="http://schemas.xmlsoap.org/soap/encoding/">
     PE
  </item>
  ...
</env:Body>
```

This message uses XML `href` elements representation, where reusable references are set up at the end of the message for any string element that is referenced more than once.

In this particular message, the large amount of space required to represent the reusable element more than wastes any of the savings that could be had. It could be worthwhile for large strings that are used many times.

Google Searches Using SOAP4R and google.rb

One of the most popular search engines particularly is Google (http://www.google.com/). Google has made available a Web Services API to allow performing programmed searches.

This is further documented at Google web APIs (http://www.google.com/apis/). To use the API, you must register for a license ID, and search requests must use this as an "authentication token." Current account arrangements limit personal usage to a maximum of 1000 queries per day.

Installation and configuration of `Google::Search` takes place as follows:

- The Ruby code may be found at Ruby/Google (http://www.caliban.org/ruby/ruby-google.shtml). The program archive, `ruby-google-0.4.1.tar.gz`, should be downloaded from that site.
- The downloaded file, `ruby-google-0.4.1.tar.gz`, is then extracted by the command: `tar xfvz ruby-google-0.4.1.tar.gz`.
- Installation normally must be done as root in order to access system directories:

```
/ruby-google-0.4.0# ruby install.rb config
/ruby-google-0.4.0# ruby install.rb install
```

- To allow the `Google::Search` class to access your Google key, you should copy the key obtained from Google into the file `$HOME/.google_key`. The file will contain a key looking something like the following (this is not a valid key and you need to get your own):

```
4COr3MEpgR06/KaxU1qIMshhaS2uH8wI
```

- Then, try out some of the sample scripts in the example directory to see how it may be used. For example, you might try the command `ruby search.rb soap wrox` and this gives the output as follows:

```
soap daterange:2452276-2452396
Result # 1

url = http://xml.apache.org/soap/
snippet =  <b>...</b> May 30, 2001 - Version 2.2 Released, <b>...</b> February 5,
2001 - Version 2.1<br> Released, Click here for a list of changes. About Apache
<b>SOAP</b>, <b>...</b>
title = Apache <b>SOAP</b>
cachedSize = 15k
relatedInformationPresent = true
directoryTitle = Apache <b>SOAP</b>
summary = Java implementation of the <b>SOAP</b> protocol. HTTP and SMTP
transmission are supported. By Apache Software...
hostName =
fullViewableName =
Top/Computers/Programming/Internet/Web_Services/SOAP/Implementations
specialEncoding =
```

```
Result # 2

...
Result # 3

...
---------------------------------
Estimated number of results is 308000.
Your query took 0.038627 seconds.
```

If you look at the examples in the `/examples` directory, you will find that after loading in the `Google` module and the classes defined therein, there are no visible references in the scripts to SOAP. All such references are confined to the internals of the `Google` module; code you write using it does not need to worry about transport details.

The `Google::Search` class has several methods, but a simple query really only requires two of then:

- `new(KEY)`
  This is the prelude function for all searches, submitting the user key (likely stored in `$HOME/.google_key`) to get a session key.
- `search(query, start, max, filter, restrict, safe, lr, ie, oe)`
  This method requests a Google search based on the query and any other parameters, returning some set of results as a `Struct::Response` object.
- There are several additional methods, including `spell()`, to do spell checking, `cache()`, to try to pull web pages from Google's cache, as well as several methods for setting up and validating more sophisticated search queries.

After the `require` 'google' call that is required to include the Google classes, your code does not involve any visible use of SOAP calls. Another simple search can be implemented as follows:

```
#!/usr/bin/env ruby
require 'google'
KEY = File.open("#{ENV['HOME']}/.google_key") {|kf| kf.readline.chomp}
google = Google::Search.new(KEY)
query = 'christopher browne wrox.com'
query << Google::Search.restrict('daterange', 2001, 1, 1)
print 'Query: #{query}'
res = google.search(query)
i = 0
res.resultElements.each do |result|
  i += 1
  print "\n[result: #{i}]\n"
  result.each do |k|
    print "#{k} = #{result.send(k)}\n"
  end
  print "-=" * 35, "\n"
end
```

This script contains no visible references to SOAP calls, and once class methods are imported, you can use them as if they were local function calls.

All you need is to generate the search criteria that actually involve assembling strings locally, and then process the results returned from Google's server.

Ruby and XML-RPC

Ruby can also be used with the XML-RPC protocol using the xmlrpc4r package, which is found at the Ruby Application Archive at http://www.ruby-lang.org/en/raa-list.rhtml?name=XML-RPC. Much like SOAP4R, it can be used with multiple XML parsers discussed previously.

The xmlrpc4r package is more featured than SOAP4R, offering additional functionalities that are not yet implemented by SOAP4R.

xmlrpc4r

The implementation of XML-RPC for Ruby is called xmlrpc4r. It is of somewhat greater maturity than SOAP4R, offering functionality as:

- Extended `FCGI` and `mod_ruby` functionality
  Servers may be assorted and implemented as standalone Ruby programs using `XMLRPC::Server`, CGI programs invoked through a web server using `XMLRPC::CGIServer` (Apache `mod_ruby`), or even FastCGI programs using `FCGI`. Both of these allow embedding the Ruby interpreter process with the web server so that an interpreter process need not be spawned for each request. This reduces the latency time.
- Introspection
  It offers an introspection API providing handlers `system.listMethods()`, `system.methodSignature()`, and `system.methodHelp()`.
- `multicalls`
  The XML-RPC addition of `multicalls`, where multiple message requests may be assembled into a single message, and submitted and returned as a single request. Some servers might support submitting a sequence of operations in a single message submission, like: `srv.multicall( ['rpc.insert', 1, 2, 3], ['rpc.delete', 4])`, which would submit these two XML-RPC messages in a sequence.
- Asynchronous RPC calls
  Clients may submit requests asynchronously, in separate threads. Thus, if there are multiple XML-RPC requests that are expected to be time-consuming, you may submit them concurrently. This allows attaching calls to multiple threads so that they take place concurrently, for example:

  ```
  Thread.new {
    p client.call_async("rpccall.insert", 4, 5)
  }
  Thread.new {
    p client.call_async("rpccall.modify", 7, 9, 11)
  }
  ```

  If there are a number of possibly time-consuming actions they can run concurrently, which may save some of the main thread's time.
- Secure connections using HTTPS and HTTP Authentication
  The xmlrpc4r package supports communication through SSL that is if the `SSL` package from RAA has been installed. It also supports HTTP Basic Authentication. Currently there is no way to use encryption or HTTP authentication headers with SOAP4R.

Of these, only system.listMethods() is particularly useful; it will return a list of all the methods supported by the XML-RPC service. The other two methods are much less useful with a language like Ruby that offers dynamic typing, where methods may accept arguments of any type.

Let's look at a sample server that exposes the functions previously defined in the Actions class via XML-RPC. We start by drawing in the class Actions, previously defined for the SOAP version, creating the class RPCActions to encapsulate those methods, and creating an instance, ActionInstance, as follows:

```
#!/usr/bin/env ruby
require "xmlrpc/server"
require "Actions"
class RPCActions
  include Actions
end
ActionInstance = RPCActions.new
```

The object server is instantiated from XMLRPC::CGIServer. This class is used when the server is to be invoked as a CGI application atop a web server such as Apache. The XMLRPC::Server class could be used instead to have a Ruby server attached to a port:

```
server = XMLRPC::CGIServer.new
```

The add_handler(name, object) call takes all the methods associated with the object, and adds them to the set of XML-RPC methods that will be accepted by the server, attaching the name to the name:

```
server.add_handler("Actions", ActionInstance)
```

The add_multicall option is added in to allow clients to submit XML-RPC messages consisting of multiple requests:

```
  server.add_multicall    # Add the ability to perform multiple calls
                          # in one XML-RPC request
```

The add_introspection function connects in an XML-RPC function called add_introspection that returns a list of all methods being supported by the server:

```
  server.add_introspection # Add in handlers for system.listMethods,
```

It also supports methods system.methodSignature and system.methodHelp. These are intended to provide meta data about the methods. Since Ruby types are associated dynamically with values, rather than with function signatures, these cannot provide much useful information, and so aren't very useful. This functionality is the XML-RPC nearest equivalent to WSDL:

```
# system.methodSignature, system.methodHelp
```

Finally, the serve method causes the XML-RPC server to accept requests. When XMLRPC::Server is used, this involves opening a socket and awaiting requests. When XMLRPC::CGIServer is used, the script will be invoked by a web server, and this method will read input from standard input, and submit results back to standard output:

```
server.serve                 # Service request(s)
```

To be consistent with the previous usage, this script should be placed in `/var/www/soap/xml-rpc.rb`.

To go along with this server, we will need a client, to try out its methods: `xclient.rb`:

```
#!/usr/bin/env ruby
require "xmlrpc/client"
host='localhost'
port = 80
bareurl = "/soap/xml-rpc.rb"
url="http://#{host}:#{port}#{bareurl}"
print "-=" * 35, "\n"
print "XML-RPC URL: #{url}\n"
```

We start by setting up a URL to point to the XML-RPC server. It points to a service invoked as `/soap/xml-rpc.rb` on the local host; if your web server is differently configured, that may need to vary:

```
server = XMLRPC::Client.new2(url)
p "All Methods Available: ", server.call("system.listMethods")
print "-=" * 35, "\n"
```

We connect to the server using the method `XMLRPC::Client.new2(fullurl)`. There is also another method, `XMLRPC::Client.new(server, url, port)`, with three arguments, if that seems preferable.

We start by calling `server.call("system.listMethods")` to see what methods are being exposed:

```
methods = server.call("Actions.listmethods")
p "Methods to be tested: ", methods
```

This has a rather larger list of methods than you might have expected; all of the methods associated with the `Actions` class were exported. In practice, it may be preferable to add methods one by one in order to only include those methods specifically intended to be exported.

Note the `Actions.listmethods` method only draws out the set of methods explicitly defined in `Actions`, which is the list we want to try out.

Now, the methods are sorted, invoked in order, and the results displayed. Watch out for `Actions.action2`, which returns a `null` value, which is not supported by XML-RPC. The XML-RPC call fails, requiring that we protect it using a `rescue` exception control structure:

```
methods.sort.each do |method|
  m = "Actions.#{method}"
  puts "Method: #{m}"
  begin
    ok, parm = server.call2(m)
    if ok then
```

```
        puts "Result: #{parm}"
        puts "Type: #{parm.type}"
      else
        puts "Error:"
        puts parm.faultCode
        puts parm.faultString
      end
    rescue
      print "Error: ", $!, "\n"
    end
  end
```

Finally, we use the `multicall()` functionality to process three XML-RPC calls together in one request:

```
  print "Combine three calls into one XML-RPC request via multicall()\n"
  print "-=" * 35, "\n"
  res = server.multicall (["Actions.action6"],
                          ["Actions.action6a"],
                          ["Actions.listmethods"])

  res.each do |item|
    print "Result: #{item} #{item.type}\n";
  end
  print "-=" * 35, "\n"
```

When using SOAP, we would have to specially design an API in order to support such a grouping of requests in a message. This is quite an attractive feature of XML-RPC.

Future of Ruby Web Services

As a relatively new language, Ruby is undergoing active ongoing development, particularly involving improvements to libraries, but even some to the base language itself. The SOAP4R implementation is somewhat immature at this point, offering only basic HTTP and CGI functionality. Interoperability testing has been leading to releases of new versions, those becoming compatible with more and more common SOAP functionality.

The release of the 'Google' library layered on top of SOAP4R has been encouraging wider spread use of SOAP4R, which should lead to further enhancements. Other relevant libraries such as XML parsers are also undergoing improvements, which bodes well for its use.

Unlike Python, where the proliferation of different SOAP libraries has made it difficult to get behind any one of them, SOAP4R has been undergoing steady improvements since its initial release in July 2000. Recent enhancements have involved making it increasingly multi-threading safe, to improve the ability for multiple threads to concurrently manage and submit messages. WSDL support will hopefully follow.

Embedded Web Services Using kSOAP

There are interesting applications of SOAP in environments that are memory constrained. Examples of these kinds of environments are devices like cell phones or PDAs (Personal Digital Assistant) where both the size of the application (the form factor) and the runtime memory requirements are crucial. Another environment is within a Java Applet, where the size of the applet is important, as it needs to be downloaded over the Internet.

There are two such lightweight SOAP implementations available in Java:

- kSOAP from Enhydra.org – kSOAP is downloadable from http://ksoap.enhydra.org/. It is available in open source via the Enhydra Public License (http://ksoap.enhydra.org/software/license/epl.html).
- Wingfoot SOAP from Wingfoot Software – this is downloadable from http://www.wingfoot.com/products.jsp. It is available for free for commercial as well as non-commercial use, but in binary form and not open source.

Both can work with Java 2 Platform, Micro Edition (J2ME) as well as Java 2 Platform, Standard Edition (J2SE) environments, and have a small client library size (under 20k bytes). While there are other SOAP implementations available for J2SE environments, the small memory footprint of kSOAP and Wingfoot SOAP make them useful for use in applets.

Since our book is focused on open source software, we will be limiting our discussion to kSOAP. For information on Wingfoot SOAP, please refer to its documentation and javadocs at http://www.wingfoot.com/res_library.jsp.

XML Pull Parser

Memory size is a major constraint for J2ME devices. These SOAP implementations optimize in this area by using XML Pull Parsers (XPP).

The more commonly used mechanisms of XML parsing are DOM (Document Object Model) and SAX (Simple API for XML). In DOM-based parsing, the XML parser builds an entire parse tree representation of the document. While this allows a lot of flexibility in manipulating complex XML documents, it is very expensive in terms of memory.

Unlike the tree-based API of DOM, a SAX parser offers an event-based API. The parser reports back parsing events, such as the start or the end of an XML element tag, to the application using a call-back mechanism. SAX has significant memory and speed advantages over DOM as it deals with XML documents on the fly, and does not need to read in the entire XML document into memory. SAX parsers are ideally suited for applications that wish to perform a few simple operations in a large XML document. However, the application code can become fairly involved if complex XML operations need to be performed. More information on SAX can be found at http://www.saxproject.org/.

XML Pull Parsers is a relatively new approach to parsing XML documents. In Pull Parsers, when an event is raised (like an element tag start) the application itself calls the next parse event from the input XML document instead of the parser calling the applications handler methods. Thus a Pull Parser is similar to a 'reader' or a tokenizer. This approach is a simpler programming style with comparable performance than a SAX parser and also has a low memory footprint. The following piece of application code (using the kXML parser) should make this clear; here the `parser.read()` method gets the next parse 'event', in this case the beginning of the XML element start tag `<FAULT>`:

```
ParseEvent event  = parser.read();
if (event.getType() ==Xml.START_TAG &&
        event.getName().trim().equals("Fault"))
{
    // Do something
```

Two major XML Pull Parsers are kXML from Enhydra (http://kxml.enhydra.org/) and XPP3 (XML Pull Parser 3) by Aleksander Slominski of Indiana State University (http://www.extreme.indiana.edu/xgws/xsoap/xpp/). Both kSOAP and Wingfoot SOAP use the kXML Pull Parser.

The drawback of Pull Parsers is that they do not support validation, and they currently lack a standard API interface. However, there is a new Java Specification Request (JSR 172) that aims to define a standard Java API called Streaming API for XML (StaAX) for Pull Parsers. The principal developers of kXML (Stefan Haustein) and XPP (Aleksander Slominski) are also working on a common implementation at http://www.xmlpull.org/.

kSOAP Tutorial

This section will present a tutorial introduction to kSOAP. We will walk through the steps for building a simple kSOAP client application that will first be deployed within an applet and then within a J2ME device.

Installation and Setup

We assume that a JDK is already installed. In case we don't have this installed, we can obtain it from http://java.sun.com/. The version used in this section is JDK v1.3.1.

We can download kSOAP from http://ksoap.enhydra.org/. The kSOAP sourcecode as well as the preverified classes are available at this site. Preverification is an extra step for developing Java classes for J2ME CLDC (Connected Limited Device Configuration). It involves running the 'preverify' tool on the class file. This does a number of sanity tests on the class file and writes out another Java class file (the preverified class). The preverified class can run on any Java Virtual Machine (JVM), however this extra step ensures that the K Virtual Machine (KVM) does not have to perform compile time checks on the class file. The K Virtual Machine is Sun's implementation of the Java 2 Micro Edition, for the Palm Computing Platform (http://java.sun.com/products/cldc/wp/).

Installation of kSOAP involves extracting the `ksoap.zip` file in a directory of choice. We don't need to download kXML as it comes bundled along with kSOAP. We need to download the optional Java file `HttpTransportSE.java` that provides the HTTP transport for J2SE.

The kSOAP Javadocs (`ksoap-doc.zip`) should also be downloaded for reference.

Building a Simple Client Application

The first step for making a SOAP RPC call using kSOAP is to create a `SoapObject` object. This class encapsulates the SOAP `Body` element:

```
SoapObject request = new SoapObject ("urn:wrox", "methodName");
```

The two parameters passed to the SoapObject are the URN (Uniform Resource Name) and the method name of the remote service being invoked. We can now add method parameters for the call using the addProperty() API call. Here, we are adding a parameter called arg0 with value 10:

```
request.addProperty ("arg0", 10);
```

Next, we construct a transport object for sending this SOAP Body to the service endpoint. kSOAP comes with two transport classes namely. HttpTransport and HttpTransportSE:

```
HttpTransport transport = new HttpTransport (serviceUrl, soapAction);
```

Or:

```
HttpTransportSE transport = new HttpTransportSE (serviceUrl, soapAction);
```

The two parameters to the HttpTransport (and HttpTransportSE) constructor are the endpoint URL for the SOAP service and the value of the soapAction HTTP header. The optional HttpTransportSE class is the desktop (J2SE) version of HttpTransport. This is the class that we would use for an applet-based SOAP client.

The HttpTransport class allows SOAP calls over HTTP using the J2ME Generic Connection Framework (GCF). The GCF provides a transport-independent mechanism to make networking and file I/O calls. It is a subset of the API calls available in the java.io and java.net packages (these packages are not available on J2ME). This also helps keep the memory footprint of the J2ME API low. The following is a brief example of the API calls in the framework. Here we show how all connections are created by one common method (Connector.open()):

```
Connector.open ("http://www.wrox.com")      // HTTP connection
Connector.open ("socket://host:80")         // socket connection
Connector.open ("file:/filename.dat")       // File
```

We are now ready to make the SOAP RPC call:

```
Object response = transport.call (request);
```

The response object is the return value from the SOAP call. It needs to be cast into the appropriate return type. For example:

```
String strResponse = (String) response;
```

Please see the online at http://ksoap.enhydra.org/software/documentation/api/ for more details.

Using kSOAP within an Applet

We will now write a Java applet that uses kSOAP to access a Web Service. The particular Web Service that we use is "Currency Exchange Rate" services hosted by Xmethods. This service has a method called getRate() that takes as input the names of two countries and returns the currency exchange rate between them. More information about this service is available at http://www.xmethods.com/ve2/ViewListing.po?serviceid=5.

In order to use kSOAP with an applet (or for that matter any J2SE application), we need to build the optional `HttpTransportSE.java` class. This, as we mentioned earlier, is a nHTTP transport implementation for J2SE, and we had downloaded it earlier from the http://ksoap.enhydra.org/ web site. This class has code (within its `call()` method) to build a SOAP envelope, do a HTTP POST to the service endpoint URL and return the response.

The `HttpTransport` class that comes by default with kSOAP is for use on J2ME only.

The following are the commands for building `HttpTransportSE.java` on Linux/UNIX. This assumes that the kSOAP classes are extracted into the `$KSOAP_HOME` directory.

```
$ CLASSPATH=$KSOAP_HOME:$CLASSPATH
$ export CLASSPATH
$ javac HttpTransportSE.java
$ mv HttpTransportSE.class $KSOAP_HOME/org/kSOAP/transport
```

The corresponding commands on Windows would be very similar, except for the `CLASSPATH` setting:

```
c:\> set CLASSPATH=%KSOAP_HOME%;%CLASSPATH%
```

In the commands above, `$KSOAP_HOME` (`%KSOAP_HOME%` on Windows) points to the directory where `kSOAP.zip` was extracted. This is for our convenience, and not required by kSOAP:

```
$ KSOAP_HOME=/path/to/kSOAP
$ export KSOAP_HOME
```

Or, on Windows:

```
C:> set KSOAP_HOME=C:\kSOAP
```

The code of the applet (`CurrencyConversionApplet.java`) is listed below. We will not go into the details of Java applet programming here:

```
import java.applet.Applet;
import java.awt.Graphics;

import org.ksoap.ClassMap;
import org.ksoap.SoapObject;
import org.kxml.PrefixMap;
import org.ksoap.transport.HttpTransportSE;

public class CurrencyConversionApplet extends Applet {

    static final String METHOD_NAME = "getRate";
    static final String SERVICE_URN = "urn:xmethods-CurrencyExchange";
    static final String SERVICE_URL = "http://services.xmethods.com:80/soap";
    static final String SOAP_ACTION = "";
```

The `paint()` method is the standard method for painting on the applet screen that is invoked by the applet viewer (or web browser) when the applet needs to be drawn. This method takes the names of the two countries as input via the `getParameter()` method. We will later show how this is passed to the applet.

Next, it calls the `getRate()` client proxy method, and displays the response that it gets from it. The response is the currency conversion rate between the two countries:

```
public void paint (Graphics graphics) {
    // Get the country names 'param' values
    String country1 = getParameter ("country1");
    String country2 = getParameter ("country2");
    // Call the client stub method
    String rate = getRate (country1, country2);
    // Display the result (the currency conversion rate)
    graphics.drawString
    ("The currency conversion rate between " + country1
      + " and " + country2 + " is " + rate, 25, 50);
}
```

The client stub method `getRate()` packages the input parameters for the SOAP request and invokes the actual remote method:

```
/**
 * Client side stub method for invoking the Web Service.
 * @param country1 Name of the first country
 * @param country2 Name of the second country
 * @return The currency conversion rate for the two countries
 */
private String getRate (String country1, String country2) {

    HttpTransportSE transport = null;
    Object result             = null;

    try {
        // Build a transport object with the endpoint URL for the
        // service and the SOAP Action HTTP header value
        transport           = new HttpTransportSE (SERVICE_URL,
                                                    SOAP_ACTION);
        transport.debug     = true;
        ClassMap classMap   = new ClassMap();
        classMap.prefixMap = new PrefixMap (classMap.prefixMap,
                                            "currency",SERVICE_URN);
        transport.setClassMap(classMap);

        // Build a SOAP body with the URN of the service and
        // the method name
        SoapObject request = new SoapObject (SERVICE_URN, METHOD_NAME);
        // Set the input parameters for the call
        request.addProperty ("country1", country1);
        request.addProperty ("country2", country2);
        // Make the SOAP call
        result = transport.call (request);

    } catch( Exception e ) {
        // In case of an error, dump the request and response SOAP
        // messages
        e.printStackTrace ();
```

```
                System.out.println ("Request: \n"  + transport.requestDump );
                System.out.println ("Response: \n" + transport.responseDump );
                result = null;
            }
            // Coax the result object into a String and return
            return "" + result;
        }
    }
```

In case of an error, this applet doesn't do a very sophisticated error handling – it just dumps the request and response. The result `Object` is then coerced into a `String` and returned back.

We compile the applet as follows:

```
$ javac CurrencyConversionApplet.java
```

We now need to build a JAR file for the applet, containing the kSOAP API classes and the `CurrencyConversionApplet.class`:

```
$ cp CurrencyConversionApplet.class $KSOAP_HOME
$ cd $KSOAP_HOME
$ jar cvf conversion.jar .
```

Applets run in a sandbox (that is an environment with security restrictions) on the client machine. This ensures that a malicious applet downloaded from the Internet doesn't do damage. Some of the restrictions on an applet are:

- Applets cannot load libraries from the client PC or define native methods. (This is why we had the kSOAP classes packaged along with the applet – having them on the client machine won't help.)
- It cannot read or write files on the host that is executing it.
- It cannot make network connections except to the host that it came from.
- It cannot start any program on the host that is executing it.
- It cannot read certain system properties.

The 'security manager' class on the client machine imposes these restrictions. Users can even implement a custom security manager.

Not being able to open a network connection to any host other than the server from where the applet is downloaded creates a problem, as sending the SOAP request requires a network connection to be opened.

To get around this problem, we could have the applet downloadable from the same server that hosts the SOAP service.

This may not be always possible. An alternative is a 'proxy' approach in which the applet gets downloaded from a server that has a 'pass through' Web Service running which acts as a proxy for the actual service. The applet then opens a network connection to this proxy service, and the proxy service forwards the request to the real web service.

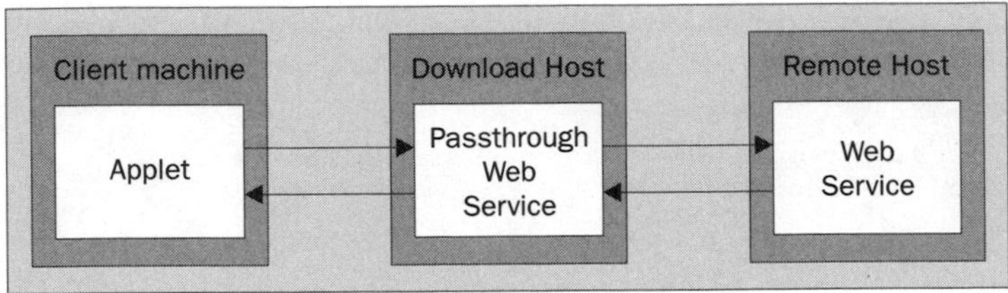

The diagram above shows the proxy approach to solving this problem. In this approach the applet is downloaded from the 'Download Host' server shown in the middle. This host also runs a proxy Web Service. The role of the proxy is to take the client request and pass it to the real SOAP service that runs on the remote host, and gather the response it gets and send it back to the applet. The proxy has the same SOAP method signature(s) as the real Web Service, but these methods do not do any real work other than passing the SOAP packets back and forth.

This approach however requires that the applet change its service endpoint URL to that of the proxy (as shown below) and that a proxy service be developed and deployed on the download host:

```
// PROXY_URL is the URL of the passthrough proxy
transport = new HttpTransportSE (PROXY_URL, SOAP_ACTION);
```

Another approach is to have a signed applet. This avoids making code changes in the applet (sending to a `PROXY_URL` instead of the real service URL), and writing the proxy.

For this, we first need to generate the private and public keys and store them in a keystore. This is done with the `keytool` command as shown below. `keytool` is a key and certificate management utility that comes along with Java Development Kits (JDK):

```
$ keytool -genkey -alias signFiles -keystore wroxstore -keypass wrox123 -dname
"cn=wrox" -storepass wrox321
```

We then make a signed copy of the applet JAR file using the `jarsigner` command as follows:

```
$ jarsigner -keystore wroxstore -storepass wrox321 -keypass wrox123 -signedjar
conversionS.jar conversion.jar signFiles
```

Next, we export the public key certificate. This certificate is distributed with the applet to authenticate the signature on the JAR file:

```
$ keytool -export -keystore wroxstore -storepass wrox321 -alias signFiles -file
wrox.cer
```

We now can write the HTML page (`CurrencyConversion.html`) with the embedded applet tags. These HTML pages can be created using any HTML editor (or even a text editor, since it has very simple HTML code).

The `archive` attribute of the applet tag is set to the signed JAR file (`conversionS.jar`), and the `code` attribute to the applet class name (`CurrencyConversionApplet.class`). The input parameters to the applet are passed via the `<param>` elements inside the applet tag as shown opposite:

```
<html>
  <head>
     <title>Currency Conversion Applet</title>
  </head>
  <body>
    <h1>Currency Conversion Applet</h1>
    <p>
    This applet gives the currency conversion rate between two countries.
    For the details of the service, see
         <a href="http://www.xmethods.com/ve2/ViewListing.po?serviceid=5">
            here
         </a>
    </p>
    <applet code="CurrencyConversionApplet.class"
       archive="conversionS.jar" width=510 height=50>
         <param name="country1" value="usa">
         <param name="country2" value="uk">
    </applet>
  </body>
</html>
```

The HTML page and the signed applet should then be copied in the /htdocs/ (or equivalent) directory of your web server. In our example, this HTML file can be accessed via the URL `http://localhost/CurrencyConversion.html`.

A user that wishes to use this applet would first import this certificate as a trusted certificate. This can be done using the `keytool` command as shown below:

```
$ keytool -import -alias signFiles -file wrox.cer -keystore userstore -storepass
user123
```

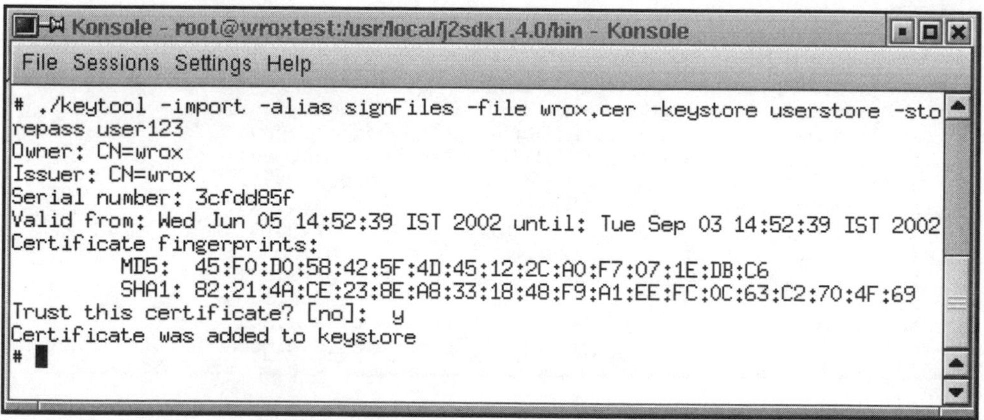

The user then creates a 'policy' file granting the applet the required permissions to do network operations. This policy file can be created either using the `policytool` application or an ASCII editor. A sample policy file (called `user.policy` here) is shown overleaf:

```
/*/* AUTOMATICALLY GENERATED ON Mon May 13 20:52:01 PDT 2002*/
/* DO NOT EDIT */

grant {
  permission java.net.SocketPermission "xmethods.com", "accept, connect, listen,
resolve";
};
```

The user can then run the applet in `appletviewer` as shown below:

```
$ appletviewer -J-Djava.security.policy=user.policy
http://localhost/CurrencyConversion.html
```

The output from the applet is as shown below:

```
The currency conversion rate between usa and uk is 0.68686
```

Further details on signed applets can be found in the Java Developer Connection article at http://developer.java.sun.com/developer/technicalArticles/Security/Signed/.

Had we not used a signed applet, and used the unsigned JAR file (`conversion.jar`), we would have got access denied errors as shown in the screenshot below.

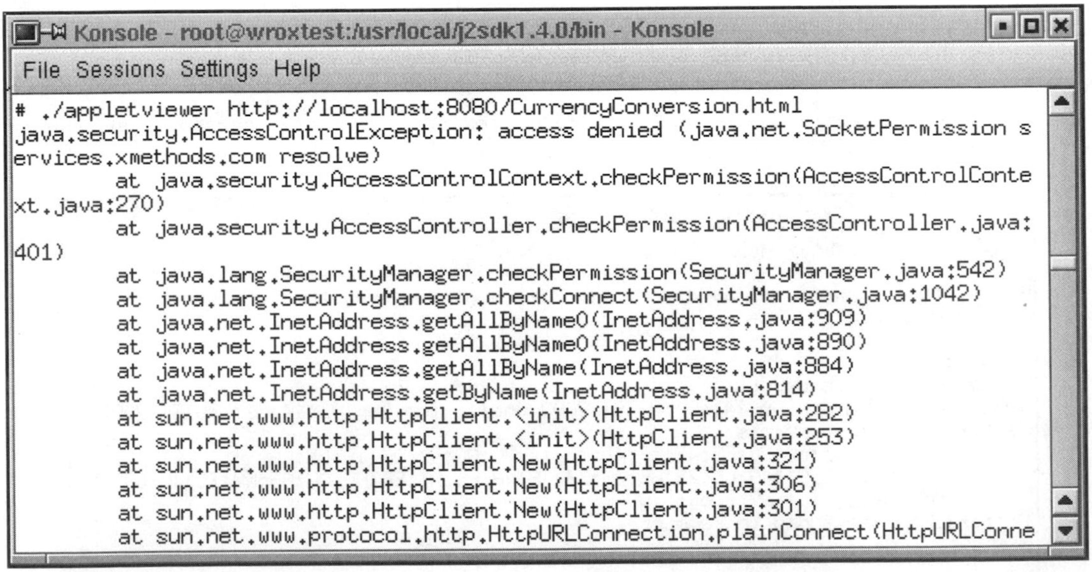

```
Konsole - root@wroxtest:/usr/local/j2sdk1.4.0/bin - Konsole
File Sessions Settings Help
# ./appletviewer http://localhost:8080/CurrencyConversion.html
java.security.AccessControlException: access denied (java.net.SocketPermission s
ervices.xmethods.com resolve)
        at java.security.AccessControlContext.checkPermission(AccessControlConte
xt.java:270)
        at java.security.AccessController.checkPermission(AccessController.java:
401)
        at java.lang.SecurityManager.checkPermission(SecurityManager.java:542)
        at java.lang.SecurityManager.checkConnect(SecurityManager.java:1042)
        at java.net.InetAddress.getAllByName0(InetAddress.java:909)
        at java.net.InetAddress.getAllByName0(InetAddress.java:890)
        at java.net.InetAddress.getAllByName(InetAddress.java:884)
        at java.net.InetAddress.getByName(InetAddress.java:814)
        at sun.net.www.http.HttpClient.<init>(HttpClient.java:282)
        at sun.net.www.http.HttpClient.<init>(HttpClient.java:253)
        at sun.net.www.http.HttpClient.New(HttpClient.java:321)
        at sun.net.www.http.HttpClient.New(HttpClient.java:306)
        at sun.net.www.http.HttpClient.New(HttpClient.java:301)
        at sun.net.www.protocol.http.HttpURLConnection.plainConnect(HttpURLConne
```

Using kSOAP in a Device

In this we will use the same Web Service that we used in the previous example. We now write a Midlet client, similar to the applet we wrote, to communicate to the Web Service.

In J2ME, a Midlet is a Java application for mobile devices. By definition, it needs to conform to the CLDC and Mobile Information Device Profile (MIDP) (http://jcp.org/aboutJava/communityprocess/final/jsr037/index.html). We will not go into the intricacies of J2ME programming in this book.

The code for the Midlet (`CurrencyConversionMidlet.java`) is listed below. A Midlet should extend the `MIDlet` class and at least define a constructor and provide implementations for the `startApp()`, `pauseApp()`, and `destroyApp()` methods. The constructor contains code that is executed only once in the Midlet's lifetime. Thus it should have all initialization code. The `startApp()` method is called each time the application goes from an inactive to an active state. The `pauseApp()` method is called when the application needs to be paused. The `destroyApp()` method is called when the application is no longer needed in memory. In our example, `pauseApp()` and `destroyApp()` do nothing:

```
import javax.microedition.midlet.MIDlet;
import javax.microedition.lcdui.Display;
import javax.microedition.lcdui.Displayable;
import javax.microedition.lcdui.Command;
import javax.microedition.lcdui.CommandListener;
import javax.microedition.lcdui.Form;
import javax.microedition.lcdui.TextBox;
import javax.microedition.lcdui.TextField;

import org.ksoap.ClassMap;
import org.ksoap.SoapObject;
import org.kxml.PrefixMap;
import org.ksoap.transport.HttpTransport;

public class CurrencyConversionMidlet extends MIDlet {

    static final String METHOD_NAME = "getRate";
    static final String SERVICE_URN = "urn:xmethods-CurrencyExchange";
    static final String SERVICE_URL = "http://services.xmethods.com:80/soap";
    static final String SOAP_ACTION  = "";

    private Display      display;
    private CurrencyView view;

    public CurrencyConversionMidlet () {
        display = Display.getDisplay (this);
    }

    // Called each time the midlet goes into active state
    public void startApp() {
        view = new CurrencyView (this, display);
        view.displayForm ();
    }

    // Called when the midlet is paused
    public void pauseApp () {
        /* do nothing */
    }

    // Called when the midlet is no longer needed in memory
```

```
    public void destroyApp (boolean unconditional) {
        /* do nothing */
    }

    public void callMethod (String country1, String country2) {
        String result = getRate (country1, country2);
        view.displayResult (result);
    }
```

The client stub that invokes the remote service is identical to that used in the applet example earlier:

```
    /**
     * Client side stub method for invoking the Web Service.
     * @param country1 Name of the first country
     * @param country2 Name of the second country
     * @return The currency conversion rate for the two countries
     */
    private String getRate (String country1, String country2) {

        HttpTransport transport = null;
        Object result           = null;

        try {
            // Build a transport object with the endpoint URL for the
            // service and the SOAP Action HTTP header value
            transport          = new HttpTransport (SERVICE_URL,
                                                    SOAP_ACTION);
            transport.debug    = true;
            ClassMap classMap  = new ClassMap();
            classMap.prefixMap = new PrefixMap (classMap.prefixMap,
                                             "currency",SERVICE_URN);
            transport.setClassMap(classMap);

            // Build a SOAP body with the URN of the service and
            // the method name
            SoapObject request = new SoapObject (SERVICE_URN, METHOD_NAME);
            // Set the input parameters for the call
            request.addProperty ("country1", country1);
            request.addProperty ("country2", country2);
            // Make the SOAP call
            result = transport.call (request);

        } catch( Exception e ) {
            // In case of an error, dump the request and response SOAP
            // messages
            e.printStackTrace ();
            System.out.println ("Request: \n"  + transport.requestDump );
            System.out.println ("Response: \n" + transport.responseDump );
            result = null;
        }
        // Coax the result object into a String and return
        return "" + result;
    }

} /* class CurrencyConversionMidlet */

class CurrencyView {

    private CurrencyConversionMidlet model;
```

```
    private Display                   display;

    public CurrencyView (CurrencyConversionMidlet model, Display display) {
        this.model   = model;
        this.display = display;
    }

    // Display the input form
    public void displayForm() {

        Form form           = new Form ("Currency Exchange Rate");
        TextField country1 = new TextField ("Country 1", null, 50, 0);
        TextField country2 = new TextField ("Country 2", null, 50, 0);
        form.append (country1);
        form.append (country2);
        form.addCommand (new Command ("Submit", Command.OK, 1));
        form.addCommand (new Command ("Exit", Command.EXIT, 1));
        form.setCommandListener
             (new CurrencyListener (model, country1, country2));
        display.setCurrent(form);

    } /* displayForm */

    // Display the result
    public void displayResult (String result) {
         TextBox textBox = new TextBox ("Currency Result",
                                              result, 256, 0);

         textBox.addCommand (new Command ("Exit", Command.EXIT, 1));
         textBox.setCommandListener (new
                    CurrencyListener (model,null,null));
         display.setCurrent (textBox);
    }

} /* class CurrencyView */

class CurrencyListener implements CommandListener {

    private CurrencyConversionMidlet model;
    private TextField country1;
    private TextField country2;

    public CurrencyListener (CurrencyConversionMidlet model,
                             TextField country1,
                             TextField country2) {
        this.model    = model;
        this.country1 = country1;
        this.country2 = country2;
    }

    // The event handling method: This gets called when the
    // user selects either the 'submit' or the 'exit' button.
    public void commandAction(Command c, Displayable d)  {
        if (c.getLabel().trim().equals("Submit")) {
            // Take the user's input and call the SOAP method stub
            model.callMethod (country1.getString().trim(),
                              country2.getString().trim());
        } else if (c.getLabel().trim().equals("Exit")) {
            model.destroyApp (false);
            model.notifyDestroyed ();
```

```
            }
        }
    } /* class CurrencyListener */
```

To build and run this Midlet, we use Sun's J2ME Wireless Toolkit. This toolkit is available for free from http://developer.java.sun.com/developer/releases/j2mewtoolkit/. The only prerequisite for this toolkit is JDK 1.3 or later.

Start the toolkit (`KToolbar`) and create a new project in it (**File->New Project** option). We name this project as `CurencyConversion`. We also are asked for a Midlet class name. Here we enter `CurrencyConversionMidlet`.

We then copy the `CurrencyConversionMidlet.java` file that we had written earlier into the new project's source directory. Here, `/path/WTKHome/` is the directory where the J2ME Wireless Toolkit is installed:

```
$ cp CurrencyConversionMidlet.java /path/WTKHome/apps/CurrencyConversion/src
```

Next, we create a JAR file with the kSOAP classes and copy them to the project's `/lib` directory. Here, `$KSOAP_HOME` is the directory where `ksoap.zip` was extracted, and `/path/WTKHome/` is the install location of the J2ME toolkit:

```
$ cd $KSOAP_HOME
$ jar cvf ksoap.jar .
$ cp ksoap.jar /path/WTKHome/apps/CurrencyConversion/lib
```

Now we are ready to build the project (**Project->Build** option):

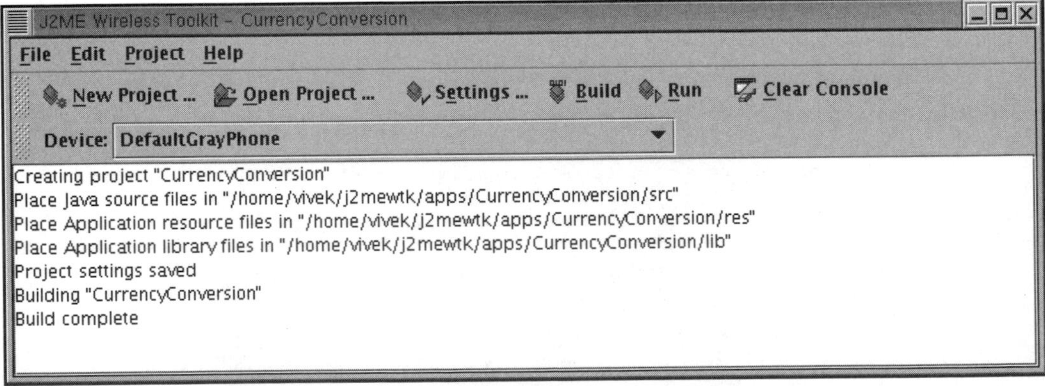

We can now test the application out in an emulator from within the toolkit itself. This can be done by first selecting the emulation device via the **Device** tab (**DefaultGrayPhone**), and then running the application on this emulator using the **Project->Run** option.

The screenshot below shows the DefaultGrayPhone emulator running the Midlet:

After entering the input values USA and UK, we can invoke the service. The response is shown in the next screenshot:

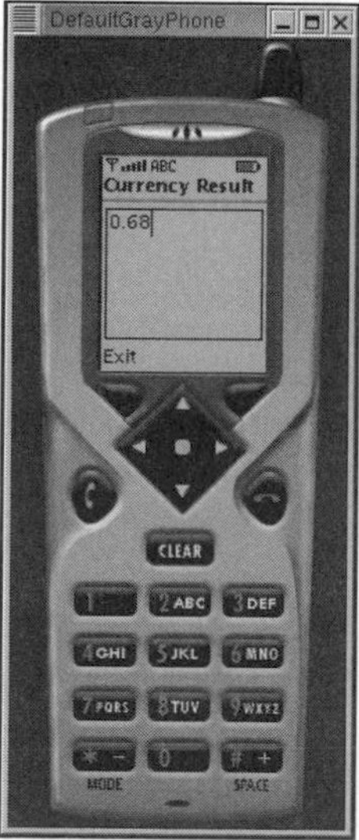

For a list of valid input values of this service, see the service description page at http://www.xmethods.com/ve2/ViewListing.po?serviceid=5.

Summary

We have explored the use of SOAP with Ruby, the 'gem of a language.' We saw the following points:

- A sample application to access public stock information was used to introduce the use of SOAP4R to write clients.
- A server application demonstrated the use of various data types, as well as how to run SOAP servers written in Ruby.
- We also saw a library layered on top of SOAP4R that allowed submitting queries to the popular Google search engine. A user code that makes use of the 'Google' Ruby class does not need to make any direct reference to SOAP classes or methods.
- Ruby's other Web Services library, xmlrpc4r, provides some useful functionality that is currently unavailable with SOAP4R.

At present, the functionality of the SOAP4R library is somewhat weak in comparison with the tools existing for other languages for Web Services. There is ongoing active development and use of SOAP4R, so it is to be expected that functionality will improve.

In embedded Web Services we were introduced to two small footprint SOAP clients (kSOAP and Wingfoot SOAP) and we explored kSOAP in some detail:

- We saw the use of SOAP in applets and in memory-limited J2ME devices.
- The Midlet that we developed was not a very complex application; the size of the JAR file was not excessive. The un-obfuscated JAR was a little over 40k in size – and this included the SOAP client and the XML parser.

But does SOAP make sense on such devices? This is a valid question, and one that has no right answer. A Web Service client on a cell phone or a PDA may look like overkill for some applications, especially if there is a large amount of XML data being transferred. However, given the number of packaged custom-developed enterprise applications that are being exposed via SOAP interfaces, it is essential that we do not dismiss them. To add to that, there are a number of devices with varied display capabilities, and to build Wireless Application Protocol (WAP)-enabled interfaces for all of them may not be practical.

11

Case Study – Designing Web Services from Legacy Modules

This chapter is a comprehensive case study that combines various technologies used for a single application. This case study will demonstrate some substantial examples of Web Services. This will involve adding some SOAP interfaces to automate data entry for an accounting application called SQL-Ledger.

In our case study, the SQL-Ledger application is being used by an Internet Service Provider (ISP). We'll automate some processes required for this ISP for its accounting department. We will look at the following three processes, in particular:

- Submitting billings on a monthly basis for each subscriber of the ISP
- Discontinuing the service for customers that have not been paying their bills for over a particular period
- Defining a number of methods to access locality information, specifically, US Zip codes, and look at their relative performance

SQL-Ledger

Before we start with automating these processes, let us get introduced to the accounting application, SQL-Ledger. Our SQL-Ledger is a web-based accounting package written in Perl, which executes as a CGI application, and stores and retrieves data using the Perl `DBI` database interface.

SQL-Ledger may not be the most sophisticated accounting solution to satisfy complex requirements, but may be suitable for small or medium-sized businesses. For exposition purposes, it has a realistic set of tables to contain accounting information, and is freely available at http://sql-ledger.org.

It provides the set of modules expected for basic business accounting, including:

- General Ledger
- Accounts Receivable
- Accounts Payable
- Order Entry (including purchasing and sales entries)
- Inventory (including management of parts, assemblies of parts, and services)

In this case study, we add some SOAP interfaces to support the needs of the ISP. Hence, it will be compatible with several web servers including Apache. The use of SOAP also allows relatively easy construction of an API connecting to SQL-Ledger that allows the ISP to automate the intended functionality. This SOAP-based functionality will add a set of SOAP methods to perform the actions.

We might illustrate the overall architecture of the system as follows:

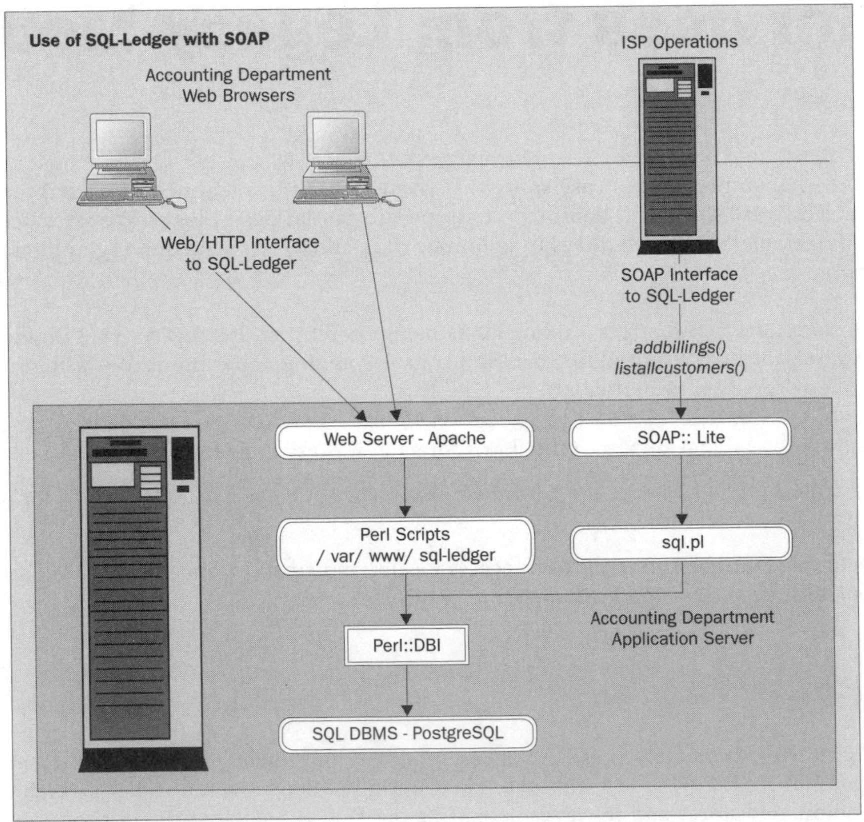

Though we will be adding additional functionality, the existing functionality of SQL-Ledger remains completely unchanged. Users in the accounting department of the ISP can access it using the standard web browser as a front-end, and the code will run as a set of CGI scripts written in Perl that access the SQL database. This approach may be described as exposing legacy applications to Web Service interfaces.

Since the application stores data in the PostgreSQL relational database, it is easy to have more tables to support additional local requirements, if required. Also, if we add an interface supporting the ISP's complete functionality, it really doesn't even need to log on to the application. It can simply schedule the interfaces to run as `cron` jobs, which will automatically execute all its tasks.

Technologies Used

As said earlier, we'll use various technologies to develop our Web Service in this case study. Here, we need to have a web server, a language to write the client and the server that can access a relational database, and a SOAP library for the language to develop the Web Service.

Configuring Apache

We need to indicate Apache the location of SQL-Ledger CGI scripts, and ensure that our Perl scripts can be run. This would involve modifying the `httpd.conf` file as shown below:

```
AddHandler cgi-script .pl
Alias /sql-ledger/ /var/www/sql-ledger/
Alias /soap/ /var/www/soap/
<Directory /var/www/sql-ledger>
  Options ExecCGI
</Directory>
<Directory /var/www/soap>
  Options ExecCGI
</Directory>
```

Here, we instruct Apache that the `.pl` files should be treated as CGI scripts. We also specify that URLs accessing `sql-ledger` and `soap` should map to the files in the respective directories. For example, the URL http://localhost/soap/something.pl will be directed to the CGI script `/var/www/soap/something.pl`. The `<Directory>` entries indicate that CGI scripts are permitted to execute in the respective directories. These entries may be augmented to include additional access controls. Once we do the desired changes to `httpd.conf` file, we need to restart Apache.

For more information on installing and configuring Apache web server, you may refer to the book *Professional Apache 2.0* from *Wrox Press (ISBN 1-861007-22-1)*, or http://httpd.apache.org/.

Configuring PostgreSQL

We'll use PostgreSQL as our database server (the SQL-Ledger is not compatible with MySQL). We may want to install `postgresql-devel` to compile Perl components from scratch, if needed. We also need to ensure that necessary PostgreSQL security configuration is done, so that connections to the database server are allowed. It is commonly found in `/etc/postgresql/pg_hba.conf`, and `/etc/postgresql/pg_ident.conf`.

You may refer to *Beginning Databases with PostgreSQL* from *Wrox Press (ISBN 1-861005-15-6)*, or http://postgresql.org, for more details on the configuration and use of PostgreSQL.

For our case study, PostgreSQL should allow Perl to access the database server over TCP/IP. By default, PostgreSQL doesn't allow remote TCP/IP access, and it may even deny local TCP/IP access. Hence, the configuration may need to be changed to allow network access. This can be carried out by modifying `postgresql.conf` with the following option:

```
tcpip_socket = 1
```

To bring the above changes into effect, we'll now restart the PostgreSQL database server.

Note that if there is any database configuration problem, the `DBI` methods are likely to fail, reporting back the faults with data similar to the following (which was achieved by shutting down PostgreSQL and running the sample client):

```
Fault actor:http://salesman:7957/
Fault code:SOAP-ENV:Server
Fault string:DB Error
```

Configuring Perl

Since we need Perl to have database access, we should have the Perl Database Independent Interface (`DBI`) that is available at http://search.cpan.org/search?module=DBI. To access the PostgreSQL database, we should also have the PostgreSQL database driver for the `DBI` module, `DBD::Pg`, which works with `DBI`. Once we have `DBI` and `DBD::Pg`, we can use TCP/IP connections to connect to PostgreSQL. To create the SOAP-based Web Services for our application, we'll need to have the Perl SOAP library `SOAP::Lite` that we covered in Chapter 6.

Installing SQL-Ledger

Now, we need to download the SQL-Ledger 1.8.4 from http://www.sql-ledger.org/. Since web applications are preferably stored in `/var/www`, we'll install the SQL-Ledger code in the `/var/www/sql-ledger` directory:

```
% cd /var/www
% tar xfvz /tmp/sql-ledger-1.8.4.tgz
```

Creating the Database

First, we need to create the database we'll use for our SQL-Ledger. The SQL scripts residing in `/var/www/sql-ledger/sql` will need to be run to populate the database with the tables required by the application.

First, let's create the PostgreSQL database `sqlleger` required for the application:

```
% createdb sqlledger
```

Once we have the database ready, we'll need to run a few more SQL scripts to build our database:

```
% psql sqlledger < Pg-tables.sql
% psql sqlledger < createindex.sql
% psql sqlledger < Default-chart.sql
% psql sqlledger < US_General-chart.sql
% psql sqlledger < Canada_General-chart.sql
```

First, we run the `Pg-tables.sql` script to create the SQL-Ledger tables, and then the `createindex.sql` script to create indices for these tables, which will improve performance of our queries.

The `Default-chart.sql` script generates a default chart of accounts, that is, a list of account numbers and descriptions to be used in the general ledger. This chart helps to classify the company activities by providing information like various categories of revenues, expenses, assets, and liabilities.

Then we run the `US_General-chart.sql` and `Canada_General-chart.sql` scripts that contain a set of accounts characteristics specific to the United States of America and Canada respectively. However, several other scripts are also available containing sample charts of accounts for other countries.

Connecting to SQL-Ledger

Once the database is present, and the web server has been configured to execute the SQL-Ledger CGI scripts, we need to connect to the SQL-Ledger application via an administration URL, http://localhost/sql-ledger/login.pl, which will also allow us to set up users who can access it. For more information on SQL-Ledger, please refer to the documentation, `/var/www/sql-ledger/doc/README`. Let's connect to the SQL-ledger application via the administration URL, http://localhost/sql-ledger/login.pl:

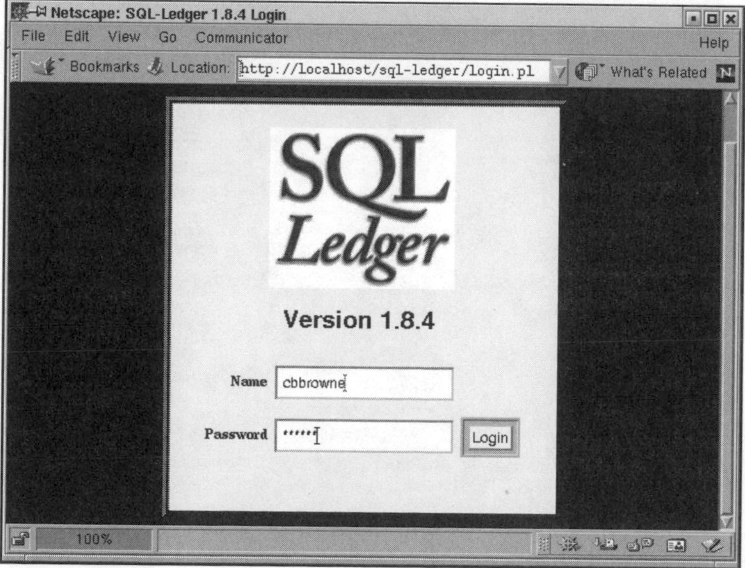

Once we enter a valid name and password, we'll see the main menu as shown in the following screenshot:

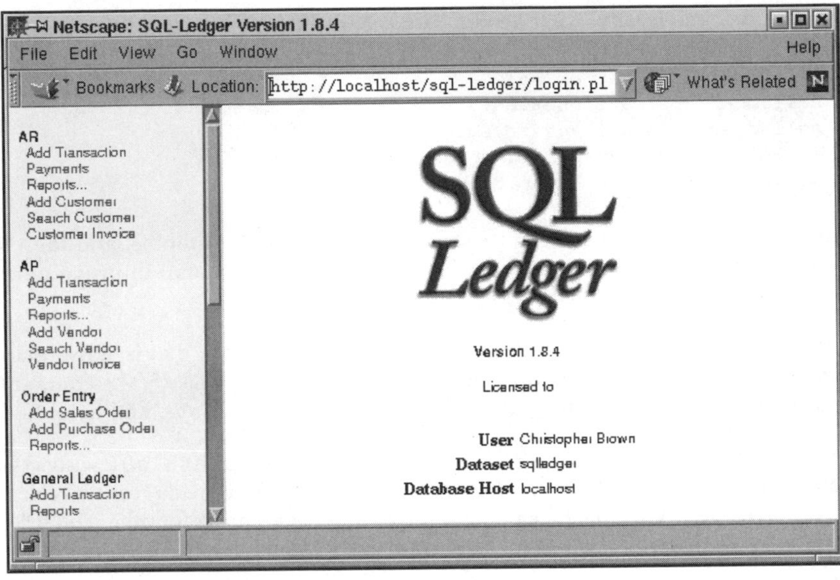

The ISP Billing Application

We'll provide three notable classes of interfaces to connect to SQL-Ledger, as shown in the following diagram:

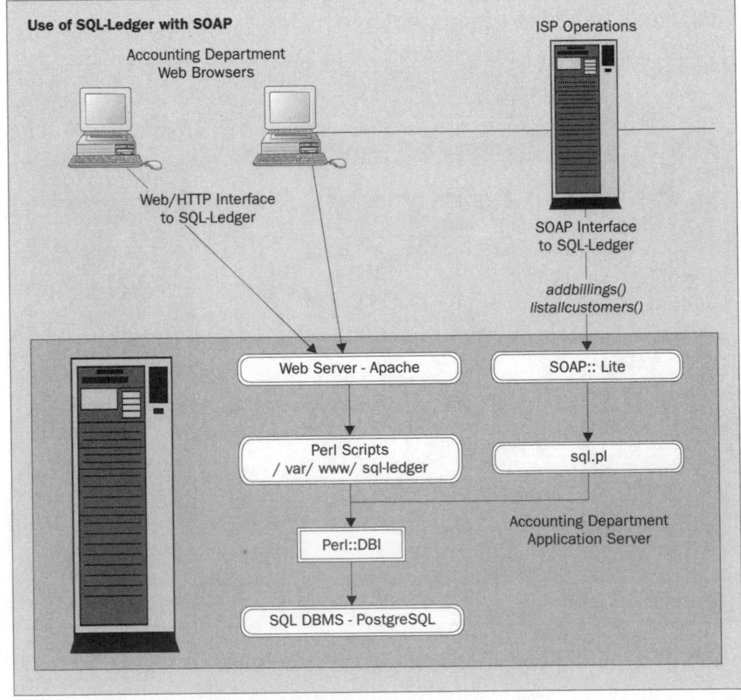

The CustomerQuery.pm module is used to find customers that have not paid their bills, and for whom the service should be discontinued at some point. For this purpose, the module provides three methods. The listallcustomers() method lists all the customers managed in SQL-Ledger, and the listcustomersoverdue() method lists the customers with overdue billings with the period for which they are overdue. The listcustomers() method is used to list further details about the customers queried for.

The AddBilling.pm module automatically submits billings for customers. There is no need for the ISP billing software to have total access to the accounting system. For instance, the system administrators will almost certainly have little to do with handling customer payments. However, they may legitimately have a need to submit customer billings. The AddBilling class contains only one public method, addbillings(), which adds billings for each customer, if an array of customers is given. There are a variety of private methods used to support addbillings(), but they are not exported as part of the SOAP interface.

In module ZipCodes.pm, we provide a set of SOAP methods for requesting information about USA Zip codes. We'll use this general-purpose module to do benchmarking, later in the chapter. This module exports six functions:

- getZipcode()
- getZipcodes()
- getZipcodeNoDB()
- getZipcodeDBNoQuery()
- getZipcodesNoRet()
- getZipcodesNoDBNoResult()

The first two of these would be useful in the normal scheme of things. The last four are variations that eliminate varyious parts of the database processing in order to allow the benchmarks to estimate what proportions of the work are associated with database-related activities as opposed to SOAP-related activities.

Here, we won't do any attempt to provide a comprehensive set of SOAP interfaces to control the complete SQL-Ledger. The environment is actually kept more secure by carefully choosing a set of necessary interfaces, and only exporting them. This will prevent the intruders from misusing any interfaces.

However, in this case study we'll not make use of UDDI or WSDL. UDDI is, as currently deployed, intended to allow publishing of the Web Services an organization offers to the public. The SOAP methods that we'll be developing for the ISP are just intended for use by the operations department, and not by the public at large.

On the other hand, WSDL that describes the Web Services would be more useful than UDDI. However, the ability to automatically generate WSDL in with SOAP::Lite is not mature yet. There is an experimental module called WSDL-Generator (http://search.cpan.org/search?dist=WSDL-Generator). We will access the SOAP services simply via a URL, which is certainly no more challenging than pointing to a WSDL definition.

Building the Server

We first need to build the sql.pl server that supports our SOAP methods. The server script has virtually no application code in it. It draws in a number of Perl classes and attaches the required methods to the SOAP server via the dispatch_to() function:

```
#!/usr/bin/perl
# $Id: sql.pl,v 1.8 2002/04/27 06:15:57 cbbrowne Exp $
use CustomerQuery;
use AddBilling;
use ZipCodes;
use SoapTools;
use SOAP::Lite;
use SOAP::Transport::HTTP;
SOAP::Transport::HTTP::CGI
  -> dispatch_to( qw(listcustomers
                     listallcustomers
                     listcustomersoverdue
                     addbillings
                     getZipcode getZipcodes getZipcodeNoDB
                     getZipcodeDBNoQuery
                    ))
# -> options ({compress_threshold => 40000})
  -> handle;
```

We have already configured Apache to treat Perl scripts as CGI scripts, so that it can execute them easily. Hence, it is normally not necessary to specify a port number. By default, web servers are configured to listen to port 80, as shown in the following /etc/services entry, and the Web Service clients will generally submit requests to port 80 unless some other port is explicitly specified:

```
www    80/tcp    http   # WorldWideWeb    HTTP
```

The real meat of the server is in the Perl class module files. As discussed earlier, we will have three classes that will provide the new functionality to the ISP's SQL-Ledger.

The SoapTools Module

Module SoapTools.pm bundles together some common utility functions, notably functions mkdata(), and reportresults() that we'll use in other modules. It also defines connect_db(), which sets up a DBI database connection to the PostgreSQL database:

```
#!/usr/bin/perl
# $Id: SoapTools.pm,v 1.3 2002/06/01 14:52:33 cbbrowne Exp $
package SoapTools;
require 5.000;
use Exporter;
use Data::Dumper; $Data::Dumper::Terse = 1; $Data::Dumper::Indent = 1;
```

```
use SOAP::Lite;
use DBI;
use vars qw(@ISA);
@ISA = (Exporter);
@EXPORT = qw(mkdata reportresults connect_db);

sub connect_db {
  my ($dbi_access, $db_user) =
    ("dbi:Pg:dbname=sqlledger;host=localhost", "cbbrowne");
  my $dbh = DBI->connect( $dbi_access, $db_user, "", {AutoCommit => 0})
    || die "DB Error\n";
  return $dbh;
}

sub mkdata {
  my ($value, $name, $type) = @_;
  $name = 'return' unless $name;
  $type = 'string' unless $type;
  return SOAP::Data -> name($name) ->type($type) ->value($value);
}

sub reportresults {
  my ($method, $ssrv_result) = @_;
  if ($ssrv_result->fault) {
    ($code, $string, $actor) = ($ssrv_result->faultcode,
                                $ssrv_result->faultstring,
                                $ssrv_result->faultactor);
    $~ = FAULT_TOP;
    write;
    print Dumper($ssrv_result->faultdetail, '');
  } else {
    print "-" x 70, "\n";
    print "Result from : $method\n";
    print "-" x 70, "\n";
    my $result = $ssrv_result->result;
    print Dumper($result, '');
  }
}

format FAULT_TOP =
=====================================================================
  Fault Found
=====================================================================
 Code:  @<<<<<<<<<<<<<<<<<<<<<<<<<<<<<<<<<<<<<<<<<<<<<<<<<<<<<<<<
  $code
 String: @<<<<<<<<<<<<<<<<<<<<<<<<<<<<<<<<<<<<<<<<<<<<<<<<<<<<<<<
  $string
 Actor:  @<<<<<<<<<<<<<<<<<<<<<<<<<<<<<<<<<<<<<<<<<<<<<<<<<<<<<<<
  $actor
.
1;
```

The CustomerQuery Module

Methods to list customer information, `listcustomers()`, `listallcustomers()`, and `listcustomersoverdue()` are implemented in the `CustomerQuery` class.

The `CustomerQuery` class begins with importing all other Perl classes that it uses, and then sets up the list of the methods it intends to export in `@EXPORT`:

```
# !/usr/bin/perl
# CustomerQuery.pm
package CustomerQuery;
require 5.000;
use Exporter;
use DBI;
use SoapTools;
use SOAP::Lite;
use vars qw(@ISA);

@ISA = qw(Exporter SOAP::Server::Parameters );
@EXPORT = qw(listallcustomers listcustomers listcustomersoverdue);
```

`%Customer_Query_Fields` is an associative array (hashtable) containing a set of fields from the SQL-Ledger table `customer`, which will be used in queries, and their types. This set of fields will be used several times both to construct SQL queries, and to indicate what data is to be marshaled as `SOAP::Data` that will be passed back:

```
# Hash table %Customer_Query_Fields centralizes the definitions to one
# spot, eliminating the risk of forgetting to update a SQL query or a
# return value. Add/remove a field here, and it automatically gets
# added/removed everywhere.

%Customer_Query_Fields =
        ( "id" => "integer", "name" => "string", "addr1" => "string",
          "addr2" => "string", "addr3" => "string", "contact" => "string",
          "phone" => "string", "fax" => "string", "e-mail" => "string",
          "creditlimit" => "float" );
```

A common alternative approach would be for each SQL query to explicitly list the fields. Reading data out of the query results would require explicitly listing each element.

Using the associative array to compute these queries and results eliminates all sorts of possible programming errors. If a field is added, modified, or deleted, the modification only needs to be done at one place in the program, that is, the definition of the associative array. The risk of accidentally overlooking a field, and leaving fields out of the returned results, or leaving fields in when they were supposed to be removed, is eliminated. This is certainly not a mandatory feature of SOAP::Lite or SQL-Ledger, but it is a very useful programming technique.

The listallcustomers() Method

The `listallcustomers()` method returns a list of all the customers. It can be depicted as follows:

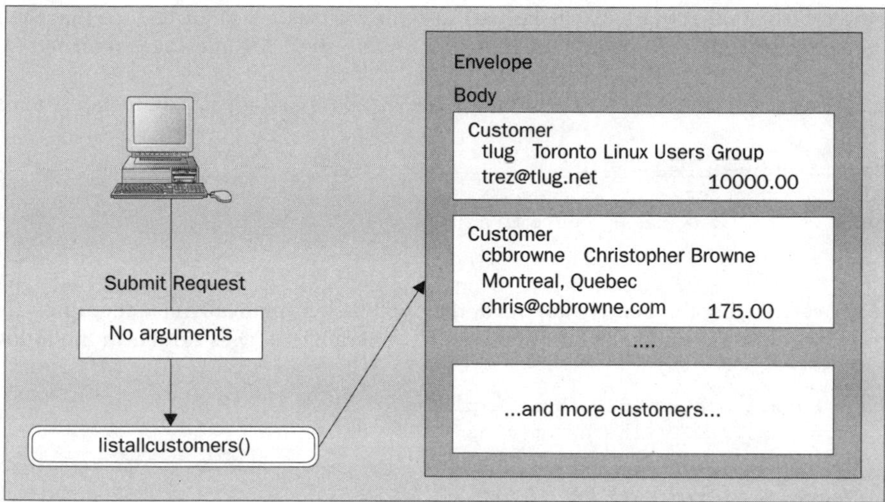

It begins by connecting to the database, generating an SQL query based on the fields in `%Customer_Query_Fields`, and executing that query using the `DBI` methods – `prepare()`, and `execute()`:

```
sub listallcustomers {
  my $DBI_H = connect_db();
  my $custquery = "select";
  foreach $fld (keys (%Customer_Query_Fields)) {
    $custquery .= " " . $fld . ",";
  }
  chop $custquery;    # Remove trailing comma for last field
  $custquery .= " from customer";
  my $QHandle = $DBI_H->prepare($custquery);
  $QHandle->execute;
```

Data for each table row is fetched and placed in `@ResultRow`, using the type indicated previously in `%Customer_Query_Fields`. Each such row is then collected into the array `@RESULTS`:

```
  my @RESULTS;
  while (my $ref = $QHandle->fetchrow_hashref) {
    my @ResultRow = ();
    foreach my $fld (keys %Customer_Query_Fields) {
      my $val = $ref->{$fld};
      if ($val) {
        push @ResultRow, mkdata($val, $fld,
                                $Customer_Query_Fields{$fld});
      }
    }
    push @RESULTS, SOAP::Data-> name('customer') -> value(\@ResultRow);
  }
```

By using `%Customer_Query_Fields` to indicate which database fields are to be collected, the errors resulting from inconsistent changes are eliminated.

Note that the returned objects are 'back-slashed', as with `value (\@RESULTS)`, so that their values are not garbage-collected until they have been transformed into the XML messages returned to the client.

Functions that access database tables should close the database and query connections before exiting:

```
    $QHandle->finish;
    $DBI_H->disconnect;
    return SOAP::Data->name('customers') -> value(\@RESULTS);
  }
```

If they are allocated using the Perl `my` keyword, they will be automatically cleaned up by the Perl garbage collection system, but the server process will generate messages similar to the following:

```
Database handle destroyed without explicit connect at
/usr/share/perl5/SOAP/Lite.pm at line 2177
```

The listcustomersoverdue() Method

The method `listcustomersoverdue()` is structured similarly to `listallcustomers()` that connects to the database, generates a query, and submits it:

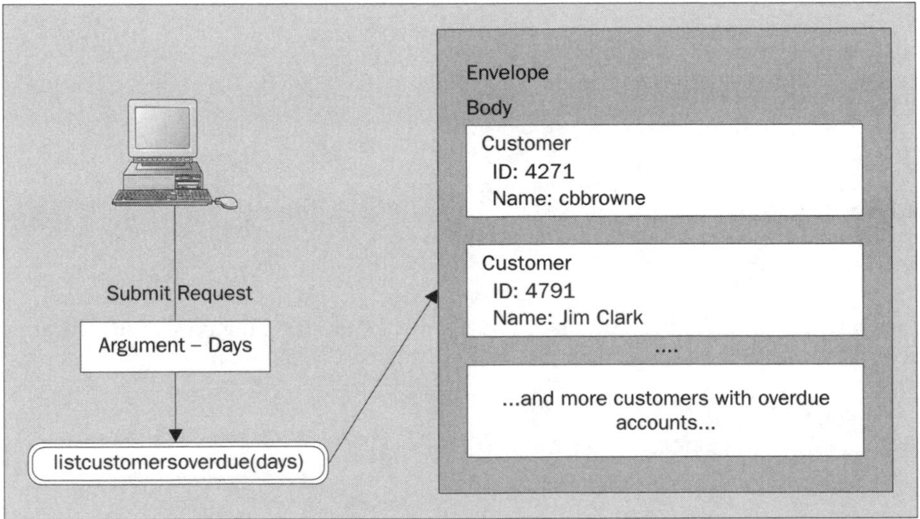

Let's write the code for the `listcusomeroverdue()` method. Here, the parameter passed to the function, `$days`, is used to find the set of customers where payments are overdue by a number of days equal to or more than `$days`:

```
sub listcustomersoverdue {
  my $days = pop;
  my $DBI_H = connect_db();
  my $overduequery = qq|
    select customer.id as id, customer.name as name from ar, customer
          where ar.customer_id = customer.id and paid != amount
```

```
            and transdate < now() - interval '$days days'
            group by customer.id, customer.name |;
    my $QHandle = $DBI_H->prepare($overduequery);
    $QHandle->execute;
```

Only two fields, the customer_id and name are returned, for each customer. Otherwise the structure is very similar to the listallcustomers() method, collecting values to be returned, and cleaning up database connection information:

```
    my @RESULTS;
    while (my $ref = $QHandle->fetchrow_hashref) {
      my ($id, $name) = ($ref->{id}, $ref->{name});
      push @RESULTS, SOAP::Data-> name('customer')
        -> value(mkdata($id, 'id', 'integer'),
                 mkdata($name, 'name'));
    }
    $QHandle->finish;
    $DBI_H->disconnect;
    return \@RESULTS;
  }
```

The listcustomers() Method

The method listcustomers() accepts a set of customer IDs as parameters, which are integers. For this set of customer IDs, it draws the same list of fields described by %Customer_Query_Fields, and returned by listallcustomers():

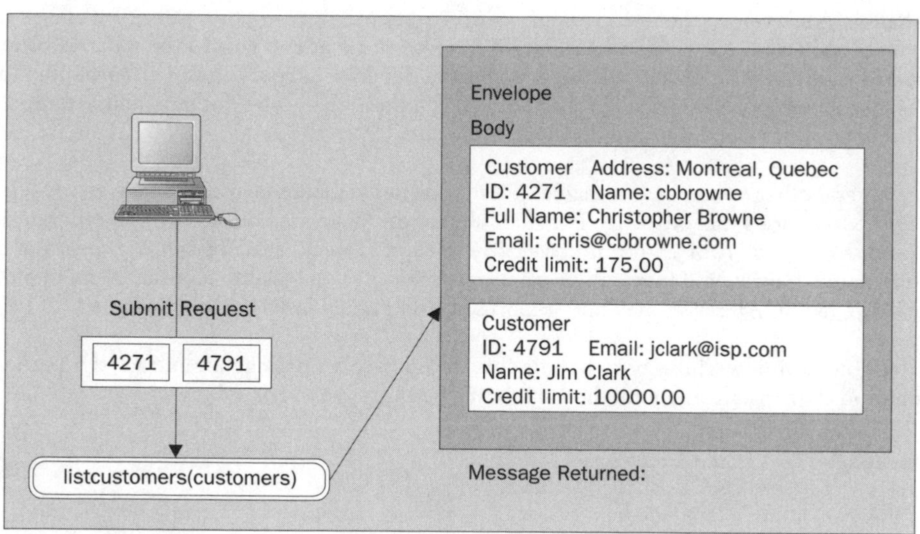

It would be unfriendly to pass in 15,000 customer IDs. The resulting SQL query would be rather large, perhaps even challenging the maximum size that the database's SQL processor can handle. The listcustomers() method is therefore set up to fail with a SOAP::Fault, if the number of customer IDs passed exceeds 400:

```
$maxcustomers = 400;

sub listcustomers {
  my $self = shift;
  my @CUSTS = @_;
  if ($#CUSTS > $maxcustomers) {
              die SOAP::Fault -> faultstring("listcustomers
              can only return $maxcustomers customers");
  }
  my $DBI_H = connect_db();
  my $custquery = "select";
  foreach $fld (keys (%Customer_Query_Fields)) {
    $custquery .= " " . $fld . ",";
  }
  chop $custquery;
  $custquery .= " from customer where id in (";
  my $last = pop @CUSTS;   # Pull out the last element
  foreach $i (@CUSTS) {
    $custquery .= $i . ", ";
  }
  $custquery .= $last . ")";  # Add the last element in, and close...
```

An alternative would be to put a loop around this, submitting a SQL query for every `1000` customer IDs; that would allow returning an essentially unlimited number of entries. However, for a really big query, the method may potentially return a totally unmanageably large SOAP message. Hence we'll limit it to `400` customer IDs.

Let's discuss in what form the results should be returned, and what methods can be used to do so.

Notice that we don't return the results in any conceivable order, using the `ORDER BY` clause in the SQL query. The SQL `ORDER BY` clause will generally impose some added cost to the database query, compared to returning the data in whatever order the database offers. On the other hand, if an `ORDER BY` can be used to impose an order on the result, it is quite likely to be the most efficient and effective way of doing so, since databases are designed to do so.

However, several other options are available. If it is known that a particular ordering is needed, a method may be set up to express that ordering. For example, we can have methods for several orderings, such as `listcustomersbyid()`, or `listcustomersbycreditlimit()`, each providing the order suggested by the method name. However, if there are many such orderings, it will lead to a proliferation of SOAP methods. Also, the SOAP server may not support some additional ordering that is needed.

A more flexible and powerful way to handle this would involve passing an extra order parameter to the SOAP method. For instance, the method might instead be invoked as follows:

```
$SoapServer->listcustomers
        ( SOAP::Data->name('IDList') ->value(@Customers),
          SOAP::Data->name('order') ->value('creditlimit descending, id'));
```

Here, the order value could be inserted directly into an `ORDER BY` clause in the SQL query, ordering the results in descending order based on credit limit, then by customer ID. Also, SOAP offers a `Map` type which is commonly used to express unordered hashtables. If values are passed as a `Map`, any ordering on the SOAP server may simply disappear between the server and the client.

The order parameter would be quite suitable to manage orderings that can be imposed by the SQL database. Databases are designed to be quite efficient at sorting things, and so this will likely be more efficient than having the client do the work.

There might be a need to have the list of customers returned in the order they occur in `@Customers`. That could be handled by doing a separate SQL query for each customer, and collecting the results in order into the result data structure. However, if the server tries to improve performance by combining the criteria into a single SQL query, there is no way to have the database return the results in that order. Maintaining results in that order would require more complex coding on the server to order the results to correspond with the original ordering.

This does not really point to the existence of a single definitive right way to deal with the ordering of elements when a SOAP method returns multiple elements. One principle that emerges is that it may be difficult to guarantee a meaningful order of the results, and the client may be considered fragile, if it can't cope with that.

Now, let's consider our example. As is shown in our example, no order might be specified. If the client needs the results to be in a particular order, it will have to explicitly sort the results after they are returned.

We'll now proceed with our `listcustomers()` method. If there was no last customer ID found, then evidently the caller did not request any customer IDs, so the SOAP method returns nothing:

```
if (!$last) {             # No results found
  $DBI_H->disconnect;     # So Disconnect
  return;                 # and return NOTHING
}
my $QHandle = $DBI_H->prepare($custquery);
$QHandle->execute;
```

This code for marshaling the results to be returned is exactly the same as the code used for marshaling return results in `listallcustomers()`:

```
my @RESULTS;
while (my $ref = $QHandle->fetchrow_hashref) {
  my @ResultRow = ();
  foreach my $fld (keys %Customer_Query_Fields) {
    my $val = $ref->{$fld};
    if ($val) {
      push @ResultRow, mkdata($val, $fld,
                              $Customer_Query_Fields{$fld});
    }
  }
  push @RESULTS, SOAP::Data-> name('customer') -> value(\@ResultRow);
}
```

The method finishes off, as always, by cleaning up the database connections, returning the backslashed `@RESULTS` array, followed by a statement returning a `true` value that is required to end a Perl module:

```
    $QHandle->finish;
  $DBI_H->disconnect;
  return SOAP::Data->name('customers') -> value(\@RESULTS);
}
1;
```

The `AddBilling.pm` module is discussed in greater detail later; this supports the `AddBilling` module that allows adding ISP billings to SQL-Ledger via a SOAP interface.

A Client To Query Customers

Now, we will develop the client, `pclient.pl`. The client starts by drawing in several SOAP-related classes, and setting up the entire configuration necessary to access the SOAP server:

```
#!/usr/bin/perl -w
use SOAP::Lite;
use SoapTools;
use Data::Dumper; ($Data::Dumper::Terse, $Data::Dumper::Indent) = (1, 1);
my $url = "/soap/sql.pl";
my $host = "salesman";
my $proxy = "http://$host$url";
my $csize = 400;
my $SoapServer = SOAP::Lite ->proxy($proxy,
                  options => {compress_threshold => $csize});

print "Soap Server: $SoapServer at $proxy\n";
print "-" x 75, "\n";
```

An associative array `%CQFLDS` sets up the list of fields that will typically be pulled in as customer information. If a field were to be added, removed, or renamed, hopefully it will only need to be modified here:

```
# Customer Query Fields
%CQFLDS = ( "id" => "integer", "name" => "string", "addr1" => "string",
            "addr2" => "string", "addr3" => "string", "contact" => "string",
            "phone" => "string", "fax" => "string", "e-mail" => "string",
            "creditlimit" => "float" );
```

Then the script starts by reading in a list of all customers by calling the SOAP `listallcustomers()` method. If something goes wrong, it uses `show_fault()` to display details of the nature of the fault:

```
# Collect list of customers into @Customers
my @Customers;
my $res = $SoapServer->call("listallcustomers");
if ($res->fault) {
  show_fault($res);
```

Once the `listallcustomers()` call works out, the following loop collects all of the customer information into the Perl table `@Customers`:

```
} else {
  my $count = 1;
  while ($res->match("//customers/[$count]")) {
    foreach my $field (keys %CQFLDS) {
      my $fval = get_field($res, $count, $field);
      if ($fval) {
        $Customers[$count-1]{$field} = $fval;
```

```
        }
      }
      $count++;
    }
```

The `match()` function calls each customer node, and then the function `get_field()` searches for the database fields within the customer record.

The above loop will leave fields that were empty in the database, and thus they will be empty in `@Customers`. After drawing the customers into `@Customers`, this code walks through all the customers, displaying the fields that are present:

```
    # Display customer list from @Customers
    print "Customers: ", length(@Customers), "\n";
    my $i = 0;
    foreach my $el (@Customers) {
      my $id = $Customers[$i]{id};
      print "ID= $id ";
      foreach my $field (sort (keys %CQFLDS)) {
        my $fld = $Customers[$i]{$field};
        if ($fld && !($field eq "id")) {
          print " $field= ", $fld;
        }
      }
      $i++;
      print "\n", "-" x 75, "\n";
    }
  }
```

Next, we call the SOAP method `listcustomersoverdue()`, to get the list of customers with overdue accounts:

```
  my $day = 30;
  my @OverDueList;
  my @OverdueIDs;
  my $query = $SoapServer->listcustomersoverdue($day);
  if ($query->fault) {
    show_fault($query);
```

Just as with the run of `listallcustomers()`, the code uses the `SOAP::SOM` `match()` function to search for the `customer_id` and name fields:

```
    } else {
    foreach my $field ('id', 'name') {
      my $count = 0;
      foreach my $value ($query->match("//$field")->valueof()) {
        $OverDueList[$count++]{$field} = $value;
      }
    }
    print "-" x 75, "\n";
    print "  Clients with accounts overdue $day days or more\n";
    print "-" x 75, "\n";
    my $i = 0;
```

```
    foreach my $el (@OverDueList) {
      my ($id, $name) = ($OverDueList[$i]{id}, $OverDueList[$i]{name});
      if ($id) {
        print "Record $i - ID=$id Name =$name\n";
        push @OverdueIDs, mkdata($id, 'id', 'integer');
      }
      $i++;
    }
    print "-" x 75, "\n";
  }
```

In this case, rather than iterating across each customer and each field for that customer, the array behavior of `match()` is used, drawing all of the `customer_id` values at once, and then drawing all of the `name` values, again all at once. This approach couldn't be used with the `listallcustomers()` method, since the potential for missing fields would lead to fields being tied to the wrong record.

Consider that the database has information about the customers as in the following table:

customer_id	name	addr1	e-mail
1	Wrox Publishing	London, England	
2	Free Software Foundation	Cambridge, MA	support@fsf.org
3	Palm Computing		
4	cbbrowne Computing Inc	Scarborough , ON	support@cbbrowne.com

The SOAP message generated for this data might look like the following:

```
<?xml version="1.0" encoding="utf-8"?>
<SOAP-ENV:Envelope attributes="simplified-away">
  <SOAP-ENV:Body>
    <companies SOAP-ENC:root="1">
      <company>
        <id xsi:type="xsd:integer"> 1 </id>
        <name xsi:type="xsd:string"> Wrox Publishing </name>
        <addr1 xsi:type="xsd:string"> London, England </addr1>
      </company>
      <company>
        <id xsi:type="xsd:integer"> 2 </id>
        <name xsi:type="xsd:string"> Free Software Foundation </name>
        <addr1 xsi:type="xsd:string"> Cambridge, MA </addr1>
        <e-mail xsi:type="xsd:string"> support@fsf.org </e-mail>
      </company>
      <company>
        <id xsi:type="xsd:integer"> 3 </id>
        <name xsi:type="xsd:string"> Palm Computing </name>
      </company>
      <company>
```

```
        <id xsi:type="xsd:integer"> 4 </id>
        <name xsi:type="xsd:string"> cbbrowne Computing Inc </name>
        <addr1 xsi:type="xsd:string"> Scarborough, ON </addr1>
        <e-mail xsi:type="xsd:string"> support@cbbrowne.com </e-mail>
      </company>
    </companies>
  </SOAP-ENV:Body>
</SOAP-ENV:Envelope>
```

Note that the empty fields are omitted, and simply don't exist in the tree represented in the XML message.

All the four queries found using `$query->match("//id")`, `$query->match("//name")`, `$query->match("//addr1")`, and `$query->match("//e-mail")` fold upwards, so that the resulting four matches for the above data in the SOAP array query would look like the following:

match("//id")	match("//name")	match("//addr1")	match("//e-mail")
1	Wrox Publishing	London, England	support@fsf.org
2	Free Software Foundation	Cambridge, MA	support@cbbrowne.com
3	Palm Computing	Scarborough, ON	
4	cbbrowne Computing Inc		

As we can see the values bubble up to the top. With the `listcustomersoverdue()` method, the ID and name values are always filled in, so no bubbling takes place, and it is fine to use this array representation. But queries based on `match("//addr1")`, or `match("//e-mail")` would provide misleading results, at least if there was any intention to try to meaningfully associate them with the companies. For example, we don't get any `addr1` value for the company with `id` equals `4`, since `match("//addr1")` does not maintain any direct association between positions in the result and positions in the original message tree.

On the other hand, if there is a process that requires all of the e-mail addresses that exist, and does not need to be concerned with any of the other data, `match("//e-mail)` will do a great job, finding e-mail entries throughout the message, irrespective of the message's hierarchy.

A more interesting example comes in the following SOAP message which has a more complex structure, where a `company` may contain multiple `e-mail` addresses, and may further contain `contact` elements that themselves contain e-mail addresses:

```
<?xml version="1.0" encoding="utf-8"?>
<SOAP-ENV:Envelope attributes="simplified-away">
  <SOAP-ENV:Body>
    <companies SOAP-ENC:root="1">
      <company>
        <id xsi:type="xsd:integer"> 1 </id>
        <name xsi:type="xsd:string"> Wrox Publishing </name>
        <addr1 xsi:type="xsd:string"> London, England </addr1>
```

```
      </company>
      <company>
        <id xsi:type="xsd:integer"> 2 </id>
        <name xsi:type="xsd:string"> Free Software Foundation </name>
        <addr1 xsi:type="xsd:string"> Cambridge, MA </addr1>
        <e-mail xsi:type="xsd:string"> support@fsf.org </e-mail>
        <contact>
          <name xsi:type="xsd:string"> Richard Stallman </e-mail>
          <e-mail xsi:type="xsd:string"> rms@fsf.org </e-mail>
        </contact>
        <contact>
          <title xsi:type="xsd:string"> Treasurer  </e-mail>
          <e-mail xsi:type="xsd:string"> treasurer@fsf.org </e-mail>
        </contact>
        <contact>
          <title xsi:type="xsd:string"> Secretary </e-mail>
          <e-mail xsi:type="xsd:string"> secretary@fsf.org </e-mail>
        </contact>
      </company>
      <company>
        <id xsi:type="xsd:integer"> 3 </id>
        <name xsi:type="xsd:string"> Palm Computing </name>
      </company>
      <company>
        <id xsi:type="xsd:integer"> 4 </id>
        <name xsi:type="xsd:string"> cbbrowne Computing Inc </name>
        <addr1 xsi:type="xsd:string"> Scarborough, ON </addr1>
        <e-mail xsi:type="xsd:string"> support@cbbrowne.com </e-mail>
        <e-mail xsi:type="xsd:string"> help@cbbrowne.com </e-mail>
      </company>
    </companies>
  </SOAP-ENV:Body>
</SOAP-ENV:Envelope>
```

A search based on `match("//e-mail")` would find all the e-mail elements, irrespective of where they may be found in the document hierarchy, and `valueof()` would return them all as a simple array containing the five e-mail addresses.

There is another problem with the `SOAP::SOM` methods; they need to walk through all elements of the message. If the message has a large number of elements, each run of `match()` walks through each of them, even though we may want to search for a single element from the message. If the message is large, the search may become too slow. We'll explore this issue in more detail in a benchmark example later in the chapter.

Let's continue with our client. After collecting the IDs into `@OverdueIDs`, the function calls `listcustomers()`, to pull the full set of customer data:

```
my @Customers;
$getids = $SoapServer->listcustomers(SOAP::Data ->value(@OverdueIDs));
if ($getids->fault) {
  show_fault($getids);
} else {
```

The customer data is attached to the SOAP request in `$getids`. Our next code snippet draws the data out of the SOAP message, and into `@Customers`:

```
my $count = 1;
while ($getids->match("//customers/[$count]")) {
  foreach my $field (keys %CQFLDS) {
    my $fval = get_field($getids, $count, $field);
    if ($fval) {
      $Customers[$count-1]{$field} = $fval;
    }
  }
  $count++;
}
```

Note that we absolutely don't have any indication as to what order the records will be returned in, as we saw in the case of `listallcustomes()`.

Similar to the code used earlier to display customers using `listallcustomers()`, this displays all customers with overdue balances:

```
  # Display customer list from @Customers
  my $i = 0;
  foreach my $c (@Customers) {
    my $id = $Customers[$i]{id};
    if ($id) {
      print "ID= $id ";
      foreach my $field (sort (keys %CQFLDS)) {
        my $fld = $Customers[$i]{$field};
        if ($fld && !($field eq "id")) {
          print " $field= ", $fld;
        }
      }
    }
    $i++;
    print "\n", "-" x 75, "\n";
  }
}
```

Function `get_field()` looks at the SOAP message to locate the specified field `$field` within customer record `$count`, returning nothing if it could not find anything:

```
# SOM search for a particular field
sub get_field {
  my ($res, $count, $field) = @_;
  my $result = $res->match("//customers/[$count]/$field")->valueof();
  if ($result) {
    return $result;
  }
}
```

Here is a rather shorter script that uses these methods to submit an e-mail to anybody overdue 30 days or more, and to shut off the accounts of anybody overdue 60 days or more:

```
#!/usr/bin/perl -w
use SOAP::Lite +trace;
use SoapTools;
my ($host, $url, $csize) = ("salesman", "soap/sql.pl", 4000);
my $proxy = "http://$host/$url";
my $SoapServer = SOAP::Lite ->proxy($proxy,
                 #options => {compress_threshold => $csize});

my $overdue = $SoapServer ->listcustomersoverdue(30);
my $info = $SoapServer ->listcustomers($overdue->match("//id"));

foreach my $e-mail ($info ->match("//e-mail")) {
  open(MAIL, "|mail -s'Overdue ISP Bill Notice' $e-mail");
  print MAIL "Hi, $e-mail.\nYour ISP billing is over 30 days overdue.\n";
  print MAIL "We would appreciate receiving payment Real Soon Now.\n";
  print MAIL "Note that our policy is to deactivate accounts after\n";
  print MAIL "they have been overdue for 60 days.\n\n";
  print MAIL "Please contact our accounting department at 800-YOUR-ISP\n";
  print MAIL "We have appreciated your business, and trust that you\n";
  print MAIL "will address this soon.\n";
  print MAIL "-- \nSigned, Your ISP\n";
  close MAIL;
}

my $longoverdue = $SoapServer->listcustomersoverdue(15);
$info = $SoapServer->listcustomers($longoverdue->match("//id"));
my %CANCELS;
foreach my $e-mail ($info->match("//e-mail")) {
  open(MAIL, "|mail -s'Overdue ISP Bill Notice' $e-mail");
  print MAIL "Hi, $e-mail.\nYour ISP billing is over 60 days overdue.\n";
  print MAIL "We are deactivating your account, in conformance with the\n";
  print MAIL "terms of service agreement.  It is unfortunately possible\n";
  print MAIL "that you may not receive this e-mail.\n\n";
  print MAIL "Please contact our accounting department if you have any\n";
  print MAIL "further concerns.\n";
  print MAIL "-- \nRegrets, Your ISP\n";
  close MAIL;
  $e-mail =~ /(^.*)\@/;
  $account = $1;
  # Use system script to deactivate the user ID
  `/usr/sbin/usermod -L $account`;
}
```

This script uses a utility called `/usr/sbin/usermod` to deactivate the user ID. Different Linux or BSD distributions may use similar scripts with slightly different names.

In an environment where a LDAP or PostgreSQL database is being used to manage authentication, this script would start with `DBI->connect()` or `Net::LDAP->new()` to connect to the database, and then update the database entries within the loop.

If authentication is being managed using `/etc/passwd`, there are two bottlenecks to be concerned about:

- If the `/etc/passwd` file is very large, and the number of users being deactivated is very large, the process could run for quite a long time, since `usermod` must read and write the full contents of `/etc/passwd` for each user being deleted.
- Each update to `/etc/passwd` using `usermod` requires getting a lock on the password file. This presents no problem within this process; the invocations of `usermod` take place one after another, with no conflicts.

However, if there are other processes that would update `/etc/passwd` concurrently with this script, locking conflicts can arise. `usermod` will fail if other updates are taking place concurrently, with the result that some accounts may not be deactivated. These bottlenecks are totally unrelated to SOAP; they relate to how the client uses the data that comes back from the server.

Also note that `shutoff.pl` script must be run by the root user to modify password files. These issues evaporate if a database system like PostgreSQL or LDAP is being used to manage authentication, since they offer compelling advantages like:

- Efficient random access to data
- The ability for multiple processes to work concurrently requesting database updates
- Transaction management, to cope with the situation where concurrent updates clash
- Access does not need to take place from the root account

Adding Monthly Billings

Now, we'll provide the ISP with an automated process for adding monthly billings for each customer. For an ISP, the list of actual customer accounts resides on the servers that control connection services, which are not the same servers that would host the accounting software and other back-office applications.

A SOAP-based web service can allow the server's managing user accounts to provide the accounting server with the list of active accounts, and a request for setting up invoices, accounts and receivable transactions for these accounts. Of course, this wouldn't offer a complete set of interfaces to control the whole accounting system. In a real-world situation, we can develop interfaces for processes like adding customers, or managing payments.

The AddBilling Module

To add monthly customer billings, we need to add a few entries to a number of SQL-Ledger tables, notably:

- `oe` – Order Entry
- `orderitems` – Order Items

- `invoice` – Invoice Entry
- `ar` – Accounts Receivable
- `acc_trans` – General Ledger line items

Adding orders also requires referencing the following additional tables:

- `chart` – Containing the General Ledger Chart of Accounts
- `tax` – Containing tax rates
- `customer` – Containing customer information
- `parts` – Containing information about the available products and services

The logical linkages between these tables can be illustrated as shown in the following diagram:

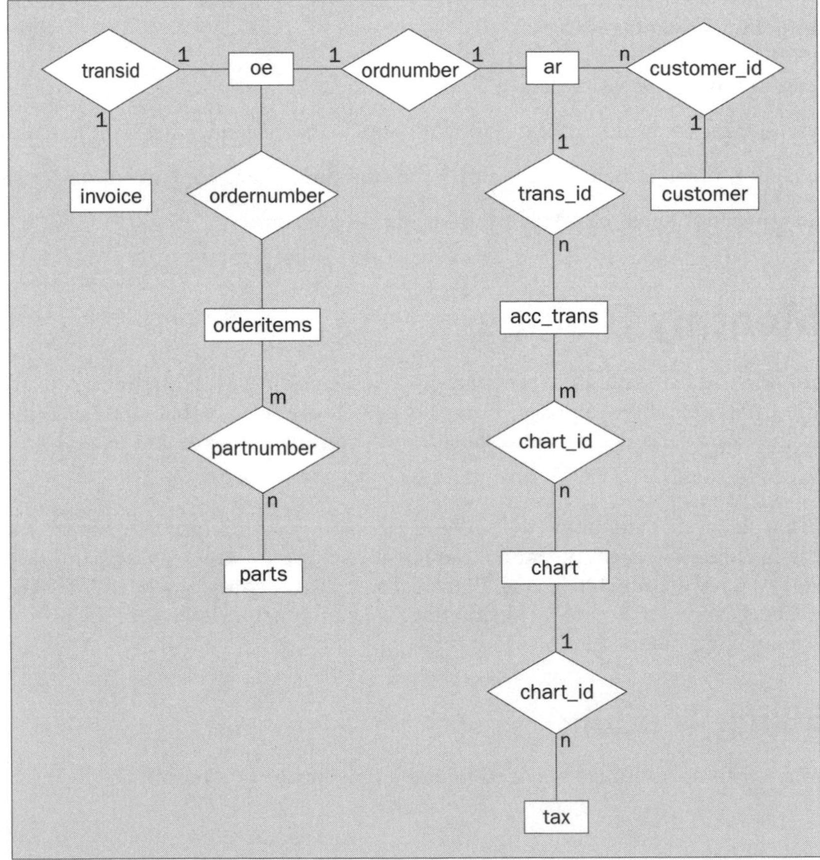

We'll export the SOAP method `addbillings()` from `AddBilling`. It accepts a sequence of billing requests, organized as shown below:

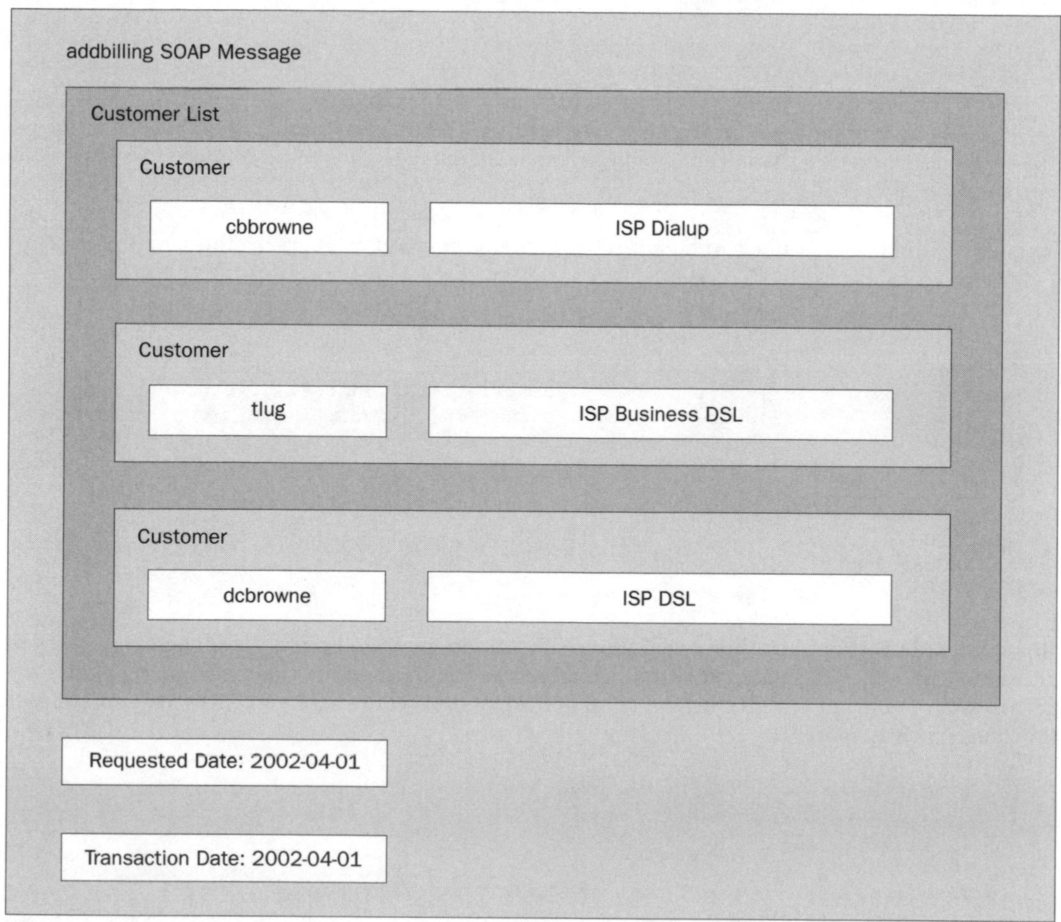

The message contains a list of customers, along with the type of ISP service subscription, and the dates associated to the billing. Pricing information is not included here; that information is stored in the accounting system.

The SOAP method reports back the prices, and some of the tax information. However, our `AddBilling` module would not supply further accounting information.

The class `AddBilling` begins with a set of Perl `use` commands that should seem fairly familiar by now:

```
#!/usr/bin/perl
# AddBillings.pm
package AddBilling;
require 5.000;
use Exporter;
use Data::Dumper; $Data::Dumper::Terse = 1; $Data::Dumper::Indent = 1;
```

```
use DBI;
use SoapTools;
use SOAP::Lite;
use vars qw(@ISA);
@ISA = qw(Exporter SOAP::Server::Parameters);
@EXPORT = qw( addbillings );
```

Two possibly unfamiliar use commands above are Sys::Hostname and Digest::MD5. These will be used by the function gen_hash() to help generate a unique key value used to look up transaction data in progress.

Next, we define the set of fields to be pulled from the parts and customer tables, and placed in %PARTSINFO and %CUSTINFO respectively. In addition, associative arrays %CUSTOMERS and %TAXRATES are defined for storing the tax information and the parameter information:

```
# Fields...
@PartsFields = ("id", "partnumber", "description", "unit", "listprice",
                "sellprice", "income_accno_id", "expense_accno_id");
@CustFields = ("id", "name", "discount", "taxincluded");

# Hash Tables used to store quasi-global information...
%PARTSINFO = ();
%CUSTINFO = ();
%CUSTOMERS = ();
%TAXRATES = ();
```

For our addbillings() method, we'll process the orders that can be processed, and collect together success and failure information. We will then return an ordinary return value containing all the success/failure information. All success/failure information is collected into @RETRES, and returned as an ordinary return value:

```
sub addbillings {
  my $transdate = pop;
  my $reqdate = pop;
  my %CUSTOMERS;
  # Take remainder of the inputs and draw them apart into pairs
  # of customer/service
  foreach my $C_ENT (@_) {
    my @CArray = @{$C_ENT};
    $CUSTOMERS{$CArray[0]} = $CArray[1];
  }
  my @RETRES;   # Return results
```

Note that this method does not try to pass back a SOAP Fault. Since the addbillings() method can process a whole host of transactions, of which some might be handled perfectly well, others might fail, and SOAP can return either the return value or Fault, but not both.

Here, notice that the addbillings() method starts by drawing the parameters out of @_. First two parameters are the requisition date $reqdate, and the transaction date $transdate. The third is an array of customer billing information, where each element itself consists of an array containing the customer's name (as found in the customer table field name), and the service name (as found in the parts table field partnumber). This data gets pushed into the associative array %CUSTOMERS for later reference.

Note that the two dates are applied in common to all the transactions. An alternative approach might be to attach individual dates to each customer billing, so that if they began service on different days of the month, monthly billings might be presented on that date within each month.

Next, we set up the database connection using `connect_db()` from the `SoapTools` module:

```
# Set up the database connection
$DBI_H = connect_db();
```

Now, a set of `DBI` queries will be set up to support the various SQL queries that get repeated over and over. This nicely introduces the sequence of database operations that will be used to add the transactions in to the accounting system. The process involves adding elements to `oe`, `orderitems`, `invoice`, `ar`, and `acc_trans` tables:

```
my $add_oe_query = $DBI_H ->prepare
                    ( qq|insert into oe (ordnumber, transdate, customer_id,
                      netamount, amount, reqdate, taxincluded, notes, curr)
values (?, ?, ?, ?, ?, ?, ?, ?, ?)| );

my $get_order_id = $DBI_H->prepare
                    ( qq| select id from oe where notes = ?|);

my $fix_oe_query = $DBI_H->prepare
                     ( qq|update oe set notes = ? where notes = ? |);

my $add_orderitems_query = $DBI_H->prepare
                            ( qq| insert into orderitems (trans_id, parts_id,
                              description, qty, sellprice, discount)
values (?, ?, ?, 1, ?, ?)|);

my $add_invoice_query = $DBI_H->prepare
                         ( qq| insert into invoice (trans_id, parts_id,
                           description, qty, sellprice,
                           fxsellprice, discount)
values (?, ?, ?, 1, ?, ?, ?)|);

my $add_ar_query = $DBI_H->prepare
                    ( qq|insert into ar (invnumber, ordnumber, transdate,
                      customer_id, taxincluded, amount, netamount, duedate,
                      invoice,notes, curr)
values (?, ?, ?, ?, ?, ?, ?, ?, 't', ?, ?) | );

my $get_ar_value = $DBI_H->prepare
                    (qq| select id from ar where notes = ?|);

my $fix_ar_query = $DBI_H->prepare
                    (qq| update ar set notes = ? where notes = ?|);

my $add_acc_trans = $DBI_H->prepare
                     (qq| insert into acc_trans (trans_id, chart_id,
                      amount, transdate)
values (?, ?, ?, ?) | );
```

Note that we have provided not just INSERT queries, but also SELECT and UPDATE queries. SQL-Ledger uses SQL sequence generators to internally generate the IDs to identify various transaction types, notably for oe and ar tables. Subsequent INSERT queries for the other tables need the ID numbers generated by those INSERTs, so the following approach is taken:

- Insert into ar, with a specially selected hash value for the NOTE field
- Select the ar record with the special NOTE value to get the ID
- Clean up ar by putting in a nicer NOTE value

At the end of this process, the ID value is available so that later INSERTs for other tables may point to the Accounts Receivable entry. The same happens with oe for Order Entry.

PostgreSQL offers an alternative method where the serial value automatically generated by the database may be requested using the database query:

```
select currval ('id')
```

This query will get the sequence number just created for the ID field, which is the value we want to use as $orderid. That would have a number of benefits, including:

- Eliminating the need for all but the final $DBI_H->commit call
- Eliminating the need for the 'fix' queries, $fix_oe_query, and $fix_ar_query

However, the currval() query only works with PostgreSQL; sequence fields have not been standardized as part of SQL, and since it's a common feature, we will find that different databases implement sequences differently.

Using the $uniquekey is certainly not pretty, but it is portable across the set of SQL implementations on which SQL-Ledger runs.

This characterizes a common dilemma found when implementing database-based applications. There is often a need to choose between techniques that are inelegant, but portable, and the techniques that allow the code to be shorter and more elegant, but with the disadvantage that the resulting application will only work with one database system.

In our case study, we'll have the following methods for reading the data needed for calculations:

- read_isp_parts_data()
- read_customers()
- read_tax_rates()
- read_chart()

Before we proceed with our AddBilling module code, let's take a look at these methods.

read_isp_parts_data() is used to populate the associative array %PARTSINFO:

```
sub read_isp_parts_data {
  my @SERVICES = @_;
  my $partquery = "select ";
  foreach my $field (@PartsFields) {
    $partquery .= " " . $field . ",";
  }
  chop $partquery;
  $partquery .= " from parts where partnumber in (";
  foreach $service (@SERVICES) {
    $partquery .= " '$service',";
  }
  chop $partquery;
  $partquery .= ")";

  my $QHandle = $DBI_H->prepare($partquery);
  $QHandle->execute;
  %PARTSINFO = ();

  while (my $ref = $QHandle->fetchrow_hashref) {
    my $partno = $ref->{partnumber};
    foreach my $fld (@PartsFields) {
      $PARTSINFO{$partno}{$fld} = $ref->{$fld};
    }
  }
  $QHandle->finish;
}
```

The fields described in `@PartsFields` are used to populate `%PARTSINFO`.

`read_customers()` is used to populate the associative array `%CUSTINFO` with more information about customers, notably the internal ID, and the customer-by-customer policies concerning discounts and taxation:

```
sub read_customers {
  my @CUSTS = @_;
  my $custquery = "select ";
  foreach my $field (@CustFields) {
    $custquery .= " " . $field . ",";
  }
  chop $custquery;
  $custquery .= " from customer where name in (";
  foreach $cust (@CUSTS) {
    $custquery .= " '$cust',";
  }
  chop $custquery;
  $custquery .= ")";
  my $QHandle = $DBI_H->prepare($custquery);
  $QHandle->execute;
  %CUSTINFO = ();
  while (my $ref = $QHandle->fetchrow_hashref) {
    my $customer = $ref->{name};
    foreach my $fld (@CustFields) {
      my $val = $ref->{$fld};
```

```
        $CUSTINFO{$customer}{$fld} = $val;
      }
    }
    $QHandle->finish;
  }
```

This function bears marked similarity to the previous one, `read_isp_parts_data()`. It would be easily possible to create an even more generic function to handle all these sorts of queries that would pass the name of the table, the desired fields, and the basis for selection. If there were a lot of tables to be read with similarly simple processing involving pulling out specific fields for specific table entries, it would be a worthwhile improvement.

Function `read_tax_rates()` pulls in the tax rates from table `tax`, with a joint to table `chart`, to indicate which accounts are involved:

```
sub read_tax_rates {
  my $taxinfoquery = qq| select rate,chart.id as id from chart, tax
                  where chart.id = tax.chart_id and link like '%AR_tax%'|;
  my $QHandle = $DBI_H->prepare($taxinfoquery);
  $QHandle->execute;
  %TAXRATES = ();

  while (my $ref = $QHandle->fetchrow_hashref) {
    my $acct = $ref->{id};
    $TAXRATES{$acct} = $ref->{rate};
  }
  $QHandle->finish;
}
```

This query isn't as generic as the previous two. Note that the scheme for determining tax rates doesn't involve any `JOIN` with customer information.

That is perfectly reasonable for a local ISP where tax rates are likely to be the same across the local region. If the activities are spread wider, there would likely need to be some regional information, and the handling of taxation would need to get a lot more sophisticated.

Finally, `read_chart()` queries the chart of accounts to see what accounts have to be dealt with as 'Accounts Receivable' and 'ISP Income':

```
sub read_chart {
  my ($AR, $INCOME);
  my $ar_query = qq|select id from chart where link = 'AR'|;
  my $in_query = qq|select id from chart where charttype = 'A'
              and category = 'I' and description = 'ISP Service'|;
  my $QHandle = $DBI_H->prepare($ar_query);
  $QHandle->execute;

  while (my $ref = $QHandle->fetchrow_hashref) {
    $AR = $ref->{id};
  }
  $QHandle->finish;
```

```
    my $QHandle = $DBI_H->prepare($in_query);
    $QHandle->execute;

    while (my $ref = $QHandle->fetchrow_hashref) {
      $INCOME = $ref->{id};
    }
    return ($AR, $INCOME);
  }
```

Alternativey, we could simply set `$ar_account` and `$income_account` to the integer values found in the chart. This would save two database queries, which isn't of any crucial importance, since they only get executed once at the start of processing.

Now, let's get back to our code where we read all of the data needed to do calculations:

```
    &read_isp_parts_data ("ISP Business DSL", "ISP DSL", "ISP Dialup");
    &read_customers (keys (%CUSTOMERS));
    &read_tax_rates();
    my ($ar_account, $income_account) = read_chart();
```

Now we get into the main loop, processing each customer as provided by the initial SOAP message. We need to check if the customer was found by `read_customers()`. If it was, then we can proceed to process the customer, else the client is informed that an invalid customer was passed in:

```
    foreach my $cust (keys %CUSTOMERS) {
      if ($CUSTINFO{$cust}) {
        # Process valid customer
        my $uniquekey = gen_hash ( $cust );
        my $soapid = "SOAP:" . `date +"%D"` ;
        chop $soapid;
        $soapid .= ":$cust";
        my ($ordnumber, $customer_id, $curr, $taxincluded, $service) =
          ($soapid, $CUSTINFO{$cust}{id}, "CDN",
           $CUSTINFO{$cust}{taxincluded}, $CUSTOMERS{$cust});
        my $nicenote = "SOAP Interface Entry - $transdate " . `date`;
        chop $nicenote;
        my $netamount = round_to_2 ($PARTSINFO{$service}{sellprice} *
                        (1 - $CUSTINFO{$cust}{discount}));
```

Next, a whole host of values are calculated. First is `$uniquekey` that uses the function `gen_hash()` written as shown below:

```
  use Sys::Hostname;
  use Digest::MD5;
  sub gen_hash {
    my @INCOMING_PARMS = @_;
    push @INCOMING_PARMS, (time(), hostname, $in, rand(), $$, $<);
    my $string = join(":", @INCOMING_PARMS);
    return join(":", ("SOAP-TEMP", Digest::MD5::md5_base64($string),
                      hostname,$$,$<));
  }
```

gen_hash() generates a temporary key that is likely to be unique. It collects a number of system parameters that vary a lot, uses the MD5 algorithm to compile this into a 128 bit value that is likely to be unique, and then assembles the result into a string that should be quite unique.

This value will be put into a note field in the database as a temporary key, allowing us to go back and search for the record that was just created. Several times there is a need to determine the internal transaction ID that is automatically generated by the database. By storing this unique value as part of the INSERT, we can go back and SELECT the ID based on this.

Ideally, we could select transaction IDs more directly from the database, but this cannot be done in a way that has been standardized in SQL standards. Many SQL databases offer some form of currval() function for this purpose.

$soapid is used as a visible 'transaction identifier'. The transaction IDs referred to above are not a public field that we see in browsing transaction lists using the web front-end of SQL-Ledger. $ordnumber uses the transaction ID, $soapid, to provide the visible transaction identifier.

Similarly, $nicenote provides a value to put into note fields indicating that the transaction was added using the SOAP interface at a particular date and time. $customer_id contains one of those invisible object identifiers, specifically the one used for internally identifying customers, and $curr identifies which currency is in use.

$taxincluded may be a little misleading; it is more likely to be properly interpreted as tax exempt. $service draws the variety of ISP service the customer is purchasing.

$netamount computes the after-discount price of the ISP service. Note that it explicitly rounds the amount to two decimal places using round_to_2() written as follow:

```
sub round_to_2 {
  my ($invalue) = @_;
  return sprintf("%.2f", $invalue);
}
```

This function will be used several times to round amounts to try to avoid some of the ill-conditioning that comes from using floating point values for financial applications.

Next, in our main module code, %TAXES and $totaltax are populated with the taxes calculated on the ISP billing. Note the computation of $dbtaxincluded; the form of the Boolean values that are put into SQL statements are t and f:

```
my (%TAXES, $totaltax);
if ($taxincluded) {
  $totaltax = 0;
} else {
  foreach my $type (keys %TAXRATES) {
    my $tax = round_to_2($TAXRATES{$type} * $netamount);
    $TAXES{$type} = $tax;
    $totaltax += $tax;
  }
}
```

```
$totaltax = round_to_2($totaltax);
my $amount = round_to_2($netamount + $totaltax);
my $dbtaxincluded = "f";
if ($taxincluded) {
  $dbtaxincluded = "t"
}
```

At last, we have enough information to start pushing transaction information into the database. The order entry data may be put into table oe. The internal ID is needed for generating entries for the table orderitems, so the process involves immediately doing the $DBI_H->commit, reading back the ID field, and then fixing up the record, so it has a note field:

```
$add_oe_query->execute
        ($ordnumber, $transdate, $customer_id, $netamount, $amount,
         $reqdate, $dbtaxincluded, $uniquekey, $curr);

# Need to get ID from OE, so commit, and read the record
$DBI_H->commit;
$get_order_id->execute($uniquekey);
while (my $ref = $get_order_id->fetchrow_hashref) {
  $orderid = $ref->{id};
  print "ID: $orderid\n";
}

# Then fix up the OE record to have the _nice_ note
$fix_oe_query->execute($nicenote, $uniquekey);
```

Next, ID and description information is drawn from %PARTSINFO, and the records are pushed out to the database for orderitems and invoice tables:

```
my $parts_id = $PARTSINFO{$service}{id};
my $description = $PARTSINFO{$service}{description};
my $discount = $CUSTINFO{$cust}{discount} * 1.0;
$add_orderitems_query->execute($orderid, $parts_id, $description,
                $amount, $discount);

my $selling_price = $PARTSINFO{$service}{sellprice};
$add_invoice_query->execute($orderid, $parts_id, $description,
             $netamount, $selling_price, $discount);
```

The ar entry, just like the oe entry, has an ID field whose value is needed to link to later entries, so this update uses the $uniquekey value, and does exactly the same 'read and clean-up' scheme previously used with oe. It could be made cleaner using some database-specific currval() functionality:

```
$add_ar_query->execute($soapid, $orderid, $transdate, $customer_id,
       $dbtaxincluded, $amount, $netamount, $transdate, $uniquekey, $curr);
$DBI_H->commit;
$get_ar_value->execute($uniquekey);
my $ar_id;
while (my $ref = $get_ar_value->fetchrow_hashref) {
  $ar_id = $ref->{id};
}
# Fix up the AR entry to have the _nice_ looking note
$fix_ar_query->execute($nicenote, $uniquekey);
```

We are now nearing the end of the process; all that remains is to add in the accounting entries to the table `acc_trans` to book all of the accruals, hitting the Accounts Receivable account, the ISP Income account. Also, if there are tax amounts, they will be associated with their respective Taxes Payable accounts:

```
$add_acc_trans->execute($ar_id, $ar_account, -$amount, $transdate);
$add_acc_trans->execute($ar_id, $income_account, $netamount, $transdate);
if ($taxincluded) {
} else {
  foreach my $taxid (keys %TAXRATES) {
    $add_acc_trans->execute($ar_id, $TAXRATES{$taxid}, $TAXES{$taxid},
             $transdate);
  }
}
$DBI_H->commit;
```

If all has gone well till now, we have just committed a complete customer transaction, and ought to report the summary information back to the client. Thus `gen_return_value()` is used to generate some `SOAP::Data` that is collected:

```
my $res = gen_return_value ($cust, $orderid, $service, $ar_id, $netamount,
$totaltax, $discount);
push @RETRES, $res;
  } else {
    my $res = gen_missing_customer($cust, $CUSTOMERS{$cust});
    push @RETRES, $res;
  }
}
```

This brings us way back to where we were checking to see if the customer was found in the database. This case handles the situation where it was not found, in which case `gen_missing_customer()` generates a `SOAP::Data` record to add to `@RETRES`.

```
  $DBI_H->disconnect;
  return \@RETRES;
}
```

After looping through all of the customers, committing those records that turned out OK, and generating a whole host of return values in `@RETRES`, we close the database connection and return `@RETRES`.

Following is `gen_return_value()` that takes its arguments and transforms them into a success record:

```
sub gen_return_value {
  my ($cust, $orderid, $service, $ar_id, $netamount, $totaltax, $discount)
    = @_;
  my @RES;
  push @RES, (mkdata($cust, 'customer'), mkdata($service, 'service'),
              mkdata($orderid, 'OrderID', 'integer'),
              mkdata($ar_id, 'ARID', 'integer'),
              mkdata($netamount, 'NetAmount', 'float'),
```

```
                 mkdata($totaltax, 'Taxes', 'float'),
                 mkdata($discount, 'Discount', 'float'));
    return SOAP::Data->name('success')
      -> type("ARRAY")
      -> value(\@RES);
}
```

Here is gen_missing_customer() that generates a SOAP::Data record for the missing customer, and adds it to @RETRES.

```
    sub gen_missing_customer {
    my ($cust, $service) = @_;
    my @RES;
    push @RES, mkdata($cust, 'customer'), mkdata($service, 'service');
    return SOAP::Data->name('missingcustomer')
      ->type("ARRAY")
        ->value(\@RES);
}
```

A Client To Generate Billings

We start with the issue of getting a list of customers and their services. The method taken here will be the simplest possible, drawing the list from the /etc/passwd file.

The assumption is that the name is based on the account name, and the kind of service may be extracted from the gecos field. This field was created on early UNIX systems at Bell Labs to control the routing of print jobs to GECOS systems used to host printer services. Only a few of us remember much about GECOS (still available from Bull as GCOS 7) and the field is now used on systems descended from Unix to store information about the user, consisting of a set of comma-separated fields typically including full name of user, room number, work phone, and home phone. These values may be changed using the command chfn.

In this application, password entries containing ISP indicate customers, and accounts that have been deactivated have their password changed to begin with.

Drawing the information out via grep ISP /etc/passwd | grep -v '/bin/false', we get the following set of passwords:

```
postgres:x:31:32:postgres,ISP DSL,,:/var/lib/postgres:/bin/sh
cbbrowne:x:500:500:Christopher Browne,ISP Dialup,,:/home/cbbrowne:/bin/sh
dcbrowne:x:1000:1000:David Browne,ISP Business DSL,,:/home/dcbrowne:/bin/sh
tlug:x:1001:1001:Toronto Linux Users Group,ISP Business DSL,,:/home/tlug:/bin/sh
flubber:x:1002:1002:Robin Williams,ISP Business DSL,,:/home/flubber:/bin/sh
roosta:x:1003:1003:Roosta,ISP Dialup,,:/home/roosta:/bin/sh
linus:x:1004:1004:Linus Torvalds,ISP DSL,,:/home/linus:/bin/sh
foobar:x:1005:1005:foo bar,ISP DSL,,:/home/foobar:/bin/sh
```

An assumption made here is that users have no access to the chfn command that would allow them to modify their gecos field; access to that is reserved to ISP staff.

Note the filter that removes entries with a `/bin/false` entry; that means the accounts that have been discontinued do not continue to get billed.

What the root user can do is this:

```
# chfn tlug
Changing the user information for tlug
Enter the new value, or press enter for the default
        Full Name [Toronto Linux Users Group]:
        Room Number [ISP Business DSL]:
        Work Phone []:
        Home Phone []:
        Other []:
```

In an ISP environment where authentication is managed using an LDAP database, the equivalent information would be pulled from LDAP. In order to support this, we need some customers loaded in. That may be accomplished manually using the `AR+` Add Customer option; alternatively, the following SQL query could be fed in via the command `cat AddCustomers.sql | psql sqlledger`:

```
insert into customer (name, addr1, addr2, addr3, addr4, contact,
phone, fax, e-mail, notes, discount, taxincluded, creditlimit, terms,
shiptoname, shiptoaddr1, shiptoaddr2, shiptoaddr3, shiptoaddr4,
shiptocontact, shiptophone, shiptofax, shiptoe-mail)
values ( 'Foobar Inc', '123 Fifth Avenue', '', '', '', 'Joe',
'613-555-1212', '', 'joe@fubar.org', '', 0.15, 't', 150000, 10, '',
'', '', '', '', 'Who', '', '', '');

insert into customer (name, addr1, addr2, addr3, addr4, contact,
phone, fax, e-mail, notes, discount, taxincluded, creditlimit, terms,
shiptoname, shiptoaddr1, shiptoaddr2, shiptoaddr3, shiptoaddr4,
shiptocontact, shiptophone, shiptofax, shiptoe-mail) values (
'cbbrowne', '123 Fifth Street', '', '', '', 'Chris Browne', '', '',
'', '', 0, 'f', 150, 10, '', 'Montreal, Quebec', '', '', '', '', '',
'', '');

insert into customer (name, addr1, addr2, addr3, addr4, contact,
phone, fax, e-mail, notes, discount, taxincluded, creditlimit, terms,
shiptoname, shiptoaddr1, shiptoaddr2, shiptoaddr3, shiptoaddr4,
shiptocontact, shiptophone, shiptofax, shiptoe-mail) values (
'flubber', '', '', '', '', '', '', '', '', '', 0.15, 'f', 444, 11,
'Robin Williams', '', '', '', '', '', '', '', '');

insert into customer (name, addr1, addr2, addr3, addr4, contact,
phone, fax, e-mail, notes, discount, taxincluded, creditlimit, terms,
shiptoname, shiptoaddr1, shiptoaddr2, shiptoaddr3, shiptoaddr4,
shiptocontact, shiptophone, shiptofax, shiptoe-mail) values (
'postgres', '42 Database Lane', '', '', '', 'Larry Gates', '', '', '',
'', 0, 'f', 100, 30, '', 'Oracleville, Ontario', '', '', '', '', '',
'', '');

insert into customer (name, addr1, addr2, addr3, addr4, contact,
phone, fax, e-mail, notes, discount, taxincluded, creditlimit, terms,
shiptoname, shiptoaddr1, shiptoaddr2, shiptoaddr3, shiptoaddr4,
```

```
shiptocontact, shiptophone, shiptofax, shiptoe-mail) values (
'dcbrowne', '429 Biz Lane', '', '', '', '', '', '', '', '', 0.1, 'f',
300, 30, '', 'Ottawa, Ontario', '', '', '', '', '', '', '');

insert into customer (name, addr1, addr2, addr3, addr4, contact,
phone, fax, e-mail, notes, discount, taxincluded, creditlimit, terms,
shiptoname, shiptoaddr1, shiptoaddr2, shiptoaddr3, shiptoaddr4,
shiptocontact, shiptophone, shiptofax, shiptoe-mail) values ( 'roosta',
'', '', '', '', '', '', '', '', '', 0, 'f', 40, 30, 'Roosta', '', '',
'', '', '', '', '', '');

insert into customer (name, addr1, addr2, addr3, addr4, contact,
phone, fax, e-mail, notes, discount, taxincluded, creditlimit, terms,
shiptoname, shiptoaddr1, shiptoaddr2, shiptoaddr3, shiptoaddr4,
shiptocontact, shiptophone, shiptofax, shiptoe-mail) values ( 'linus',
'', '', '', '', '', '', '', '', '', 0.85, 'f', 100000, 40,
'Linus Torvalds', '', '', '', '', '', '', '', '');

insert into customer (name, addr1, addr2, addr3, addr4, contact,
phone, fax, e-mail, notes, discount, taxincluded, creditlimit, terms,
shiptoname, shiptoaddr1, shiptoaddr2, shiptoaddr3, shiptoaddr4,
shiptocontact, shiptophone, shiptofax, shiptoe-mail) values ( 'tlug',
'100 Yonge St', '', '', '', 'Drew', '', '', '', '', 0, 't', 150, 10,
'Toronto Linux Users Group', 'Toronto, Ontario', '', '', '', '', '',
'', '');
```

Now, let's begin with writing the client. The first few lines are typical, as we do while setting up the connection to the SOAP client:

```
#!/usr/bin/perl -w
use SOAP::Lite;
use SoapTools;
use Data::Dumper; ($Data::Dumper::Terse, $Data::Dumper::Indent) = (1, 1);
my ($host, $url, $csize) = ("salesman", "soap/sql.pl", 400);
my $proxy = "http://$host/$url";
my $SoapServer =
   SOAP::Lite -> proxy($proxy, options => {compress_threshold => $csize});

print "-=" x 35, "\n";
print "Soap Server: $SoapServer at $proxy\n";
print "=-" x 35, "\n";
%SERVICES = ();
my @CUSTOMERLIST;
read_password_file();
foreach my $cust (keys %SERVICES) {
  push @CUSTOMERLIST, SOAP::Data -> value([$cust, $SERVICES{$cust}]);
}
$reqdate = "2002-04-21";
$transdate = "2002-05-01";
$res = $SoapServer->addbillings(@CUSTOMERLIST, $reqdate, $transdate);
print Dumper($res->valueof());
```

In the above code, the function `read_password_file()` reads customer information from `/etc/passwd`, parsing the fields using regular expressions, and placing the values in `%SERVICES`. Then we marshal the customer information into `@CUSTOMERLIST` for transmission over to the SOAP service, send it over to `addbillings()`, and then dump out the values passed back.

The `read_password_file()` can be written as shown below:

```
sub read_password_file {
  # Search for lines containing 'ISP' where the second field
  # doesn't start with "!"
  open(PW, "grep ISP /etc/passwd | egrep -v '^[^:]*:[^!]' |");
  my $line;
  while ($line = <PW>) {
    # Split the password line into a set of fields; we want the
    # name and GECOS fields
    $line =~ /^([^:]*):[^:]*:[^:]*:[^:]*:([^:]*):/;
    my ($name, $gecos) = ($1, $2);
    # Now pull the GECOS field apart to get the account type
    $gecos =~ /^[^,]*,([^,]*),/;
    my $acct = $1;
    print "ID: $name Account Type: $acct\n";
    $SERVICES{$name} = $acct;
  }
}
```

Benchmarking with Zip Codes

Now, we'll look at general-purpose functionality that can obviously be used with SQL-Ledger. Let's have few methods for pulling US Zip codes out of a relational database, providing methods that take out the information about the city, state, latitude, and longitude.

The goal of this exercise is to explore the differences in performance between several different implementation approaches. The data is the same; we vary the method that the data is requested. The table contains data that includes the following Zip code information:

Zipcode	State	City	Latitude	Longitude
76155	TX	FORT WORTH	32.8247	-97.0503
75028	TX	FLOWER MOUND	33.0383	-97.0745
75010	TX	CARROLLTON	33.0304	-96.8777
75019	TX	COPPELL	32.9673	-96.9805
75057	TX	LEWISVILLE	33.0532	-96.9999
75063	TX	IRVING	32.9247	-96.9598

We can add this table to our database by using the following SQL query:

```
CREATE TABLE "zipcode" (
        "zipcode" character varying(5) NOT NULL,
        "city" character varying(30) NOT NULL,
        "state" character(2) NOT NULL,
        "longitude" real,
        "latitude" real,
        Constraint "zipcode_pkey" Primary Key ("zipcode")
);
```

A corresponding SQL script containing a large collection of Zip codes may be found at http://www.cbbrowne.com/downloads/.

In this Zipcodes module, we'll introduce two main SOAP methods:

- getZipcode() – Pulls information about one Zip code
- getZipcodes() – Pulls a list of Zip codes, based on an array that is passed in

Here, the objective is to see how performance differs between the two methods. The initial expectation is that it should be quite a lot faster to submit larger requests, but the question is how big the difference will be, and what parts of the system most control that difference.

Let's take a look at the server that implemented the ZipCodes module:

```
#!/usr/bin/perl
package ZipCodes;
require 5.000;
use Exporter;
use SoapTools;
use SOAP::Lite;
use vars qw(@ISA);
@ISA = qw(Exporter SOAP::Server::Parameters);
@EXPORT = qw(getZipcode getZipcodes getZipcodeNoDB
             getZipcodeDBNoQuery getZipcodesNoRet
             getZipcodeNoDBNoResult);
```

The module, of course, begins with the "paperwork" for setting up the module linkages. Here, we define the set of database fields that are to be pulled from the database:

```
%ZIPFIELDS = ( "zipcode" => "string", "city" => "string",
               "state" => "string", "latitude" => "float",
               "longitude" => "float" );
```

Method getZipCode() is written here; it establishes a connection to the database, draws the requested Zip code, and passes back an array representing the resulting data:

```
sub getZipcode {
  my $self = shift;
  my ($zip) = @_;
```

```
    my $DBI_H = connect_db();
    my $zipquery = "select * from zipcode where zipcode = '$zip'";
    my $DBI_H = connect_db();
    my $QHandle = $DBI_H->prepare($zipquery);
    my @RESULTS;
    $QHandle->execute;
    print " getZipcode: ",  $zipquery, "\n";
    while (my $ref = $QHandle->fetchrow_hashref) {
      my @ResultRow = ();
      foreach my $fld (keys %ZIPFIELDS) {
        my $val = $ref->{$fld};
        if ($val) {
          push @ResultRow, mkdata($val, $fld,
                                  $ZIPFIELDS{$fld});
        }
      }
      push @RESULTS, SOAP::Data-> name('zipcode') -> value(\@ResultRow);
    }
    $QHandle->finish;
    $DBI_H->disconnect;
    return SOAP::Data->name('zipcodes') -> value(\@RESULTS);
  }
```

Method `getZipcodes()` is very similar to `getZipcode()`, but draws in a list of Zip codes as input and passes back a tree of results:

```
  # Maximum number of zip codes queryable
  $MaxZips = 400;

  sub getZipcodes {
    my $self = shift;
    my @ZIPS = @_;
    if ($#ZIPS > $MaxZips) {
      die SOAP::Fault
        -> faultstring("getZipcodes can only draw $MaxZips zip codes");
    }
    my $DBI_H = connect_db();
    my $zipquery = 'select * from zipcode where zipcode in (';
    my $last = pop @ZIPS;
    foreach my $i (@ZIPS) {
      $zipquery .= "'". $i . "', ";
    }
    $zipquery .= "'" . $last . "')";
    print "Zip code query: $zipquery\n";
    my $DBI_H = connect_db();
    my $QHandle = $DBI_H->prepare($zipquery);
    $QHandle->execute;
    my @RESULTS;
    while (my $ref = $QHandle->fetchrow_hashref) {
      my @ResultRow = ();
      foreach my $fld (keys %ZIPFIELDS) {
        my $val = $ref->{$fld};
        if ($val) {
```

```
          push @ResultRow, mkdata($val, $fld,
                                  $ZIPFIELDS{$fld});
        }
      }
      push @RESULTS, SOAP::Data-> name('zipcodeEntry') -> value(\@ResultRow);
    }
    $QHandle->finish;
    $DBI_H->disconnect;
    return SOAP::Data->name('zipcodes') -> value(\@RESULTS);
  }
```

Lastly, a set of variations on `getZipcode()` and `getZipcodes()` are defined. The function `getZipcodeNoDB()` returns a fixed value regardless of what is passed in; it does not connect to the database at all:

```
  sub getZipcodeNoDB {
    my @RESULTS;
    my @ResultRow = ();
    push @ResultRow, mkdata('75063', 'zipcode', 'string');
    push @ResultRow, mkdata('Irving', 'city', 'string');
    push @ResultRow, mkdata('TX', 'state', 'string');
    push @ResultRow, mkdata(-42, 'latitude', 'float');
    push @ResultRow, mkdata(-35, 'longitude', 'float');
    push @RESULTS, SOAP::Data-> name('zipcode') -> value(\@ResultRow);
    return SOAP::Data->name('zipcodes') -> value(\@RESULTS);
  }
```

The `getZipcodeDBNoQuery()` function returns a fixed value regardless of what is passed in. Unlike `getZipcodeNoDB()`, it does connect to the database, but it does not submit a query.

Timings for this function may be compared with `getZipcode()` to estimate the time required to establish database connections:

```
  sub getZipcodeDBNoQuery {
    my @RESULTS;
    my @ResultRow = ();
    my $DBI_H = connect_db();
    push @ResultRow, mkdata('75063', 'zipcode', 'string');
    push @ResultRow, mkdata('Irving', 'city', 'string');
    push @ResultRow, mkdata('TX', 'state', 'string');
    push @ResultRow, mkdata(-42, 'latitude', 'float');
    push @ResultRow, mkdata(-35, 'longitude', 'float');
    push @RESULTS, SOAP::Data-> name('zipcode') -> value(\@ResultRow);
    $DBI_H->disconnect;
    return SOAP::Data->name('zipcodes') -> value(\@RESULTS);
  }
```

The following function `getZipcodesNoRet()` is based on `getZipcodes()`, but does not bother returning the results of the query:

```
sub getZipcodesNoRet {
  my $self = shift;
  my @ZIPS = @_;
  if ($#ZIPS > $MaxZips) {
    die SOAP::Fault
      -> faultstring("getZipcodes can only draw $MaxZips zip codes");
  }
  my $DBI_H = connect_db();
  my $zipquery = 'select * from zipcode where zipcode in (';
  my $last = pop @ZIPS;
  foreach my $i (@ZIPS) {
    $zipquery .= "'". $i . "', ";
  }
  $zipquery .= "'" . $last . "')";
  print "Zip code query: $zipquery\n";
  my $DBI_H = connect_db();
  my $QHandle = $DBI_H->prepare($zipquery);
  $QHandle->execute;
  my @RESULTS;
  while (my $ref = $QHandle->fetchrow_hashref) {
    # Don't bother returning SOAP results...
  }
  $QHandle->finish;
  $DBI_H->disconnect;
  return SOAP::Data->name('zipcodes') -> value(\@RESULTS);
}
```

This lets us determine how long it takes to process the rather large SOAP message that is returned.

Then we have a function `getZipcodesNoDBNoResult()`, which is based on `getZipcodes()`, but does not connect to the database or return any results. This method allows us to determine how long it takes to process the SOAP messages containing the query:

```
sub getZipcodesNoDBNoResult {
  my $self = shift;
  my @ZIPS = @_;
  if ($#ZIPS > $MaxZips) {
    die SOAP::Fault
      -> faultstring("getZipcodes can only draw $MaxZips zip codes");
  }
}

1;
```

Building the Zipcodes Client

To go along with this, here is the client script to do a simple benchmark based on this set of methods:

```
#!/usr/bin/perl -w
use SOAP::Lite;
use SoapTools;
use Data::Dumper; ($Data::Dumper::Terse, $Data::Dumper::Indent) = (1, 1);
my ($host, $url, $csize) = ("salesman", "soap/sql.pl", 400);
```

```
my $proxy = "http://$host/$url";
my $SoapServer =
  SOAP::Lite ->proxy($proxy, options => {compress_threshold => $csize});

print "-=" x 35, "\n";
print "Soap Server: $SoapServer at $proxy\n";
print "=-" x 35, "\n";
```

As always, the usual bookkeeping is involved in setting up the connection to the SOAP server. Note that this sets up the client to support the data compression that SOAP::Lite supports. It might be interesting to try it out with compression turned off to see how that influences performance. That would be done by eliminating the `compress_threshold` parameter from the options.

The database fields will be then set up as an associative array so that later code can pull the set of fields without needing to hard code field names into the code:

```
%ZIPFIELDS = ( "zipcode" => "string", "city" => "string",
               "state" => "string", "latitude" => "float",
               "longitude" => "float" );
```

We'll set up a range of Zip codes that are to be queried, from `09301` to `09601`:

```
# Range of zip codes to search through
($from, $to) = (9301, 9601);

# Data structures to collect timing info
my (@DESC, @TIMING, @QUANT, $testno);
```

Before we move ahead with our client code, let's take a look at a couple of methods we'll be using.

The arrays `@DESC`, `@TIMING`, and `@QUANT` will be used to collect the timing data:

```
sub collect_stats {
  my ($pos, $string, $start, $count) = @_;
  my $elapsed = time() - $start;
  $DESC[$pos] = $string;
  $TIMING[$pos] = $elapsed / $count;
  $QUANT[$pos] = $count;
}
```

The method `collect_stats()` does the work of collecting information about a particular test into these arrays. The standard function `time()` provides date stamps accurate to the second, so any tests that run less than a second will not be reported to a useful degree of accuracy without running them several times.

The function `Lots_of_Queries()` accepts the range `$from` and `$to`, as well as the name `$method` of the SOAP method that is to be used to access Zip codes, one at a time. It drops the results into `@Zipcodes`, which is the return result for `Lots_of_Queries()`. This function will be used three times to see how long it takes to run `getZipcode()`, `getZipcodeDBNoQuery()`, and `getZipcodeNoDB()`:

```
# Lots_of_Queries invokes a SOAP request for each zip code
# and allows selecting the method via the third argument
sub Lots_of_Queries {
  my ($from, $to, $method) = @_;
  my @Zipcodes;
  for (my $i = $from; $i <= $to; $i++) {
    my $count = 1;
    $getids = $SoapServer->call($method => SOAP::Data
                             ->value(sprintf("%05d", $i)));
    if ($getids->fault) {
      reportresults($method, $getids);
    } else {
      foreach my $field (keys %ZIPFIELDS) {
        my $fval = $getids->match("//$field")->valueof();
        if ($fval) {
          $Zipcodes[$count-1]{$field} = $fval;
          #print $field, $fval, "\n";
        }
      }
      $count++;
    }
  }
  return \@Zipcodes;
}
```

Let's come back to our client code where we'll use the above methods. Three runs of `Lots_of_Queries()` collect comparative performance statistics for the three variations of the Zip code queries:

```
# Run the Singleton SOAP Queries
$tstart = time();
my @RES = Lots_of_Queries($from, $to, "getZipcode");
collect_stats(++$testno, "getZipcode", $tstart, 1);
$tstart = time();
@RES = Lots_of_Queries($from, $to, "getZipcodeDBNoQuery");
collect_stats(++$testno, "getZipcodeDBNoQuery", $tstart, 1);
$tstart = time();
@RES = Lots_of_Queries($from, $to, "getZipcodeNoDB");
collect_stats(++$testno, "getZipcodeNoDB", $tstart, 1);
```

We compare these three queries to find out if a kind of database connection pooling can be used to cut down on the number of established connections. The succession of `$t2`, `$t3`, `$t4`, and so forth will be used to record the time consumed by successive phases of processing:

- `getZipcode()` – Collects real data from the database.
- `getZipcodeDBNoQuery()` – Establishes the database connection, but does not bother doing any database query. The method returns useless data, but returns the right amount of useless data, so that the work done marshaling results on client and server and transmitting the SOAP message should be comparable to `getZipcode()`. This function is used to determine how the database queries are time consuming.

- getZipcodeNoDB() – Does no database work. This is intended to measure how expensive it is to establish database connections, distinct from the queries. As with getZipcodeDBNoQuery(), the data is completely worthless, but since it is again of realistic size, work done transferring and processing the SOAP messages will be comparable to getZipcode().

The program now proceeds to set up a query that will use getZipcodes() to pull Zip codes 09301 through 09601. Zip code values are not numbers, and require the leading zero, so sprintf("%05d", $i) transforms this into a string, ensuring that leading zeroes are kept, to be passed on via SOAP:

```
my @ZIPS;
for (my $i = $from; $i <= $to; $i++) {
  push @ZIPS, SOAP::Data->value(sprintf("%05d", $i)) ->type("string");
}
foreach my $i (0..9) {  # 10 times to give better precision...
  $getids = $SoapServer->getZipcodes(SOAP::Data ->value(@ZIPS));
}
collect_stats(++$testno, "getZipcodes", $tstart, 10);
$tstart = time();
```

Since this method runs quite quickly, in only few seconds, it is invoked ten times so that the average time may be determined to a greater level of precision.

As it turns out, performance of the SOM code that draws the Zip code data out of $getids is very interesting to examine. The following code walks through the data in $getids using the SOM function match(), to extract the Zip code data, and collects the time statistics:

```
my @Zipcodes;
my $count = 1;
#print Dumper($getids);
while ($getids->match("//zipcodes/[$count]")) {
  #print "Count: $count\n";
  foreach my $field (keys %ZIPFIELDS) {
    my $fval = get_field($getids, $count, $field);
      if ($fval) {
        $Zipcodes[$count-1]{$field} = $fval;
      }
  }
  $count++;
}
collect_stats(++$testno, "SOM Collection", $tstart, 1);
$tstart = time();
```

It turns out that this approach to the extraction of data from $getids, using a whole lot of match() calls, is extremely expensive.

We'll use the manual_parse_query() method that takes an alternative approach, walking through the data in the complex data structure in $getids. $getids contains a nested set of arrays and associative arrays arranged in a particular manner. The main object, $getids is an associative array where the main contents of the message are contained in the _content entry. Within that content element, there is an array of size 7, as shown in the following table:

Name	Description
name	string
attributes	associative array
children	array
undef	Unused
values of children	array
lname	string
namespace information	associative array

@RESULTS is set up with the set of results using manual_parse_query(), and the final time statistic is collected. It turns out that this function runs very quickly, completing regularly in a tiny fraction of a second, the minimum resolution of the timer. As a result, it is run 1000 times to get a much more precise estimate of the timing:

```
foreach my $i (0..999) {
  my @RESULTS = manual_parse_query($getids);
  #print "Dump results: ", Dumper(@RESULTS);
}
collect_stats(++$testno, "parse query manually", $tstart, 1000);
$tstart = time();
```

Next, the methods getZipcodesNoRet() and getZipcodesNoDBNoResult() are run. These SOAP methods work in a similar manner as getZipcode():

```
foreach my $i (0..9) {
  my $nores = $SoapServer->getZipcodesNoRet(SOAP::Data ->value(@ZIPS));
}
collect_stats(++$testno, "getZipcodesNoRet", $tstart, 10);
$tstart = time();

foreach my $i (0..9) {
  my $nores = $SoapServer->getZipcodeNoDBNoResult(SOAP::Data ->value(@ZIPS));
}
collect_stats(++$testno, "getZipcodesNoDBNoResult", $tstart, 10);
$tstart = time();
```

getZipcodesNoRet() does not bother returning Zip code results as a SOAP message. The goal of this is to determine the amount of time taken to marshal and return the results.

getZipcodesNoDBNoResult() does not bother doing any database query nor does it return any Zip code results. Essentially, all it does is to parse the incoming SOAP message. Comparing that to getZipcodesNoRet() will give us a good idea as to how much time is consumed by the database query.

Since these methods run quite quickly, they are each executed several times to get better precision. Now we'll use the DBI class to set up a direct connection to the database, not using SOAP at all:

```
foreach my $i (0..10) {
  &dbi_query_many_queries();
}
collect_stats(++$testno, "DBI: Many Queries", $tstart, 10);
$tstart = time();
foreach my $i (0..10) {
  &dbi_query_one_big_query();
}
collect_stats(++$testno, "DBI: One Big Query", $tstart, 10);
$tstart = time();
foreach my $i (0..10) {
  &dbi_query_one_little_query();
}
collect_stats(++$testno, "DBI: Ranged query", $tstart, 10);
$tstart = time();
```

The `dbi_query_many_queries()` query uses the `DBI` interface directly, generating and invoking a query for each element:

```
# Submit a DBI query
sub dbi_query_many_queries {
  my $DBI_H = connect_db();
  foreach my $zip (9301..9600) {
    my $zipquery = "select * from zipcode where zipcode = '$zip'";
    my $QHandle = $DBI_H->prepare($zipquery);
    $QHandle->execute;
    $QHandle->finish;
  }
  $DBI_H->disconnect;
}

sub dbi_query_one_big_query {
  my $DBI_H = connect_db();
  my $zipquery = 'select * from zipcode where zipcode in (';
  foreach my $i (9301..9600) {
    $zipquery .= "'0". $i . "', ";
  }
  $zipquery .= "'09601')";
  my $QHandle = $DBI_H->prepare($zipquery);
  $QHandle->execute;
  $QHandle->finish;
  $DBI_H->disconnect;
}

sub dbi_query_one_little_query {
  my $DBI_H = connect_db();
  my $zipquery = qq|select * from zipcode where zipcode >= '09301' and
                    zipcode <= '09601'|;
  my $QHandle = $DBI_H->prepare($zipquery);
  $QHandle->execute;
  $QHandle->finish;
  $DBI_H->disconnect;
}
```

Finally, the timing measurements are displayed:

```
print "-=" x 35, "\n";
print "  Timing Results\n";
print "-=" x 35, "\n";
print "Proxy: $proxy\n";
print "-=" x 35, "\n";
foreach $i (1..$testno) {
  printf "%52s   %4d   %7.3f\n", $DESC[$i], $QUANT[$i], $TIMING[$i];
}
print "=-" x 35, "\n";
```

The results of a run of this may be a little surprising; on a 266 MHz AMD K6 host, the final results look like:

```
-=-=-=-=-=-=-=-=-=-=-=-=-=-=-=-=-=-=-=-=-=-=-=-=-=-=-=-=-=-=-=-=-=-=-=
Soap Server: SOAP::Lite=HASH(0x838b848) at http://salesman/soap/sql.pl
=-=-=-=-=-=-=-=-=-=-=-=-=-=-=-=-=-=-=-=-=-=-=-=-=-=-=-=-=-=-=-=-=-=-=-
-=-=-=-=-=-=-=-=-=-=-=-=-=-=-=-=-=-=-=-=-=-=-=-=-=-=-=-=-=-=-=-=-=-=-=
  Timing Results
-=-=-=-=-=-=-=-=-=-=-=-=-=-=-=-=-=-=-=-=-=-=-=-=-=-=-=-=-=-=-=-=-=-=-=
Proxy: http://salesman/soap/sql.pl
-=-=-=-=-=-=-=-=-=-=-=-=-=-=-=-=-=-=-=-=-=-=-=-=-=-=-=-=-=-=-=-=-=-=-=
                                          getZipcode      1   813.000
                                 getZipcodeDBNoQuery      1   875.000
                                      getZipcodeNoDB      1   725.000
                                         getZipcodes     10    81.300
                                      SOM Collection      1   476.000
                                parse query manually   1000     0.076
                                    getZipcodesNoRet     10     4.100
                            getZipcodesNoDBNoResult     10     4.200
                                   DBI: Many Queries     10     1.600
                                  DBI: One Big Query     10     0.700
                                   DBI: Ranged query     10     0.100
=-=-=-=-=-=-=-=-=-=-=-=-=-=-=-=-=-=-=-=-=-=-=-=-=-=-=-=-=-=-=-=-=-=-=-
```

Benchmarking

There are some very interesting conclusions to be drawn from the results.

The tests that pull data for one Zip code at a time demonstrate quite clearly that requesting information about 300 Zip codes using 300 SOAP requests takes a lot of time. A communication scheme that will take several minutes to complete is certainly not what we want to use.

When lesser database work is done, several '`null` loads' are performed to analyze how much of the overhead for the single item-oriented methods are associated with the (often time-consuming) task of establishing database connections.

It is quite common for Java applications using JDBC to use classes that share database connections as much as possible in order to save the efforts of setting up new context objects. If that is valuable for Java servlets, we might expect the approach to be valuable here.

In this case, the cost of database connections seems to represent about 10% of total time, while the cost of performing the database queries is a little bit larger than that. Hence, the value of connection pooling seems fairly limited, offering a maximum theoretical improvement of 10%, and much less than that would likely be possible in practice.

The SOAP query using `getZipcodes()` is vastly faster than the queries that request one Zip codc at a time. That shouldn't come as much of a surprise, and demonstrates the importance of trying to have SOAP requests submit multiple results, when possible.

On the other hand, a quite astounding result is the long time required to remap the results from `getZipcodes()` using the `SOAP::SOM` methods.

That takes considerably longer than the individual SOAP calls to `getZipcode()`. The reason for this result is that each and every `match()` call walks through the whole `$getids` structure. There being 123 Zip codes, and five fields to search for, `match()` walks through the entire set of 123 Zip codes 615 times, which is distinctly not what we desire.

The `SOM` search is followed by a direct walk through `$getids` using `manual_parse_query()`, which does just one run through the data in `$getids`, extracting all of the data in a fraction of a second. This does not imply that the `SOAP::SOM` methods should never be used, only that they must be used carefully. Each time they are used, they may walk through the whole message, so running them many times on large messages is a poor idea.

Another implication that is somewhat surprising, and fortunately, encouraging, is that the major bottlenecks we find are on the client-side. The notable client-side bottleneck is with the `SOM` methods, and can be resolved by manually walking through the `SOM` data structure.

The last three measurements access the data directly using the `DBI` interface, making no use of SOAP. Even the slowest one, which processes an SQL query for each element, runs considerably faster than even the fastest SOAP call. This tells us that SOAP is enormously inefficient in comparison with the `DBI` interface. That principle may be applied quite widely. XML messages are quite verbose, compared to binary formats, and parsing XML messages is quite costly.

Just as with `SOAP::SOM`, there are places and ways of using SOAP that will be wise, and others that are not. It is easy enough to link `DBI` or some other such interface into an application, which will often provide much more efficient communications than SOAP can offer.

A direct `DBI` query is fairly faster than the fastest of the SOAP queries, nevertheless `getZipcodes()` does run quickly enough to be reasonably acceptable even when used in an interactive process.

SOAP is used for a number of reasons. If SOAP is used as a common protocol to connect to the servers, the only libraries required are those for SOAP, regardless of how many kinds of services may be added. The SOAP interface does not expose nearly as much of the database as the `DBI` interface would, simplifying managing security.

Each SOAP interface only exposes the specific data and methods it is designed to expose. In case of the methods that have been implemented in this chapter, this includes specific sorts of information about customers. There is no way for the ISP to use these SOAP methods to access payroll information or accounts payable information, as no methods exist to support access to those sorts of data.

Securing PostgreSQL against unauthorized accesses using a generic access scheme like DBI is likely to be rather more challenging than securing SOAP interfaces that only provide the precise set of operations that are intended to be allowed.

There are further performance comparisons that could prove useful:

- Comparing the behavior for different network configurations, such as having the SOAP client separated from the server via various slower sorts of network links
- Varying the configuration or nature of the network protocol, changing the use of message compression, or using substantially different protocols such as HTTPS or Jabber
- Varying the message schema further

The examples included just two data representations, one for `getZipcode()` and one for `getZipcodes()`; it would be interesting to try alternative representations such as:

```
$outgoing_message = SOAP::Data
-> value ( SOAP::Data ->type('string') -> value('75063'),
           SOAP::Data ->type('string') -> value('Irving'),
           SOAP::Data ->type('string') -> value('TX'),
           SOAP::Data ->type('float'),
           SOAP::Data ->type('float')
         );
```

This representation treats the result as an array with a fixed number of fields; in effect, the names become irrelevant.

Traditional data interchange applications have long used much the same approach. Mainframe-based applications typically set up the records as fixed-length sets of fields, often exactly 72, 80, or 132 characters wide, corresponding to common sizes for punched cards or screen widths:

```
$outgoing_message = SOAP::Data
-> value (SOAP::Data ->value(SOAP::Data->value('zipcode'),
                             SOAP::Data->value('75063')->type('string')),
          SOAP::Data ->value(SOAP::Data->value('city'),
                             SOAP::Data->value('Irving')->type('string')),
          SOAP::Data ->value(SOAP::Data->value('state'),
                             SOAP::Data->value('TX')->type('string')));
```

This representation has each real element treated as an array composed of a string which is the name, followed by the element's value.

It is a rather less space-efficient way of transmitting the data, since rather than having the name as part of the element, it sets up an extra element, and roughly doubles the size of messages. It has the significant merit that it simultaneously exposes both names and values in native form in various languages:

```
 # Perl
@Resulting_Message =
  [['zipcode', '75063'],
   ['city', 'Irving'],
```

```
    ['state', 'TX']];

# Python
Resulting_Message = (('zipcode','75063'),('city','Irving'),('state','TX'))

# Ruby
Resulting_Message = [['zipcode','75063'],['city','Irving'],['state','TX']]
```

This representation may not be particularly efficient in terms of message sizes, but working with the result requires no special SOAP-specific APIs or code, and that is quite useful. In most languages, it is by far most convenient to access data in whatever native form it is provided in. The nested arrays shown above are quite a convenient form, requiring no SOAP-specific code. In contrast, consider the following XML structure:

```
<location>
  <zipcode>75063</zipcode>
  <city>Irving</city>
  <state>TX</state>
</location>
```

When the result is extracted from that message by these languages, the resulting value is likely to simply look like `['75063', 'Irving', 'TX']`. The names of the elements, `zipcode`, `city`, and `state`, disappear unless you use language-specific SOAP APIs to expressly extract that information.

Summary

We have looked at some more realistic examples of the use of SOAP in this chapter, based on interfacing with the SQL-Ledger accounting system. We developed a web service (a SOAP interface) to supply information about customer accounts, including methods to query customers individually or in groups, as well as requesting lists of customers with overdue payments. We added a SOAP interface to add billing documents to the accounting system.

We created a SOAP interface to query the system about US Zip codes. Several different query approaches were examined to see how the performance of SOAP queries varies. Poorly designed interfaces may perform very badly.

Configuring Tomcat with Apache

Tomcat can be used as a standalone web server. We can also use it along with Apache. In such a configuration, Apache would serve up the static HTML pages and Tomcat would handle the JSP pages and servlets. Why do we want to use Apache for the static HTML pages instead of Tomcat's HTTP/1.1 connector? We do this because we get a better performance by using such a configuration.

Tomcat 4.0 provides for two means of allowing communication between Apache and Tomcat – through the AJP protocol and through the new WARP protocol. The AJP protocol requires the use of `mod_jk`, which is a component that enables communication between Apache and Tomcat. This component replaces the older `mod_jserv`, and has a better architecture allowing support for Tomcat 1.3.x as well as Tomcat 1.2. It also provides better SSL support. The `mod_webapp` connector provides WARP support.

Before we start discussing the configuration of either of them, remove any `AjpServMount` directives from `httpd.conf`, as these directives would exist if Apache were previously set up with JServ. These are not compatible with `mod_jk`. The configuration setup described below will work for both Apache 1.3 as well as Apache 2.0.

AJP Connector

The AJP `Connector` directive (shown below) should be present by default in Tomcat's `server.xml` file:

```
<!-- Define an AJP 1.3 Connector on port 8009 -->
 <Connector className="org.apache.ajp.tomcat4.Ajp13Connector"
            port="8009" minProcessors="5" maxProcessors="75"
            acceptCount="10" debug="0"/>
```

Next, we install and configure mod_jk. This is available either in binary or in source form from the Jakarta web site. The mod_jk binary is available for some platforms (such as Linux and Windows) from Tomcat binary download location. The Tomcat 3.3 binary release location (http://jakarta.apache.org/builds/jakarta-tomcat/release/v3.3/bin/) has this too. mod_jk is independent of Tomcat versions.

In the source form, it is available as the Jakarta Tomcat Connector module, downloadable from http://jakarta.apache.org/builds/jakarta-tomcat-4.0/release/v4.0.3/src/. The code for mod_jk is in the jk directory under the Tomcat connectors' source tree. This directory also contains a README.txt with the build instructions.

We use the new Tomcat-Apache auto-configuration mechanism as it simplifies our configuration. Using this mechanism, all we need to do is to include the mod_jk.conf-auto file in Apache's httpd.conf, and then add directives to Tomcat's server.xml to get it to generate the mod_jk.conf-auto file.

A sample include directive for httpd.conf is shown below.

On UNIX:

```
include /usr/local/jakarta-tomcat-4.0.3/conf/jk/mod_jk.conf-auto
```

On Windows:

```
include "c:\Apache Tomcat 4.0\conf\mod_jk.conf-auto"
```

We can configure Tomcat so that it automatically generates a mod_jk.conf-auto file when it starts up. Since we have this file included in Apache's httpd.conf, this is all that we need to do.

To get Tomcat to generate this file, we need to add an ApacheConfig directive in Tomcat's server.xml file. The syntax of this directive is:

```
<ContextManager ...>
   ...
   <ApacheConfig options />
   ...
</ContextManager>
```

The options mentioned above can be one or more of the following:

- configHome
  Default parent directory for the following paths. If not set, this defaults to CATALINA_HOME. Ignored whenever any of the following paths is absolute.
- jkConfig
  This specifies the path to write apache mod_jk conf file. If not set, defaults to conf/auto/mod_jk.conf.
- workersConfig
  Path to workers.properties file used by mod_jk. If not set, defaults to conf/jk/workers.properties.

- `modJk`
  This specifies the path to Apache `mod_jk` plugin file. If not set, defaults to `modules/mod_jk.dll` on Windows, `modules/mod_jk.nlm` on Netware, and `libexec/mod_jk.so` everywhere else.
- `jkLog`
  This directive specifies the path to log file to be used by `mod_jk`.
- `jkDebug`
  This specifies the JK `Loglevel` setting. May be `debug`, `info`, `error`, or `emerg`. If not set, defaults to no log.
- `jkWorker`
  `jkWorker` specifies the desired worker. Must be set to one of the workers defined in the `workers.properties` file. `ajp13` or `inprocess` are the workers found in the default `workers.properties` file. If not specified, defaults to `ajp13`.

The `worker.properties` file defines the properties for a Tomcat worker, which is an instance of Tomcat that executes servlets on behalf of some other web server (such as Apache in this case). The following is a sample of a `worker.properties` file. The AJP port number (8009) specified in the `workers.properties` should be the port number for the AJP connector in `server.xml`:

```
workers.tomcat_home=/usr/local/jakarta-tomcat
workers.java_home=/usr/java
ps=/
worker.list=ajp13

worker.ajp13.port=8009
worker.ajp13.host=localhost
worker.ajp13.type=ajp13
...
```

- `forwardAll`
  If `true`, forward all requests to Tomcat. This helps ensure that all the behavior configured in the `web.xml` file functions correctly. If `false`, let Apache serve static resources. The default is `true`. When `false`, some configuration in the `web.xml` may not be duplicated in Apache. Review the `mod_jk` conf file to see what configuration is actually being set in Apache.
- `noRoot`
  If `true`, the root context is not mapped to Tomcat. If `false` and `forwardAll` is `true`, all requests to the root context are mapped to Tomcat. If `false` and `forwardAll` is `false`, only JSP and servlets requests to the root context are mapped to Tomcat. When `false`, to correctly serve Tomcat's root context we must also modify the `DocumentRoot` setting in Apache's `httpd.conf` file to point to Tomcat's root context directory. Otherwise some content, such as Apache's `index.html`, will be served by Apache before `mod_jk` gets a chance to claim the request and pass it to Tomcat. The default is `true`.
- `append`
  Append to the current configuration file.

A sample entry from `server.xml` is shown below:

```
<ApacheConfig forwardAll="false" noRoot="false"
       jkConfig="conf/mod_jk.conf-auto" jkDebug="error" />
```

After we complete this configuration, we should restart Tomcat and Apache. Now, Apache will serve up all static content (HTML pages, images, and so on) and Tomcat will handle the dynamic content (JSP pages and servlets). The static content will be served from Apache's `DocumentRoot`, and the JSP and servlet requests to the root context will be served from Tomcat's `ROOT` web application. We may need to update Apache's `DocumentRoot` to point to Tomcat's `ROOT` web application; otherwise any static reference in a JSP/servlet (such as a `.gif` or `.jpg` file) would not be displayed.

We can create custom configurations by first enabling auto-configuration (as shown above), and then using the generated `mod_jk.conf-auto` as a template.

If we do this, we must remember to save the resultant config file as some other name (other than `mod_jk.conf-auto`) and include that file in `httpd.conf`. This is because the `ApacheConfig` directive in `server.xml` would cause Tomcat to create this file each time it starts up, overwriting our changes.

The directives that can go into `mod_jk.conf` are shown below. These directives can be placed either at the root section or inside `VirtualHost` sections. These directives can also be placed inside the `httpd.conf` file instead of including `mod_jk.conf`:

- `LoadModule/AddModule` directives for loading `mod_jk.so`

  On UNIX:

```
AddModule  mod_jk.c
LoadModule jk_module  libexec/mod_jk.so
```

- `JkLogFile` directive for specifying the log file
- `JkLogLevel` directive for specifying the log level. The level could be one of `debug`, `info`, `error`, or `emerg`.
- `JkLogStampFormat` for specifying the date/time format for log files.

  The example below shows these setting for UNIX:

```
JkLogFile         /usr/local/apache/logs/mod_jk.log
JkLogLevel        info
JkLogStampFormat  "[%a %b %d %H:%M:%S %Y] "
```

- `JkMount` directive for assigning URLs to Tomcat.

  The syntax for this directive is:

```
JkMount <URL prefix> <Worker name>
```

  The example below sends all requests for JSP pages and servlets to Tomcat for processing:

```
JkMount /*.jsp ajp13
JkMount /servlet/* ajp13
```

- `JkWorkersFile` directive for letting `mod_jk` know the location of our `workers.properties` file.

  A sample `JkWorkersFile` directive is shown below:

```
JkWorkersFile /usr/local/jakarta-tomcat/conf/workers.properties
```

WARP Connector

WARP is a new protocol for enabling communication between Apache and Tomcat. We need to use mod_webapp for WARP. mod_webapp doesn't support some of the functionality provided by mod_jk, such as load balancing. The configuration steps for setting up mod_webapp are detailed below.

Configure Tomcat

The <Connector> directive for the WARP Connector in server.xml file is shown below:

```
<Connector className="org.apache.catalina.connector.warp.WarpConnector"
 port="8008" minProcessors="5" maxProcessors="75"
 enableLookups="true" appBase="webapps"
 acceptCount="10" debug="0"/>
```

Take a note of this port number (8008). We will be using this later in Apache's configuration.

Install and Configure mod_webapp

WARP uses the mod_webapp module to connect Apache with Tomcat. This module can be obtained in source form as a part of the Jakarta Tomcat Connectors module, downloadable from http://jakarta.apache.org/builds/jakarta-tomcat-4.0/release/v4.0.3/src/. The code for mod_webapp is in the webapp directory under the Tomcat connectors' source tree. This directory also contains a README.txt with the build instructions.

After building the mod_webapp DSO, we would need to configure Apache to load the module. This would need the following lines to be added to Apache's httpd.conf configuration file:

```
LoadModule webapp_module libexec/mod_webapp.so
AddModule mod_webapp.c
```

The above settings are for UNIX. For Windows, the LoadModule directive would look like this:

```
LoadModule webapp_module modules/mod_webapp.so
```

We can use the apachectl command (in Apache's bin directory) to ensure that the Apache configuration is correct:

```
$ apachectl configtest
```

Finally, we add our web application connections and context into the Apache configuration. The directives for these are WebAppConnection, WebAppDeploy, and WebAppInfo.

```
WebAppConnection [connection name] [provider] [host:port]
```

`connection name` is a unique name for the connection to be created between Apache and Tomcat, `provider` is the name of the provider used to connect to the servlet container (currently only the `warp` provider is available), and `host:port` are the host name and port number to which the WARP connection must attempt to connect. The port specified in our `server.xml` file for the Warp connector:

```
WebAppDeploy [application name] [connection name] [url path]
```

`application` name is the application's name as present in our `webapps` directory in Tomcat. For example, if we want to deploy a WAR-based web application, our application name would be something like `myApplication.war`. `[connection name]` is the name of a previously declared WebAppConnection directive. `[url path]` is the URL path where this application will be deployed:

```
WebAppInfo /path
```

This directive shows information on all configured connections and deployed applications. These are made available at the URL http://server.name:port/path/.

The following is an example of configuration statements added to Apache's `httpd.conf`:

```
WebAppConnection conn      warp  localhost:8008
WebAppDeploy     examples  conn  /examples
WebAppInfo /webapp-info
```

Here, we are instructing the `WebApp` connector to connect to the servlet container waiting for requests on the current `localhost` host and bound to port 8008. The 8008 port is the port specified earlier in Tomcat's `server.xml` file for the `org.apache.catalina.connector.warp.WarpConnector` connector.

server.xml Attributes for Tomcat Configuration

server.xml is an XML document. Most elements correspond to Tomcat modules, with Java setters being automatically associated with element attributes. The Javadocs that accompany Tomcat will contain more details but this document focuses on the common behaviors.

Parent Configuration Elements

The purpose of server.xml is to define the configuration of an instance of the Tomcat web server. The parent configuration elements in server.xml represent that instance.

Server

This is the main element in server.xml. It has a single child describing the Tomcat configuration, <ContextManager>.

Examples

```
<Server>
  <ContextManager >
    ... ( tomcat configuration )
  </ContextManager>
</Server>
```

ContextManager

Description

This is the main tag, used to set generic Tomcat options. The following are some of the children it supports:

- `<module_name>`
  Adds a module to the configuration. Module names are defined in `modules.xml`, where each tag is associated with a class name that implements the module. Each element attribute corresponds to a setter method in the implementing class.
- `<Context>`
  Defines a web application. This is a legacy method of specifying a web application. It is included for backward compatibility with older Tomcat versions. As a rule, applications should be defined in separate config files, named `apps-`*name*`.xml`. This way you can configure your web applications without modifying your `server.xml` file.
- `<Property name="`*property_name*`" value="`*property_value*`">`
  Adds arbitrary name/values to `ContextManager`. The properties can be used for variable substitutions, instead of attributes.
- `<module name="`*module_name*`" javaClass="`*full.class.name*`">`
  Adds a module to the configuration. All modules included in the standard distribution are defined in `modules.xml`, but you can define additional tags and their associated class in `server.xml`. This behaves like `taskdef` in ant.

Attributes

Attribute	Description	Default
`installDir`	Base directory for Tomcat installation. It is typically guessed by the startup program, but you can override it here.	`CATALINA_HOME` or one level above the location of the startup script or `tomcat.jar` (if "java -jar" is used for startup).
`workDir`	Directory where temporary files will be created. Relative paths are interpreted as relative to `CATALINA_HOME`.	`work`
`home`	Base directory for the Tomcat instance. While `install` is used to find the libraries, home is used to resolve almost all relative paths – `webapps`, `work`, and so on.	`CATALINA_HOME` or the value guessed by the startup program.

Example

```
<ContextManager install="/opt/tomcat" workDir="/var/tomcat" home="/var" />
```

C

TcpTunnelGui and Tcpmon

The Apache Soap implementation includes the `TcpTunnelGui` tool, which is used to monitor TCP requests and responses. This tool is used for debugging SOAP programs. Often, it is useful to see the actual SOAP messages traveling between client and server. This helps in understanding the working of SOAP protocol and in debugging live applications. The GUI-based tool opens a port on the machine on which it was started, and channels traffic to a remote host/port combination. On running this tool, two windows are displayed, which show data originating from the client and from the server.

The command to start this tool is:

```
java org.apache.soap.util.net.TcpTunnelGui listenport tunnelhost tunnelport
```

As seen from this command, the `TcpTunnelGui` tool requires three command-line parameters:

- `listenport`
  The port to which the SOAP messages are sent.
- `tunnelhost`
  The hostname of the SOAP server. Set this to `localhost` for local installations.
- `tunnelport`
  The port that the SOAP server is running on. Set this to 8080 for Jakarta Tomcat.

AXIS provides a similar utility class, `tcpmon` for monitoring requests and responses to any TCP port. This tool can be used to act as a TCP router redirecting messages to the desired host and port. It can be used to monitor/redirect any traffic passing over TCP. This tool can be run as shown below:

```
java org.apache.axis.utils.tcpmon
```

On running `tcpmon`, a window is shown with the title **TCPMonitor**. It displays two options: **Listener** that is the default and **Proxy** that is used to specify the details of HTTP proxy server.

D

JBoss Installation

To simplify our installation we'll use the JBoss/Tomcat bundle provided for us. JBoss downloads are available at http://jboss.org/downloads.jsp. At the time of this writing the most current versions available as **stable** releases were JBoss 2.4.6 and Tomcat 4.0.3. This is listed at the JBoss download site as `JBoss-2.4.6_Tomcat-4.0.3.zip`. Download this file to a convenient location.

Install the Software

Once the file is downloaded, installation is straightforward. Open the Zip file you just downloaded. In our examples we are using `/tmp`. Again substitute your actual download directory. Extract the files to your desired location, for example `/usr/local`.

All files will extract to a subdirectory labeled `JBoss-2.4.6_Tomcat-4.0.3`. Installation of JBoss and Tomcat is now complete.

Create an environment variable for the JBoss distribution called `JBOSS_HOME`. This should point to your extracted folder, in our example `/usr/local/jboss-2.4.6_Tomcat-4.0.3`.

Test the JBoss Tomcat Installation

We'll test the installation by starting JBoss. Execute `$JBOSS_HOME/jboss/bin/run_with_catalina.sh`. JBoss will start. The output should contain no error or exception and be similar to that shown overleaf:

Konsole - root@wroxtest:/usr/local/JBoss-2.4.6_Tomcat-4.0.3/jboss/bin - Konsole
File Sessions Settings Help
[INFO,RMIConnectorService] Starting
[INFO,RMIConnectorService] Started
[INFO,MailService] Starting
[INFO,MailService] Mail Service 'Mail' bound to java:/Mail
[INFO,MailService] Started
[INFO,ServiceControl] Started 48 services
[INFO,STDERR] JBoss-2.4.6 Started in 0m:30s.498
New
Konsole

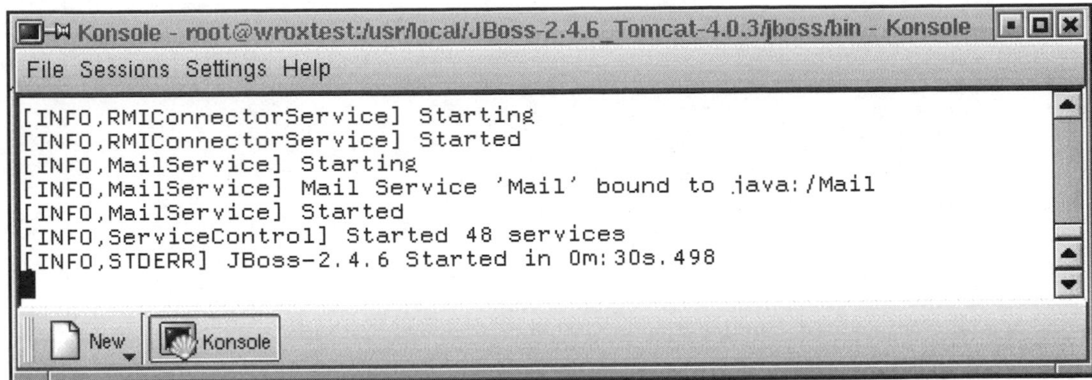

Additionally, you can test Tomcat by pointing a web browser to the installation. Type http://localhost:8080/index.html into your browser and you should see the default Tomcat page as shown below:

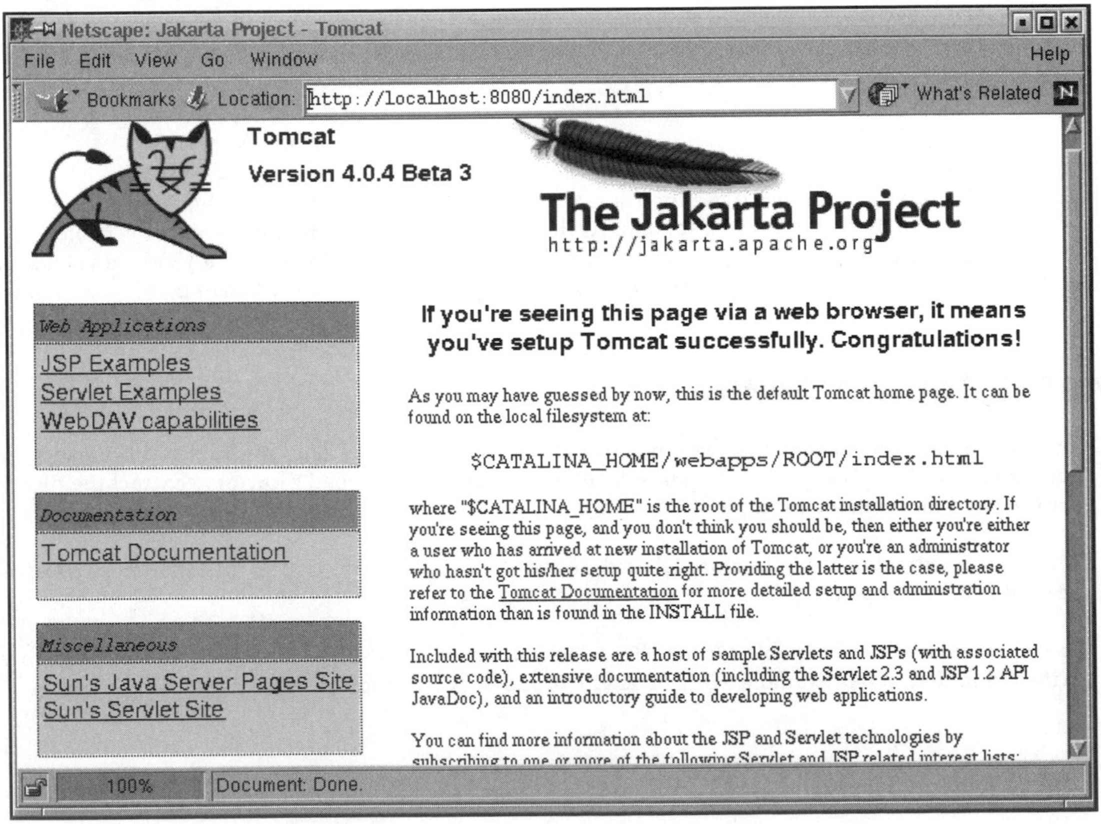

Netscape: Jakarta Project - Tomcat
File Edit View Go Window
Help
Bookmarks Location: http://localhost:8080/index.html
What's Related
Tomcat
Version 4.0.4 Beta 3
The Jakarta Project
http://jakarta.apache.org
Web Applications
JSP Examples
Servlet Examples
WebDAV capabilities
Documentation
Tomcat Documentation
Miscellaneous
Sun's Java Server Pages Site
Sun's Servlet Site
If you're seeing this page via a web browser, it means you've setup Tomcat successfully. Congratulations!
As you may have guessed by now, this is the default Tomcat home page. It can be found on the local filesystem at:
$CATALINA_HOME/webapps/ROOT/index.html
where "$CATALINA_HOME" is the root of the Tomcat installation directory. If you're seeing this page, and you don't think you should be, then either you're either a user who has arrived at new installation of Tomcat, or you're an administrator who hasn't got his/her setup quite right. Providing the latter is the case, please refer to the Tomcat Documentation for more detailed setup and administration information than is found in the INSTALL file.
Included with this release are a host of sample Servlets and JSPs (with associated source code), extensive documentation (including the Servlet 2.3 and JSP 1.2 API JavaDoc), and an introductory guide to developing web applications.
You can find more information about the JSP and Servlet technologies by
100%
Document: Done.

E

WSDL2Java Options

The list of options for WSDL2Java is as follows:

Option	Description
`-d, --deployScope <argument>`	Add scope to `deploy.wsdd`: "Application", "Request", or "Session"
`-h, --help`	Print a usage message
`-m, --messageContext`	Emit a `MessageContext` parameter to skeleton methods
`-N, --NStoPkg <argument>=<value>`	Namespace mapping to package
`-n, --noImports`	Generate code for the immediate WSDL document
`-o<directory>, --output`	Output directory for emitted files
`-p<name>, --package`	Package name to put the emitted files
`-s, --skeleton`	Emit a skeleton class for web service
`-t, --testcase`	Generate a client-side JUnit test case
`-v, --verbose`	Print information messages

F

Java2WSDL Options

The list of options for Java2WSDL is as follows:

Option	Description
-h, --help	Show this screen and exit
-H QN, --header QN	Add a header with this qname to each method
-m M, --mapping M	Map SOAP types to existing Java types
-o N, --output N	The name for the resulting WSDL file
-O, --oldschema	Use the older XML Schema namespace
-r A B, --rename A B	Rename the method with signature A to name B
-S N, --serializers	Custom serializers config file
-t N, --types N	Mapping of Java types to custom SOAP types
-u N, --url N	URL to which service is bound (SOAP server URL)
-x N, --exclude N	Exclude method with signature N from compilation

G

SOAP::Lite Classes

The Perl implementation of SOAP is done using SOAP::Lite. This module is in `/SOAP/Lite.pm` and contains the following classes.

`SOAP::Lite.pm`:

Module	Function
`SOAP::Lite`	Main class that provides all the integration
`SOAP::Transport`	Supports all transport architecture (TCP, SMTP, POP3)
`SOAP::Data`	Provides extensions for data type serialization architecture
`SOAP::Header`	Provides extensions for SOAP header serialization
`SOAP::Parser`	Parses an XML file into an object tree
`SOAP::Serializer`	Serializes all data structures to a SOAP package
`SOAP::Deserializer`	Deserializes the results of `SOAP::Parser` into objects
`SOAP::SOM`	Provides access to the deserialized object tree
`SOAP::Constants`	Provides access to SOAP constants
`SOAP::Trace`	Provides fault-tracing facilities for various events
`SOAP::Schema`	Provides access and stubs for schemas

Table continued on following page

Module	Function
SOAP::Schema::WSDL	Provides a WSDL implementation for SOAP::Schema
SOAP::Server	Handles all server-side incoming requests
SOAP::Server::Object	Handles objects-by-reference
SOAP::Fault	Provides support for Faults generated on the server

SOAP::Transport::HTTP.pm:

Module	Function
SOAP::Transport::HTTP::Client	Client interface to HTTP transport mechanism
SOAP::Transport::HTTP::Server	Server interface to HTTP transport mechanism
SOAP::Transport::HTTP::CGI	CGI implementation of server interface
SOAP::Transport::HTTP::Daemon	Daemon implementation of server interface
SOAP::Transport::HTTP::Apache	mod_perl implementation of server interface

SOAP::Transport::POP3.pm:

Module	Function
SOAP::Transport::POP3::Server	Server interface to POP3 protocol

SOAP::Transport::MAILTO.pm:

Module	Function
SOAP::Transport::MAILTO::Client	Client interface to SMTP/sendmail

SOAP::Transport::LOCAL.pm:

Module	Function
SOAP::Transport::LOCAL::Client	Client interface to local transport

SOAP::Transport::TCP.pm:

Module	Function
SOAP::Transport::TCP::Server	Server interface to TCP protocol
SOAP::Transport::TCP::Client	Client interface to TCP protocol

SOAP::Transport::IO.pm:

Module	Function
SOAP::Transport::IO::Server	Server interface to IO transport

The SOAP::Lite module contains the following member functions:

Function	Description
new()	This is an optional method that accepts a hash with method names as keys
transport()	Provides access to the SOAP::Transport object
serializer()	Provides access to the SOAP::Serialization object
proxy()	Loads the required module and specifies the address of the service
endpoint()	Changes the endpoint without changing/loading another protocol
outputxml()	Allows returning of the raw XML packet from all method calls
header()	Shortcut for SOAP::Serializer->header()
on_action()	Sets a handler for on_action event (while creating SOAPAction)
on_fault()	Sets a handler for on_fault event
on_debug()	Sets a handler for on_debug event (for debugging)
on_nonserialized ()	Sets a handler for on_nonserialized event (generated when items cannot be serialized)
call()	Provides shortcut for calling remote method calls
self()	Returns the object reference to global default object specified with the use SOAP::Lite call

The SOAP::SOM module contains the following member functions:

Function	Description
match()	Returns true/false after matching nodes
valueof()	Returns the value of the matched node from match()
dataof()	Same as valueof(), but returns a SOAP::Data object
headerof()	Same as dataof(), but returns a SOAP::Header object
namespaceuriof()	Returns the URI of the matched element

Table continued on following page

Function	Description
`root()`	Same as `valueof('/')`
`envelope()`	Returns the value (as hash) of the `Envelope` element
`header()`	Returns a hashtable of the `Header` tag element
`headers()`	Returns all the headers inside the `Header` tag element
`body()`	Returns a hashtable of the `Body` tag element
`fault()`	Returns a hashtable of the `Fault` tag element including `faultcode`, `string`, `actor`, and `detail`
`faultcode()`	Returns the `faultcode` element if present
`faultstring()`	Returns the `faultstring` element if present
`faultactor()`	Returns the `faultactor` element if present
`faultdetail()`	Returns the `detail` element if present
`method()`	Returns input parameters or result (response) of the method element
`result()`	Returns the `result` of the method call
`paramsin()`	Returns all input parameters
`paramsout()`	Returns all the output parameters
`paramsall()`	Returns the result and output parameters in an array

The `SOAP::Data` module contains the following member functions:

Function	Syntax	Description
`name()`	`SOAP::Data->name(mytype => 123)`	Used to serialize SOAP elements: `<mytype>123</my type>`
`value()`	`SOAP::Data->name('mytype')->value(123)`	Specifies a value for a SOAP element
`uri()`	`SOAP::Data->name('abc')->uri('http://foo.com')`	Specifies a URI
`type()`	`SOAP::Data->type(base64 => $string)`	Specifies a SOAP data type
`attr()`	`SOAP::Data->name('abc')->attr({xmlns => 'mynamespace'})`	Specifies an attribute and its value for the name tag

The `SOAP::Serializer` module contains the following member functions:

Function	Description
`autotype()`	Specifies whether the serializer will try to make autotyping or not
`readable()`	Specifies the format for the generated XML code
`namespace()`	Specifies the default namespace for generated envelopes
`encodingspace()`	Specifies the default encoding namespace for generated envelopes
`typelookup()`	Gives access to the type lookup table that is used for autotyping
`uri()`	Specifies the URI for SOAP methods
`multirefinplace()`	Puts values for multi-references in the first occurrence of the reference
`encoding()`	Changes encoding for generated envelopes in the XML declaration
`header()`	Specifies the header for generated envelopes

The `SOAP::Serializer->envelope()` method and its parameter values:

Values	Syntax	Description
`method`	`envelope(method => 'name', @params)`	Builds a request/response envelope
`fault`	`envelope(fault => 'fcode', 'fstring', $details)`	Builds a fault envelope
`freedom`	`envelope(freeform => 'something')`	Builds custom payload inside a SOAP envelope

The `SOAP::Trace` module's available events are:

Event	Supports	Description
`transport`	Client	Access to request/response for transport layer
`dispatch`	Server	Shows full name of dispatched call
`result`	Server	Result of method call
`parameters`	Server	Parameters for method call
`headers`	Server	Headers of received message
`objects`	Both	New/`DESTROY` calls
`method`	Both	Parameters for `'->envelope(method =>'` call
`fault`	Both	Parameters for `'->envelope(fault =>'` call
`freeform`	Both	Parameters for `'->envelope(freeform =>'` call
`trace`	Both	Trace enters into some important functions
`debug`	Both	Details about transport

kSOAP API Reference

Here, we'll take a look at a summarized version of the kSOAP API. For a complete listing, please refer to the kSOAP javadocs at http://ksoap.enhydra.org/software/documentation/api/.

The org.ksoap Package

The `org.ksoap` package contains the basic set of SOAP serialization and deserialization classes.

org.ksoap.ClassMap

The `ClassMap` class provides methods, such as `addMapping()` for defining the mapping between Java classes and the XML element names. This method defines the mapping from a namespace and name to a Java class and vice versa. An overloaded version of this method also allows for marshaling mechanism to be specified. The `ClassMap` class also has SOAP properties for serialization and deserialization:

```
public class ClassMap {

  public ClassMap ()
  public ClassMap (boolean legacy)
  public Object readInstance (SoapParser parser, String namespace,
                              String name, ElementType expected)
                              throws IOException
  public Object [] getInfo (Object type, Object instance)
  public void addMapping (String namespace, String name,
                          Class clazz, Marshal marshal)
  public void addMapping (String namespace, String name, Class clazz)
  public void addTemplate (SoapObject so)
}
```

org.ksoap.Soap

The Soap class contains only some constants, such as the encoding (http://schemas.xmlsoap.org/soap/encoding/), the namespace (http://schemas.xmlsoap.org/soap/envelope/):

```
public class Soap {

   public static final String ENV;
   public static final String ENC;
   public static final String XSD;
   public static final String XSI;
   public static final String XSD1999;
   public static final String XSI1999;
   static PrefixMap basePrefixMap;
   public static final PrefixMap prefixMap;
   public static final PrefixMap prefixMap1999;

   static boolean stringToBoolean (String s)
}
```

org.ksoap.SoapEnvelope

The SoapEnvelope class, as the name suggests, encapsulates the SOAP Envelope. It has setEncodingStyle() for setting the SOAP encoding style attribute, and a getBody() method to get the SOAP Body. The listing of the methods is given below:

```
public class SoapEnvelope {

   public SoapEnvelope ()
   public SoapEnvelope (ClassMap classMap)
   public Object getBody ()
   public Object getResult ()
   public void parse (AbstractXmlParser parser) throws IOException
   public void parseHead (AbstractXmlParser parser) throws IOException
   public void parseBody (AbstractXmlParser parser) throws IOException
   public void parseTail (AbstractXmlParser parser) throws IOException
   public void setEncodingStyle (String encodingStyle)
   public void write (AbstractXmlWriter writer) throws IOException
   public void writeHead (AbstractXmlWriter writer) throws IOException
   public void writeBody (AbstractXmlWriter writer) throws IOException
   public void writeTail (AbstractXmlWriter writer) throws IOException
   public void setBody (Object body)
   public void setClassMap (ClassMap classMap)
}
```

org.ksoap.SoapObject

Client applications use the SoapObject class for building SOAP RPC method calls. This class gets mapped to the SOAP Body. It has methods such as addProperty() for adding parameters to the method call. The name of the remote method and its namespace is set via the SoapObject() constructor. This class implements the KvmSerializable interface (described later). Client applications can provide their own custom class by implementing this interface:

```
public class SoapObject implements KvmSerializable {

  public SoapObject (String namespace, String name)
  public boolean equals (Object o)
  public String getName ()
  public String getNamespace ()
  public Object getProperty (int index)
  public Object getProperty (String name)
  public int getPropertyCount ()
  public void getPropertyInfo (int index, PropertyInfo pi)
  public SoapObject newInstance ()
  public void setProperty (int index, Object value)
  public SoapObject addProperty (String name, Object value)
  public SoapObject addProperty (PropertyInfo pi, Object value)
}
```

org.ksoap.SoapParser

`SoapParser` is the parser class for SOAP messages. It currently supports only local `hrefs`, and doesn't support partial arrays, and multi-dimensional arrays:

```
public class SoapParser {

  public SoapParser (AbstractXmlParser parser, ClassMap classMap)
  public Object read () throws IOException
  public Object read (Object owner, int index, String namespace,
                      String name, ElementType expected)
  protected void readSerializable (KvmSerializable obj)
  public Object readUnknown (String namespace, String name)
                             throws IOException
  private int getIndex (Attribute attr, int start, int dflt)
  public void readVector (Vector v, ElementType elementType)
                          throws IOException
}
```

org.ksoap.SoapPrimitive

The `SoapPrimitive` class encapsulates the primitive data types:

```
public class SoapPrimitive {

  public SoapPrimitive (String namespace, String name, String value)
  public boolean equals (Object o)
  public int hashCode ()
  public String toString ()
  public String getNamespace ()
  public String getName ()
}
```

org.ksoap.SoapWriter

The `SoapWriter` class writes objects based on the SOAP section five encoding rules:

```
public class SoapWriter {

  public SoapWriter (AbstractXmlWriter writer, ClassMap classMap)
  public void write (Object obj) throws IOException
  public void writeObjectBody (KvmSerializable obj) throws IOException
  protected  void writeProperty (Object obj, ElementType type)
                               throws IOException
  protected void writeVectorBody (Vector vector, ElementType elementType)
                                throws IOException
}
```

org.ksoap.SoapFault

`SoapFault` is an exception class encapsulating SOAP Faults. It implements the `java.io.Serializable` and the `org.kxml.XmlIO` interfaces:

```
public class SoapFault extends IOException implements XmlIO {

    public String faultcode;
    public String faultstring;
    public String faultactor;
    public Vector detail;

    public void parse (AbstractXmlParser parser) throws IOException {
    public void write (AbstractXmlWriter xw) throws IOException {
    public String toString () {
}
```

org.ksoap.Marshal

The `Marshal` interface is provided for allowing custom serializers and deserializers:

```
public interface Marshal {

  public Object readInstance (SoapParser parser, String namespace,
                              String name, ElementType expected)
                              throws IOException;
  public void writeInstance (SoapWriter writer, Object instance)
                             throws IOException;
  public void register (ClassMap cm);
}
```

The org.ksoap.transport Package

The `org.ksoap.transport` package, as the name suggests, contains the underlying transport classes.

org.ksoap.transport.HttpTransport

The `HttpTransport` class provides methods for HTTP calls over the J2ME generic communication framework. The `call()` method sends a request envelope to the service endpoint, and returns the SOAP response. The endpoint URL and the `SoapAction` HTTP header can be set either via the constructor, or by using the `setUrl()` and `setSoapAction()` methods. This class has a `debug` property that can be set to `true` for enabling tracing. When it is `true`, the `requestDump` and `responseDump` data elements get filled up with the request and response SOAP messages:

```
public class HttpTransport {

  public boolean debug;
  public String requestDump;
  public String responseDump;

  public HttpTransport ()
  public HttpTransport (String url, String soapAction)
  public void setUrl (String url)
  public void setSoapAction (String soapAction)
  public void setClassMap (ClassMap classMap)
  public void call () throws IOException
  public Object call (SoapObject method) throws IOException
  public void reset ()
}
```

org.ksoap.transport.HttpTransportSE

`HttpTransportSE` provides the same functionality as `HttpTransport`, but for J2SE. Hence, it can be used in PC-based SOAP client applications or even within an applet. This is an optional class, and is not packaged along with the kSOAP binary download.

The org.ksoap.marshal Package

The `org.ksoap.marshal` package contains optional implementations of the `org.ksoap.Marshal` interface. This, as mentioned earlier, allows for custom serializers and deserializers.

org.ksoap.marshal.MarshalBase64

This is a serializer and deserializer implementation class for Base64 objects.

org.ksoap.marshal.MarshalDate

This class is a serializer and deserializer implementation class for `dates`.

org.ksoap.marshal.MarshalFloat

This is a serializer and deserializer implementation class for `float`, `double`, and `decimal`. This works only in a J2SE environment, as CLDC does not have floating point arithmetic support.

org.ksoap.marshal.MarshalHashtable

Serializer and deserializer implementation class for `Hashtables`.

The org.kobjects.serialization Package

CLDC does not have support for Java reflection. The `org.kobjects.serialization` package is thus required for serialization support.

ElementType

The `ElementType` class encapsulates type information.

PropertyInfo

This `PropertyInfo` class is used to store information about each property that an implementation of `KvmSerializable` interface exposes.

KvmSerializable

The `KvmSerializable` interface provides the `set` and `get` methods for properties.

Index

A Guide to the Index

The index is arranged hierarchically, in alphabetical order, with symbols preceding the letter A. Most second-level entries and many third-level entries also occur as first-level entries. This is to ensure that users will find the information they require however they choose to search for it.

A

B

D

E

F

G

H

I

J

K

L

M

N

O

P

Q

R

S

T

U

V

W

X

Z

Registration Code : 74695N8S8H2P5YY01

Wrox writes books for you. Any suggestions, or ideas about how you want information given in your ideal book will be studied by our team. Your comments are always valued at Wrox.

Free phone in USA 800-USE-WROX
Fax (312) 893 8001

UK Tel.: (0121) 687 4100 Fax: (0121) 687 4101

Professional Open Source Web Services– Registration Card

Name ______________________

Address ______________________

____

____

____

City __________ State/Region __________

Country __________ Postcode/Zip __________

E-Mail ______________________

Occupation ______________________

How did you hear about this book?

❒ Book review (name) ______________

❒ Advertisement (name) ______________

❒ Recommendation ______________

❒ Catalog ______________

❒ Other ______________

Where did you buy this book?

❒ Bookstore (name) __________ City __________

❒ Computer store (name) ______________

❒ Mail order ______________

❒ Other ______________

What influenced you in the purchase of this book?

❒ Cover Design ❒ Contents ❒ Other (please specify):

____

How did you rate the overall content of this book?

❒ Excellent ❒ Good ❒ Average ❒ Poor

What did you find most useful about this book? ______________

____

____

What did you find least useful about this book? ______________

____

____

Please add any additional comments. ______________

____

____

What other subjects will you buy a computer book on soon?

____

What is the best computer book you have used this year?

____

Note: This information will only be used to keep you updated about new Wrox Press titles and will not be used for any other purpose or passed to any other third party.

7469 Check here if you DO NOT want to receive support for this book ❒ 7469

Note: If you post the bounce back card below in the UK, please send it to:

Wrox Press Limited, Arden House, 1102 Warwick Road,
Acocks Green, Birmingham B27 6HB. UK.

Computer Book Publishers

NO POSTAGE
NECESSARY
IF MAILED
IN THE
UNITED STATES

BUSINESS REPLY MAIL

FIRST CLASS MAIL PERMIT#64 CHICAGO, IL

POSTAGE WILL BE PAID BY ADDRESSEE

WROX PRESS INC.
29 S. LA SALLE ST.
SUITE 520
CHICAGO IL 60603-USA